The
Beatitudes

The mountain on which the Beatitudes were preached
as a part of the Sermon on the Mount, is not identified.
For many centuries the traditional site near the Sea of
Galilee has been called the Mount of Beatitudes. A
drawing of this site is used on the cover.

The Beatitudes

A Commentary on Matt. 5:1-11; Luke 6:20-26

The Pursuit of Happiness

Spiros Zodhiates

AMG
PUBLISHERS
Chattanooga, TN 37421

The Beatitudes:
The Pursuit of Happiness

Originally published as
The Pursuit of Happiness

ISBN 0–89957–508–0

Printed in the United States of America
03 02 01 00 99 98 –D– 6 5 4 3 2 1

PREFACE

Did the Lord Jesus Christ promise happiness to His followers? I was astounded to discover that the Greek words that are the exact equivalents for the English word "happy" do not occur in the New Testament at all. Yet there is a popular notion that the New Testament is a Book that deals with the happiness of man.

This book will point up the basic difference between the two words "blessed" (*makarioi* in Greek) and "happy." To put it briefly here, "blessed" refers to the one whose sufficiency is within him, while "happy" refers to the one whose sufficiency comes from outside sources. The New Testament says that he is "blessed" who is God-sufficient, in whose heart Christ dwells, whom he has accepted as his Saviour. For such a one, the outside circumstances of life do not affect his inner peace and poise. By contrast, the happy person depends on good fortune to keep him smiling. "Happy" comes from the word "hap," meaning "chance." It is therefore incorrect to translate the word *makarioi* (which we find repeatedly in the Beatitudes) as "happy." It means something far different, in its real sense; it means "blessed."

The Lord Jesus and the New Testament, therefore, do not promise us good fortune, on which happiness depends, but blessedness, which is a direct result of God's work in our hearts through His Son.

The message of the New Testament is that you may have everything that this world has to offer and still not be blessed (or call it happy, if you wish, as long as you mean by it an inner peace of soul). But when you have God in your heart through Jesus Christ, then good or bad fortune is incidental; in fact, it is hardly fortune any more; it is Divine Providence.

This book, then, deals with a consideration of what it means to be blessed. The Beatitudes as we find them in Matthew 5 and Luke 6 contain a wealth of instruction that will repay careful study.

May the Lord enable you to experience the height and depths of blessedness, His blessedness, as you read this book and meditate upon His Word.

—SPIROS ZODHIATES

The Study
Ridgefield, N. J.

(*Note: For the convenience of the reader, the bibliography is included right in the textual matter in each instance where reference to it occurs.*)

CONTENTS

Chapter

THE CONDITIONS OF BLESSEDNESS

The Constitution of the United States guarantees every citizen the right to "life, liberty, and the pursuit of happiness." To the Founding Fathers, these seemed basic rights, and surely without them we would be most miserable. And yet we are a little concerned about modern man's interpretation of that word "happiness." If it could be realized, would it be the treasure he is really seeking? Is it the highest state of well-being to which he can attain? Is there anything superior to it? To this latter question we must answer, Yes, if only for the obvious reason that "happiness" is a sometime thing, here today and gone tomorrow. But God offers us something far better—that includes all the good we could hope for in achieving happiness and infinitely more: a permanent joy that is not affected by the ups and downs of life— a condition called "blessedness."

In Matthew 5:3-10, we have a prescription for blessedness from the Lord Jesus Christ. He had already commanded men to repent and believe the Gospel (Matt. 4:17, Mark 1:15). That was His first commandment and the only one addressed to the unconverted. Then came His commandment to Peter and Andrew to follow Him and become fishers of men. We must first experience the new birth: regeneration, repentance, and faith in the redemptive work of Christ on the cross of Calvary. When we repent and believe, we are saved from our sins and forgiven by God. After we experience this forgiveness, we become anxious for others to have the same experience. This is what moves us to become fishers of men. Being forgiven by God is such a joyful experience

1

that we must share it with others, so that they, too, may repent and believe and be saved.

Now the Lord Jesus tells us that the person who has experienced forgiveness of sins and who shares this experience with others is a blessed person. But in order that his blessedness may reach its peak and become a unique experience, he must fulfill certain conditions. Christ gives us eight steps that we must climb in order to reach the summit of heavenly blessedness upon this earth. There are evidently degrees of blessedness, or the Lord would not have given us this prescription.

Some people think that the Beatitudes merely describe the characteristics of those who have repented and followed the Lord Jesus Christ, that they tell us what these people are instead of what they should become. Of course, there is some truth in this; for when a person is converted to Christ his whole nature changes and he becomes a new creature in Christ Jesus. This corresponds to the life a child receives at birth. But nevertheless, the Christian must aim at growth, maturity, and a full expression of the dormant qualities that lie within. We cannot assume that man becomes perfect the moment he is saved and his sins are forgiven. If that were so, why should anyone preach to the converted? And most of the preaching in the New Testament, and in our pulpits today, is addressed to those who are already saved. No, the truth is that, though we receive life—the life of God, eternal life— when we receive the Lord Jesus Christ as our Saviour, we have a great deal to assimilate and do before we can grow to maturity. There is no place, at least in this life, where we can say that we have reached the ultimate in the Christian life, the ultimate of God's standard for us. This will be reached only when we go to be with Him and are no more encompassed by earth's penetrating clouds of sinfulness.

What the Lord is giving us here is guidance on how to grow to that mark He has set before us, even though we cannot fully attain it down here. There is blessing in the way, whatever the degree of accomplishment may be.

In the original Greek text, no verb is used in conjunction with the word "blessed," which appears a total of eight times in Matthew 5:3-10. The English translation reads, "Blessed *are* the poor in spirit," "Blessed *are* they that mourn," etc. You will notice that the word "are" is in italics in your Bible, which means that it is missing in the Greek. What we actually have in Greek is "Blessed the poor in spirit," "Blessed those that mourn." We could very well place an exclamation mark after the adjective "blessed," for it is as though the Lord shouted to His disciples, "Here is the way to blessedness! Be ye poor in spirit, be ye mourning, be ye meek, be ye thirsting and hungering after righteousness, be ye merciful, be ye pure in heart, be ye peacemakers, be ye persecuted for righteousness' sake."

This is the prescription for blessedness. Be all these things, once you have repented of your sins and stepped forward to follow Christ. This is why I am including these Beatitudes among the commandments of Christ. They are not commandments for us to be blessed, but commandments to fulfill the conditions of blessedness. In the Christian life there is a process of cause and effect just as in everything else. If you do not eat, you will be hungry, undernourished, and eventually die of starvation as a natural consequence. If you are not humble enough to acknowledge your ignorance of certain things, you will never ask questions in order to learn. Everything has a cause and an effect. And the degree of our blessedness is determined by our meeting of the conditions laid down by the Lord Jesus Christ here. If we fulfill only one condition out of the eight, we shall attain to only a fraction of the

3

blessedness that could be our share. The farmer reaps what he sows. If he sows one acre of wheat, he will reap only as much wheat as will grow on one acre of land. There is a parallel in the Christian life.

Actually, the adjective "blessed" in the Beatitudes could be rendered "blessedness of." Jesus our Lord did not speak the Beatitudes in Greek but in Aramaic, a language very similar to Hebrew, spoken by the people of His day. Aramaic and Hebrew have a common kind of expression that is, in fact, an exclamation, meaning "Oh, the blessedness of!" That expression (*ashere* in Hebrew) is very common in the Old Testament. It is as if the Lord were saying, "Oh, the blessedness of those who are or do these things that I am about to enumerate!"

In their basic concept, the Beatitudes are neither a prophecy concerning some future state nor a wish concerning the possibility of a present state. They are mere statements of fact concerning the process of spiritual cause and effect in the Christian life. They tell of the natural consequences of our attitudes as Christians in this life. They are laws of the spiritual life, of the life of the Christian. And it is only to the Christian that they apply, because to the non-Christian they make no sense.

God has set certain laws to apply to certain people. To the unconverted He says, "Repent," and has promised to forgive their sins. But to a man whose sins are not forgiven, who is not regenerated by the Spirit of God, these laws do not apply, for he is outside the sphere of the citizens of the Kingdom of God. The laws of America do not apply in Greece, and vice versa. Only the Greeks who live in the United States are under the laws of the United States, not those who live in Greece. As long as you are outside a country, and have no connection with it, its laws do not apply to you. These laws of blessedness, then, are for citizens of Christ's Kingdom only. To those

4

outside of Christ, they are not only foreign but will seem ridiculous as well. Those outside of Christ seek their happiness aggressively. They reach after pleasure, money, fame, power—all in pursuit of happiness. The Christian is different. He does not seek happiness as such. In the Christian market place, happiness as a distinct commodity does not exist. You cannot go and buy it by the pound. It is not available for sale or for conquest. It is merely a by-product. And the Christian's blessedness is fundamentally different from the happiness that the unconverted seek. Blessedness depends on God and happiness depends on circumstances. This is the basic difference between those who are outside of Christ and those who are in Christ.

We do not repent so that we may be made blessed but that we may receive forgiveness of sins. Blessedness comes as a by-product, as a natural consequence. We do not mourn so that we may be made blessed; but, when we mourn for our own sins and the sins of others, blessedness in our own souls and possibly the souls of others is the natural result. A Christian is what he is, and does what he does, not for any ulterior motive, but through Christ and for Christ. In Christ we find our blessedness. It would be entirely contrary to the spirit of Christ and to the whole concept of His teaching to be and do certain things for selfish purposes, that is, for our own blessedness. This is not the spirit of the Beatitudes. It is not, "I want to be blessed; therefore let me be humble or poor in spirit," or "I want to be blessed; therefore let me mourn, let me weep, let me be meek." All the spokes of my activity and being do not have my own life as their center, for the purpose of contributing to my own blessedness, but revolve around Christ; and it is in Christ that my blessedness and joy are found. As we shall see in our studies, the right motivation of all our activities is the all-important thing in the Christian life and in the Christian philosophy of life, as opposed to other religions.

Thus the basic concept here is "What blessedness is the share of the humble, of the meek," etc. But don't try to be all these things so that you can be blessed yourself, but be these things and do these things because of Christ, and for Him, because in them He is pleased. The more we endeavor to please Him, the more blessed we shall be.

What we have in the Beatitudes, then, is not a prescription for blessedness, but a prescription giving the conditions of blessedness, which are valued, not for the result which they produce, but for their own intrinsic worth.

HOW CAN WE BECOME WHAT GOD IS
— BLESSED?

As God through Moses gave men a code to regulate their lives, so Christ has given a code, particularly for Christians, to remind them constantly of the guiding principles necessary to secure without conscious intention the blessedness that the world misinterprets as happiness and so consciously strives after.

Many people are under the impression that three chapters comprising what is commonly known as the Sermon on the Mount, Matthew 5-7, are actually one discourse, given by our Lord at one sitting and in one place. Now it may be that He gave every one of these principles as He sat on the mountain, or on several mountains at different times. This teaching in Matthew was most probably given on several consecutive occasions, as the people and disciples kept coming back to the same place to be taught. But it is hardly conceivable that the Lord preached such a long sermon at one time. It contains far too much for anyone to absorb all at once. Our Lord, from every evidence we have, was not a long-winded preacher.

It is quite possible that this is also a compilation of what the Lord had been saying to His disciples over and over again. Perhaps He had to remind them every day of these fundamental rules of the Kingdom of God, governing the conduct of His citizens. This is in accord with the fact that the verbs in Matthew 5:2 and Luke 6:20 are in the imperfect tense in the original Greek. They are *edidasken*, "was teaching," and *elegen*, "was saying." This tense describes repeated, continuous, or habitual action at different times in the past, rather than a single performance. What we have in these chapters is what the Lord was telling His disciples time and again. Naturally, it was not the entire three chapters, but parts of them, which occupied each day's or each week's lesson. This places great importance upon this passage of Scripture, compiled for us by Matthew in one complete section.

We do not find any absolute continuity of thought in these three chapters, but fragments of consecutive teachings on various subjects. We have a discourse on the conditions of blessedness, another on the purpose of the Christian in the world, a discussion of the relationship of the Christian and Christ to the ethical laws of the Old Testament, etc. If you observe carefully, however, you will discover two passages that seem especially out of context, although we believe they were placed there for a purpose. One is Matthew 5:31, 32, which deals with divorce and remarriage. Preceding it we have the teaching on how to behave when we encounter the outward temptations of life; and following it we have the teaching on oath-taking. The other passage is Matthew 7:7-11, which speaks of asking and receiving. It is preceded by the advice not to throw our pearls before swine and is followed by the Golden Rule, so called, to do unto others as we would have them do unto us.

Scattered through the Gospel of Luke, not necessarily in consecutive order, and with some variations, we find a number of the items in these three chapters of Matthew. Here are a few of the parallels:

Matthew 5:13	Luke 14:34, 35
5:15	8:16
5:18	16:17
7:1-5	6:37-42
7:7-12	11:9-13

These were indeed important pronouncements that our Lord was constantly making to His disciples. One further

8

indication of their importance is that Matthew tells us that the Lord Jesus gave them sitting down (Matt. 5:1). They were *ex-cathedra* pronouncements, given with authority by virtue of His office. Casual instruction by a rabbi was usually given as he was strolling around or standing, but official teaching was given from a seated position. That is why so much is made of the *ex-cathedra* pronouncements of the Pope, which are considered by his followers to be infallible, while those made otherwise are not so considered.

Let us, then, consider our Lord's pronouncements with all seriousness, for they concern the conditions of our blessedness in this world and the ultimate realization of that state when we shall be with Him forever.

The first thing for us to determine is the meaning of the word "blessed," as it is used here in the Beatitudes and throughout the Scriptures. What does it mean to be "blessed"? The word in Greek is *makarios*, used in its plural form, *makarioi*, in the Beatitudes. The word occurs in classical Greek as *makar*, an adjective describing the gods as opposed to mortals. It was a divine quality. Philo, in *de Sacrificiis Abelis et Caini*, p. 147, speaks of "God who was not born, incorruptible and unchangeable and holy *and only blessed*" (author's translation of text as quoted in Moulton and Milligan, *The Vocabulary of the Greek Testament, illustrated from the Papyri and other non-literary sources*, Eerdmans, 1957, p. 386). Later it came to be used also of men, and especially of the blessed dead, who were liberated from the influences of the outside world. The Greek historian, Herodotus, even uses this word of an oasis in the African desert, thus vividly bespeaking its later meaning in the Scriptures (Liddell and Scott, *A Greek English Lexicon*, Oxford, 1958. p. 1073).

Behind the original usage of this word by the Greeks lay the idea that the gods were blessed in themselves, unaffected by the outside world. This condition of blessedness is ascribed to the gods, for instance, by writers such as Homer and Hesiod, who spoke of the gods as distinct from men who are liable to poverty and death. Thus, one general conclusion we can draw is that the word *makarios* originally meant that state that is neither produced nor affected by outside circumstances, but is intrinsic within. This is the underlying principle in the use of the word in the Septuagint and the New Testament.

Makarios, "blessed," is that person in whose heart God Himself dwells. That's what it means to be a Christian. You are miserable and sinful. Looking within yourself, you are utterly disappointed, because there you see the devil enthroned as a result of man's fall in his federal representative, Adam. Looking around you, you soon become completely depressed, for blessedness is nowhere to be found in a world of sin and sinful men. Finally, when you realize that blessedness can be found neither within nor without, you look upward, beyond yourself, beyond man, beyond things, to God Himself—the only possessor of real blessedness, in that His blessedness is woven into His character and is not an acquired characteristic. You long to share in that divine blessedness. But how? In order to have this nature of God within you, you must become a child of God. Yet you cannot do this by your own effort or that of anyone else. "But as many as received him [the Lord Jesus Christ], to them gave he power [or authority] to become the sons of God" (John 1:12). By receiving the Lord Jesus Christ, you enter into the family of God, acquire the nature and character of God, and enthrone God within your heart and life. As a natural by-product of that miraculous transaction, you acquire the blessedness of God, that blessedness that belonged originally and still belongs to God Himself, which the Greeks even in their pagan state understood to be an attribute of deity.

It is high time we, the advanced people of this generation, understood one simple fact about personal blessedness. It is fundamentally a distinct quality of God, our Creator, and cannot be acquired apart from Him. We cannot have what God has without having God Himself. That is why we so often fail in our quest for blessedness. My earnest advice to you is not to try to seek blessedness (or what you may call happiness—although they are not the same) apart from God, but to seek God; accept Him as your Heavenly Father through the Lord Jesus Christ, who died to reconcile you, a sinner, with a holy God. Only then will you experience that blessedness that the world cannot give or take away. It is only as we thoroughly understand the meaning of this word *makarios*, "blessed," that the words of the Lord Jesus Christ in the Beatitudes and elsewhere will have any real meaning for us.

CAN WE KNOW BLESSEDNESS HERE, OR ONLY IN THE HEREAFTER?

In our last study, we saw that it is impossible to have *makariotees*, that blessedness that is a distinct quality of God, without having God Himself within our hearts through faith in the Lord Jesus Christ.

But the adjective *makarios* was also used by the Greeks to describe the blessed dead. The idea behind this was that the dead were not annihilated, as some modern religious cults would have us believe, but were carried over from one medium or sphere into another, where they were unaffected by misery and suffering. The world beyond was the world of the gods for them, and therefore the world of blessedness. This is why they often referred to the dead as the *makares*, using the word as a substantive.

This is significant because it shows how real the world beyond was to the Greeks, that realm where the dead had a far greater chance of being blessed than the living. They believed that there was no suffering after death. In the life of the Christian, this hope of complete blessedness and greater likeness to God is most apparent as he reads the teachings of the Lord Jesus and the entire New Testament.

But the teaching of Christ goes beyond this promise of blessedness after death. He tells us that we need not wait until we cross over beyond the shores of human life to experience this blessedness, which the Greeks imagined belonged only to the gods and the after-life. For Christians, the blessedness beyond the grave is only an extension and heightening of our present state and condition. We need not wait until after death to be blessed

12

and become partakers of the character of God. We can experience that here and now. This, in fact, is what the Lord is trying to make clear to His disciples by giving them the Beatitudes. We can be poor, hungry, persecuted, distressed in every way, and still be blessed; for nothing that happens to us from without can take from us the character of God that dwells within.

The Beatitudes, then, are a description of the true Christian. He is a person who is blessed in this life, not because of what happens to him, but sometimes in spite of it. He does not need to wait until after death for that blessedness. No other religion, besides Christianity, offers such a philosophy of life; and, because it does, its philosophy of death is also a philosophy of life in the true sense of the word. There is a definite relationship between our state in life and in death. Our condition after death is determined by what we are and do down here on earth. We cannot be and do anything we please while alive and expect to be blessed after death. Our physical conduct determines our metaphysical destiny, as illustrated by our Lord's story of the rich man and Lazarus in Luke 16. Blessedness after death is not automatically conferred upon us; it can only come as the extension of our present living blessedness. If we are sinful and miserable down here, we can expect no blessedness in the world to come. That which a man sows he shall also reap.

It is most interesting to trace the development of certain words from Classical to Modern Greek. In Modern Greek, whenever we refer to a dead person, we say *ho makaritees,* "the blessed one." By this expression we convey the blessedness of his memory and our hope that he is enjoying his present state. It is in just this way we must refer to Christians who are living under the conditions described in the Beatitudes, as given to us by Matthew and Luke. Let us consider these in order:

Oh, how blessed are the humble Christians, the poor in spirit and in pocketbook! (Matt. 5:3 and Luke 6:20). This cannot be said of any who are not Christians. In the first place, they could not be truly humble in spirit, and secondly they would not subject themselves to voluntary poverty, as indicated in Luke.

Oh, how blessed is the Christian who mourns, either over the death of a loved one or over his own sins! (Matt. 5:4 and Luke 6:21). Only the Christian considers self to be dead and Christ alive in him, and only the Christian rejoices over the death of self. This cannot be true of anyone else, whatever his religion or belief. Luke tells us that Christians who shed tears for the sake of Christ are blessed indeed. This is a strange paradox. Generally we are directed toward laughter instead of tears. Yet the Christian who is blessed himself because of the indwelling Christ is the only one who can see the unhappiness of those without Christ and feel sorry for them. Our sorrow for others is a proof that we are different from the world around us. If we were in a similar sorry state, we could feel no sorrow for the sinful world in which we live. This, therefore, is a distinctive of Christian blessedness.

Oh, for the blessedness of the meek! (Matt. 5:5.) Those who are constantly angry at God and the world because they feel they have been badly treated cannot possibly be blessed. It is only the Christian who san say, "And we know that all things work together for good" (Rom. 8:28). He alone can accept his lot cheerfully as God's will for his life, and try to use his crutches for, instead of against, God and his fellow beings. This is Christian blessedness.

14

Oh, for the blessedness of the Christian who is righteous because of Christ within! (Matt. 5:6 and Luke 6:21.) Such a one does not think he has all the righteousness he will ever need but constantly seeks a new supply. He who does not have the nature of God within feels no need of righteousness, much less hungers and thirsts for it. To seek righteousness despite the fact that it may not secure advancement or success for you is distinctively Christian, and this is a characteristic of real blessedness. A person who uses any means to achieve his selfish ends cannot be blessed.

How blessed is the Christian who does not think of himself only, but of others, and tries to help them all he can! (Matt. 5:7). The truly merciful man is the one who has experienced mercy in his own life, the mercy of God in his heart. That is the Christian.

What blessedness there is in the man whose heart is pure! (Matt. 5:8.) But man cannot possibly purify his own heart. It comes as a result of God's work in his innermost being. Thus here we have again the demonstration of God's activity in man's heart resulting in blessedness.

What blessedness there is in being at peace with one's Creator! (Matt. 5:9.) The man who has not been born again is at constant war with his Maker. But as the Christian experiences the peace of God in his own heart, he is possessed with a great yearning, if not a compulsion, to share that peace with others. And only as men live at peace with God can they live at peace with one another. Only the Christian starts aright in this business of bringing about peace. Today we speak of peaceful co-existence, and that is all it is at best. This is not what the Christian has. He does not try to persuade God to be tolerant of man's warring spirit against Him, nor to persuade man to tolerate God, but to bring man to an awareness of his

15

need of reconciliation with God. Only as man is reconciled to God in Christ can he be reconciled to his fellow man. Men reconciled with God can live like brothers in one family instead of enemies on the same earth. Only the Christian has such a philosophy of peace for his fellow men. Hence the missionary spirit in the Christian.

What blessedness there is in persecution as a result of being faithful to the Lord Jesus Christ! (Matt. 5:10-12; Luke 6:22, 23.) No pressure from without can ever keep down the elation within that comes from Christ. This is Christian blessedness. This is what happens to an individual who allows Christ to live within his heart. This is the only way one can be blessed in a world of unhappiness and pressures beyond man's ability to bear.

DOES GOOD LUCK AFFECT BLESSEDNESS?

Many people today are happy only because they have been lucky. As far as they are concerned, there are only two classes of people: those who are happy because they have had good fortune and those who are not happy because they have had ill fortune. Their philosophy is that happiness is conditioned by outward circumstances. They know nothing of the inner resources that can counteract what they call "bad luck."

Our Lord must have had this in mind when He gave us the Beatitudes, especially in His choice of the word *makarioi*, "blessed." He wanted to show us how little effect the outside world can have upon the inner self, and how differently it can be interpreted by a "blessed" Christian. The state and disposition of our souls is the most important thing in the world. We can darken the world around us by wearing dark glasses, in a physical and a spiritual sense. It acquires the colors we see it through. This is the essential teaching of the Beatitudes.

"Fortune," either good or bad, has nothing to do with a Christian's happiness. He can be poor and yet rich, persecuted and yet blessed and blessing, hungry and yet satisfied, empty and yet full. The Christian is a paradox. He is dependent upon God who created Him and independent of the world in which he lives, as far as his relationship with his Creator is concerned; and this alone determines his happiness or unhappiness.

We have seen that *makarios*, "blessed," was formerly used to denote a state belonging to the ancient Greek gods, who were thought to be exalted above earthly suf-

17

fering and the limitations of this life. Aristotle contrasted the *makarios*, or "blessed one," to *ende-ees*, "the needy one." If the opposite of the one who is blessed is the one who is needy, *makarios* is the one who needs nothing, who has no need of the outside world. Although he is in the world, he is independent of the world. This is evidenced by the peculiar use the Greeks made of the adjective *makarios*, when they designated the island of Cyprus (which happens to be the author's birthplace), *Cyprus hee makaria*, "Cyprus the blessed one." What did they mean by that? That Cyprus was a lovely, fertile island, whose people did not need to go outside its coastline to find all they needed for sustenance and happiness. The island was blessed because it provided everything needful. Thus it is with the Christian, our Lord tells us. He has everything within him that will make him happy. His happiness is not dependent upon luck, but upon the divine resources within.

Strictly speaking, we should not translate the word *makarios*, used in the Beatitudes and elsewhere, as "happy," because the English word "happy" comes from the root word "hap," meaning "chance." We say, "This is what happened to me," meaning this is what came to us by chance. A person's "happiness," then, depends upon the happenings of life, upon the influences of the outside world. This is not the case with those whom the Lord describes as *makarioi*, "blessed." No one can take their joy from them. The world around them can neither give them this joy nor deprive them of it (John 16:22). Christians are not blessed because of what the world may give them but because of what God has given them through His Son, the Lord Jesus Christ. He is all-sufficient.

18

If our joy as Christians were to depend upon the effect of the outside world upon us—the effect of riches or poverty, sickness or health—then Christ within would no longer be sufficient. Nothing in the Christian's life must detract from the sufficiency of the Lord Jesus Christ. If our joy depends in any way upon what we can get out of the world, then the Lord Jesus Christ will be less than satisfying. Either He must satisfy us fully, or He cannot satisfy at all.

What the Lord wants us as His disciples to understand is that our joy and blessedness are not conditioned by the world without but by Christ within. After all, we must realize that the things that happen to us happen also to the Lord who indwells us. And as He viewed His crucifixion day as His crowning day, so must we. There are no accidents in our lives, just providences; and whatever touches us touches Him first.

Roland V. Bingham, founder of the Sudan Interior Mission, was seriously injured in an automobile collision in his sixtieth year. His head was severely cut and a number of bones were broken. When he regained consciousness in the hospital next day, he asked the nurse what he was doing there. "Be very quiet," she replied. "You've been in a frightful accident." "Accident?" Dr. Bingham exclaimed. "There are no accidents in the life of a Christian. This is an incident." And he was right. There are no accidents in a Christian's life, just incidents of God's work within.

That great scholar, Herman Cremer, in his discussion of the Old Testament Hebrew equivalent for *makarios,* sums it up beautifully thus: "It is the state wherein one enjoys the favor and salvation of God. Earthly as is the manifestation of this blessedness, it is essentially more than this, it is the gracious and saving effect of God's favor, but is enjoyed only when there is a corresponding behaviour towards God; so that it forms the hoped-for good of those who in the present life are subject to oppression . . . Inwardly it exists in the enjoyment of grace and fellowship with God, even where the outward condition does not correspond." (*Biblico-Theological Lexicon of the New Testament*, T. & T. Clark, Edinburgh, 1954, p. 777.)

He then goes on to speak of the use of *makarios* in the New Testament, saying that it expresses "the life-joy and satisfaction of the man who does or shall experience God's favor and salvation, his blessedness altogether apart from his outward condition" (*ibid.*). This is why the Christian is indifferent to the praises or curses of men. All he cares for is to please God, for he knows that on this his blessedness depends. Blessedness for the Christian does not depend on his being on good terms with everyone, at the sacrifice of godly principles, but on being in harmony with God. This is why a Christian can be persecuted and happy, poor and happy, hungry and happy, assailed as a malefactor and still give praise to God. Only a Christian can do this. And such a man God calls blessed, for he views what the world calls disappointments as God's appointments for his life, and he is satisfied with them.

> "Disappointment—His appointment,"
>   Change one letter, then I see
> That the thwarting of my purpose
>   Is God's better choice for me.
> His appointment must be blessing,
>   Tho' it may come in disguise,
> For the end from the beginning
>   Open to His wisdom lies.

"Disappointment—His appointment,"
  "No good will He withhold";
From denials oft we gather
  Treasures of His love untold.
Well He knows each broken purpose
  Leads to fuller, deeper trust,
And the end of all His dealings
  Proves our God is wise and just.

"Disappointment—His appointment,"
  Lord, I take it, then, as such,
Like the clay in hands of potter,
  Yielding wholly to Thy touch.
All my life's plan is Thy molding,
  Not one single choice be mine;
Let me answer, unrepining—
  "Father, not my will, but Thine."

If you as a Christian can say that, you are blessed, no matter what may happen to you from without. The Lord never actually promised us happiness, because that depends upon chance. He promised us blessedness, for that depends upon Christ within and is the portion of those who have no will but God's will, which they accept and rejoice over.

A fortunate person may be happy, but a happy person is not necessarily a blessed one. We cannot always have good luck, but we can always be blessed, for our Lord said, "Lo, I am with you alway" (Matt. 28:20). "In the world ye shall have tribulation: but be of good cheer; I have overcome the world" (John 16:33). Fortune cannot always be on our side, but Christ can. The indwelling Christ cannot be affected by the world that He created and governs. It is indeed blessed to possess Him and be possessed by Him.

President Theodore Roosevelt, who was very near-sighted, always carried with him two pairs of glasses of different strength, one for near and one for far vision. Bifocals were unknown at that time. During his last great political campaign, while in the city of Milwaukee, he was shot by a man called Schrenk. The surgeon who examined his wound handed him his steel spectacle case with the remark that its presence in his vest pocket had saved his life. The case had broken the force of the bullet and deflected it from his heart.

"Well, now, that's strange," said Mr. Roosevelt as he took the case with the shattered spectacles. "I've always considered the burden and handicap of having to carry those two pairs of glasses, especially these heavy ones that were in this case, as a very sore one, and here at last they have been the means of saving my life."

We may not always know in this life the reasons for the handicaps with which we have been afflicted. Quite often they turn out to be blessings in disguise. Milton, blind, was more of a poet than when he had his full sight. The imprisoned Bunyan wrote for the ages to come. A man may be slowed up by lameness so that he lives much longer to continue his work. We have countless evidences that God is in the events of our lives to a greater extent than most of us imagine.

It may be that you should thank the Lord for some failure, loss, bereavement, or sickness in your life. Perhaps it was more of a blessing than you realized at the time. It may have been that God was working within you instead of the devil working against you as you thought. To be blessed is to live in a dark world with the light of Christ within. Do you have that light? Without it you cannot find your way.

CAN MAN BLESS GOD?
AND HOW DOES GOD BLESS MAN?

⟨∾⟩

How can man bless God and at the same time be blessed by Him? How can God be at the same time the subject and object of man's blessing?

It is unfortunate that two distinct Greek words in the New Testament have been translated by the one English word "bless" in most cases. The first is *makarizoo*, the verb from which we get the adjective *makarios*, "blessed," used in the Beatitudes. The second is the verb *eulogeoo*, which does not appear in the Beatitudes in its adjectival form. Man is never said to *makarizei* (bless) God, using the Beatitude word, but to *eulogei* (eulogize) Him. Since blessedness as expressed in the Beatitudes is a quality of character belonging intrinsically to God, it is impossible for man to impart it to Him. Only God can impart blessedness; no one can make Him blessed. It is not in this sense that we can bless God. Nothing that man can do or say can add to the already perfect character of God.

But there is a sense in which man can bless God in a manner pleasing to Him, and that is when he eulogizes Him. This is really the meaning of the verb *eulogeoo*, commonly translated "to bless." It literally means "to speak well of." And certainly we ought to speak well of God, which is equivalent to praising and thanking Him. We must do this at all times, under all circumstances, and never "blame" Him for anything that may befall us.

Also, when we ask God to bless us, we do not ask Him to do it in the sense of the word *makarizoo*, as used in the Beatitudes, but in the sense of the verb *eulogeoo*. It is never said in the New Testament that God

23

makes us "blessed," *makarious*. Why? Because, as we have seen in our previous studies, the "blessedness" spoken of in the Beatitudes is not a commodity to be sought from God or to be given by God at our request, but is the by-product, the result, of the fulfillment of certain conditions that the Lord has set before us.

Only twice does the verb *makarizoo*, "to bless" as used in the Beatitudes, occur in the New Testament.

The first occurrence is in Luke 1:48, where Mary the Virgin, on becoming aware of the fact that she was to be the mother of the Lord Jesus, says, "For he hath regarded the low estate of his handmaiden: for, behold, from henceforth all generations shall call me blessed." Actually, it is the future tense of the verb *makarizoo* that is used here; and what is declared is that Mary has become the recipient of the life of God, since blessedness is an exclusive characteristic of God that He conveys to man when He indwells him.

The second use of this verb in the New Testament is in James 5:11, which speaks of the afflicted and the persecuted. "Behold," says James, "we count them happy which endure." The Greek word for "happy" here is the verbal form *makarizomen*, which should better be translated "we declare them blessed," we declare them as having the life of God. When men are afflicted, we should not conclude that they are devoid of the life of God. When God is within, we may expect pressure from without.

When we pray, we never ask God to make us "blessed" (*makarious*), in the sense of the word as used in the Beatitudes. The blessings of God that we seek have nothing to do with the blessedness that our Lord spoke about in the Sermon on the Mount. What do we mean, then, when we ask God to bless us and others? The Greek word that conveys our actual meaning here is

24

eulogeoo, "to bless, to speak well of."

It is obvious that when we pray "God, bless me," we make God the Subject who bestows the blessing and ourselves the object of it. He is the Giver and we are the recipients. Now, how can God speak well of us, and why should we ask Him to do so? Isn't it rather presumptuous and beside the point for man to ask God to speak well of him?

In His Word, God gives man certain general promises. These promises are like money in the bank. They are in the reservoir of God. They can become ours only as we claim them, and this we can do only as children of God who have the right of free access to Him. Stating it as simply as possible, we might say that, whenever we ask God to bless us, we actually ask Him to personalize His blessings to us. "Bless us, Lord"—make Thy promises applicable to us individually.

What we actually seek from God when we ask Him to bless us is His favor and grace. The fact that we realize our need for it presupposes a realization of our emptiness and sinfulness. It is as if we realized that God would be justified in speaking evil of us, so we beseech Him instead to speak well of us. "Lord, speak a good word for me; I know I do not deserve it."

In several places in the Septuagint (Greek) Version of the Old Testament, this word is used in connection with other promises of God. As we examine them, we shall come to realize a little closer the meaning of the word "blessing."

In Genesis 12:2, we read of the promise God gave to Abram, "And I will make of thee a great nation, and I will bless thee, and make thy name great; and thou shalt be a blessing." Here the blessing of God is synonymous with the making of Abram's name great. Abram did not seek to make his own name great, as so many are desperately trying to do. A great name is not something we deserve or can achieve, but is the gift of God conferred upon us. Let us cease striving for greatness. It has to come from God.

Then, in Genesis 17:20, we have the promise of God to Ishmael, "Behold, I have blessed him, and will make him fruitful, and will multiply him exceedingly." And to Abraham the angel of the Lord said, "In blessing I will bless thee, and in multiplying I will multiply thy seed as the stars of the heaven, and as the sand which is upon the sea shore" (22:17). Our ability to multiply and increase is a direct blessing of God and not our achievement. Here is an instance of the sovereign grace of God becoming particularly individualized.

We could give many more references in which the blessing of God is sought, but these will suffice to show that when we pray for blessing on our lives we confess our emptiness and invite God to fill us.

Though the actual Greek word refers to God speaking well of us, we must remember that God's words are God's actions. Whenever God speaks, energy is released. Read the first chapter of Genesis to see how much power there is in everything God says. "And God said, Let there be light: and there was light" (1:3). When God speaks concerning us, something happens in our lives.

It is interesting to note that the same word, in its adjectival form, is used in Matthew 25:34. "Then shall the King say unto them on his right hand, Come, ye blessed of my Father, inherit the kingdom prepared for you from the foundation of the world." In the original Greek, the word translated "blessed" is *eulogeemenoi*, and it means those for whom the promises—these specific promises of God concerning the Kingdom— were made. Here Christ was speaking of the time for the fulfillment of His promises.

Do you remember how Peter concludes his sermon concerning the covenants or promises of God? "Unto you first God, having raised up his Son Jesus, sent him to bless you, in turning away every one of you from his iniquities" (Acts 3:26). This was spoken to the Jews whom Peter was seeking to lead to a belief on the Lord Jesus Christ. How could God bless them? In fulfilling His promise of a Messiah to them. This is what is meant by the phrase, "Sent him to bless you." It was to fulfill His promise to them. And truly, the Lord Jesus Christ was God's fulfillment of His promise to the Jews.

Next consider that marvelous verse, Ephesians 1:3, "Blessed be the God and Father of our Lord Jesus Christ, who hath blessed us with all spiritual blessings in heavenly places in Christ." Paul here is speaking of the heavenly life that God has promised to each believer through Christ.

In all these instances, *eulogeoo,* in one form or another, is the word used, and it invariably refers to God's activity in our lives. That is exactly what is meant by our asking God to bless us: we beseech Him to demonstrate His activity in our lives. We must clearly recognize, however, that His promises for us do not always assure us of receiving what we want, but what He wants for our lives. We assume a great responsibility when we ask God to bless us. In so doing, we show a willingness to accept His will for our lives, rather than to impose our will on Him for our own purposes. When we realize that, we may not always be too anxious for the blessing of God upon us. But from experience we can say that His blessing upon us, whether it brings something we want or do not want, is best for us, since it helps to conform us to His heavenly image. If the Captain of our salvation was made perfect through suffering, how much more do we need life's purifying and chastening experiences! (Heb. 2:10.) What He chose for Himself, as the perfect way, may be the perfect blessing for us. He knows best, and that is what we acknowledge when we ask Him to bless us.

A Persian legend tells us that a certain king needed a faithful servant and had to choose between two candidates for the office. He took both at fixed wages and told them to fill a basket with water from a neighboring well, saying that he would come in the evening to inspect their work. After dumping one or two buckets of water into the basket, one of the men said, "What is the good of doing this useless work? As soon as we put the water in one side, it runs out the other." The other answered, "But we have our wages, haven't we? The use is the master's business, not ours." "I am not going to do such fool's work," replied the other; and throwing down his bucket he went away. The other man continued until he had drained the well. Looking down into it he saw something shining at the bottom, which proved to be a diamond ring. "Now I see the use of pouring water into a basket!" he exclaimed. "If the bucket had brought up the ring before the well was dry, it would have been found in the basket. Our work was not useless." Remember, when God's blessing does not fully coincide with your expectations, wait until the well is dry. There may be a diamond ring at the bottom.

Think twice every time you ask God to bless you. You are asking for His promises to be fulfilled in your individual life, and they bring both sunshine and rain. Both are needed. They are both God's actions to promote our spiritual well-being.

IS IT RIGHT FOR US TO ASK GOD
TO BLESS "THINGS"?

When we pray, we ask God not only to bless us and our friends, but also the food that is set before us on the table and many other things that relate to life. Can inanimate things also be blessed?

When we ask God to bless certain things, we are asking Him to consecrate them as instruments in the ultimate accomplishment of His will. God does not ask us to consecrate ourselves only, but all that belongs to us. It was the Lord Himself who said to Israel, "And ye shall serve the Lord your God, and he shall bless thy bread, and thy water; and I will take sickness away from the midst of thee" (Exod. 23:25). There is a blessing for our bread and water. What does that mean? That even the material means of life may contribute to the exaltation of the Lord in our lives.

We ask God to bless our food, our work, everything that affects our lives. But let us take care that in so doing we are not interjecting our desire to have our own way with things. Those who do not acknowledge God in their lives do not stop to ask His blessing on the food they eat or the water they drink. Why? Because they take the common things of life as matters of course instead of as gifts from God. They do not recognize their possessions as instruments through which God can work and accomplish His purposes. The food that I take can make me strong to do either good or evil. I have power to take and eat it, but it is only the grace of God that enables the food that my hands bring to my mouth to contribute to my ultimate good, which is the glory of God my Creator.

29

As we have seen, the Christian religion presents a paradox that the world cannot understand: that a person may be poor and blessed and also rich and blessed. On the other hand, he may be poor and miserable and also rich and miserable. In Luke 6, the Lord tells us that those who are poor and hungry for Jesus' sake can be blessed. This leads us to believe that God may not always give riches and prosperity in answer to our prayers for blessing upon the material things of life, but poverty and adversity. God can be exalted through these and work in our lives through them. When we acknowledge that what we are and what we have are only what God permits us to be and have, we can then ask His blessing upon them. Thus we can pray, "Lord, use my poverty, my riches, my health, my sickness." The Christian is the only person who can do this.

By blessing our handiwork, God may sometimes spoil our plans. But we shall be happy if we accept His actions. Let us not ask Him to bless the things we undertake for Him unless we are willing to have Him interfere—either in accordance with or contrary to our expectations. God does not have to conform His blessings to our expectations. Our knowledge of life is very limited, but God always takes the long-range view. He does not look upon failure as the end of our hopes, but as a stepping-stone to the accomplishment of His purpose in our lives. Deprivation of a luxury or even a necessity may turn out to be a blessing for us. The spoiling of our human plans may spell the salvation of our lives for higher and mightier things.

When Sir James Thornhill painted the cupola of that world-famous structure, St. Paul's Cathedral, in London, he was obliged to work while standing on a swinging scaffold far above the pavement. One day, when he had finished a detail on which he had spent days of painstaking effort, he paused to evaluate his work. So well had he succeeded in his task that he was lost in wonder and admiration. As he stood there gazing at the structure, he began to move backward to get a better view, forgetting where he was. Another artist, becoming suddenly aware that one more backward step would mean a fatal fall, made a sweeping stroke across the picture with his brush. The bemused artist stopped and rushed forward, crying out in anger and dismay; but when his companion explained his strange action, he burst into expressions of gratitude.

This is an excellent illustration of how God blesses the material things in our lives and why we should ask Him to bless them. We thus acknowledge His partnership. Before we leave for work in the morning, we may pray, "Lord, bless everything I do today," perhaps going into particulars and mentioning certain activities individually. There are two possible outcomes: Either our plans will turn out as we hoped or they will fail. Having asked God to bless, we asked Him to be a partner. We realized that we could not possibly accomplish anything of our own power and will. It is as if we were saying, "Lord, take over; use me as Thy instrument in accomplishing Thy purpose."

Only if that is our attitude shall we have the grace to praise God whatever the outcome may be. If we succeed, we shall give Him all the credit. If we fail, we shall take it that He has something different in mind for us. Immediately, we shall seek the lesson that is hidden in the failure, though what we did was what we believed to be proper and right according to the general counsel and direction of God in our lives.

There is a danger in success that we sometimes fail to recognize, as in the case of this famous artist. God directs us to ask for His blessing upon our work so that we may not be tempted to take too much credit for the outcome, but give the glory to God. What we admire, God sometimes has to use His brush upon in order to save our very lives. God's brush of effacement is more of a blessing than we think.

A gentleman of wealth, but a stranger to a personal knowledge of God, was walking alone through his grounds one evening. Coming to the mean hut of a poor man with a large family, who earned their bread by his daily labor, he heard the continuous sound of loud speaking. Curiosity prompted him to stop and listen. The man of the house happened to be at prayer with his family. As soon as he could distinguish the words, he heard him give thanks to God for the goodness of His providence in giving them food to eat and raiment to put on, and in supplying them with what was necessary and comfortable in the present life. He was immediately struck with astonishment and confusion, and said to himself, "Does this poor man, who has nothing but the meanest fare, and that purchased by hard work, give thanks to God for His goodness to himself and family; and I, who enjoy ease and honor, and everything that is pleasant and desirable, have hardly ever bent my knee or made any acknowledgment to my Maker and Preserver?" This incident was the means used by God to bring this rich man to a realization of his lack of what makes a person really blessed. And it was not long before he accepted the Lord Jesus Christ, whose blessing is evidenced in both poverty and riches.

In the feeding of the four thousand, we find that the Lord Jesus took the seven fishes and blessed them (Mark 8:7). The word here is *eulogeesas*, "having spoken well of." He did the same thing when He fed the five thousand. Why was that? Why did the bread and fish need blessing in the hand of the Lord Jesus Christ? John, in his Gospel, instead of *eulogeesen*, "blessed," says *eucharis-*

teesas, "having given thanks." This shows that, when the Lord asked His Father to bless this little food, He was at the same time thanking Him for it. Here is the interaction and perfect cooperation of heaven and earth. Man's little in the hands of God becomes sufficient so that we can give thanks for it. Thus, when we ask God to bless the food that we have, it is the same as thanking Him for it, for we recognize that it is only through Him we have received it and will find it sufficient to meet our needs and even exceed them. There is sufficiency in thankfulness and there is sufficiency when God is recognized as the Giver.

The Talmud says with great wisdom, "He who enjoys aught without thanksgiving is as though He robbed God." Therefore, in asking God to bless whatever pertains to life, let us remember that we are asking Him to have His way and must therefore be satisfied with whatever He brings about. By asking God to be our partner and bless all we have and do, we are asking Him to interfere. And when He does, let us thank Him, whether the results please or displease us. Don't ask God to bless anything unless you really mean what you say.

33

WHAT MAKES A MAN RICH?

The Lord Jesus realistically acknowledged the existence of both poverty and riches—in the physical realm as well as the spiritual. One may be poor in matters of the mind and spirit as well as in material possessions, or one can be rich in mind and spirit as well as in material possessions.

The Lord Jesus never sought to abolish these two classes of people. He accepted them as part and parcel of the framework of society, inherent in the nature of things. It may be that we view the matter differently, that we feel people and things should be equal in all respects, that there is some inequity here. We are dissatisfied with the *status quo*. If it is because we feel we are living selfishly, and should be more willing to help our less fortunate neighbor, all well and good. But if we feel resentment toward God for this state of affairs, we have not thought it through.

God created man sinless and perfect; but man from Adam on down chose to disobey God and run his own life. This present world of inequity is a result of man's mismanagement. Yet, in a sense, God's will does prevail, for the natural laws of cause and effect are His, and He does not suspend them even when the results are evil. Man has sinned, and in consequence must learn that he has to live with the results of sin. Blaming God for the poverty and tragedy of life is to reason like a child, petulantly complaining that God should let us reap good where we have sown evil. What kind of Father would He be to do that? He would simply be encouraging us to go ahead and live as selfishly and immorally as we pleased.

As we read the New Testament carefully, we do not

find the Lord Jesus commanding us either to embrace poverty or pursue riches. He is deeply concerned about what we are; but what we possess interests Him only insofar as it affects what we are or could become. There is, of course, a relationship of cause and effect between what we are and what we have, as well as between what we are and what we do.

What the Lord Jesus teaches in the Gospels is that it is possible to be happy or unhappy whether one is rich or poor. Neither riches nor poverty should be pursued for their own sake. It is a sin for the poor man to have as his ruling passion in life the desire to become rich, as well as for the rich man to set his heart on the preservation of his wealth.

Search the Scriptures as you will, you cannot find a Beatitude reading, "Blessed are the rich." Why? Because to most men this is self-evident. It is a generally held belief that the rich are fortunate, that favorable circumstances are equivalent to blessedness.

Here is where the teaching of the Lord Jesus fundamentally differs from the viewpoint of the world, for He taught that blessedness depends, not upon the circumstances of life, but upon the relationship of man's spirit with the Spirit of God. He sought to show men that the Christian is not circumstance-conditioned but God-conditioned. Whatever his circumstances may be—riches or poverty—as long as his spirit is united with the Spirit of God, as long as God dwells in his heart through Jesus Christ, he is blessed. Blessedness is not an inner reaction to external conditions, but is the work of God's grace in the human heart.

If the Lord had said, "Blessed are the rich," people would have thought He meant, "Blessed are ye because of riches." He would have given the impression that riches are what bring blessedness. This is what the natural man expects and believes. But the Lord came to introduce a new state of affairs, the kingdom of the spiritual man within the physical world, a King-dom within a kingdom. The general tenor of the Word of God is that it is possible to be blessed in spite of one's riches.

But if there is one thing more than another that wears people down, it is physical poverty. The great masses of people—past, present, and future—have been, are, and will be poor, despite all man's efforts to bring in a golden age. To this majority the Lord Jesus came with the message, "A man's life consisteth not in the abundance of the things which he possesseth" (Luke 12:15). Poverty is just one of the adversities of life, and Scripture tells us that no adversity can rob a man of his divine blessedness.

As William Hubbard said, "In the Bible the word 'poor' is sacred. It is one of the holiest words in the Holy Book. It is, I think, never used in a bad or depreciatory sense, nor as a term of reproach and contempt . . . The Bible, whatever else it is not, is, beyond doubt or question, the poor man's friend." (*The Christian World Pulpit, Vol. XV, p.* 49.) Why? Because it combats the generally held notion that the poor are always miserable. That which the world considers miserable is blessed when it is God-controlled and God-ordained. The rich man should not feel proud of his riches, for they produce no blessedness; and the poor man should not bewail his poverty, for it in no way hinders blessedness. This is the fundamental teaching of the Lord Jesus on poverty and riches.

In Matthew 5:3, the Lord Jesus says, "Blessed are the poor in spirit: for theirs is the kingdom of heaven." Then in Luke 6:20 we find Him saying, "Blessed be ye poor: for yours is the kingdom of God." Why are the two renderings different? Did one of the two evangelists report our Lord's words inaccurately? Are the historical records mistaken?

36

Scholars have argued interminably over whether the Beatitudes as we find them in Matthew's Gospel refer to the same utterances of our Lord as those found in the Gospel of Luke; or whether Matthew and Luke record similar but different teachings. We do not have time or space to go into these arguments, but our own conclusion, based on considerable study, is that the pronouncements that we find in the Beatitudes of Matthew and Luke, although similar, were spoken at different times and on many occasions. In Luke 6:20 it is quite evident that the Lord is speaking about the physical circumstances of life —poverty, hunger, tears—as contrasted with material riches. The passage in Luke does not refer to spiritual values but to physical circumstances. Matthew 5:3, however, speaks of the spiritual condition of man. In Luke the Lord speaks of physical poverty, and in Matthew of poverty of the spirit, which means humility. Why should not the Lord Jesus Christ have spoken about both at different times? He was concerned about both body and soul, the stomach and the mind, the pocketbook and the heart. He was always realistic. He recognized that the body can be the tabernacle of the Holy Spirit, and that souls are created in bodies and are not independent of them. When He saw the multitudes physically hungry, He fed them with bread and fishes, not with spiritual counsel only. The Lord Jesus knows that it takes food for the body and the Word of God for the soul. He does not confuse the two. He recognizes that man is composed of both matter and spirit. He has something to tell us about both, and about how their interaction may or may not affect our blessedness. He says, "You can be physically poor and still be blessed. But you must be humble in spirit if you want divine blessedness to dwell in your heart."

We must bear clearly in mind the meaning of the Greek word *makarioi*, "blessed." It is not synonymous with the word *eutucheis*, "happy," those who have good luck or enjoy favorable circumstances. The word *makarioi*, as explained in detail in previous studies, refers to a condition created in the Christian's heart by God, through Christ's indwelling. This blessedness is not affected by riches or poverty. As they were powerless to effect this blessedness, neither can they alter it. Happiness, as the world understands it, is conditioned by circumstances, but blessedness is God-conditioned. Therefore we cannot say that riches are a blessing and poverty a curse. If the one possessing them is a Christian—and therefore a blessed person—they will not be his masters but his servants. Both states can be used to the glory of God. The rich Christian, through the sanctification of his wealth, can use it to increase the by-products of blessedness. The poor believer can demonstrate by his cheerfulness that God's grace makes any state in life a blessed one. No one is blessed because he is rich; he is blessed because he is a Christian. And because he is, his riches are not a curse but a blessing. Nor is anyone blessed because he is poor; he is blessed because of the presence of Christ in his heart. Therefore his poverty can never detract one iota from his blessedness. It may even add to it by causing him to depend more wholly upon the Lord, thus producing the conditions of greater blessedness.

Too much stress cannot be placed on the fact that blessedness in either case is not the result of a conscious and voluntary striving for riches or poverty, but is the by-product of fulfilling the conditions of a Christlike life. We should not throw ourselves into the clutches of abject poverty, nor should we court persecution, so that we may obtain greater blessedness. We must be wary of selfish motives even in our obedience to the commands of the Lord Jesus. Christian ethics frowns on giving so that we shall some day receive a reward from the Lord. Such rewards may and will come, our Lord has assured us; but our actions should be inspired, not by hope of reward, but by love of the Lord Jesus, who first loved us and gave Himself for us. What parent would want children who obeyed him only for what they could get out of him? We want our children to obey us because they love us. Don't you think God expects the same thing?

THE TWO KINDS OF POVERTY

We have said that some scholars try to reconcile the Beatitudes as given by Matthew and Luke by saying that they represent identical principles given on identical occasions. But is this conclusion justifiable?

Consider the preacher of today. Sometimes he preaches a whole sermon to meet a particular need in his audience. But nothing is to hinder him from repeating some of his thoughts, especially the outstanding ones, in identical or varied words, in exhortations that he may give at other times and places. We believe that this is what produced these two accounts.

In the Gospel of Matthew the Lord gave a complete message, or it may be several messages on various occasions, perhaps in the same place. Matthew compiled these into the three chapters we know as the Sermon on the Mount. But Luke, with a particular audience in mind, selects from the multiplicity of Christ's teachings only those Beatitudes that will meet the need of those to whom he writes.

It is our conclusion, therefore, that the Lord must have said both "Blessed are the poor in spirit: for theirs is the kingdom of heaven" (Matt. 5:3) and "Blessed be ye poor: for yours is the kingdom of God" (Luke 6:20). Can not both be true? Does not the word "blessed" apply to both conditions? Why say that Matthew and Luke meant the same thing, but that one or the other altered our Lord's words to suit his own particular purposes?

We must remember that Matthew wrote primarily, but not exclusively, for the Jews, and that Luke wrote primarily, but not exclusively, for the gentiles. The primary purpose for which each wrote had a bearing on their selection of specific incidents and sayings in our Lord's ministry. Matthew wrote to prove that the Lord Jesus was the expected Messiah of the Jews, the Anointed One of the Lord. The Jews thought that the Kingdom of God would be a literal, earthly kingdom. But Matthew presents the Lord Jesus as One whose kingdom is primarily, but not exclusively, spiritual. The time will come for a literal Kingdom of God upon earth, but this will be in connection with the Second Coming of the Lord and not the first. His first coming was for the purpose of establishing the Kingdom of Heaven in men's hearts. But His disciples could not or did not want to understand this.

In the 14th chapter of Matthew, we read that the Lord crossed the Sea of Galilee to find a solitary place for rest and meditation. But the crowds heard where He was going and walked around the seashore to meet Him. They would not let Him alone. He cured their sick and performed other miracles. When it began to grow dark, His disciples asked Him to dismiss the people so that they could go and find something to eat. But the Lord decided to feed them Himself by the miracle of multiplying the loaves and fishes. There were five thousand men, not counting the women and children. What a crowd!

Now we come to something very strange indeed. Nowadays, after an evangelist preaches the Gospel, he tries to leave his assistants behind to follow up those who have in some way responded to his message. The disciples of the Lord Jesus were available to do this work. But we do not find Him telling them to stay on with the crowd and instruct them further regarding the Kingdom of Heaven. Instead He sends them away. Verse 22 tells us, "And straightway Jesus obliged (or forced) his disciples to get into the boat, and to go before him to the other side, until he dismissed the crowds" (author's translation from the Greek). Why? It is not hard to surmise. The miracle of the feeding of the thousands of hungry people had impressed everyone so much that they were probably eager to declare the Lord Jesus Christ as their political leader and liberator.

"Here is the Kingdom of God come to us in actuality," they must have reasoned. "Let us make this man King over us. No one ever manifested such power among us." And how would the disciples respond to this? They were human, too. No doubt many of them looked for personal aggrandizement. They showed it on more than one occasion. It would have been natural for them to think, "If the Master is made King, then we shall surely be given prominent places in His government on earth. After all, why wait any longer for the Kingdom to come, when we can wield power here and now? A bird in the hand is worth two in the bush. Let us have the earthly Kingdom of the Messiah right now." Perhaps they were in the vanguard of those who egged on the crowds to begin agitating for Jesus Christ to assume His throne as an earthly King.

The Lord could not allow them to proceed further in their ignorance and carnality. But are we any better than they? We seek exalted positions here instead of waiting for our heavenly glorification. The Lord must have grown angry with their shortsightedness. This is implied by the use of the verb *eenangasen*, which means "forced them, compelled them," possibly even by physical means. "Go away," He must have said to them, "you who seek to make me King so that you can have prominent positions of authority. The Kingdom I have come to establish at this time is a spiritual one."

Thus, Matthew selects those Beatitudes that stress the spiritual conditions necessary for the disciples of Christ to enjoy the highest possible blessedness available here on earth. Note the following qualities emphasized in Matthew, and you will find that they are all spiritual.

Poverty of spirit, i.e., humility

Mourning, i.e., sorrow of soul

Meekness, i.e., gentleness of spirit

Hunger and thirst for righteousness or justice

Mercy, pity for others

Purity of heart

Peace-making

Endurance under persecution

Is there anything physical about these conditions? No, they are all qualities of the mind and heart. A person having these spiritual qualities is divinely blessed. But the possession of these qualities is not independent of Him who gave them. God's blessing upon man, which is actually to be equated with God's grace and salvation, is never the result of what we are or do, but solely the result of what God did and does for us, freely offered to us in Christ. To be *makarios*, "blessed," is to have the character and qualities of God in us, through the indwelling of Jesus Christ in our hearts as a result of the miracle of the new birth.

Blessedness is life, the life of God in us. But that life has to grow. We must become aware of the One who gave us life. Every one of these spiritual conditions can only be fulfilled by a child of God who is already blessed by having God in him through Jesus Christ. These eight steps that Matthew gives us are eight rungs on a ladder, as it were, to make our blessedness more blessed. Just as sin can become more sinful, so blessedness can become more blessed. There is progress in the Christian life, and that progress depends on the fulfillment of certain spiritual conditions. Matthew stresses these in order to counteract the earthly-mindedness of the Jews, to whom he is primarily addressing his Gospel. We remember that the disciples also were Jews. This explains the stress on the spiritual conditions and qualities of Christ's spiritual Kingdom, a Kingdom of blessedness.

But Luke wrote primarily to bring out the humanity of the Lord Jesus. He wrote mainly to gentiles, who were not possessed with a yearning for the political kingship of the Messiah. It was a matter of complete indifference to them. But they were attached to material things. They wanted to be rich, feeling that this in itself would be a blessed state. The Lord wants to disabuse them of this notion.

The disciples, too, had to be impressed with the humanity of the Lord Jesus Christ as they experienced hunger, physical poverty, and bodily suffering. Luke presents the Lord as most interested in our physical afflictions for His sake. He tasted deeply of physical affliction, and our taste of it should not make our Christian blessedness less blessed, but more blessed. This is the message of Luke.

The Gospel of Luke can truly be called the Gospel to the poor. Only Luke mentions the Lord's declaration of purpose in the synagogue in Nazareth: "The Spirit of the Lord . . . anointed me to preach the gospel to the poor" (Luke 4:18). When the Lord Jesus received the disciples of John the Baptist, who at a time of great physical affliction doubted the deity and messiahship of the Lord, He told them to go and tell their imprisoned master, "To the poor the gospel is preached" (Luke 7:22). Only Luke tells of the rich man and the beggar (Luke 16:19-31). And in quoting some of the Beatitudes uttered by the Lord Jesus, Luke selects those that deal with physical suffering. He does not choose the Beatitude in which our Lord says, "Blessed are the poor in spirit," as Matthew does, but quotes the one in which Jesus says, "Blessed be ye poor"—poor in material things.

Blessedness comes to us both as a result of our state
44

of mind and heart and as a result of the state of our bodies. We are a union of both, and the Lord Jesus recognized it. He spoke about the relationship of both as they influence our communion with God within us, for that, after all, is what blessedness means.

IS THERE ANY MERIT IN BEING POOR?

It is our purpose in this series of studies to examine both physical and spiritual poverty to see whether they are a blessing or a curse. Let us first consider the blessing of physical poverty as spoken of by Luke (chapter 6, verses 20-26). Here is his account of the Beatitudes of the Lord Jesus referring primarily to physical hunger and privation. We say primarily, because it is impossible to separate the spirit from the body and the body from the spirit. One reacts on the other. Our bodies react to mental strain and our minds and hearts react to physical strain.

> And he [the Lord Jesus] lifted up his eyes on his disciples, and said,
>
> Blessed be ye poor: for yours is the kingdom of God.
>
> Blessed are ye that hunger now: for ye shall be filled.
>
> Blessed are ye that weep now: for ye shall laugh.
>
> Blessed are ye, when men shall hate you, and when they shall separate you from their company, and shall reproach you, and cast out your name as evil, for the Son of man's sake.
>
> Rejoice ye in that day, and leap for joy: for, behold, your reward is great in heaven: for in the like manner did their fathers unto the prophets.

And then the Lord turned to the rich in the company and said,

> But woe unto you that are rich! for ye have received your consolation.

Undoubtedly, by rich here He did not mean rich in spiritual qualities, but rich in material possessions.

He then turned to those who made their stomachs their main concern and said to them,

> Woe unto you that are full! for ye shall hunger.

Full of what? Of physical food, naturally.

> Woe unto you that laugh now! for ye shall mourn and weep.

Why were they laughing? Because they had everything that could satisfy their physical desires, acquired, in many cases, no doubt, by dishonesty and oppression. Laughter and weeping are physical reactions to outside circumstances. We look upon laughter as an indication of happiness. But it is possible to weep and be blessed. This blessedness, however, is caused by the indwelling Christ.

> Woe unto you, when all men shall speak well of you! for so did their fathers to the false prophets.

It is easy to buy favorable publicity. Men speak well of the rich man far more often than of the poor. Who pays any attention to him? Men may not, but God does. This is what Christ came to tell us.

Are we to assume from this that the Lord Jesus commends poverty and suffering in our lives, in the lives of His disciples? Is poverty in itself a blessing? Is physical hunger desirable and beneficial? Are we to seek to bring sorrow and persecution upon ourselves?

A great deal of misunderstanding has arisen as to the practical teachings of the Lord Jesus Christ. Some believe that He condemned outright the possession of wealth and demanded that we renounce everything we possess, become poor, go hungry, and constantly mourn, as the

47

price of going to heaven. This is what makes some people take to the monastic life, a life of privation and asceticism. And yet, despite their self-imposed poverty, many of these men and women have not fully enjoyed the blessedness of which the Lord spoke so clearly. We can never enjoy the blessedness of the Lord to its fullest extent through self-imposed privation that has a selfish motive.

We live in a world of relative values, and everything in it must be judged, not as having intrinsic worth but for its relative value. Poverty, voluntarily embraced, is of no value in itself. Its value depends on its motive and purpose. If we embrace poverty to please the Lord Jesus Christ and to accomplish the purpose for which He came to the world—to seek and to save the lost—then it acquires value, and its by-product is blessedness.

The Lord does not felicitate people for being hungry, poor, and mournful. His approval depends on the reason for their being in such a state. The secret of this whole passage in Luke is in the closing words of verse 22, "For the Son of man's sake." We are blessed if we are poor, hungry, weeping, hated, isolated, persecuted, maligned, not through our own fault, not as a result of some crime we have committed, not because of laziness, but for the sake of the Son of man, the Lord Jesus Christ.

A similar expression is found in Matthew 5:11. This, we believe, is the foundation on which all the Beatitudes rest. The conditions mentioned by Luke and Matthew are of value and produce blessedness only if they are fulfilled for the sake of the Lord Jesus Christ, and not for our own sakes. If we live a life of poverty so that we can boast of our self-sacrifice, causing others to commend our fine example instead of exalting the Lord Jesus, then it is not for the sake of the Son of man at all.

This is the way the Lord Jesus places Himself in the center of our lives and circumstances. No one but God

48

has a right to make such a sweeping claim on our lives and loyalties. In so doing, the Lord Jesus proclaims His deity and His right to take the place of God in our hearts. When He becomes central in our lives, then we fully enjoy His presence within us, for that is the meaning of blessedness. What we actually have in the Beatitudes is Christ's claim to pre-eminence and man's contrasting lowliness. In order that we may fully enjoy God in our lives, we must voluntarily make Christ the end, the object, the inspiration, and motive of all we attempt or do.

Actually, by giving us this motive as the basis of our lives, the Lord Jesus pays a great tribute to us as human beings. All creatures possessing intelligence act from some consideration or other. They act for the sake of something. Only material things have no set and conscious purpose. The end they serve is one outside and beyond themselves. Sun, moon, and stars revolve and shine for no "sake" that they can comprehend, though they blindly accomplish, under the Divine Hand, the most benign purposes. For His pleasure they are and were created.

When you rise higher and come into the sphere of animal life, you begin to see the idea of "sake" appearing. It may be simply instinct, but still it is clearly something very like what is found in the region of humanity. You see, for example, that an animal does things for the sake of its offspring. The mother will seek food for the sake of her offspring. She will deny herself for the sake of her offspring. Natural affection is prompting animals every day to do and endure for the sake of their offspring what, apart from them, they would neither do nor endure.

And when from animals we come to man, we enter a region in which the element of "sake" is to be even more extensively in operation, for we are in the presence of intelligence, will, and moral affections; and a being so richly endowed must act for the sake of something or someone, and that which constitutes his sake, or motive, or spring, or impulse, that on account of which he acts or forbears to act, suffers or forbears to suffer, must determine the quality of his life. In other words, the higher the sake, the higher the man. If the sake is God, then the man is godly.(See Enoch Mellor, *The Hem of Christ's Garment and Other Sermons,* London, 1883, pp. 87-109.)

But can we really always act in our lives for the sake of the Lord Jesus Christ? Does the Lord speak of mere actions here in the Beatitudes, or does He speak of character—the character of blessedness? This we shall see in our next study.

CAN WE ACCEPT CHRIST'S TEACHINGS
WITHOUT ACCEPTING CHRIST?

❧⚬✦⚬❧

Different individuals react differently to the circumstances of life, but every action we perform has some motive. We may not be fully conscious of many of these motives, but underlying our life as a whole is some pervading moral concept that governs our actions, growing out of the nature of the influences most generally brought to bear upon us.

You may challenge this assertion because, on reviewing your life as a whole, you notice many inconsistencies. Nevertheless, underneath it all is a oneness that can be traced to some master consideration. Occasional ripples may be seen at times on the surface of your life that do not all lie in the same direction, and still less in the direction of the main current; but they are nothing more than the ripples you can see on a gusty day upon the surface of a river, which not only do not go very deep, but do not interfere with the settled, constant, irresistible movement of the river towards the sea. Our lives have a general tendency and direction that no mere superficial disturbances will ever avail to arrest, and that general tendency or direction indicates what is the motive—the "sake"—by which our lives are controlled.

It is a common practice, when we wish to give a condensed and summary expression of what we think about a man, to do it in a single word or phrase. We say of one, he lives for money. Meet him when you will, his one idea is money. Converse with him when you will, his talk is of money. He estimates men by their money. If he speaks to the living—What have they in the shape of money? And if he speaks of the dead—How much have they left in the shape of money? He rises early, retires late, and eats the bread of carefulness for the sake of money. And though you will find him at times performing actions that have no connection with the main drift of his life, they do not at all alter your conviction that this main drift is money.

Thus, in the Beatitudes, Christ delineates the general areas of activity in life in which we have the opportunity of demonstrating to the world the One for whose sake we live, and move, and have our being. Within these general areas, some disturbing ripples of inconsistency may arise, for we are imperfect and still in the flesh of human weakness; but, by acting generally in the way set forth in the Beatitudes, we demonstrate that God dwells within us, we show forth our blessedness.

Remember that the Greek word *makarioi*, "blessed," is used in the Beatitudes as if it were an exclamation. "Oh, the blessedness of those who are hungry for the sake of Jesus Christ! Oh, the blessedness of those who are humble because of the Lord Jesus!" And who makes this exclamation? Of course, God foretells it and forthtells it. He tells us ahead of time the result of a certain attitude on our part, and He tells us to acquire that attitude. When we are willing to go hungry, and do so for His sake, He foretells what the result will be: blessedness. And since He knows the result of the action, He commands the action. But He also wants those who observe our lives to recognize our blessedness. Others must see how we act when we go hungry for the sake of Jesus Christ and exclaim, "That man has God in him; he is blessed! He is not unhappy because he is poor or because he goes hungry for a purpose."

They must see how we act in a quarrel and say, "That man, that woman, has Christ the Peacemaker in his heart!" When the world sees a Christian humbled, mourning, gentle, hungering and thirsting after justice, merciful, pure in heart, peace-making, persecuted, hungry, poor, weeping, spoken evil of, excommunicated, all for the sake of the Lord Jesus Christ, they cannot help exclaiming with astonishment, "Oh, the blessedness of such a person! I wish I could feel the way he does when these things happen to me." And the more we act like Christ, the more of Christ people will see in us. The Lord put it very plainly when He said, "Let your light so shine before men, that they may see your good works, and glorify your Father which is in heaven" (Matt. 5:16). Observe that He said "your" Father and not "their" Father. God is not their Father. He is only the Father of those who have accepted His Son, and have thus become "blessed."

Some people have superficially concluded that the Beatitudes are merely a set of moral principles, which if a man is able to keep will assure him of heaven, eternal bliss, and salvation. Nothing is farther from the truth. We cannot isolate one verse, one Beatitude, but must consider them as a whole and let them stand on their proper foundation, on that all-important phrase, "for the Son of man's sake." This means that these principles, apart from the person of the Lord Jesus Christ, will not yield the fruit of blessedness. Happiness is circumstance-conditioned and blessedness is God-conditioned. Circumstances can make you happy, but there is only One who can make you blessed, and that is God through Jesus Christ. Happiness fluctuates with circumstances, but blessedness remains unaffected by them, for it was not produced by them in the first place.

The Beatitudes are not a mere exposition of certain truths that have an intrinsic value apart from Him who gave them. A fundamental difference between the Lord Jesus Christ and other teachers is that they teach what is true independently of themselves, while He teaches what is true because of what He is in Himself. Newton was a teacher, a great teacher of truth; but none of the truths that he taught owes its existence to him. It existed myriads of years before him, would have been discovered by others, and would be the same if Newton had died before discovering it. He uplifted a veil and disclosed what had previously been hidden; he did not create it. Apart from him, the world would go on just as it does now: light would shine, gravitation would still attract, the sun would still rise and set, the moon would still wax and wane, and the tides still throb with their mighty measured pulse from shore to shore. We have a world of scientific lore, rich, deep, varied, and ever increasing; but not one of the truths of which it consists has any personal quality, or depends in any wise for its value on the man whose genius first flashed upon it his searching light.

But while the truths of nature are not Kepler, or Newton, or Herschel, or Faraday, or Einstein, and have no vital connection with these men, the truths of Christianity are Christ. They are not revealed by Him; they are made by Him. They once did not exist at all. They constitute a world that is as much a creation as the natural universe itself. They are not true except in Christ. They express Him; He is their fountain; and apart from Him they die.

Men have striven, and do still strive, to cast off the personal from Christianity and retain what they deem essential truth. But what essential truth can you retain when you have dismissed all that pertains to the person and work of Christ? How futile, for instance, to take any one of the Beatitudes, either in Matthew or Luke, apart from their general context, and say, "Christ declared that all you need do to inherit the Kingdom of Heaven is to be humble"; or something far easier, "Become poor, physically poor, and you will secure the Kingdom of God. All you have to do is sell all you have, wear a pair of sandals, go to a monastery, and you are all set; the Kingdom is yours."

Nothing could be further removed from what the Lord Jesus Christ taught than this. You cannot retain any essential truth in any one Beatitude if you divorce it from the person and work of Christ. This is true of all doctrine. Would you retain the doctrine of the incarnation and reject God manifest in the flesh? Would you retain the doctrine of the atonement and reject Him who died as a propitiation for our sins? Would you retain the doctrine of the resurrection and reject Him who was buried and on the third day rose again? Would you retain the doctrine of heavenly blessedness and reject Him who said, "I go to prepare a place for you?"

You cannot retain the essential and reject the personal. The essential is the personal, and the personal is the essential. You cannot retain the water and reject the sea, nor light and reject the sun, moon, and stars, no more than you could retain your health and reject the atmosphere you breathe. Christianity, so far as it embodies spiritual force and motive, so far as it meets man in his sin, weakness, sorrow, and despair, is Christ—nothing less than Christ, nothing more than Christ, nothing else than Christ. It is not merely a creed, any more than a man is merely a painted skeleton. It is not a system of morals, any more than trees without roots would form a garden. Christianity has a personal voice—the voice of one person to another—the voice of Christ to man—and its voice is "for My sake, for the Son of man's sake." Take this out of the Beatitudes, and they hold no truth. (See *The Hem of Christ's Garment*, by Enoch Mellor, Second Edition, Richard D. Dickinson, London, 1883, pp. 87-109.)

WHAT DOES POOR IN SPIRIT MEAN?

Let us now look at the actual Beatitudes dealing with poverty—first as given by Matthew and then as given by Luke.

"Blessed are the poor in spirit: for theirs is the kingdom of heaven," says our Lord in Matthew 5:3.

We have already dealt extensively with the meaning of the term "blessed"—*makarioi,* in the original Greek text. "Blessedness" (*makariotees*) was a quality attributed by the ancient Greeks to the gods. The Gospel writers used this Greek word to convey Christ's teaching about the inward condition of the soul of man when it is indwelt by God through the Lord Jesus Christ in the new birth. This term was used to express the joy and happiness experienced by the dead. But Christ came to tell us that it is not necessary to wait until we are dead to enjoy the fullness of God—we can do it right here and now by having God in us—and death is merely an extension of the blessedness of life.

The ancient Greeks also used the word *makarios* to denote someone or something that is self-sufficient, that neither needs nor is dependent on the outside world for its essential sustenance. Of course, we cannot say that the Christian is self-sufficient; but, since he is indwelt by God through Jesus Christ, he becomes God-sufficient. The outer circumstances of the world can neither create the inner joy and satisfaction of his life nor can they really affect or cancel them. The Christian is God-sufficient and not circumstance-conditioned. That, in brief, is the meaning of the word *makarioi*, "blessed," as used in the Beatitudes. Don't ever equate it with the words "hap-

56

piness" or "happy," because these come from "hap," which refers to chance. The joy of the Christian's life does not depend on chance but on Providence. Chance may make you happy, but it will never make you blessed. Only God can do that.

The Lord tells us in Matthew 5:3 that those who are "poor in spirit" are blessed. The verb "are" is not found in the original Greek text, but it can be understood. The construction, however, intimates an exclamation similar to the Hebrew *ashere* that we find in Psalm 1:1 and other Psalms. "Blessed" is the opposite of *ouai*, the Greek for "woe." We could very well translate it as "Oh, the blessedness of those who are poor in spirit!"

Who makes this exclamation? First, the Lord Jesus Christ, who states that blessedness is the natural and inescapable outcome of a certain condition. It is similar to a doctor's saying, "If you rest, if you take this medicine, the result will be thus and so." That is what the Lord does here. He says that where the condition of poverty of spirit exists, the result is blessedness. This is the pronouncement of One who knows. He diagnoses, He prescribes, and He foretells the result.

What is our Lord's diagnosis of the state of the person who is asked to be poor in spirit? We can discover this as we understand the meaning of the Greek word used here, *ptoochoi*, "poor." There are two Greek words that refer to poverty, *penia* and *ptoocheia*, and their corresponding adjectives, *penees* and *ptoochos*. *Penees* occurs but once in the New Testament, in II Corinthians 9:9, and is a quotation from the Old Testament (Psalm 112:9). *Ptoochos*, however, is used between thirty and forty times. There is a distinction in the meaning of these two words. *Penees* comes from the verb *ponomai*, which is related to *ponos* ("pain") and *poneomai* ("to suffer pain"). *Penees*, therefore, means the person who is poor but earns his bread by his own labors. He has to work until he is tired to satisfy his poverty. But he *can* satisfy it himself. That is why Hesychius calls such a person *autodiakonos*, "a deacon to himself, one who can minister to himself." This word does not indicate extreme want, or that which verges upon it. It is the opposite of the rich, who needs not work to satisfy his needs.

Penees is not the word used in the Beatitudes, either in Matthew or Luke, but *ptoochos*. This is significant, because *ptoochos*, unlike *penees*, is one who is poor but does not satisfy his own needs. He depends upon other people's alms. He is like a beggar. His help and rescue must come from outside. Such was Lazarus in the story of the rich man and the beggar in Luke 16:20. He is called *ptoochos* because he was an object of charity. He depended on the mercy of others. The ancient records tell us that Plato would not endure such a man in his ideal state (Legg. XI 936c). Furthermore, *ptoochos* is also related to the verb *ptoossein*, which means "to crouch." It is the person who in his abjectness needs to crouch in the presence of his superiors.

Why did the Lord select this particular word? It was to convey His diagnosis of man. He is empty, poor, helpless. He cannot work for his own salvation. He is *ptoochos*, not *penees*. He needs crutches. He needs mercy from outside himself. And since this is the general condition of fallen man, no one from his own level, his horizontal environment, can help him. His help must come from someone who is superior, from above, from God.

Now take the meaning of the word *ptoochoi*, "poor," in conjunction with the meaning of the word *makarioi*, "blessed," as we have explained them, and you will see the beauty of the picture that unfolds before us. Man is empty. He is totally dependent upon the grace and mercy of God. But how can he acquire them? He can become blessed, which means to have God in his empty heart. But this can take place only as a result of the work of the Lord Jesus Christ. Here we have the fulfillment of the words, "for my sake," of the Lord Jesus in Matthew 5:11. It is on account of the Lord Jesus Christ, because of what He is and has done for man, that man can become blessed, full of the salvation and mercy of God.

What this Beatitude actually says is that unless man realizes his poverty (*ptoocheia*), his complete emptiness and inability to fill the void, he will not be filled. If you don't realize you are sick, you will not seek a doctor nor will you take the medicine he might prescribe. Emptiness is necessary before fullness can take place. Only as we empty ourselves of ourselves can God fill us with Himself because of Christ and on account of Him. Thus we become whole, we become blessed. With the emptying of self and the filling of Christ, blessedness ensues, the blessedness of heaven in the human heart even while here on earth. For though this earth may produce distressing circumstances, they will not affect the condition of the soul in any way. Thus we have the diagnosis, the medicine, and the result.

But it is not only the Lord Jesus who tells us we are blessed. When we become full of God, blessed, whole, and spiritually sound, the world will know it, too. They will not say, "See how happy these Christians are," but "How blessed they are! They are not happy because of the good fortune they experience but because of the presence of God in them." This blessedness is not only assured by Christ, but it is also noticed by our fellow men and will be acknowledged in exclamatory remarks to the glory of the One who made us spiritually whole.

To show that man's emptiness is spiritual and not material, that his suffering is not a physical problem but one of the soul, Matthew adds *too pneumati*, "in spirit."

"Blessed the poor in spirit." This is a locative dative, indicating the area of the emptiness. It is not the poor in material things that the Lord can satisfy but those who realize that their spiritual self is empty. (See A. T. Robertson, *A Grammar of the Greek New Testament*, p. 513.) It is as if the Lord were saying that the primary need He came to meet was that of our spirits and not of our bodies. Our bodies are important, but only insofar as they are the dwelling places of our spirits, of the immaterial but real part of our personalities. God is Spirit, and He communicates, not with our bodies, but with our spirits. We may think that our primary problems are material, but it is not so. They are spiritual, and once they are solved all will be well.

Man thinks with his mind, with his spirit. He can recognize his emptiness and his need only through his spirit, his "think part," as one little girl called it. Thought is necessary in order to come to Christ. You think of the consequences of your emptiness, that it will lead you to death. Unless you seek mercy, you are done for. Even as thought was the first thing implied in the first commandment of Christ to man, "Repent," so is it in the first Beatitude. When you think, you will discover how empty you are, how unable you are to satisfy that emptiness, and will realize that you must go to your Creator to satisfy it. You need spiritual crutches. You need a Saviour and His mercy; you need the Lord Jesus Christ.

In its final analysis, the term "poor in spirit" means humble. Only those who are humble will ever seek God and receive from Him His blessedness through Jesus Christ. It does not mean base or poor in intellectual gifts or attainments. If that were so, Christ would have been proclaiming idiots the happiest creatures in the universe, and ignorance the most blissful of all states. The man who is poor in spirit can think, and he thinks so well and so wisely that he comes to the conclusion that he is absolutely empty without God.

It is foolish not to be able to discern that the creature is unable to live independently of His Creator and stay alive. A wise man is always poor in spirit; were he full and satisfied, he would not be wise, nor would there be any chance that he should become so. When a man knows everything, nothing remains for him to learn; when he is full, he has no room for more. Very likely that man knows most of all who, after search and research, after years of application and industry, is convinced that he knows very little and must still work with might and main. That is the greatest secret a man can find out, the most helpful and the most hopeful. He is poor in spirit when he has found that out, and will soon enter upon a kingdom.

The true man of science walks with bare head bowed in the presence of his great mistress—Nature. He does not brawl to her of what he knows—not he; but in lowly attitudes he woos her still, meekly praying her to teach him more and more. However unceremoniously he may brush past our opinions and beliefs, he is reverent and humble before Nature; and when he is perfected she gives him the keys of her kingdom. Poorness in spirit is that humility which looks away from self, and depends upon the strength that is stronger and the wisdom that is wiser than we.

"Blessed are the poor in spirit: for theirs is the kingdom of heaven."

"To this man will I look," says the Lord, "even to him that is poor and of a contrite spirit, and trembleth at my word" (Isa. 66:2). Humility is the first step into the Kingdom of Heaven. Pride is the wall that keeps man out.

WILL ONLY THE POOR INHERIT
THE KINGDOM?

Having established the underlying principle that the Beatitudes are inseparably attached to the person of the Lord Jesus Christ who pronounced them, we can further assert that the primary purpose for which they were given was to show forth what He was in His essence and work.

Moses, in urging the people of Israel to an obedient and godly life, never added, "For my sake." Joshua never, in any address to the people of Israel, urged their loyalty to God for his sake. Isaiah never enforced his expostulations and exhortations by saying, "For my sake." John the Baptist never obtruded a personal consideration and said, "For my sake." There was a man who stood before judges and kings as a witness for the Gospel, who was in labors more abundant, who penned the records that for the most part have guided and sustained the faith and life of the Christian Church in all ages, who was beheaded in Rome as a martyr; but even Paul never said, "For my sake." And angels have come from heaven, and have brought messages from God, messages of warning, of instructions, of consolation; but angels never sought to strengthen the force of their communications by saying, "For my sake." Whether men or angels, they have contented themselves with fulfilling the behests of heaven, they have accounted themselves as servants of God, have hidden themselves behind the majesty of Him who alone is great, and have felt that to stand presumptuously in advance of God, or even co-ordinately at His side as if they were His co-equals, and to draw attention to their own persons by saying, "For my sake," was to insult the glory of Him who will not give His glory to another. The Lord Jesus Christ stands alone when He bids us be partakers of His grace and thus become blessed "for his sake."

The Greek word thus translated is *heneken* or *heneka,* which actually means "because of, on account of, for the sake of." The Lord says, "Because of Me you can be blessed." In other words, His declaration is twofold: 1) "Here is what I am—God incarnate." 2) "Here is what I can do for you—make you blessed, bring God to you, and cause Him to dwell within you. Your becoming blessed means that you acquire the eternal quality that belongs to God, you receive the life of God in you. And when you do that, there are certain conditions under which the blessedness that I have given you will shine forth most brightly before the world. In addition, your own blessedness will become more blessed."

Essentially, then, through the Beatitudes, the Lord Jesus declares His essence and His work. He is God incarnate. He thought it not robbery to be equal with God. He is the brightness of His Father's glory and the express image of His person. He is the Word made flesh. When He says "on my account," or "because of me," or "for my sake," He interferes with no higher authority. There is none above Him who can forbid the homage that He seeks. The Lord Jesus came to point us to God, and by pointing us to Himself He does exactly that. He is the Alpha and the Omega, the beginning and the ending, the first and the last. It is because he that hath seen the Son hath seen the Father also that we can bow at His feet and, like Thomas, when his doubts and fears were scattered and his faith established, can exclaim without fear of idolatry, "My Lord and my God!" (John 20:28). That is what the Lord Jesus is, and only as we accept Him as God can we accept His work on our behalf. The miracle of His incarnation presupposes His eternal Being as God and is necessary for the effectiveness of His redemption.

Not only is He God, but He has brought to us the possibility of having God in us by dying for us. This is the service that Christ rendered for us, our redemption. Here, by saying "on my account," or "because of me," or "for my sake," it is as if He were pointing out first of all what He did for us on the cross and through the empty tomb, as reasonable ground for asking of us the sacrifices of His Beatitudes. It is only in His doing that we can do anything at all, be blessed and fulfill any of the conditions for our growing in the life of divine blessedness.

Only as we bear this in mind can we truly understand the first Beatitude found in Matthew concerning the humble spirit and the first two in Luke concerning physical poverty and hunger.

The life of Christ was predominantly characterized by two things—humility, the emptying of His glory that He had with the Father in eternity, and sacrifice on our behalf. The first Beatitudes in Matthew and Luke tell us that we cannot be like Him unless we, too, are humble and learn to sacrifice "for his sake." If we are blessed by having Him within us, we cannot but act like Him in these two respects. When Christ spoke these words, He did not preach a blessedness that He did not enjoy.

The reason these Beatitudes are not interpreted correctly by most modern preachers is that we are afraid of their implications. We do not want to humble ourselves. We project the Beatitude about humility to the millennium instead of practicing it right here and now; expecting, of course, to experience it in its complete and perfect form only in the millennium. To take the first two Beatitudes of Luke literally for what they unmistakably mean would frighten us, lest they induce pangs of conscience for not sacrificing and if needs be going physically hungry for the sake of the Lord Jesus Christ. These Beatitudes are often preached by men who know nothing about them from actual experience, and who seem as far removed as possible from the bliss that the words of Christ insure. Many of us exert all our powers to escape them by resorting to spiritualization and by claiming that they do not apply to our present age. This is a bliss from which we run with all our might, and the further we can remove our heels from it the more blessed we esteem ourselves.

No wonder, then, that those who closely follow our lives, as they become aware of our blessedness not because of the circumstances of life but in spite of them, exclaim with wondering conviction, "Oh, the blessedness of the humble Christians! Oh, the blessedness of the Christians who go poor and hungry for the sake of their Master and His Gospel!" Humility and sacrifice are relegated to Christ only, for us to admire, instead of being considered as virtues we should allow Him to work out in us. Most Christians seem to be quite willing to do without these blessings of poverty of spirit and pocketbook.

The Saviour said, "Blessed are the poor," never "Blessed are the rich." "Blessed be ye poor!" are His words of benediction. By contrast He warns, "Verily I say unto you, That a rich man shall hardly enter into the kingdom of heaven. And again I say unto you, It is easier for a camel to go through the eye of a needle, than for a rich man to enter into the kingdom of God" (Matt. 20:23, 24). The rich man incurs enormous risks, and yet how many of us, if we had the chance, would not be eager to run them? It is frequently reckless, unChristian courage that dares to be rich; but I suppose not many of Christ's followers, despite His warning words, are without this trait. On the other hand, it is a demonstration of Christian courage to be possessed of heavenly humility and earthly poverty for the sake of the Lord Jesus Christ.

Remember, however, that the Lord Jesus Christ never taught that the poor, simply because they are poor, are the possessors of God's Kingdom. Nor are the rich, merely because they are rich, outside the Kingdom. Scoffers at the Gospel have used this Beatitude as a taunt and a gibe. The Emperor Julian, writing derisively of the Christians of his day, said that he "only wished to confiscate their goods in order that, in the character of poor men, they may enter the kingdom of heaven."

Very many, very early in the history of the Church, took this Beatitude literally, in all sincerity, and voluntarily renounced all rights of wealth or property as inconsistent with the highest claims of Him whom they called Lord, and as incompatible with the full joy and privileges of the sons of God. But we have no ground for supposing that the poor are blessed to the exclusion of the rich; nor that those in poverty are heirs of God's Kingdom irrespective of their relation to Jesus Christ. Indeed, there are poor who are utterly unblessed; and there are rich who—as did Abraham, Isaac, and Jacob— live in the smile and favor of God. We must not magnify literal poverty as if it were all, nor drop it out of sight as if it were nothing. The doctrine of voluntary poverty is not all a lie; men must often dare to be poor for Christ's sake, and such poor are certainly blessed. Seasons and conditions may make it essential, but it is not essential in itself. It may be indispensable as an accident of earthly government, or of social or commercial surroundings, but not an absolute necessity of the Christian spirit and character. Were it so, no Christian would be well-to-do, no Christian might succeed in business or commerce, nor be the possessor of lands, or houses, or cattle, nor might he engage in any productive pursuit whatever. Poverty would be a universal obligation. The supposition is a violation of common sense.

Poverty is a possibility of the Christian life as such, but not an absolute necessity, and the willingness to accept it must always be present should conditions and necessities demand it. A businessman who is a Christian must endeavor to increase his business and profits so that He can help the work of Christ that much more. The purpose sanctifies the increase of possessions. And the more man gives to God, the more God gives to man. But God's shovel is always bigger than man's. In actuality, the giving up of property to God may be of less use to Him than if we faithfully and conscientiously and profitably exploited it, so that the flow of help to God's work might be more permanent and continuous.

What Christ actually meant by these pronouncements in the Beatitudes is that the richest man in the Church must dare to be poor, should the circumstances of his generation challenge his allegiance to the Saviour on that ground. If that be, as it has been in ages gone, the true test, clearly he must consent to it.

Outward poverty, then, is not essential to this blessedness, nor is outward wealth incompatible with it. A man with a full purse may be "poor in spirit"—humble and rich in faith and an heir of the Kingdom of Heaven. On the other hand, a man poor in purse may be proud of his poverty and resentful of those who have full purses. A rich man, with his houses and lands, may still be one of the beggars to whom Christ pledges the Kingdom of Himself and the Father. He may be one of the poor whom nothing but God can satisfy, and may live holding nothing in his own right, and counting

67

himself to have nothing, but in the will and by the permission of God. Such a man, however much he owns, is one of Christ's blessed poor. Unless a person is possessed of the blessedness of the poor in spirit, unless he is humble before God, the Giver of all good and perfect gifts, though he be rich or poor in material things, he cannot be truly blessed.

The two, humility and voluntary poverty when demanded by the circumstances and exigencies of God's work, go together. The first is essential to secure the blessedness of the second, and the second is null and void without the first. God does not want proud paupers nor does He want boastful and tight-fisted men of wealth. Poverty and riches must always be a means to an end and never the end in itself. The end and purpose must be the glory of Christ. As He could not redeem us if He were not what He was—God—so our becoming poor for His sake will avail us nothing if we are not humble in heart and spirit. That is why one Gospel writer reported the blessedness of humility (a blessedness of being), and the other the blessedness of becoming poor (a blessedness of doing).

WHAT IS MEANT BY THE KINGDOM
OF HEAVEN?

Uncertainty as to the result of our actions can be torture. When we take medicine, we want to know whether it is going to help us or not. We would not take an aspirin if we did not believe it would clear up our headache. We seek out a doctor who not only knows how to diagnose our illness, but also to prescribe something that will be effective. Our eyes are constantly on the outcome of our every action. We are made that way. The habit of anticipating the end of an effort seems to be written deeply into the constitution of our beings.

The Lord Jesus Christ is fully aware of our thought processes, because, after all, He is the One who made us. He knows what is in us. He is the Master Psychologist. If we understand Him and His teaching, we shall need very little else to tell us how to order our lives aright. When He gave the Beatitudes, He did three things: He diagnosed the case, He prescribed for it, and He foretold the result of taking the prescribed medicine. There is no uncertainty whatever about the outcome. The promise of what is going to happen is given with the utmost assurance, with no "maybe's" or "but's." Take a look at these promises of the Lord Jesus in the Beatitudes:

For the humble: the Kingdom of Heaven.
For the mourning: comfort.
For the meek: an inheritance.
For the hungry after righteousness: fullness.
For the merciful: mercy for themselves.
For the pure in heart: the sight of God.
For the peacemakers: the sonship of God.
For the persecuted: the Kingdom of Heaven.

So much for the Beatitudes in Matthew. Now for those in Luke:

For the poor: the Kingdom of God.
For the hungry: fullness.
For the weeping ones: laughter.

In similar manner, there are promises of condemnation as well as promises of blessing. A doctor not only has the right to tell a patient who takes his medicine that he will get well, but also the one who refuses to take it what consequences he will suffer. Here, too, the Lord Jesus knows what He is talking about.

Since we are examining Matthew 5:3, let us look at the promise given in this first Beatitude. "Blessed are the poor in spirit: for theirs is the kingdom of heaven."

We are especially interested in the Greek word *hoti*, translated "for," which occurs in each of the eight Beatitudes in Matthew and three times in the Beatitudes given by Luke. There is no doubt that in all these instances the conjunction is causal, meaning "because." It explains the reason. Now what does it explain here? What does the clause, "for theirs is the kingdom of heaven," mean? Does it explain the word "blessed" or does it explain the condition that forms the first step toward that blessedness—poverty in spirit, humility? In other words, are we blessed because ours is the Kingdom of Heaven, or is the Kingdom ours on the condition of our being humble?

We saw that blessedness is in itself the natural consequence of humility. Not humility *per se*, but that quality of humility that causes its possessor to realize his emptiness and run to Jesus Christ. Don't forget that everything is connected to "for my sake," which the Lord pronounced at the end of these Beatitudes and which applies to all of them. Humility is the first step

70

that leads to Jesus Christ, and it is the Lord Jesus Christ as the incarnate God who confers this blessedness. The whole accomplishment revolves around the person of the Lord Jesus. All we need do is allow Him to fill us.

Actually, the first result that the Lord promised for us in these Beatitudes is His blessedness, His indwelling. This runs through all the Beatitudes. Why, then, does He give us the added promise, "for theirs is the kingdom of heaven"? Because He wants to further explain the nature of this blessedness. Your blessedness means the Kingdom of Heaven within you. "You are blessed because God dwells in you through Me," the Lord said, "and when that happens I am there as King and Lord of your life. I am there, not as a guest, but as a permanent Ruler. And, since I come from heaven, My coming into you has brought heaven to you." That's exactly what happens when a man humbles himself before God and goes to the Lord Jesus Christ for salvation. God comes into his heart and takes over His rule within him. This, succinctly, is the whole plan of God for man. This is what it means to be saved, to be born again into the Kingdom of Heaven, to have the Christ of heaven come to you, and consequently heaven itself, even while you live on this earth.

Thus, in the first of the Beatitudes in Matthew, we could really state that the conjunction *hoti* has a dual meaning; it is causal and also epexegetical—it further interprets the term "blessed." From this we conclude that the humility that leads to the Lord Jesus has two interrelated results: it makes us blessed and it brings the Kingdom of Heaven to us. We say "interrelated" because, in reality, blessedness and the Kingdom of Heaven in the human heart actually mean the same thing. They simply stress two different aspects of the total situation. Blessedness shows what God does for the humble ones who go to Christ. It describes our benefit from the transaction. This fills us with joy and peace unspeakable. But when the Lord Jesus enters our hearts, we must always recognize that we are not to order Him around, but He is to command us. We are not to establish Him as a King and then act as prime ministers, but allow Him to run both the constitutional and executive government within us.

Two more things must be said in connection with the clause, "for theirs is the kingdom of heaven." First, the verb used here is in the present and not the future tense, as in every other Beatitude in Matthew 5 that does not refer to the Kingdom of Heaven or God. In Matthew, then, only the first and the eighth Beatitudes, which refer to the Kingdom of Heaven as the promise, use the present tense: "For theirs *is* the kingdom of heaven." In Luke, only the first Beatitude is in the present tense. Why is this? All three Beatitudes whose promise is in the present tense speak of the Kingdom of Heaven or God, and, when a Beatitude promises something other than the Kingdom, the promise is always in the future tense. This is indeed suggestive. May we venture an explanation?

You will recall what we said about the meaning of the word *makarioi*, "blessed," among the ancient Greeks. It referred to the bliss of the dead, those who had departed from this earth. The Jews were predominantly looking forward to a set time when the outward Kingdom of God would be established upon this earth. And the Christians' blessed hope is that this Kingdom will be established. But the Lord does not want those who receive Him as Saviour and Lord to think that He relegates all blessing to the distant future. There is blessing for us here and now. The Kingdom of Heaven or God will be fulfilled in its literal sense in the future,

72

but it is also among us and in us now. It starts here and now and continues world without end. The moment you humble yourself, recognize your unworthiness, and go to the Lord Jesus Christ, He makes you blessed and establishes His eternal rule in you. He becomes your King.

This is further made clear by the fact that our Lord does not say, "for the world's is (or will be) the kingdom of heaven." The Lord does not speak here of the relation of heaven and earth as such. He is not referring primarily to the establishment of the Heavenly Kingdom upon this earth and of imposing His rule over believers and unbelievers, but He says, "theirs is the kingdom of heaven"—theirs individually, personally. He refers to people who have humbled themselves and come to Him.

Secondly, we believe that the particular meaning of the term "Kingdom of Heaven" or "Kingdom of God" must be sought each time in the cultural background of the speaker and the hearers, plus a consideration of the intention revealed in the total message. Sometimes these terms do refer to the millennial Kingdom and sometimes they do not. But that the two terms are equivalent in their basic meaning any serious student of Scripture cannot doubt. A clear demonstration of this is found in Matthew 19:23, 24. "Then said Jesus unto his disciples, Verily I say unto you, That a rich man shall hardly enter into the *kingdom of heaven*. And again I say unto you, It is easier for a camel to go through the eye of a needle, than for a rich man to enter into the *kingdom of God*." The Lord could not have been referring to two different kingdoms. (See discussion of this problem in article by Dr. Eugene A. Nida, in "Meaning and Translation," in the *Bible Translator*, Vol. 8, No. 3, July 1957, published by the United Bible Societies. Also see Erich Sauer, *The Triumph of the Crucified*,

73

A Survey of Historical Revelation in the New Testament, The Paternoster Press, London, 1951.)

One more thought: Not only does humility lead to Christ and therefore to blessedness and the coming of the Kingdom of Heaven within us, but it is perfected as the Lord exercises within us His full power as King. It may be that the very reason the life of the Lord Jesus within us is described as the life of a King is to make us realize that we are mere subjects. Once we have acquired our blessedness in Christ, let us not revolt and seek independence. Humility is not only the first step but also the last, and there can be no step toward the perfection of the blessedness within us without this humility. It is the basis for everything that is to follow. In the Beatitudes in Matthew, the Lord begins with Himself as the King in verse 3 and ends as the King in verse 10. Our humility and subjection to the Lord as King is the one thing that will make His stay in us comfortable and truly blessed. The very fact that we are told that the desired place of Christ within is that of a ruling King presupposes the idea that there may be outbursts of revolt. This will simply reduce the degree of our blessedness. Let us, therefore, crown Him Lord of Lords and King of Kings from start to finish. This is what is meant by the first Beatitude.

SHOULD WE EXPECT GOD TO PRAISE US?

We have finished our consideration of the first Beatitude as given by Matthew concerning poverty of spirit, humility. This concerns the spiritual aspect of man. Luke, however, deals with the material. We must face that as well.

"Blessed be ye poor: for yours is the kingdom of God" (Luke 6:20). We have already proved that this refers to physical poverty. Now let us proceed to determine its exact meaning. In what way is the man blessed who is poor in material things? This we have already covered to a great extent.

In Matthew, the Lord uses the third person when He says, "for theirs is the kingdom of heaven." But in Luke He uses the second person, apparently because He is speaking directly to His disciples. This we infer from the possessive pronoun "yours," *humetera* — even though it is not clear in the first phrase, "Blessed the poor." The word "ye" is not in the original Greek text. The literal translation is "Blessed the poor," and it is exactly the same in both Gospels, except that Matthew adds "in spirit."

Much may be learned from these differing constructions. We should remember that on both occasions there were three kinds of people present while the Lord was speaking these words. First there were the crowds of men and women who were just listeners. We do not read that the Lord or the disciples dismissed the crowds that followed Him. He had healed many among them and performed wonder-arousing miracles. Crowds are the same in every age. Surely, after witnessing such activity, no one would want to leave as long as they knew that the miracle-working Jesus was still around. Today it takes the police to disperse a small crowd that gathers around the scene of an accident. Just imagine what would happen if it were the scene of a miracle. No, the crowds were still there. But the Lord did not speak directly to them, although He wanted them to hear what He was saying to His disciples. And who would not listen who had this divinely given opportunity to eavesdrop, if you can call it that?

Secondly, there were the larger group of disciples composed of those who became adherents of the Master, those who believed on Him as their Messiah and Lord. And thirdly, there was the smaller and more intimate circle of disciples, His apostles. We believe it is to these two groups of believers that the Lord spoke directly. But although the principles He enunciated in the Beatitudes applied particularly to the lives of the disciples, they could apply also to the lives of those outside the fold of believers. Every preacher addresses himself primarily to the disciples of Christ, to the believers, but that does not mean that he does not extend an invitation to those outside of Christ to come to Him and enjoy the same blessedness that is experienced by those who have received the Son of God as their Saviour and Lord. We believe this is why the first part of these Beatitudes was phrased in a general manner and so recorded by both Matthew and Luke: "Blessed the poor in spirit," and "Blessed the poor." This is true of those who have believed, but it can also become true of all who will believe.

When the Lord spoke the words recorded in Matthew, He did not want to address the disciples in front of the listening crowds and extol their virtue of humility. The Lord is far wiser than to turn to any of us and say, "My child, congratulations on your being so humble."

We ought to be humble, but we ought not to be aware of it. If we are humble and know it, we are not humble at all. No matter how humble the Lord considers us, if we look hard enough we shall still find some trace of pride that will lead us to ask Him to humble us further. We should never be like the Pharisee who thanked the Lord for his humility. That's one thing the Lord does not ask us to thank Him for. We should always beg Him for humility, for we can never have enough. Let our actions demonstrate it, rather than our mouths proclaiming it.

There is an interesting incident in the account that Luke gives us in his 7th chapter. John the Baptist had been imprisoned for the sake of the Lord Jesus Christ. He sent his disciples to ask whether the Lord Jesus was truly the Messiah or if they were to expect One who would not permit His followers to suffer imprisonment for His sake. The Lord answered first with actions, by continuing to perform miracles, thus demonstrating to John's disciples that He was indeed a miracle-working God, the true Messiah, in spite of the fact that He allowed John to suffer for His sake. And then He sent a message to John in jail. But in verse 24 we find that the Lord waited for the disciples of the Baptist to leave before He began to praise John. He gave no praise in front of them, lest the report of it make John proud. But He voiced His praise, after John's disciples were gone, to others who could not communicate it to him.

That is why, in Matthew 5:3, the Lord speaks in the third person. Otherwise, it would have been as if He were saying right to His disciples' faces, "You are humble, you are poor in spirit: therefore you are blessed; therefore yours is the kingdom of heaven." He would certainly not do that.

But when we come to Luke, the situation is a little

different. Everybody knew that those closest to Jesus
Christ were the poorest in material possessions. A pauper
doesn't have to speak of his poverty. It is apparent. It
was probably something His followers were derided for.
"Look at these disciples of Christ. Neither their Master
nor they have anything, nor can He do anything for
them." Poverty causes our fellow men to look down on
us. The disciples needed no comfort for their spiritual
humility. That caused them no suffering from the world
in which they lived; but it is different with physical poverty and hunger. There are no pangs of humility, but
there are pangs of physical poverty and hunger. The
Lord realizes it. He experienced the same thing in His
own life, for He had nowhere to lay His head. Therefore He speaks straight to the disciples and says:

> Blessed the poor: for *yours* is the kingdom of
> God.
> Blessed the hungry: for *ye* shall be filled.
> Blessed the weeping ones now: for *ye* shall
> laugh.
> Blessed are *ye*, when men shall hate *you*, and
> they shall separate *you* from their company,
> and shall reproach *you*, and cast out *your*
> name as evil, for the Son of man's sake.
> Rejoice *ye* in that day, and leap for joy: for,
> behold, *your* reward is great in heaven: for
> in the like manner did their fathers unto the
> prophets.

This is all in the second person. But all the Beatitudes in Matthew, with the exception of verse 11, are in
the third person. Of course, these are two distinct occasions recorded by the two evangelists. And why does
not our Lord, as quoted by Matthew, use the second
person and speak directly to the disciples? Because

each of the conditions referred to, for which the natural outcome is blessedness along with something else, is a spiritual condition, which should develop in us unconsciously as a result of the grace of God within. That is why we find Matthew saying:

"Blessed are the poor in spirit: for *theirs* is the kingdom of heaven." This is humility. Only God can give it to us.

"Blessed are *they* that mourn: for *they* shall be comforted." This is soul and spirit sorrow. Only the Holy Spirit can cause it.

"Blessed are the meek: for *they* shall inherit the earth." This is the gentleness of heaven and can come only from there.

"Blessed are *they* which do hunger and thirst after righteousness: for *they* shall be filled." This is desire for the things of God and can only be divinely instilled.

"Blessed are the merciful: for *they* shall obtain mercy." This is having the same pity for men and women that God Himself has and can give.

"Blessed are the pure in heart: for *they* shall see God." This is redemption and can be accomplished only by the blood of Jesus Christ.

"Blessed are the peacemakers: for *they* shall be called the children of God." This is the peace which is the gift of God.

"Blessed are *they* which are persecuted for righteousness' sake: for *theirs* is the kingdom of heaven." This is the possession of righteousness, which is a divinely acquired quality.

The companion Beatitude, which is found in verse 11, is different. "Blessed are *ye*, when men shall revile *you*, and persecute *you*, and shall say all manner of evil against *you* falsely, for my sake." This is very much like

79

the one we find in Luke 6:22. This concerns open attacks by the world that hates Christ. Then we need the direct comfort of the Lord Jesus Christ, and He does not want us to feel that the world has the last word in our lives. This last word of Christ's is not something that would puff us up when told to our face, as would the others. It can produce no pride, but only comfort and endurance.

This, then, is the secret of why the Lord turned directly to the disciples in Luke 6 and spoke to them in the second person. It is not easy to go poor and hungry, to weep and be persecuted for the sake of the Lord Jesus Christ. We cannot help but know it. Others know it because they cause a great deal of it. But best of all, the Lord Jesus Christ takes note of it and He has something to tell us. We shall see what that is in our next study.

HOW POVERTY CAN MAKE YOU RICH

When the Lord Jesus Christ speaks of sacrifices on His behalf, we have a tendency to spiritualize His meaning. We are reluctant to make a literal and personal application. This is the most pathetic aspect of modern Christianity—the watering down of the requirements of discipleship. We have a way of getting around the obvious intent of Christ's teaching and assuaging our consciences at the same time. We want to feel we have done our utmost for Christ and at the same time retain the utmost for ourselves.

The consistency of one's daily life is the truest reflection of the state of his spirit. The Lord will not accept words as a substitute for the works of faith. Faith that is not manifested in works is dead. Now works justify no one; we are justified by faith and faith alone; but this must be a living faith that manifests itself in the works of faith. Good works must always be the product of faith, if they are to be acceptable in God's sight.

An old Methodist preacher once offered this prayer in a meeting: "Lord, help us to trust Thee with our souls." Many voices responded with a hearty, old-fashioned "Amen!" "Lord, help us to trust Thee with our bodies," he continued. Again the response was a vociferous "Amen!" Then with still more warmth he said, "And, Lord, help us to trust Thee with our money." Not an amen was heard in the house, except that of an impoverished old lady.

"Blessed the poor," the Lord said. "Blessed the hungering ones now. Blessed the weeping ones now." What's all this? Poverty, hunger, tears! What is blessed about

81

them? No political leader would dare to campaign on this platform, for he would surely be defeated. The people have rendered their verdict that man's life consists in the abundance of his possessions. They place little faith in what Christ said.

But was Christ such an idealist that He divorced Himself completely from the realistic issues of life? To the worldly man, these seem to be riches, a full stomach, and the enjoyment of pleasure and laughter. Are these three elements missing from the Christian's life? Are they sinful in themselves? Will they keep us out of the Kingdom of God and cause us to perish eternally?

Before we classify Christ as a naive idealist, let us try to understand Him. The Lord was facing a concrete situation at this time. He and most of His disciples were poor in this world's goods. It may be that on this special occasion the poverty and hunger of the disciples had provoked disparaging comments from the crowd. "Well, if Jesus Christ is God as He and you claim, why on earth does He not give you enough to eat; why does He not allow you to live decent lives and have at least the essentials of life?" This is what many Christians hear today from the world. This was a realistic situation that the Lord met. And undoubtedly this was not the only time He encountered it. As we pointed out, He must have spoken these words to His disciples repeatedly, as suggested by the imperfect tense of the verb *elegen*, "was saying," in Luke 6:20. The world has praise for riches, but not for poverty. Jesus' conception of blessedness clashes with the common maxims of the world. What does society say? Happy is the man who has abundance of wealth; whose jovial face is wreathed with smiles; who, holding his head high, can indulge his passions and crush his enemies; whose heart burns hot, and whose hand strikes hard, and whose conscience does not know how to plague him! Sentence for sentence, Christ says exactly the opposite.

But did He mean that poverty, as such—the poverty that abridges pleasures, hinders usefulness, limits generosity, multiplies cares, and exposes to temptation—is in reality a blessed state? Poor men will find it difficult to believe this, and, when they remember that poverty is threatened as a divine judgment upon idleness and upon ill-chosen society, their hesitation will seem justified.

Yet let us take a look at poverty. The condition of the poor man is, perhaps, more blessed than that of his wealthy neighbor. This view seems to be gradually developed as we advance through the Bible. In the writings of Moses, poverty is regarded as constituting a claim to pity; but the conception is greatly modified in the prophets. And, when we reach the incarnation, we find the Son of God selecting the condition of a poor man as that in which He, at least, could most effectively do His appointed work. He could have chosen wealth, for He owns the cattle on a thousand hills, but He chose poverty. He was not ashamed to accept charity from those who ministered to Him, and He called public attention to the fact that He had not where to lay His head. That's more than the pride of many of us would allow us to make public. In like manner, His apostles were poor. Moreover, His warning that it is harder for a rich man to enter into the Kingdom of Heaven than for a camel to pass through the eye of a needle, and His advice to the young ruler, must not be forgotten.

Probably the safest and happiest condition is that of a modest sufficiency; and we do well to echo the prayer of Agur, "Give me neither poverty nor riches; feed me with food convenient for me" (Prov. 30:8). But if the

83

choice lay between absolute poverty or absolute wealth, it would certainly be more blessed to be poor. Thus we can see that there is truth in the general statement of the Lord, "Blessed the poor."

In relation to Gospel blessings, the statement is historically true. Not only did the Lord turn from the rulers of Israel to the poor populace, dropping His doctrine as the rain, and distilling His speech as the dew along the streets and highways, where thronging crowds appealed for His compassion, but also He pointed to this very fact as evidence that He was the promised King of Righteousness. "Go and shew John," He said, "these things which ye do hear and see: the blind receive their sight . . . the deaf hear, the dead are raised up, and the poor have the gospel preached to them" (Matt. 11:5).

And in every age of the Church's history, as by some subtle law, the Beatitude has been fulfilled. It seems to be the will of the loving Father that they who know most of physical privation through the sin of the first Adam shall be most susceptible to spiritual enrichment through the grace of the Second Adam. Indeed, we can see how that will accomplishes its ends. In the state of poverty there is absence of much that tends to hinder the acceptance of the Gospel; absence of the snares of Mammon—absence of the self-sufficiency, pride, and fullness of bread that harden the hearts of many rich men, and which in such instances as David, Hezekiah, and the wealthy fool of the parable, are often vividly illustrated in the Scriptures.

Moreover, there are strong inducements for the poor to welcome the story of redeeming love. Who knows so well what it is to be tried and crushed, and what wonder if for them the invitation has a peculiar fascination, "Come unto me all ye that labour and are heavy laden, and I will give you rest"? Who feels like them the instability of worldly possessions, the painful uncertainty of human friendships, the need of divine sympathy? All this helps them to welcome the pitying message of eternal love. Never in the Scriptures do we read of a poor man raised to wealth that he may be brought nearer to God, but repeatedly, in such instances as Manasseh, Nebuchadnezzar, and the prodigal son, we note the reverse process, until we begin to echo the Master's word, "Blessed the poor."

Our Lord had a reason for making this general proclamation. What He meant primarily is that those who are materially afflicted seek God far more readily than those who live in favorable circumstances. We know this to be true in our own experience. Of course, we must not make the mistake of thinking that there is an intrinsic value in poverty. It is simply the condition that makes man accept divine blessedness more readily.

We must further remember in this connection that pious men are not always poor. Nicodemus and Joseph of Arimathea were rich; so, apparently, were Philemon, Gaius, and Stephanas; and among the believers in Berea were "also of honourable women which were Greeks, and of men, not a few" (Acts 17:12). Men of wealth are advised by Jesus, "Make to yourselves friends of the mammon of unrighteousness; that, when ye fail, they may receive you into everlasting habitations" (Luke 16:9). Sometimes only by failure do we turn to the Lord Jesus Christ. Let us therefore see the blessing of failure. And Paul echoes this exhortation when he bids Timothy, "Charge them that are rich in this world . . . that they be rich in good works, ready to distribute, willing to communicate, laying up in store for themselves a good foundation against the time to come, that they may lay hold on eternal life" (I Tim. 6:17-19). It would be ungenerous, unjust, and ungrateful to forget how often the consecrated wealth of munificent believers has been used for the glory of God.

Contrariwise, the poor are not all pious. Penury does not always acquaint them with their dependence upon the Giver of all good. They often fail to become rich in faith, but instead are embittered with discontent, and inflamed with envy, or betrayed into crime. While, therefore, there is reason for affirming that poverty is not without recompense of blessing, it is obvious that some additional factor or factors remain to be considered. (See "The Heirs of the Kingdom," by the Rev. W. J. Woods, in *Christian World Pulpit*, Vol. 38, 1890, pp. 3-6.)

The Lord, then, looks upon poverty and physical hunger as conditions more favorable to the acceptance of the Divine than the opposite conditions. This, however, is not a hard and fast rule. Thus, as you look upon your poverty that favored the acceptance of the Lord Jesus Christ and led to your becoming truly blessed, praise God for it. If, on the other hand, your riches have been the condition under which you turned to the Giver of all to find the true peace that passeth all understanding, praise the Lord for them and use them for Him. What the Lord gives us in this Beatitude is the most likely and probable condition in which we will be moved to turn our eyes upward. It is the condition of poverty, hunger, and tears.

WHAT IS PARAMOUNT IN YOUR LIFE?

How can a person be poor and at the same time blessed? The Lord Jesus Christ gives us the answer in Luke 6:20: Because "yours is the kingdom of God." Can there be any other explanation? You can be joyful even in a state of poverty—whether it is self-chosen or others have imposed it upon you for the sake of the Lord Jesus Christ—simply because you have the Lord Jesus in your heart. If you did not have Him, then poverty would be a cause of uneasiness and complaint.

The Lord did not say that poverty produces blessedness or that it brings the Kingdom of God to you. That is not what He meant to be understood by His words, "Blessed the poor: for yours is the kingdom of God." To make our Lord's words absolutely clear, let us first see what He did not mean by this statement and then what He did mean.

He did not mean that poverty is a necessary condition for obtaining the Kingdom of God, that is, for becoming a child of God and going to heaven.

He did not mean that poverty is a necessary condition for becoming blessed.

He did not mean that blessedness and the Kingdom of God are two separate and distinct things. They are two aspects of the same state. When are you blessed? When you receive the Lord Jesus Christ as your Saviour and thus have God dwelling within you. You acquire His character, which is self-sufficient and not dependent upon external factors for its satisfaction. You then become God-sufficient rather than world-sufficient. Poverty will not affect this condition within, nor riches either. Further to explain this miracle that has taken place within the human heart, the Lord adds, "For yours is the kingdom of God."

This does not mean that you are poor simply because you are blessed and because you have the Kingdom of God. When you become a Christian, a born-again believer, a child of God, you are not immediately characterized, nor should you seek to be characterized, by material poverty. Don't deliberately go about shabbily dressed and penniless. That's not the idea at all. Neither blessedness nor the possession of the Kingdom of God is the result of material poverty.

The conjunction that is used in Luke 6:20 is *hoti*, correctly translated "for." This is causal, answering the question "why?" You are joyful even though it is necessary for the cause and sake of Christ to be poor. This is a paradox in the life of a Christian. What makes it possible and actual? It is because you are blessed and because you have the Kingdom of God. Though you are poor, you are the host of a King. This is indeed strange, isn't it? What king would seek refuge in a poverty-stricken dwelling? You may lack the riches from without, but you have within you the One who owns all things. It isn't things that satisfy you, but He who made things and people, He who made all things, visible and invisible. Poverty, therefore, does not confer upon you either blessedness or the Kingdom of God.

What our Lord gives us here is an explanation of the joy of the Christian in the midst of poverty. He is joyful because God is within him, and He is sufficient. When God is within the believer, He is the absolute Ruler and King. His divine kingdom is established within the human heart. This is sufficient reason to be joyful and happy in the midst of poverty and lack of material things. This is in the same category as the declaration that Christ is the Bread of Life. Things do not bring real satisfaction to us, but a person can, and that Person is the Lord Jesus Christ when He is enthroned as King.

A speaker at an International Student Volunteer Convention said he had received a letter from a college chum whose life was devoted to money making. He wrote, "Bob, poverty is hell!"

Bob replied, "Bill, to be without the love of Christ is hell!"

Bob was right. Christ came to tell us that man's greatest joy and satisfaction are not to be found in things, or in his fellow human beings, but in God, his Maker. And the reason why Christ came to earth, why Deity became humanity, is so that humanity might share in Deity and be blessed, be what God is. When Christ is central, it is immaterial whether you are poor or rich.

The story is told of a painter whose heart was so full of love for the Lord Jesus Christ that he was willing to sacrifice his own fame and the praise of men for his Master's glory. He painted a picture of the Last Supper, putting his best effort into the work. He lavished time and pains and love upon it, working out every detail with the greatest care. Even the cup that stood on the table was painted with as much perfection as the more important parts of the picture. It was a beautiful cup, richly set with jewels that held the light in their ruby depths and seemed to sparkle and flash, so cunningly were they wrought. When his great picture was finished and hung, the painter concealed himself that he might hear, unobserved, the comments of those who came to see his masterpiece. And behold, one after another as he looked would cry out, "What a wonderful cup! How it sparkles!" "The cup is surely made of gold and precious stones!" "Such a cup was never painted before!"

Out from his hiding place came the disappointed artist and with a few strokes of his brush painted out the lovely cup, to the dismay of the onlookers. In its place he drew a common cup of clay, such as peasants use, and colored it in dull and sober tints. When the people upbraided him, saying, "Why did you destroy the jewelled cup?" he replied sadly, "Because it did not fulfill its purpose. I made the cup beautiful because it was for the Master's use, and nothing can be too rich or too carefully wrought that has to do with Him. But if your eyes are holden by the beauty of the jewels so that you cannot see the face of the Lord Jesus Christ beyond, the goodly cup must be sacrificed."

That is exactly how it should be in the life of a Christian. When people look at us, they must not say, This man, this woman, is happy because of riches or poverty, but because of Jesus Christ. He must be the secret of our joy in life. We must know this ourselves and we must consciously or unconsciously demonstrate it to the world around us. "Blessed the poor: for yours is the kingdom of God." When they see your joy in poverty, they will know that it is because you are blessed, because you have Jesus Christ within and therefore He is King of your life. Then people will not credit either your poverty or your riches as the cause of your happiness, but your Christ.

In one of his books, Archdeacon Wilson tells a significant story. Some of the best and ablest of the students at a women's college opened a class for teaching the poorest of the men in a neglected suburb. They were fired by the noblest impulse—to give themselves to work for their unfortunate brothers. After some months, they asked the men whether there was anything in particular they wanted to hear more about. There was silence, and then a low whisper was heard from among them. One of the women went up to find out who had spoken. "What was it you wished especially to hear about?" she asked. "Could you tell us something about the Lord Jesus Christ?" asked one of the men. Here it is. These men, as they looked upon these college students, did not covet their money, or their education, or their social position, but longed for that which made them what they were, Jesus Christ. This is what the world should be impelled to crave as they look upon us—not the things about us, or the lack of them, as the cause of our happiness—but rather the Lord Jesus Christ.

Observe that the verb is in the present indicative tense here: "For yours is the kingdom of God." This suggests that the possession of the Kingdom of God is not something that is future, but something that is here and now and will continue to be our possession. Our fellowship with God begins the moment we believe in Christ and continues until its consummation, when we shall see Him face to face. In Luke 6:20 the Lord was not making a promise, but a statement: "You are poor for My sake. But you are blessed, not because of your poverty, but because of Me. Furthermore, I am in you as your King and I shall continue to be." These words were more particularly addressed to the disciples, who had actually experienced the joy of salvation in Christ. Have you experienced it also?

GOING HUNGRY FOR CHRIST'S SAKE

"Blessed are ye that hunger now: for ye shall be filled" (Luke 6:21a).

❧✺❧

Poverty is a relative state, as are so many conditions in life. Absolutes pertain to God, that which is relative to the life of man. When a person says, "I am poor," what does he mean by it? Usually, that he is below the average in his financial possessions and earnings. In such an appraisal, one's environment must be taken into account. A person who considers himself poor in the United States might really be quite rich in Greece. The standard of living in a particular environment must be taken into consideration at all times. And this is as it should be. We must never try to assume the absoluteness of God in anything that pertains to us. Your holiness and mine cannot be absolute, our knowledge cannot be absolute, our love cannot be absolute. They are all relative, as is poverty.

Thus, when the Lord Jesus said to His disciples, "Blessed the poor: for yours is the kingdom of God" (Luke 6:20), He did not refer to utter, absolute poverty that leads to physical death. The Lord does not want us to exist in such an abject state that our usefulness in His service is diminished or lost. Oh, that extremists would acquire a Scriptural balance of values! What our Lord actually meant by the term "poor" is the state—the relative state—of being dependent on God and not adopting an independent attitude. As our riches cannot be absolute, so our poverty—voluntary or involuntary—cannot be absolute either. Poverty is actually that state in which we feel a sense of privation at not having what the rich have. In this statement of our Lord's it is the personal voluntary sacrifice on the part of the believer of the luxuries that others crave for.

Let us take an example. You may have money. In order to experience this blessedness of which our Lord speaks, you do not have to give it all away. But instead of living in the most luxurious place you could afford in order to maintain status, you could deny yourself that luxury and use the money you save to provide others with some of the very essentials of life. It is thus that we who are Christians can demonstrate the spirit of Christ, who being rich became poor for our sakes. Poverty, then, in its relative sense, means a sense of lacking something that others may possess and consider precious. We as Christians do not need to have all that the world can offer us. Let us be willing to do without some things. What we do without is again relative. For those who live in a country with high standards of living, it may mean giving up a luxury; for those who live in a poorer country, it may mean giving up something essential. Poverty for the Christian is the voluntary relinquishment of the right to possess as much as the most he might have.

In order that the Lord might make more tangible what He meant in Luke by physical poverty, He gave a specific illustration of it. He said, "Blessed the ones now hungering." From poverty He deduces hunger, physical hunger, not the spiritual hunger we find referred to in Matthew. There is blessedness in both kinds, but we want to consider first the Beatitudes as recorded in Luke and then proceed to those in Matthew.

"Blessed those who are now hungering" (Author's translation). What is hunger? It is the discomfort or pain produced by the need for food. Hunger in its primary sense is physical. It is usually the natural result of poverty, although a person may decide to go hungry when he doesn't have to. A person who has enough

93

money can buy food to eat and does not need to go hungry. The reason the Lord proceeded to elaborate on poverty by speaking of hunger was to show us what He meant by the state of poverty.

Poverty is a state, while "hungering" is an action of the Christian's will. Very interestingly, in the first Beatitude in Luke, "Blessed the poor," the word "poor" is an adjective used as a noun. But in the second Beatitude, Christ uses the present participle *hoi peinoontes*, "those who are hungering." The Lord undoubtedly refers to those who voluntarily go hungry for the sake of His Gospel. We must understand this Beatitude as including the condition in verse 22 that modifies all the Beatitudes, "For the Son of man's sake," so that it would read in its totality, "Blessed the hungering ones now . . . for the sake of the Son of man . . . for ye shall be filled." The will of the Christian is involved here. It is not an involuntary state of poverty in which he finds himself, caused by oppression and adversity. Being poor because one cannot help it is not what the Lord is referring to here. Rather He speaks of being poor because one wants to for the sake of the Lord Jesus Christ. To point up the voluntary aspect of the physical privations that we should be willing to undergo for the sake of Christ, He went on to say, "Blessed those who are hungering now." It is as if He were saying, "There will be occasions when you will have to make a choice, to go hungry in order to be or bear a witness for Jesus Christ." He does not refer to a constant state of hunger but to voluntary occasions when hunger should be endured for the sake of the Son of man.

I witnessed a vivid illustration of this one day when I visited the little room where one of the missionaries of the American Mission to Greeks lives in Athens, Greece. This man is an invalid who was condemned to execution by the Nazis during the occupation of Greece in World

War II. Seven bullets went through his body and he was left for dead, but he escaped the ordeal alive. Through this experience, and the personal witness of a servant of Christ, he found Christ as his Saviour. After becoming blessed in the Lord through the new birth, he did not want to keep the good news to himself but was anxious to share it with others. Although he suffered eighty per cent incapacitation and constant excruciating pain, so that he had to remain in bed most of the time, his great rejoicing in the midst of affliction attracted attention. A radio announcer came to visit him and told his story over the air in Athens, inviting afflicted people to write to this invalid who knew the secret of being joyful in the midst of affliction. The same thing happened with respect to one of the leading newspapers in Athens. As a result, this consecrated missionary now has a congregation of about nine thousand people all over the world who write to him asking the secret of his joy. He has written about thirty-eight thousand letters to individuals thus far.

On the day I visited him, I found him and his wife with a bundle of letters ready to mail to people who were in desperate need of the message of salvation. He said to me, "Brother Zodhiates, yesterday my wife and I had a bundle of letters and Scriptures to mail out to anxious souls but we had no money to buy stamps. We only had enough money for food for that day. We had to make a decision—to eat or to mail the message of hope and salvation to others. We decided to go hungry." And they did. Now here they were with another bundle of letters to mail but neither food nor money. They were simply waiting on the Lord. Here is a real example of what Christ meant by "Blessed the hungering ones now." Blessed are those who, when occasion arises, do not hesitate to go hungry for Christ's sake, to make Him known or be true to Him.

This viewpoint is born out by the fact that the article is used before the participle, and when this is done the present participle has often the iterative sense. (A. T. Robertson, *A Grammar of the Greek New Testament,* Doran, 1923, p. 892.) "The hungering ones" does not necessarily mean those who are in a constant state of poverty and hunger, but those who are willing to go hungry repeatedly as the occasion demands it. There is no suggestion here of the deification of poverty or hunger. These must not become ends in themselves but only the means for glorifying Christ. We, as the disciples of Christ, should not seek poverty and hunger as if these were in themselves virtuous states, which would atone for our sins and save our souls.

Consider St. Francis of Assisi. He was a partner with his father in the mercantile trade, as well as the prospective heir of considerable wealth. At the age of twenty-five he went to the local bishop with his father to make a legal renunciation of his inheritance. He stripped off the robes he wore and gave them to his father, that his renunciation of earthly goods might be complete, saying, "Hitherto I have called you father on earth; but now I say with more confidence, Our Father who art in Heaven, in whom I place all my hope and treasure." He wore no shoes or girdle but contented himself with one poor coat, girt with a cord. Was his attitude right or wrong? Of course, God is the judge, but if he did all this in order to attain blessedness, it was a gross misunderstanding of the words and commandments of Christ. Logically his actions could be taken to mean that those who did not do as he did must not be blessed. No degree of poverty and hunger has any intrinsic value. They serve only as occasions for demonstrating our fidelity to the Lord Jesus Christ.

Our point about the iterative sense of the participle *hoi peinoontes,* "the hungering ones," is born out by the conjunction used in verse 22, *hotan,* meaning "whenever." Actually, *hotan* is made up of two words, *hote,* meaning "when," and *an,* meaning "if." The real meaning, then, of this particle or conjunction is "whenever" or "when if." To put it in simpler language, "when the occasion demands it," be ready to go hungry for the sake of Jesus Christ. You don't have to be poor or go hungry in order to be blessed; but, whenever it is necessary, don't hesitate to incur such sacrifices as often as the occasion demands it. Do not sacrifice Christ and His work for riches or food at any time. This is the meaning of the words of Christ in Luke 6:20.

CHRIST SATISFIES THE UNSATISFIED

How and why is hunger a blessing? Or did the Lord Jesus Christ not know what He was talking about when He said, "Blessed those hungering now: for they shall be filled"?

Hunger is a real and universal fact. We experience it three or more times a day. It will help us if we remember that the Lord in all probability spoke this Beatitude soon after He had finished His forty-day fast in the wilderness. As a man, the Lord felt the pangs of hunger. He knew what it was like. He was speaking out of His own personal experience.

Hunger is a natural desire for food. God made us in such a way that we must eat to live. If we stop eating, we die. These are natural laws. Some people wish they did not have to eat, especially housewives, who seem to spend most of their time in the kitchen. Others wish they had nothing else to do but eat. These people usually do not have to cook! But whatever our attitude toward eating, it is an essential process and it is not of our own making. Why should the Lord Jesus tell us that it is blessed to be deprived of that which is naturally essential?

There is a delicate point to be considered here concerning the relationship that should exist between us and the Lord. Most of us boast about what we are doing for God, but if we are honest with ourselves we must admit that what we give Him is usually out of our abundance and not out of our need. We give, but we do not go without. We feed others, but we ourselves do not go hungry. In our giving there is no element of privation or voluntary going without on our part.

Most of the disciples were poor to begin with. They were simple fishermen who did not have much to give, nowhere near as much as the least of us. There were some who were better off, like Barnabas who sold his property and gave the revenue to God and His service. But the Lord established a principle as to what constitutes acceptable sacrifice in His sight. He does not look upon the amount we give or the service we actually render; but He looks at these things in relation to what we are actually able to give or do. A person may give large sums, but these may be far less in the sight of God than the little another person gives. Our privation of essential and natural wants in our lives is God's criterion of our sacrifice on His behalf.

The Apostle Paul clearly demonstrated this in II Corinthians, chapter 8. He compares two groups of Christians. The first were the Corinthians, who were well-to-do. Naturally they could and did give great amounts. On the other hand, there were the Macedonians, who were poor and could naturally give very little. Because the Corinthians gave more, they esteemed themselves above the Macedonians. Paul seeks to correct this by saying, "How that in a great trial of affliction the abundance of their joy and their deep poverty abounded unto the riches of their liberality" (v. 2). It is possible for one to be poor and yet abound in giving. This was the case with the Macedonians. Paul goes on to say, "And beyond their power they were willing of themselves" (v. 3). One person may give much, but what he gives is below his power; and one gives little, but the little he gives is beyond his power. Now, which is greater in the sight of God? The one who gives much suffers no lack, but the one who gives little goes hungry to give even that. It is this principle of sacrificial giving that the Lord is establishing with this Beatitude, "Blessed the hungering ones now: for they shall be

99

filled." He stresses the privation of the essential and not of the surplus. In order to go hungry, we must give that which was meant to satisfy our natural hunger.

This reminds me of a bit of verse I read the other day:

A big silver dollar and a little brown cent,
Rolling along together they went,
Rolling along the smooth sidewalk,
When the dollar remarked—for the dollar can talk—
"You poor little cent, you cheap little mite,
I'm bigger and more than two times as bright;
I'm worth more than you—a hundredfold—
And written on me, in letters so bold,
Is the motto drawn from the pious creed,
'In God we trust,' which all can read."

"Yes, I know," said the cent, "I'm a cheap little mite,
And I know I'm not big or good or bright.
And yet," said the cent, with a meek little sigh,
"You don't go to church half so often as I!"

How true. In God's sight, the cent must often look bigger than the dollar.

There are some Christian ministers who preach tithing, as if that is a Christian principle. It may shock you to learn that I do not believe it to be. It is an Old Testament principle unworthy of Christians. The Lord said, "Blessed the hungering ones now." That does not mean the rich man who gives only one tenth of his income to God. He won't suffer hunger by doing it. Actually, very few of us have an excuse for stopping at one-tenth. If we do that, we belong to the Old Testament dispensation and are not New Testament Christians. If we stop at the tenth, and give our surplus only, we shall lack the Christian blessedness of which our Lord speaks. There is blessedness in depriving oneself of the essential and natural things of life. It is blessed to go without dessert, perhaps, but it is even more blessed to go without a meal, when and as the necessity arises—not just for the sake of denying ourselves, but that we may serve Christ or relieve the hunger of another.

What would we do without hunger in the physical world? We would never feel like eating. A person who never gets hungry is actually sick. The feeling of hunger is a sign of health. It is true that we would die without food, but also we might die without the desire for food. So, actually, hunger is a great blessing in our lives, even as our Lord said. Hunger is essential to life, just as food is.

Complete and absolute satisfaction with food and the material things of life can be dangerous for the Christian. Satisfaction creates sterility and stagnation. J. R. Miller tells of Thorwaldsen, who wrought long and with earnest enthusiasm upon his statue of Christ. But when at last it was completed a deep sadness settled over him. When asked the reason for this he replied, "This is the first of my works with which I have ever felt satisfied. Till now my ideal has always been far beyond what I could execute; but it is no longer so. I shall never have a great idea again." Satisfaction with his work was to him the sure indication that he had reached his best achievement. He would grow no more, because there was now no longing in his soul for anything better. He recognized this, and hence his pain of heart. Actually, then, what this Beatitude means is, "Blessed those who are now unsatisfied." The person who is satisfied with what he is and what he does is useless in the hands of God. God cannot fill him. The disappearance of the sense of hunger is a very dangerous thing indeed.

How can we sympathize with the poor and hungry of this world, of whom there are far too many, if we never experience want ourselves? Many of us are indifferent to the needs of the poor because we do not know what it means to be poor. But it is possible to experience hunger occasionally—the hunger that the poor must have as their constant companion—so that we may sympathize with them. Hunger is a specific element of poverty that everyone can experience. It will be a blessing to us, for it will move us to alleviate the hunger of others; and through giving we become more blessed than through receiving.

For those who voluntarily go hungry for the sake of Jesus Christ there is a reward. The Lord says, "Ye shall be filled." In the Greek this is *chortastheesesthe*, the future passive of the verb *chortazoo*. The meaning of this verb is "to feed, to fill, to satisfy." The Lord tells us that we are going to be filled by a source other than ourselves. This is what the passive voice indicates. "We shall be filled, we shall be satisfied." There is no satisfaction in hunger, but, when we go physically hungry for the sake of Jesus Christ, He will satisfy us. There is no satisfaction either in the hunger itself or in ourselves, but in Jesus Christ. He can make up for physical hunger.

Each time we go hungry for the sake of Christ, there will be comparable satisfaction from Him. Now what kind of satisfaction will that be? What kind of filling will it be? Not necessarily material. If the sacrifice is material, the reward need not be material. After all, the material sacrifice was prompted by a spiritual principle, and therefore the satisfaction should be spiritual. The Lord does not promise us that the moment we decide to deprive ourselves of food for His sake He is going to send His ravens to feed us. No, He promises spiritual satisfaction for material sacrifice. This is evident from the use of the future tense here. Its futurity is not immediate but remote, as we can see from verse 23. "For, behold, your reward is great *in heaven*." "Ye shall be

102

filled," or satisfied, when and where? Not here in fullest measure, but in heaven, when you depart from this material world. This, of course, in no way excludes the spiritual satisfaction that a Christian experiences when he sacrifices and goes hungry for the sake of Jesus Christ. Heaven is only an extension of the blessedness that the Lord gives in this life. But it is a distinct characteristic of the Lord Jesus that He rarely promises material blessings for material sacrifices, but primarily spiritual blessings. If He gave us earthly riches as a reward, He would be making us what He desires us not to be—rich and selfish persons who keep everything for ourselves. The Lord never intended us to be surfeited with material things. But He promised, whenever we went materially empty for His sake, that He would fill us and satisfy us spiritually, here and now and forever after.

THE BLESSING OF TEARS

"Blessed are ye that weep now: for ye shall laugh" (Luke 6:21b).

⟨⟨✦⟩⟩

"Blessed are those who are now crying, for ye shall laugh." This is how the second part of Luke 6:21 reads in the original Greek text. It constitutes the third Beatitude of Christ as given to us by Luke. Here we have the blessedness of tears for the sake of the Lord Jesus Christ.

Usually the world considers that those who laugh are happy, rather than those who weep. Is this saying of the Lord Jesus, then, another of His paradoxes? One can laugh as long as every prospect pleases, but is life an unbroken series of pleasant experiences? Is there anyone whose life has never been characterized by tears and sorrow? Joy, as the world understands it, has its source in the outside world, instead of springing up from within the heart and soul of man.

A poor nervous wreck of a man once called on a famous London doctor. Said the doctor, "You need to laugh. Go down and hear Grimaldi, the famous clown. All London is holding its sides laughing at him." But the visitor straightened himself and said, "Doctor, I am Grimaldi." Laughing when looking at the comic strips is not real fun. Even those whose profession it is to make us laugh are not necessarily happy.

What the Lord Jesus Christ tells us in this Beatitude is that it is possible for man to shed tears and yet be happy. Actually, we should not use the word "happy" but "blessed." Blessedness is that condition in which God dwells within your heart through Jesus Christ. Your happiness then depends on the working of God within and not the pleasantness of life without. But in order to arrive at that state where God will consent to come and

104

live within you, you must shed tears; you must weep for your sin, and repent, and go to Christ, and accept Him as your Saviour and Lord. Then you will have an inner spring of joy within. Your joy and laughter will not depend on what others may do to make you happy, but on what Christ has done for you and in your life.

Despite the fact that sorrow and tears accompany the repentance that brings blessedness, you will also experience a state of permanent joy that is born within you. Blessedness is born in sorrow for one's sins, followed by joy over sins forgiven. It actually makes no difference whether the circumstances of your life are such as to produce tears or laughter. They will leave your inner blessedness unaffected, for that depends entirely on Christ.

The Lord did not say, "Blessed are the laughing ones," but "Blessed are the weeping ones." To have said the former would have been to state the obvious in the eyes of the world, because that is what they naturally think. Although even then it would have been more correct to say, "Happy are the laughing ones." You are "happy" when things go well with you and your outer circumstances are laughter-producing. But you are unhappy when sorrow surrounds you. It is possible, however, to be blessed regardless of laughter or sorrow outside you, and even in spite of it.

"Oh, the blessedness of those who are now weeping!" This was a general statement applicable to all who heard Jesus Christ, both His disciples and the multitudes. When you look at your sin, you cannot help being ashamed and sorrowful. You realize that you are hopeless. You cry for mercy. God visits you with His eternal salvation. Once you are saved, you experience another kind of crying. It is for the sins of others who have not yet known the forgiveness you have enjoyed. We believe this is the

105

crying our Lord refers to in this Beatitude. There is a ministry in tears, the tears that a Christian sheds for others.

"Blessed are those now weeping . . . for the sake of the Son of man . . . for ye shall laugh." This does not mean that the Christian should be morose and gloomy. We are not supposed to wear a long face or black clothes. That is not the idea of this Beatitude at all. Here, as in the previous Beatitude, we do not have an adjective used as a substantive, but a participle preceded by an article. It is *hoi klaiontes*, "the crying ones." There are several things that this form suggests.

First, it speaks of voluntary acts of weeping. This does not mean that the Christian should be in a perpetually tearful state or should never laugh. That would be contrary to the general injunctions of Scripture to be joyful in the Lord and sing praises to His name. But there are times when the sins of our fellow human beings and the state of the world bear so heavily upon our hearts that we cannot help weeping. These times of weeping are, as in the case of the previous Beatitude concerning hunger, voluntary acts. They do not imply a habitually sorrowful attitude in life, but refer to occasions when we are moved to deepest pity and sympathy—not by any lack in our own lives but by the lack of the joy of Christ in the lives of others.

Secondly, this participle preceded by the article has the iterative sense. This sorrow, in other words, is not constant and uninterrupted but an occasional act, repeated as often as necessary, as the Lord burdens our hearts for the sins of others.

Undoubtedly, as the Lord spoke these Beatitudes, He had in mind three classes of listeners: those who persecuted the Gospel, those who believed it, and those who preached it. What should be the attitude of the Christian toward his persecutors? Should it be one of revenge or of pity? We should shed tears for our enemies, for if they knew the Lord in His fullness they would not be opposed to us. Our tears for them can become the water that will cause the seed of the Gospel to grow in their hearts.

Next to the joy of one's personal salvation is the joy of seeing someone else saved from sin. Charles H. Spurgeon said, "Even if I were utterly selfish, and had no care for anything but my own happiness, I would choose if I might, under God, to be a soul-winner; for never did I know perfect, overflowing, unutterable happiness of the purest and most ennobling order till I first heard of one who had sought and found the Saviour through my means."

The St. Bernard dogs in the Alps who seek out travelers lost in a storm take their mission very seriously. One of these dogs returned late one afternoon, wearied from fighting his way through the drifts. He went to his kennel, lay down in a corner, and acted thoroughly despondent, despite the efforts of his master to encourage him. Was he sick? Well, no—not in body, but in heart. He had failed to find anyone to help and had come back ashamed. It is such sorrow of heart, resulting in outbursts of tears on behalf of others, that should characterize the Christian.

> I do not know how soon 'twill be
> Ere I will cross life's darkest sea;
> But when on earth my life shall end,
> I hope in heaven to meet a friend
> That I did help, by act or word,
> To follow Christ, the Risen Lord.
> No greater joy to man can come
> Than just to know he's helped someone.

There is a blessing in the tears we shed for others. We shed them because we are blessed, because we have Christ in our hearts. Otherwise, when we looked at the sins of others, we might shrug them off as no concern of ours, or even laugh at them. Sometimes that which causes the world to laugh causes the Christian to cry. When you cry at what the world laughs at, you demonstrate that you are blessed, that you have God in you. You do what God would do because you are what God is—blessed. And your blessedness does not depend on the wisecracking antics of others but on the heavenly joy within. This is how blessedness and tears can go together—the first producing the second, and the second not stealing from the first. You cry because of your own blessedness and as a result of the lack of blessedness in others.

In the Christian life there is a ministry of laughter and joy and there is a ministry of tears. Of the Lord Jesus it was never said, "Jesus laughed," but "Jesus wept." People took notice of His tears and not of His laughter. Shall we be like Him? Why did He weep? We shall see that in our next study.

WHY JESUS WEPT

One of the greatest sermons Henry Ward Beecher ever preached was on the subject, "Why the Saviour Wept." As I read it, my own heart was so greatly edified that I want to share its thoughts and some of its words with you. In Luke 6:21, the Lord Jesus asks us to weep for His sake. He was willing to weep for ours. We must examine not only His words but His example.

Luke tells us that Jesus wept as He looked out over Jerusalem (19:41-44). He had come into the city from Bethphage and Bethany, seated on a colt, after a most triumphal procession. Shouting themselves hoarse, the people had acclaimed Him as a king. "Blessed be the King that cometh in the name of the Lord," they shouted. "Peace in heaven, and glory in the highest." It was a great hour, an hour such as kings might covet. Yet, as the procession moves on, a strange depression comes over Jesus Christ. Turning at an angle of the Mount of Olives where Jerusalem comes into view, He breaks down into sad and bitter tears, saying, "If thou hadst known! If thou hadst known!"

What feelings were in Christ's heart toward those who had injured Him and were about to destroy Him? It was in Jerusalem that He had received His greatest rebuffs. There was a conspiracy under way to put Him to death. He was marked, yet, knowing it, He voluntarily returned. He knew that His time had come. He was entering the city that had murder in its heart toward Him, where the shouts of "Crucify Him!" would soon resound. This was the city that had persecuted the prophets and covered itself with guilt. Yet, in view of all this, He was so moved by compassion that He could not repress tears; He beheld the city without one stirring of wrath. With the full consciousness of doom, He felt only sympathy for these wicked men and this great community stained with the blood of the saints.

In Christ's attitude we see the attitude of God toward a hopeless humanity that will not turn to Him. We have a revelation of the inner feelings of God. The tears of Christ are not tears of human weakness but of divine compassion. We see that God is sorry for the hopelessly lost. He is sorry for you. He weeps as He looks at you, unrepentant and unhappy. The fleeting happiness you do experience may only be due to the temporarily favorable circumstances of life. But that is such a flimsy thing; it is here today and gone tomorrow. You lack Christ's blessedness, which He is so anxious to impart to you once you believe on Him and accept Him as your Saviour. Think of it—God weeping over you! Your heart should melt with wonder at the thought. God is not as stern and unsympathetic as you may think. He weeps over your lost condition.

One Sunday night, D. L. Moody preached in a big circus tent from the text, "The Son of man is come to seek and to save that which was lost" (Luke 19:10). After he had finished, a little boy was brought to the platform by an officer who had found the child wandering in the aisles. Mr. Moody took him in his arms and asked the crowd to look at the lost child. Said he, "The father is more anxious to find the boy than the boy is to be found. It is just so with our Heavenly Father. For long years He has been following you still."

There is not a shred of meanness in the person and character of God. If anything reveals His feelings toward an unrepentant humanity, it is the tears of Christ over Jerusalem. The voice of the Old Testament is, "I have no pleasure in the death of him that dieth." "Why will ye die?" (Ezek. 18:32, 31.) "Let the wicked forsake his way . . . and let him return unto the Lord" (Isa. 55:7). "Though your sins be as scarlet, they shall be as white as snow" (Isa. 1:18). How the Lord yearned for Jerusalem to know and experience His salvation. He was in no way responsible for their plight. God's nature is such that it yearns over men that have destroyed themselves and whose destruction is irremediable. There is no revenge here; no wrath, no smoke of indignation, and no heartless, hating rejoicing over the sufferings of any creature. A being that can look upon intense suffering that has no remedial power in it—suffering without any other end than that they shall suffer—a being that could look upon that and snuff it up as sweet incense ought never to be called God. Nor can you be called a godly person, a Christian, if you rejoice in any way over the sufferings of others. You ought rather to weep over them. Christ wept over Jerusalem when there was no remedy for her. The remedy was there, but they would not receive it. What Christ weeps over is the refusal of men to receive Him. He knows the consequences of this refusal. And that is why He weeps. He knows what the end of that refusal will be. And if you only knew, you would weep, too.

An Indian Christian was convulsed with heartbroken sobs. A Christian worker went up to him and putting his arms around his shoulders said to him, "The blood of Jesus Christ . . . cleanseth us from all sin." He thought the Indian was weeping because of his sins. But the weeping man looked up and said, "Praise the Lord for that, but, oh, what an awful vision I have had of thousands of souls in this land of India being carried away by the dark river of sin! They are in hell now. Oh, to snatch them from the fire before it is too late!"

You know what the tears of the Lord Jesus Christ over Jerusalem proved? The certainty of God's law—that all

111

things will follow the lines laid down for them from the beginning. There is an inexorableness about the laws of God. And the certainty of moral law is just as great as the certainty of physical law. We know perfectly well that certain courses pursued in regard to bodily health will terminate in a certain way; there is an inevitableness about physical laws in the physical world. The result of breaking or keeping the moral law is just as certain. As Christ looked upon Jerusalem in her rejection of her Redeemer, He knew what the consequences of that rejection would be. He could not help but weep.

But why didn't our Lord change Jerusalem's attitude toward Him, rather than weep over her? Was it because He was unable to do so? No. But we do not find in the whole history of Christ's miracles one instance in which He wrought a miracle to change a man's mind. He had control of the physical laws by which He changed their bodily conditions, but He never worked a miracle that would change the will or the purpose of men's hearts. That was one realm He never invaded or touched. There are a great many instances in which He influenced and incited, but never one in which He interfered with man's free choice, his own status as a free agent with the right to care for himself. Therefore we have no grounds for supposing that at any time on earth there will be such an intervention of the divine will as will prevent the legitimate consequences of the violation of great spiritual and natural laws in the moral kingdom. Our own experiences will help us to some extent to comprehend this state of the divine mind. We mourn for and have compassion over friends whose every step is downward, whom no considerations of friendship, household love, business prosperity, nor any motive of pride or self-respect can hold back. Have you never felt such compassion for one that you knew to be doomed? And what must be the compassion of the divine mind when that process of destruction is going on in countless millions of souls, for generations and centuries? If we have the character of God, and that which characterizes deity—the quality of blessedness—we must manifest the same sorrow for the inevitable eternal destruction that will come upon those who refuse to accept the love and tender mercy of God. Tears are the only outlet for our inability to change men and women and make them experience what has made life worth living for us and death worth waiting for.

But the question that now arises is, "Why does not God save people against their wills?" This we shall consider in our next study.

WHY DOESN'T CHRIST CHANGE US, INSTEAD OF WEEPING OVER US?

The Scriptures declare without reservation that God's will and desire is for all men to know Him and experience His salvation. When a man wants something, he usually goes ahead and gets it. Where there is a will there is a way, they tell us. Cannot God, then, find a way to effect His will for the salvation of men and women?

Why did Christ weep over Jerusalem instead of saving her from her sin and unbelief? He knew that Jerusalem was doomed, yet He could do nothing about it. He turned the burden of His grief upon Himself and wept, instead of manifesting His miraculous power by imposing His will upon the people of Jerusalem. He poured out His heart over the inevitable. And He still does. Is this a weakness? In acting thus, God presents Himself as a Father who, instead of forcing His will upon His erring child, chooses to weep over his sinfulness and insistence on following his own way. Such a God, such a Father, is given to us in the Scriptures, and yet many choose to continue in their unconcern. He could punish us and yet, instead of executing summary justice, He exercises long-suffering and weeps over us. He sorrows because He knows full well what our ultimate end will be—eternal destruction.

We might comprehend man's defiance against a God who is stern, arrogant, and peremptory, but it is hard to understand man's callousness in the face of such tenderness and loving-kindness as that of a Saviour who would rather weep than whip; who, instead of letting men perish in their own sin, gave Himself as a ransom for them—even for those who would crucify Him.

God influences but does not compel moral states, even as a human father. You can influence your child morally, but you cannot possibly imbue him with your high ethical standards against his will. And when he does not choose to follow in your footsteps, if you are a godly and high-principled parent, it can break your heart. You are impotent, though you stand cloaked with the strength and legal authority of a father. And that is the way that a Christian feels toward those who refuse to follow Christ. He wants everyone to experience the joy and satisfaction of knowing and following Christ, but he stands impotent at their refusal to do so. In such a case, he can do nothing, the Lord says in this Beatitude, but weep. When sinners accept Christ, the Christian rejoices and heaven with him, but for those who reject Christ, as Jerusalem did, he cannot help but cry his heart out. This is the kind of weeping that is blessed, our Lord says. He experienced it Himself.

"But," you continue to argue, "if God can do anything, why does He leave the world to work out its own destruction? Why does He not compel men to do right?" No one knows the answer to this ever-difficult question. Christ invites men to repent. Some receive Him and become the children of God. Some prefer to continue in their sinful state. When they make that choice, Christ weeps over them instead of exercising His omnipotence to change them. For some reason, He chooses not to violate the prerogative of those who insist on remaining in their sin. But how this breaks the heart of the Saviour!

As Beecher says, "No man can tell what a machine is by seeing the scattered wheels lying around. No man can tell what a picture is going to be by seeing the canvas and the mere ground rubbed in. No man can tell of this world, which is part of God's universe, what relation it holds to other worlds; and it is the completed administration of God over the whole universal, when all the various beginnings—the genesis in this world and in that world, and in the other world—when all these various colours and development of the power of the soul shall have been marshalled and be come together, and you see the totality of the administration of God; then perhaps a man may be in such a position that he can form some judgment why God did or did not. But one thing is certain: that, so far as the world is concerned, there are certain great laws that lead to righteousness, to safety, and to happiness, and certain great laws that lead through transgression to dishonor, disgrace, and suffering immeasurable."

Why, then, did not Christ interfere to save Jerusalem from destruction? Because then He would have intervened to cancel the very laws that He made, the laws of cause and effect. These people in Jerusalem chose to follow a way of unbelief, refusing the redemption that is offered in Christ and by Christ. They had to suffer the consequences of their own choice. In forcing His salvation upon them, Christ would have been violating the foreordained consequence of unbelief. Why does not God interfere? No one really knows. But the fact remains that He does not; and in His choice not to interfere with our choice of receiving Him or rejecting Him, His heart is broken. He weeps bitterly yet continues to stretch forth His hands to rescue as many as will still receive Him. His mercy is to the very last.

Christian parents often weep bitter tears over wayward sons and daughters, asking God why in His omnipotence He could not have preserved them from evil. On the desk in my study, I have a little thought that my wife gave me, which I look at constantly. Here it is: "Never despair of a child. The one you weep the most for at the mercy seat may fill your heart with the sweetest joys."

116

There is wooing in our tears for the sins of others, for our children who are astray. Although they may not force the sinning ones into the family of God with the power of a rescue operation, they may make him realize that there is divine wooing in the tears of the concerned believer.

A man was severely attacked by another, who sought to kill him. The face of the injured man was badly scarred for the rest of his life. He cherished no enmity, however, against the person who made the attack, and later sought to have him pardoned. The announcement was made to the prisoner. As he read the pardon he said, "I want something more than pardon, sir; I want friendship." "What kind of friendship do you want?" asked the warden. "I can do without anybody else's friendship but that of the man I injured." The man with the scarred face came to see him and assured him with tears in his eyes of both his pardon and friendship.

That is what Christ did. He could not change the result of the sin of Jerusalem, but He could weep over its coming doom; and there must have been some who saw not only pardon in the tears of Jesus but also eternal friendship. Our tears for others can have a greater influence on their hearts than our condemnation of them for refusing to follow Christ. The world craves for concern, not for condemnation. To condemn is human, but to be concerned is indeed divine.

"There is a sacredness in tears," said Washington Irving. "They are not the mark of weakness, but of power. They speak more eloquently than ten thousand tongues. They are the messengers of overwhelming grief, of deep contrition, and of unspeakable love."

Leigh Hunt said there are four kinds of tears. "Some tears belong to us because we are unfortunate; others because we are humane; many because we are mortal.

But most are caused by our being unwise. It is these last, only, that of necessity produce more."

Believers know yet another kind of tears. They come from the compassionate hearts of those who weep for others who do not know Christ, and because they do not know Him persecute them. As Sir Walter Scott observed, it is these tears that become the softening showers that cause the seed of heaven to spring up in the human heart. Let us remember, then, that "Every tear of sorrow sown by the righteous springs up a pearl" (Matthew Henry). Because Christ wants us to have pearls in our crown, He asks us to weep. "Oh, the blessedness of those who are now weeping, for ye shall laugh." Therefore let us weep now, so that others may rejoice in the possession of salvation in Christ; and one day we shall laugh over the tears we shed while here on earth. There is a real ministry in our tears.

THE MINISTRY OF TEARS

Tears now, laughter later; laughter now, tears later. That is how it often works. Those who repent in tears find their hearts full of laughter the moment they are forgiven. But those who laugh over their sins instead of shedding tears will one day lament over their laughter. Both tears and laughter are God's creation. "God made both tears and laughter, and both for kind purposes," said Leigh Hunt. "For as laughter enables mirth and surprise to breathe freely, so tears enable sorrow to vent itself patiently. Tears hinder sorrow from becoming despair and madness; and laughter is one of the very privileges of reason, being confined to the human species."

What did the Lord mean when He said in Luke 6:21, "Blessed those who are now weeping, for ye shall laugh"? He was referring to the disciples who were weeping because of their persecutors—not because of the harm that came to them personally; this produces joy rather than tears—but because of the spiritual state of these enemies of the Gospel. They shed tears of pity and compassion for their souls and over their ultimate destruction. We should rejoice over the privilege of suffering persecution, but we should weep over our persecutors in pitiful love.

The reason why you as a Christian are moved to weep over your persecutors and in general those who do not follow Christ is that you are blessed, you have God within your heart. You are not blessed because you are persecuted. Persecution in itself cannot make anyone blessed. It may even be caused by other things than your personal righteousness and fidelity to the Lord Jesus Christ. You may be persecuted because you are an evil character and a menace to society. You may be persecuted because you deserve it. However, you have a firm promise from God, if you are persecuted because He indwells your heart and manifests Himself in your life, that one day you shall laugh.

Here again the Lord put the first clause in general terms: "Blessed those now weeping." He did not say, "Blessed are ye now weeping." He wanted the crowds who were listening in to what He was telling the disciples to know that tears were good for them, too, as they are for anyone who will shed them in sincerity and faith. For the unregenerate they should be tears of repentance, for they make possible the entrance of God into one's heart. But even when we experience the joy of salvation we shall continue to shed tears of recurring repentance for our failures and sins. First we shed the tears for sin, and then, later, the tears for sins.

But of course, in the case of the disciples, the Lord meant these sayings to have a special application to them. That is why, in the second clause, He turned to them, possibly pointing His finger at them, and said, "For ye shall laugh." This is an assured promise, for their choice to follow Christ to the end of their days had already been made. They were already believers. Nevertheless, the Lord uses the future tense when it comes to laughter, although He speaks in the present tense about weeping. Weep now, and ye shall laugh in the future, He tells His disciples.

How far off is this future time of our laughter? Undoubtedly the Saviour refers to the bliss of the believer in heaven, since He so clearly states that in verse 23. Some of us are in a great hurry for laughter in this life. We weep today and we expect to laugh tomorrow. We must exercise patience in regard to our heavenly laughter. It will be laughter without tears, as we are told in the Book of the Revelation. "God shall wipe away all tears from their eyes" (7:17).

Laughter in heaven, then, will be unmixed with tears, but our tears down here on earth are mixed with laughter. There is a certain amount of joy in the tears of the believer. T. DeWitt Talmage, in his exquisite sermon, "The Ministry of Tears," has an opening paragraph that deserves to be quoted in full.

"Riding across a western prairie, wild flowers up to the hub of the carriage wheel, and while a long distance from any shelter, there came a sudden shower, and while the rain was falling in torrents, the sun was shining as brightly as ever I saw it shine; and I thought, What a beautiful spectacle this is! So the tears of the Bible are not midnight storm, but rain on pansied prairies in God's sweet and golden sunlight. You remember that bottle which David labelled as containing tears, and Mary's tears, and Paul's tears, and Christ's tears, and the harvest of joy that is to spring from the sowing of tears. God mixes them. God rounds them. God shows them where to fall. God exhales them."

And then Talmage goes on to tell us why tears are precious and what their real ministry is. First, they keep this world from becoming too attractive. If it were not for tears, we would not be willing to quit this world of ours. We would want it to become our eternal abode. If it were not for tears, this world would be considered a good enough heaven for all of us. But the believer in particular knows that this world is not good enough for him. He looks for a better city not made with hands, where tears shall be no more. Tears make heaven desirable. And the Christian sheds tears because he sees that people think this earth of tears more blessed than heaven. No man wants to go out of this world, or out of any house, until he has a better place. It is the ministry of tears to make this world worth less and heaven worth more. We believers shed tears over the wrong values placed on things by the people of the world.

Secondly, our tears make us feel our complete dependence on God. If an omnipotent and miracle-working Christ would weep over an unrepentant Jerusalem, how much more must we feel our inability to do anything about the spiritual indifference of men and women all around us. Where our words and our counsel fail, our tears before God may prevail. They are tears of human inability expressing our dependence upon the wooing of God's Holy Spirit. We may think we can do great and mighty things in the world in which we live. We can circle our earth and travel in weightlessness; but no man can actually change a human heart. That is a work of God and His Spirit. No psychological method, no oratorical preaching, no invitation can change a sinner into a saint. Only Christ can do that. We can influence the decision of a person, but we cannot bring it about ourselves. And those that we think we bring about ourselves have the unmistakable look of man-made conversions. Our tears on behalf of those who do not know Christ demonstrate our impotence and our dependence on the Triune God when it comes to their salvation.

In the third place, our tears on behalf of others will enable us to remember the degradation from which we have been saved ourselves. Only those who recognize the height of their salvation will recognize the pit of the unsaved and will cry for them. If we do not cry and weep for those in the pit of sin, we need to be cried over ourselves. Weeping for others means we have been wept over ourselves. The Christian cannot laugh at sin. If he does, he shows that he likes it. But if he cries over it, it means he abhors it.

God carefully keeps these tears that we shed for the sin of the world and the unrepentant. Our laughter in heaven will depend to a great extent on the tears we have shed on earth. Let us pray with the Psalmist, "Put thou my tears into thy bottle" (Ps. 56:8). Let us recognize that this Beatitude is an interpretation of what we find in Psalm 126:5, 6: "They that sow in tears shall reap in joy. He that goeth forth and weepeth, bearing precious seed, shall doubtless come again with rejoicing, bringing his sheaves with him." The Apostle Paul, speaking to the elders of the Church at Ephesus, said to them, "Serving the Lord with all humility of mind, and with many tears" (Acts 20:19). Had you realized that there is a blessing in being not only a minister of the Word but a minister of tears? To this ministry let us give ourselves when our words avail little. Tears will make the Word more effective.

GOD'S REACTION WHEN MEN HATE US

In the first three Beatitudes of Christ in Luke's Gospel (6:20, 21), we have a set of three double statements. The first statement in each set is general and the second is particular.

> Blessed the poor: for *yours* is the kingdom of God.
> Blessed the hungering ones: for *you* shall be filled or satisfied.
> Blessed the weeping ones now: for *you* shall laugh.

The first statement in each case applies to anyone who is blessed. And who are the blessed? The ones who have accepted the person and work of the Lord Jesus Christ. All the Beatitudes are based on the phrase, "for the Son of man's sake" (Luke 6:22), and also on the phrase in Matthew, "for my sake" (5:11). If you are blessed, you will be willing to be poor, go hungry, and shed tears for the sake of your Saviour, the One who made you blessed, so that others may know His blessedness, too. Others will never know His blessedness without personal sacrifice on the part of the already blessed ones. This privilege of being poor, going hungry, and weeping for Christ's sake on behalf of others is general. But of course its generality is limited by its very nature, for it applies only to those who belong to Jesus Christ. It is not limited just to the disciples who were listening to Christ at that particular moment when He was speaking to them.

The Lord never sugar-coated His Gospel. He did not make wild promises but spoke the truth, that the Christian life is one of great privileges and blessings but that it is also a life of grave responsibilities. Following Christ may entail poverty, hunger, and tears. And the Lord wanted even those who were outside the fold of His redeemed, who were listening in at that time, to be fully aware of the responsibilities as well as the blessedness of the Christian life. You will be blessed, indeed; God will dwell within you; but at the same time this will entail your doing what God would have done; for, after all, He acts on your behalf when He is in you.

But at that particular moment, the disciples to whom Christ was speaking were characterized by poverty, hunger, and tears. They had experienced these already for the sake of Christ and they were resolved to experience them in the days to come. So the Lord changes from the general statement, in each of the three Beatitudes in Luke, to the particular. He says, "Yours is the kingdom of God; you shall be filled; you shall laugh." For theirs was the experience of poverty, hunger, and tears. You cannot reap where you have not sown.

But observe a shift in the way the Lord gives the fourth Beatitude in Luke. He does not say, "Blessed the hated ones," but "Blessed are *ye*, when men shall hate you" (v. 22). The Lord is speaking to the disciples personally now. He descends from the impersonal tone of the statement of general fact to the warmth of individual application. Nothing causes our Saviour so much concern as to see us hated for being blessed, for having been made righteous by Him. An attack against a child of God is considered an attack against Christ. "Here you have me at your side," He says to us. "I'll tell you the truth directly and openly about what you can expect."

It is quite possible that the reason more people did not follow Christ during His earthly ministry was His forthrightness about the persecution of the Christian believer and the sacrifices that he would be expected to make for the sake of Christ. Today when we invite people to believe on the Lord Jesus Christ, we make it seem as if there were everything to gain and nothing to lose, as if it were all privilege and no responsibility. This is not the Gospel.

Probably, as the disciples faced the fury of opposition from those among whom they lived and to whom they preached and manifested love and beneficence, they were deeply disappointed. They showed the love of God to others, yet all they got in return was hatred. This is enough to throw anyone into despair. The Lord could see that these disciples needed a personal word, a direct word, and He gave it to them. "Blessed are ye, when men shall hate you, and when they shall separate you from their company, and shall reproach you, and cast out your name as evil, for the Son of man's sake."

Here these disciples were, poor, hungry, and weeping for the sake of others, trying to help others spiritually and materially; yet all they received in return for their sacrifices was hatred. It is not only dogs who bite the hand that feeds them, but human beings also. It happened then and it is happening today. To the child of God, this is the most shocking experience of all. It is the hardest to take. And this may be why the Lord did not mention it until the very end.

I have in mind a report from Greece concerning the spiritual work of a dear old man named Andrew who, at his own expense, went through the islands of Greece to distribute copies of the Gospel of John and other Christian literature, to point men and women to the Lamb of God. Nearly every place he went he was arrested by the police. And this in a country like Greece, where freedom was born! But it just goes to prove the eternal truth of the words of Christ. They were true then, in the case of the disciples, and they are true today.

126

Brother Andrew was arrested on the island of Corfu. At the police station, they said to him, "What are these?" pointing to the Gospels of John he was distributing. "You are proselyting. You will be sued." "No, sir, I am not doing anything evil. I am trying to help the work of you policemen by making it possible for people to read the Word of God," was Andrew's reply. "I hate you," responded the policeman. "I did not bring you here to give me instruction. I don't want to see you again. Get out of here!"

"Blessed are ye, when men shall hate you." It applied to the disciples of old and it applies to modern disciples, too, who fearlessly proclaim the Gospel. But it hurts when we find that people hate us simply because we love them with a love that they cannot understand, a love divine that we have acquired as a result of our blessedness in Christ.

We notice that the eighth Beatitude in Matthew is characterized by the same grammatical shift, from the general to the particular. There, too, the Lord said, "Blessed are ye, when men shall revile you, and persecute you, and shall say all manner of evil against you falsely, for my sake" (Matt. 5:11).

One more thing that makes this fourth Beatitude in Luke and the eighth in Matthew so very precious is that the Lord replaces the term, "the kingdom of God" or "kingdom of heaven," with something even more personal. He proceeds from the Kingdom to the King Himself. He says, "For my sake, for the Son of man's sake." When we are hated by our fellow men for the sake of Jesus Christ, we have one very special comfort, and that is the proximity of the Son of God. God is never so near us as when we suffer for His sake. Then it is not the abstract Kingdom that belongs to us, but it is the living King Himself. The love of Christ for us becomes

127

more affecting when we experience men's hatred for His sake.

A little eight-year-old girl was sent on an errand by her parents. On the way, she was attracted by the singing at an open air Gospel meeting and drew near. The leader was so struck with the child's earnestness that he spoke to her and told her of Jesus. When she returned home, her father asked her what had detained her. She looked up into his face and told him where she had been. He beat her and forbade her ever again going to such a place.

Some weeks later she was sent on another errand. She passed the same spot and saw the same speaker, who again told her of Jesus. She became so deeply interested that she quite forgot her errand, and on returning home told her father that she had brought Jesus. The enraged father kicked and beat the poor little creature until the blood trickled down her face and fell upon her dress.

She was put to bed by her kind mother, never to recover from her father's ill treatment. Just before she died, she called her mother and said, "Mama, I have been praying to Jesus to save you and Daddy." Then, pointing to the dress, she said, "Mama, cut me a bit out of the blood-stained part." The mother did so. "Now," said the dying child, "Christ shed His blood for my sake, and I am going to take this to Jesus to show Him that I shed my blood for His sake."

The trusting child passed away, not, however, before she had sown the seed that in after years ripened into the fruit of salvation for her father and mother. It is with full justification that the Lord draws closer to those who, like the little girl in this true story, are willing gladly to lay down their lives for Jesus' sake. This is the coronation of Christian blessedness, when you are hated and persecuted simply because you love others to death —not their death, but your own.

If others, by hating us, make us angry, they are the victors. But they utterly fail when they cause the King of Kings and Lord of Lords to love us that much more and embrace us all the more warmly. This is our due, and Christ cannot be counted as a respecter of persons for comforting and rewarding us in this way.

WHY DOES THE WORLD HATE CHRISTIANS?

The Lord certainly did not mean the fourth Beatitude in Luke to apply in any way to those outside the immediate circle of His believing disciples. It could not possibly apply to those outside of Christ, and that is why the Lord used the personal pronoun in speaking to the disciples, "Blessed are *ye*, when men shall hate you, and when they shall separate you from their company, and shall reproach you, and cast out your name as evil, for the Son of man's sake."

The fact that the Lord used the present tense of the verb is an indication that the disciples were experiencing these things at that particular time. This was not a temporary state of affairs, but one that would recur in the days to come, for them and for all future disciples of Christ. This we gather from the fact that the verbs "hate, excommunicate, reproach, and cast" are all in the future tense. "You are blessed now for all that is happening to you now and for all that you know will happen to you in the days to come, as long as you remain faithful to Me," the Lord said.

The word "blessed," *makarioi* in Greek, shows why the disciples were hated and why they would be hated in the future. "You are blessed" means you have Christ within you. Your primary concern in life is not the circumstances of life but how to please God within you. He is your sufficiency. This makes the world around you angry. It interferes with its business and pleasures. What would happen if every living person were converted to Jesus Christ? Don't you think that the shape and practice of things would radically change?

The Christian is not primarily concerned with "things,"

while the world is. This creates a conflict of interests, resulting in two different reactions. The reaction of the Christian has already been described in the previous Beatitudes, as given in Luke. The world's concern for things and circumstances makes the Christian sacrifice, endure poverty, gò hungry, and weep as he realizes what the world misses by not having Christ. The other reaction is that of the worldly person. It is one of hatred for the Christian, because somehow he considers him a roadblock to the fullest enjoyment of the pleasures of the world. Here, then, we have the tears of the Christian for the worldly person, and the hatred of the worldly person for the Christian. What is the fundamental cause of all this? The blessedness of the Christian, the fact that he has God within him and is trying to please Him. Thus the word "blessed," *makarioi,* in this fourth Beatitude in Luke gives us right from the outset the cause of the hatred of the world, as it gave us the cause for the poverty, the hunger, and the tears of the Christian.

Let us take an example. The Christian believes that the Lord's Day should be spent in rest, meditation, and worship of the Lord. On the other hand, the world believes it should be spent in pleasure. There is a concerted effort on the part of many businessmen now to make Sunday just another day for business—the best day, since people would have more time to shop. That is why there is such a battle to keep the stores open on Sunday and carry on business as usual. Here is the conflict. The Christian opposes such a thing. This hurts the possible profits of the worldly businessman. Will this cause him to love the Christian or hate him? And the tragic thing is that some so-called Christians try to find excuses to justify their actions.

A servant who had recently experienced the blessedness of faith in Christ was ordered by his master to per-

131

form a certain piece of work on the Lord's Day. "But," said the servant, "it is the Lord's Day." "Does not Christ say, if a man have an ox or an ass that falls into a pit on the Sabbath Day he may pull it out?" replied the master. "Yes," said the servant, "but if the ox has a habit of choosing the Sabbath Day to fall into the pit, then the man should either fill up the pit or sell the ox." How many unbecoming deeds we Christians do under the cloak of our Lord's words, so that we may not offend those around us. We do not want to arouse their hatred by standing true to Him and therefore we fall into all kinds of compromises. No wonder the world does not hate the Christians any more, because there is almost complete conformity of Christianity with the world, instead of just the opposite.

A Christian Chinese, paying a visit to a so-called Christian country, at once noticed the nearness to the world of many professing Christians. Later on, when alluding to the matter, he said, "When the disciples in my country come out from the world, they come clear out." What a sharp indictment that is of our modern Christianity, a Christianity that does not arouse the hatred of even the worst enemies of Christ. We do not shed tears for the world around us, nor do we make the world angry at us. A truce of co-existence has been effected. We possess a very low estimation of Christianity when we try to see how near to the world we can live and yet be Christians. We are commanded to come out and be separate from the world when we take upon ourselves the duties of a Christian. Not, of course, that we must go to a monastery to live; but our life must be a life of separation from sin while we are in the world. While surrounded by sin and the world, we must live the life of Christian blessedness, and this in itself must bring conviction to the world around us. Sin, in other words, must not be made comfortable in our presence but must become disturbed. We cannot rightly serve God and yet love and cling to the frivolities of the world; but our lives should so shine with the illumination of the light of Christ's love that the world will not have to examine us closely to see if we are Christians.

The true Christian reflects the light of Christ in his daily walk in life and never finds it necessary to go through the world sounding a trumpet and crying out, "A Christian! A Christian!" We should feel very humiliated when people have to ask us whether we are Christians or not. Stop and think why this is not apparent from just one look at us. Would it not be much better if, as we walked the streets of our town and visited the stores, the people pointed to us and said, "There goes a Christian"? Our very presence should make them conscious of the influence of Christ, a Christ who is such a censor of sin that inevitably some will hate Him. Not everyone will hate us, of course, but those who would rather embrace sin than Christ, who alone can make them blessed.

Indeed, our evident blessedness in this world of sin can have one of two effects—that of drawing people to the Christ who made us blessed, or of hating Him and us because our very presence is a reproof to their evil works. Take a good and searching look at your blessedness to see whether it makes people react to you, either with love or hatred. If it leaves people indifferent, there is something wrong with it.

An English traveler in Jerusalem was trying to find someone who could speak both English and Arabic. He heard of an American missionary who lived near by. Accosting an Arab boy who knew a little English, he asked him if he could direct him to the missionary's home. The face of the boy lit up, and he said, "You mean the lady who lives next door to God?" If an uncouth street urchin could detect one who walked with God, why cannot we so live that the world can see Jesus in us, see that we are indeed "blessed"? And remember that "blessed" does not mean "happy"; it means having God in us; while "happy" means having the circumstances of life favorable to us. Our happiness will never make anyone come to Jesus; it will only fix his attention upon the things of the world, since happiness is dependent upon them. Our blessedness, however, will either attract them to Jesus or will repel them and make them hate us.

The Lord Jesus very clearly told us, "If ye were of the world, the world would love his own: but because ye are not of the world, but I have chosen you out of the world, therefore the world hateth you" (John 15:19).

ARE YOU HATED FOR THE RIGHT REASONS?

You are blessed; therefore sinful men insisting on the enjoyment of their sin hate you and will continue to hate you. The reason they do so is that your blessedness is a reproof to them in their sinful state.

The message of the fourth Beatitude in Luke is that, some time in your Christian walk, if you are really and truly blessed, you will be hated, excommunicated, made fun of, and slandered. This is inescapable. The adverb used here is *hotan*, "when," which involves certainty and not merely a possibility of occurrence. It is not "Blessed are ye, *if* ye shall be hated," but "Blessed are ye, *when* ye shall be hated." It is true that the word *hotan* is made up of the Greek adverb *hote*, meaning "when," and the conjunction *ean*, meaning "if." The correct meaning of it is "whenever." But it is not "if ever." There is, however, a slight distinction between *hote* and *hotan*. *Hote* is merely "when" as a point of time. For instance, *Hote touto poiee, hamarteesetai* means "He will be wrong when he does this." However, *hotan*, "whensoever," indicates time as a condition of the action, with the additional notion of the probability of its happening. *Hotan touto poiee, hamarteesetai* means "Whensoever he does this, he will be wrong." (See William Edward Jelf, *A Grammar of the Greek Language*, Vol. II, Syntax, 1859, p. 568.) In other words, *hotan*, which is used here, denotes a definite probability of occurrence. It is not merely possible though improbable, but it is possible and probable.

Jelf tells us something more about this conjunctive adverb: "It is used when there is some connection of cause and effect between the clauses; when some particular fact is spoken of, not only as taking place when

135

the action of the temporal clause takes place, but depending for its realization on the event to take place at the indefinite time so signified" (*Ibid.*, p. 567). What does this mean? It means that whenever we are hated, excommunicated, slandered, and ridiculed for the sake of Christ, more of the blessedness of God is realized in our hearts.

Notice the beautiful interaction of the Christian life and the world. You are hated by the world because of the indwelling Christ. He is the One who arouses the hatred of the people as they are reproved for their evil works. But this hatred caused by your blessedness as a Christian also has an effect upon you. It makes you more blessed and not less, as probably would be expected by the natural man. Men ordinarily are unhappy when they are hated by their fellow men. Their happiness depends on the love of others. It is not so with the Christian. He is not merely "happy," circumstance-conditioned, but "blessed," God-conditioned. Therefore the external love or hatred of others leaves him unaffected as far as his blessedness is concerned. That is why the hatred of others can increase his blessedness rather than decrease it, but only when it is for the sake of Christ. Under no circumstances can we experience an increase in our blessedness when others hate us. If they hate us because of something that we have done wrong to them, we are miserable. If those around us hate us because of our sinfulness and misconduct resulting in the common harm, then we derive nothing good from it. Let us be careful to put things in their rightful perspective. Let us also be careful as Christians not to needle those outside of Christ simply to make them hate us and hate Christianity as a whole for the sake of increasing our own blessedness.

Two sisters who had been living in different cities came home for a visit. While away from home, one of the girls had become a Christian. After a few days, the other girl said, "I don't know what causes it, but you are a great deal easier to live with than you used to be." Our blessedness must not make us difficult to get along with. Holiness of life should not create difficult characters. If you as a Christian are difficult to get along with, those around you will automatically blame Christ.

Let us not then deliberately try to arouse the hatred and malice of others by what we do wrong or even by the way we do the right thing. Sometimes the way we tell the truth and even preach it is as bad as telling an untruth. When we preach, does our manner cause people to believe that we love them or that we hate them? Do we present the Gospel in such a way that it will attract, or is there so much of self in it that people cannot help but hate us? Let us in all things imitate Christ, and when we have done that some will surely hate us. But let us be sure it is not because of anything that deserves hatred, but that it is for Christ's sake.

A minister was asked by a Quakeress, "Does not thee think that we can walk so carefully, live so correctly, and avoid every fanaticism so perfectly, that every sensible person will say, 'That is the kind of religion I believe in'?" He replied, "Sister, if thee had a coat of feathers as white as snow, and a pair of wings as shining as Gabriel's, somebody would be found somewhere on the footstool with so bad a case of color-blindness as to shoot thee for a blackbird."

When the Lord says, "Blessed are ye, when men shall hate you," He does not mean that all men will hate us. There is a definite article in front of *anthroopoi*, which literally should be translated "the men." This is done to distinguish one class of people from another. (See A. T. Robertson's *Grammar of the Greek New Testament*, pp. 757-58.) It is as if He were telling us that there are two

137

classes of people who will react to our blessedness of life and character: those who will love us for it and be influenced by it and those who will hate us. But not all men will hate us. Some will, and it is to this particular class of haters of the Gospel and those who live and preach it that the Lord is referring. This leads us to the conclusion that, if everybody hates us, there must be something wrong with us. Then it's time to examine, not others, but ourselves.

The story is told of a man and an angel who were walking along together. The man was complaining of his neighbors. "I never saw such a wretched set of people," he said, "as are in this village. They are mean, greedy of gain, selfish, and careless of the needs of others. Worst of all, they are forever speaking evil of one another." "Is it really so?" asked the angel. "It is, indeed," said the man. "Why, only look at this fellow coming toward us! I know his face, though I cannot just remember his name. See his little shark-like, cruel eyes, darting here and there like a ferret's, and the lines of covetousness about his mouth! The very droop of his shoulders is mean and cringing, and he slinks along instead of walking." "It is very clever of you to see all this," said the angel, "but there is one thing that you did not perceive; that is a mirror we are approaching."

Examine yourself, Christian friend, when everybody seems to hate you. Is it possible that you may be hating everybody? If all men hate you, don't expect to have your blessedness increased. Perhaps you were not blessed to begin with. Stop; take inventory of your soul. Is Christ there? Does He manifest Himself to others?

YOUR COMPANY IS NOT DESIRED

What is hatred? It is a violent dislike. It is a strong feeling of the will that is the opposite of love. It is a quality of the soul. Everybody hates. Even God hates. In the Bible we find God presented not only as a God of love but also as a God of wrath. "The wicked and him that loveth violence his [the Lord's] soul hateth" (Ps. 11:5b).

In one of Aesop's fables he tells of an ape who had a great desire to partake of the honey that was deposited in a rich beehive and yet was afraid to meddle with it because of the sharp sting of the bees. "How strange," reflected the ape, "that a bee, who prepares a delicacy so passing sweet and tempting, should also carry with him a sting so dreadfully bitter!" "Yes," answered the bee, "equal to the degree of sweetness in my better work is the bitterness of my sting when my anger is provoked."

Hatred, then, is not intrinsically bad, nor is love intrinsically good. It all depends upon what we hate or love and why. God continues both to love and hate when He indwells the human heart. He is never apathetic toward good and evil. He loves the one and hates the other.

What, then, does Christ do when He enters into the human heart and makes a person blessed? He reaches down to the old roots of our love and hatred, destroys them, and replaces them by a new love, a new hatred, exactly the reverse of the love and hatred of the old nature. Let us seriously consider whether this marvelous change has really taken place in our individual lives. The reversal of these mighty mainsprings of all thought and action is not such a small event that it can happen with-

139

out our knowledge. "I love the things that once I hated, and I hate the things that once I loved," was the answer of a young girl when asked if she knew she had been born again.

Our hatred for evil should be the outcome of our love for God. Hatred should have no selfish motive. As Christians, let us be careful that in our expression of hatred we do not become hateful, vindictive, or spiteful. Let us be very sure we hate as God hates, and not out of hidden hostilities and frustrations, or an unconfessed resentment that the sinner we condemn is getting away with something we cannot or dare not. Let not our expressions of hatred for evil be so censorious that others, looking at our pursed lips and listening to our shrill denunciations, feel that we are making the sins of others an occasion for exhibiting our own self-righteousness. Let us feel sorrowful at the necessity of condemning, eager for the redemption of the sinner, in the spirit of Him who said, "Love your enemies, do good to them which hate you, and pray for them which despitefully use you" (Luke 6:27).

David, speaking of the enemies of God, says, "I hate them with perfect hatred: I count them mine enemies" (Ps. 139:22). In the unbeliever, hatred is imperfect; in the believer it attains perfection. There is a righteous hatred of evil that proceeds from love. But this is not the kind of hatred the Lord refers to here, that shown toward those who love the Lord and sacrifice their all for Him. Such hatred is based on selfishness. The unrighteous hate the Christian because He is a fly in their ointment of pleasure, spoiling their enjoyment of sin. On the other hand, the Christian is to demonstrate hatred for what causes evil. God and His people do not really hate the sinner but the sin that causes so much misery. It is not a selfish hatred but an altruistic one. God's hatred for evil led Him to the cross. We can acquire such hatred for evil only as we acquire God's love for the sinner and are possessed with a superhuman desire for his liberation from the evil that imprisons him. Hatred is perfect when it stems from our concern over what a person could become in and through Christ.

The Lord in His fourth Beatitude in Luke told us very definitely that a certain class of people would hate us, not because of the evil we do but because of the blessedness and holiness that characterize us. When this happens, we can know that they are unregenerate men. One really wonders whether some so-called Christians who hate their own brethren in Christ actually possess any of the blessedness of Christ. Friends of the same Lord cannot hate each other. If they hate each other, that means that they are also enemies of the One they claim to love. Ask yourself very seriously, whom do you hate and why?

The Lord also tells us that when we live a godly and active life of love for the Master we shall not only be hated but also excommunicated. Notice that I said, "When we live an active life for the Lord." Only an active and witnessing Christian will be willing to be poor, go hungry, and shed tears for the sake of Christ. An inactive Christian does not care whether others are going to hell, and therefore no one will bother him. It is the Christian who constantly lives and witnesses for Christ who gets into hot water. But that should cause him no dismay; hot water helps to keep him clean.

This hatred that is in the heart of the unconverted person against an active, witnessing believer is not merely envy, or dormant hatred, but a very active one. The Lord tells us what expressions that hatred will take: excommunication, ridicule, and slander. Let us examine each of these in turn.

141

The word *aphorisoosin*, translated "they shall separate you from their company," is a very intriguing one in Greek. It is made up of the preposition *apo*, meaning "from," and the verb *horizoo*, meaning "to fix, to set, to determine, to appoint." The compound verb *aphorizoo*, then, means "to set away from one's self," or, literally, "to separate." This word is related in meaning and sound to the word "Pharisee," which also meant "a separated one." Actually, in this context, the word means "excommunicate." Excommunication is the separation of someone from the synagogue or the particular company that they consider their own. In Modern Greek, this is the identical word that is used for "excommunication" —*aphorismos*. The Pharisees of old not only separated themselves from the rest of the world but also were ready and eager, in the intensity of their hatred, to separate those who believed in Christ and were propagating His Gospel.

What Christ tells us here is that those who are going to hate us will not always be the irreligious or unreligious. They may well be those who are organized into closely knit religious systems, and they will claim to hate us in the name of God. These people can hate most viciously. "They shall separate you from their company," the Lord said. And this may be a religious company. But if they do this to you who, for the sake of Christ, are poor, go hungry, and shed tears as you seek to witness and win others to Him, it is not a company you should be eager to remain in anyway. What, then, have you lost? Absolutely nothing. Separation from such company brings you closer to Christ.

This is what happened to the blind man to whom the Lord restored sight in the 9th chapter of John. Before that, he was blind both spiritually and physically. Nevertheless, he was an acceptable member of the synagogue.

But after his physical and spiritual eyes were opened and he began to tell people about his Saviour, they cast him out. They excommunicated him. Excommunication from a pharisaic community may become a real blessing to you if it is for the sake of Jesus Christ. Don't try to fight it. Rest on the bosom of the Saviour. It is more blessed to be Christ's than to cling to any religious system that has no use for real Christian holiness. They want you out because your very presence is a rebuke to their consciences.

The real and the artificial exist side by side in the religious world of today. The presence of the real live Christian in a congregation of pharisees cannot be tolerated. It is related of the Queen of Sheba that she sent two wreaths of roses to Solomon, one real and the other artificial. To test his reputed wisdom she defied him to detect the genuine from the artificial. Solomon at once directed that some bees be brought into the room. Immediately they flew to the real flowers and ignored the counterfeit. The real disciples of Christ are known by the bees that cluster round to sting them. Artificial flowers don't attract stinging bees. Rejoice, therefore, when you are excommunicated from the organized world of artificial religion.

WHY DOES THE WORLD RIDICULE
THE CHRISTIAN?

❦

Sin and religious falsehood cannot possibly tolerate the company of holiness and truth. They are ill at ease. Pleasure must have compatible companions for its full enjoyment. The pharisee separates himself from others, believing himself to be a special object of God's love and attention. A group of pharisees will cast out those who are not equally pharisaical. And those who become blessed in the Lord cease from that moment to be pharisees. Therefore the active believer in Christ will inevitably find himself cast out by the pharisees.

As we study the life of Christ, we see Him constantly rebuffed by the Pharisees of His day. Nevertheless, He continued to go among them—not to be part of them (for they would have nothing to do with Him), but to witness to them. He never gave up on them. When He could do nothing else for them, He wept over them and their city of Jerusalem. How we need to follow the example of our Lord! Men may excommunicate us from their well-organized religious society, but that does not mean we should cease all association with them. This, of course, should involve no compromise of principle on our part. We must continue to let our light shine among them. We should never abandon those who excommunicate us, but prayerfully and constantly seek to win them to Christ. It is possible, you know. The Lord never gave up on Saul of Tarsus but persevered until he became Paul of the gentiles. Though the pharisees give us up, for the sake of Christ we must never give them up.

The verb *aphorisoosin,* meaning "They shall separate you from their company, or excommunicate you," is in the active voice. The Christian is not to bring this excommunication and separation upon himself, but it will be imposed by the religious or worldly community. It is the world and false religion that cannot tolerate the Christian. The Christian should tolerate the world—even the pharisees—so that he may win them for Christ. This follows the principle of being in the world but not of the world. The fact that the Christian is ousted from the company of unbelievers, worldly or religious, is evidence that he is in no way compromising his principles by seeking to please men rather than Christ. If the Christian were willing to compromise, why should they ask him to leave their worldly or pharisaic company? The Christian should remain in the world, without compromising, until the Lord takes him out of it. Try as hard as he will to be friendly, he will find that those who hate the Gospel will barely tolerate him. A girl who accepted the Lord Jesus as her personal Saviour was worried about her future course of conduct. "Shall I have to give up all my friends?" she asked. "They will give you up, before you have an opportunity to give them up," was the reply. But we should be careful never to give up when it comes to seeking their souls for the Saviour.

The world, both the secular and more especially the religious, will not be satisfied with simply excommunicating us but will also revile or reproach us. They will heap insults upon us. They will say all manner of evil against us. The Greek word used here is *oneidisoosin*, "reproach," the same word that was used in Matthew 27:44 to tell us of the reproach uttered against the Lord Jesus by the two thieves who were crucified with Him. This was because He claimed to be the Son of God. In the King James Version it says that they "cast the same in his teeth." The primary meaning of the Greek word for "revile" actually is "to cast in one's teeth." This is the outward expression of their reviling. If the thieves did that to the Lord Jesus Christ while He was hanging on the cross, don't be surprised if the unbelieving world does it to you when you follow Him and make Him known to them. It is a unique distinction.

Ridicule is a great weapon in the hands of the world, especially of the religious pharisees who persecute and hate true Christians. Do you recall what happened to the Lord in Capernaum? He had just landed there when Jairus, the ruler of the synagogue, besought Him to come and heal his daughter. The heart of this father was filled with agony for his twelve-year-old daughter. But there was a great crowd in the way. The Lord Jesus was delayed, having stopped to perform another miracle in between. Meanwhile, a messenger came to say that Jairus' daughter had already died. Nevertheless, Jesus went and entered the house with Peter, James, and John. There was great confusion because of the people milling around. The Lord said, "Weep not; she is not dead, but sleepeth." What was the reaction of the people? "And they laughed him to scorn." (Luke 8:52, 53.) Why? Because He had said that she was asleep, while they were sure that she had died. One moment nothing was to be heard but weeping and wailing, and the next the shrill lament was drowned in laughter.

As G. H. Morrison writes: "How often was Jesus assailed with ridicule. Our Lord had to suffer more than bitter hatred. He had to suffer the sneering of contempt. When a man is loved, his nature expands and ripens as does a flower under the genial sunshine. When a man is hated, that very hate may brace him as the wind out of the north braces the pine. But when a man is ridiculed, only the grace of heaven can keep him courteous and reverent and tender; and Jesus was ridiculed continually. 'Is not this the carpenter's Son? Do we not know

His brothers?' 'He is the friend of publicans and sinners.' Men ridiculed His origin. Men ridiculed His actions. Men ridiculed His claims to be Messiah. Nor in all history is there such exposure of the cruelty and bestiality of ridicule as in the mocking and taunting at the cross, with its purple robe, and its reed, and crown of thorns. Think of that moment when, all forspent and bleeding, Jesus was brought out before the people; and Pilate cried to them, 'Behold your king! Is not this broken dreamer like a Caesar?' That was the cruel ridicule of Rome, often to be repeated by her satirists, and it was all part of the cross which Jesus bore. It is not enough to say Christ was hated, if you would sound the deeps of His humiliation. There is something worse for a true man than being hated, and that something worse is being scorned; and we must never forget that in the cup, which Christ prayed in Gethsemane might pass from Him, there was this bitter ingredient of scorn.

"Nor should we think that because Christ was Christ He was therefore impervious to ridicule. On the contrary, just because Christ was Christ He was most keenly susceptible to its assault. It is not the coarsest, but the finest natures that are most exposed to the wounding of such weapons, and in the most sensitive and tender heart scorn, like calumny, inflicts the sorest pain . . . Think of Christ, uncoarsened by transgression, exquisite in all faculty and feeling, and you will understand how, to a soul like His, it was so bitter to be laughed to scorn. I thank God that the Saviour of the world had not the steeled heart of a Roman Stoic. I thank God He was so rich in sympathy, and so perfectly compassionate and tender. But I feel that the other aspect of that beauty must have been exquisite susceptibility to pain, and not alone to pain of spear and nail, but the more cruel and deep-searching pain of ridicule." (*The Wings of the*

147

Morning, Hodder and Stoughton, London, 1907, pp. 256-59.)

Is it not natural, then, for the Saviour to tell us what we, who receive Him into our hearts, and become blessed, and actively witness for Him, and sacrifice for Him, must expect from others? Would they treat us any differently than they treated Him? How could that be possible, since they continue to treat Him and not us thus, because it is He who lives within? If a class of people does not ridicule us for Christ's sake, then we have something to be concerned about.

Why was it that the Lord Jesus was ridiculed? Certainly not because He was ridiculous. Let us look at the occasion of His coming into Jairus' home. He told those present that the girl was asleep. Lacking imagination, they took His words literally. They could not understand His mystic and heavenly language. Here we have the ridicule that springs from ignorance rather than intelligence. The so-called intelligent men must beware lest they display their ignorance rather than their knowledge and human wisdom when it comes to ridiculing what is Christ's.

The same thing happened on the birthday of the Christian Church at Pentecost. There came a sound as of a mighty rushing wind, and the Spirit of God fell on the little company. They were marvelously exalted by the gift of the Holy Spirit and went out in the glory of it to preach Christ. The people, blind to the source of their enthusiasm and power, mocked at them as though they had been drunk. "These men are full of new wine," they said (Acts 1:13). It was an argument; it was a sneer. And thus we see ridicule becoming the convenient weapon of the ignorant. It is not always a token of superiority or cleverness. It is far oftener the mark of incapacity. The non-blessed cannot understand the blessed ones. It

148

takes the Spirit of God within to discern the things of the Spirit of God. "But the natural man receiveth not the things of the Spirit of God: for they are foolishness unto him: neither can he know them, because they are spiritually discerned" (I Cor. 2:14). A sneer at the Christian, then, is the apology for argument made by a man who does not understand. And that is why, though you find Christ angry, you never find Him ridiculing anybody, for every secret of every human heart is perfectly understood by the Redeemer.

This is why we must consider ourselves blessed when men ridicule us for Christ's sake, because there is something heavenly in us that they neither understand nor want to understand. But be careful lest people ridicule you with justification, because you are naturally ridiculous, instead of ridiculing you for the supernatural possession within you that is incomprehensible to them. This gives us so much more reason to thank God for having it revealed to us. On the other hand, our reaction to others' ridicule, when it is for the sake of Christ, must be like that of Christ: "Forgive them; for they know not what they do" (Luke 23:24). We must be willing to die if needs be for those who ignorantly ridicule us.

HOW SHOULD A CHRISTIAN REACT TO SLANDER?
". . . and cast out your name as evil, for the Son of man's sake"
(Luke 6:22d).

What would you do if you saw a false report about you in the newspaper? Suppose it was a deliberate attempt on the part of the enemies of Christ to discredit the Gospel by discrediting you. Your immediate reaction would probably be to take legal action to make the person who wrote this story retract his lie. We are always ready to defend our reputation, especially when we are of good and exemplary character.

But the Lord Jesus has told us we must expect such treatment if we are active Christians. Our blessedness will result in others casting out our "name as evil, for the Son of man's sake." Why be surprised, then? It is part of the blessing that the Lord said would come along our way.

We can make certain fundamental deductions from this Beatitude in Luke 6:22.

First, we should not believe all that the enemies of Christ say against a fellow Christian. The world is out to discredit the Gospel and will attain its purpose when it makes its lies so credible that even Christians believe them.

Second, it is a credit to us when they maliciously cast out our name as evil, because that is a proof that it is good. The world is expert in taking facts and drawing wrong conclusions from them. They do not need to find something wrong in order to speak evil of us. They can take the good things we do, twist them around, and draw the wrong inferences from them. They may see you coming out of a tavern where you have gone to distribute tracts and speak to souls about Christ, and the next day

150

publish as fact that you were seen coming out of a tavern drunk. They may see you sitting with an unbeliever for the purpose of witnessing to the saving grace of God, and next day discredit your name by saying that you no longer believe in the fundamentals of the Bible because you were seen with a notorious sinner. The facts may be correct, but the inferences are maliciously wrong.

Was it not the same with the Lord Jesus Christ? How beautiful was His life on earth! He did not mention a single condition of blessedness that He Himself did not experience. He became poor for our sakes. He went hungry many times. He wept. He was hated. He was ridiculed and slandered. The Lord never asks us to go through experiences that He Himself did not have as man. His accusers said, "The Son of man is come eating and drinking; and ye say, Behold a gluttonous man, and a winebibber, a friend of publicans and sinners!" (Luke 7:34). This is the sort of thing they were spreading around about Him.

The hostile attitude and activity of the world against the Christian is a progressive thing. First they hate the active Christian who does all in his power to spread the Gospel. Hatred may be hidden in the heart, but it can also manifest itself externally. This Beatitude gives us two manifestations of this hatred, the first of which is ridiculing the Christian to his face, making fun of him. That's hard to take, especially for young Christians. From that they proceed to another manifestation of hatred, and that is widespread calumny—trying to defame one's name, to ruin one's reputation by as great a slander as possible.

What did the Lord do when He was maligned? Certainly, spreading the word that He was a glutton and a drunkard was an unthinkable slander against the perfect Son of God. The more perfect the character of the one who is slandered the worse the slander. If there was

151

anyone who had the right to resist and fight back, it was the Lord Jesus. But we read that when He was reviled He reviled not again (I Pet. 2:23). If He ever alluded to the slanders against Him, it was for the benefit of the people who were harming themselves by uttering them.

It is true that the Lord Jesus both ate and drank, for otherwise, as a human being, He could not live. He set the pattern of normal physical life for us. He did not resort to asceticism. His enemies listened to His claims as God. They looked at Him eating and drinking as a regular perfect human being. There was nothing wrong with that. But they put together His claims of deity and the facts of His normal human actions and came to the conclusion that if He were really God, as He claimed, He should neither eat nor drink. They knew perfectly well that He claimed to be God and also man, for the Word became flesh, but it did not pay them to allow their full knowledge of the case to sway their minds in the slander launched against Him.

So it is with people as they look at us. They take half the truth. They look at facts, but because of their muddy thinking and prejudice they see them refracted and distorted. Here, then, we find that in the life of Christ the facts were true. He did indeed eat and drink for the sustenance of His human body, and He made friends of publicans and sinners, not participating in their sins, but for the sake of winning them to Himself. If you are at all like Christ, human but with the life of God within you, you cannot help being slandered, too. Either you will have to cease being a man who engages in the normal activities of life while engaged in witnessing for Christ, or else you will have to accept the slanders of those who hate Christ. It is not actually you that they are after. The real target is the Lord Jesus Christ who gave you this blessedness that you possess and exhibit.

Just recently, as a result of my publishing Gospel messages in nearly all the secular Greek press, as well as helping the Greek people through the American Mission to Greeks, of which I am General Secretary, I was anathematized in an encyclical that called me "arch-heretic and nationally dangerous." This was not issued by an irresponsible group but by the official State Church of Greece. All I had done was to obey the injunction to clothe the naked, feed the hungry, heal the sick, and preach the Gospel of God. They freely acknowledged this in the encyclical, of which 640,000 copies were printed and distributed far and wide among over eight million people. But the inferences drawn were slanderous. They claimed that I was interested in proselyting the people to a particular church, or engaging in relief work for the sake of attracting the people to myself or to a particular denomination. At first I was greatly disturbed about this. It was surely casting my name out as evil. But as time went on I began to see what great blessing came out of it.

One example of this was a letter from a man on the island of Corfu. He had decided to commit suicide but first thought he would pay one last visit to his village church. That morning in church they distributed the encyclical against me. He decided to see what it had to say. It told him not to read my Gospel messages in the newspapers and to burn any Evangelical publication that he might have. This aroused his curiosity. "After all, in the sermon that I am forbidden to read, I may find something to brighten my life," he reflected. He hurried out and purchased a newspaper and read the Gospel message for the first time. Instead of going ahead with his plans to commit suicide, he wrote to us asking for a New Testament, which we gladly sent him. Was the slander against me a blessing? Of course it was and continues to be. If it were not for my activity for Christ, I would not have been

153

in this slanderous publication. If you are never slandered, you are probably not very active for God.

Since slander is bound to come, how should we face it? Rowland Hill was once shamefully attacked in the public press. He was urged by a friend to start a libel action and to seek justification in a court of law, but he replied: "I shall rather answer the libel, not prosecute the writer: 1) Because in doing the one I might be led into unbecoming violence. 2) Because I have learned from long experience that no man's character can be eventually injured but by himself. It requires particular but supremely attractive grace to return good for evil, to meet a censorious person with unruffled patience, to face criticism uncritically. But the Spirit of God instructs us to render to no man evil for evil. The victory we feel we need over others is often to be found in conquering ourselves."

As Christians who are blessed and who therefore seek to lead others to the same blessedness in Christ, let us not attach too much importance to the slander launched against us. Lincoln declared that, if he read all the criticisms directed at him, he would have had time for nothing else. Another man when severely criticized said, "I hit him with a chunk of silence." An indignant Bostonian rushed into the office of Edward Everett Hale, excited and angered over some criticism that had appeared in a newspaper. Mr. Hale said to him, "Now calm yourself; not half the people in this city take that paper, not half of those who take it read it, not half of those who read it saw that particular item, not half of those who read the statement believed it, and not half of those who believed it are of any consequence."

The most important thing that you should take into account when your name is cast out as evil is that even if some believe the slander, God does not. He knows that it is for His sake.

154

WHAT IS THE WORLD'S MOTIVE FOR SLANDERING THE CHRISTIAN?

"What's in a name?" Something very real. In the case of a man, it is his character, his personality, what he does, and what he believes. "The name is a mark or sign of him who bears it; it describes what is, or is said to be, characteristic of the man, and what appears as such." (Hermann Cremer, *Biblico-Theological Lexicon of New Testament Greek*, T. & T. Clark, p. 454.)

When our name is cast out in public as evil, the most precious thing we possess is defamed. It is an attempt to ruin not only our name but also what it stands for, the total person. It is an effort to degrade us as persons and thus to destroy what we are doing. And, since the Christian's primary characteristic is that Christ indwells him, and his foremost task is to make that Christ known to others, the attack is really aimed at Christ and His avowed purpose to work through the Christian in the lives of others. A certain class of people specializes in that sort of attack upon Christians. It is not that they are really interested in one individual Christian more than another, but they are interested in defeating Christ. Christ is their target; but because He is not here to be maligned personally, they seek out those in whom He dwells, those who represent Him on this earth. And thus the war is on.

Let us remember, however, what we said concerning the definite article before the word *anthroopoi*, "men." The Lord said, "Blessed are ye, when men shall hate you, and when they shall separate you from their company, and shall reproach you, and cast out your name as evil" (Luke 6:22). The translation of the word that indicates who does all these things should be "the men," indicating not all, but only a certain class, of men. When the whole world speaks evil of you, beware, take stock, examine yourself. But do not expect to avoid the unavoidable, that a class will cast out your name as evil. They are the enemies of the Christ within you. This slander is the result of your bold and active witness for Christ.

Someone once told the amiable poet Tasso that a malicious enemy spoke ill of him to all the world. "Let him persevere," said Tasso. "His rancor gives me no pain. How much better it is that he should speak ill of me to all the world than that all the world should speak ill of me to him."

A nobleman once wrote outside his castle gate: "They say. What do they say? Let them say." Write these words on your door, too; write them on your heart.

The Lord attests that your name is good. Otherwise wicked men would not speak evil of it. The word translated "cast it out" in the original Greek is *ekbaloosin,* literally "to drive out, to expel, to throw out more or less forcibly." Your name as a Christian is likely to become a public football. It will travel from one lip to another, and from one paper to another. Blessed are you, the Lord assures you. This verb is in the aorist future, indicating an act in a historical setting complete in itself. This is not something that will happen constantly, but there will be frequent attacks upon your name. When these attacks come, you will be made to realize more fully your blessedness in Christ. Do not shy away from certain activities because they are likely to make your name a public football. Stand up for Christ whatever others may think of you. There is a principle established here: Never give up a task for Christ simply because you are likely to be misunderstood and have your name cast out as evil. Never be guided by expediency, as so many Christians are today, but by principle and a fiery enthusiasm for Christ. We note here that all the other verbs are in the same tense, the aorist future, referring to outbursts of hatred and excommunication and to periods of making fun of you as a Christian. These occasions cannot be avoided in your Christian life.

How is the name of the Christian presented? "As evil," the Lord tells us. The word that is used in the Greek text is interesting and deserves special consideration. There are two words in Greek that can be translated "evil"— *kakos* and *poneeros*. *Kakos* affirms of that which it characterizes that qualities and conditions are wanting there that would constitute it worthy of the name it bears. For instance, we say, "He is a bad doctor" (*kakos iatros*), meaning that he lacks the qualities and skill that characterize a good doctor. But *poneeros* is descriptive of the person who, as Ammonius calls him, is *ho drastikos kakou*, "the active worker-out of evil." He is one that puts others to trouble. In *poneeros*, the positive activity of evil comes out far more decidedly than in *kakos*. In other words, someone who is *kakos* is just bad without spreading it to others, while *poneeros* describes one who is actively bad, evil not only in his make-up but also in his work and activities. (See R. C. Trench, *Synonyms of the New Testament*, Eerdmans, 1953.)

It is the word *poneeros* in the accusative neuter that is used here in the fourth Beatitude as given to us by Luke. They cast out your name as "evil," *poneeron*, not claiming that it is evil in itself only, but that it causes a great deal of trouble and pain to all those around. In a sense, they are right. The Christian through his life and preaching is a real trouble-maker in the world. That's why they want to get rid of him. His very presence is a knife in the soul of the world. The Christian's presence and testimony are a constant check against the tendency of sin to overwhelm the world. Without the Christian, there would be no restraint on evil-doing. Thus, those who are really evil consider the saints as evil because they disturb their evil works. It is significant that the first author of all the mischief in the world, Satan, is called *ho poneeros*, "the evil one" (literal translation in Matt. 6:13, Eph. 6:16). If the devil is actively bad, we must be actively Christian, even if our activity disturbs the world and is considered evil by them.

Who is actually the party responsible for all this hatred, excommunication, ridicule, and slander? Not we, because we neither merited nor achieved our present state of blessedness. It is by God's grace and His alone that we became blessed when we received Christ as our Saviour. And it is He who enables us to go poor and hungry, to shed tears, to be hated, to be excommunicated, to be ridiculed, to be slandered for His sake, and to consider it well worth while. All these adversities and more cannot steal one iota from our blessedness but rather serve to increase it.

We examined the expression, "for the Son of man's sake," quite extensively in several previous studies. What arrests our attention here, as well as throughout the New Testament, is how often the Lord calls Himself, and is called by others, "the Son of man." He is more commonly known as the Son of man and more infrequently as the Son of God. A. B. Bruce, in his book, *The Kingdom of God* (T. & T. Clark, 1909, pp. 166-186), gives a most perceptive and thorough treatment of the terms, "the Son of man" and "the Son of God," in reference to the doctrine of the Kingdom of God or the Kingdom of Heaven. In summary he writes: "As Son of Man, Jesus stood in a relation of solidarity and sympathy with men. As Son of God, He stood in a similar relation to God. As bearing both titles, He was in intimate fellowship with both God and man, and a link of connection between them. In His person the kingdom was thus realized in germ, as a kingdom of grace in which God is related to men as Father, and men are related to God as sons—a kingdom of filial relations."

The most important reason for His choice of this name, the Son of man, was to give admirable expression to His connection with the human race. In this instance, He says "for the Son of man's sake" because He wants us to be aware of His identification with human suffering and want, except for sin. He became man; He became poor; He went hungry; He shed tears; He was hated; He was excommunicated; He was reproached; He was slandered. Why? All for our sakes, so that we might become blessed. Now that we are blessed, we must be ready to suffer all these things for His sake. And He understands what we are going through each time we suffer, for He is predominantly the Son of man when we are experiencing these reactions of the world to our Christian life and witness.

NOT WANTED — YET JOYFUL

Although the Christian has God in him, he does not cease to be human. Here is the picture the Lord presented of him in the Beatitudes as given in Luke. He willingly became poor, went hungry, shed tears, was hated, excommunicated, reproached, and slandered for the sake of the Lord Jesus Christ. It's a sad picture, isn't it? These are the consequences of active blessedness—blessedness that has a burning passion for others to become blessed, too, through experiencing Christ. At the same time, these are also the *conditions* of blessedness and of an increase in blessedness. Because the Lord knew that we in our human state are more likely to regard these as unpleasant consequences of blessedness rather than as conditions of increased blessedness, He gives us four encouraging notes.

First He says, "Rejoice ye in that day, and leap for joy." Second, He tells us the reason for rejoicing (other than our resultant blessedness): "For, behold, your reward is great in heaven." Third, He tells us to take a look at history. "For in the like manner did their fathers unto the prophets." He bids the disciples to look forward and then to look backward. There is no hope like the future, and there is no confirmation of that hope like the past. Fourth, He bids us look at the rich around us and think of their future. "But woe unto you that are rich! for ye have received your consolation." (Luke 6:23, 24.)

Don't bemoan your lot at having a large segment of the world against you because you follow Christ and dare to testify for Him. Rather rejoice, the Lord says. This verb "rejoice" is in the aorist imperative tense, *chareete*, which should be translated "you will rejoice"

160

at a definite time in the future. When is this to be? It is the time when we shall appear before the judgment seat of Christ for the distribution of rewards for service. (See Matt. 16:27, Luke 14:14, Rom. 14:10, I Cor. 4:5, II Cor. 5:10, Eph. 6:8, II Tim. 4:8, Rev. 22:12.)

Let us not confuse this, however, with salvation, which is ours the moment we believe. The Lord did not say here, "Rejoice now," but "You will rejoice" at some future date. Now you are fully satisfied in the enjoyment of your blessedness in Christ as you endure the physical privations of life and the hatred of the world. All condemnation in the matter of sin is past forever for the Christian. Our redemption is complete. We shall never come into judgment concerning our sin. (John 3:18, 5: 24, 6:37; Rom. 5:1, 8:1; I Cor. 11:32.)

Therefore the judgment seat of Christ deals wholly with the matter of rewards for service and has nothing to do with the question of sin. In the New Testament, God offers salvation to the lost, here and now (Luke 7:50, John 3:36, 5:24, 6:47), and to the saved, rewards on the Day of Judgment, in the future, at the coming of the Lord (Matt. 16:27, II Tim. 4:8, Rev. 22:12). Salvation is a free gift of God (John 4:10, Rom. 6:23, Eph. 2:8, 9), while rewards are earned by our works (Matt. 10:42; Luke 19:17; I Cor. 9:24, 25; II Tim. 4:7, 8; Rev. 2:10, 22:12). Read carefully the two extended passages bearing on the doctrine of rewards, I Corinthians 3:9-15 and 9:16-27, and also look up the passages on the various crowns: I Cor. 9:25, Phil. 4:1, I Thess. 2:19, II Tim. 4:8, James 1:12, I Pet. 5:4, Rev. 2:10, 3:11.

The Lord, therefore, does not declare that heaven will be gained by being poor, going hungry, or inflicting pain on one's body, or being persecuted, hated, excommunicated, reproached, and slandered. Heaven is a gift of God to those who believe on the finished work of Christ on

Calvary's cross. But there will be a day of reckoning as to what we have done after we were saved by His free grace. For the Christian who really sacrificed while here on earth, that will be a great crowning day of rejoicing. It is to that specific time that the Lord is referring by the use of the word *chareete,* and not to this present time.

The Lord is most realistic about the physical pains produced by the adversities of life. When people hate us, He does not expect us to laugh and find pleasure in it. Hunger produces very real physical pangs. The Lord is not trying here to reverse the natural reaction of a human being to the laws of nature. What He puts before us is the reaction of the spirit to the physical influences and forces of this world.

Let us look again at our Lord as man confronting the adverse elements of nature. Did you ever make a careful study of Mark 1:13? It says of our Lord, "And he was there in the wilderness forty days, tempted of Satan; and was with the wild beasts; and the angels ministered unto him." Here the Lord was experiencing poverty, hunger, the wiles of the devil, loneliness—all for our sakes in His desire to seek and to save that which was lost.

"This was a meeting of extremes—the wild beasts and the angels. Two ends of the ladder of creation rested on the Son of Man! His human nature had never been so lowly, never so near the ground. He was experiencing what we all at times experience—a sense of the desert. The sheen had faded from the waters of Jordan; the dove had departed; the crowd had deserted; again as in His infancy He was with the beasts of the field. Yet it was now again that the angels came. It is always in His depression that we read of the angels coming—in the manger, in the wilderness, in the garden. Why do they come in His depression? Because there is a virtue in depression? No, the reverse—because there is a danger in it.

162

God will not let me have a cross without the alabaster box; He fears the effect on me of unqualified pain. There is not in all His providence a night without a star. He plants a flower on every grave, and that flower is the boundary line beyond which grief cannot go. Therefore it is, O Father, that I do not die. I could not have lived with the wild beasts if the angels had not come. I have often marvelled that I did not die in the desert. When I saw it from afar I said, 'I could not live there.' Yet I have passed through, and my life is preserved. The moment I entered the desert I felt a nameless strength. It was Thy nameless angel, O Father—the angel that struggled with Jacob to keep him standing when he seemed to fall. So should I have fallen but for Thy nameless angel— Thy strength that passeth understanding. It was not that my anticipation of the desert proved false; it was as bad as I expected it to be. If I had been left to myself, I should have grovelled on the ground. But the nameless hand upheld me, the unseen Presence saved me, the indefinable Peace supported me. It was an incomprehensible peace. It came where it had no right to be. By all the laws of nature I ought to have fallen; the gravity of the whole earth was dragging me down; wherefore did I stand! It was Thy veiled arm that held me. O Peace irrational, O Strength invisible, O Rest inexplicable, O Power that movest through shut doors, I have lived by Thee! Thy staff in the valley, Thy rose in the desert, Thy star in the night, Thy crown in the cross, Thy bells in the snow, Thy voice in the storm, Thy print in the wounds, Thine angel with the beasts of the field—it is they that have comforted me." (George Matheson, *Leaves for Quiet Hours*, James Clark, 1904, pp. 99-101.)

No, the Lord is a realist. He does not expect the Christian to be free from natural reactions to natural actions in this life. But where there are wild beasts and the devil,

His angels are there, too. As we undergo these experiences, in our natural beings we shall feel distressed, but in our spirits we are blessed, for our blessedness depends on Him and not on what the world does to us.

Another verse to ponder is Hebrews 12:2, which tells of our Lord's reaction to the cross of Calvary. "Looking unto Jesus, the captain and perfecter of faith, who for the joy that was set before him endured the cross, despising the shame, and hath sat down at the right hand of the throne of God" (author's translation). "For the joy that was set before him." The joy was future, but the shame was present. It is the same with us. What is joy for us? It is the sense of active cooperation with the laws of God's world. For Christ, it was active cooperation with the plan of salvation for man. Joy for us is always the glad feeling that we are, for the time at least, in harmony with the mind and purpose of God, that we are, in however small degree, thinking God's thoughts after Him and doing what He wishes to see being done. Joy is the spontaneous elevation of mind that rewards all good work.

"The poet feels joy when he has translated a beautiful idea into beautiful language; the artist feels joy when he has reproduced on canvas some lovely vision that floats before his mind's eye; the man of science, when he has discovered some long-hidden secret of nature's laws; the craftsman, when he contemplates a piece of skillful and honest work that he has turned out; and we feel it when we have faithfully obeyed the voice of Christian conscience and done an action with which we hope that God will be pleased. In every case, it is as creators of something that we feel joy. It is the satisfaction of the deepest need of our nature, that of doing or making something that is intrinsically right and good, which gives us joy."

We must distinguish between joy and pleasure. Pleasure is the product of circumstances. Joy is the product of harmony with the divine will. This is why the Christian may have all kinds of experiences from the outside that, while they do not produce pleasure, produce real joy within—a joy, nevertheless, that is often mixed with physical pain, but that will turn into a joy free of pain on the great Day of Judgment. This joy is the result of our love both for the Redeemer and the sinner. It is this love that makes sacrifice joyous. Love imparts enough joy to assure us that we are doing what we were meant to do. Our Maker, in His kindness to us, has ordained that every difficult task we perform successfully shall have its accompanying thrill of joy that is far deeper than pleasure. This joy for the Christian is permanent, unaffected by circumstances, while the world's pleasures are temporary and at the mercy of every wind of change. I'll take the joy still incomplete, the sunshine that falls through tears now but will be without tears "in that day." How about you?

SHOULD THE CHRISTIAN SERVE JUST FOR THE SAKE OF THE REWARD?

❦

When the Christian appears before the judgment seat of Christ, he will be in for a good many surprises. Some of these surprises will be joyful and some extremely sorrowful. But they will be irrevocable. No one will have the opportunity of coming back to have another chance at being faithful to the Lord. When we appear before Him on His judgment seat, the chapter of work and sacrifice, or leisure and sunshine, will be over. A new chapter of our existence will be opened.

In Luke 6:23 the Lord shows that He is first concerned with those who have labored and sacrificed. He tells them that, besides their blessedness in this life, there will be more to come; and that more will entail the perfection of joy. How could the Lord adequately describe this great joy that will be the reward of sacrifice? After saying, "You will rejoice in that day," He adds something else, another word that is descriptive of the greatness and completeness of that joy. It is the verb *skirtaoo*, in Greek, which occurs but three times in the New Testament. It means "to leap, to spring about as a sign of joy." This was used of sheep gaily skipping about. In other words, the Lord tells us that when we hear His "Well done, good and faithful servant," we shall not be able to contain ourselves in His presence, we shall skip about like little lambs. The word used here occurs also in Luke 1:41 and 44 in reference to the unborn John the Baptist in the womb of his mother, Elisabeth. This leaping is actual and literal; it can be witnessed by others. How sadly mistaken are those religious cults that teach that at death everything ceases to be, that there is no consciousness of being. The Lord tells us that a day is coming when we shall leap with joy for everyone to see. This will be the perfect complement of our tears and sorrow while on earth.

Is it possible that the rewards destined for the sacrificing Christian will be far greater than he can ever imagine? Again the verb is in the aorist imperative (*skirteesate*), including definiteness of time in the future. Actually, I believe, it refers to the time when the Lord will make the announcement to us of the reward of our faith and sacrifice. There will be astonishment. There will be such a pleasant shock that we shall begin skipping about like little lambs, leaping like unborn babes. And observe the announcement that the Lord will make: "Behold, your reward is great in heaven." It is at the time of this announcement of the awarding of the incorruptible crown that we shall leap for joy. Something greater than we expected will be revealed. The Lord will take us by surprise. It will be greater joy than we think in heaven if we belong to this first category of those who fulfill the conditions of the first four Beatitudes in Luke. But not otherwise, as we shall see later on.

Very interestingly, the demonstrative particle *idou*, "behold," is actually the aorist middle imperative of the verb *eidon*, except that it has the acute accent when used as a particle. The verb *eidon* is used to demonstrate perception by sight; it means "to perceive, to see something, to experience it." The particle that comes from this verb is used to arouse and enliven the attention of hearers or readers. It is used to emphasize the size or importance of something. (See *eidon* and *idou*, in Arndt and Gingrich, *A Greek-English Lexicon of the New Testament and Other Early Christian Literature*.)

It is evident that the Christian described by the Lord in the preceding few verses of the four Beatitudes in

Luke will come face to face with something very important and far greater than he had ever expected. It is going to be something very real that will make him leap with joy.

All this leads us to believe that this future reward has never actually been the motivating force for the sacrifice of the actively witnessing Christian. It is not the size of the reward that has made the Christian willing to be hungry, poor, tearful, hated, excommunicated, reproached, slandered. The true Christian has never been selfishly motivated. If he had been, the Lord would not have told us that he would be surprised when he experienced the joy of receiving the rewards of heaven; he would not be so overwhelmed. Rather, he would complain that he did not get his just share. Isn't that the attitude of those whose sole motivation is the pay at the end of the day, at the end of the week, month, or year? If a person is working for money alone, you can never give him enough to satisfy him. But the person who has a motivation other than "pay" will never complain; he will consider it a privilege to be given the opportunity of doing the work he loves. Whatever pay comes to him at the end of the road, he will receive with surprise and gladness, with no thought of complaint. Unfortunately, the idealism and higher motivation of work has almost completely vanished from our materialistic world. That is why there is constant trouble between management and labor, and always will be as long as man has the sin of Adam in his heart and life.

On the other hand, the Lord is a just and reasonable Master. He is conscious of His responsibilities, of reason and justice. Don't look at this promise of the Lord as constituting a motive for man's sacrificial labor for Christ, but as Christ's expression of reasonable justice. That is why the greatness of the reward comes as a surprise that makes the Christian at the judgment seat leap for joy. The objection is sometimes raised that the Christian ought not to think of rewards at all in the Christian walk and race, that he ought to have no interest in rewards. The person who makes much of the rewards of the Christian life really turns the Christian faith into a kind of glorified selfishness. So speak the critics of the Christian Gospel. But the fact that the Lord speaks of the rewards does not in any way indicate the motivating power of the Christian but the intention and justice of Christ.

It is as if the employer were to call in his employee and say, "Now I want you to undertake to do certain tasks for me. We have to explore the world of germs so that we can rid humanity of their death-dealing blows. Your salary or your reward for this discovery will be so and so. But I don't want you to do it for what you will get out of it, but for the benefit you will be able to confer on suffering humanity." Suppose two doctors offer their services for this task. One is interested in conquering germs and the other in becoming rich. Whom do you think the employer will engage? And who do you think will come through with the greatest achievements? But what would we think of the employer who did not give any reward to the person who was so dedicated to the task of conquering disease?

The Christian described in these Beatitudes is not the one who works for reward but for love. The reward is incidental and speaks more of the character of the employer than the employee, if we may use such commercial terminology in describing the relationship between the Christian and his Master. Our Lord repudiated selfish discipleship when He roundly charged the people with following Him, not because they saw signs, but because they ate of the loaves and were filled. A man who follows for the sake of reward is not a Christian in the true sense at all. For the Christian, the object of love and the reward of discipleship are one and the same. Christ is the object of our love. We do what we do because He indwells us. And Christ is the end of our striving. He wants us to have the assurance that blessedness is ours here and now in the midst of all life's afflictions, afflictions that come to us as a result of our voluntary sacrifice and love for the Master. But He also wants us to know that He is a just God who rewards sacrifice when all is said and done. And He waits till then for the full manifestation of the reward, lest we be tempted to fix our eyes upon the reward instead of the rewarder. Knowing Christ as we do, seeing what He has done for us down here, we know that He will not disappoint us. In fact, our verse tells us that we shall be surprised. He will reward us far more generously than we can ever imagine. By saying, "For, behold, your reward is great in heaven," He wants to assure us of His equitable and generous character. We sacrifice for Christ, not for what we shall get from Him —although that is a foregone and reasonable expectation—but for what He is.

We notice that there is no verb in the clause, "for your reward *is* great in heaven." The word "is" is supplied by the translator, as indicated by the fact that it is in italics in the Bible. I believe the understood verb here should rather be "will be," since the whole context is that of futurity. This reward, in other words, is not already determined as the Lord speaks of it, but we have a chance yet to determine its size by the amount of sacrificial service we are going to perform for the Lord in the course of our lives, The word that is translated "great" in its more literal sense means "much." Therefore, it is not really the fact of the reward that the Lord is stressing here, but the "muchness" of it. It is the plenitude implicit in the word that the Lord is stressing. After the

170

plenitude of service and sacrifice comes the plenitude of reward. The Lord will not requite us from a heart of justice, in reasonable measure, but out of a heart of love, in the abundance of generosity. What a glorious surprise heaven will be for the Christian! What a contrast with this earth! Sacrifice here, saturation of heavenly joys and blessings there.

A LESSON FROM HISTORY

There is no better teacher than history. A wise man never ignores its lessons. The Lord Jesus Christ asks us to look at the history of the righteous prophets, to see how they were treated. This will prove especially helpful to us at times when people treat us unkindly or hate us for the sake of the Gospel of the Lord Jesus Christ.

Thus, when He bids us look forward to the reward of sacrifice in the Day of Judgment, He asks us to look backward, "For in the like manner did their fathers unto the prophets" (Luke 6:23). The Greek expression used here, *kata ta auta*, means "in just the same way." In just the same way were the prophets treated.

Now why did the Lord call attention to the prophets of the past who suffered for the sake of their testimony? There were probably several reasons.

First, the Lord wanted to show that the pattern of God is unchangeable even as He is unchangeable. God cannot treat us now differently than He treated the prophets of the past, because that would be unjust. He did not choose to spare them the fiery furnace of heathen affliction, nor does He always choose to spare us from the hatred, slander, and persecution of His enemies. He told us that a greater prophet than John the Baptist was never born of woman; and yet He let him suffer imprisonment and death at the hands of a wicked emperor. Christ's reference to the prophets of the past is equivalent to saying, "I am 'the same yesterday, and to day, and for ever'" (Heb. 13:8). Let us not consider this verse as referring only to the power of God demonstrated in the past in the victories He gave to His saints, but also as referring to the permissive will of God for His saints to suffer for His

172

sake. He does not want to give us the idea that He is a respecter of persons—especially of us.

The second reason the Lord referred to the prophets of the past may have been to remind us that He is not unkind to us particularly. No matter how great a work of grace God does in our hearts through His Spirit, some trace of selfishness always remains. We want special consideration from God, especially when we have sacrificed for His sake. A good example of this attitude is found in John the Baptist. While he was in prison, his disciples reported to him that the Lord Jesus Christ was still performing mighty miracles across the Dead Sea. He healed the sick, gave sight to the blind, raised the dead, and evangelized the poor. John must have begun to think within himself, "Here I am in jail for the sake of Jesus Christ, about to be executed by evil men. My ministry is being prematurely terminated. The Lord Jesus could do something about it if He chose; and yet He does nothing for me." He became so upset that he sent two of his disciples to ask Jesus a very distrustful question, "Are you the Coming One, or do we expect *another of a different quality?*" This is the meaning of the Greek word *heteros* in Matthew 11:3 and the alternate readings of Luke 7:19, 20. John began to doubt whether the Lord Jesus, whom he came to know and whose coming he had announced and whom he had baptized, was really the expected Messiah, the Son of God. In jail he had second thoughts about Christ and the kind of person that He should be. He cannot be One that disregards me, and allows me to remain in jail, and be killed so ignominiously, while He has power to liberate me from the hands of my enemies. I want a Christ whose center of attention is His suffering servant, John the Baptist.

Don't we all feel that way at times? We want a God who centers His attention upon us individually. After all,

John did nothing wrong. He was like the blessed person that the Lord describes in this section of the Beatitudes. Why should the righteous suffer, when Jesus Christ has the power to free him from such sad experiences? We have a subjective view of God most of the time, especially in the hour of testing and trial. But the subjective view is the smallest view. God is not only powerful when I am the supreme object of His care and attention, but also when His power is shown to others even through my affliction. The greatest view of God is the objective view. Think of God as dealing with the whole creation of billions of people and then you will begin to realize how great He is. If He centered His attention only upon you, disregarding others and His general plan and purpose, He would indeed be a small God.

It is significant that a man like John the Baptist, who doubted even the identity of the Lord Jesus because of concern with self, was commended by the Lord as the greatest of the prophets. "Verily I say unto you, Among them that are born of women there hath not risen a greater than John the Baptist." Then He adds something else that may include you and me as blessed Christians. "Notwithstanding he that is least in the kingdom of heaven is greater than he" (Matt. 11:11; also see Luke 7:28). The prophets of the past were not perfect, nor are we as we witness and suffer for Christ. We shall have our moments of doubt and human exasperation, but it is good for us to remember how God dealt with the prophets of old and what Christ said of them. Their opportunities and privileges of suffering can be ours as well, and thus their greatness.

There is yet a third reason, I believe, why the Lord made mention of the prophets of the past in this connection of suffering for His sake. He realized that man does not want to stand alone. Two can face death together much easier than if they were alone. Company makes life more worth while and death easier. We all seek important and glorious associations. You like to be able to say that you are the friend of some famous person. If you have an ancestor who distinguished himself in the annals of history, you like to talk of him. A feeling of fame comes to you from famous associations. That is why the Lord wants to remind us that, as we are hated, excommunicated, reproached, and slandered, we are in glorious company. Part of the glory of our blessedness is that it is shared by the heroes of the cross. Even shame can be borne when it is endured in a bright and gallant band, such as the prophets of the past. Persecution and death may be magnanimously met when suffered in company with the goodly fellowship of the prophets, with the glorious company of the apostles, with the noble army of martyrs, with all that purely lived, with all that faithfully fell, and above all with Jesus, the great Captain of the Faith, who left us an example that we should follow His steps.

What martial music is to men marching to battle should such thoughts be to us. What a glorious company we are classified with. If God were to treat us differently, He would have to assign a different and an inferior glory to us. This, I am sure, no sensible child of God would want. Paul knew what he was talking about when he said, "For I reckon that the sufferings of this present time are not worthy to be compared with the glory which shall be revealed in us" (Romans 8:18). Would you change your eternal association with the greatness of the past, with Moses, Isaiah, Jeremiah, Daniel, Paul, Peter, and above all the Lord Jesus Christ, just so that you could enjoy for a time the pleasures of this world, the so-called love of sinners, a full stomach, laughter, and flattering

175

publicity? Frankly, which would you rather have? Which association is most worth while?

Observe that the verb that is used in Luke 6:23 is *epoioun*, "they were doing." It is not as the King James Version has it, "For in the like manner *did* their fathers unto the prophets," but "were doing." This progressive form of the verb indicates that this was repeated action, not just a single act of persecution. Persecution and suffering for the sake of Christ was an oft-repeated experience in the lives of the prophets. They did not give up witnessing and telling forth the oracles of God after an outburst of persecution against them, but their lives were a series of episodes of witnessing and persecution, one succeeding the other.

The word "fathers," of course, was and is used with the meaning of "ancestors." The Lord used it with the implication that their descendants were the same kind of people. Human nature is the same. We should not be surprised when, in the midst of an unparalleled civilization, we as Christians are just as furiously maligned. In fact, the attacks upon Christians may have grown more subtle. Why did the Lord speak of the fathers as the ones who ill-treated the prophets? He wanted to indicate to us that those who should take a loving fatherly interest in us may become our greatest and fiercest enemies, and this should not surprise us in any way. It is possible that your own father and mother may hate you when you take a stand for the Lord Jesus Christ. That will not make you happy, of course, but it will make you feel in a more real sense your blessedness in Christ. The Lord told us in Matthew 19:29 what to expect from our closest relatives. "And every one that hath forsaken houses, or brethren, or sisters, or father, or mother, or wife, or children, or lands, for my name's sake, shall receive an hundredfold, and shall inherit everlasting life." Sometimes those who are closest to us become our bitterest enemies when Jesus Christ takes the first place in our lives. But it is worth while putting Him first, no matter how others feel toward us. It is His opinion of us that counts for real blessedness.

WOE UNTO
YOU CHRISTIAN HYPOCRITES!

A blessing becomes much more valuable in our eyes when we know its opposite. As a father I say to my child, "Son, if you do this I will reward you by giving you something I know you will like very much. But if you do not obey me and do what I ask, then the punishment will be thus and so." It is good to think of the reward but it is also advisable to know the punishment for failure to do what we should. The punishment from which we escape makes the reward far greater by contrast. Because the Lord knows that it is in our make-up to want to know what the future holds, He tells us of the brightness and the darkness that lie ahead as a result of our choices.

In Luke 6:20-23 He tells us of the blessedness of sacrifice for the sake of the Son of man. Initially we are blessed indeed when we accept Jesus Christ as our Saviour. Then our blessedness increases as we are willing to be poor, go hungry, shed tears, and endure hatred, excommunication, reproach, and slander for His sake. The reward for all this is, first, a greater sense of our blessedness in Christ, a realization that our peace and joy depend on the indwelling God and not on what we have or have not, or on what people in the world think of us. And, secondly, we shall receive a great reward on the Judgment Day of Christ.

The contrast to this blessedness is found in Luke 6:24-26. If we refuse to act as dedicated Christians, with a passion to share Christ with others at any cost, what will our lot be, what are we to expect? Our study of the Beatitudes would be incomplete if we did not examine this antithetical passage. What about the person who is unwilling to accept poverty, go hungry, shed tears, and endure hatred, excommunication, reproach, and slander when called upon to do so for the sake of Christ? Is it fair for him to receive as much as the Christian who has sacrificed and suffered for the cause of the Lord Jesus Christ? No, indeed, for then Christ would be unjust. His justice requires Him to render rewards to some and withhold them from others. We shall reap as we have sown. That is God's inviolable law. He leaves us free to sow whatever we wish, but He rewards us on the basis of what we sow. In the Christian life, we have freedom of choice and action, freedom to get rich or be poor, freedom to enjoy all that the physical world can give us within the sphere of what is God-pleasing, or to go without some things. But by our doing or not doing, we bind God as far as our present blessedness and our future reward are concerned.

Thus, after giving us the Beatitudes of sacrifice, our Lord goes on to give us the woes of self-centered enjoyment. He says:

> But woe unto you that are rich! for ye have received your consolation.
> Woe unto you that are full! for ye shall hunger.
> Woe unto you that laugh now! for ye shall mourn and weep.
> Woe unto you, when all men shall speak well of you! for so did their fathers to the false prophets.

179

Immediately the question arises whether it is sinful to be rich, to eat well, to laugh, and to enjoy the esteem of men. How are we to understand these words of Christ? Shall we become ascetics and go about with long faces? Surely this is not what Christ meant.

In order to understand the antithesis of the Beatitudes, we must recall all that we have said about the blessings that precede these woes. The Beatitudes as we find them in Luke were given to show the sacrifices entailed in Christian living for the sake of the Lord Jesus Christ. When we go without certain things so that others may acquire the blessedness of Christ – their salvation – we appreciate our own salvation even more. But if, instead of sacrificing for Christ and others, we concentrate on selfish enjoyment, we experience less of the joy of our salvation, of our blessedness in Christ. That which we hold most precious and worthwhile, we are to sacrifice and even die for. Would you not do that for your wife, your mother, your child, whoever is nearest and dearest to you in this world? What you are willing to do for a person shows how precious that person is to you. It is not what you say, your flowery protestations of love, that count, but what you do for the person you love. So it is with Christ. We say He has blessed our souls by joining us to our Creator. But if we are not willing to give up everything for His sake to make Him known to others, we simply reveal our hypocrisy. We demonstrate that Jesus Christ is really not as precious to us as we say He is.

As in the Beatitudes we have the conditions of blessedness, so in the woes pronounced by Christ we have the conditions that will lead to a lack of blessedness in our Christian lives. Here we have the difference between Christian sincerity and Christian hypocrisy—those who really put Christ first in their lives and those who only profess to do so. The first thing, then, that our Lord wants to show us here is how miserable, how scantily blessed are those who consider themselves happy because of their earthly treasures. And the second thing He wants to impress them with is what awaits them in the world to come.

Since the Beatitudes in Luke concern our physical sacrifices for Jesus Christ, the woes logically have to do with the enjoyment of physical blessings to the detriment of the cause of Christ. The Lord Jesus is not against riches, food, laughter, and a good reputation; but He condemns all these if they are secured and held at the expense of the cause of Christ. If the Gospel of Christ is not advancing because of our unwillingness to sacrifice for the Lord, then woe unto us! Human values are always relative, and this applies to what we do or fail to do. The absolute standard is God Himself.

To be rich is not wrong, but to be rich and have the Gospel suffer in consequence is wrong. To enjoy food is natural, and God is never against the natural enjoyment of the things He has made. But if we eat heartily and fail to share with others who have nothing, if we let the Gospel suffer because we want to have the best and nothing less than the best, then woe unto us! If we go about laughing unconcernedly, despite the sinful state of the world, instead of weeping over it, and trying to do something about it, then woe unto us! If we seek to ingratiate ourselves with others so that they will speak well of us at the sacrifice of truth and to the detriment of the saving Gospel of the Lord Jesus, then woe unto us!

It is not sinful to be rich, to be full, to laugh, to be well spoken of, but it is sinful to seek all these things if and when the result is the limitation of the Gospel or the nullification of its power. The Lord wanted to impress upon us that what we do or fail to do affects Jesus Christ and the blessedness of others, and only in that relationship do riches and poverty, hunger and satisfaction, tears and laughter, slander and a good reputation acquire their relative value. It is the relative as related to the absolute that makes an action good or bad.

We believe, therefore, that these words included in the woes of Christ are actually addressed to believers — those who made a profession of faith, secret or open, but a reserved commitment to Christ in acts. They represent those who were saved without showing any appreciable growth in the way of blessedness, in contrast to the wholehearted, out-and-out disciple of Christ. Our Lord spoke of what some of the disciples did for Christ, how much they were willing to go without for the sake of the Son of man. And then He spoke of what some Christians were not willing to go without for His sake. Therefore the expression, "for the Son of man's sake," constitutes the basis of both the Beatitudes and the woes, the first in a positive manner, the second in a negative. Blessed are we when we do these things for the sake of Christ, and woe unto us when we do not do them.

Therefore the woes are for Christians, too. They are for those who think that a mere profession of faith will entitle them to all that heaven has by way of reward for those who go there. The Lord warns them through these woes that some Christians will get to heaven by the skin of their teeth; they will just barely make it. And even this will come, not as a result of any merit of their own, but as a result of trusting Christ and accepting Him as their personal Saviour. Their faith has not been developed in any way; they are just barely blessed. On earth they did not experience the fullness of Christian blessedness, and in heaven they will not have the fullness of the Christian's reward.

It is quite possible that among those to whom the Lord Jesus was speaking as He pronounced these woes were disciples who were selfish, whose first aim was not to spread the Gospel but to enjoy all that God gave them. They forgot that one reason God gives is that we may be enabled to give. Who knows but what among these were Joseph of Arimathea, who only came out for Christ after His death on the cross, when he went to Pilate to ask for the body of Jesus that he might bury it in his rich garden? He was afraid of the ridicule of his fellow-members in the Sanhedrin. Or Nicodemus who came to Jesus by night? Or Barnabas, the Cypriot, who quite possibly decided afterwards to sell his property and place it at the feet of Jesus for His service? Who knows but what among these were Ananias and Sapphira, who by their premature death proved what they were – selfish rich who wanted to give the impression that they had given all to Jesus when they had given only a part? And who knows but that the Lord wants to speak to you and me through these woes? Christian, take a good look at yourself. Are you characterized by hypocritical avowals or by actual and active sincerity? It is not what you say that proves how much you love Jesus Christ. You prove your love by the degree of your identification with Him and by what you do for Him.

YOU'VE HAD IT, YOU SELFISH RICH!

Our last study was a general introduction concerning the woes pronounced by Christ in Luke 6:24-26. It will be helpful to us to examine each one separately. These are negative counterparts of the Beatitudes. As the Beatitudes express the conditions for receiving the riches of blessedness in Christ here and hereafter, so the woes express the conditions that lead to poverty of blessedness in Christ here and hereafter. Christ sets before us blessedness in its highest and lowest degrees. The Holy Spirit will indicate to each one of us exactly where we stand on the ladder of Christian blessedness. The Lord pointed out the two ends, the top and the bottom. Where are you?

We have already examined the conditions for being at the top rung of the ladder. Now we shall descend to see what is at the bottom. After we discover what is there, I trust you will resolve to fulfill the conditions for top blessedness. God would like to take you to the top, but it does not depend on Him. It depends entirely on you. At the top are the sacrificing Christians, at the bottom the selfish Christians.

Let's look at the first woe. "But woe unto you that are rich! for ye have received your consolation." The Lord begins these warnings with an interjection that occurs mainly in Matthew and Luke. It is the Greek word *ouai*, "woe," denoting pain or displeasure. You make a similar sound, "Ow!" or "Ouch!" when you stub your toe. Something has hurt you. You have experienced pain. This is in direct contrast to the blessedness

185

that the sacrificing Christian experiences. And to make the contrast more apparent, this section of woes is introduced by the conjunction *pleen*, meaning "but, nevertheless, however." The succeeding woes are not preceded by "but." Therefore it is evident that the contrast is between two classes of followers of Christ, the one class who live for Him and are willing to sacrifice anything for Him, and the other who live for self even though they believe in Christ and have acquired forgiveness of sins and that initial step of blessedness, their salvation. These are the woes pronounced upon Christian selfishness.

The Lord addressed these woes to a particular class of people. This is readily seen from the adjectival substantives we find in the Greek text that have the definite article before them just as in the case of the Beatitudes. (A. T. Robertson, *A Grammar of the Greek New Testament*, Doran, 3rd edition, p. 757.) "But woe unto you *the* rich... *the* full ones, *the* laughing ones." The Lord did not refer to all the rich, to all the full ones, to all the laughing ones, but only to that particular group of His disciples whose riches, whose fullness, whose laughter were detrimental to His cause. He issues no general condemnation of the rich, the full, and the laughing ones; just as He gives no general promise of blessedness to all who are poor, hungry, tearful, hated, excommunicated, reproached, and slandered, but only to those who undergo these experiences for the sake of Christ. The only rich, full, laughing ones that are condemned here are those whose condition is detrimental to the cause of Christ.

The first class, then, upon whom the Lord pronounces

woe is the rich. This surely refers to the rich in material things. How illogical to claim that the Beatitudes in Luke are exactly like those in Matthew, that both refer to spiritual poverty and spiritual riches. If Luke 6:24 refers to the spiritually rich (and it must refer to them if verse 20 refers to the spiritually poor, since it is in contrast to it), why should Christ say, "Woe unto you"? Why should a spiritually rich person be so severely warned and alarmed? There is no reason for it. He should rather be commended.

Now when is it wrong to be rich? When your riches hinder in any way the progress of the Gospel of Jesus Christ. It is not wrong to be rich and to engage in business so that you can use the profit for the glory of God and the promotion of His Gospel. If it were wrong to possess money, then no Christian would ever be in business, and the work of the Lord would actually suffer and not gain as a result of it. If I understand the spirit of Christ's teaching, it is that the Christian should be diligent in business and in handling what God has given Him, but never for selfish purposes. No Christian should become rich for the purpose of showing off or wielding earthly power but for the purpose of using what God has given him for the progress of the Gospel. This does not mean giving away everything that you have, but using your possessions in such a way that the greatest good will result for Christ and His work.

Supinely accepting poverty can be wrong, too, if this state does not contribute to the glory of the Son of man. If all Christians were ragged and lazy, what kind of testimony would that be for Christ? Unless the purpose and cause of poverty or riches are Christ and His work, they are wrong and produce woe and not a blessing. Of course, we must recognize that poverty may be due to ill health or natural shortcomings in making a living. What we speak of here is voluntary poverty, being poor for the sake of Christ when you could have been rich, because you see that your riches would not have contributed as much as your poverty. Using your unusual talents for the cause of Christ, for instance, instead of for enriching yourself, is to follow the course many dedicated Christians have chosen. And you will be blessed for it. The one general basic criterion is that Christ be first in your every consideration, and not self.

Not only do selfishly used riches result in little blessedness in this life, but they should produce dread in us as far as the future is concerned. "Woe unto you the rich!" Why? "For ye have received your consolation." The verb that is translated "have" in the original Greek text is most intriguing. No one English word can adequately convey its meaning. It is not *echein*, which simply means "have," but the verb *apechein*, which in ancient Greece was used to indicate that a sum was received in full and was receipted as such. The verb is composed of the preposition *apo*, meaning "from," and the verb *echein*, "to have." A debt is paid off in full. The creditor can have no further claims on the debtor. The account is closed in a manner satisfactory to the recipient.

This is the verb that is used three times in this sense in Matthew. In the first instance, Matthew 6:2, the Lord is referring to those who give alms for the purpose of being seen and commended. He says of them, "They have their reward in full." And what is that reward? The fact that they have been seen by others.

In the second instance, Matthew 6:5, the Lord speaks about those who like to pray loudly in public so that everybody may know that they are men of prayer. Of them He says, "They have their reward in full." There will be no answer to those prayers from God the Master says. These people got all they asked for, favorable human comments that they were men of prayer.

And the third case is in Matthew 6:16, those who fast, not for the sake of pleasing God, but of impressing men. Of these the Lord said, "They have their reward in full." They impress men but not God.

In all three cases, the verb *apechousin* is used, exactly the same word that is used here in Luke 6:24. If we were to put it in colloquial English, we would say that this verb means, "You have had it all." "Woe unto you, the rich, for you have had it all." You have had what? Your consolation. The word in Greek is *parakleesin* and is akin to the word *parakleetos*, which is one of the names of the Holy Spirit in the New Testament. (See John 14:16, 26; 15:26; 16:7.) In this context it means "comfort," implying comfortable circumstances. In other words, the Lord says to the rich Christians who live selfishly, who use their riches not for Christ but for attaining every possible comfort of life, thinking in this way to increase their blessedness, "You have had your comforts in full. You will have nothing more coming from Me when you appear before Me on the Judgment Day." Naturally, this refers to a future day of Judgment. When these selfish rich Christians appear before the Lord in expectation of reward, He will say to them, "You have had it, brother. Remember all the comforts of your earthly life? You sought them, and I did not stand in your way. You were free to use the money you made with My enabling as you pleased. You used it selfishly. Now don't come to ask for a reward that you don't deserve. You have had your reward. It was the comforts of life."

The verb *apechein*, "to have in full," is in the present tense here, which fits perfectly with the whole pattern of thought. You have your comfort in full now. You live for the present and your reward is here and now. You may live more comfortably than the one who sacrifices for Christ, but the one who gives lends to the Lord and will receive it back with interest. Your comforts neither add to your blessedness, nor do they obligate the Lord to give you a reward in the Day of Judgment. How meaningless it is to live just for the present, with no expectation of something better in the future. The elimination of a better future darkens the most brilliant present.

One morning a minister found a folded paper on his pulpit containing the words, "The prayers of this congregation are requested for a man who is growing rich." Truly, the rich need our prayers — not because they are rich, but that they may have wisdom not to use it all for self. Riches for the sake of self are a curse, but riches for the sake of Christ are a blessing. In the first instance, its owners have no reward coming, but in the second, they will receive abundance. "How much did he leave?" asked one, referring to a millionaire who had just died. "Every cent," was the reply. If you are a wise and provident Christian, you will not leave everything behind but will send some ahead to wait for you.

WHAT ROLE DOES YOUR STOMACH PLAY IN YOUR LIFE ?

Is it wrong to eat until your hunger is satisfied? Isn't God the One who created food? Why should we not enjoy it? The Lord often feasted while on earth; why shouldn't we? Why, then, did the Lord Jesus say, "Woe unto you that are full! for ye shall hunger" (Luke 6:25) ?

This is in direct contrast to the Beatitude, "Blessed those now hungering: for ye shall be filled." On the one hand, we have the Christian who is willing to go hungry for the sake of the Son of man, and on the other the Christian whose primary concern is to fill his stomach, regardless of the need of the world for Christ.

There is no doubt that the Lord speaks here of physical food and physical filling, even as it was of physical hunger that He spoke in the previous corresponding Beatitude. Again we see that it would be nonsensical to spiritualize this passage of Luke's Beatitudes and woes. It just would not make sense.

This does not necessarily mean that the people on whom the Lord Jesus pronounced this woe had just eaten to satiety. He was referring rather to their attitude toward the role food should play in their life. To eat until one's stomach is satisfied is only natural, and God does not condemn the natural enjoyment of His gifts. The stomach with its functions and the food we put in it are God's gifts. He would not give them to us and then forbid us to use them for the purpose for which they were intended.

What the Lord is concerned about is what we put

first in our lives as Christians. A predominant characteristic of our Adamic nature seems to be to put last things first and first things last, to consider the important trivial and the trivial important. We see this every day in our children's lives. Most of our problems with them originate in their habit of not tackling first things first. Any teacher will tell you the same thing. Give a child something to do, and tell him it is important and ought to be tackled right away before anything else; but if other unimportant but attractive distractions are around they will present a great temptation and will almost inevitably claim his attention first. That is human nature.

It is so in our relation to Christ. Natural desire so often supersedes supernaturally imposed duties. We feel that it is far more important for us to overfill our empty stomachs than it is to reach others with the blessedness that is in Christ. It is this that our Lord is condemning in this woe – consideration for our own stomachs over and above the souls of men and women all around us and in the wide world in which we live. Let us be frank with ourselves. If it came to the point where we had to choose, which would we do – satisfy our empty stomachs or sow the seed of the Gospel of the Lord Jesus Christ? The question boils down to this, "Who or what is first in our lives? Is it our stomachs or Christ and His cause?" If it is the stomach, then the Gospel will suffer loss. Woe unto us, if that is the case! Especially are we condemned if we give the impression by our words that Christ comes first, when we know that it is really our stomachs that receive first consideration. When we speak of the satisfaction of our stomachs we do not refer to the God-given desire to

192

eat to live, but rather to the desire to live to eat. This is a denunciation, not of a normal appetite, but of gluttony, which is all too prevalent among us today.

"How much is your salary?" a Mohammedan asked a mission school teacher who had once followed the crescent instead of the cross. "Fifty cents a week," was the answer. "Why, you could get ten times that in a government school!" "Yes, but I do not teach for money; I teach for God." "Well—are those all the clothes the missionaries provide? Don't you have a robe also?" The humble teacher looked down at his cotton shirt and trousers. "No, these are sufficient," he replied. The Moslem shook his head. "I never thought there was anything to this Jesus religion," he observed thoughtfully. "but there must be, if a man will give up his robe and his lawful wage for it." Could it be that the Gospel is impeded because we are more concerned about a bulging stomach than reaching others with the Gospel of the grace of God? This is what Christ meant when He said, "Woe unto you that are full!"

The word *empepleesmenoi*, "full," is a participle used as a substantive and is preceded by the definite article. As we indicated with similar word constructions in this passage, this makes the word refer to a particular class, and not, in this instance, to everybody who eats until his stomach is satisfied. It does not refer to the non-Christian whose God is really his stomach. What does he care? On what will he spend his money other than his body, and especially his stomach? He will buy whatever is most expensive and satisfying. Nor does this woe apply to everybody who satisfies his appetite. This in itself is in no way sinful. The sin is not in the satisfaction of the body but in the disposition of the heart and mind.

The application of this woe narrows down to the Christian who has accepted the Lord Jesus Christ as his Saviour and for whom the propagation of the Gospel should be of primary concern. This woe, like all the Beatitudes and woes of Luke 6, must be related to the central and basic phrase, "For the Son of man's sake," of verse 22. Otherwise there is no explanation of these words of Christ, either grammatically or exegetically.

The verb *empepleesmenoi*, "full," is in the passive voice, which indicates that this filling is attributed not to self but to an outside agent. In other words, there is a recognition here that we are filled, that we have no real ability to fill ourselves. This is indeed suggestive. We have no ability to fill or satisfy ourselves even as far as our physical appetite for food is concerned, and there is no reason why the basic meaning of this word could not be extended to all the physical appetites of our body. The appetites have been given to us by God to begin with. The food is given to us by God originally. What could we produce if it were not for God? Everything is God's. Therefore, in recognition of God's part in giving us our appetites and what it takes to satisfy them, we must place the Giver first instead of His gifts.

What a paradox we have here! We sit down at a table spread with an abundance of food. We bow our heads to thank God for it, and then we tackle it as if there were no God over us watching our actions. We entertain not one serious thought of Him who comes first, even as we enjoy His physical filling of our physical needs. How important it is for us to remember that the real satisfaction of our bodily appetites belongs also to Him, and He must come first and the thoughts of Him must preoccupy us even as we become the recipients of His physical blessings.

The contrast is sharp in this woe, as in the previous one. But in verse 24, the word "now" is expressed by the present indicative of the verb *apechete*, "ye have (now) in full" your comfort. In verse 25, the word "now" is expressed by the adverb *nun*, to make us realize that our preoccupation should not be with the present only but also with the future. Only a fool lives for the present and cares nothing about what lies ahead. Let us remember that the future is but the consequence of the present. If "now" is all you care for, the "hereafter" is going to cause you a great deal of concern.

Charles H. Spurgeon once wisely observed, "If a man might have a cottage on a hundred years' lease, he would prize it much more than the possession of a palace for a day." Of course he would; and this is what adds so much preciousness to the joys of heaven, for they are eternal. The pleasures of this world, however bright they seem, are but for this one day of life. If they were all they profess to be, and a thousand times more, they would not be worthy to be mentioned in comparison with "pleasures for ever more" at God's right hand.

The first thing that should cause concern to the Christian whose stomach and bodily appetites come first in this life is that his blessedness is at a minimum. But there is something else that will cause him concern in the Day of Judgment, to which definite reference is made both in the Beatitudes and the woes. The Lord says, "For ye shall hunger." The verb "hunger" here indicates that the real meaning of the previous verb, "be filled," is the filling with food. By it the Lord implies the temptation that even the Christian has of putting his stomach first.

But in what way will the Christian hunger hereafter, whose first concern is for food for his stomach in this life? Will he be physically hungry in the world to come? Will there be physical appetites in the hereafter? We are not told in Scripture. But our resurrection bodies will be like that of the Lord Jesus Christ when He arose from the dead (Phil. 3:21). It was real but glorified. In the same manner our resurrection bodies will be real although glorified. They will be characterized, we can presume, by corresponding appetites. In the degree of their make-up, our glorified, transformed bodies will have both physical and spiritual appetites.

The expression "ye shall hunger" refers to a sense of need, a need that cannot be satisfied. It has to do with the degrees of bliss in heaven, which are determined by the rewards that Christians will receive on the Day of Judgment. The lack of reward for some believers is here presented as unsatisfied hunger. The rich man who put his own needs first will be told that he has had it all on earth. The glutton, the Christian who sought the best for his stomach with complete disregard of the consequences to the cause of Christ, has had it all. There will be "food" in heaven that he will desire but cannot have. This "food" can be presumed to be as glorified and transformed as his resurrected body. He will see the Christians who deprived themselves on earth enjoying this heavenly "food," and he himself will crave it, but he will not be able to satisfy this "heavenly" hunger. How terrible it will be to want something and not be able to have it, especially when you are in the state of general blessedness.

The verb *peinasete*, "ye shall hunger," is in the future active indicative, which fully agrees with the rest of the verbs in the Beatitudes, especially "ye shall be filled" in the second Beatitude. It speaks of a specific time in the future when this shall take place. No doubt it refers to "that day" of verse 23 when all Christians shall appear before the Lord for the judgment of their works, as we saw in a previous study in our series on verse 23. What a shock that Day of Judgment will be to many Christians who sought above all else to satisfy their stomachs and then expected to receive the full enjoyment of heaven as well. The announcement of their unsatisfied hunger will be given to them at a definite time in the future, and the consequence of that announcement will be present with them forever. Choose, therefore, whether it really pays to place the stomach first in your life as a Christian.

WHEN IS IT WRONG TO LAUGH?

Is there anything wrong with laughter? Should Christians be distinguished by their lack of laughter or by their smiling faces? A deacon, scrutinizing passengers as they alighted from a train, was trying to pick out the visiting minister, whom he had never seen, Selecting a likely fellow, he asked, "Pardon me, but are you the minister?" "No," came the curt reply, "it's my indigestion that makes me look like this!" Well, fellow ministers, is this the impression that we have given the world. that we are incapable of laughter? Is this how we interpret the words of Christ, "Woe unto you that laugh now! for ye shall mourn and weep" (Luke 6:25)?

Many people today basically misunderstand the teachings of Christ and because of that they often do the exact opposite of what the Lord intended. Understanding Christ and His teaching is essential before we can mirror Him to the world as He meant us to do.

Perhaps the greatest cause of misunderstanding Christ and much of the Scriptures is the habit of taking words out of context. Preachers take a verse and preach on it in complete isolation from its historical background and general context. One might easily leap to the conclusion on reading this woe pronounced by Christ that He was opposed to laughter, but that is not the case. He attended the wedding at Cana of Galilee, and that was certainly a joyous occasion. He attended feasts and was accused of being a glutton and a winebibber. That does not mean that the accusations of His enemies were true, but it is certain that the Lord was not a joy-killer but a joy-producer. Ask anyone who receives the Lord Jesus Christ as his Saviour. He can hardly contain himself for joy. Heaven comes to dwell in his heart, and even in the midst of terrible affliction he can smile victoriously. His joy is abiding because it is not produced by the outward circumstances of life but by the indwelling Christ.

What, then, did the Lord mean by this third woe in Luke 6:25? "Woe to the laughing ones now! for ye shall mourn and weep." We must seek its meaning in relation to the third Beatitude, of which it is the direct contrast. "Blessed the weeping ones now: for ye shall laugh... Woe to the laughing ones now! for ye shall mourn and weep." The Beatitude and the woe, taken independently as declarations irrelevant to a context, have no real meaning. We must remember that every one of these Beatitudes and woes is related to the person and work of Christ. The foundation on which they stand is that one phrase, "for the Son of man's sake," in verse 22. Otherwise the structure is up in the air. It cannot stand of itself. The Lord desires the blessed Christian to increase his blessedness, the reality of Christ within him, by weeping over the sins of others who are outside of Christ. In doing this, he will one day have occasion to laugh joyously when, in the Day of Judgment, he meets many who are there because of the tears he shed while on earth. Tears related to Christ and His work are precious indeed in His sight. But tears shed as a consequence of the punishment of sin are simply the sinner's due. Not all tears produce or multiply blessing. It is the same with laughter. It is neither good nor bad in itself. What is the criterion by which we are to judge? It is the Lord Jesus Christ.

Stop to think why you laugh when you do. What is the motive of your mirth? Only fools laugh just for the sake of laughing. Our laughter must be intelligent; it must have motive and purpose. What should its motive be? The glory of Christ. Laugh only at those things that are pure and wholesome in their connotations. Never laugh at anything that will bring shame to Christ. It sometimes happens that in a college classroom the professor will make fun of Christian beliefs. He will even crack jokes about the Lord Jesus Christ in order to make the students laugh. Smart professor. He thinks that the more he ridicules revealed religion the more enlightened he will appear to his students. Suppose you are a Christian student among many godless fellow students. When everyone else bursts out in laughter, what should you do? Join in the laughter, to show that you are broadminded even though you are a Christian? Would that not be a betrayal of the Lord Jesus in whom you believe? That is the kind of laughter that the Lord forbids. It is the laughter of His children that would besmirch His glory and be detrimental to their witness to the world of what He really is to them and what He can be to those who accept Him as their Saviour.

A similar incident occurred in the life of Christ. It is recorded briefly in the eighth chapter of John's Gospel. The scribes and Pharisees brought a woman to the Lord Jesus who had been caught in the very act of adultery. Have you ever thought of how men would comport themselves in such a case? Would they come to the Lord in a sorrowful manner or in a frivolous and laughing mood? What were they really trying to do here? Their primary motive, no doubt, was to betray

Christ into a repudiation of the Mosaic Law as it governed those taken in adultery. But a secondary motive, I believe, was to tempt Jesus to laugh with them at this exhibition of human sin. The woman became a verbal football to them, the butt of their coarse jests. Quite possibly those who had brought her to Jesus Christ were the very ones responsible for her sinful degradation and yet had the animal audacity to make fun of her. They wanted to cause Christ to side with them in their laughter at sin. Who knows the conversation in full and the scene in its every detail? The Evangelist prefers to give it to us briefly and to allow us to read between the lines. What did the Lord do? He pretended that He did not hear what they were saying. He stooped down and wrote on the ground so that He might not look at her and them. He refused to laugh at sin, for then His whole ministry would have been brought into ridicule.

Do we realize what actually happens when we laugh with those who laugh because of sin? What do we accomplish by it? We simply bring reproach upon the name of Christ. We cause the Gospel of Christ to be brought to naught. The harm Christians can bring to the cause of Christ is incomparably greater than that which the world can inflict. Frankly, I am never afraid of the laughter of the world at Christ, but I shudder when Christians laugh at sin.

A young Buddhist who had made a careful study of Christianity, and particularly of Christ, said to a Christian, "Your Christ is wonderful—oh, so wonderful—but you Christians are not like Him." Without knowing it, he had put his finger on the greatest need of present-day Christianity—more of Christlikeness in those

201

who bear His name. When we see others laughing as a result of sin and the degradation that sin has brought about, do we laugh with them or do we weep? The Lord does not forbid legitimate laughter; and actually the Christian has far more joyous and wholesome things to laugh about than the world has. But let us make sure that our laughter does not give those around us the wrong idea of Jesus Christ, or bring shame to Him. Let this be our criterion for laughter.

In this third woe, the Lord does not use the pronoun *humin*, "unto you," as He did in the two previous woes. The only explanation we can suggest is that, at the moment the Lord spoke these words, no one was laughing. These words were given in an atmosphere of great seriousness. Then, too, He did not want to limit their application to those present but to make it as general as possible. It was the general attitude of laughing to the detriment of the Gospel that the Lord wanted to warn all Christians against.

In using the adverb *nun*, "now," He did not necessarily mean that particular moment but the whole course of this earthly life in contrast with futurity, as vividly expressed in the future tenses of the verb "shall mourn" and "shall weep." A little laughter now at the expense of Christ will bring calamitous results in the Day of Judgment. It will keep us from laughing then. While others will be rejoicing, those who put Christ to shame on earth will mourn and weep.

That the two verbs, *pentheesete* ("mourn") and *klausete* ("weep"), refer to the Judgment Day of verse 23 cannot be doubted, because they also are in the aoristic future as are the others in the Beatitudes. What a sad day that will be for those Christians who laughed on earth when they should have wept. Perhaps this sounds strange. We have always thought of heaven as a place of joy. And indeed there will be a basic joy; but there can be no sameness in the degrees of joy. This would be completely contrary to the idea of the justice of God. Sacrifice must be rewarded in all its degrees. Surely the Lord had two reasons for speaking so constantly of our behavior as Christians: the effect it would have while here on ourselves aud others, and also its consequence in the hereafter. Therefore I am justified in asking you, Christian, do you find your joy in the things of the world or in the things of Christ? You show forth what you are by the things you laugh at and the things you weep at.

Pentheesete is the strongest word for mourning in the Greek language. It is used to express mourning for the dead, a passionate lament over one who was loved. You will mourn over your dead opportunity to weep over sin, you who once laughed at it.

We are reminded of the serious words of our Master in Matthew 10:32, 33 (cf. Luke 12:8, 9). "Whosoever therefore shall confess me before men, him will I confess also before my Father which is in heaven." This may be taken as an exegesis of the third Beatitude and woe as they are given in Luke 6:21 and 25.

POPULAR CHRISTIANS

Truth is illuminated and attains greater clarity when stated both positively and negatively. The Lord Jesus Christ, in addressing His disciples, told them they would be blessed when a certain class of people hated them, made fun of them, excommunicated and slandered them, as they sought to live a Christ-centered life and witness to the saving power of the Son of man. That was the negative reaction to the disciples of those who hated the Gospel. But the Lord wanted to warn them also against the positive reaction to their lives and deeds. We should beware, not only of the adverse reaction of the world toward our Christian witness, but also of its approbation. Applause is sometimes as dangerous as hatred. Stop to take stock of yourself, not only when men hate you, but also when they praise you. This is surprising advice, isn't it? It is one of those divine paradoxes given for the life of the Christian down here on earth.

The Lord stated this positive reaction of the people toward us as Christians in these words: "Woe unto you, when all men shall speak well of you! for so did their fathers to the false prophets" (Luke 6:26). Here is Christ's pronouncement of woe against Christians who seek worldly popularity.

Yet throughout the Bible we are told to watch our every step as we come in contact with others, so that their judgment of us and our Lord may be favorable. As Christians we should never disregard the judgment of others. We should show real concern as to what others think of us and our Lord. If this is the general teaching of Scripture, why did the Lord Jesus pronounce this woe? Here again we have a case here examining the text independently and superficially will lead to misunderstanding of the One who gave us these words. The Lord Jesus never meant His disciples to seek the hatred of others and to shun the love and admiration of society. If others do not have admiration and praise for the Christian who lives a righteous life, for whom then will they have it? The verse has to be considered in context and the text has to be carefully analyzed. As we study the Scriptures, we stand not so much in need of sermonizing as interpretation to help us understand what is meant. Then we must ask the Holy Spirit to help us to practice it.

Again this woe, which is the negative counterpart of the "blessed" of verse 23, is to be taken in relation to the basic phrase, "for the Son of man's sake," of verse 22. These Beatitudes and woes have no value taken independently. They must all be understood in relation to the person and work of Christ. This is our first principle of interpretation. And since this is so, we must logically conclude that this woe refers, not to those who do not know the Lord Jesus, but to those who have received Him and tasted His salvation. It refers to Christians. It refers to you, if you belong to Christ. However, if you are not a born–again believer, it means nothing to you. Quite naturally you will find your happiness in what others think of you. The more they praise you the happier you will be. If people do not think that you are the best fellow or the best girl imaginable, you will be miserable.

The Lord Jesus never disputed this philosophy as far as the unregenerate man is concerned. If you belong to the world, then it is only natural that you should seek the world's popularity. If you belong to the world, then it is all right to seek riches, an abundance of food, lots of fun, and the applause of as many as possible. Your happiness is found in these external factors of life. But you do not possess true happiness, as God understands it. You think of happiness as depending on what you have, but God knows that true happiness depends upon what you are, and even more on what He is. Therefore He does not seek to give you all you want, but to make you something that you are not. He wants to make you blessed, to dwell in your heart, to make you a new creature. This He can do if you will allow the Lord Jesus Christ to come and dwell in you. If you will receive Him as your Saviour by faith, then you will become blessed; not happy as the world understands happiness, but as God has determined it from all eternity. Blessedness, then, is what we can call real Christian happiness.

If, however, you belong to the Lord Jesus Christ and are consequently blessed, it is indeed wrong for you to seek those things that are not directly related to your blessedness but only to happiness as the world understands it. It is like a cow looking for meat to eat instead of grass. Meat will not satisfy a cow. There must be a correspondence between the nature of the individual and what he seeks to acquire. If you are a Christian, a blessed person, yet all you seek is money, food, fun, and popularity, then you are the most miserable of all creatures. You are a person of divided loyalties, a spiritual schizophrenic. You seek that which cannot feed or increase your blessedness, but rather diminishes it. You belong in your entirety neither to the Lord Jesus Christ nor to the world. You hold on to Christ with one hand and to the world with the other. You know neither the real value of blessedness nor the happiness that the world has to offer. You have the joy of Christ, and yet you seek joy also in riches, food, fun, and popularity. Yet when you get it, you feel scruples of conscience, for you have not been true to your blessedness. It depends, then, on what you are in relation to Christ whether these woes of our Lord apply to you or make sense to you.

This woe pronounced by Christ must also be understood in relation to the effect your conduct will have on the person and work of the Lord Jesus. As a Christian, it is up to you to examine your every action for the motive behind it. You may protest that this is not always practical, that we often do things more or less as a matter of habit. We do things a certain way as we are generally inclined. But it is precisely this general inclination, this general motivation of our actions and words, that I refer to when I speak of our motive each time. Do we generally do things so that men may applaud us, or so that they may be attracted to the Lord Jesus Christ? When we are elevated in the eyes and minds of people, what happens to the Lord Jesus? Is He exalted or does He suffer disgrace? The whole question is one of how our actions affect what people think of Christ. Is He more loved because of us, or less? What happens to Him when men applaud us and speak well of us? This speaking well of us is not the real point at issue, but speaking well of us in relation to how these same people (or others) speak and think of Him. Actually, as I understand this woe and the general tenor of Scripture, it is not a sin to be well-spoken of; it is sin when it shames the Lord Jesus. In our endeavor to be well-spoken of, we may bring great shame to His name.

Need I make the application of this solemn thought? It especially ought to come home to us who preach the Word and witness to the power of the Gospel. Are the methods that we use usually those that tend to make us popular or even to make Christ acceptable to the worldly minded? Let us beware lest we try to make the Lord Jesus more popular than He wants to become. Is there a secret and unacknowledged desire for our own popularity in our efforts to make Christ popular? We should be careful lest we try to change the character of Christ and His teaching by adopting popular frivolities in our witnessing for Him.

May I invite you to put yourself in the place of the Lord Jesus Christ as He stood in His humanity on the pinnacle of the temple in Jerusalem? This is the highest place around, the vantage point from which all men can see you. Here comes the devil. He is more anxious than you are to have you receive greater popular acclaim. The devil is the only one who always thinks there is yet a higher pinnacle for you to climb, the pinnacle of immediate popularity and praise. "Throw yourself down," he tempts you. "You possess supernatural powers. Nothing will happen to you. You made the law of gravitation; you can also control it. Do something out of the ordinary to win extraordinary praise. The goal is a holy one. By performing a public miracle you will make people believe in you as the Son of God." Would you have thrown yourself down? And yet how many of us do this every day by choosing expediency in preference to principle, immediate success in preference to patient labor, psychological reaction in preference to the conviction of the

Holy Spirit? Are we using our blessedness, that which God has given us, the supernatural life within, to tickle the natural fancy of people, to attract their attention, to win their applause? There were two paths that lay before the Lord: immediate popular acclaim or the cross. He chose the cross and with it the permanent crown of the resurrection for Himself and for all of us. Did His ministry, then, end in failure or success? The success of expediency and applause is temporary; the success of principle and sacrifice is permanent and glorious. Let us think seriously of what our success and the applause of men will do to the character and work of Christ. Is our aim to please Him or to please others so that they may applaud us?

WHEN IS IT WRONG TO BE POPULAR?

"Woe unto you, when all men shall speak well of you! for so did their fathers to the false prophets" (Luke 6 : 26). We have seen that these words of the Lord Jesus Christ were spoken to Christians, and they have value only as they are related to His person and work. Having laid this foundation, we are now ready to examine their meaning.

Who is the one upon whom this woe falls when men speak well of the Christian? To whom is the woe addressed? In the Greek text there is no direct object here. Christ does not say, "Woe unto you, or woe unto those who," but simply "Woe." This is to express the horror, the displeasure, of whom? I believe first of all of the Lord Jesus Christ Himself. Woe, horror, when all men speak well of you! This is a horrifying, a displeasing experience to the Lord Himself. And this fact ought to be horrifying to us also, for what displeases Him should automatically displease us.

There are few things that grieve the Lord more than for us to receive glory from men as a result of which He is put to shame. Our success can be His displeasure. The underlying thought in this woe is that if we receive all the applause and praise of men there will naturally be very little left for the Lord Himself. One thing God will not tolerate is to share His glory with another. He must be God and we must be men. This is indicated in the second commandment God gave to Moses: "For I the Lord thy God am a jealous God" (Exod. 20 : 5). The more glory we receive as we serve and witness for Christ the less He receives. If all men praise us, there are none left to praise Him. Sometimes it seems that the closer we come to Christ the greater the danger is, and the more likely we are to steal from Him the glory that belongs to Him.

It may be that this woe is addressed to us preachers more than anybody else. It is meant for those who are popular and who thrive on popularity. How we need to remember the words of the Apostle Paul, "Let us not be desirous of vain glory, provoking one another, envying one another" (Gal. 5:26). The curse of the Christian witness in our day is that every one of us believes himself to be the closest to Jesus Christ. Out of that feeling arises a contempt for our brethren whom we consider far removed from the bosom of the Saviour. God save us from the woes that are involved as a result of our supposed proximity to the Lord we so adore.

A Persian fable tells about a gourd that wound itself around a lofty palm and in a short time climbed to its very top. "How old mayest thou be?" asked the vine of the palm. "About a hundred years," answered the tree. "A hundred years, and no taller? Only look! I have grown as tall as you in less than a hundred days." "That may be true," replied the stately palm. "Every summer of my life a gourd has climbed around my body, as proud as thou art, and as short-lived as thou wilt be." This is a natural result to those of a proud, vainglorious spirit – short-lived and disastrously ended; but the humble are not so, for God protects them from the storms of temptation and gives them grace to battle against the withering blasts of the evil one, while the proud wither and droop under the pressure.

211

Oh, Lord, the pride in me remove;
My selfish will displace.
Fill Thou the vacancy with Thy love;
Uphold me by Thy grace.

Therefore we see that the woe applies both to the
person and work of the Lord Jesus Christ. What a disappointment it is to the Lord when we are spoken well
of by all men. But how blessed we are when they speak
well of the Lord, whose witnesses we are and who indwells
our hearts. The trouble with the church, as we see it, is
that it has too many admirers of men instead of devotees
of God. And the tragedy is that we preachers have our
ears attuned more to the applause and praise of men
than to the voice of God. Someone who heard Bramwell
speak asked another in the audience how it was that
Bramwell had something that was new to tell every time
he preached. "Why," said he, "you see, Brother Bramwell
lives so near the gates of heaven that he hears a great
many things that we don't get near enough to hear anything about." Is that true of you and me? If it is not,
God help us!

The more I labor for God the more persuaded I
become that, in order for God to be able to work, we,
His servants, must keep out of His way. If we seek our
own glory, then we shall accomplish only the human
and ordinary. But if we seek His glory and His alone,
then He will accomplish through us the humanly
impossible but divinely possible. Billy Dawson, one of
the great preachers of yesteryear, entered his pulpit once
and gave out as his text, "Through this man is preached
unto you the forgiveness of sins." Then he dropped down
behind the pulpit, so that nothing could be seen of him

and only his voice could be heard saying, "Not the man in the pulpit; he is out of sight; but the Man in the Book. The Man described in the Book is the Man through whom is preached unto you the forgiveness of sins."

This woe, then, is both for Christ and for us. He is displeased when all men speak well of us. And it is horrible for us, too, because it does harm to our spiritual state and our relation to the Lord Jesus Christ. Nor does it cause people to become attached to the Lord when they are so attached to us that all they can say is how good we are instead of how wonderful our Saviour is.

The following epitaph on John Bacon's grave is a challenge to thought: "What I was as an artist seemed to me of some importance while I lived; but what I really was as a believer in Jesus Christ is the only thing of importance to me now." We may be tempted actively to seek the praise of men while on earth. But what good will that do us when our eyes are closed and our work is done? Is it the praise of men, or the praise of God dwelling in men that will count then? When you stand at the end of life's road and look back, which do you think will be most important, the praise that you received from men or your fidelity to the Lord Jesus Christ? Watch lest on that day you say to yourself, "Woe unto me! All that has happened to me was that people thought I was a jolly good fellow!" That will be a tragedy.

The ancient historian points out this difference between Cicero, the polished speaker, and Demosthenes, the burning orator: After a great speech in Rome, every tongue was loud in praise of Cicero; but the people who listened to Demosthenes forgot the orator. They went home with hurried stride, lowering brow, clenched fist, muttering in a voice like distant thunder, "Let us go and fight Philip." Let us consider ourselves a failure when people say of us, "What a wonderful speaker he is," instead of being moved to love the Saviour more, so that they would be willing to die for Him if necessary.

HOW CAN ALL MEN SPEAK WELL OF US?

In our last two studies we found that the woe which our Lord pronounced concerned Christians and not those who have no connection with the Lord Jesus Christ. Then we saw that popularity is wrong for the Christian only as it adversely affects the person and work of Christ. We also discovered that, first of all, such popularity is horrifying and displeasing to the Lord Himself, and then it does the person who received it absolutely no good. When all men speak well of us as Christians, it brings woe to Christ and His work and woe upon us.

Now it is impossible for all people to praise us constantly. As in the case of poverty, hunger, hatred, slander, etc., which we find described as our occasional portion in the Beatitudes of the Lord Jesus in Luke, so here in Luke 6:26 the Lord does not refer to a continuous state but to occasional periods of popularity. He does not expect us voluntarily to go hungry all the time, but only when and if our witness for Christ makes this necessary for the glory of the Son of man and the spreading of His Gospel. What He is referring to in this woe is occasional times when men will praise us as Christians. This we gather from two words in this verse. The first is the adverbial conjunction *hotan,* which refers to a definite time, "whenever, or whensoever," as we explained in a previous study (see chapter on "Are You Hated for the Right Reasons?" in booklet entitled *Persecution).* It is both possible and probable that this will happen to you. You cannot help it or control it. The second word is the verb *eipoosin,* "they shall speak," in the aorist tense, which also indicates a definite time. The element of constancy is missing here. It is not the same as if Luke had used the verb *legoosin*, "they speak," which would indicate constant speaking. In other words, in the aorist *eipoosin*, "they shall speak," we have an indication that there are certain times in our lives when people will speak well of us, and rightly so. They cannot help but speak well of us, when we demonstrate the love, compassion, and sacrificial spirit of Jesus Christ. But is it to these times that this woe has reference? We doubt it very much. When we live Christlike lives and harm no one, a great many people will speak well of us, and this is as it should be.

But the Lord spoke about certain other times when all men will speak well of us. What are these times? I believe the answer to this is to be found in the second part of our verse, "for so did their fathers to the false prophets." It is when we are false prophets and people speak well of us that it brings woe unto us and unto the Lord. It is wrong to be popular when that involves the sacrifice of principle. If we are true prophets of God and still popular, well and good. But woe unto us if we act or speak falsely, to the shame of the Lord Jesus Christ, for the sake of being popular. When we are popular because we are true to God, then people will become attached to the Lord Jesus Christ more than to us. When we are popular because we are false prophets, then people will become more attached to us than to the Lord. If people are more attached to Luther than to the Lord Jesus Christ, then Luther enjoys the wrong kind of popularity. If people are attached to Calvin, or Arminius, or Chrysostom, or Augustine, or St. Francis, or any saint, more than they are to the Lord

216

Jesus Christ, then these saints of God have failed as far as they are concerned.

Here again we have a woe pronounced against hypocrisy. What is actually implied in this verse is that we are false for the sake of popularity. That is hypocrisy. When we are willing to sacrifice principle for the sake of personal popularity, then we do not value the truth: our lives have not been wholly conformed to the image of the Son of God. When we are true to Christ, some people are bound to speak evil of us. But the false prophets of whom Christ speaks were constantly praised by their fathers. This constant praise is indicated by the imperfect tense of the verb *epoioun,* "did," the correct translation of which should be "were doing." There was a continuity about it. If the false prophets had been true to God, they would have incurred some adverse comments, but this they could not take. There was only one way they could enjoy the constant praise of men and that was to sacrifice principle for applause, to say anything that would satisfy their listeners. It is cowardice, as well as hypocrisy, constantly to preach or to say only that which will please people, whether it is the truth or not. We must preach not to please men but to please God, not to be applauded but to convict in the power of the Holy Spirit.

The Lord speaks of the false prophets as being constantly applauded by their fathers, or by the people surrounding them, but He speaks of us Christians as being only occasionally spoken well of by all men. It is sad but true that, no matter how strong we are in faith and principle, there are times when we fall for the desire for public esteem. This desire for popularity is so much a part of our Adamic nature that it pops up from time to time even after we become Christians. We are not as bad as the false prophets. They were deceivers all the time and therefore received the constant applause of men. But we receive their applause only occasionally, as we yield to the temptation to please men instead of God.

Frankly, haven't there been times like that in your life, or am I talking about myself only? We are Christians, of course. We are blessed, certainly. That is, if we have received the Lord Jesus as our Saviour. But when we prepare a sermon, or discuss our religious beliefs with others, is it always so that people may look straight in the eyes of the Lord Jesus Christ, or also that they may fix their admiring glances on us? Do you say what you do and do what you do because it is the truth revealed in the Word of God, or because you want to hear people say how good you are and how well you speak?

If you are a false prophet, you don't horrify the Lord Jesus by your false words and pretentious life. That's all He expects of you. He experiences horror when He does not get what He expects from one of His own, when He looks to you to uplift Him and you uplift yourself. Then the Lord is horrified. And when you realize it yourself as a Christian, you are horrified, too. The sooner we realize it the better for the Lord and for us. This horror is good. It has medicinal and remedial effects. Let us beware of these moments of self-exaltation that creep into our lives, often quite unconsciously.

Parmenides, the Greek philosopher, was reading a philosophical discourse one day before a public assembly at Athens, when he observed that the whole company had left him except one, Plato, the great philosopher. He kept right on reading, saying that Plato alone was sufficient audience for him. To a really wise man, the well-weighed approbation of a single judicious character gives more heartfelt satisfaction than all the noisy plaudits of ten thousand ignorant though enthusiastic admirers. It is so much better to have the approbation of God than the approbation of all men. When it comes to a choice, says our Lord in pronouncing this woe, take the approbation of God and despise the applause of all others.

How can all men speak well of us? Isn't that an impossibility? Is this merely a hypothetical case? As perfect as the Lord Himself was, not everybody spoke well of Him. Nor do all men speak well of the devil. You could be as perfect as Christ or as evil as the devil and still not achieve this universal approval of which the Lord spoke. Was He then adducing an impossible situation? Not at all. We will understand this better when we examine what He meant by this woe.

First let us consider the expression, "all men," in the Greek text. This is *pantes hoi anthroopoi*. Again, as in this entire section of the Beatitudes and the woes in Luke, the generic noun *anthroopoi*, "men," is preceded by the definite article, making this word refer to a certain class of people only. Certain people will always speak well of the false prophets. Humanity is divided into two classes as far as every one of us is concerned, those who love us and those who do not. It is the same thing with the Lord and with the devil. It is impossible to have everybody love you or everybody hate you. When you are a false prophet, those who are faithful to God will not speak well of you, but those who are not

219

faithful to God will praise you. It is to this latter group that the words *hoi anthroopoi*, "the men," refer.

But how shall we understand the pronoun *pantes*, "all," preceding "the men"? I believe this refers to the individuals within this specific group. Liddell and Scott, the leading Greek lexicographers, say, "When this pronoun is used of the several persons in a number, it means *every*, like the Greek *hekastos*." (Greek-English Lexicon, 1889, p. 1160.) If we were to paraphrase this phrase, we might put it this way: "every one in this particular group of men." Now this is quite possible, isn't it? In our Christian walk we find a person here and there who is not a Christian. We want to please them somehow. If we stand true to the Lord Jesus Christ and tell them the truth about God and themselves as well as ourselves, they will not pat us on the back. But if we tell each one what he wants to hear and flatter them according to their varied desires, then surely they will say with one accord, "What a wonderful person you are!" Reference is made here to the approbation of individual members within a certain class of people.

There is a corresponding phrase to this one in the second part of this verse in the words, "their fathers." Again, the word "fathers" *(pateres)* is preceded by *hoi*, "the." Who spoke well of the false prophets? Not all the people, but their fathers, a particular class, those who agreed with their falsehoods and lying prophesies. They made them prophets in the first place because they were anxious to have some justification for their sinful lives. There are many ministers today, but not all are ministers of God. There are many prophets, but some are declared prophets by God and some by their fathers, the fathers of falsehood and evil.

Are you a man-made or a God-made prophet? If you are God-made, you will seek to please God, and as a natural consequence those who also seek to please Him will speak well of you. But if you are a man-made prophet, then you will go about patting men on the back so that they may do the same to you. Far too many of our congregations today have become mutual admiration societies instead of places where the prophets of God speak with divine power for the conviction of sinner and saint alike.

ARE ALL MOURNERS BLESSED?

God's greatest desire is that He may be as perfect in us as He is in Himself. What happens to us the moment that God indwells the human heart as a result of the miracle of regeneration, the new birth? What does it mean when we speak of a person as having been saved or converted? Not that he acquired religion or became religious, but that God came to dwell in his heart when man by faith invited Him to do so. It means the meeting of God with man and man with God. Who performs the introduction? The Lord Jesus Christ. And why is He necessary? Because He, being God, is holy, and having become man He became sin for us, so that in Him the holiness of God and the sinfulness of man met. The holiness of God was satisfied through His death on the cross, and the sinfulness of man was atoned for in His person.

When God is invited into the human heart, what happens? Does man become perfect? No, but he is redeemed from the guilt, the penalty, and the power of sin, and receives a new life from God. In this sense, man becomes a new creature. A little baby does not know how to treat a perfect thing when it is handed to him, nor do we expect him to. We recognize that babyhood is the first and necessary stage of life. But a baby is born to grow. So it is with man when he is born into the Kingdom of God. As a babe in Christ he hardly knows what to do with the perfect God indwelling him in the person of the Lord Jesus Christ. The conformity of man in his weakness and humanity to the Lord Jesus in His perfection and deity may be called the subjective perfection of God within us. This is what is meant by our growing spiritually, or dying to self, so that the Lord Jesus may have full and absolute reign within us. This

222

is also the highest degree of blessedness that man can attain – his conformity to the God of heaven within.

The Lord Jesus, in the Beatitudes as presented by Matthew, gives us eight conditions for the attainment of this perfect blessedness – God's subjective perfection within us, if we may call it that. Our imperfections, however, deprive us of the full enjoyment of the perfect Christ within us in the same way that a baby cannot enjoy all that an adult can. This is why we must constantly grow in Christ, and our enjoyment of Christ must increase as we live in Him and He in us. This thought is clearly and beautifully brought out in Hebrews 6:1, 2. "Therefore leaving the principles of the doctrine of Christ, let us go on unto perfection; not laying again the foundation of repentance from dead works, and of faith toward God, of the doctrine of baptisms, and of laying on of hands, and of resurrection of the dead, and of eternal judgment."

I firmly believe, from my study of the New Testament, that the relative degree to which we enjoy the Lord Jesus Christ within us here and now will be the degree of our enjoyment of Him in heaven. Not all who are saved will enjoy Christ to the same degree. If they were merely babes in Christ, they will know and enjoy Him as babes; but adults in Christ will be able to enjoy Him as such. It is inconceivable that a non-dedicated Christian would enjoy the same degree of everlasting bliss as a saint of God whose primary interest and concern were Christ.

Therefore the Lord is anxious for us to fulfill the conditions of the utmost blessedness possible for us in this life. At the same time, He gives us in each instance an idea of the woes that will be ours in the world to come if we fail to fulfill the conditions of blessedness. Our conduct, our conformity to Christ in this life, will determine our eternal destiny. The Lord is concerned that we have the utmost of Him here and now, so that we may have the utmost of Him in heaven. There must be degrees of punishment in hell and there must be degrees of joy in heaven.

We have already examined in detail the first condition of this supreme blessedness the Lord wishes for us in conjunction with the study of the first Beatitude in Luke. The first Beatitude in Matthew has to do with poverty of the spirit, that is, humility, and the first one in Luke has to do with poverty of the body.

To be humbled before the Lord Jesus Christ is the first step toward ascending the ladder of full conformity to Him. We have seen that humility by itself has absolutely no value as far as our acquisition of the blessedness of God in us is concerned. Humility does not give us a ticket to the Kingdom of God. This Beatitude as well as every other must stand on the foundation of the Lord Jesus Christ. The foundation of the Beatitudes in Matthew is indicated in the two words with which chapter 5, verse 11, ends – "for my sake." This indicates, as we saw in previous studies, that every Beatitude has to be considered in relation to the person and work of the Lord Jesus Christ. Our humility is of value only when it makes us turn from self to the Lord Jesus. To realize we are helpless does not help us to be rescued. It is the first step but not the final and saving step. It is the going to Christ in humility that counts.

These conditions of the blessed life of the Christian are related in a most wonderful way. It is a staircase of eight steps, so to speak. You cannot take the second and succeeding steps without taking the first. It must be step by step that these conditions of blessedness are fulfilled.

In our desire, then, to acquire the perfection of conformity to Christ, we enter upon the study of the second condition of the blessed life. Here is what our

Lord said about this second step: "Blessed are they that mourn: for they shall be comforted" (Matthew 5:4). It is our purpose to discover what the Lord meant by these words.

It is true that He was speaking to the disciples in particular, but here we have a general statement the universality of which cannot be doubted. "Blessed are they that mourn: for they shall be comforted." Our Lord did not say to His disciples, "Blessed are ye when ye mourn: for ye shall be comforted." The application of this statement universally apparently takes precedence over its particular application for the disciples.

This Beatitude, however, cannot be divorced from its foundation, "for my sake." The fact that you mourn has no intrinsic value. There is no comfort in mourning, but there is comfort in Christ. This Beatitude, then, in its total perspective ought to be read, "Blessed are those that mourn for my sake: for they shall be comforted by me." And let's not forget that it is the Lord Jesus Christ, the source of all comfort, who is speaking.

The first thing we must determine in our consideration of this Beatitude is the meaning of the word "mourn." In the Greek, the expression used is *hoi penthountes*, "the mourning ones." We shall not tackle the syntax or grammar of this, but must analyze the meaning of the word itself. The verb *penthein*, "to mourn," was used by the ancient Greeks, and is used today, to express lamentation and extreme sorrow for the dead. Later it came to mean any other passionate lamenting. In fact, *penthos*, "mourning," was considered by Plutarch a form of *pathos*, "passion." (See Plutarch, Cons. ad Apoll 22). To mourn, then, means to grieve with a grief that so takes possession of the whole being that it cannot be concealed.

In the New Testament this word is used nine times. Two of the most important examples of the use of the word are in Matthew 5:4 and Luke 6:25. (Also see Matt. 9:15, I Cor. 5:2, II Cor. 12:21, James 4:9, Rev. 18:11, 15, 19.) There is no stronger word of mourning in the Greek language than *penthein,* used in the second Beatitude. According to St. Chrysostom, the respected Father of the early Church, the *penthountes,* the "mourning ones," are those who so grieve that their grief manifests itself externally *(hoi met'epitaseoos lupoumenoi).* Mourning, then, as used here in the New Testament, is overt or manifested sorrow.

The question that immediately arises in our minds is, "What is blessed about sorrow?" We usually conceive of sorrow as a blight upon human experience. Sometimes it is and sometimes it is not. When we mourn for the sake of the Lord Jesus Christ, that is, when our mourning is related to His person and work, then there is blessing in our mourning and the result of it will be joy. There is a definite limitation as to who will get blessing out of sorrow. Let us not misunderstand this Beatitude as meaning that all those who sorrow are blessed.

Who can deny that there is much sorrow of one kind or another in this world of ours? We have all seen it; we have all felt it. Man is born to sorrow. Even our pleasures are sullied with pain. Even such a joyous occasion as marriage means separation from old loved ones. Surely, if they that mourn are blessed, then each of us may claim a part in this Beatitude. Can we thus appropriate the blessing? Definitely not. Sorrow apart from Christ is a curse, but sorrow for the sake of Christ becomes a blessing untold. Grief, sorrow, pain of heart, mourning, in Christ, erect no wall of partition between man and God. In Christian sorrow there is no evil.

When was God most real to us as Christians? Stop and think about this for a moment. Was it when our bankbook showed such a comfortable balance that we felt secure in the knowledge that we could provide for almost any emergency? Was it when our health was perfect? Was it when we had just been commended by the boss, or our friends and neighbors, for some piece of work well done? Was it when all was well with us, when nothing threatened our way of life or our self-esteem? No, at such times the soul is tempted to slumber, to relegate God to church services on Sunday and a perfunctory prayer at bedtime.

When is God most real to us? Be truthful about it. When the grave opens at our feet and we see a loved one laid into the earth with heartbreaking finality. When sickness strikes and the doctors confess the limitations of medical science to restore us quickly to health and strength. When we're out of work, and the rent is due, and all our plans and hopes have come to nought. When our friends walk by on the other side of the street, and our nearest and dearest can do nothing but heap reproach on us. When our own sin, and shame, and guilt, and humiliation, and pain seem more than we can be‾r. And make no mistake about it, the Christian is not only not exempt from such agony of heart, he is specifically admonished by his Lord that "in the world ye shall have tribulation."

But is it not true, Christian, that at the moment when our hearts seemed too full of anguish to bear any more, and we flung ourselves down before the Lord in utter defeat of spirit, we heard Him say, "It is I, be not afraid"? It was but for a moment, perhaps, but it was real, as real as the law of gravitation for Isaac Newton. And oh, the comfort, the strength of it! Did it not recreate us? Did it not swell our souls with faith, and hope, and joy? Did not heaven come nearer to us? And did we not rise to walk the earth as seeing Him who is invisible? Christ can be seen the clearest in the darkness. You may be far nearer God than you suppose when a thick cloud shrouds you in mourning. Be calm in God! Listen for thy soul's comfort, oh, listen to this: "Blessed are they that mourn: for they shall be comforted." (See "The Mourning Heart," by Walter Wynn, in *The Christian World Pulpit*, Vol. 39, 1891, pp. 179-181.)

HOW SHOULD CHRISTIANS REACT TO SORROW?

When is suffering a curse and when is it a blessing? This is the question that arises in the mind of any thinking person as he reads the second Beatitude in Matthew, "Blessed are they that mourn: for they shall be comforted."

There is a pretty story about the gravel-walk and the mignonette. "How fragrant you are this morning," said the gravel-walk. "Yes," said the mignonette, "I have been trodden upon and bruised, and it has brought forth all my sweetness." "But," said the gravel-walk, "I am trodden on every day, and I only grow harder." That is similar to the effect sorrow has on people. It hardens some and makes others fragrant. What makes the difference?

Before we answer that, let us ask another question: Is blessedness the result or the cause of mourning? "Blessed are the mourning ones." Are they blessed because they mourn, or do they mourn because they are blessed?

Blessedness is not necessarily the result of mourning. Every time you are sorrowful you must not expect that you will automatically be blessed. The Greek word *makarioi*, "blessed," sheds light on this. It means to possess the quality that distinguishes God, to be Godlike. In order for you to become Godlike, God must indwell your heart in the person of the Lord Jesus Christ. This is the basic teaching of the New Testament. We can be saved in no other way than by faith in the finished work of Christ on Calvary's cross. If you want to become blessed, you must believe on the Lord Jesus Christ and you will be saved. Since this is the only way we can become *makarioi*, "blessed," we must

229

exclude the possibility of mourning bringing us this blessedness.

This, however, does not hinder mourning from being a step on the ladder of blessedness, a condition under which blessedness can be appropriated by man. Let me give you an illustration from everyday life. I have a check in my hands that would enable my child to have a college education. I say to him, "Son, if you will step over here, I'll give it to you." Where does the real value lie – in the check, in the step, or in me? First it is in me, and then the check, and then the step.

So it is in our relationship with God. Without Him there could be neither the offer nor the possibility of salvation. Next comes what He offers: salvation, forgiveness of sin, blessedness. And then there must be certain attitudes on our part. The first is that of humbling our hearts before Him. The greatness of God in our experience will be proportionate to how small we consider ourselves. The second attitude is that of sorrow, of mourning. Remember, however, that there is no actual salvation in this sorrow, as there is no intrinsic value in faith. A lot of people preach faith, but everything depends on the object of your faith. If you have faith in a swindler, you will be disillusioned; but if you exercise faith in the Lord Jesus Christ you will be saved. Yet it is not the faith that saves you, but Christ. The faith is merely a means to an end. It is the end that is important in the final analysis.

The first thing we are to understand by this word mourning, no doubt, is the sorrow implied in repentance. Repentance means sorrow for our sins and turning to Christ who can save us. Repentance is the condition under which God will come to dwell within us, and since mourning is part of repentance it thus becomes a condition of blessedness. You humble yourself by admitting you are lost. This is followed by sorrow

230

for your lost state. But neither your realization nor your sorrow can help you apart from Christ. What is the use of realizing that you are in a burning building, if you don't know of a way of escape?

The mourning of which our Lord speaks is the second step or condition of the blessedness that comes to man from Christ and because of Christ. If you recognize that you are a sinner, and are sorry for your sinful state, it is because you have already ascended the first step, that of humility. A strange thing, isn't it? By going down you ascend — not in your own strength but by the power of Him who knows how to elevate the humble. No proud man is ever sorry because he has brought failure upon himself. He will find a thousand excuses, but he will never say, "I am wrong." You cannot fulfill the second condition of blessedness unless you fulfill the first. Recognize who you are and then weep. This is the meaning of the first and second Beatitudes as we find them in Matthew. A paraphrase of the second Beatitude, then, would be, "The mourning ones! They are blessed. Their tears have brought them to the Lord Jesus Christ."

Why do you suppose these two particular words, "blessed" and "mourning," were chosen by the Holy Spirit in the Greek to express the thought that our Master must have put forth in Aramaic? We saw that the word *makar*, from which we get *makarioi*, "blessed," was used to designate the blessed dead. The living, in the minds of the ancient Greeks, had little chance of acquiring blessedness in this life. They felt that the pain and suffering of daily existence were inconsistent with *makariotees*, that blessedness could not be ours while we had to mourn down here on earth. And when would we cease to mourn but after this earthly life was over? The Lord wanted to dispel this misconception. He wanted His disciples and the whole wide world to know that suffering does not block our way to God nor

231

does it cease to exist after we become blessed. So many of us say, in the midst of great affliction, "Oh, I wish it were all over, so that I might not have to suffer any more!" And when we hear of someone who has died after a long and painful illness, we sigh with relief and say, "He is much better off, poor man."

"Now, just a minute!" the Lord says. "I want you to know that there is a definite relationship between the blessedness that I give and the suffering that I permit." This is why He couples two such incongruous words as "blessed" and "mourn." "No one," He says, "can attain to the blessedness that I give unless he mourns in repentance. This is the first thing." But it is not exclusively to this mourning of repentance that He is referring. He wants us to let our light shine in this world, here and now, and not wait until our eyes are closed in death. The purpose of life is not to die but to make others live in Christ and acquire this blessedness that we possess.

It is in this life that the Lord wants us to show that our blessedness received from God is not affected by sorrow. As Christians, we do not cease to be blessed when sorrow strikes at the very root of our lives. The world looks at it differently. It is as natural for man to shrink from trouble as it is for the African to try to escape the bite of a serpent. We hunt for bubbling pleasure, pant for unruffled ease, and long for such a worldly status as will deliver us from all care. We pursue those objects which we fondly dream are able to rock to sleep our care. Here we have Christ linking blessedness to mourning. He plows through the furrows of our common conceptions. He asserts that in men's spiritual experiences mourning can become the river on whose surface sails one portion of life's highest blessedness.

The people who are merely happy, that is, those whose joy in life depends on fortunate circumstances, will cease to be happy when sorrow and adversity strike. Sorrow in the life of the Christian does not strike the chord of discontent and dissonance but the chord of blessedness, and brings forth music. The world will be astonished when they see joy in the house of sorrow. This can happen only in a Christian – a blessed – home. The world does not consider mourners, the afflicted and sorrowful, happy or blessed. The happiness hunters do not look for joy in the shadow of grief.

Legend has it that a German baron made a great Aeolian harp by stretching wires from tower to tower of his castle. When the harp was ready, he listened for the music. But it was in the calm of summer, and in the still air the wires hung silent. Autumn came with its gentle breezes, and there were faint whispers of song. At length the winter winds swept over the castle, and now the harp answered in majestic music. This is a very good illustration of what our Lord meant when He said, "Blessed the mourners." Their blessedness is more apparent at times when adversity and sorrow strike. When as a Christian you can laugh and be jovial when everything goes well, the world will think nothing of it. But they will be deeply impressed when the harp of blessedness plays music in the time of storm. This is why the Lord associates blessedness with mourning and sorrow in this life. He wants people who are strangers to this blessedness to know that, although sorrow is inevitable, it can bring forth praise rather than sighs. A blessed Christian is one who can see purpose in sorrow and use it. He saw it in the first place when, in his sinful state, he realized his lost condition and the necessity of going to Christ. Now that he is in Christ, he is not exempt from sorrow, but sorrow brings out the brilliance of his blessedness for all the world to see.

THE TWO KINDS OF SORROW

When the Lord said, "Blessed are they that mourn: for they shall be comforted," He meant primarily those who are sorry for their sinful state and go to Him for salvation. But He also meant that in sorrow our blessedness in Christ shines forth most brilliantly before the world.

It is sorrow that leads us to Christ, and it is sorrow born triumphantly that points people to Christ most vividly. This is the real message of the second Beatitude in Matthew. Christianity is different from any other religion because of its attitude toward sorrow. We could truthfully say that the depth of a man's Christian experience may be measured by his willingness to endure grief and his capacity to feel the right sort of grief.

It is instinctive to avoid pain and sorrow; it is instinctive to hug to ourselves the comforts of an advantageous position, and to experience no grief that by a reasonable amount of effort and selfishness we can avoid. And this sort of instinct is strengthened in us as the result of the false supposition that Christ suffered in order that we might not have to suffer. There is some truth in this, of course. It is the constant testimony of the New Testament that Christ, in pain and anguish of body and mind, offered Himself a sacrifice to the Father in order to bring us back to God. Thus to redeem us from sin is to release us from the worst sort of pain, the pain of a conscience alienated from God, the pain of the worm that dies not and the fire that devoureth. But it is wrong to assume that the suffering of Christ was meant to exempt us from the suffering and sorrow consequent to salvation. Christ suffered in order to bring us to God, in order that when we are brought near to God we might each in our own time and place suffer as He suffered. There is nothing, as far as we can certainly know, that Christ endured that we, His redeemed, are not required to endure – only now with a new hope, with a new intelligence, with a fresh redemptive purpose.

Is it the death of the body? Christ by dying took the sting out of death, but He left us to die. The death of the Christian is mournful in a way, but it does not deprive him or the Christians remaining behind of the blessedness that Christ gives. It is on the cross that Christ shone the brightest. It is on his deathbed that a Christian shines the brightest, too. It was the song at midnight in the Philippian jail that led the jailer and others to take note of the blessedness of the Christian. Christ has taught us to see in Him the truth that "whom the Lord loveth he chasteneth, and scourgeth every son whom he receiveth" (Heb. 12:6).

The fact that a man's Christianity is measured by his willingness, his deliberate willingness, to endure pain does not mean that he is to go about seeking pain as if pain were a good and as if joy were an evil. That would be a morbid philosophy of life. That is not the true spirit of Christ. All Christ's sufferings were because of others. Only once do we find our Lord imposing pain upon Himself and that was during the forty-day fast in the wilderness. But this self-sought pain that Christ endured occupied a very small place in all His sufferings.

What the Lord endured and suffered sprang from a threefold root. It was the pain that belongs to innocence and sinlessness in a world like ours; it was the pain that came of obedience as He learned more of the meaning of obedience through the things that He suffered; it was the pain that came of sympathy in a world of anguish like ours. So it was only by the pursuing of His course that suffering came. Suffering did not become the course itself. It became part and parcel of His sinlessness, of His obedience, and of His sympathy. In this manner pain is unavoidable for us, too, but not as an end in itself. The Lord never appoints a way before us and says, "Here is the way of suffering and sorrow; follow in it." He appoints the way of blessedness, of Christlikeness, of obedience to the will of the One who indwells us, and of sympathy and service for those around us who are in sin. Sorrow is not service but the concommitant of service. When sorrow is regarded as service, it ceases to be good and becomes evil; it ceases to be acceptable to God and of use to our fellow men.

The Lord lived about thirty-three years on this earth. Thirty of them were spent for the most part in the quiet and happy atmosphere of the little town of Nazareth. It was when He plunged into His public ministry that His sufferings increased. For Him to have sought to avoid suffering and sorrow would have been disobedience in service. We know that He would never have given up service because of sacrifice. And it may be that His service as well as ours would never bear the results that God expects without the willingness to suffer the sorrow that accompanies service.

The Lord came to do the will of His Father. He foresaw and deliberately accepted the burden of that pain that His Father had chosen for Him. He accepted with the manfulness of a perfect human will, as the God-Man, the burden that obedience to the Father had laid upon Him. This is what He in turn expects of us. His desire is not for us to suffer but to serve; but can there be effective service without suffering? Sorrow seems to be an intrinsic part of effectual service and obedience to God.

The Christian is one who also feels the right sort of pain and grief. Look around at the people of the world. How amazingly they differ in the sort of things that hurt them. You touch this man through his pocket, that man through his family affections, the voluptuary and sensualist through his lusts and appetites, the proud man through his honor, the man of letters through his reputation, the good man through his conscience. Are there not differences? Are they not amazing? Is not one man altogether unhappy under circumstances where another would feel nothing, and another bowed down to the dust by a burden that would be imperceptible to his fellow? So different are we in the things that make us grieve, and this difference is substantially a difference in the ideals and thoughts that move our lives.

A blessed person is content in whatever state he finds himself, while a person who has never experienced God is never content no matter how much he has. The ideal of the one is to please God with whatever he possesses – and God is pleased with much or little – while the worldly person seeks to please himself. But he can never adequately do that, for self always seeks something more. Selfishness has no saturation point. There are sorrows brought about by selfishness of which the blessed person knows nothing. In one way, therefore, the sorrows of the blessed person are far less than those of the worldly person. In the sorrow of the godly there is purpose; in the sorrow of the ungodly, no purpose at all.

The Lord never meant by this Beatitude that all mourning carries a benediction with it. He distinguishes between the two kinds of mourning: that which leads to repentance, to the Lord Jesus Christ, and has a purposeful end, on the one hand, and that which is the natural consequence of sin on the other. There is no blessing in feeling the sorrow that results from sin. Even the beasts of the field feel this kind of sorrow. They violate the laws of nature and suffer for it. Man violates the laws of God, the spiritual as well as the physical, and he suffers for it. This is not the sorrow of which

237

the Lord speaks. There is a sorrow that is demonic, that chafed ambition or disappointed vanity writhes under. There is also a sorrow that is the evidence of a sanctified and regenerated heart. The Lord Jesus makes the distinction between these two kinds of suffering and sorrow clear in this second Beatitude. The one causes despair, the other brings joy.

The Attic Greeks used the word *makarioi*, "blessed," to apply also to those who belonged to the upper classes, because it was thought they lived in a region untouched by a breath of pain. When a person becomes blessed in Christ, the things over which he sorrows are not the trivialities of life. He has the capacity for the right kind of grief, which is always lost in God's comfort. There is no cheapness about his grief. There is an aristocracy about it, for it is godly grief. What grieves God grieves him. Is that the case with you, or do you grieve over a million and one things? It depends on whether you are merely happy, circumstance-conditioned, or blessed, God-conditioned.

WHAT IS GODLY SORROW?

Sorrow comes to all men, but it does not affect all men alike. If it is not the right kind of sorrow, it not only does not bring blessing with it, but it leads to death. When our Lord gave the second Beatitude in Matthew, He did not promise a benediction on all kinds of sorrow. "Blessed are they that mourn: for they shall be comforted," He said. But He did not refer to all kinds of tears and mourning.

The Lord speaks here of a very distinct group of mourners, of a particular sorrow. In fact, the phrase, "they that mourn," is expressed in Greek by the participle of the verb *pentheoo* preceded by the definite article. As we saw in previous studies, this is done to distinguish one class from another. (See A. T. Robertson's *Grammar of the Greek New Testament*, p. 757.)

This sorrow is for sin rather than for the consequences of sin. The distinction is vital and practical. A man may live in immorality. As a result he contracts a loathsome disease, his children are mentally retarded, and a number of other calamities befall him. This naturally causes him sorrow, but he mourns only because of the consequences of sin and not over the sin itself. He may go right on living in sin, or give it up only because he is afraid of further consequences. Any man is bound to mourn deeply over the consequences of his sin when the inevitable overtakes him; but only a Christian feels poignantly the inherent bitterness of the sin, quite apart from its consequences.

Judas mourned over his sin, but only because of its evil effects. Peter mourned after committing sin, not because of its effects, but because it was the sin itself that he deplored. Pharaoh did not actually repent, though he wept when he cried in his agony, "Take away the frogs," that is, the judgment. But David mourned rightly when he said, "Take away my iniquities, I beseech thee." The sorrow that is sanctified by the Saviour's benediction exists in the heart – often as a principle, occasionally as a passion, which mourns and grieves because of sin as a thing hateful in itself, rather than because the consequences of that sin are injurious to his comfort and peace.

The sorrow that the blessed person feels extends not only to sins that are known, or public, but to secret sins. There is no more striking or indisputable proof of a regenerate heart than sorrow because of sins that the world knows nothing about. David sorrowed for numbering the people, which the world did not think of as a sin, as well as for the murder that he committed, which all men hated. And David prayed most spiritually and fervently when he said, "Cleanse thou me from secret faults." These often cause greater sorrow to the Christian than the open and observable sins. If they don't, then he is guilty of hypocrisy.

Godly sorrow—that which distinguishes the blessed person – is not only felt as a passion, or has power as a principle, but also shows itself long after in the tone, the temper, and the conduct of the whole man. When Pharaoh was under the judgments of God, he owned and regretted his sin; but as soon as the judgments passed away, he returned to his wickedness again. Saul persecuted David and deplored what he had done. But when there was no more sign of judgment, he commenced his bloody persecution again. But we read that when Job sorrowed over his sins he said, "If I have done iniquity, I will do no more" (Job 34:32). The sorrow that not only acknowledged bitterly the iniquity that was perpetrated, but was able to add, "I will do no more," was a sorrow of a godly sort; was a sorrow that the Apostle describes when he says, "Godly sorrow worketh repentance to salvation not to be repented of: but the sorrow of the world worketh death. For behold this selfsame thing, that ye sorrowed after a godly sort, what carefulness it wrought in you, yea, what clearing of yourselves, yea, what indignation, yea, what fear, yea, what vehement desire, yea, what zeal, yea, what revenge! In all things ye have approved yourselves to be clear in this matter" (II Cor. 7:10, 11). Here is the sorrow that is the inspiration of grace, and on whose brow there is written the benediction that cannot be effaced, "Blessed are they that mourn: for they shall be comforted."

The sorrow experienced by the blessed Christian arises from sin seen in the light of Christ's countenance. This is why I insist that none of the Beatitudes can be separated from the person and work of the Lord Jesus Christ. The foundation of the whole structure of the blessed life is expressed in the phrase, "for my sake," in Matthew 5:11. Sin seen in the flash and splendor of Sinai will make us perceive and feel that it is an awful and a perilous thing; but seen in the light of that countenance that looked in agony from the cross, it will make us feel it poignantly and as a bitter thing. Hence it is stated, as strikingly illustrating the sentiment before us, "They shall look upon me whom they have pierced, and they shall mourn" (Zech. 12:10). Again it is said, "Him [Christ] hath God exalted . . . a Prince and a Saviour, for to give repentance," that is, godly sorrow, "and forgiveness of sins" (Acts 5:31). A sorrow that drives us from Christ, or does not originate with seeing Christ, will not be blessed nor will it end in joy.

Godly sorrow always ends with joy for it ends with Christ. That sorrow for sin that drives to despair is from beneath. But that sorrow for sin that prostrates us at the feet of Jesus is an inspiration from above. As long as the heart beats, and the sun shines, and the day of grace lasts, there is no sorrow that should drive us from Christ. It is nearer to go to Jesus than to go away from Him.

Furthermore, godly sorrow not only weeps over its own sins and runs to Christ, but also weeps over the sins of others, the world, the Church in her present state. Jeremiah, when he looked around him, said, "Oh that my head were waters, and mine eyes a fountain of tears, that I might weep day and night for the slain of the daughter of my people" (Jer. 9:1). And David said, "Rivers of waters run down mine eyes, because they [that is, the world] keep not thy law" (Ps. 119:136). No Christian can read his newspaper, or listen to some modern sermons, without crying bitterly. If we are human, we must be sorry. If we are Christian, we must in bitterness of heart mourn over the indifference of the world toward the things that count – the Lord and His Gospel – and over the worldly and unbelieving state of the Church.

When the Apostle Paul visited Athens, surprisingly he was not impressed with what would have probably impressed everybody else. If he had been a mere philosopher, he would have been so charmed with the Parthenon and other monuments of that most magnificent city that he would have written poetry, or pronounced an oration upon it. But we read that, when there, he had no eye for its statuary, no time to listen to its philosophers. It was not that he had no taste, not that he was no scholar, not that he had no aesthetic susceptibilities, but that he had a heart so charged with the grace of God, and with sympathy and sorrow for man's ruin, that he saw nothing but a city wholly given to idolatry.

Though there is much outside the Christian to make him shed tears, there is a bright sunshine within that makes him rejoice when all the world is dark. A Christian, when he looks around him, must be sad. When

242

he looks within himself, he cannot but see elements of sorrow; but when he looks above himself, and learns what his destiny is, and what the price of it was, he must rejoice with joy unspeakable and full of glory. (See John Cumming, *Benedictions: or the Blessed Life,* John Jewett and Cò., 1854, pp. 72 - 83.)

IS GOD THE AUTHOR OF SORROW ?

We have seen thus far that there are two kinds of mourners and two kinds of mourning and sorrow: one that leads to destruction and the other to repentance and the joy of deliverance. There is no doubt that our Master meant the latter when He said in the second Beatitude in Matthew, "Blessed are they that mourn: for they shall be comforted."

But how are we to analyze sorrow — a tear, a human tear, a good tear, if we may call it that? It is child's play to analyze a medical compound compared with the analysis of a tear. Science is of no value when you desire to discover the root causes of a tear. In a passage of unsurpassed beauty, Amiel, the French philosopher, remarks, "One may guess the why and wherefore of a tear, and yet find it too subtle to give any account of. A tear may be the poetry of many feelings passing through the soul at the same time, the essence of so many opposing thoughts. Sometimes a tear simply expresses the overflow of the soul, the result of memory. But a tear can express all that one cannot or will not say, even all that one refuses to say to oneself. Confused conflicts, secret troubles, suppressed grief, smothered conflict, voiceless regret, the emotions we have struggled against, the pain we have sought to hide, our fears, sufferings, our restless doubts, our unrealized dreams, the wounds inflicted upon our ideal, our hopes, and a multitude of ills which slowly accumulate in one corner of the heart like water dropping noiselessly on the roof of a cavern, together with the mysterious movements of the inner life, all these things will sometimes end in an instant of emotion, and the emotion concentrates itself in a tear just visible on the edge of the eyelid." This is an exquisite description of your tears and mine and what is behind them, but in reality it only gives us a faint idea of the depths of human sorrow. It is the common heritage of humanity, of the ungodly and the godly, but there is a difference in its cause and its end. The sorrow of the ungodly, if it is not followed by true repentance, leads to death, and the sorrow of the godly leads to life. The one is caused by the distressing consequences of sin and the other by the conviction of the Holy Spirit.

Although the cause and the end of sorrow are different in the ungodly and the godly, yet sorrow is sorrow, and tears are tears. Constitutionally, whether we are Christians or not, we shrink from them. It is the joyful experiences of life that we welcome, not the sorrowful ones. You and I would rather go to a wedding than to a funeral. Sorrow is not an essential good like love, in spite of the fact that it will mingle with any good thing, and is even so allied to good that it will open the door of the heart for any good. It is true that there are always more sorrowful than joyful men standing about the everlasting doors that open into the presence of the Most High. It is true, also, that joy is in its nature more divine than sorrow; for although man must sorrow, and God share his sorrow, yet in Himself God is not sorrowful, and the glad Creator never made man for sorrow, and to claim that He did would be an affront to His very nature and inconsistent with His ultimate purpose for His creatures. Sorrow is but a stormy strait through which man must pass to his ocean of peace. He makes joy the last verse in every song.

But it is generally true, nevertheless, that a man in sorrow is brought nearer to God than a man in joy. Gladness may make a man forget to be thankful; misery drives him to prayer. For we are not yet perfect, we are only becoming. And to become what God wants us to be we must pass through the valley of sorrow. The

245

endless day will at length dawn, whose every throbbing moment will propel our hearts Godward; we shall scarce need to lift them up: now there are two doorkeepers to the house of prayer, and sorrow is more on the alert to open than her granddaughter Joy.

The gladhearted child runs farther afield; the wounded child turns to go home. The weeper sits down close to the gate; the Lord of life draws nigh to him from within. God loves not sorrow, yet rejoices to see a man sorrowful, for in his sorrow man leaves his heavenward door on the latch, and God can enter to help him. He loves to see him sorrowful, for then He can come near to part him from that which makes his sorrow a welcome sight. So good a medicine is sorrow, so powerful to slay the moths that infest and devour the human heart, that the Lord is glad to see a man weep. He congratulates him on his sadness. Grief is an ill-favored thing, but she is Love's own child, and her mother loves her. (See Dr. George Macdonald's sermon, "Sorrow, the Pledge of Joy," in the *Christian World Pulpit*, 1892, Vol. 42, pp. 478 - 480 tr.)

The most wonderful thing we discover through sorrow is that, though God is not its author, as He is not the author of evil, He uses sorrow for our good. Because of the universality of sorrow, and its visitation upon both the godly and the ungodly, we tend to forget that its origin is not in God but man. God actually is not responsible for our sorrow and suffering. These are the direct and original result of evil and God is not the author of evil. Death and mourning came upon man as a result of his disobedience toward his Creator in Adam. True, God created man with the power of choice, but this was a necessity, for if disobedience were not possible, then obedience would be a sham and a mockery. It would be like holding elections with only one candidate, as they do in the communist countries. Evil is the concommitant of good, and good could not be conceived of without the existence of evil. This evil was the consequence of our disobedience, of our wrong and deliberate choice. We therefore became the immediate cause of evil and God permitted it. What one permits, he does not become the cause of. What an unjust God He would be if He had foreordained joy for obedience and no sorrow for disobedience. The consequence of our own evil choice in Adam is part and parcel of God's justice.

Therefore there can be no life exempt from sorrow and mourning, since there is no life exempt from sin, original sin. The Apostle Paul declares it in unequivocal terms when he says, "For all have sinned, and come short of the glory of God" (Rom. 3:23). "And God saw that the wickedness of man was great in the earth, and that every imagination of the thoughts of his heart was only evil continually" (Gen. 6:5). "For there is no man that sinneth not" (I Kings 8:46). "They are all gone aside, they are all together become filthy: there is none that doeth good, no, not one" (Ps. 14:3, cf. Ps. 130:3). "Who can say, I have made my heart clean, I am pure from my sin?" (Prov. 20:9, cf. Ecc. 7:20). "All we like sheep have gone astray; we have turned every one to his own way; and the Lord hath laid on him the iniquity of us all" (Isa. 53:6). "But we are all as an unclean thing, and all our righteousnesses are as filthy rags; and we all do fade as a leaf: and our iniquities, like the wind, have taken us away" (Isa. 64:6, cf. Mic. 7:2). And then finally John, speaking even of the believing Christians, says, "If we say that we have no sin, we deceive ourselves, and the truth is not in us" (I John 1:8, cf. I John 5:19). As sin therefore is our common heritage, so is sorrow. Sin is the mother of sorrow, but there is a sorrow that is the

247

mother of joy, and it is of this sorrow that the Lord Jesus is speaking in the second Beatitude.

We repent because of sin, and in repentance one of the main elements is godly sorrow. We mourn because of sin. And when we do, the result is joy, the joy of forgiveness and deliverance by the Lord. But the person who enjoys sin will not weep over it. He will indulge in it as freely as he can as long as he can make it trouble free. But inherent in sin is sorrow, terrible sorrow, deathly sorrow, that man can do nothing about, except perhaps be completely disgusted with himself. But it is only the person who feels the guilt and penalty of sin who will mourn over it.

Of course, the sinner experiences a certain amount of pleasure in sin. But there is no joyful state in sin. As for the Christian, he experiences mourning over the constant harassment of sin from within and without. He mourns over the very presence and possibility of sin, not necessarily over its performance only. But the Christian turns to the Christ within him who is ever present, and in Him he finds comfort and succor. Here is where there can be a reconciliation between two irreconcilables — blessedness, a state of holiness, and mourning, a state produced by sin — in one and the same life, the life of the Christian here and now. Blessedness is not produced by either joy or sorrow, as the world knows them. But neither is it affected by the circumstances of life, joyful or sorrowful, for blessedness is the result of man's fellowship and communion with Christ consequent to his sense of sin and sorrow over sin.

WHY IS SORROW A BLESSED THING ?

Exactly what does the Lord mean by "mourning," as we find it in the second Beatitude? It is not just shedding tears or inflicting physical harm on ourselves. Church history tells us of a group of men called the Anchorites, who lived in the fourth century. They dwelt in solitude, fasted, and injured the body. The nearer they could bring themselves to the level of the animals the better pleased they were. One sect of Anchorites grazed with the common herds in the fields of Mesopotamia, and they were hence called *boskoi,* or "shepherds." They acquired a great reputation for holiness because of their mournful attitude toward life. One of the most famous of these monks was Simeon Stylites (395 - 451), so called from his standing for years on the top of a column sixty feet high until his muscles became rigid. Some of these hermits hung weights on their bodies; others kept themselves in cages; all endeavored to make themselves miserable.

The motive of many of these men may have been a truly honorable one, a desire to escape from the vices of the great cities. But the greater the corruption of society the more need for holy men and women to live in that society. The world can only become darker by the withdrawing of its lights and more corrupt through the gathering away of the salt scattered over it. Had Simeon Stylites gone forth as a missionary to preach the Gospel, instead of standing on his pillar, surely his reward in heaven would have been greater and the burden on men's hearts lighter. These men failed to see that there is nothing in sorrow that is in any sense expiatory. No matter how many tears you may shed and how many afflictions you may impose upon yourself, how many stairs you ascend on your knees, or how many miles you walk, your penances will never cancel any of your sins. All the penitential sorrows that ever pierced the agonized heart never secured, by their merit, the forgiveness of one transgression. A humble and a broken heart is indeed a sacrifice, but it is not a propitiation; it is a spiritual offering.

The Greek word for "mourning," *penthos,* as we said in a previous study, takes the form of a passion. It is feeling, especially over the loss of a loved one. It is not just grief; it is the manifestation of grief. In Modern Greek we still use exactly the same word to indicate bereavement. The word has not lost or changed its meaning since very ancient times. When we say of someone in Greek *penthei,* we indicate that she is wearing a black dress if it is a woman, or a black tie or band around the coat sleeve if a man. When we see these external signs, we know that they represent bereavement.

But we do not believe that the Lord in this Beatitude referred merely to expressions of sorrow and mourning, but rather to a state of mourning, a condition of the heart. We arrive at this conclusion first of all by noting that the present participle of the verb is used here. It is *penthountes,* "those who are mourning." It does not say *hoi pentheesantes,* "those who did mourn once in the past." Nor is it in the future to indicate mourning to come. It refers to those who "are mourning." Now the present participle, like the present infinitive, is timeless and durative. If we were to render this phrase correctly from the Greek, we should say, "Blessed are those who once mourned, those who now mourn, and those who will continue to mourn." "Blessed! the mourning ones." (See A. T. Robertson, *A Grammar of the Greek New Testament,* p. 891.) What does that mean? It means that this mourning extends to the past, to the present, and to the future. It is timeless.

There is a starting point to our blessed mourning. It started when we mourned unto repentance. But it did not end there. It continued after our conversion to Christ and will continue for all the days of our blessed state in Christ. However, Christ indwells us only during our earthly lives. When we see Him face to face we shall be with Him. There are two verses of Scripture that make this very clear. The first is Colossians 1:27, "Christ in you, the hope of glory." And what is this hope of glory? That one day we shall no more have Christ in this mortal sinful body of ours, but our bodies will be glorified and we shall be with Christ. The second verse is Philippians 1:23, "For I am in a strait betwixt two," says the Apostle Paul, "having a desire to depart, and to be with Christ; which is far better." Our state of blessedness, that is, of God within us, starts with our conversion experience and continues throughout our lives.

Now, when the present participle is used with the article, as is the case here, it is often iterative. In other words, it is an experience that recurs constantly, and it becomes a state, a condition, a second nature with us. The Christian, in his state of blessedness, cannot but constantly feel sad over sin, whether in him or outside of him. The moment he loses the sense of sorrow over sin and takes joy in sin, a break occurs in the fellowship of the two I's within him, Christ and self. The Lord is actually telling us that, in order for us to enjoy His blessedness, His presence within us, we must always be in a state of mourning. Why? Because we live in a world full of sin. The greater the light is within us the greater the darkness appears without. The holier our lives are the greater will be our discernment of sin in and around us. A blessed person is not blind to sin. If he is, he is just deceiving himself.

This fully agrees with the fact that repentance, as

taught in the Scriptures, is not a once-and-for-all experience. It has a beginning, but it is continuous. The moment we repent, we begin to acquire a sense of the holiness and majesty of God. As we grow in the life of blessedness, our view of God's holiness continues to increase along with our view of our own sinful unworthiness. The holier we see God to be the more sinful we consider ourselves. There is an aristocracy of spiritual discernment as we grow more Christlike. The more Christ is esteemed the more self is abhorred. We rejoice over Christ but we mourn over sin. Things that before were not sinful become so when they are placed in view of the holiness of God. It is then that we understand that we constantly fall short of God's expectation for our lives. Before conversion, we are mostly aware of our sins of commission. Then, as we grow in Christ, we not only mourn over the sins committed (which are now on the decrease), but we also mourn over our sins of omission and sins of disposition. Our sense of right and wrong is greatly sharpened as we grow in the state of blessedness in Christ, and therefore we grow in our experience of mourning. We mourn over things that we would never have blinked an eye at before.

It can therefore be safely said that the state of blessedness of the Christian is proportionate to his state of mourning. Satisfaction with what we are and what we do spells stagnation and mediocrity of blessedness. That is the trouble with many Christians. They are sorry for their sin initially, but when they fall into sin again they think nothing of it. The man who is not conscious of sin in his life is hopeless. He will be happy in his sin. And this is the tragedy of our flippant, superficial, modern-day Christianity. So many of us are happy in our sinfulness while we call ourselves Christians and profess a once-and-for-all experience of godly sorrow in repentance. Every time we feel the sense of our own sin, no matter how big or how small, we become more blessed, for we come to Christ. The sense of sin produces sorrow, and sorrow makes us run to Christ. In this, sorrow is a blessed thing.

COMFORT FOR THE SORROWING

God does not comfort all who mourn. Only those who mourn in Christ, and for His sake, are promised the comfort of Christ. The fact that the second Beatitude in Matthew refers to a special kind of mourners is apparent from its second clause. "Blessed are they that mourn: *for they shall be comforted.*" Actually, in Greek, the second clause says, "for these ones shall be comforted." Not all mourners shall be comforted, but this particular class of mourners whom we described quite extensively in our previous studies. There is no comfort for those who mourn as a result of their own sin, those who reap the natural consequences of their sinful lives. Nor is there comfort for those whose sorrow is of the world. That leads to death, as the Apostle Paul declares in II Corinthians 7:10. There is comfort only for godly sorrow.

The first thing that we note in this second clause of the Beatitude is that the comfort of God is for those who come to His Son, the Lord Jesus Christ. And this comfort is for individuals. The situation itself may be sorrowful, but the individual who experiences sorrow and mourning will find comfort in it. Comfort is only possible when we are in situations of sorrow. All godly sorrow is so medicinal that many of us can sympathize with Augustine's passionate prayers for the "grace of tears." Affliction's showers dash the blossoms from the branches but fertilize the roots and enrich the fruitage of autumn. Bereavements and disappointments prune the vine but swell the grapes. Tribulations tear but unclog the soil. Adversity opens the gates of heaven to visions which prosperity is never privileged to see. Often they come home with heaviest sheaves who went forth weeping with the precious seed. All these benefits of sorrow are obtained in full measure by those who mourn the guilt of sin. The agonies of their repentance are sanctified that they may "rise on stepping stones of their dead selves to higher things." And like as in physical disease, the time when a man feels weakest is not when the fever is upon him, but when it is passing away (wherefore when he is most distressed he has really most reason to be cheered): so with such as mourn their sins, when convictions of guilt are deepest and hearts most heavy, they are drawing nearest to that spiritual health which is the beginning of everlasting life. (See William J. Wood's sermon, "The Heirs of the Kingdom," in *The Christian World Pulpit,* Vol. 38, 1890, pp. 95 - 96.)

As blessedness is the natural result of our mourning over our sins, so also is the comfort that comes from the Lord Jesus Christ. Sorrow for sin brings us to that Man of Sorrows who came forth from God to bear our sorrows and carry our griefs. Just when we most truly mourn our sin against the loving Father He comforts us with the message of His grace, with the vision of that Christ, once crucified, but now throned in all power and might, who is saying, "Thy sins, which are many, are all forgiven thee. Go in peace." It is the Incarnate God who speaks — that is the comfort. It is a finished work of atonement He proclaims — that is the comfort. It is the word of complete reconciliation and assured peace — that is the comfort. It is joy unspeakable and full of glory. It is union with Christ Himself — that is the comfort. And there is no comfort in the whole wide world which can compare with this. It is worth all the mourning and the weeping to have the enjoyment of such comfort, for it means God within us and the fullest realization of that. *(Ibid.,* p. 96.)

Very interestingly, the word that is used in the Greek for "comfort" is the same word from which one of the names of the Holy Spirit is derived, *parakleetos,* the Paraclete, or the Comforter. It is the basic verb *parakaleoo*, which means "to summon, to call to one's side, to call upon for help, to appeal to, to request, to encourage, to comfort, to cheer up." Stop to think of the ministry of the Holy Spirit in the life of the believer and you will know why He is called the Comforter so many times in the New Testament. The Holy Spirit is the One who brings conviction of sin in the first place. Without His power you could never feel sorrow over your sinful estate or of coming short of the perfect stature of Christ after you are saved. The Holy Spirit is the energizing power in the human heart. The moment you realize your helplessness and cry out for help, you do so in the power of the Holy Spirit. In yourself you are absolutely dead in trespasses and sins. You don't know anything. But in the Holy Spirit, the Third Person of the Trinity, you know that you are a sinner and that there is a fountain of blood at the cross where your sins can be exchanged for the joy of forgiveness and salvation.

The declaration of this second Beatitude, then, is that the person who mourns for his sin and looks to Christ for forgiveness does so in the power of the Holy Spirit. The moment you humble yourself and mourn for your sin and go to Christ, the Holy Spirit takes up His abode in you. He is your comfort, He is your joy, He is your victory. You cannot take any credit for yourself, for it all belongs to God working within you. This is why the circumstances of life from without can never affect your blessedness, for the things God creates or permits cannot affect Him.

It is also worthwhile to note that this verb *paraklee-theesontai*, "shall be comforted," is in the passive voice, which indicates that the comfort is not intrinsic in the sorrow, nor does it find its source in us, but it comes from outside ourselves. Here we have a statement of the objective reality of God the Holy Spirit. God is not a creation of our minds, He is not an idea, but a Person outside of ourselves and independent of ourselves. There are some today who try to tell us that in ourselves we have a storehouse of comfort, we can pull ourselves up by our own boot straps. You will never be able to do that. There is only One who can pull you up and that is God, by an action independent of yourself.

And then, finally, we must point out that this verb *parakleetheesontai* is in the future tense – actually the aoristic future – and as A. T. Robertson observes it is an effective aoristic future. *(Grammar of the Greek New Testament*, p. 872.) Its primary purpose is not to indicate the time of the action but the effectiveness of the action of God in our lives when we mourn. It is more or less of a *fait-accomplit*, an accomplished fact of the past, experienced in the future. This is actually what an aoristic future is. It denotes certainty; it speaks of an accomplishment. And this accomplishment is not only for the present time but will continue in the future. This aoristic future is not merely punctiliar, that is, referring to moments of the future when we shall experience the comfort of God, but refers to a constant experience of the comfort of God. It does not refer to occasional visitations of the Holy Spirit when we need Him in times of trouble, but the constant and uninterrupted effective indwelling of the Holy Spirit within us. The Christian life is not one in which we play hide and seek with God, but it is God taking up His constant comforting abode within us. Since the participle *penthountes*, "the mourning ones," is in the present tense, which indicates constancy of mourning, the verb *parakleetheesontai* must also refer to a constant effective experience.

There is, however, a sense in which the fullness of our comfort will be in the future. We are comforted right along, but the day will come when the worth of the indwelling God will be fully realized. There is comfort

257

now and there will be comfort later on. As the skeptic, Ernest Renan, confessed, "After all, the Bible is the one great book of consolation for humanity." One thing that we shall not carry with us in the world to come is mourning. That we shall leave behind. God shall wipe away all tears. But our future state of blessedness will not be characterized merely by the absence of sorrow. We are not blessed here on earth in spite of sorrow but because of sorrow and mourning. Our blessedness in Christ here and hereafter does not involve the absence of mourning but the presence of Christ. And the presence of Christ will be fuller when we see Him face to face than at any other time.

There is a wonderful scene in chapter 7 of the Book of the Revelation, where we find the redeemed singing the praises of God. Among them were some who appeared to have special glory — a great multitude which no man could number, gathered out of all nations, standing in the place of honor before the throne, wearing white robes and carrying palms in their hands. When the question was asked, "Who are these highly favored ones and whence came they?" the answer was, "These are they which came out of great tribulation." This joyous multitude came from homes of sorrow. They were the suffering ones on earth who had passed through a baptism of tears. In heaven they wear white robes, stand nearest to the throne, and bear the emblems of completest victory. How strikingly this vision interprets this second Beatitude, "Blessed are they that mourn!" Earth regards suffering as a misfortune. The world pities those who are called upon to endure sorrow. The condition of mourning is one from which men shrink. But in the Kingdom of Heaven those are the favored ones who are called upon to suffer. Instead of being the unfortunate, they are the blessed. (J. R. Miller, *The Master's Blesseds*, London, pp. 44 - 46.)

We must finally remember that blessedness is not found in the mourning or the sorrow but in the comfort. Sorrow in itself is not a blessing. Sickness, pain, affliction, trial, are not favors in themselves. These experiences can be nothing else but hard and bitter. It is only in their fruits that the blessing comes. So it is with the mourning for our own sins and with the suffering that comes to us as a result of Adam's sin and the sins of others. How marvelous that God can take what is really an evil, the misery of sorrow, the consequence of sin, and make it the condition of the greatest joy and comfort that we can know. How can we help but pray in the Spirit with William J. Woods, "Wound us, oh! Thou Lord Jehovah! until we sorrow with godly sorrow for the sin wherewith we have wounded Thee; yea, until we come to Christ the Saviour, suffering with Him now that hereafter we may reign with Him. Then wilt Thou heal us, and the bones which Thou hast broken shall rejoice." *(The Christian World Pulpit,* Vol. 38, 1890, p. 96.)

There are blessings (which actually mean God's plans for us) which we cannot obtain if we cannot accept and endure suffering. There are joys which can come to us only through sorrow. There are revealings of divine truth which we can get only when earth's lights have gone out. There are harvests which can grow only after the plowshare has done its rough work. "Blessed are they that mourn: for they shall be comforted." Not to be willing to endure pain and suffering is not to be able to get the best things of grace. (J. R. Miller, *Ibid.,* pp. 55 - 56.)

> We must live through the weary winter
>   If we would value the spring;
> And the woods must be cold and silent
>   Before the robins sing.

The flowers must lie buried in darkness
  Before they can bud and bloom;
And the sweetest and warmest sunshine
  Comes after the storm and gloom.

DOES MEEKNESS RULE OUT ANGER ?

We usually think of human improvement in terms of upward steps on the ladder of life. But in the spiritual realm man must take three steps downward if he wants to be blessed, that is, to experience the presence of God within him. These are the steps of humility, mourning, and meekness. The grace of God is poured out abundantly in this world, yet relatively few enjoy its benefits. Why is this? Because its life-giving waters are available only to those who will place themselves in a lowly position, as a cup is placed under a fountain. In Christianity there is only one way up, and that is down.

The Beatitudes of Christ in Matthew 5 prescribe the conditions of blessedness. The first three denote poverty of spirit, that is, humility, mourning for our sins, and meekness of heart. We have already examined the first two in detail, and now we proceed to the third.

These Beatitudes must be taken as consecutive — especially the first three, which deal primarily with our attitude toward God. If we want God to come into our hearts and live through the Lord Jesus Christ and make us blessed, we must first of all humble ourselves, recognize our sinful state, and then mourn or cry over it. But this is not the cry of despair and hopelessness, but the cry of a soul going to the Lord Jesus for help. We become blessed the moment we go to Him, for it is then that God consents to take up His abode in us.

The fact of Christ's indwelling immediately becomes apparent to ourselves and to others. The first characteristic of God's presence in us is this virtue called meekness in Matthew 5:5. Although this is truly a condition of blessedness, it also becomes a result of blessedness, a result of the new birth in Christ.

We must differentiate between the basic conditions of blessedness—those that lead to our salvation—and those that are the consequence of our blessed state and also the conditions of further blessedness. It is impossible, for instance, for man to obtain salvation and forgiveness of sin unless he first humbles himself, is sorry for his sin, and runs to Christ. Humility and mourning are the first two basic conditions of blessedness. But after a person is saved and indwelt by God through the Lord Jesus, he does not cease to be humble and to sorrow over the many perplexing sins that spring from within and from without. There is a difference in quality and degree between the humility and mourning that lead to Christ and the humility and mourning that continue to exist and are partly the result of the state of blessedness. Our humility and mourning grow and are sanctified as we grow in Christ. Our sense of what constitutes pride and sin becomes far sharper and more penetrating after Christ comes to dwell within us than before.

Now we come to meekness, in the third Beatitude. This is a condition of blessedness, but not the initial blessedness that a person experiences the moment he invites Christ to come into his heart and life. It is the result of that initial work of God within us, and it then becomes the condition of our growth in blessedness. In other words, it is possible to be blessed, to be a Christian, and still not be characterized by the virtue of meekness. This is not a step necessary to salvation but to Christlikeness. As we go down the steps of blessedness so that we may experience the heights of blessedness, at the second step we find what is necessary for the basic blessedness of man. You cannot be blessed unless you take the step of humility and the step of sorrow for your sin. But meekness, which is found on the third step, is not a condition of salvation but is rather one of the fruits of salvation, or, as the Apostle Paul calls it, a fruit of the Holy Spirit. This explains our assertion that this third Beatitude, as well as all the following Beatitudes in Matthew, is first the consequence of our blessed state and then the condition of a higher degree of blessedness.

We shall see this more clearly as we examine the exact meaning of the word "meekness," *praotees*, in Greek. There are many qualities or elements that go to make up meekness, some of which may be startling to our preconceived notions. This virtue of meekness was known and discussed extensively by the ancient Greeks. Aristotle, the moralist philosopher, devotes an entire discussion to this word *praotees*. He considered meekness a virtue. His general principle in describing a virtue was to place it between two extremes. For instance, who is a generous man? The person who stands in between the spendthrift and the miser. A generous man, according to Aristotle, is one who does not waste his money, but at the same time does not keep everything for himself. Virtue, for Aristotle, was the middle ground between two extremes. Sometimes it might be well for us to remember this.

In discussing meekness, he said it is that which stands between *orgilotees*, "excessive anger," and *aorgeesia*, "angerlessness." This is the first meaning of the word *praotees*, "meekness," that we shall consider. It is neither constant anger nor total absence of anger, but seasoned, controlled anger. In further studies, we shall see what else meekness includes.

This, then, immediately disposes of the idea that the meek are passive persons who never get angry. There is no passivity in meekness. When the Lord Jesus Christ comes into our hearts, He does not go to sleep and put us to sleep. He becomes aggressively active within us. The apathetic Christian can hardly be considered a Christian at all. You remember how the Lord described the Spirit of God to Nicodemus that memorable night when this ruler of the Jews sought Him out? He likened Him to the wind, which blows where it pleases (John 3:8). The blowing wind is a force that makes itself felt. When Christ indwells the human heart, something happens within us that must manifest itself without as a result of Christ's indwelling Spirit.

According to this Beatitude, a Christian does and should get angry. But he must be careful to get angry at the right things and refrain from getting angry at the wrong things. Before he was saved and became blessed, his anger was sinful. Now it must be righteous. Meekness is the sanctification of anger. It includes patience and long-suffering for personal affronts, with the willingness to speak out vigorously in defense of the Gospel. To get angry at what we should and when we should is a definitely Christian characteristic.

But can we have confidence in our ability to distinguish the things and the times that call for anger? We have two voices within us, the voice of God and the voice of self—the latter a remnant of our inheritance from Adam. If God within us has the predominance, then our blessedness is at a high level; but if our unregenerate nature is in control, the blessedness that we possess is at a low ebb. You can tell how close a person is to the Lord, and to what extent the Lord lives in him and self is dead, by noticing what he gets angry at and when. Anger betrays a great deal. But let us never think that a person who never gets angry is an ideal Christian character.

What this third Beatitude in Matthew actually says is, How blessed is the person who always gets angry at the right time, at the things he should be angry at, and never angry at the wrong time. Examine the record of our Lord's life and you will see that this was so with Him, the perfect One.

In Christianity, meekness ought not to be interpreted as passive acceptance of all the evils that sinful men and Satan try to bring upon us and upon the world in which we live. We Christians ought not to be doormats. This is not what being meek means. It means long-suffering and patience, true. But in a world such as ours there is a place for strife, a place for anger, for strong speech and strong action. We have no business trying to pass through a world of conflicting forces without taking sides. We are simply cowardly when, in order to save ourselves possible discomfort or unpopularity, we cautiously forbear uttering a word of censure upon some powerful evil or abuse. We cannot sympathize very strongly with the right if we can see it overborne without coming forward in its defense; just as you would not give very much for the alleged friendship of anyone who could hear you slandered and held up to scorn without quickly and warmly protesting. The truth is stated in two famous lines by Browning:

> Dante, who loved well because he hated,
> Hated wickedness that hinders loving.

It was the divine pity and tenderness in Jesus that filled Him with divine indignation against the hypocrisy and hardness of the professional religionists of His day. His was the wrath that has been described as "the second, hotter flame of love" — and those who have never felt the like anger when face to face with some great wrong have small claim to be His disciples. No vested abuse has ever been routed until men's hearts were stirred to a generous anger against it and they determined that it must not continue. You can argue round and round some evil, show that it is wasteful of life and happiness, convince the intellect that it is unnecessary and could be remedied – and get no forwarder; but let a spark of feeling be kindled – let men and women once say with conviction, "This is wicked, and we won't have it" – and the days of that abuse are numbered. "Be ye angry, and sin not," says the Apostle Paul in Ephesians 4:26. By all means let us refrain from sinning, but by all means let us be angry upon the right occasion, when some meanness has to be exposed, some injustice to be redressed, some conspiracy against the light to be unmasked. This is the primary meaning of meekness, and blessed are we if we understand it and practice it. (See J. Warshauer's sermon, "Nabal and Abigail," in *The Christian World Pulpit*, Vol. 83, Feb. 10, 1913, p. 117.)

DOES MEEKNESS MEAN
TOLERANCE OF EVIL?

In our previous study we saw that the primary meaning of meekness, as understood by Aristotle, was the virtue that stands between *orgilotees*, which is excessive anger, and *aorgeesia*, which is no anger at all, or very little anger. Aristotle saw the necessity of anger at the right time and over the right things. And so did our Lord, both in word and practice. Therefore the most ancient and basic meaning of this word *praotees*, "meekness," used in the third Beatitude, must include the idea that we are to stand up and be counted for the Lord Jesus Christ, passionately to rebuke what He is displeased with and to commend that which exalts Him.

We must now examine Aristotle's motive in arriving at this definition of *praotees*, "meekness," as opposed to the Christian motivation. Here is where we shall find a difference and discover in what way the meaning of the word has been ennobled and lifted from earthly origins to heavenly heights. As Archbishop R. C. Trench says in his *Synonyms of the New Testament*, "The great moralist of Greece set *praotees*, meekness, as the *(mesotees peri orgees)* thing that stands between the two extremes, excessive anger *(orgilotees)* and no anger *(aorgeesia)*, with, however, so much leaning to the latter that it might very easily run into this defect; and he finds it worthy of praise, more because by it a man retains his own equanimity and composure, than for any nobler reason. The word is associated by Plutarch with moderating one's passions *(metriopatheia,* De Frat. An. 18); with occupation *(ascholia,* Cons. ad Uxor. 2); with forbearance *(anexikakia,* De Cap. ex In. Util. 9); with fortitude *(megalopatheia,* De Ser. Num. Vind. 5):

with ready obedience *(eupeitheia,* Comp. Num. et Lyc. 3)*;* with contentedness or ease *(eukolia,* De Virt. et Vit. 1)."

The fundamental difference, then, between the classical Greek writers and the writers of Scripture with regard to the meaning of the word *praotees,* "meekness," is that there was rather a tendency among the ancient Greeks not to get angry at all, even when they should have for righteousness' sake and in defense of that which was right. This attitude is wrong, according to the New Testament. This we gather not only from the meaning of words spoken by our Master but from His deeds. To understand a man's words, we should always put them side by side with his life and deeds. Remember to do this as you seek to determine the meaning of difficult words spoken in the Scriptures. As far as our Lord is concerned, we are not simply to take what the Epistles say about Him but also what the Gospels tell us He did. There may be doubt, there may be dispute, about His meaning; there can be none about His action. Our Christian faith is founded not so much upon words as upon deeds, not so much upon a doctrine that has been preached as upon a life that has been lived and sacrificed for us.

Let us then consider our Saviour and the things that made Him angry. The first instance of His anger is in Matthew 12:9-14, Mark 3:1-6, and Luke 6:6-11. The Lord entered the synagogue in Capernaum on the Sabbath day and there met the man with a withered hand. All around him were Scribes and Pharisees, the strict religionists of that day. They were looking to see whether the Lord would heal this man on the Sabbath so that they could accuse Him of breaking the law. The Lord showed no false meekness here but boldly acted as He thought right. He healed him. There is no day or moment when His mercy and love cannot be applied. When He asked the watchful gathering, "Is it lawful to do good on the sabbath days, or to do evil? to save life, or to kill?" they kept quiet. The Lord, however, was burning with anger. Mark tells us that He "looked round about on them with anger, being grieved for the hardness of their hearts." This is the same Lord who said, "Take my yoke upon you, and learn of me; for I am meek and lowly in heart: and ye shall find rest unto your souls" (Matt. 11:29). How can we reconcile the two utterances? Does a meek person also get angry? Our Lord did, and He should be our example.

Wouldn't it have been easier for the Saviour to refrain from action? He knew that the healing of this man with the withered hand would arouse the fanaticism of the Pharisees. But through fear of them and for the sake of peaceful and amiable relations with them, should He have let the man go on suffering without offering him divine help? This is a real-life problem that often confronts Christians today. A mistaken concept of what constitutes true meekness may hinder us from doing what is right and proper in the sight of God. We should dare to be merciful toward one needy individual to the dismay and hatred of many religionists. As Christians, we must not seek peace at any price. This is not meekness, nor did it characterize that perfect example of meekness, the Lord Jesus Christ. The man who cannot be angry at evil lacks enthusiasm for good.

The Lord chose to perform the miracle of healing on the Sabbath rather than to please the Pharisees. Had He chosen to please the Pharisees, it would have been an act of selfishness. Not to do good because many will hate you for it is to do evil. The Lord was hated because He chose to do, not what was expedient for Himself, but what was needful for suffering and sinful humanity. After all, the very reason He came to this earth was to seek and to save that which was lost. And He was determined to do this no matter what the Pharisees thought of His actions. When they objected to His doing good, He did not hesitate to become angry with them. This was part and parcel of the character of His meekness, for He was angry at the right people and for a justified cause. It would have been easier not to have performed the miracle and not to have opposed the Pharisees, but then He would not have accomplished His divinely appointed duty.

This is where Aristotle's philosophy failed in even approaching the interpretation that Christianity has attached to meekness. Aristotle said that it is the middle way between excessive anger and no anger at all, but his philosophy inclined toward not getting angry at all if that were to promote personal ease. This should never be our principle as Christians. We can never be blessed if that is the kind of meekness we possess – a meekness that prefers inaction rather than risk arousing others against us, a meekness that steals from us the emotion of resisting evil with all the strength of our souls, at any cost.

As Dr. J. H. Jowett says, "A life incapable of anger is destitute of the needful energy for all reform. There is no blaze in it, there is no ministry of purification. If a city is to be purged from its filth it will have to be by souls that are burning with moral resentment. It is the man who is 'fervent in spirit' who will most assuredly 'serve the Lord.' 'The grass withereth... because the spirit of the Lord breatheth upon it.' The Church needs more of this withering breath and consuming energy that is born of holy wrath against all established wrong. We are taught in the New Testament that this power of indignation is begotten by the Holy Spirit. The Holy Spirit makes us capable of healthy heat, and it inspires the fire within us. The Holy Spirit never creates a character that is lukewarm, neutral or indifferent." *(The Christian World Pulpit,* 1913, Vol. 83, p. 158.)

Therefore let us not hide behind a false conception of the meekness of our Lord and of the meaning of His teaching about meekness. How can you be blessed if at the same time you tolerate evil, saying nothing about it and doing nothing about it because you want to appear meek? Meekness is not passive; it is active; it calls for activity, angry activity against evil. As Alexander Maclaren wrote, "The nature that is incapable of being touched with generous and righteous indignation is so, generally, either because it lacks fire and emotion altogether, or because its vigour has been dissolved into a lazy indifference and easy good nature which it mistakes for love. Better the heat of the tropics, though sometimes the thunderstorms may gather, than the white calmness of the frozen poles. Anger is not weakness, but it is strength." *(Gospel of St. Mark,* p. 96.) Does your meekness possess such strength of unselfish action and anger?

THE ANGER OF THE MEEK
AND LOWLY JESUS

Thus far we have seen that meekness concerns first of all our attitude and activity toward evil; it includes being angry at the right things and people at the right time. We have also seen that only that anger that emanates from selfless interests and motives can truly be said to be part and parcel of Christian meekness. You are not meek when you tolerate evil and do nothing about it because you do not want to stir up trouble or disrupt the existing peace. Our Lord said, "Blessed are the meek: for they shall inherit the earth." But we saw that He got angry at the Scribes and Pharisees because they did not feel He should have healed the man with the withered hand in the synagogue of Capernaum on the Sabbath day.

There are several instances in our Lord's life that show His anger. We must determine the real motive of His anger in each case in order to understand the proper motivation of the anger of meekness.

We see the Lord in the temple at Jerusalem. Certain men had turned the house of God into a market place, buying and selling various wares. This desecration greatly angered our Lord. He was so indignant that He overthrew the tables of the money changers and the seats of those that sold doves. And He said to them, "It is written, My house shall be called the house of prayer; but ye have made it a den of thieves." (See Matthew 21:12-14.) The Lord did not utter these words in a calm and dispassionate manner. He spoke vigorously, with righteous indignation.

What motivated the Lord's anger at these merchants? The last thing that some preachers of today would dare to do is to express anger at a rich merchant. Look what we stand to lose if we scold them, and what we stand to gain if we pat them on the back. Let God judge them; why should we? Perhaps if the Lord had not overturned their tables, these merchants would have given Him a little gift of money or a dove. He acted in this case also against His personal interests. He did not show that meekness that operates with an eye to selfish advantage. He acted as the Prophet of God. The cleansing of the house of God was far more important to Him than any personal advantage.

How many of us act that way today? We come and go in our churches very quietly, lest we disturb anyone. A preacher may reason, "After all, if I speak up they may not pay my salary; they may cast me out as a heretic." This is devilish meekness, selfish meekness, that keeps quiet when the house of God is turned into a den of thieves. We have too much of that kind of meekness. We need Christlike meekness that is not afraid to upset established evils even in the house of God. Do you have that daring meekness of the Lord Jesus? Or does your meekness acquiesce in evil? If so, no wonder you are not as blessed as you once hoped you would be. It was the same Lord who said of Himself "I am meek and lowly in heart" who upset the tables and called the merchants in the temple thieves. You are not meek when you refrain from calling sin by its proper name lest you offend someone.

But the Lord Jesus was not angry only at the Pharisees in the synagogue of Capernaum and the merchants in the temple of Jerusalem. He was also angry at one of His own disciples, Peter, who belonged to the inner circle. Peter urged the Lord not to expose Himself to the suffering and dangers that He was told awaited Him the next time He went to Jerusalem. Peter loved his Master so much that he wanted Him to avoid any evil that might threaten Him. How did the Lord feel about this? Did He politely express His appreciation for Peter's concern? Did He praise him for his love toward Him? No, the Lord was angry. He showed it by the words He spoke to Peter, "Get thee behind me, Satan: thou art an offence unto me: for thou savourest not the things that be of God, but those that be of men" (Matt. 16:23). Think of it! The Lord called Peter "Satan." This was the same rebuke He gave to the devil in the wilderness. Then the Lord warmly urged the doctrines of self-denial and taking up the cross, and threatened the loss of life to those who would basely save it, reminding them of the just retribution that awaited them on the Day of Judgment. The Lord was angry because Peter had attempted to make Him act selfishly. Peter wanted the Lord to be passively meek, to hide somewhere and not speak out against the established religion and customs of the day — just to keep quiet and not go near Jerusalem at all. But the Lord chose the "meek" course of going to Jerusalem and speaking up about the evils then prevalent, declaring His deity and the purpose of His coming to earth without fear. Here again we have meekness manifested in action, an action that involved danger to self but that would result in the salvation of man.

I think that we make God really angry when we conceive of Him as being capable of condoning a course that is selfish, a course that would place our own ease and safety first. God's actions are always selfless, and His manifestations through us are always consistent with His character. His meekness among us was characterized by His entrance into Jerusalem to be crucified. That is the kind of meekness that should characterize our blessedness. That is the way that the Lord within us

274

wants to act in our everyday lives. If we, like Peter, advise Him to take a different course, the course of avoiding duty because it will be painful, then we become Satans in His sight. It is part of meekness to dare to do the unselfish task instead of interpreting meekness as retirement from duty when our ease is threatened.

Another instance in which we find the Lord Jesus protesting was when He was examined by the high priest as to His doctrine. One of the officers that stood nearby struck the Lord with the palm of his hand. Upon this, the Lord said, "If I have spoken evil, bear witness of the evil: but if well, why smitest thou me?" (John 18:23). There are some historians who say that this officer was Malchus, whose ear Peter had cut off and the Lord had miraculously restored at the time of His arrest. If this is so, then no rebuke could be more justifiable. Here we have a piece of illegal cruelty that the high priest should have checked. Here the Lord shows us through His example that meekness does not mean we cannot protest when we are illegally treated. To protest is our privilege and duty and is not contrary to meekness. Being meek does not mean submitting to all the indignities and whims of the world and God's enemies. But of course, after we have protested, we must place ourselves under the providence and care of our God. In this instance the Lord had the power to strike His enemies dead and to escape from the death they planned for Him, but He did not do it, because He was aware of the fact that this was part of the divine plan for His life in the redemption of mankind. Meekness is not simply giving in, without declaring the truth. True meekness calls for the fearless and passionate declaration of the truth and then leaving the results in the hands of God.

Why did not our Lord's meekness cause Him to

practice His own words on this occasion, "Whosoever shall smite thee on thy right cheek, turn to him the other also" (Matt. 5:39)? Isn't it strange how many of us find ourselves unable to understand these words of Christ? We can see His example, however, and we must interpret what He said by what He did. In reality, there is full agreement with what the Lord said in Matthew 5:39 and what He did and said in John 18:23. Matthew 5:39 speaks of retaliation for personal injury, but John 18:23 deals with indignation at an attack upon what the Lord represents — in this case, His position as the Son of God, the Messiah of the Jews. Christian meekness does not permit retaliation for personal injuries, but it does demand that we protest when the doctrine and person of the Lord Jesus Christ are attacked.

We must not forget that this Beatitude, as well as every other, is inseparably connected with the person and work of the Lord Jesus. The basis of this edifice of the blessed life stands on the foundation, "For my sake," of verse 11. "Blessed are the meek for the sake of the Lord Jesus: for they shall inherit the earth." And in the light of the meaning of the word "meekness," as we have seen, we could very well paraphrase this Beatitude thus: "Blessed are those who never get angry for their own sakes (i.e., at personal affronts), but who do not hesitate to show righteous anger for the sake of the Lord Jesus Christ." We must also be careful lest our anger becomes improper or excessive and therefore harms instead of benefits the cause of the Lord Jesus. This is what Christian meekness means: to react to evil as the Lord did, for His sake.

MEEKNESS—A NATURAL GIFT
OR A SUPERNATURAL GRACE?

One question that arises out of this study concerning Christian meekness expressing itself as righteous anger against evil is, how shall we know when to get angry and to what degree? We need some safeguards. We are likely to mistake evil for good, and vice versa. What are the criteria for righteous anger that should characterize Christian meekness?

First of all, if anger is to be righteous, it must be controlled anger. If you were to go out in the street and see a drunken man beating his wife and children, what would your duty be as a Christian? Just to stand there and look at them apathetically? Of course not. Your righteous anger would be aroused. If it was uncontrolled anger, you might become so furious as to kill that man. But controlled anger would act decently, and circumspectly. Uncontrolled anger is always weak, but controlled anger is an element of strength. As Alexander Maclaren says, "Where a man does not let his wrath against evil go sputtering off aimlessly, like a box of fireworks set all alight at once, then it comes to be a strength and a help to much that is good."

We see an example of the majesty of meekness in our Lord's conduct in Gethsemane. A cohort of Roman soldiers came to arrest Him. He had them reeling backward to the ground. There the Lord demonstrated meekness, but not in weakness. All the strength in heaven and on earth was present with the Lord, but it was manifested in righteous anger, deliberate yielding, through strength, not weakness. And this proved to be a moral dynamic of immeasurable force.

Let there be no mistake; meekness can smite when

the occasion demands; and there is no more terrible phrase within the covers of Sacred Writ than "the wrath of the Lamb." The world has yet to learn that the highest expression of power is the control of power. This is the supreme test of character — not self-declaration and self-assertion, but self-restraint. The truth is that all anger is sinful that causes us to lose our self-control. A poor cobbler who was accustomed to attend the public disputations in Latin at an academy was asked if he understood that language. "No," he replied, "but I always know who is wrong in the argument." "How?" asked his questioner. "Why," came the answer, "by noting who loses his temper first!"

In fact, the word *praus*, "meek," in ancient Greece was used to denote a wild animal that had been domesticated. Previously it had known no restraint as it lived in the open fields and forests, but now it had a master to obey, to be guided and directed by. It is the same animal, but in a different environment and with a different disposition. This is exactly what the Lord does to us when we accept Him and become His children. He takes our wild natures and domesticates them. We accept God's control over us. And that control operates from within and not from without. The Lord within holds the reins. We go where He wants us to go; we do what He wants us to do; we say what He wants us to say. In other words, to be meek in the full meaning of the word is to be God-controlled and not self-controlled. Of ourselves we are unable to control our anger and emotions, but when we become blessed through the indwelling of God then we are placed under His control.

This meaning of meekness being our "God-control" agrees beautifully with the Scriptural meaning of the word *praotees*, "meekness," which is not evidenced in a man's outward behavior only, in his relations to his fellow men, nor in his mere natural disposition, but which is rather an inwrought grace of the soul; and the exercises of it are first and chiefly toward God. (See R. C. Trench, *Synonyms of the New Testament*, p. 152.)

There are several fundamental lessons we can learn about meekness as taught by our Lord. First, it is not a natural attribute of man. Naturally we are possessed of an uncontrollable temper. We are wild beasts. Observe how men treat each other and you will see that this is so. Do you realize that in the United States, where the influence of Christianity is probably greater than anywhere else, for every dollar that is dropped in the offering plates of our churches, all the churches of all denominations, nine dollars are spent for crime? This is man in his wildness, uncontrolled in his passions. Meekness is what he needs. But this can only come through blessedness. And blessedness is the coming of the Lord Jesus into our hearts to bring the whole power of the Godhead to control us. We cannot control ourselves, nor can anyone else control us. It takes God, our Creator, to do this through His Son, the Lord Jesus Christ. We can never truly understand this Beatitude unless we understand the true meaning of the word "blessed," *makarioi* in Greek, and relate its teaching to the phrase, "for my sake," for the sake of the Son of man, the Lord Jesus Christ, in verse 11. Self-control is an impossibility; therefore God-control must take over.

Actually, in this third Beatitude we have the manifestation of the work of God within us. This is why the Apostle Paul calls "meekness" one of the fruits of the Spirit of God (Gal. 5:22, 23). It surely is. It is not one of ours. We have no capacity to develop it.

Furthermore, in this Beatitude the Lord is not speaking of actions of meekness but of the inner state

279

of heart. This is why our Lord said of Himself, "I am meek and lowly in heart." Meekness does not refer exclusively to our outward behavior but also to our state of heart. The Lord makes us meek, and then our actions cannot help but reflect this meekness. This is the general disposition of the soul. It is not a natural disposition but an acquired one. It is possible, of course, to trespass on our state of meekness with acts that do not demonstrate divine control of our lives, but these are only isolated exceptions. Sometimes we say of our child, he is a good child, but occasionally a bit headstrong. Well, sometimes God says that of us. That wild nature keeps coming back, and we kick against our cage and hate the feel of the reins. But we are under control, and praise the Lord it is His control.

Remember, this meekness is primarily concerned with our relationship with God and not with men. God's primary concern is not with our relationship to our fellow men but with our relationship to Him. Our blessedness has nothing to do with the horizontal relations of life but only with the vertical. But when our vertical relation to God is right, our horizontal relations with men cannot help being Godlike. If we are meek toward God, we will be meek toward men.

Being meek, then, is not merely the outward manifestation of controlled anger; it is actually the spirit of loyal and unquestioning submission to – or rather willing concurrence with – the mind and purpose of God. It is the temper and attitude of consenting accommodation to those plastic circumstances, those shaping and controlling Hands, "that reach through nature, moulding men." Meekness toward God on our part is willingness to know God's will for us individually, and not only to know it, but also to surrender our own will to it. Only as we show God that we will to do His will, will He show us what to do. Meekness, then, is a state of willingness to accept at all times His will for us. Only then will His blessedness be at its highest peak in our lives.

ARE THE MEEK AWARE
OF THEIR HUMILITY?

"Blessed are the meek: for they shall inherit the earth." The meek are not the weak but the strong. Their strength has been given to them by the One who has made them blessed, the Lord Jesus Christ. In His strength they resist evil, they become angry at it. Their hearts and minds are so attuned to the mind of Christ that evil will not go unchecked in their presence.

But meekness is a quality that we acquire as a gift of the Spirit of God and refers primarily to our attitude toward God. "It is the temper of spirit in which we accept his dealings with us as good, and therefore without disputing or resisting." (R. C. Trench, *Synonyms of the New Testament*, p. 152.) The meek life, then, is the God-controlled life. It is impossible to live it outside the family of God. Before God can control us, He must take up His reign within us as Saviour and Lord in the person of His Son. In a sense, then, we could very well equate this quality of meekness with our faith in God. Meekness toward God is faith toward God. Our acceptance of Him must also mean our acceptance of all that He directs and permits to come our way, as the product of His omnipotence, omniscience, and absolute love for us. Meekness does not mean mere acquiescence in the sorrow and loss that come our way. Nor is it accepting the inevitable in a sullen and despairing mood. We are not meek when we say, "Well, what can't be cured must be endured." Such an attitude will bring no blessing to our hearts, for our trials will teach us nothing. Nor is meekness merely recognizing the unpleasant experiences of life as part of God's over-all plan for life's highest development. Meekness is a step further.

It is what the Apostle Paul meant when he said, "We glory in tribulations also; knowing that tribulation worketh patience" (Rom. 5:3). Discipline does not necessarily bring man's character into correspondence with the divine. The same furnace that turns the precious metal into a molten mirror that reflects the refiner's face only hardens into a more stolid stubbornness the worthless clay. We have seen the same dark bereavement or financial loss, under which one marriage partner grew more spiritual and withdrawn from earth, stiffen the other into an unbending obstinacy and a more obdurate resistance to all that was meek and lowly in heart.

The attitude we take in trouble will determine the moral result that will accrue. The great end that God is aiming at is perfection of character. But no character ever yet came to perfection in the fields of prosperity. Perpetual sunshine would inevitably shrivel its beauty and arrest its growth. Cloud and darkness are not more necessary to the golden plenty of the harvest than are discipline and distress to the perfecting of the soul. Only in the forges of trial and bereavement can the iron of our nature be wrought by God into steel for the service of Him who made us blessed and who wants to make others blessed, too.

> Life is not as idle ore
> But iron dug from central gloom,
> And heated hot with burning fears,
> And dipt in baths of hissing tears,
> And battered with the shocks of doom
>   To shape and use.

Meekness, then, is not only to tolerate God within you – for there is no alternative for the blessed life – but to glory in His presence and providences, no matter what happens.

We have seen thus far that meekness involves our willing and joyful submission to the will of God for our lives. Meekness Godward is faith in God. But the blessed person, the person who has been born into the family of God, has to contend with himself in relation to his meekness. What is the attitude of a meek person toward himself? Being meek is seeing ourselves as God and others see us. A woman with a drunken husband resolved to reveal him to himself. She knew what he was, and so did the children — alas, too well! But he did not seem to grasp it. One night, when he returned home and sank to disheveled slumber in his chair, she had him photographed and laid the result beside him at breakfast next morning. The disclosure is said to have caused his reformation. If we who are blessed in the exercise of our meekness could see ourselves as others see us and as God sees us, we would be restrained from flaring up into excesses of anger and passion. We cannot be proud when we see ourselves as God sees us. We cannot but be meek and humble when we realize what we are in the sight of God, no matter how far along in the Christian life we may be.

At the time Phillips Brooks was made a bishop, a friend was staying at the house. They were chatting together, when Phillips Brooks said, "R —, if you see any difference in me, you'll tell me, won't you?" It was the vigilance of a great soul who knew the peril of success and prosperity. We must recognize that there is a real peril in becoming blessed. First we humble ourselves and then we become exalted; but we ought not to be aware of our exaltation and become proud of it. Imagine becoming proud of the very humility that caused God to elevate us! Blessedness is not a state

284

of having once received the grace of God and needing it no more. We need constant elevation, and in order to have that we must have constant humbling. This is what meekness means.

Did you know that only the smaller birds sing? You will never hear a musical note from the eagle in all your life, or from the turkey, or from the ostrich. But you will hear music from the canary, the wren, and the lark. "Big birds" in the family of the blessed cannot sing. No matter how big God makes us, we must always think of ourselves as small, for that is how we look in the presence of His majesty.

Being important in our own eyes will create in us an attitude of demanding our "rights" before God. In this connection, it is interesting to note the distinction between the word *praotees*, or *prautees*, "meekness," and another Greek word, *epieikeia*, translated "gentleness." These two words occur together in II Corinthians 10:1, "Now I Paul myself beseech you by the meekness [*prautees*] and gentleness [*epieikeia*] of Christ, who in presence am base among you, but being absent am bold toward you." The word for "base" here in the Greek is *tapeinos*, "humble."

The word *epieikeia*, translated "gentleness," has no exact English equivalent. It always contains the implication of a superior condescending to an inferior, while *praotees*, "meekness," implies nothing of the sort. Some people who think of themselves as meek seem to have a high idea of themselves, as though in their self-conscious humility they are superior to those with whom they condescend to co-exist. Do we give men the idea that we are honoring them with our presence among them? This is not meekness at all; it is gentleness in the sense of the Greek word *epieikeia*, implying the condescension of a superior to an inferior. If we have such a spirit of superiority, we evidence it even when we come to God. We claim His special attention, feeling that we have more rights than others. It is a sad day in the life of a Christian when he regards a gift of God as an exacted and demanded right. Surely, we have legal rights when we become children of God, but how much better God and others will think of us, and how much more blessed we shall be, if we consider them at all times as gifts of His grace. Meekness, then, is not an attitude of condescension toward those to whom we think ourselves superior.

One more great difference between *praotees*, "meekness," and *epieikeia*, "gentleness," is that meekness has its inner spirit, while gentleness must needs embody itself in outer acts. A gentle person acts humble while he may think himself superior, but a meek person thinks of himself as nothing apart from God, and acts accordingly. A gentle person may be a hypocrite, but a meek person acts what he is. It is in this state of realization of our smallness that our blessedness is realized in greater measure. Thinking yourself big and acting small is not being meek at all. Meekness consists in thinking yourself small and acting in that spirit.

When Sammy Morris, a Kru boy from Africa, came to America to be trained for Christian service, he presented himself for matriculation at Taylor University. He revealed a spirit all too rare among Christians. When the President of the University asked him what room he wanted, Sammy replied, "If there is a room nobody wants, give that to me." Of this incident the President later wrote: "I turned away, for my eyes were full of tears. I was asking myself whether I was willing to take what nobody else wanted. In my experience as a teacher, I have had occasion to assign rooms to more than a thousand students. Most of them were noble, Christian young ladies and gentlemen; but Sammy Morris was the only one of them who ever said, 'If there is a room that nobody wants, give that to me.'" This is what being meek is, to consider yourself before God and others as worthy of nothing but their mercy. And though others may not always understand your motives, God at least will appreciate this and will make your life that much more blessed. Our legal rights never cause our hearts to overflow, but the mercy of God always does.

It is good to remember this: "When God intends to enrich a soul, He first makes it poor; when He intends to exalt a soul, He first makes it sensible of its own miseries, wants and nothingness." (Flavel.) God, in the person of the Lord Jesus Christ, asks us to be meek because of His desire to be our superior, instead of permitting us to feel superior and demanding. A superior person must reach up to God, yet he will find Him unattainable; but a meek person will be reached down to by God. A superior person does not attract his inferiors by condescending to reach down to them; and those whom he considers his inferiors will never want to reach up to him. Meekness, then, is an inner state; it is what we think of ourselves before God and in our innermost being.

MEEKNESS TOWARD OTHERS

We have seen that meekness toward God is a life and a disposition of faith and dependence upon God. Realizing that we are not worthy of any of His benefits, we do not consider ourselves privileged characters, or try to make Him a respecter of persons where we are concerned.

And in our estimate of ourselves, we shall find no grounds for superiority in meekness. To be meek is not merely to think ourselves great and act humble, but to realize we are nothing and to act accordingly; for whatever good there is in us is by the grace of God and for the glory of God. If you want to find out if you are meek, look first into the face of God and see what you think of Him, what He thinks of you, and then what you think of yourself. Be honest about it.

Now meekness concerns not only our disposition toward God and our estimate of self, but it concerns also our disposition toward others, the evil and the good. It is not always what we are able to do or not do for others that counts, but what we would have liked to do or not do, if it were in our power. Men's outward actions are often controlled by fear of punishment or lack of reward, but dispositions show the true character of a person.

Thus *praotees*, "meekness," has to do with our dispositions, as well as our actions toward others, as the word *epieikeia*, "gentleness," implies. You are gentle to others because if you weren't you wouldn't get along well in society, not because you necessarily like or love people. Meekness is something more than the gentleness imposed by duty and selfish motives. Meekness replaces the selfish motive in our disposition toward others with a benevolent motive. Meekness toward others makes us love them in spite of what they do to us. It may be that they are God's chastening and purifying agents for us, who are His blessed ones. In II Samuel 16:5-14, we read of an incident in the life of David in which Shimei cursed him and flung stones at him. It is amazing to note David's reaction. "Let him alone, and let him curse," he said, "for the Lord hath bidden him. It may be that the Lord will look on mine affliction, and that the Lord will requite me good for his cursing this day" (verses 11 and 12).

We saw in a previous study that one criterion of righteous anger is whether it is under the control of God. There is yet another criterion that fits here perfectly. It is the absence of malice, which is the negative aspect of love. Though we are right in feeling abhorrence toward the evil that others contemplate against us, we should look with love upon those who are contemplating it.

But is not this love toward others at all times, and especially toward the evil ones, contrary to the principle of righteous anger and justice? Should not the meek person seek to bring punishment upon the culprit against humanity? A perfect example of righteous anger in love is the one that our Saviour showed toward the Scribes and Pharisees when He healed the man with the withered hand in the synagogue in Capernaum. We read that the Lord "looked round about on them with anger, being grieved for the hardness of their hearts" (Mark 3:5). Here is an insight into the soul of the Lord Jesus – anger mingled with grief. This is meekness toward others. This is anger that may impel to punish but is not malicious. Its reason for punishment is the passionless impulse of justice or the reformation of the wrongdoer, not a getting even with him. This is pure anger, the anger of love. It is the anger of the parent toward the naughty child. In this incident the Lord has revealed to us the nature of God – a God whose heart is moved by emotions, not passions. In God's anger there is no self-regarding irritation, no passion, no malice. And that is how it should be with us, since God has taken up His dwelling place in us when we became blessed. In God's anger we find the necessary displeasure and aversion of infinite purity at the sight of man's impurity. The fact that a judge pronounces a wrongdoer guilty and imposes the punishment due him does not mean that he hates him. A God who was all mercy would be an unjust God. The judge is condemned when the wrongdoer is acquitted; and he that strikes out of the divine nature the capacity for anger against sin, little as he thinks it, is degrading the righteousness and diminishing the love of God. A God such as that would be neither worth loving nor worth trusting. The Gospel is not only the revelation of God's righteousness for faith, but is also the revelation of His wrath against all ungodliness and unrighteousness of men.

Our meekness should arouse in us, as it did in the heart of the Saviour, both anger and compassion. There should be anger against the sin and compassion for the sinner. He looked upon those Scribes and Pharisees sitting there with hatred in their eyes; and two emotions, which many men suppose as discrepant and incongruous as fire and water, rose together in His heart: wrath, which fell on the evil; sorrow, which bedewed the doers of it. The anger was for the hardening of their hearts, the compassion was for the hardeners. Meekness, then, toward others can be said to be, among other things, that quality of the Christian which is intolerant of evil around him, but compassionate of the evil-doer. Meekness looks at sin as a thing to be frowned on and also as a thing to be wept over. Meekness regards evil-doers as persons that deserve to be blamed and to be chastised, and to feel the bitterness of their evil, and not to interfere too much with the salutary laws that bring down sorrow upon men's heads if they have been doing wrong, but on the other hand, it takes care that our sense of justice does not swallow up the compassion that weeps for the criminal as an object of pity. Public opinion and legislation swing from the one extreme to the other. We have to make an effort to keep in the center, and never look round in anger, unsoftened by pity, nor in pity, enfeebled by being separated from righteous indignation. (See Alexander Maclaren, *Gospel of Mark*, pp. 94-104.)

The Greeks contrasted this word *praotees*, "meekness," with *hupseelokardia*, which means "lofty or high heartedness." It is the opposite of pride. And it is in this sense that we should think of meekness, especially in our relations with others. It is a significant thing that we are warned so constantly in the Word of God against pride. If we are to show forth our blessedness to our fellow men and women, it is essential that we be humble before them. It is true, of course, that we have something that they do not possess, but we must not give the impression that it is any of our own doing. The relationship of the meek Christian to the unconverted world should be similar to that of the parent toward a prodigal son, not like the attitude of the elder son toward his erring brother. The father did not condone the sin of his son. He simply received him lovingly when he came back dirty and unlovable. But the elder brother was angry and would not enter the house. So many of us acquire an air of pride when we receive the Lord Jesus and are distinguished from our fellow men by that blessedness that comes from heaven. But think of what we were when God received us! In unregenerated men and women, let us not see what they are — sinners — but what they can become, if we only show them in humility what Christ has done in us.

"He is impossible to get along with, because he thinks he's impossible to get along without," was said of a Sunday school teacher. No wonder the result was a dismal failure for the would-be indispensable. The worst idea a Christian can have is that he is absolutely necessary in the world in which he lives and to the work in which he is engaged — that his absence would mean the collapse of the world, of the Kingdom of God, and of the whole undertaking. A meek person is one whom others may consider indispensable, but who never considers himself so.

In the exercise of meekness, undoubtedly you and I will be taken advantage of. In spite of our meek anger, the world will not stop harassing us. Protest we must; but we must also accept the unjust treatment of others with meekness. A Brahmin compared the Christian missionary to the mango tree. It hangs all its branches with fruit. It is then assailed with stones and clubs by passers-by. How does it respond? By dropping down fruit at every blow at the feet of those who assail it. At the close of the season, it stands scarred and battered, its leaves torn off, its branches broken. But next year it bears more fruit than ever. That is what our meekness should do in the world — not try to conserve its self-esteem but bear fruit, fruit that descends low at the impact of clubs and stones. Christian meekness cannot be exercised in isolation. It must be manifested within the framework of society, a society that hates the Lord Jesus Christ, openly or subtly, and all who stand for Him. Isn't that true of our world? How greatly we need Christian meekness to live in it.

NOT BY CONQUEST
BUT BY INHERITANCE

One of the strangest and most paradoxical statements ever made by the Lord Jesus is found in the third Beatitude as given to us by Matthew (5:5). "Blessed are the meek: for they shall inherit the earth." What does that mean? How can the meek inherit the earth? Have you ever seen it happen? If this promise were intended only for the ages to come, we might understand it better. One of the pitfalls of Scriptural interpretation is to relegate all the real blessings of Christ to some distant future date, possibly the Millennium. Here we are told that we inherit the earth. How can it mean the earth on which we now live? We forget that eternal life and its full enjoyment become ours the moment we receive Jesus Christ as Saviour and Lord. He has told us that it is now, at this present time, that God is made real to us, though the perfection of His reality will not be reached until that great day when we shall go to abide with Him forever. But how can the meek inherit the earth here and now? Have you found this to be true in your own experience or that of others? What does this Beatitude mean?

It is the same as saying that in the animal kingdom rabbits and sheep shall dominate all other animals, and that nightingales and canary birds shall rule over owls, vultures, and eagles. If this Beatitude had said, "They shall have quiet," everybody would have responded, "Oh, yes, they shall have quiet." If it had said, "They shall have a pure heart," everybody would have conceded, "Yes, they shall have a pure heart." Men would have admitted these things; but to say that the meek are to govern; to take that which is regarded as springing

293

from weakness, and that which has in it less overtness, apparently, than any other quality, and to elect it to supremacy, and declare, "It shall be magistrate, it shall rule, it shall possess the earth," with this great roaring race, red with blood, flashing with arms, combining with all forms of victorious plans, rolling through time as the waves, storm-driven, roll through the ocean — that is too much for anybody. Men cannot understand how meekness is going to inherit the earth.

The main reason for the world's astonishment at these words of Jesus is their misunderstanding of the meaning of meekness. They believe that it refers to passivity instead of activity, to the conquering of the Christian by the world instead of the conquest of the world by the Christian. Meekness is the highest form of power; but it is of the Spirit and not of the flesh. The person who is blessed because he has the Lord Jesus in his heart is meek, that is, he is characterized by the power of the Spirit. God within him is power, and that power has the ability to conquer and never to be conquered. The Lord here declares the superiority of the Spirit over the flesh, the superiority of God over man, and the superiority of activity undertaken in calmness over outbursts of passion.

Men believe in physical strength. They believe in arms and armies. They believe in craft and cunning. They believe in energy, and will, and perseverance. They believe in things. They believe in matter. They believe in influencing their fellow men, working upon them by threats, by pain, by fear. There are very few people who believe that man is using himself in the strongest possible manner who is governed by his highest nature, in perfect accord with the divine nature within him as a result of his new birth in Christ.

In saying that the meek shall inherit the earth, our Lord declares the potential accomplishment of the man who is indwelt by Christ, by the Spirit of God within man. Observe that I did not say, the spirit of man, but the Spirit of God within man. The spirit of man in its sinful state is corrupt. It does not drive man much higher than his flesh and the fullest enjoyment of it.

There have been men who conquered the world by the mere force of arms. Their conquest, however, was only temporal. It did not inscribe itself permanently on the annals of history and produces no thrill in the hearts of men and women everywhere. Who are the men whom time could not slay? It was not the oriental emperors of Medea, and Babylonia, and Assyria. They were the richest, the strongest, the most successful for their time. All the world poured tribute into their coffers to support their luxurious self-indulgence. But what became of them? Who can tell? How did time treat them? They have been effaced from the memories of men. Time sits upon the ruins of the mighty things which they built, muttering; but we cannot hear even the name it pronounces. "The memory of the wicked shall rot." The memory of Hitler has rotted, though he conquered country after country by military might. So did Stalin, yet his corpse was unearthed and moved to a less honorable place by his successor. These have been the conquerors of as much earth as they could by the power of the flesh. It is not to them that the Beatitude refers, for they were neither blessed nor did they make anyone else blessed through their conquests.

Observe that the Lord said, "For they shall inherit the earth," not "They shall conquer the world." That Christian who is most blessed does not view the world with the idea of conquering it. It is the unregenerate man who seeks to conquer and possess as much as possible. The regenerate man leaves the apparent and temporary conquest of the earth to the mighty of earth, while he is satisfied with inheriting it.

What you inherit, you have not necessarily worked for. It represents the conquest of someone else. When you inherit, you enter upon the labor of another; while when you conquer you do it in your own strength. How marvelously these words fit the total concept of the Beatitudes. A blessed person is one who has God in him. God is the Creator and Sustainer of the entire universe. Why should someone who has the Creator within himself actively seek that which already belongs to his Father? By receiving the Lord Jesus Christ as our Saviour and becoming blessed, we become the children of God and heirs of His kingdom. The Apostle Paul has told us clearly, "The Spirit itself beareth witness with our spirit, that we are the children of God: and if children, then heirs; heirs of God, and joint-heirs with Christ" (Romans 8:16, 17). It is in this sense, then, that we are actually the heirs of the earth, because the earth is the Lord's and the fullness thereof. This is why the Lord admonishes His disciples to seek first the Kingdom of God and the material things of life shall be added unto them. Our only pursuit should be that of God, and He is the One who will take care of our earthly needs. This does not mean that man should not work for a living or seek to better his lot. It means that he should put first things first, that spiritual values should be preeminent and material considerations secondary. The Christian's conquest is only through Christ; it is the enrichment by inheritance.

How has the Lord Jesus Christ come to His throne? Not by the might of the flesh but by the meekness of His Spirit. He emptied Himself and by becoming man He was exalted and was given a name which is above every name. This contemplation of the Holiest among the mighty and the Mightiest among the holy, who made Himself of no reputation that He might bridge the moral distance that sin had made between us and God, slays our pride, burns up our selfishness, and humbles us into penitence and tears.

In meekness, then, we find the meeting place of both right and might – the right and might of moral and spiritual kingship. The coronation of meekness is the declared supremacy of goodness – the enthronement of moral force.

Graduates in meekness, through surrender of the will and affections to the Supreme, realize their birthright. They are "begotten ... again unto a lively hope by the resurrection of Jesus Christ from the dead, to an inheritance incorruptible, and undefiled, and that fadeth not away" (I Pet. 1:3, 4). This inheritance is an acquired moral right through the laws and lines of spiritual descent. The heirs are the sons and daughters of the Highest – the children of the King. They are princes and princesses of the blood, whose right it is to rule.

He lives and is immortal, not who conquers the world for himself, but who liberates the world from its self-imposed sin and calamity. A conqueror sweeps the earth for selfish purposes. It is by killing others that men usually enthrone themselves over them, never by killing themselves. The Lord Jesus won the earth unto Himself, not by killing others, but by sacrificing Himself. He lives, then, and is immortal, who lives to do good to others besides himself.

Other men have gone up, but they have come down again. The meek were at the bottom when the race began. They had conscience, they had scruples, they had delicacy of thought and feeling; and they could not consent to be gainers at the expense of the destruction of other men. They rather pitied them and helped them. They could not exercise hatred here and there. They must wait patiently for their success. They must live right, whether they were successful or not. But little by little they grew and advanced. It is the weed that

297

springs up quickly on the dunghill; but it seems as though corn would never get out of the ground. So men, laying the true foundations of life, seem to develop slowly; but there is steady progress in their growth, and finally their faith and patience are rewarded, and on their passage up they meet those who outstripped them at the beginning. We meet everybody twice. First as he goes by us on his way up, laughing at us as we plod on behind him, and again, as he comes down, while we are still plodding on and up.

Men who believe in right instruments, in a right temper, in that wisdom which is in concord with God, in purity, in sympathy, in loving-kindness, and in well-wishing for every human soul, and who square all their measures by these divine qualities – such men go steadily on and up; and when you come to make up the account, and balance the books, they always come out on the credit side; they are always ahead.

(See Henry Ward Beecher's sermon, "Meekness, a Power," in *The Christian World Pulpit*, vol. VII (1875), pp. 179-84. Also, "The Raiment of the Soul," by Henry Howard, pp. 160-1.)

INHERITANCE A MATTER
OF RELATIONSHIP

Why does Matthew 5:5 say that the meek shall inherit the earth? Is it because they are meek or because they are blessed? Is there some intrinsic value in the spiritual quality of meekness that entitles us to inherit the earth? We do not feel that this is the meaning our Lord meant to convey in this Beatitude.

We have seen in previous studies that all the Beatitudes are related to the person and work of the Lord Jesus Christ. They are based on that foundational phrase of Matthew 5:11, "for my sake." Therefore the third Beatitude in its total perspective actually reads, "Blessed are the meek: for they shall inherit the earth for my sake." The phrase, "for my sake," is to be understood as applying to every part of the Beatitude. People are blessed for My sake, said the Lord, because of what I am and what I have done for them. Blessedness is the indwelling of God in man. It can come about only through what Christ has done for man.

A basic prerequisite of the state of blessedness is a high degree of human meekness. Then, when Christ comes into our hearts, we become what He is, truly meek. Before we received Christ, we saw ourselves as God saw us, and after our conversion to Christ we continue to see ourselves as He sees us. So meekness is both a condition of blessedness and a result of it.

But real meekness, in the sense in which the Lord Jesus meant it, is impossible to those who are not blessed. It is impossible for the unregenerate man consistently to hate sin, and get angry at it, whether it be found in himself or others. Man's capacity to discern the sinfulness of sin comes from God within him. It is not mere human meekness that entails the promise of inheriting the earth, but blessedness.

Blessedness involves relationship – the relationship of man to God, of children to the Father. And heirship is commonly regarded as a privilege of relationship. After you are gone, strangers will have no claim on your estate. It is your family who can claim the right of inheritance. However, no man likes to feel that his children are respectful and obedient only because they want to inherit his wealth. You would not want a child who thought more of your possessions than he did of you. Then how must God feel toward those of His children who are constantly praising Him for His blessings in this life and the heritage of heaven to come, but never for Himself? How this must grieve the heart of the One who redeemed us through the precious blood of His Son, the Lord Jesus Christ. We are preoccupied with the enjoyment of earth, instead of looking to heaven which has made earth enjoyable for us. This Beatitude reminds us that we shall derive the greatest enjoyment from earth when God and heaven are our first concern. By aiming at that which is first and highest, relationship, we shall secure that which is secondary, heirship. Let us not seek God for the earthly blessings He can bestow upon us, but for Himself alone and the privilege of being related to Him.

If you had the choice of inheriting a million dollars or of being legally adopted by the owner of the whole earth, which would you choose? He who owns the whole earth is characterized by omnipotence and permanence that none can steal. Would it not be folly to prefer money to such a personal relationship? Relationship is far superior to heirship. If you seek to become related to God only for what you hope to get in return, the relationship will seem so drab, and He so small, that you are sure to be disappointed. Blessed are they who seek God for Himself – for the relationship alone – rather than the blessings that are the natural outcome of the relationship.

A nobleman worked for many years as a porter in a railway station because he did not know his true position in the world, until one day a gentleman approached him and said, "Sir, may I ask your name?" "John — ," was the reply. "Well, then, I have come to tell you that you are the Earl of — and entitled to a large estate," replied his visitor. Do you think that man stood about the station touching his cap for tips any longer? Not he. He took possession of his inheritance at once. His inheritance was the outcome of a relationship.

Generally speaking, in the Scriptures a person who becomes acquainted with God by receiving the Lord Jesus Christ as his personal Saviour is promised heavenly riches. In the first Beatitude, we are told that if we humble ourselves and go to Christ, we shall possess the Kingdom of Heaven. Nothing is said about possessing the earth. When we become Christians, we are said to become citizens of heaven, temporarily living upon this earth. Philippians 3:20 says, "For our conversation is in heaven; from whence also we look for the Saviour, the Lord Jesus Christ." The word translated "conversation" should actually be "citizenship."

Taking the Beatitudes in Matthew as a whole, we note that the predominating element of promise, as in all the New Testament, is not material prosperity and possessions but heaven and its riches. Since heaven is spiritual, its riches must also be spiritual. In Matthew 5:3 we are told, "Blessed are the poor in spirit: for theirs is the kingdom of heaven." This speaks of something definite possessed by the person who is blessed, who has God within him. It is the Kingdom of Heaven, not the kingdom of earth. In verse 10, the Kingdom of Heaven is mentioned as the definite possession of those who are persecuted for righteousness' sake. In the whole series of Beatitudes, our Saviour promises nothing concrete except in verse 5, where He tells us we shall inherit the earth. This stands in great contrast to the Kingdom of Heaven. Then in Matthew 5:12, which concludes the Beatitudes, He tells us beyond the shadow of a doubt that our reward will be in heaven and not on earth. "Rejoice, and be exceeding glad: for great is your reward *in heaven:* for so persecuted they the prophets which were before you." Three times our Lord refers to heaven in the Beatitudes in Matthew.

How about the other promises? Let us look at them: comfort, filling, mercy, the sight of God, the privilege of being called the children of God. What are all these but characteristics of the soul rather than the body? They speak of what happens within us rather than what happens without. They are the result of heaven's descent to earth, especially in our own hearts. They are spiritual qualities that become part and parcel of our lives, in addition to our being blessed when we have God in us and fulfill the other more specific conditions outlined in the Beatitudes.

The only promise of something that is not a quality of the soul, other than the Kingdom of Heaven, is the earth in the third Beatitude. Why is the earth mentioned here midway between the two promises of the Kingdom of Heaven and among all these spiritual qualities of the blessed Christian life? What does this inheritance of the earth really refer to? We shall examine this in detail in our next study.

WHAT IT MEANS TO
INHERIT THE EARTH

When Christ said, "Blessed are the meek: for they shall inherit the earth," He gave us no small promise, if words mean what they say. It sounds like an easy way of becoming rich quickly, doesn't it?

Does the Lord speak here of those who by their courteous and gentle manners persuade the rich to remember them in their wills? If you are meek and humble and subject yourself to a rich father or other relative, perhaps you will inherit all he has. Does this Beatitude refer to those who are meek for the ulterior motive of possessing all that belongs to someone else some day?

A young man asked his minister to officiate at his brother's funeral. "Let me see," said the minister. "Your brother was thirty-two years old?" "Yes." "He worked hard for twenty years, didn't he?" "Yes." "Well, what did he get out of it?" "He left eighty acres of fine land, money in the bank, and thousands of dollars in insurance." "Yes, that's what you get out of it; but what did he get out of it?" "Oh, we are going to buy him an expensive oak casket!"

In order to determine the true meaning of the word "earth," in this context, let us first of all find out what it cannot mean. We shall be able to do this by keeping in mind the total teaching of the Lord Jesus Christ. Earth here cannot possibly mean riches. The Lord never promised an abundance of material things if we followed Him. He very definitely told us not to have our eyes fixed upon this earth or the things of earth. Hear His words: "Lay not up for yourselves treasures upon earth, where moth and rust doth corrupt, and where thieves break through and steal: but lay up for yourselves treasures in heaven, where neither moth nor rust doth corrupt, and where thieves do not break through nor steal" (Matt. 6:19, 20). This is clear. The Lord Jesus would not volunteer to give us by inheritance that which He considers evil for us to acquire in our own strength and through our efforts. His commandment is that we may not seek after riches or the acquisition of the earth. Why, then, would He turn around and promise us that which we are forbidden to seek after? If we are citizens of heaven as Christians, why promise us the earth as a reward for the spiritual quality of meekness? The Lord is consistent in His teaching. He does not say one thing in one place and something else in another.

Earth here could not mean material benefits, because that would not correspond ethically with the character of those whom the Lord promises to compensate and crown. The character that is designated as blessed throughout the Beatitudes and all of Scripture is not that of the man who has great possessions but the one who is unaffected by what he possesses. He may be rich and blessed or he may be poor and blessed. Neither riches nor poverty bring blessedness. That comes as the result of God's activity in man's life because of what the Lord Jesus is and what He did for man. When we possess heaven, earth is incidental. It would therefore be contradictory for the Lord of Heaven to promise the earth, the incidental, as His inheritance for us. The Lord would not bequeath us anything but the best. Material benefits, although they come from God and are essential, are not the best. They are not conducive to true happiness.

The very reason the Lord gave us the Beatitudes was to persuade us of this great truth. He would not, then, bring His teaching to nought and depreciate the purely spiritual character He wants us to have by bequeathing to us that which made the young ruler reject Christ and go away sorrowing. Why would the Lord promise us what might become a hindrance to our perfect relationship with Him? A philosopher has rightly said that, though a man without money is poor, a man with nothing but money is poorer still. Worldly gifts cannot bear up one's spirit under trials and troubles, any more than headaches can be cured by a golden crown or toothaches by a string of pearls. Earthly riches, as Augustine has truly said, are full of poverty. This cannot be what the Lord promised as the inheritance of the meek.

The world's notion of riches seems to include the idea that a man who has $100,000 must be twice as happy as the man who has $50,000. Riches, though honorably come by, are yet like manna; those who gathered less had no want; and those who gathered more found it to be trouble and annoyance to them. It would therefore be completely out of character for the Lord to bequeath us trouble and annoyance by literally bequeathing us the earth.

The earth that we inherit as a result of our relationship to Jesus Christ and through our disposition of meekness is not riches or material possessions. These are inconsistent with the character of those who have attained Christian blessedness. The reward must be relevant to the character of the one receiving it.

Suppose that you want to please a friend and make him happy. You know that he loves books but does not like to swim. Books are his life; water is his phobia. Knowing the framework of his character, you decide to build a swimming pool in his yard. How much happiness will that bring him? You should donate a library of good books to him. The gift must be suited to the character of the person for whom it is intended.

Think of the incongruity of a missionary to the South Sea Islanders addressing a group of savages thus: "We bring you the Gospel of Jesus Christ, which teaches love and forgiveness and the abandonment of all your cruel and horrible practices. If you will accept this teaching, and turn your back upon all your savage customs, you shall be rewarded at the end of the year with a cannibal feast." Yet this is no worse than what some people understand by this Beatitude. They would make the Saviour say, "Blessed are the unworldly – those who have renounced the material in favor of the moral and the spiritual, the kingdom of earth for the Kingdom of Heaven – for they shall inherit mere earth!" That is, the thing they have been weaned from, the thing that they have been taught to regard only as a means to larger and sublimer ends, is to turn out after all to be itself the end, the highest good! Could anything be more absurd than this?

But isn't the meek Christian supposed to enjoy the earth on which he lives? Yes, indeed he is. In fact, he is the only one who does truly enjoy it. Just ask yourself, what is the use of having money if you do not have the opportunity of spending it, or food if you do not have the capacity to enjoy it? The really rich person is he who can relate what he has to the satisfaction of his need. What good would it do you to possess the earth if you did not have the capacity of enjoying it in the real sense of the word? What would you do with billions of dollars on an island where there were no markets to buy anything?

It seems to us that this inheritance of which the Master speaks is the ability He gives the meek to enjoy to the fullest whatever material and spiritual blessings He permits them to have while here on earth. This ability is something only a true Christian can have. In this Beatitude, the Lord is not promising much or little, prosperity or poverty. He is promising the spiritual capacity to enjoy whatever He gives, much or little. What would a rich man do with a table full of the best food if he did not have the capacity to enjoy it? He may have less than the poor man who finds hearty satisfaction in a meager plate of beans. But this ability to enjoy our inheritance can be ours only if we have an attitude of complete resignation to God's will for us on earth. A meek person is one who is totally resigned to God's will and allows for no compromise with sin; he gets angry at it.

The author has known of Christians who have been imprisoned because of their testimony for Christ. Is such a person an heir to the earth? You say, "How can he be? If he were, he would not be in prison." He is there because the Lord permitted him to suffer for His sake. A Christian in jail for the sake of Christ is freer than his persecutors who enjoy their so-called liberty, thinking that they own the world. He who thinks he owns the world is not necessarily the true heir of it. Dr. Payson was asked if he could see any particular reason for his great bodily affliction. "No," he replied, "but I am as well satisfied as if I could see ten thousand reasons; God's will is the very perfection of all reason."

"The earth is the Lord's, and the fulness thereof." He may have given you a small or a large portion. Be satisfied with it and enjoy it, remembering that He has said you cannot enjoy the earth unless you relate it to the One who gave it to you. Without Him, the abundance of the rich is nothing and the little of the poor leads to despair. The wise man of Proverbs put it well and succinctly when he said, "Give me neither poverty nor riches; feed me with food convenient for me: lest I be full, and deny thee, and say, Who is the Lord? or lest I be poor, and steal, and take the name of my God in vain" (Prov. 30:8, 9).

"And they shall inherit the earth." Do you know what this actually says? Do not be over-anxious about riches or poverty. Be content with the state of your material possessions. You become content when you become a Christian. When you become blessed, your attitude toward God is one of meekness, of absolute submission to His will.

HOW TO ENJOY LIFE TO THE FULL

In our last study we saw that when the Lord Jesus said, "Blessed are the meek: for they shall inherit the earth," He was not speaking merely of the Millennium, nor yet of physical and material possessions here and now, but of the ability to enjoy to the fullest whatever He in His wisdom sees fit to give us.

We are not to complain to God that He does not bless us when He does not load us down with material benefits. Unfortunately, many people think this is what Christ meant when He promised us the earth, and for that reason they decide to follow Him. Who would not like to be adopted by a rich father? Those who have joined the Christian Church with such motives have been utterly disappointed and have brought great shame to the cause of Christ. What the Lord Jesus promises to the believer is eternal life, inner peace, and satisfaction. And this satisfaction evidences itself in our attitude toward the possessions of life. It makes no difference whether you are a poor man who will own only the six feet of ground in which you are buried or a rich man who owns many thousands of acres. Ultimately both of you will occupy just six feet of ground anyway.

Leo Tolstoy, the famous Russian writer, had a deep insight into human nature. In one of his books he speaks of a Russian peasant who was told that he could have all the earth he could measure in one day, from sunrise to sunset. He envisioned great holdings. Early in the morning he began walking; but as he realized that every foot of land on which he trod was his, he began to run at a feverish pace. The agreement stipulated that by sundown he must have returned to his starting point. His greed was so great, however, that more than half his time had elapsed before he turned back. He had to run at top speed to beat the setting sun. It was a real struggle. If he were not at the appointed place, he would lose all. He finally made it. But even as his foot touched the starting point, he fell dead from exhaustion. All that he gained in the end was sufficient land for his dead body. Six feet of earth. That was his final inheritance.

People do not always enjoy what they struggle so hard to attain. Many times the effort kills them. There is a kind of relentlessness in the price exacted for the possessions we strive to earn. What we must learn to do is to accept the inheritance God gives us and to enjoy that. Life itself cannot be earned; it is a gift. Let us consider all that pertains to life in the same way, as God's bequest to us. Anything that is divorced from God cannot bring full joy and satisfaction.

We know that the Lord gives more to some men than to others. Some of His children have great possessions and some do not. Who are we to question His wisdom? What the Lord wants to impress upon us in this Beatitude is that whatever we have is a bequest from Him. We do not deserve, nor can we claim by right, even the plot of ground where our bodies are finally laid to rest. The rich man must acknowledge his possessions as a bequest from God, and the poor man must do the same. Much or little, it makes no difference; we all have some part of earth for which we must thank God. How about the air we breathe, the water we drink, the food we eat? Their full enjoyment comes from a realization that they are God's bequests to us.

What the Lord is actually telling us in this Beatitude is to recognize His hand in everything we have on earth, whether it be much or little. Yet how reluctant we are to do this. We feel that when we receive Christ

He must prosper all our undertakings. He must fill our barns and our account books. He must heal us of all our sicknesses and afflictions. If you feel that way, you have never entered upon the full enjoyment of your inheritance from God.

A poverty-stricken woman was found on Christmas Day eating a dinner that consisted of a piece of bread and a small fish. A minister who visited her spoke commiseratingly of the poverty of her fare, to which the old woman, with face aglow, replied, "Poor fare? Dear heart, don't you see that the Lord has laid tribute on land and sea to feed me this blessed Christmas Day?" This woman owned the earth, though she ate only bread and herring for Christmas dinner.

This Beatitude should teach us not only to recognize that all good and perfect gifts come from God, but also to think of our inheritance as the best for us and to thank God for it, without trying to compare our share of earth with what others have. We must have an appreciation for our lot on earth, and the Lord tells us that only as we are clothed with His meekness will we have it.

A man who owned a small estate sent for an agent and asked him to write an advertisement offering it for sale. When the advertisement was ready, the agent read it to him. "Read that again," said the owner. The agent read it once more. "I don't think I will sell after all," said the man. "I have been looking for an estate like that all my life and did not know that I owned it." Have you praised the Lord for what you now possess on this earth? You wouldn't have had it if the Lord had not given it to you.

One night during an evangelistic meeting, a paralytic was wheeled down the aisle and placed just before the platform. In the preliminary part of the service, the song leader caught sight of him and asked, "What is your favorite hymn?" He immediately answered, "Count Your Blessings!" There was no wail of complaint from the handicapped man, just a vivid sense of the goodness of God. This paralytic was surely heir to a greater part of earth than many a millionnaire. Our submissiveness to God spells satisfaction for our lot on earth. This is the lesson of this Beatitude, "Blessed are the meek: for they shall inherit the earth." Meekness, in this sense, is a power – the power to feel satisfaction with what God gives, the power not merely to suffer it but to enjoy it to the full and to use it for His sublime purposes.

Why are we surprised at the hardships that are ours as Christians? The Lord has told us that, as a result of our following Him, we may be deprived of a great many things on this earth – even home and loved ones. Hear Him speak: "There is no man that hath left house, or brethren, or sisters, or father, or mother, or wife, or children, or lands, for my sake, and the gospel's, but he shall receive an hundredfold now in this time, houses, and brethren, and sisters, and mothers, and children, and lands, with persecutions; and in the world to come eternal life" (Mark 10:29, 30). We are rewarded here and now and in the hereafter. If you lose your mother for the sake of Christ, you will have a hundred mothers. How can this be? In the loving fellowship of Christian believers you will find many dear saints of God who will be mothers in Christ to you. You lose one to gain a hundred. And these you can truly enjoy. Now, you are not to expect that for every person or thing you lose you will receive a hundred literal replacements; but it is a general principle that the life that is lived for God and in submission to Him is never wanting in enjoyment. You may miss the natural family ties that were yours by blood, but you will enjoy the spiritual brotherhood of so many more. Nothing that is given up for Christ is ever lost. The loss becomes a gain – gain now and gain later – when it is incurred for the sake of the Lord Jesus. Who but the meek, the submissive to God's will, can enjoy their losses for Christ's sake?

Who can be truly said to possess the earth – he who owns a thousand houses, none of which is actually a home to him, or he who, without one house to call his own, has ten in which his knock at the door would rouse instant jubilation? Who is the richer – the man who, his great wealth spent, would have no refuge; or he for whose necessity a hundred would sacrifice comfort? Which of the two truly possessed the earth – King Agrippa or the tent-maker, Paul? It was from personal experience that Paul wrote to Christians, "For all things are yours; whether Paul, or Apollos, or Cephas, or the world, or life, or death, or things present, or things to come; all are yours" (I Cor. 3:21, 22).

When we receive Christ as our Saviour, we become blessed indeed. We receive the life of God in us. But when we become meek in our daily walk, as our Lord tells us, we acquire the ability really to enjoy this God-given life. If we rebel against life as God has given it to us, how can we possibly enjoy it? The condition for enjoying God's gifts to us, beginning with life and embracing all that pertains to life, is meekness, submission of our will to His. That is why the Lord is not content to stop with blessedness, but goes on to advocate meekness as the condition for our inheriting the earth. In this life we cannot enjoy God or His gifts unless we learn to be submissive to Him, not passively submissive but actively so.

Benjamin Franklin once said, "The sentence which has most influenced my life is, 'Some persons grumble because God placed thorns among roses. Why not thank God because he placed roses among thorns?' I first read it when but a mere lad. Since that day it has occupied

313

a front room in my life, and has given it an optimistic trend." To be meek is to have a disposition to see the roses among the thorns, rather than to complain about the thorns among the roses. Which do you see? Your answer will help you to judge whether you possess that meekness of which our Saviour spoke.

"Two men looked out from prison bars. The one saw mud, the other stars." You, too, are a prisoner of earth, no matter how much of it you possess or have inherited from the hand of God. But when you look at that piece of earth that you consider yours, do you see mud or stars? When our Saviour promised us the earth in this Beatitude, He was not speaking quantitatively but qualitatively. As Howe said, "I take him to be the truly rich man that lives upon what he has, owes nothing, and is contented; for there is no determinate sum of money, nor quantity of estate, that can make a man rich, since no man is truly rich that has not so much as perfectly satiates his desire of having more, for the desire of more is want, and want is poverty." Be careful, therefore, lest, possessing the world, you are not really heir to it because you lack the ability to enjoy it in relation to its Maker. To possess whatever you have and consider it not really your own but the One's who gave it is to have the ability to enjoy it in its fullest sense, no matter how small or great it may be.

"But," you say, "God has given me nothing. I haven't inherited a bit of this earth." This reminds me of an incident told by the Earl of Cairns, who did so much to improve mental asylums and to better the conditions of the insane. He says that once he was laid hold of by a madman.

"Have you ever thanked God for your mind?" cried he.

"No," said the Earl.

"Then get down on your knees and do it now!" insisted the strong maniac, forcing him to his knees.

Think twice – ten times – before you say that you are not heir to the earth. You are heir to as much as you are meek enough to recognize as coming to you from God for your enjoyment.

THE ENJOYMENT OF LIFE,
HERE AND HEREAFTER

We have seen that Christ's first meaning when He promised that the blessed meek would inherit the earth was not that they would receive large estates but a capacity for enjoying earth's blessings. Of all men, the meek have the greatest capacity for this.

Does the miser, the churl, the sybarite enjoy this fair earth? Do not the very passions in which these men depart from meekness mar their peace and blur their vision, so that no landscape, however bright, nor any sky, however soft, can charm the trouble from their heart? Does not the fever of their worldliness dry up the sweet springs of life, until discontent has desolated everything? From whom comes the querulous question, "Is life worth living?" Not from the honest peasant living his simple, healthy, natural life of contented poverty, but from the sons and daughters of sated abundance and jaded ambition. The truth is that the children of ambition never do inherit the earth. Their portion is always a something not yet attained. Each is a fresh example of the line so often quoted, and of them so true, "Man never is, but always to be blest." But the man whom Christ has taught lessons of meekness – the humble, lowly, contrite man, to whose poverty of spirit the Kingdom of Heaven has been revealed, and whose mourning the Holy Ghost has comforted – he inherits the earth! For him the fair day breaks, and the soft sky shines, and all the wonders of the glorious world appear; and none can steal his joy in the fellowship of Nature, or the deep content of his peace with God. His also are the joys of home, sweet faces and dear voices of his own beloved, pleasures of honest toil, delights

316

of intellectual inquiry, opportunities of blessing and being blessed in the service of humanity, and glad assurance of divine protection, as if the tabernacle of eternal God were spread above him. Ah! my friends, the germs of all the difference between heaven and hell lie in the dispositions men nourish in their breasts. And blessed are the meek, for here and now they inherit the earth.

To inherit the earth, then, is to inherit all that the earth symbolizes and stands for. It is not the mere possession of material earth, but what matter stands for in our hearts and minds. It is true that the word "inherit" has a forward look, but just as the heir to material possessions is permitted during his minority to draw upon his future inheritance for his present needs, so an earnest of the promised inheritance comes even here and now to those who have graduated in the school of meekness, and have thus acquired the moral qualities which render them eligible to realize in part their birthright as the sons of God. In meekness there is a considerable element of reverence to God, the sense of awed submission to an overmastering purpose and power. Thus it comes to pass that the men who get the most out of the earth here and now – the men to whom Nature most readily yields up her secret – are the men who are meek and lowly in heart. For the careless and flippant she has no disclosures. She does not admit them to her sanctities nor unfold to them her thought. The secret of Nature, like the secret of Nature's Lord, is with them that reverence her, and to them alone does she unveil. It is the child-spirit of meekness, that teachableness of disposition, that will secure our being led

> Into regions yet untrod,
> To read what is still unread
> In the manuscripts of God.

The moral qualities necessary to the best work, even in the realm of physical research, have long since been recognized, even by men who have stood aloof from the churches, and made no pretense to orthodoxy of faith. Think of the patience, the persistence, the courage, the loyalty to facts, the absolute candor and self-restraint, the freedom from passion and prejudice, and the score of other qualities which are essential to accurate observation and successful experiment in the way of scientific research.

Only he who comes in meek and lowly mood and puts himself to school at Nature's feet will hear her speak. Her messages will tremble to him on the midnight starbeam, and whisper in the evening breeze. The waving forest will be vocal with their music, and the ocean will break the secret in myriad accents to the hearing ear and the understanding heart. Hence it is that through meekness man comes into the inheritance of Nature's inner thought and purpose, which is the thought and purpose of God. Physical science, rightly interpreted, is the "thinking of God's thoughts after Him." It is the unraveling of the divine purpose, the disclosing of His method, the rendering back of matter its forces into terms of mind and will.

But matter is never constant; it is in perpetual flux. It is mind alone that abides. Behind and beneath all phenomena pulses and beats and burns the changeless will of God; and the man who can pierce through the passing show of things, who can push behind and beneath mere semblances, and lay hold of the essential and underlying soul of them, is alone the true possessor of the earth, and not the man who merely holds its acreage in hand. The only abiding inheritance is that which passes through moral and mental appropriation into the structure of character. Of this, nothing can rob us. Our stored mental impressions, our intellectual and moral acquisitions, no moth or rust can corrupt, no thief break through and steal. Into this inheritance we come through the gateway of meekness, and the moral discipline that this involves supplies us with the subjective factor of value upon which the worth of everything objective depends. It is what we bring to a thing in the way of mental and moral appreciation that imparts to it its value.

All the laws and forces of the material world are spread out before the mind of the savage as they are before that of the scientist, but with what difference of result. To the one they are nothing but a series of unrelated phenomena, while to the other they are the ordered processes of a system whose courses can be accurately traced, and whose issues can be definitely forecast. The difference does not lie in the system, but in the contemplating and interpreting mind.

Give a savage ink, paper, and a pen, and he will probably drink the ink, hang the pot round his neck as an ornament, and add the paper and pen to the pantheon of his household gods. Give similar materials to Shakespeare, to Milton, to Bunyan, and behold a moving tragedy, a mighty epic, or an immortal dream!

Look at it in another way. Have you ever thought how meager and inexpensive are the materials which go to make a great picture? Just a few oils, a bit of canvas, and a brush or two – the whole of which can be purchased for a few dollars. But when these are handled by a great artist, who pours his soul into his work, you get a production that may be valued in thousands of dollars. It is, then, this inner and plus quality which everywhere creates value.

That which makes the world a better place today for you and me to live in than it was in the grey beginning of years, is not that man has added a single ounce to its gold or silver, its copper or coal. He has not created one of the forces which sweep majestically around him and bend their necks to his yoke. They were all here before he came, and were waiting for his appropriating and utilizing brain. But he has brought to them that without which their scientific, artistic, or industrial value would be nil, namely, the cultured brain, the seeing eye, and the skillful hand. The obedience which these acquirements have necessitated on his part, the self-denial, the finely-disciplined accuracy, the trained power of observation, and the delicacy of adjustment in conducting experiments, are all expressive of moral qualities, without which no man can intellectually enter the kingdom of earth. The man who has qualified for this Beatitude and truly inherits the earth is he who has penetrated to the very heart of Nature; to whom she whispers her secrets, and whom her forces stand ready to obey. It is not the man, then, who merely annexes territory that has earned this blessedness, any more than the man who merely owns a library is heir to all the knowledge it contains. He, and he alone, is the true possessor who transfers the contents of his books to his brain, and stores his mind with the best thoughts of the world's best thinkers. You may burn that man's library, but you can never disinherit him of his mental stores. They are a permanent possession, and will survive when all that is merely material will have suffered ruin and decay. Thus, we see that through meekness alone we enter into the possession of that which endures.

Let us therefore cultivate meekness, submission to God. Violence and ill temper, impatience and unkindness, may snatch the scepter for a season; but no gains of that kind carry with them ability to enjoy God's earth. "The earth is the Lord's, and the fulness thereof" (Ps. 24:1). The true abiding possession of it He gives only to His children. Blessed are they who have learned of Jesus, who is "meek and lowly in heart," the lessons of submission to God, courtesy to men, forbearance with evil doers, steadfast loyalty to principle! Blessed! for the very lessons are an endowment of grace. Blessed! for they who practice them shall find rest to their souls. Blessed! for they grow like unto their Lord, and they shall see Him as He is. Blessed! for in that likeness they shall conquer, and by that meekness they shall prevail. Through time and in eternity, "Blessed are the meek: for they shall inherit the earth." (See "The Heirs of the Kingdom," by William J. Woods, in *The Christian World Pulpit*, August 27, 1890, Vol. 38, pp. 135-6, and "The Enthronement of Meekness," in *The Raiment of the Soul*, by the Rev. Henry Howard, pp. 170-6.)

By many, this sentence is regarded as a quotation from Psalm 37:11, where David is speaking of the land of Canaan – an acknowledged type of heaven. So understood, the promise means that the meek will be rewarded in the world to come. Whatever they now suffer on account of their meekness will be more than made up to them then. Thus the Apostle writes to the Hebrews, "For ye . . . took joyfully the spoiling of your goods, knowing in yourselves that ye have in heaven a better and an enduring substance" (10:34). No doubt this is good doctrine; but may we not also read the passage literally? Not one of the promises attached to the other Beatitudes is figurative, and there seems no necessity for treating this as an exception. According to the promise of our God, "We . . . look for new heavens and a new earth, wherein dwelleth righteousness" (II Pet. 3:13). Stupendous changes are to come upon this globe in the great day of the Lord; its destruction is to be followed by reconstruction; the new heavens and the new earth are to surpass the old alike in material excellence and in moral beauty; and who shall be the inhabitants of that renovated world? To whom shall it

321

belong? For whom shall it be prepared? And who are they that shall inherit it? It shall belong to Him who made and remade it. It shall be prepared for the saints who are to reign with Him in glory; and blessed are the meek, for they shall inherit the earth. (William J. Woods, *Ibid*). The Apostle John declares it in unmistakable terms when he says, "And I saw a new heaven and a new earth: for the first heaven and the first earth were passed away; and there was no more sea" (Rev. 21:1). Read carefully the third chapter of Peter's Second Epistle and the 21st chapter of the Revelation, and you will be informed of this new earth and new heaven. Peter very clearly tells us that, as in past ages great and renovating changes were brought about by the agency of water as regards this earth, so, vast and extensive changes will be effected in the future by the agency of fire, which is both a purifying and destructive element, and probably still greater changes in the more distant future, when the new heavens and the new earth are created, which are to remain before the Lord for evermore. (See also Isaiah 65:17; 66:22.) Most significantly, Peter predicts that the conflagration of this present earth will occur through the splitting of the elements, which man has now accomplished and through which he builds his devastating atom and hydrogen bombs.

Thus the blessed meek in Christ are the ones who fully enjoy this earth and their life on it, and are assured of their full inheritance of the new earth, where "God shall wipe away all tears from their eyes; and there shall be no more death, neither sorrow, nor crying, neither shall there be any more pain: for the former things are passed away" (Rev. 21:4). No wonder the Lord calls such persons blessed. Are you one of them?

ARE OUR PHYSICAL DESIRES EVIL ?

"Blessed are they which do hunger and thirst after righteousness: for they shall be filled" (Matt. 5:6). These words from the lips of the Lord Jesus were meant primarily for His disciples. But all around Him were a multitude of people who had come from that whole area, some from as far as sixty miles away. These included peasants from the fields of Galilee, fishermen from the Gennesaret shore, men and women from Jerusalem, maybe even some from beyond the Jordan in Moab. No doubt many of them were tired and hungry and thirsty, after traveling so far in the hot sun.

Perhaps some who came from a distance had brought their lunches with them. As time went on there on the hillside, it is quite possible that they opened their lunches and began to eat. It was perfectly legitimate for them to sit down and satisfy themselves. The Lord was conscious of their hunger and thirst, and in accordance with His custom of using the physical needs of men and women as the means of impressing upon them the still deeper needs of their spiritual natures, He turned to His disciples and said, "Blessed are they which do hunger and thirst after righteousness: for they shall be filled." However, He spoke loudly enough so that everyone could hear Him; for though the Beatitudes were addressed specifically to the disciples, their application was not exclusive to them.

Was this a denunciation of the natural satisfaction of the body? Not in the least. The Lord fully recognizes man's instinctive bodily needs, for He gave them to us as our Creator. If He had not given hunger and thirst to animals and men, they would die. Almost the first thing a baby cries for is food. God made us with an inbuilt safety valve. Whenever the body needs food or liquid, the alarm bells of hunger and thirst ring. If it were not for these God-given signals, how would we manage to regulate our intake of food and water for the replenishment of our bodies? There is no particular blessedness, however, about being physically hungry and thirsty. It is an instinctive desire that man satisfies along with animals, fish, birds, and all living things.

Since God made hunger an integral part of our beings, it must be a good thing. God is not the Creator of evil. He only permits its existence as the necessary concomitant of free will, in consequence of which we may choose to obey or disobey His will, that is, His law.

In creating man, God endowed him with both physical and spiritual appetites and desires. The only condition for the proper satisfaction of these desires was obedience to His command. And in giving man free will, God gave him the possibility of disobeying Him. Otherwise man's obedience to God's specific command would have brought no pleasure either to man or God. The satisfaction of all man's desires, physical and spiritual, depended upon his response to God's desire for obedience. That was the goal of God for man. But man rebelled and disobeyed God, and in so doing lost the desire to please God and obey Him. He was left with only his sinful nature, which seeks to satisfy primarily the desires of the flesh. Man, apart from the desire to obey God and reach the goal that He has set for him, is distinguished by a craving to satisfy his physical appetites, which have become lusts.

This is evident today and has been throughout all history. Man has concentrated most of his efforts on the satisfaction of the hunger, not of the soul and spirit, but of the flesh. He strives to produce more food, and to find release from his passions, in complete disregard of the laws God has established for his full and proper enjoyment and satisfaction. There is a distinct difference between a Christian – a godly, blessed man – and one who does not recognize God in his life and conduct. Both have physical and mental appetites. When a person becomes a Christian through the new birth, he does not lose his constitutional appetites and desires. But unlike the non-Christian, he no longer habitually makes the satisfaction of these desires an end in itself. He has but one ultimate end in life, and that is obedience to God. He does not as a rule seek the satisfaction of his flesh or his mental desires, appetites, and thoughts outside the prescribed laws of virtue clearly instituted by God in His Word. The Christian puts the Giver of his physical and mental appetites first, while the non-Christian puts the satisfaction of his appetites first and makes them an end in themselves, regardless of how God feels about them or whether they violate His laws.

"But," someone may object, "does not the natural man have other appetites than the physical? Does he not often evince a desire for honesty and integrity in public and private life? Does he not work to promote law and order, progress, culture, science, humanitarian causes – even apart from God?" And we would answer that it all depends upon the basic motivation. If they have their roots in self-seeking, self-exaltation, self-satisfaction, they are carnal appetites in the sight of God. Does this seem a harsh judgment? My neighbor works for good government. Shall I not commend him for this? Does God condemn him for it? It is a sad but incontrovertible fact that man's efforts to make this a better world apart from God are really an affront to Him; for they seek to substitute man's righteousness for God's righteousness, man's program for God's program, man's glory – we might even say man's deification – for

God's glory and praise. The Christian will often find himself in the position of having to commend good works, to assist in them, and to benefit from them, without being able in his heart to approve their basic motivation: the demonstration of man's goodness apart from God. This is part of the price we pay for having our citizenship in heaven and our residence on earth, for being in this world but not of it, for renouncing all claim to "natural" goodness and recognizing in Christ our only claim to righteousness. It takes a discerning Christian to preserve his spiritual perspective and equilibrium in a world that seeks to deify man.

It is well to remind ourselves that in the Beatitudes the Lord gives us both the conditions and the characteristics of a blessed life. He says in this Beatitude, "Blessed are they which do hunger and thirst after righteousness." This might be paraphrased, "Oh, the blessedness of those who have spiritual hunger and thirst!" Christ was contrasting the natural man with the spiritual. Natural man — fallen and sinful — hungers and thirsts for physical satisfactions — food, water, the things of this earth. Of course, there have been ascetics who have rejected the physical appetites and have substituted for them equally sinful religious and intellectual desires. They are sinful because their beginning and end is not the glory of God. Any attempt of man to save himself through the satisfaction of his physical or intellectual desires is sinful. On the other hand, the spiritual person possesses, in addition to the natural physical and mental appetites, another kind of appetite — spiritual hunger and thirst. The difference between the two is that one is governed by his sinful appetites, while the other is governed by Christ and hence by his spiritual appetites. Thus in turn he can govern his sinful appetites. This is a valid test as to whether we are spiritual persons or not. Our desires and physical appetites will demonstrate that to us and to others. To understand a man's character we have only to know the things he delights in. If all he lives for is to satisfy his animal instincts, he reduces himself to the animal level. And even if he also lives merely to satisfy the intellect apart from Christ, he is not a child of God. But if he lives to please and glorify God, who has given him both a body and a spirit, if he submits his reason to Christ, then that is a sign that he is a child of God.

We must recall the basic meaning of the Greek word *makarioi*, "blessed." It refers to those persons who are indwelt by God, who are characterized by what characterizes deity — blessedness. They are the people who have been fully restored to the image of God by accepting the Lord Jesus Christ as their Saviour. The price of sin and disobedience against God is death. But instead of letting us pay the penalty for our sins, the Lord Jesus, the incarnate God, died for us on the cross of Calvary. The debt for our restoration before God has thus been paid. If and when by faith we accept this payment on our behalf, a miracle has taken place, a miracle as great as that of our original creation. It is the miracle of spiritual re-creation. Once again we become the children of God. God establishes His throne in our hearts. And since God is within us, and our desires are conformed to His, we cannot but hunger and thirst after righteousness.

As in all the Beatitudes in Matthew, then, this spiritual desire is both the condition of divine blessedness for man and also the result of blessedness, God's indwelling of the human heart.

How is spiritual desire the condition of man's blessedness? Before he can be blessed, man must come to a realization of the emptiness of his own soul and turn to the One who can satisfy Him, the One who can save him, the Lord Jesus Christ. He recognizes that he is governed by his physical appetites as well as an unholy intellectual appetite and will, that he lacks the appetite for spiritual things that man had in Adam before the fall. This is the interest engendered by the power of the Holy Spirit in the heart of man. It is the same with the other Beatitudes in Matthew. Natural man must be made poor in spirit, humbled, must mourn, become sorry for his sinful state, become meek in order to go to Christ. The proud person, who rejoices in his sinfulness, will never be so disgusted with himself that he will seek Christ. As long as you consider yourself as having a righteousness of your own, you will never seek the righteousness that is in Christ. To hunger and thirst for righteousness means that you are seeking something outside yourself, something that you do not primarily and originally possess — a spiritual appetite.

This desire for righteousness is equivalent to the desire to have Christ. This Beatitude stands, like all the others, on the foundation of the phrase in verse 11, "For my sake." Blessed are they who hunger and thirst after righteousness. But whose righteousness? Certainly not their own —for who would seek something that he already possesses — but Christ's, which no one possesses to start with. Therefore this hunger and thirst after righteousness is the condition, the prerequisite, of blessedness in Christ. Since Christ and Christ alone makes us blessed, it has to be His righteousness that is meant here, a righteousness that the sinner in his sinful state knows nothing about, but which he will seek as he reaches the end of himself and cries to Christ for mercy and salvation. And this he does as the Holy Spirit convicts him of his need of the righteousness of Christ.

THE NATURALNESS
OF HUNGER AND THIRST

Who are the blessed? Those who hunger and thirst after righteousness. This righteousness referred to in Matthew 5:6 is surely the righteousness of Christ rather than self. Blessedness is the state of God indwelling man through the miracle of the new birth when man goes to Jesus Christ for salvation. This going to Christ by the sinner is described by the Lord in the fourth Beatitude as hungering and thirsting after righteousness.

This Beatitude, as are all the previous ones, is connected with the phrase, "For my sake," of verse 11. Taken in its proper perspective in context, this fourth Beatitude would read, "Blessed are they which do hunger and thirst after righteousness for my (Christ's) sake, for they shall be filled by me." As we look at it thus, this Beatitude takes on real meaning. Spiritual hunger is shown to be primarily the condition of blessedness. If you do not have the appetite, the desire to go to Christ in the first place as you realize your sinful condition, you will never be blessed. Only those who seek the Lord will find Him.

But hungering and thirsting after righteousness is also the result of blessedness in Christ. You must hunger for Christ initially, but once you have gone to Him and tasted of Him as the eternal Bread of Life, you will feed upon Him continually. Here, as in the preceding Beatitudes, the state, or trait, or characteristic is a necessary condition for acquiring the blessedness that is in Christ, after which it becomes the second nature of the believer, so to speak. You have to become poor in spirit (humble), mourn over your sinful state, and become meek in order to go to Christ and acquire this divine blessedness; but once you have become blessed in Christ, you are automatically all these things: humble or poor in spirit, mournful over sin, and meek. So it is with righteousness. You don't have it as a sinner, but you want it when you realize that it is the only way in which you can become blessed. Consequently you go to Christ and acquire it in and through Him; and then you are righteous, not of yourself, but simply and merely for the sake of the Lord Jesus Christ.

The Lord had a reason for using the terms "hunger and thirst" here. These are inborn characteristics of man's physical being, not subject to voluntary control. You don't say, "Now I will be hungry," and then become hungry, or "Now I will be thirsty," and then become thirsty. Hunger and thirst are automatic and recurring states, woven into the very structure of being. The only person who does not get hungry and thirsty is the person who is sick or dead. This has a parallel in the spiritual realm. You can tell whether a person is alive in Christ by whether he hungers and thirsts after Christ. After one becomes blessed in Christ, he does not have to try to become hungry and thirsty for the things of God. He is that constitutionally, by nature, not by effort. You can tell a healthy Christian by the hunger and thirst he demonstrates for God. If you see him needing all kinds of appetizers, you can rest assured that he is sick.

A basic characteristic of the healthy person is hunger and thirst for what is necessary to sustain life. This is exactly what the Lord had in mind when He said, "Blessed are they which do hunger and thirst after righteousness." This is why it is futile to force religious exercises on people. Unfortunately, many take this

Beatitude as a command from Christ to make people want to pursue righteousness in spite of their inner contrary desires. A cow will never crave meat, nor will a sinner ever crave after the things of God. You will crave feverishly for those things that correspond to your nature. Christ did not come to teach us to do righteous deeds without being righteous. This is impossible. You cannot do what you are not. His command in this fourth Beatitude is not merely to pursue righteousness, to try to live up to what Christ wants you to do. Try as hard as you may, you will never succeed in this. If you are a sinner, you will want to feed on the pleasures of sin. But if you are a Christian you will want Christ. You want that which you are.

How tragic is the prevalent theological teaching of *trying* to do good, of *trying* to live righteously. Christ never told us to *try* to do the right thing. He knew it would be impossible without first being made right ourselves. To say, therefore, that in order to be blessed we have to hunger after righteousness is sheer nonsense. We are hungry in the physical world because it is our nature to be so. Human endeavor to do good while we remain in our natural evil state is condemned in Isaiah 64:6, "But we are all as an unclean thing, and all our righteousnesses are as filthy rags."

That is why, in the Scriptures, this blessedness in Christ is also called conversion. It is not merely a matter of acting differently but of being made new creatures in Christ Jesus, with entirely new appetites built into our spiritual constitution, as physical hunger and thirst are built into our natural bodies. A person who has acquired this blessedness in Christ does not hunger for the same things that he did before coming to Christ. Anyone who does has never been converted. It is related of Augustine that after his conversion he was met by a fallen woman who had known him in his sin. As he passed her by, she stopped him and said to him, calling him by his familiar name, "Austin, it is I." Augustine turned and said, "But I am not Austin. I am not the man you once knew, for I have become a new creature in Christ Jesus."

A certain prisoner, most cunning and brutal, was singularly repulsive even in comparison with other prisoners. He had been renowned for his daring and for the utter absence of all feeling when committing acts of violence. The chaplain had spoken to him several times, but had not succeeded even in getting an answer. The man was sullenly set against all instruction. At last he expressed a desire for a certain book, but as it was not in the library the chaplain pointed to the Bible, which was placed in his cell, and said, "Did you ever read that Book?" He gave no answer but looked at the good man as if he would kill him. The question was kindly repeated, with the assurance that he would find it well worth reading. "Mister," said the convict, "you would not ask me such a question if you knew who I am. What have I to do with a book of that sort?" He was told that his character was well known to the chaplain and that for this reason he recommended the Bible as a book which would suit his case. "It would do me no good," he cried. "I am past all feeling." Doubling up his fist, he struck the iron door of the cell and said, "My heart is as hard as that iron; there is nothing in any book that will ever touch me."

"Well," said the chaplain, "you want a new heart. Did you ever read the covenant of grace?" To which the man answered sullenly by inquiring what he meant by such talk. His friend replied, "Listen to these words: 'A new heart also will I give you, and a new spirit will I put within you' (Ezekiel 36:26)." The words struck

332

the man with amazement. He asked to have the passage found for him in the Bible. He read the words again and again; and when the chaplain came back to him the next day, the wild beast was tamed. "Oh, sir," he said, "I never dreamed of such a promise! I never believed it possible that God would speak in such a way as that to men. If He gives me a new heart, it will be a miracle of mercy; and yet I think He is going to work that miracle upon me, for the very hope of a new nature is beginning to touch me as I never was touched before."

What was the consequence of that new heart, of that new nature in that prisoner? He became gentle in manner, obedient to authority, and childlike in spirit. When he became righteous in Christ, he craved after righteousness, he became hungry and thirsty after the One who made him righteous.

THE CHARACTERISTICS
OF HUNGER AND THIRST

Hunger and thirst in themselves, if unsatisfied, are unpleasant experiences. Yet like all appetites of the body and the soul, they are prerequisites of physical or spiritual satisfaction. If it were not for hunger, no one would seek food. Stop to think what life would be like without the process of eating day after day, and all that is involved in it. In the last resort, man works that he may eat and live. Many people, of course, are toiling for luxuries, but the overwhelming majority are working for their daily bread and are kept at work by the fear of losing it. Here, then, we have pain that leads to pleasure, hunger that leads to food, thirst that leads to water. The real and ultimate value of these appetites lies in their satisfaction and not in the appetites themselves, necessary as they may be.

So it is with our spiritual natures. Once we have been born into the kingdom of God, we are possessed of a natural appetite for spiritual things. This is built in, just like physical hunger. Spiritual hunger is a demonstration of spiritual health. Conversely, the absence of spiritual hunger is an indication of spiritual illness.

What do you do when you feel hungry and thirsty? Do you call upon the resources within yourself to satisfy that hunger and thirst? Ask some of our overweight brethren how satisfying that would be. Try it yourself and see what happens. To satisfy hunger and thirst, you must go outside yourself. Man can neither find food within himself, nor does he have the ability to produce it. All he can do is exert strength and intelligence to obtain the food and water to satisfy his hunger and thirst, but he does not actually and originally produce it. If the raw materials were not there, he could never satisfy his natural appetites, no matter how hard he worked. This is a perfect illustration of what happens in the spiritual realm. The food, the water, the grace and satisfaction our soul and spirit are seeking are outside of ourselves. Yet to us is left the effort to obtain and receive them. The fountain is yonder, and if we want to quench our thirst we must go to it and drink. God who made hunger a universal desire also made food universally available. But to appropriate it individually requires individual effort. All the food in the world is absolutely useless unless you take some of it and eat it. The grace of God and forgiveness of sin are available, but you must individually appropriate them.

Spiritual hunger is of two kinds. First you have an initial sense of emptiness when you realize you are a sinner. You feel like the prodigal son, far from the father's house. "And when he came to himself, he said, How many hired servants of my father's have bread enough and to spare, and I perish with hunger!" (Luke 15:17). He came to a moment in his life when he realized that he was hungry, empty. He was dead as far as his father was concerned. He knew that unless he went somewhere where there was food, he would perish. You are hungry without Christ. Yet some passage of Scripture, some sermon, gives you hope that this spiritual emptiness can be filled, if you will go to the source where it can be satisfied. You go to Christ and become blessed, for you are indwelt by God through Christ.

The prodigal son realized many times the emptiness of his life, but when he reached the end of his own rope he decided to go to his father. There was a power outside himself acting upon him to activate his rising and going to his father. There was a voice within him speaking — the voice of the Spirit of God — telling him that he would find acceptance with his father. There is a distinction, then, between the sense of hunger and thirst and the decision to do something about it. Without the rising and going, hunger means despair. Resist not the Holy Spirit urging you to go where your empty soul can be filled. The arms of your Heavenly Father are open to receive you if you come to Him in repentance, acknowledging that your own efforts to fill yourself have utterly failed, and that the best this world has to offer is empty husks.

There is yet another parallel between the satisfaction of physical hunger and that of the spirit of man. A man may stand in the saddest and deepest need of God's forgiveness. He is more or less conscious of his need, and in a way would like to have it met, but he cannot bring himself to accept God's provision for it. He cannot summon the will to do what is necessary to become a partaker of God's grace, and by his spiritual inanition and atrophy chooses death rather than life in Christ. Spiritual hunger not only requires the grace of the Holy Spirit to make it hopeful, loving, longing, but also the faithful, eager search for that freely offered pardon that is its food.

The second hunger is not really and primarily a hunger of the will, as is the initial hunger when the Holy Spirit operates in your soul and causes you to run to Christ for salvation. It is constitutional hunger. If grace does not quicken your initial desire for righteousness into loving faith; if loving faith does not seek eagerly and by all appointed means for the offered food; surely it is not a hunger that can be blessed or result in your being filled, nor can it lead to anything but starvation, famine, and death. When you receive

336

the life that is in Christ, you become constantly hungry. You eat for the strengthening of your weakened personality, which has just recovered from sin as from an illness, but you also eat for normal growth. And this is a good thing, because then you can be constantly filled. The recurrence of hunger is blessed because it brings the recurrence of satisfaction. But this second hunger can never be satisfied by anything within yourself. It, too, must be satisfied by an element outside yourself. Our sufficiency even after our new birth is never in ourselves but in Christ. When we submit to Christ, we do not just submit our appetites to Him for satisfaction but ourselves. Some people think that by receiving Christ they will have a certain emptiness in their lives filled, certain appetites satisfied, but they do not commit their whole selves to Christ. This is a perversion of the Gospel. When Christ saves, He does not save us from a limited number of needs, but He saves our whole personality; He saves us. He does not merely give us the ability to do certain good deeds; He makes us good. We do not come to God just to satisfy our hunger and emptiness, but to acquire a perpetual hunger for Him, in whom alone there is spiritual satisfaction.

This is beatifully illustrated by an incident in the life of the Greek philosopher, Socrates. He had a trusted servant who, seeing others giving presents to his master, came to him one day and said, "Because I have nothing else to give thee, Master, I here give thee myself." Socrates saw the earnestness of the servant and said, "Do so." After bestowing upon him gifts, and advancing him to the head of his servants, he called him one day and said, "I now give thee back to thyself better than when I received thee." Our betterment is simply an inbuilt hunger for God.

The Lord did not want to give us the idea that the blessed Christian life is one of stagnant self-perfection. Therefore He did not say, "Blessed are those who were once hungry and came to me," but, "Blessed are they which do hunger and thirst." In the Greek, two participles are used here, *hoi peinoontes kai dipsoontes*, "the ones hungering and thirsting." Both of these participles are in the present durative tense, which indicates durative action. They indicate that this hunger and thirst after righteousness is continuous. No one is blessed, for instance, who once went forward to the altar to accept Christ, showing some kind of hunger after God, and since then has no appetite for Him. Just as in marriage, you would not go to the wedding with the chosen one of your heart, then afterward have no desire to be with her, saying that the marriage contract is enough. Far too many people seem to feel this way when it comes to their supposed union with Christ. They point to their contractual experience, if we may call it that, when they first demonstrated the desire to receive Jesus Christ as Saviour and Lord, as proof of their salvation. But this is not sufficient proof, the Lord says. The reality of your experience of salvation is shown by the hunger that naturally resulted and continues to exist in your heart for the Lover of your soul, the Lord Jesus Christ. Oh, the blessedness of those who had, not a once-and-for-all feeding upon Christ, but, having started to feed upon Him, have never come to the end of their hunger for Him.

Hunger and thirst can never be permanently satisfied. We feel hungry, we eat, and in a little while we are hungry again. A peculiar characteristic of hunger is that, once you satisfy it, you begin to look forward to what you are going to have to satisfy it when it reappears. You no sooner finish one meal than you start planning another. The more you enjoy food the more you look forward to the moment when you will be hungry again. Actually, the Lord did not pronounce His blessing upon the satisfaction of our hunger, but upon the hunger itself. He did not say, "Blessed are those who possess righteousness," but, "Blessed are they which do hunger and thirst after righteousness" (Matt. 5:6). The obvious inference is that it is impossible for man, any man, to have all of God and His righteousness. Man has a built-in sense of insufficiency and dissatisfaction. No man feels that he has enough. Before he is born again, he never feels that he has enough of what the natural world can offer him, and when he is born again and becomes a child of God he still never feels he has enough of his Father, God. The unregenerate man finds his happiness, not in the possession of earthly things, but in the pursuit of them, for he can never possess all that he desires. After he reaches a goal, he looks ahead to still another goal.

The historian, Gibbon, tells us that Abdulrahman, of the Moslem Califfs of Spain, built for his pleasure the city, palace, and gardens of Zehra, beautifying them with the costliest marbles, sculptures, gold, and pearls. He had 6,300 persons, wives, concubines, and eunuchs at his service. His guard had belts and scimitars studded with gold. At his death, the following authentic memorial was found: "I have now reigned above fifty years in victory or peace . . . . Riches, honours, power, pleasure have waited on my call . . . . I have diligently numbered the days of pure and genuine happiness which have fallen to my lot: they amount to fourteen."

As a distinguished author wrote: "Those who consider want of money the worst of evils are fools; there is a far more painful one, and that is penury of desires." That is true also of the Christian. The least blessed Christian is the one who thinks he has received all that

339

there is to be had of God and His righteousness and desires no more. The most blessed Christian is he who is possessed of a constant desire for the righteousness of God, who feels that he can never get enough of it. The more he desires it, the more he receives.

HOW HUNGRY ARE YOU ?

Hungry and thirsty people are actually unsatisfied people. Therefore what we really have in the fourth Beatitude of Christ, in Matthew 5:6, is a declaration that the unsatisfied are blessed.

There are, however, two kinds of unsatisfied people. The first are those who do not know the Lord Jesus Christ, and hunger and thirst after earthly treasures and pleasures. They make these their goal. They can never acquire enough to satisfy them. The goal is forever unreached; therefore they never possess true happiness. God created us for one purpose: to enjoy Him as our Creator and to commune with Him. Everything else is meant to be merely the means to that end. When the end becomes the means and the means the end, the result is sheer misery. When we desire God for the material benefits that we hope He will bestow upon us, then even these material things will not carry with them the blessing that could have been ours if they were merely incidental to the main purpose of our lives.

Here, then, we have a class of people who find no sufficiency or satisfaction in all created things because they put the creation before the Creator. A man whose goal in life is the possession of things never feels he has enough or derives perfect satisfaction from what he has. What seemed just the thing that he wanted when viewed from a distance is found, once possessed, to be no satisfaction at all, but a new stimulus that makes him long, and thirst, and hunger for something more, till at last the man who pursues most eagerly, and possesses most largely, the best things of this world, learns eventually, amidst tears and bitter regrets, that he was

341

spending his money for that which was not bread, and his labor for that which has satisfied not.

On the other hand, we have a class of unsatisfied ones who find satisfaction because their sufficiency is in Christ, the Creator of all things. Whether they have much or little of this world's goods, it is sufficient, because in it they see the hand of God. Their sufficiency is not in things created but in the Creator.

This is clearly brought out by the grammatical construction of this Beatitude in the original Greek text. Ordinarily, in Greek, verbs of hungering and thirsting are followed by the genitive case. In English, this Greek genitive case would often be indicated by the preposition "of." For instance, when I say, "This is part of the whole," the phrase "of the whole" is in the genitive case. Now the genitive that follows verbs of hungering and thirsting in Greek is called the partitive genitive, which indicates that part of the whole is meant. For instance, when I say, "I hunger for of bread," it means that I am hungry for part of a loaf of bread that I may be looking at. In other words, in Greek, when a verb expressive of hunger or thirst is used, the genitive case is used. If, therefore, this hungering and thirsting spoken of by the Lord was meant to express desire for only a part of the righteousness of Christ, the word righteousness would have been in the genitive case. But strangely enough it is in the accusative case. It is *teen dikaiosuneen* and not *tees dikaiosunees*. (See William Edward Jelf, *A Grammar of the Greek Language*, John Henry and James Parker, Oxford and London, 1859, p. 196.) The action of the hunger and thirst are transferred upon the object, which here is the righteousness of Christ.

The Lord is thus telling us that he is blessed who is constantly evidencing hunger and thirst, not for just part of the righteousness of Christ, but for His whole righteousness. This desire for complete righteousness is impossible for man to possess or demonstrate in and by himself.

When Alexander the Great offered to do any favor that the Greek philosopher Diogenes might ask, Diogenes simply requested the conqueror of the world to step aside, and not stand between him and the sun. However rude we feel such an answer to be from the lips of the cynic philosopher, it is the best answer you and I could make to any and every object that would steal our hearts from Christ and His righteousness. Let Him, who is all your salvation, be all your desire. If there is anything standing between you and Christ, you cannot be said to desire the whole righteousness of Christ. Unfortunately, that is the position of most Christians today. That's why the righteousness of Christ, as possessed and demonstrated by us, is so ineffective in this world of unrighteousness.

But before we go on, we must determine what is meant by righteousness in this Beatitude. This is one of the basic words of the Bible. It takes us to the courtroom, where we stand as the accused. Our sin is disobedience to God. The punishment for this sin has been predetermined. It is death, separation from God. As creatures separated from God, we have made His creation the object of our desire, rather than union with and enjoyment of God, the Creator. Our blessedness and satisfaction can be reclaimed only as we acquire this lost relationship with God. But God is a just God. He cannot pronounce punishment on a sin and then not apply His Word. This would make Him a liar. Here, then, we find a God who must be true to His Word and at the same time wants to reconcile man to Himself. He finds a way. His Son, the Lord Jesus Christ, One of the Three Persons of the Trinity, volunteers to stand between man and God. He takes upon Himself the penalty of our sin, which is death. Righteousness is the very name of Christ in prophecy, "This is his name whereby he shall be called, THE LORD OUR RIGHTEOUSNESS" (Jer. 23:6). He became man in order to die on the cross. Through His death two things are accomplished. First, the justice of God is satisfied. He is proven true to His Word. And secondly, man, on acceptance of this voluntary act of sacrifice of Christ, is set free from sin and brought back into fellowship with God, his Creator. Then man is said to be justified before God. But note how this is done. Only through the person and work of the Lord Jesus Christ.

As the Apostle Paul says in I Corinthians 1:30, "Of him are ye in Christ Jesus, who of God is made unto us wisdom, and righteousness, and sanctification, and redemption." The only reason the Lord Jesus Christ could pay the penalty of our sin was that He had no sin of His own. Our sin was laid on Him but was never in Him. He was absolutely righteous. In other words, He never broke a law of God, either in His pre-incarnate or incarnate existence. Righteousness is the opposite of sin or lawlessness. Therefore the only absolutely and inherently righteous One is God. Christ is entirely righteous and unimpeachably holy in Himself, and He has in His holiness offered Himself a sacrifice without spot to God for our sins. In consequence God mercifully looks upon us as righteous in Him, imputes His righteousness to us, calls it ours, treats us as if it were ours, pardons us because of it, though it be altogether His, and not ours. We, by faith in Him claiming this pardon, coming boldly in the strength of His sacrifice to the throne of grace, wrapping ourselves round in faith in the divine mantle of His holiness, and therein being forgiven for His holiness' sake. This is the first, greatest, chiefest way in which Christ is our righteousness. In this His righteousness we trust to be pardoned for our original inherited sin and also for the sins which we continually commit, and continually repent of. In this righteousness we trust that, weak and wilful as we are, we are still God's children in Christ, accepted in the Beloved. In this, and in this only, we trust to stand before the judgment-seat of Christ, knowing no righteousness but His, for His sake forgiven finally and for ever, for His sake admitted into the full fruition of His joy, heirs not in title only then and hope, but in actual and strong righteousness, – righteousness outward, forensic, imputed, – righteousness consisting in pardon, – the only righteousness which is real, thorough, trustworthy, which can stand when He appears, and endure the severity of His judgment. (George Moberly, *Sermons on the Beatitudes*, Oxford, 1860, pp. 63-4.)

This righteousness is not something that we could ever have earned for ourselves; we acquire it only as we believe on Christ who is our righteousness. The Apostle Paul put it clearly and succinctly in II Corinthians 5:21, "For he [God] hath made him to be sin for us, who knew no sin; that we might be made the righteousness of God in him [Christ]." As our sin was placed on Christ, Christ's righteousness is imputed to us. It is not in us. We are righteous only because He is righteous and only as long as He dwells within us. As when a child travels in his father's company all is paid for, but the father himself carries the purse; so the expenses of a Christian's warfare and journey to heaven are paid for and discharged for him by the Lord in every stage and condition.

We must not separate this Beatitude from its foundation phrase, "for my sake," of verse 11. "Blessed are they which do hunger and thirst after righteous-

345

ness . . . for my sake." In effect the Lord Jesus is saying here, "The only reason you can have any spiritual appetite at all is because of what I am and did for you. I am the One who intervened between your sin and the righteousness of God. I have taken your sin and I have given you the righteousness of God." And the mystery of mysteries is that the Lord has not become sinful as a result of this transaction, but we have become righteous.

A blessed person is not one who seeks merely to perform a few acts of righteousness here and there, not one who desires only a part of the righteousness of Christ, but who wants all that is to be had of Christ. And this is not something inherent to his nature but comes from outside himself.

Why does the Christian constantly hunger for the righteousness of Christ — the whole of His righteousness? Because even in his blessed state of the new birth he feels the constant impact of sin upon himself. His desire for the righteousness of Christ indicates the constant struggle he experiences against sin. The Christian is blessed and can continue to be so even as he lives in a world of sin and unrighteousness. His desire for the whole righteousness of Christ is a fervent desire for freedom from sin, in Christ and through Christ. The sin is all around, but the blessed person has no desire for this aura of evil in the world, but for the righteousness of Christ.

Unfortunately, many Christians desire only part of the righteousness of God in Christ. They want to lead lives of compromise. With one part of their natures they desire sin, and with the other the righteousness of Christ. However, our degree of blessedness, we are told in this Beatitude, depends on how much of the righteousness of Christ we earnestly desire. The more satisfied we become with the righteousness of Christ the more we shall desire it. And the more we desire it the more of it we shall have. The holier we become the less willful desire we shall have for sin. Our constitutional desire for righteousness is proportionate to our holy living.

SATISFIED TO OVERFLOWING

"Blessed are they which do hunger and thirst after righteousness: for they shall be filled," our Lord said. He was not speaking of human righteousness, a sense of justice as understood by men, but of the righteousness of God, of the total commandments of God. Merely to possess a sense of justice and righteousness in this world is far from enough to make us blessed. In the original Greek text, the definite article precedes the word *dikaiosuneen*, "righteousness." Literally translated, this Beatitude should read, "Blessed those hungering and thirsting after the righteousness." Not any righteousness, but the righteousness of the One speaking, of the Lord Jesus Christ Himself.

But, you say, does not this make the Gospel very narrow? Yes, it does. Now let me ask you a question. What can satisfy hunger? Only food — nothing else. What can satisfy the need of your lungs to breathe? Life itself is very narrow. And so is Life with a capital L. It can only be found in Christ. The tragedy of our modern age is the desperate need for something to fill the emptiness of the human heart and the multiplicity of suggestions for filling it. Blessedness can be found only in the righteousness of Christ, and nowhere else. Hungering after any man's righteousness, even your own, will do you no good. It will not make you blessed but will simply increase your sense of need and emptiness.

Here, as in all the preceding Beatitudes, a specific class of people is spoken of. Who are blessed? Those who evidence hunger and thirst for the righteousness of Christ. The participles "hungering and thirsting" (peinoontes kai dipsoontes in Greek) are preceded by the definite article. Only one article appears here, that in front of hungering, but it may very well be taken to apply to both. (See A. T. Robertson, *A Grammar of the Greek New Testament*, Doran, pp. 757, 785-8.) Therefore, not only is a specific and exclusive righteousness spoken of here, but also a special class of hungering and thirsting folk. Our Lord refers to those who are blessed and who, as a result of their blessedness, are characterized by this intense spiritual yearning for the righteousness of Christ. It is not those who occasionally show signs of spiritual hunger, but those who are so spiritually constituted that they cannot live without constantly feeding upon the righteousness of Christ.

And this class of people is further emphasized by the word *autoi* in Greek, translated "they." Usually the "they" in Greek verbs is indicated by a suffix attached to the verb. But here the pronoun *autoi* is a separate word, as if to emphasize the exclusiveness of the group. "For they themselves shall be filled."

Now what is this filling that is promised? There is a paradox here. On the one hand we have the participles hungering and thirsting, which indicate continuous and repeated desires, and on the other hand we have the verb *chortastheesontai*, "shall be filled," which is in the future indicative passive. This is usually punctiliar or momentary. Thus we see that the hunger and thirst are durative or continuing, while the satisfaction and filling are punctiliar or momentary. How can we reconcile these two? Some profitable lessons are suggested by this.

The blessed will never have a once-and-for-all filling. To be filled is to be satisfied, and to be satisfied is to cease from hungering and thirsting. But Christ cannot mean that the sacred craving shall be appeased in the sense that all aspirations shall come to an end, and the

349

longing that is so blessed shall never be felt again. Satiety is not to be the outcome of man's holiest endeavors. The extinction of his craving for righteousness for himself and the world would be the worst calamity that could befall him. There is no annihilation of pure desire in Christianity, no cessation from the divine task of growth in grace and in likeness to God. And yet, paradoxical as Christ's promise is, who can say that He does not fulfill it? Those that hunger and thirst most, have most. Those who are foremost in the craving for good, find it most. They have meat to eat that others know not of. They find meat where others neither see it nor suspect it. These are they who can look on by faith and see of the travail of their souls and be satisfied.

If we are blessed, we experience a continuous process of being hungry and thirsty for the righteousness of Christ, and every time we go to Christ to be fed we are filled. But this filling does not guarantee that we shall not get hungry and thirsty for Him again. Nothing could more adequately express this constant desire for Christ and His instantaneous filling each time we desire Him than the sense of hunger and thirst. The fact that we have to eat again does not mean that we are not satisfied each time we eat. The fact that we will have to eat at noon does not steal from us the pleasure of eating our breakfast. Each filling is complete in itself, yet each filling is new every mealtime. Every breakfast, lunch, and dinner has new value. Those responsible for cooking may think it would be wonderful if this constant need to keep filling our stomachs and quenching our thirst could be eliminated. But would it really be better if we could eat once and for all? Under the stimulus of a recurring appetite, we really look forward to the next meal, nor does one meal detract from the anticipation of the next. A loving wife looks forward to preparing it, and a loving and hungry husband looks forward to consuming it. A loving mother delights to put food before her children, and healthy children plunge into it with keen enjoyment. It is the same with the children of God. Our Heavenly Father is constantly preparing food for us, and it is fresh each time we receive it. Each time we partake of it, we experience new enjoyment; and we look forward to getting hungry again so that He can satisfy us again. His satisfaction of us is complete each time and yet not ultimate. Isn't that wonderful?

This verb also has the impact of an effective aorist (A. T. Robertson, *A Grammar of the Greek New Testament*, p. 872.) It emphasizes the end or the accumulation of action. We are filled each time we hunger for righteousness and this is effective filling. We have no sense of dissatisfaction or emptiness, but at the end of the road we shall have a cumulative satisfaction, so that when we finally appear before the throne of God's judgment our satisfaction will be complete. As we look back, we shall say, "It has really been a full life, full of righteousness, not our own but Christ's."

Thus we see that the promise reaches beyond the present. Its cumulative, absolute, and true fulfillment belongs to the hereafter. It is no delusion, that dream of a perfect world, wherein dwelleth righteousness; that inspiring dream which even now can lead us on from strength to strength, can make us work with God now, and in our measure learn to feel with Him to hate that which He hates, to love and pray for that which He loves. One day it shall be realized, for it is not only "the consummation that eager hearts expect," but the one far-off divine event to which the whole creation moves. Yes, those who are hungering and thirsting after righteousness are no visionaries: they are fed upon a hope which cannot fail; they are hungering and thirsting for the one reality in the universe, for that which is the true law of life in this world, and the eternal law and the unfading joy of heaven.

God gave us a direct illustration of being fed by Him when He provided manna for the hungry Israelites. The manna had to be gathered every day. No one can store up God's food. He does not give out frozen food, but fresh, not ice cubes, but flowing water. He said that out of us living waters shall spring up. When God gives us spiritual manna, we cannot afford to miss gathering it daily, for we cannot keep one day's supply over to the next. Sufficient for each day is the food thereof. The morrow must take thought for the things of itself. The Christian who does not daily hunger for his spiritual bread, and daily ask for it, is likely to starve. He will find no freezers in the Kingdom of God. He doesn't need them. The Lord taught us to pray, "Give us this day our daily bread." Yesterday's prayer will not do for today, nor today's for tomorrow. Every day, night and day, must he who is in earnest in hungering and thirsting for the sacred food of righteousness, seek it, gather it, and feed upon it for his soul's health. It lies about his path and about his tent; it is in His Bible; it is in his chapel, if he will kneel down and ask for it; it is everywhere.

As far as the manna was concerned, each person had to gather it for himself. You cannot delegate to any other, be he minister or priest, parent or brother or child, the work of feeding your soul with the food of God. As the children of Israel could not send one to gather for many, nor employ those that were younger, or poorer, or less noble, to gather instead of them, so is the work of feeding on the sacred food of God, now and for ever, a strictly personal one. None can do it for another. It is a lonely, inward work. We may advise one another, we may pray for one another; but to act for one another, to hunger spiritually, or feed for one another, to reach or touch each other's soul, we are totally powerless. The work is to be done in the solitude and depth of each separate soul by itself and for itself.

Claim for yourself all that God has. Don't think that this food belongs in abundance only to those who have been in the faith a long time. Sometimes it seems that the older we get in Christ the more lax we become in our hunger for Him. We must act starved for Christ all the time. That's the meaning of this Beatitude.

"Why do you insist upon having the largest piece of pie, Harry?" asked a mother reprovingly. "Isn't your big brother entitled to it?" "No, Mama, not the way it looks to me," replied Harry. "He was eating pie three years before I was born." Is that the actual observation that younger Christians make of us who have been feeding on Christ for so many years?

The fact that the verb *chortastheesontai*, "they shall be filled," is in the passive voice means that this filling is caused by an outside agent. We are the objects of the filling, but God in Jesus Christ is the One who fills us. We are filled by Him and Him alone. This Beatitude is one that emphasizes throughout the grace of God. The great doctrine of the atonement of Christ is its very heart.

When people recognize our constant hunger and thirst after righteousness, and see how wonderfully Christ satisfies us, they cannot but be impressed. True Christian hunger for righteousness is infectious. Men and women around us know that life is as hard for us as for them. But they see our overcoming Christian lives. We become a mystery to those around us. We don't have to open our lips for our righteousness to radiate to others.

Righteousness is caught before it is taught. Those in the world around you will know whether you met God in His Word and in prayer before your head-on encounter with them. One who truly hungers and thirsts for the forgiveness of God has helped to win others to the like holy longing by the secret radiation of his own Spirit-lighted heart, before he knows or suspects that he has been noticed or observed at all.

Let us not forget that the words of the wise are as nails (Eccles. 12:11), but their examples as hammers. When Lord Peterborough lodged for a season with Fenelon, he was so delighted with his piety and virtue that he exclaimed at parting, "If I stay here much longer, I shall become a Christian in spite of myself!"

Don't try to preach righteousness to your children. Practice it first. If you preach it without practicing it, you simply show that this business of Christianity is a sham, a hypocrisy. A man going from his house to the barn one snowy morning heard a voice behind him, "I'm coming along, too, Papa," and looking back saw his little son lifting his feet and planting them carefully in his footsteps. So the children imitate us. "No man liveth unto himself." Our children walk in our footsteps of righteousness or unrighteousness. Don't ask the children to demonstrate hunger for Christ, His Word, His Church, prayer, if you do not do so yourself. Don't send them to the school of Christ's righteousness; take them there and stay there yourself.

Some folk eat because they have to and consequently don't enjoy it; and some eat and love it. So it is in our spiritual lives. A good criterion of whether you are a healthy child of God is whether you enjoy God's food, God's water, the fellowship of His Church and His people, prayer, and His Word. Tell me what you enjoy most in life, and I'll tell you what place Christ's righteousness has in your life.

CAN THE HELPLESS SHOW MERCY?

"Blessed are the merciful: for they shall obtain mercy" (Matthew 5:7).

In the eight Beatitudes as given in Matthew, we are climbing the ladder of Christian blessedness. On the first rung we find those who in a humble spirit have recognized and confessed their helplessness and have called upon the Lord Jesus Christ for help and salvation. "Blessed the poor in spirit: for theirs is the kingdom of heaven . . . for the sake of the Lord Jesus Christ." Every Beatitude is incomplete without resting on the foundational phrase, "for my sake," in verse 11. Helplessness does not do anyone any good. A recognition of it is merely the first step leading to Christ. But without the person and work of the Lord Jesus, no one can possess the Kingdom of Heaven.

Man thus becomes *makarios*, "blessed" (not "happy," as so many interpret this word). Happiness springs from favorable circumstances, while blessedness is the acquisition of God within the human heart. If you are blessed, you have God. If you are happy, you have good luck. If you are blessed, you will not be affected by circumstances but will make the circumstances of life serve God's central purpose in your life.

On the second rung of the ladder of blessedness, we find those who, on looking within themselves, find much to cry over and for God to rejoice over. "Blessed the mourning ones: for they shall be comforted . . . for the sake of the Lord Jesus." This sorrow for self does not originate in self-pity, but is of Christ and for Christ. Sin brings sorrow, but forgiveness brings joy. And forgiveness is found exclusively in Christ. Therefore this

355

Beatitude cannot be separated from its foundation, "for my sake," from the person and work of the Lord Jesus.

As we climb the third rung of the ladder of blessedness, we find those who have recognized their helplessness and gone to Christ, who do not consider themselves sinless, but forgiven sinners, and who do not remain passive in the presence of sin. They are in active opposition to it. That's the first meaning of "meekness," *prautees*, in Greek. And the counterpart of that is complete submissiveness to the will of God. "Blessed the meek: for they shall inherit the earth." Here the Christian has grown to the place where he can really enjoy God's earthly will for him, not merely suffer it. This does not mean that Christians are obliged to enjoy the actual temptations, sins, or adverse circumstances of life. But they can look forward with joy to the end result of these experiences, or even rejoice in the knowledge that the end result will mean the glory of God and consequently their own blessedness in Christ.

Helplessness, sorrow, meekness: these are not blessed in themselves. It is the rewards that are blessed: the Kingdom of Heaven, comfort, enjoyment of the earth. The rewards stand in joyous contrast to the experiences.

On the fourth rung we experience the blessedness of hungering and thirsting after righteousness, the righteousness of Christ. When we discover we have nothing of our own to be proud of, we will naturally hunger for that which is not ours, the righteousness of the One who made us blessed. "Blessed the hungering and thirsting ones after righteousness: for they shall be filled . . . because of Christ (for my sake)."

But let us go on to the fifth rung of the ladder of blessedness. Here we have those who are merciful. Observe that now it is not the things they lack that are supplied by God; but they are given more of what they have and show forth. They have and show mercy; they will experience mercy. Here we do not have contrasts between their states and lack of possessions and what God supplies, but rather confirmations of that which they already manifestly have. They have and show forth mercy; therefore God's mercy toward them will increase.

This is also true of the sixth and seventh Beatitudes. The pure in heart shall see God, who is pure; and the peacemakers are proclaimed children of God, who maketh peace. Mercifulness, purity of heart, peacemaking, are qualities, virtues, which are God-given in the first place. They are not conditions of want and emptiness for God to fill. They are the result of God's provision for hunger already experienced.

Thus, the three lower rungs of the ladder of blessedness are on this side of those who hunger and thirst after the righteousness of Christ. There we find those who are helpless, sorrowing, and meek – all conditions not blessed in themselves, but prerequisites for blessedness. They are like empty glasses that the Lord fills. And then, on the higher rungs of the ladder of blessedness, the other side of those who hunger and thirst after righteousness, are the merciful, the pure in heart, and the peacemakers. All these graces that follow the fourth Beatitude of hungering after righteousness assume the possession of that righteousness. The graces that precede the fourth Beatitude are those of persons in whose hearts there is a deep and conscious sense of poverty, ignorance, error, and sinning.

These three Beatitudes on each side of spiritual hunger pair beautifully into a trio of contrasting states. Take the first pair, the first and fifth Beatitudes:

"Blessed the poor in spirit – the helpless ones."

"Blessed the merciful – those who show mercy."

In the first Beatitude, we have those who need

mercy, and in the fifth we have those who show mercy. But we could not climb to the fifth rung of the ladder unless we had begun with the first one. When we remember this simple principle, all the difficulties in connection with this fifth Beatitude disappear. What is the main difficulty people find with this verse? The assumption that this fifth Beatitude teaches that in order for us to experience the mercy of God we must first show mercy. But we cannot show mercy unless we have first experienced it. We have to climb the first rung of the ladder before we reach the fifth. Some people think they have long enough legs to reach the fifth rung before they step on the first one. They think that all they need to do to experience God's mercy is to show mercy to others. But you cannot give what you do not have, and you do not have what you have never received. In the first Beatitude, we have man's helplessness and Christ's salvation. And the salvation of Christ incorporated in that all-important phrase of verse 11, "for my sake," involves the experience of mercy.

The Lord selects mercy as the first grace exhibited by the justified believer on which to pronounce His benediction. "Blessed are they which do hunger and thirst after righteousness: for they shall be filled," and then, "Blessed are those who, having that righteousness, exhibit mercy: for they also shall obtain mercy." Don't be afraid that by giving to others the mercy given to you, you will be impoverished. He who gives will receive more than he gives. God's shovel is always bigger than ours. To whom much is forgiven, by such much will be forgiven. They who have received the richest mercies will themselves exhibit, not for a reward, but as a grateful and instinctive response, the richest mercies to mankind. There may be nothing in the hand – this we cannot help – but there may be much in the heart, and this we are responsible for. God's grace puts mercy in the heart; God's providence puts the means of unfolding it in the hand. These are not always and everywhere joined. One has a full hand, and has an empty heart. Another has a compassionate heart, of whose compassion tears are the only available exponents, and whose good wishes, often more precious than the gold of others, are all they can give to denote how deeply they feel. If we have, mercy draws on it; if we have not, mercy expresses our sympathies, retires, and is silent. (See John Cumming, *Benedictions or The Blessed Life,* John P. Jewett and Co., Boston, 1854, pp. 138-9.)

A Christian who has been helped in his helplessness will help others in a similar plight. If he is helpless himself, how can he help anyone else? It is like expecting one drowning man to save another. You've got to be saved to save someone else, if we may put it that way. Your showing of mercy to others is not the cause of your experiencing the mercy of God, but the result of it. You show mercy because you have experienced mercy. You do not experience that first mercy of the Lord in your helplessness because you show mercy. You show mercy because you are merciful, but you do not become merciful because you show mercy.

A great many commentators and theologians seem to confuse our initial experience of the grace of God in the helplessness of our sinful state with the need of the mercy of God after our salvation. There is a way in which the mercy of God after our new birth and initial forgiveness is proportionate to our mercifulness. When, for the first time, we experience the mercy of God, it is absolutely an undeserved mercy; it is of grace and of grace only, and not of works, lest any should boast. Ephesians 2:8 and 9 stand eternally true: "For by grace are ye saved through faith; and that not of yourselves:

it is the gift of God: not of works, lest any man should boast." But Ephesians 2:10 is just as eternal and just as true: "For we are his workmanship, created in Christ Jesus *unto good works,* which God hath before ordained that we should walk in them."

First comes the unmerited grace of God – faith, as James calls it – followed by the works of grace and faith. If these do not follow, that is definite proof that grace is lacking. In Scripture, therefore, we have two kinds of mercy and grace: first, the unmerited mercy of God, which the Lord Jesus gives us in our helplessness when we go to Him by faith; and after that the merited mercy of God through our works of mercy to others. The thesis here is that a man who has experienced the mercy of God cannot help but show mercy to others. And the more mercy he shows the more mercy he receives from God. The order, then, is that helplessness attracts mercy; and mercifulness, once mercy has been experienced, attracts more mercy.

The best commentary on this Beatitude is that masterly verse in James 2:13 that says, "For he shall have judgment without mercy, that hath shewed no mercy; and mercy rejoiceth against judgment." What does that mean? We shall see in our next study.

GOD'S MERCY, UNDESERVED
AND DESERVED

No man in his sinful state deserves the mercy of God. In fact, the very connotation of the word "mercy" rules out any idea of merit. What we receive through merit is not mercy; it is pay for work accomplished.

God in His great and immeasurable love toward us never confines Himself to giving us only what we deserve, but far more than that. Whenever God acts, it is always in man's favor. Even our reward for obedience and service is so much greater than what we deserve that it passes the limits of wages and becomes mercy. Thus, the judgment of works could very well be said to be a judgment of mercy, both in this life and the life to come. No one who understands the heart of God would want Him to be merely a paymaster. We want Him to act like a father to us. And a father never pays his child; he showers upon him the largess of his heart, all that is his. Some may consider this to be merely the execution of fatherly duty toward the son, but it is actually the overflowing of fatherly love, which is always full of mercy. The mercy of God overshadows all His other characteristics and attributes. He seems to have found a way to interweave constant threads of mercy through all His other attributes, including His justice. God loves the sinner, yet He cannot trespass against His own law, which states that "the wages of sin is death." Therefore someone must die for the sin of man. God's justice demands it. At the same time, His mercy finds a way to satisfy His justice through the sacrifice of His Son for man, so that mercy may be shown to man. Thus, even in the justice of God and its expression, there is mercy.

On the other hand, God would be unjust if He allowed His mercy to cancel out His sense of justice. And He would be utterly unjust if He disregarded the sacrifices of His consecrated and dedicated children by rewarding the worldly and selfish Christians just as much. Not every Christian is on the same level. When we appropriate the initial mercy and grace of God for salvation, we are all on an equal footing before Him, and are afforded the same privileges and responsibilities. according to our individual capacities. The mercy of God unto salvation is the same for everyone living upon the face of this earth. But from that moment on, the race begins – the race of the Christian life, in which we have the opportunity to fulfill the various conditions of the blessed life in Christ. Heaven depends upon our appropriation of the initial grace of God, but the enjoyment of heaven is proportionate to our enjoyment of Christ here on earth. The Beatitude, "Blessed the merciful: for they shall receive mercy," and every other passage of Scripture that deals with the expression of mercy and the giving of rewards to man, refer not to the unbeliever but to the believer. It is of the believers that the Apostle Paul writes, "Now he that planteth and he that watereth are one: and every man shall receive his own reward according to his own labour" (I Cor. 3:8).

God's mercy for the believer, both in this life and the life to come, is sometimes entirely undeserved. How we thank God for every undeserved mercy of His! What would we do without them? Every breath we take is through the undeserved mercy of God. But when God has given us all that He chooses to as undeserved mercies, He then proceeds to give us the just reward of our labor for Him, for His sake. Nevertheless, this reward is also full of mercy; it is not the reward of an austere paymaster but of a Heavenly Father. It is of this that the fifth Beatitude speaks. "Blessed the merciful: for they shall receive mercy."

Exactly the same message is contained in James 2:13. In James 2:12 we have an admonition to bathe our lives and action in love: "So speak ye, and so do, as they that shall be judged by the law of liberty." This is the law of God's liberality, God's law of mercy. But it is mercy that does not cancel justice but is based on justice. Observe what James says in the next verse: "For he shall have judgment without mercy, that hath shewed no mercy; and mercy rejoiceth against judgment." This means that to the believer who has not shown mercy to others while on earth, God will not show mercy in the day of judgment. And that will be the time when he will need it most desperately. Woe unto him if God should deal with him according to His justice without mercy! The amount of mercy then shown to us as Christians in heaven will be proportionate to the amount of mercy we have shown down here on earth.

This is exactly what the fifth Beatitude means. While God showers upon us His undeserved mercies, He cannot disregard those who deserve His special mercies for the mercy they have shown while on earth. God's distribution of deserved mercies to His children is written deep in the very fiber of His character. His undeserved mercy springs from the exigencies of His unyielding justice, and His deserved mercy is to fulfill justice toward the various degrees of fidelity on the part of His children. Otherwise, why should we sacrifice, toil, and labor, if those who do not are going to receive the same reward? (For a full exegesis of James 2:13, see the author's book, *The Work of Faith*, Eerdmans, 1960, pp. 190-3.)

When we speak of deserved mercy, we do not mean that the sacrificing and merciful Christian does what he does for the sake of the reward, from selfish motives. The reward actually reveals the character of the Rewarder, rather than the recipient. The father who tells his child that he will reward him for certain things, first of all manifests what kind of father he is and secondarily what he thinks of the child. There may be other children living and acting far more worthily, and yet they receive no rewards from their parents. As we are merciful to others, as this Beatitude commands us to be, we should not be motivated by the reward but by our love and devotion to the Lord Jesus. This Beatitude, as every other one, is linked with that ever-important phrase, "for my sake," of Matthew 5:11.

Let us come back to the illustration of the relationship between father and child. The child who realizes the proper duties of his relationship to the father acts in obedience, in a manner worthy of his father's name, simply because he is his father. What he does at home is neither in the expectation of wages nor of a reward. And the same is true of the Christian when he is declared to be in the state of blessedness. He belongs to the family of God. God is his Father. He has to walk worthily of Him, expecting neither wages nor rewards. It would be as far below the dignity of a father to pay his son mere wages as it would be if everything he gave him was a reward, with no recognition of the worth of his work.

The same principle provides the solution to other difficulties in Scripture, such as that oft-repeated sentence in the Lord's Prayer, "And forgive us our debts, as we forgive our debtors" (Matt. 6:12). What does that mean? Exactly what it says, that God's mercy toward us as Christian believers will be proportionate to the degree of our mercifulness. This has nothing to do with the forgiveness of our sinful state and our receiving the new birth. This has to do with our life after we become children of God. For if it were not so, then we would not have addressed God as a Father. "But as many as received him, to them gave he power to become the sons of God, even to them that believe on his name" (John 1:12). God's forgiveness for us in our Christian lives here and now, and later in the world to come, will not entirely depend upon our spirit of forgiveness; but the degree of our forgiving others will certainly influence the Lord to exercise a greater or lesser measure of mercy toward our failures. Leniency by us toward our fellow believers will be met with leniency by God, without the least sacrifice of justice, but rather in the proper execution of justice.

God does not choose to divorce His actions from their relationship to ours. He can and does act independently, as He did on Calvary's cross, where His Son died for us. But that action of redemption does you and me no good unless we relate it to ourselves, unless we appropriate it by faith. He acts independently, but His actions affect us only as we appropriate them. His general mercy and grace become our particular mercy. The same relationship between God's actions and ours, His dispositions and ours, continues to hold good after we appropriate His grace for our salvation. Right after giving us the model prayer, He says, "For if ye forgive men their trespasses, your heavenly Father will also forgive you: but if ye forgive not men their trespasses, neither will your Father forgive your trespasses" (Matt. 6:14, 15). Now remember that the Lord speaks to us as Christians; otherwise He would not have called God our Father. How absolute is this? Does God's forgiveness and mercy depend on our forgiveness and mercy for others? Is this what the fifth Beatitude, "Blessed the merciful: for they shall receive mercy," really means? We shall consider this further in our next study.

MERCIFULNESS THE GAUGE
OF CHRISTLIKENESS

Take a good look at the fifth Beatitude, "Blessed the merciful: for they shall receive mercy." Did the Lord mean to say to us, "You show mercy to others, and I'll show mercy to you; don't show mercy to others, and I'll not show any mercy to you"? No, it is not as simple as that. This mercifulness is related to the law of forgiveness, which requires careful study.

When Peter asked the Lord how many times he was obligated to forgive his brother, the Lord told him there was no limit. That is the meaning of "seventy times seven." Then the Lord gave the parable of the unmerciful servant. His master forgave him his debt of ten thousand talents, but he would not forgive a debtor of his who owed him only a hundred pence. The Lord therefore said to him, "All right, if that is the principle you apply to others, I will apply the same principle to you. You don't forgive; I don't forgive either. You don't show mercy; I don't either. I took the initiative to forgive you, but you did not exercise the forgiveness I gave you. Your life of enjoyment of forgiveness depends upon your exercise of forgiveness." That is why we have the eternal words of Christ, "So likewise shall my heavenly Father do also unto you, if ye from your hearts forgive not every one his brother their trespasses" (Matt. 18:35).

Note very carefully that the offer of the Lord's forgiveness is not dependent upon the exercise of forgiveness by man. The exercise of forgiveness entails the possession of forgiveness. You receive much, you can afford a little. If you cannot afford a little, that means you have not really appropriated that which has been given to you. If you do not possess for the purpose of giving, then you don't possess at all. This is a fundamental law of God written in the very nature of things, of all His creation. If a rich man, who possesses a great deal, keeps it all and does not use it for its intended purpose, it becomes a burden to him. That which is not used dies. Hold your arm still for a few months and you won't be able to use it at all.

This is the law set forth in the fifth Beatitude. "Blessed the merciful: for they shall receive mercy." Actually, as we have said in previous studies, there is no verb in the first part of the Beatitude. The Greek text says, "Blessed the merciful." A far better translation of this, taking into account the exegesis of the statement, is, "Oh, the blessedness of the merciful ones!" God looks upon His children who exercise mercy toward others. The first thing He says about them is that they are blessed. The statement that they are blessed explains why they are merciful. If it were not for their blessedness in and because of Christ, they would not be merciful. That is the first and fundamental teaching of this Beatitude. The mercifulness of man is a direct result of his blessedness, of the person and work of Christ for and in man. To be blessed means to have God in our hearts, and when He is there we become God-sufficient. To be God-sufficient is to have a proper evaluation of our circumstances. God becomes man's acquisition for the sake of the Lord Jesus Christ, because of what He is and what He has done for man. Therefore we conclude that man's mercifulness is the direct result of man's blessedness in Christ. To be blessed is to have experienced the mercy of God through Christ, and you cannot possibly experience it without showing the same kind of mercy to others.

Mercifulness, therefore, is due to the work of Christ in the first place. It is not a natural inclination of man. And is it not true that mercifulness is essentially a Christian grace? In proportion as men are destitute of evangelical righteousness before God, they are strangers to tender compassion and mercy toward mankind. The Scribes and the Pharisees had a righteous ness that was their own, and it was only fit to be their own; they had, therefore, a hardheartedness, a cruelty, and an indifference to the wrongs and the sufferings of others, which were notoriously and publicly their own also. None are so tender in their compassion to their brethren as those who have felt in their own hearts most richly and fully the compassion of God toward them. As a church ceases to be evangelical in its creed and spiritual in its convictions, it comes to be bigoted, exclusive, and cruel. Hence, wherever the righteousness that is by faith is lost in a professing Christian church, there mercy to the souls, and compassion to the bodies of men, seem to be altogether quenched and extinguished. In the purest church there is most of missionary action, because there is most of tender compassion in the heart; in the corrupt and apostate church, there is selfishness and exclusiveness, because they have lost the light, and the softening influence of that salvation through faith in the atonement of the Lamb, which lies at the very foundation and root of all Christian character. (See John Cumming, *Benedictions or The Blessed Life*, John P. Jewett Co., Boston, 1854, pp. 137-8.)

Nobody can travel far without being impressed by the gulf that yawns, at this point, between the sentiments that prevail in a predominantly Christian country on the one hand and in heathen lands on the other. You

369

may, of course, see cruelty under the shadow of a church spire, and kindness amid pagan temples. But the general trend of things is in the opposite direction. In lands that have not as yet capitulated to the authority of the Cross, there is very little respect for the feelings of animals and humans. In a crowded Eastern bazaar, it is not uncommon to see a native sitting beside the road tearing a live fowl limb from limb, and evidently enjoying the hideous struggles of his writhing victim; yet the great crowd surges by unmoved, seeing nothing extraordinary and nothing deplorable in his horrible amusement.

The world would have been a pitiless place if Jesus had never come into it. It is, of course, sublimely true that millions of men and women who make no profession of Christianity perform deeds of mercy almost daily. It does not affect the question. The point is that, had it not been for the influence of Christianity upon their lives, upon their homes, and upon their ancestors before them, such men and women would never have seen any need to be kind, pitiful, or charitable; they would never have formed those merciful ideals, would never have felt within their breasts those tender instincts. They are acting quite unconsciously under the divine impulse of Christianity, and following blindly and unwittingly in the footsteps of the Nazarene.

The idea of showing kindness and pity to a stranger or a foe never entered the old world until Christianity emphasized the obligation; and it has only been found in the track of Christian apostles and teachers ever since. We can never forget that the neglect, exposure, and murder of innocent babes was a common practice throughout the whole world – even amidst the philosophy of Rome and the culture of Greece – at the time when Christ appeared to show men a more excellent way.

370

There has never been discovered a solitary trace of such an institution as a hospital in the whole wide world prior to the dawn of the Christian era. Even the *Encyclopedia Brittanica* conceded that only the germ of the hospital system may be seen in pre-Christian times. And not one has ever been established since, except under the direct or indirect influence of Christian teaching. Christlessness in any society means mercilessness. Rome in the full pomp of her glory, and in the unshaded light of her culture, had for her chief amusement and delight the combats between man and man, and between men and wild beasts, in the Colosseum. And rich and poor — with even the vestal virgins among them — looked on approvingly, applauding tumultuously. Heathendom is pitifully destitute of that mercifulness which is so universally and beautifully evidenced by the hospitals, orphanages, schools, asylums, homes for the aged, and similar institutions with which we are so familiar in the Christian world.

This is predominantly true of the individual. Christian mercifulness is derived from Christ. Therefore the degree of a man's mercifulness is the degree of the measure of mercy that he has received from Christ. The more merciful a Christian is the more blessed he is. The converse is also true. The more blessed he is the more merciful he is. A Christian woman who was engaged in work for the poor and degraded met a friend who was well acquainted with those she sought to reach. "It does seem wonderful to me that you can do such work," her friend said. "You sit beside these people, and talk with them in a way that I do not think you would if you knew about them, just what they are, and from what places they come." Her answer was, "Well, I suppose they are dreadful people. But, if the Lord Jesus were now on earth, are they not the very people

He would strive to teach? Would He feel Himself too good to go among them? And am I better than my Master?" A poor illiterate person, who stood listening to this conversation, said with great earnestness and simplicity, "Why, I always thought that was what Christians were for."

As the world looks upon our Christian practice and sees our mercifulness, they cannot but exclaim, "They must be Christians." And as they see our blessedness in the exercise of mercy, they cannot but be attracted to the Saviour whose mercy we manifest. Isn't that what Christians are for? The answer that the Lord gives is, Yes, "Blessed the merciful: for they shall receive mercy."

Love and mercy are Siamese twins. One cannot exist without the other. John says, "Beloved, let us love one another: for love is of God; and every one that loveth is born of God, and knoweth God. He that loveth not knoweth not God; for God is love . . . . Beloved, if God so loved us, we ought also to love one another. No man hath seen God at any time. If we love one another, God dwelleth in us, and his love is perfected in us . . . . If a man say, I love God, and hateth his brother, he is a liar: for he that loveth not his brother whom he hath seen, how can he love God whom he hath not seen? And this commandment have we from him, That he who loveth God love his brother also." (I John 4:7. 8, 11, 12, 20, 21.)

"Hereby perceive we the love of God, because he laid down his life for us: and we ought to lay down our lives for the brethren. But whoso hath this world's good, and seeth his brother have need, and shutteth up his bowels of compassion from him, how dwelleth the love of God in him?" (I John 3:16, 17.)

This is what Christ meant when He said, "Blessed the merciful: for they shall receive mercy."

WHAT MERCY IS NOT

We are talking about being merciful, but we must take care that we fully understand the meaning and implications of the word. Like many other important words, it has often been misunderstood and therefore misapplied. As we examine the word "mercy," *eleos,* in the Greek text, let us first consider it negatively, that is, what it is not.

It is not the opposite of justice, as it is often thought to be. The Lord would not tell us in the fourth Beatitude that we are blessed if we hunger and thirst after righteousness (or a just and holy life) and then in the next breath repudiate the principle of justice by telling us that we should be merciful. Being merciful, as it concerns us and as far as God is concerned, does not mean not being righteous and just. The law from Sinai proclaims truth without mercy, and the unrenewed heart desires mercy without truth. The one would result in the perdition of men; the other in the dishonor of God. Truth alone would honor God's law but destroy transgressors; mercy alone would shield the transgressors but trample on the law. If there were only truth, earth would no longer be a place of hope; if there were only mercy, heaven would no longer be a place of holiness. On the one side is the just Judge, on the other the guilty criminals. If He gives them their due, there will be no mercy; if they get from Him their desire, there will be no truth. You may get one at the expense of casting out the guilty multitude; you may get the other at the expense of putting to shame the Holy One; but apart from the Gospel of Christ, both cannot be. They meet in the Mediator. In Christ the fire meets the water without drying it up;the water meets the fire without quenching it. Truth has its way now, and all the desert of sin falls on Him who bears it; mercy has its way now, and all the love of God is poured out on those who are one with His beloved Son. Iniquity is punished in the substitute sacrificed, and so purged from the conscience of the redeemed. "There is therefore now no condemnation to them which are in Christ Jesus." The blood of Jesus Christ cleanseth from all sin. This is the Gospel. There is no salvation in any other. (See William Arnot, *Illustrations of the Book of Proverbs*, Nelson and Sons, London, 1858, pp. 68-73.)

Mercy is not something that merely softens the hard lines in the judge's face, and tinges with leniency the sentence he pronounces. In order to understand mercy, we must first look to the heavens, to God Himself, who truly exercises it, before we look around us to the world that needs it. We must take this problem of justice and mercy to Him. God is just. He is never anything less than just. As He looks upon His world, there are no weak or blind moments in that omniscient contemplation. And every day of our lives we face this justice of His. We suffer for our sins. The laws that we break never forget that we have broken them, and sooner or later they exact the penalty. This is justice, but this is also mercy. It is for our highest good that we should suffer when we do wrong. Thus we learn not to do wrong. Thus we learn that sin is a terrible thing. If God played with His laws, He might give to individual lives momentary ease, but He could not give to His world eternal salvation.

So, then, mercy is a strong, firm word. There is no weakness in it, no blindness. The truly merciful man does not think to exercise mercy at the expense of justice. He knows that such a thing is impossible. To

374

be less than just, as far as we are able to perceive justice, is in the end to be less than merciful. Mercy without justice becomes morally dangerous, as does free forgiveness, which many wrongly see in the words of Christ: "If ye forgive not men their trespasses, neither will your Father forgive your trespasses" (Matt. 6:15). It seems to imply an insufficient recognition of the evil of wrongdoing. If people could count on free forgiveness or mercy every time they transgress, they would become morally lax, and in order to sustain the majesty of the moral law and the moral health of society it is necessary that penalties should follow wrongdoing. In fact, such mercifulness and free forgiveness would lead to universal moral anarchy.

We must pass into that great mystery of love in the heart of which justice and mercy dwell together, living one life and doing one work. How do we come there? We find that God never refuses us forgiveness, and never grants us escape from punishment – the punishment we call consequences. A sinner comes to the mercy of God, with his broken body and wasted years, and that mercy fails him not, and he goes out to live a forgiven and victorious life; but it is the life of a man who has been a sinner. There are consequences of his sin that he cannot remedy and that God does not remedy either. As a result of sin, for instance, a man may have lost his sight. When God saves him from the guilt and punishment of sin, He does not necessarily eradicate all the consequences of his sin.

And here we come to the necessity of bringing out the distinction that exists between two important New Testament words, "grace" *(charis)* and "mercy" *(eleos).* Grace is the free gift of God, which is never earned or merited by man. It has reference to the sins of men and is that glorious attribute of God which these sins call out and display. Mercy, however, has a special and immediate regard to the misery which is the consequence of these sins. (R. C. Trench, *Synonyms of the New Testament*, p. 169.) The nails are removed from the board by grace, but the scars are there. Mercy is for the scars of sins forgiven. Mercy is God's comfort for the consequences of past sin. The consequences of forgiven sin necessitate the ever present mercy of God in our lives. Mercy, therefore, springs from our proper view of sin and the calamitous consequences of it in our own lives and in the lives of others. We see that the world is full of the bitter and painful consequences of wrongdoing; but to each man in his own sin God reveals the law of mercy. It is written across our sky; it is the background of our human lives. There are hours when it is the only thought we can take heart to think upon. We have sinned, and our sin admits of no palliation or excuse. All we have left us is this: God is merciful and we need His mercy. Yes, and in those hours when life seems to be much as it should be, we dare not forget the unseen faultiness, the wrong that is folded in our very satisfactions, and that makes mercy the one word that fits our lives.

Mercy, then, or free and immediate forgiveness of wrongdoing, does not mean simply letting the sinner off, doing nothing about the matter, condoning his sin. That would lead to disaster. That would be cruel. It would lead many persons to become confirmed offenders, because it would lead them to suppose that there is nothing wrong in what they do. What is really needed for the sinner is that he should come to a sense of his own sin. That, for him, is the only way of hope. And a careless, merely goodnatured treatment of his sin leads him just the other way. Mercy or free forgiveness cannot mean "doing nothing about it."

It is only as we feel our own need of mercy that we

develop in our lives the truly merciful spirit. The mercy that we show toward a wrongdoer must be the outcome of a true view of sin. Consider the man who says soft words about his neighbor's sin because he does not want to say hard words about his own sin. That is not mercy. It is self-deception. We must not read this Beatitude, "Blessed are they who condone the faults of others, for their faults shall be condoned." The truly merciful spirit comes to us, not as we seek to minimize our sin, but as we learn to magnify God's love. The mercy that we show toward a wrongdoer must not be the result of a light view of his sins, but rather the result of a true view of our sin and of that great love of God that is able to forgive. The wrong my brother does me wrongs me. It is not mine to measure and judge his sin. That I must leave with the heaven above him. As far as my personal relation to him is concerned, I can only remember that I also have sinned and wronged the love of the Father-heart. Some day his sin and mine will come home to us, maybe.

But it is not for us, brothers and sisters in need and sin, to judge one another in the things wherein we have offended. We can only forgive fully and freely as we hope to be forgiven. The merciful shall obtain mercy, not simply because they show mercy to others, but because in showing it they have proved that they have some true sense of the need for mercy in every sinful life, most of all in their own life, and have testified thus to their faith in that Infinite Love that deals not with us after our sins, neither rewards us according to our iniquities. (See Percy C. Ainsworth, *The Blessed Life*, Charles H. Kelly, London, 1915, pp. 117-123.)

DOES MERCY PRECLUDE PUNISHMENT?

In our previous study we saw what mercy is not. It is not apathy toward evil in the lives of others. Permitting evil to continue unpunished and unchallenged is not mercy; it is complicity in crime and is extremely dangerous, both to the perpetrators of evil and to the victims of it.

On the other hand, mere punishment is usually quite useless as far as changing the sinner is concerned. Locking up a thief in jail to separate him from the environment that would permit him to steal is not being merciful to him. Mercifulness involves the responsibility of doing something for the sinner while limiting the harmfulness of his sin. Mercifulness is concerned with people and their need of the grace of God and not merely with the restriction of evil. Actually, evil can only be restricted by the conversion of evildoers into children of God, "blessed ones." There must be personal and humane interest behind the social restriction of evil. Otherwise the evildoer is angered and hardened that much more. The law has no power to convert the evildoer, for it cannot change people for the better. This feature of it makes it merely restrictive, not remedial. In our demonstration of mercy we must always bear in mind the sinner as well as the evil he causes to others. Punishment divorced from a genuine interest in the person punished makes bad people worse.

The Lord Jesus gave us a perfect example of mercifulness. How did He treat those who sinned? How did He administer His forgiveness? He was known as the Friend of publicans and sinners. He hated their sin while continuing to love them. Their sin was repulsive to His holiness and purity, but their needy souls made Him seek them out. The Pharisees wanted Him to separate Himself from sinners, but He would not. When He was with them, He rarely needed to condemn them. His presence was sufficient to make them condemn themselves. They discovered a wonderful thing about Him, totally unlike the attitude of their human religious leaders, which was that, though He knew all the vileness of their sin, He did not withdraw from them. His soul and theirs were far apart as far as spiritual fellowship was concerned, but He insisted on going where sin abounded because only in that way could grace and mercy abound even more. He remained their friend – perhaps even more their friend than ever, because they needed Him more.

What the Lord saw in an individual was not merely a bad person who ought to be punished and made to smart, but a son or daughter of God who had wandered from the path of life and needed to be brought back. This attitude is divine by its very nature. What is the natural, physical and sinful instinct of man? He is apt to take an almost fierce pleasure in seeing bad people suffer. When we read a novel, we long for the chapter where the villain shall be exposed and get what he deserves. We want to hear that he was flung down a precipice, or tormented by cannibals, or horsewhipped till he could not stand. These are the feelings of the natural man and not of the blessed man who has God in him. Those who feel this way care not at all that the villain should cease to be a villain; they simply want to see him suffer. They are a little like spectators at a gladiatorial game.

That was not the way that the Lord Jesus acted or felt. He did not wash His hands of those who hated Him and sought to harm Him. If we want to be characterized by His mercy and forgiveness, we have no right, and we should not even have the desire, to wash our hands of evildoers. Punishment is necessary to restrict the spread of evil. Otherwise our mercy toward one, if mercy means not checking and punishing the evildoer, will deprive many others — those whom the evildoer might hurt — of mercy. But we have no right to wash our hands and rest in peace once we have shut him within prison walls. That's what the law does, but not the mercy of God.

God punishes the evil but seeks to redeem the evildoer and does not rest until He has used every possible means to that end. Mercy acknowledges and discerns what people are but sees with the eye of hope and faith what they could become by the grace of God. That was how the Lord Jesus once looked upon us. Mercy wears a special kind of divine spectacles. It sees every sinner as a would-be saint and treats him that way.

If mercy did away with punishment, it would defeat its own purpose, because in most instances it would embolden the sinner to continue in his evil ways. God never did away with punishment for evil. His laws are inviolable. The wages of sin is death; it always has been and always will be. But Christ volunteered to die instead of us. And only by accepting what He did for us do we go free of the punishment for sin. But punishment must fall on someone. And that someone must be you, the evildoer, unless you accept the work that the Lord Jesus did for you.

The Greek word for merciful is *ele-eemoon*. In Hebrew, the word for mercy is *chesedh*, which is difficult to translate into English. It does not merely mean sympathy as we usually think of it, that is, feeling sorry for someone in trouble, but empathy, the ability to get right inside another person's skin, so that we see things with his eyes, think things with his mind, and feel things with his feelings. This, then, is more than an emotional outburst of pity. It demands a quite deliberate effort of the mind, of the will. It involves our identification with the other person until we see things as he sees them and feel things as he feels them. (See William Barclay, *Gospel of Matthew*, Vol. 1, The St. Andrew Press, Edinburgh, p. 98.)

Isn't this what the Lord Jesus did? He identified Himself with us sinners. He was not a sinner Himself, but He took upon Himself our own sin and He tasted the consequence of sin, death, in His own body. In being merciful to us, the Lord Jesus actually crept under our skin of flesh and blood and became a man.

Try being merciful in this manner when you meet a person without Christ. You can well see how miserable he is, but do not stop at that. Try imaginatively to live his life, to think his thoughts. We are often tempted to dismiss the misery we hear about in the world as sob stories. Stop a minute. Get under the skin of that widow who wrote the author from Greece asking him to find a home, a family that would adopt her only child, a four-year-old boy, because she could no longer bear to hear him cry constantly, "I am hungry." When the Lord tells us to be merciful in such a case, He tells us to get under the skin of that widow and feel what she feels as those heartbreaking tears roll down her child's cheeks because of hunger. Put yourself in her place. Would you want to part with your child? What makes you think that she loves her child any less than you do yours?

Life may be dark for you, in spite of all your possessions, because you have never tried to brighten the path of another by showing mercy.

381

A wealthy woman who happened to be out in the snow one night was so very cold that she cried out, "Oh, those poor people that have so little money; how little heat they have, and how pinched they must be! I will send some coal to twenty families, at least." But when she reached her own parlor, there was a fine fire burning, and she sat there with her feet on a stool, and enjoyed a cup of tea. She then began to say to herself, "Well, it is not very cold after all. I don't think I shall send that coal, for the time being, anyway." Mercy means deeply felt sympathy, and that means suffering with the sufferer, living his life under his skin.

Queen Victoria was a close friend of Principal and Mrs. Tullock, of St. Andrews. Prince Albert died and Victoria was left alone. Just at the same time, Principal Tullock died and Mrs. Tullock was left alone. Quite unexpectedly, Queen Victoria came to call on Mrs. Tullock when she was resting on a couch in her room. When the Queen was announced, Mrs Tullock struggled to rise quickly from the couch and to curtsey. The Queen stepped forward. "My dear," she said, "don't rise. I am not coming to you today as a queen to a subject, but as one woman who has lost her husband to another." She put herself in her friend's place. That is what God did for us. That is what we should do for others. Mercy is the voluntary experience of the sufferings of others by getting under their skin and then seeking to do for them what we should like to have done for us if we were in similar plight.

WHICH COUNTS MORE,
THE MOTIVE OR THE DEED?

In the booklet preceding this (*Mercy: God's and Ours*), we saw that mercy is sorrow at the suffering of a fellow creature. But it is more than sorrow. It is an earnest desire to relieve suffering wherever possible. It does not ask such questions as, "Is the sufferer of my nation, sect, party, or church? Does he speak my shibboleth, wear my robes, advocate my cause?" In its purest form, it sees nothing but the suffering; in its noblest exercise, it recognizes nothing in the expressions of its liberality but a sufferer, wherever and whoever that sufferer may be.

The outstanding illustration of this that we find in Scripture is our Lord's parable of the Good Samaritan. Samaritans and Jews were traditional enemies, yet this Samaritan stopped to help a wounded Jew. He did this, not out of kinship or abundance, but out of a sense that he ought to help where need existed, regardless of the person involved or the sufferer's own ability. Thus mercy is a duty that is required of us all, unto all. No other consideration than the need should serve to call forth our mercy.

This mercy, or compassion with legs under it, not only overflows the puny distinctions of party, nation, or tribe, but it even overflows the broad, lofty, and awful wall of sin itself. It does not say of the sufferer, does the man deserve relief? It simply asks, does he suffer? In showing mercy, the merciful man looks less at the sins of the sufferer than at the depth of his want and the agony of his heart. He leaves the suffering man's sins with God, for Him to pardon or punish; he takes the suffering man's sorrows for himself to pity, to compassionate, and to relieve.

When an applicant comes to us for pecuniary relief, we should not ask, as we are so apt to do, "What are your antecedents?" but, "What is your need?" Do not, however, feel that this means you must allow yourself to be imposed upon. If you detect evidences of hypocrisy, sham, and pretense, uncloak it, rebuke it, and dismiss it; but if you discern real misery, even though it be the consequence of real crimes, leave the crimes with God and with the man's own conscience, and hasten to bind up his wounds, supply his wants, and give relief as you are able. We are not only to show mercy in spite of a man being a stranger, a foreigner, but in spite of his being a sinner.

How hard this strikes at the insularity and selfishness of some Christian denominations that say, "Denominational money for denominational missions only." As if the evil of our divisions were not enough, we compound it by restricting the people to whom we shall show God's mercy. The same holds true of those who say, "America for the Americans, Britain for the British," etc. Let us beware lest we be found faithful to a denomination, to a nation, to a clan, and unfaithful to Christ. In the last analysis, it is our fidelity to Him that will count. The Lord did not say, "Blessed are the merciful who show mercy to their own creed and nationality, for they shall experience the same from them."

Some may object that the erring are not worthy of our sympathy and help. One man wrote me after hearing my appeal for the ten starving children of a family in Greece, where we minister, "They should practice birth control, and not have so many children."

He objected to showing mercy to them, clothing them, feeding them, loving them — as if these children were in any way responsible for their plight. Let me ask you a frank question, friend. If God were to show mercy only to the innocent, where would you be? If the Lord Jesus, born of a Jewish virgin, were to have mercy only on His own people, the Jews, where would you be? Did you in any way deserve the mercy of God when He showered it on you? Do you now deserve any of the mercies of God? With what measure we mete to others it shall be meted to us. Make no mistake about that.

We are to go a step further and pity the sufferer as a sinner; to show mercy to him simply because he is a sinner. We are not only to show mercy to him by relieving his wants in spite of his being a sinner, but to show mercy to him just because he is a sinner. Since all have sinned and come short of the glory of God, our mercy ought to be all-inclusive. It should extend not only to the poor but to the rich, not only to the depressed but to the jovial — to everyone. For mercy is not only for the person who is in need of material blessings, but above all for the one who is lost and on his way to hell. He has lost the way to heaven. Being merciful to him means pointing out the way to him.

And who on earth is most in need of pity? Surely the sinner. We need to abhor the sins and errors of the one who has gone astray, but at the same time we need to feel compassion over the awful position into which he has fallen. It is God's prerogative to ascend the judgment throne and pronounce retribution; it is my privilege, and my duty, too, to bow the knee at the throne of grace and to pray for mercy and forgiveness for the fallen one. God passes judgment on the character of the man; I, as a fellow sinner, pity the misfortune of the man; and, because he is suffering, I must try to relieve him; he has gone astray, I will try to put him right; he is a sinner, I will seek to lead him to the Lamb of God who taketh away the sin of the world.

When Jesus shed tears over Jerusalem, He wept over its great sins and its approaching calamity. The slaughter of the innocent babes by Herod did not occasion so much sorrow to Jesus as the approaching destruction of Jerusalem. The death of those innocents simply meant their translation to glory; but the ruin of Jerusalem was awful beyond description, because at the Day of Judgment it would be more tolerable for Sodom and Gomorrah than for such a capital surrounded by such privileges.

It is remarkable that mercy, which is so frequently enjoined in the Gospels, and especially in the fifth Beatitude, on the followers of Christ, is one of those graces that ancient heathen philosophy repudiated as indicating weakness of character. The Stoic, as personified in Zeno, allowed you to relieve the suffering, but forbade you to feel the least compassion for the sufferer. Human nature, in the eyes of the Stoic, reached its culminating grandeur in proportion as it became petrified into ice or consolidated into stone. You might relieve the needy, if you met with them; but to shed a tear, or to be penetrated by a deep and tender compassion, was denounced as unworthy of a great man and a good philosopher.

Ancient philosophy placed importance on the act, while the Gospel places importance on the motives and dispositions of the heart. "Blessed the merciful ones," the Master said. He referred to a special class, since the adjective is preceded by the definite article, as we have seen all along in these Beatitudes. Only the

Christian could really feel true mercy toward all humanity. This adjectival substantive does not refer to every kind of mercy, to mere acts of helpfulness, but to hearts disposed to help and to weep over the sufferings of others as Christ did. These are so merciful, they possess such a Godlike mercy toward others, because of what Christ is and what He has done for them. It is all for His sake (Matt. 5:11). Here we have the exhibition, not of mere humanism, but of divinity. It is not the mercy of Zeno and the Stoics that Christ is speaking about, but the very same mercy that He bestowed on those who received Him as their Saviour and Lord.

When we relieve a poor, destitute, starving beggar that appeals to us for aid, the money, the food, the clothes that we give him, most precious in their place, are not so comforting to his heart as the spirit and the manner in which we give them. If we help a destitute orphan child, but at the same time coldly say that he should never have been born, we render what we give null and void in God's sight. Some feel, when a needy person applies for relief, that when they have given a trifle they have done all that is really required. The way in which we give is often more effective than the sum that we give.

A man who once stopped to bestow alms on a beggar found to his dismay that he had nothing in his pockets. He began stammering out his apologies. "I am sorry, Brother," he said, "but I have nothing, Brother." That word, "brother," meant more to the beggar than any money he could have given. "Never mind, Brother," was the beggar's reply; "that, too, was a gift, Brother."

The Apostle Paul, in Romans 12:8, amplifies this Beatitude of Christ by saying that we should show mercy with cheerfulness. In fact, the Greek word translated "cheerfulness" is *hilarotees,* which in English is transliterated "hilarity." Hilarity is a sort of exuberant joy, boisterous mirth, jollity. This indicates how important the manner and motive of mercifulness are. There is a right and wrong way of doing even good things, such as showing mercy. Second only to the character of the deed is the way in which we do it. Giving, when not inspired by the single motive of love and a desire to help, ceases to be giving at all. The Christian is to show mercy with hilarity, as if he were finding tremendous joy in it.

In other words, it must be fun to be merciful. And frankly, there isn't any greater pleasure. Try it. If mercifulness is fun to us, then we shall make the recipient feel that he is not only receiving a blessing, but by the act of receiving he is also conferring one upon the giver. A good thing like mercifulness must also be beautiful and radiant. The way in which we do a good thing is almost as important as the thing itself.

(See J. D. Jones, *The Inevitable Christ,* Hodder and Stoughton, pp. 299-316; and Percy C. Ainsworth, *The Blessed Life,* Charles H. Kelly, pp. 117-127.)

WILL ALL GOOD WORKS BE REWARDED ?

We find two classes of merciful people in this world: those who are moved by humanitarian instincts, who do good because they are human beings, and those who are merciful because of what Christ is to them (a quite restricted group.) Nearly everyone, even the worst criminal, is characterized by at least some acts of mercifulness in his life. A thief who embezzles large sums of money will yet have compassion on a poor widow and her orphaned children. All of us know people like that. Not all that is in man is absolutely evil. In human evil we find some traces of good, and in all human good there is some taint of evil. Our moral values and actions are relative.

But this is not the kind of person our Lord is speaking about in the fifth Beatitude. No matter how many or how great the acts of mercifulness this person may perform, as long as the basic make-up of his heart and life is sinful, he will never experience the mercy of God. Forgiveness is not for him until he repents and experiences the grace of God. Then he becomes a new creature, who does not simply perform occasional acts of mercy, but is merciful even as the One who saved him. His whole disposition and outlook on life are those of mercifulness. His acts of mercy are not merely humanitarian, but are divine acts wrought through him. This second class of people is counted merciful, not because of sporadic acts of mercy, but because of the presence of God within them. They allow God to act on their behalf. Their actions are not their own, even as their dispositions are not their own. They are divinely motivated. There is a tremendous difference between these two groups. The first man, the unsaved one, acts purely as a human being; the second man acts as a redeemed human being, made a partaker of the divine nature by God's grace. This latter is what the Lord calls the blessed person throughout the Beatitudes. And this latter group is the restricted one upon which the Lord pronounces the wonderful promise that "they shall obtain mercy."

The restricted nature of this group is manifested not only in the definite article *hoi* preceding the adjective *eleeemones*, "merciful," but also in the use of the demonstrative pronoun *autoi*, meaning "they." (See A. T. Robertson, *Grammar of the Greek New Testament*, p. 757.) In Greek, the third person plural of a verb (and, in fact, all the inflections) is indicated, not by a pronoun as in English, but by distinctive endings. For instance, in order to say "they shall obtain mercy" in Greek, we do not need the pronoun "they." The verb *eleeetheesontai* is sufficient by itself. The word "they" is indicated by the suffix of the verb. In the Greek text, however, in addition to the verb ending, this clause contains the Greek demonstrative pronoun *autoi*, meaning "they." This is placed there for emphasis and distinction. It is as if the Lord wanted to distinguish between the humanly merciful and the divinely merciful: those who perform acts of mercy because they are human, and those who are merciful because they are blessedly Christ's.

For the first, the expressions of mercy are exceptions to their human character; for the second, mercifulness is part and parcel of their divinely acquired nature. It is this latter group that shall obtain mercy. And this fully agrees with the general principle of rewards for the Christian. Verses like I Corinthians 3:8, "Every man shall receive his own reward according to his own

390

labour," do not really refer to every human being, but to every person within a certain group, a certain specified class, as in the Beatitudes. This special class is that of those who have been born again and have become blessed. No man can earn or buy the mercy of God with his good works. But God will reward the mercifulness and sacrifices of His own children because He delights in them. That's what Christ is talking about in the fifth Beatitude.

The verb that is used in the original Greek text is *ele-eetheesontai*, translated commonly, "they shall obtain mercy." This is in the passive voice. In fact, a better translation would be, "they shall be shown mercy." The receiving of mercy on their part does not imply accession to a demanded right, but rather the bestowing of an unexpected privilege amounting more or less to a surprise. The mercy that they shall experience will come to them as a bonus. While they were merciful, their hearts and minds were not upon the reward but upon their duty to be Christlike. The Christian never is what he is, or acts the way he does, simply because of the reward he hopes to receive from Christ, but because of what Christ means to him. It is all because of Christ. "For my sake," says the Lord; and His disciples surely should be what they are and do what they do simply and primarily for His sake. If we are merciful for the sake of experiencing mercy from God, we shall always consider His mercy far less than we deserve. The Christian who acts from a selfish motive is a complaining Christian. But the one who acts from love of Christ always considers whatever he receives from his Master as more than he deserves. The satisfaction of the reward does not actually depend on its size, but on our inner attitude toward it. Our evaluation and appreciation of self are the gauge of our evaluation and appreciation of God's relationship and mercy toward us.

We have a marvelous illustration of this Beatitude in the 25th chapter of Matthew, where our Lord speaks about the judgment of the nations. The Lord wants to show us here that what is done for our fellow human beings is actually done for Him, and implies that in making up His accounts He records none of our words but all of our works. He speaks of two classes of surprised people here. The first class is astounded when they hear the Master Judge say to them, "Come, ye blessed of my Father, inherit the kingdom prepared for you from the foundation of the world: for I was an hungred, and ye gave me meat: I was thirsty, and ye gave me drink: I was a stranger, and ye took me in: naked, and ye clothed me: I was sick, and ye visited me: I was in prison, and ye came unto me" (vv. 35, 36). These people never even saw Jesus Christ in person. But they had acted for His sake while on earth.

Here is His answer: "Verily I say unto you, Inasmuch as ye have done it unto one of the least of these my brethren, ye have done it unto me." Who is the rewarder here? The Lord Jesus Christ. Who actually received the mercy shown by these people who are rewarded? Not the Lord Himself, but men, women, children in need. These people, so merciful in their lives, were little conscious of it. It was no special effort for them to be merciful. It was a matter of course. Mercifulness became natural in their supernaturally blessed state. Their reward was a surprise to them. And the reward was from the eternal Judge, from the Lord Himself. We who have acted out of love for Him toward our fellow men shall indeed be surprised with the abundance of mercy we shall receive from Him at the Judgment Day. This is exactly what James says in chapter 2, verse 13: "For he shall have judgment without mercy, that hath shewed no mercy; and mercy rejoiceth against judgment."

And then the Lord gives us the opposite picture, that of those who did nothing for their fellow human beings in His name. How could they, since they did not know or recognize Him? Their eternal punishment is not the result of their lack of mercifulness toward others, but of their non-recognition of the Lord Jesus Christ. How could they see Christ in others and do for them what He would have done, if they did not know Him at all? What they did not do was the result of what they were not, and what they were not was the thing that led them to eternal condemnation. They were not acquainted with the Lord Jesus Christ. If they had been merciful, but not as unto the Lord Jesus Christ, it would not have counted. In order to receive Christ's reward, our mercifulness must be related to Him. In order to be the rewarder of mercifulness, He alone must be its inspirer. This is what the fifth Beatitude, "Blessed the merciful: for they shall obtain mercy," means.

This Beatitude, then, is not as all-inclusive as people think it is. It is quite restricted. But I hope it includes you; and the only way it can do that is if you are acquainted with the Lord Jesus Christ and therefore act as He would. You must first receive mercy from Him in your sinful state and become born again. Then you will show the same mercy to others. And in return you will receive more mercy, and this mercy will have the quality of reward rather than of regeneration and salvation.

REWARDS — NOW OR HEREAFTER ?

While God is the primary rewarder of the believer, extending him divine mercy for the mercy he has bestowed on others, there is a sense in which the merciful believer also receives mercy from his fellow men, believers and unbelievers alike. There is a disposition even in the minds of the unsanctified masses of mankind to respect, revere, and love the merciful, the compassionate man. No matter how cruel it may be, the world will never forget our Christian mercies.

A certain family had two sons. The older said he must make a name for his family and so turned his face toward Parliament and fame. The younger decided to give his life to the service of Christ and so turned his face toward China and duty. He was Hudson Taylor, the missionary, who died beloved and known on every continent. "But," someone wrote, "when I looked in the encyclopedia to see what the other son had done, I found these words, 'the brother of Hudson Taylor.'" It may be that some were inclined to ridicule him when he went to the mission field. But finally he was respected and admired. His mercifulness had not been in vain, even as far as the world was concerned.

But the merciful also receive recognition and reward from God Himself. And this takes place both in this world and, in its full measure, in the world to come. The merciful man may not be able to enjoy all the physical comforts of this life. He may not make as much money as his selfish comrade, but the rewards of mercifulness in this life are far superior to comforts and riches. The day of grace is not the day of judgment; yet even in this world enough retribution occurs to show that God reigns, while enough confusion exists to make us long for a judgment day when all wrongs will be rectified.

David declares in Psalm 41:1, 2, "Blessed is he that considereth the poor: the Lord will deliver him in time of trouble. The Lord will preserve him, and keep him alive; and he shall be blessed upon the earth: and thou wilt not deliver him unto the will of his enemies." The Lord will often raise up people entirely unknown to us to show us mercy, even as we showed it unto others. I can personally testify that I have found this true in my Christian experience. We can never outdo the Lord in our giving. Give generously and with joy in His name, and He will shower you with mercies. God is no man's debtor.

Two boys who were working their way through Leland Stanford University found themselves almost without funds. One of them conceived the idea of engaging the great Polish pianist, Paderewski, for a piano recital, and devoting the profits to their board and tuition. The pianist's manager asked for a guarantee of $2,000. The boys proceeded to stage the concert, but the proceeds totaled only $1,600. The boys sought the great artist and told him of their efforts. They gave him the entire $1,600 and a promissory note for $400, explaining that they would earn the balance and pay it off at the earliest possible moment.

"No, boys, that won't do," said Paderewski. Then, tearing up the note, he returned the money to them, saying, "Now take out of the $1,600 all of your expenses, and keep ten percent of the balance for each of you for your work, and let me have the rest."

The years rolled by. The war came, and Paderewski was striving with might and main to feed the starving thousands in his beloved Poland. There was only one man in the world who could help Paderewski. Thousands of tons of food began to come into Poland for distribution. After the starving people were fed, Paderewski journeyed to Paris to thank Herbert Hoover for the relief sent them.

"That's all right, Mr. Paderewski," was Mr. Hoover's reply. "Besides, you don't remember how you helped me once when I was a student at college, and I was in a hole." Remember the words of the Master: "With what measure ye mete, it shall be measured to you again" (Matt. 7:2).

A discouraged young doctor in one of our large cities was visited by his father, who came from a rural district.

"Well, son," he asked, "How are you getting along?"

"I'm not getting along at all," was the reply.

The old man's countenance fell, but he spoke courage and patience and hope. Later in the day he went with his son to the free dispensary. He sat in silence while twenty-five poor unfortunates received help. When the door had closed upon the last one, the old man burst out, "I thought you told me you were doing nothing. Why, if I had helped out twenty-five people in a month, I would thank God that my life counted for something."

"There isn't any money in it, though," objected the son.

"Money!" the old man shouted. "What is money compared with being useful to your fellow men?"

How true! Mercifulness carries within it its own reward and joy. The person who helps someone else helps himself first. That is why this Beatitude has been called the one with the double blessing. It blesses the giver and the receiver. And when we remember the words of the Master, that it is more blessed to give than to receive, we shall know that mercifulness has a built-in reward. When was the last time you did something for someone in need? I don't know whether you have ever given a morsel of bread to a hungry child, or placed a warm garment over his shivering body, or a pair of shoes on his bruised feet. Try it and see what happens, not necessarily to the person you have helped but to yourself.

I prayed: "O Lord, bless all the world,
    And help me do my part."
And straightway He commanded me
    To bind a broken heart.

I prayed, "Oh, bless each hungry child,
    May they be amply fed."
He said, "Go find a starving soul,
    And share with him your bread."

"Oh, stir the hearts of men," I prayed,
    "And make them good and true."
He answered, "There is but one way—
    They must be stirred through you."

Dear friend, unless you really mean
    Exactly what you say,
Until you mean to work with God,
    It's dangerous to pray.
                    — *Leola Archer*

Selfishness is as corrosive to the heart as poison; but mercy, charity, benevolence, spread a glow of beauty over the face, and create in the heart serenity, thanksgiving, and peace. If we could get rid of that selfishness which thinks pityingly of its own sufferings, however little, and nothing of a brother's, however great – which is ever jealous lest it fail to get what it deserves, and is even afraid lest we do not defer to it with all, and that not a little, which it thinks is its due – how calmly would our hearts beat, how truly would we illustrate what all history is teaching, that in proportion as Christianity spreads over the mass of mankind, does the desert begin to rejoice, and the wilderness to bloom even as the rose. But when we fall into that horrid state, which some think the very perfection of common sense, "The world cares nothing for me, and I care nothing for the world," we shall feel it sounds very grand, but we shall be very miserable. We know there is no happiness in any such feeling. There is no help but for us to love, if we would be happy. Hate men, and you will be more miserable than they; love men, and they will be blessed by your love, and its reflex operation will bless yourself also.

And then, in a more real and a fuller way, mercifulness will be rewarded in heaven. The Beatitudes end with a crowning commandment given to us in Matthew 5:12, "Rejoice, and be exceeding glad: for great is your reward in heaven." Death does not create character. It fixes it forever. If mercy be an evidence of grace, the character it indicates is perpetuated by death. The waters of death are not waters of ablution; they simply carry him who is placed in their current to the judgment seat and leave him just as they found him.

Does not this Beatitude indeed lead us to believe that there are special blessings in the world to come which are assigned to special characters distinguished by special graces? These blessings in the world to come are not the rewards according to deserts of graces we have developed here, but they are the assignment of spheres and fields for the exercise of these peculiar graces in their maturity, the seeds of which have been sown upon earth, and have been more or less developed in the growth of our character here below. There may be a sphere in the future rest where the meek shall reign; another sphere where the peacemakers shall be manifested as the sons of God; another where the merciful shall shine in that beautiful light. Heaven is not one vast monotony: it is composed of varied characters with varied degrees of development, of sanctification and expansion; each will have his place, a place contingent upon the peculiar character which, through the Spirit of God, he developed in his conduct in this present world; and thus in the age to come there may be benedictions fitted for each Christian, according to what he was, through grace, in the world of the living.

(See John Cumming, *Benedictions: or The Blessed Life*, John P. Jewett Co., Boston, 1854, pp. 136-161.)

The Apostle Paul wrote concerning his friend Onesiphorus, who often helped him and was not ashamed of his chains, "The Lord grant him that he may find mercy of the Lord *in that day*" (II Tim. 1:18). What day? The Day of Judgment. Our destiny on that day depends on our behavior in this present day.

Out of this life I shall never take
Things of silver and gold I make.

All that I cherish and hoard away
After I leave, on the earth must stay.

Though I have toiled for a painting rare
To hang on my wall, I must leave it there.

Though I call it mine and I boast its worth,
I must give it up when I quit the earth.

All that I gather and all that I keep,
I must leave behind when I fall asleep.

And I wonder often what I shall own
In that other life, when I pass alone.

What shall they find and what shall they see
In the soul that answers the call for me?

Shall the great Judge learn, when my task is through,
That the spirit had gathered some riches, too?

Or shall at the last it be mine to find
That all I had worked for I'd left behind?

– Edgar A. Guest

"Poor Robert! I understand that he did not leave much property," said a friend commiseratingly of one who had just died, as he drove home with the minister from the cemetery. "Too bad! He worked hard, and made money, but he was too tenderhearted. I think every beggar in town must have known him."

The minister listened politely. "I suppose what you say is right about his having no property, but I imagine, from what I have known of his life, that he must have considerable property to go to."

Do you? Have you sent anything ahead? It may be that you don't have too much time left to do so. You'd better get busy. Your mercifulness here will be stored up there with compound interest.

WHAT MAKES US DO GOOD TO OTHERS?

Being blessed means having God within us. If we possess Him, then we shall demonstrate His dispositions and actions. God delights in nothing so much as the showing forth of His mercy. The condemnation of a sinner grieves Him, but to forgive without violating His justice gladdens Him. "As I live, saith the Lord God, I have no pleasure in the death of the wicked; but that the wicked turn from his way and live: turn ye, turn ye from your evil ways; for why will ye die, O house of Israel?" (Ezek. 33:11). God is not a sadistic judge. He condemns when He must, but His necessity does not always coincide with His will. The condemnation that He brings upon man is a duty imposed upon Him by the unrepentant state of man, but the demonstration of His mercy is the natural outcome of His character. It is the concomitant of His will, His desire, His yearning for all men.

In nothing does God delight more than in the exercise of mercy. "Who will have all men to be saved, and to come unto the knowledge of the truth" (I Tim. 2:4). "The Lord is . . . not willing that any should perish, but that all should come to repentance" (II Pet. 3:9). We are most like God when we are merciful. It should be the natural outcome of our blessedness in Christ. Our mercifulness is in direct proportion to our blessedness. The more truly holy we are, the more merciful we are. The zenith of mercifulness is found in God. And this is because of His holiness. The strongest is the gentlest, and the purest is the most pitying.

In Hosea 11:9 we find a sublime statement about God's attitude toward the sin of Israel's ingratitude. He says, "I will not execute the fierceness of mine anger . . . for I am God, and not man" – an indication that the more human we are the more merciless we are, and, conversely, the more divine we are the more merciful we shall be. And God is most merciful "just because he most condemns the disease, most feels its virulence, most sees its ravages. Your brother man overestimates your power of resistance; he has less sense of sin's horror. To the eye of Divine Love sin has crippled even your power of will; and Divine Love pities you." (See George Matheson, *Rests by the River,* Hodder and Stoughton, London, 1906, pp. 115-118.)

In this Beatitude, then, we see how both God and men measure our godliness. It is by our genuine mercifulness. If you are not characterized by mercy, a Godlike mercy, you are neither blessed nor holy. Your whole religiosity and salvation are a mockery and a delusion.

Actually, there is no such thing as human mercy. The flow of the stream of human mercy must be traced back to the fountainhead of the mercy that is divine. It has its source in the very nature of God. Every merciful thought and purpose and intention existing in men is simply an evidence that God, being a fountain of unfailing mercy, created man in His own image, in His own likeness. Mercy is of the very essence of Deity. And the main characteristic of God's mercy is that it is undeserved by man. We often mistake the repayment of a kindness as mercifulness. Because some one at some time did us some good, we feel we must do likewise. This is a human concept of mercy. It lacks divine motivation. True mercy is beneficent even to our enemies and never expects repayment in kind. True, there is a reward for every merciful act, but no merciful act should be done for the sake of the reward. It should be the natural outcome of God's divine nature within us, and then and only then is it Godly and Godlike mercy. "And whosoever shall give to drink unto one of these little ones a cup of cold water only in the name of a disciple, verily I say unto you, he shall in no wise lose his reward" (Matt. 10:42.) "In the name of a disciple" means to demonstrate the nature, the divinely motivated nature, of a disciple of Christ.

Plutarch tells us that the Rhodians appealed to the Romans for help, and one suggested that they should plead the good turns which they had done for Rome. This was a plea difficult to make strong enough, very apt to be disputed, and not at all likely to influence so great a people as the Romans, who would not readily consider themselves to be debtors to so puny a state as that of Rhodes. The Rhodians, however, were wiser than their counsellor and took up another line of argument, which was abundantly successful. They pleaded the favors which in former times the Romans had bestowed upon them, and urged these as the reason the great nation should not cast off a needy people for whom they had already done so much.

If this is the character of our pleading for mercy from God, simply because it is His nature to be merciful, let this same virtue characterize us. We show mercy to others, not because they deserve it, not because we hope for reciprocation either from them or from God, but because we are blessed, that is, Godlike, merciful. This nature was marred in the fall of Adam. Soon after that we find that brother kills brother over a most trivial matter. The presence of sin encourages merciless- ness. But now, with the restoration of man to God through the Lord Jesus Christ, for His sake (Matt. 5:11) mercifulness has also been restored in man. The Divine again takes residence in the human, so that

God's mercy is expressed through redeemed man.

Mercifulness as an attitude of heart is governed by certain principles that we shall do well to observe. The first one is that we should not be quick to suspect. It is a fundamental principle in our courts of justice that the prisoner should get the benefit of every doubt, and that if the judges err at all it must be on the side of leniency and mercy. Justice never sentences on suspicion. But, in the secret tribunal of our hasty and passionate hearts, the judgment-seat is often swept by fiercer and sterner principles. The face of a friend appears before our mind under a hint of suspicion. Without further evidence, we convict and pass hasty sentence, and he stands perpetually exiled from our hearts and homes. "Be merciful!" the Saviour pleads. Never, never condemn on the strength of a suspicion. Be slow to arrive at a harsh conclusion, even when there is strong presumptive evidence; and even when the evidence is conclusive, be merciful, be merciful, be merciful!

> Judge not! The workings of his brain
> And of his heart thou canst not see.
> What looks to thy dim eyes a stain,
> In God's pure light may only be
> A scar brought from some well-won field
> Where thou wouldst only faint and yield.

Two thoughts should lead us to think mercifully even of those who have been convicted of the most atrocious offenses and revolting crimes. We must say to ourselves:

1) They never enjoyed my opportunities, friendships, and privileges. If they had, perhaps they would be much better than I am.

2) I was never exposed to their environment, dis-

advantages, and temptations. If I had been, perhaps I would have been far worse than they.

It is the tongue that needs a double portion of mercifulness. If I could paraphrase our Lord's Beatitude, I would say, "Blessed the Christian with a merciful tongue." An unmerciful tongue may be more cruel than the most terrible instrument of torture ever forged. It can stab more keenly than a dagger, and cut more deeply than a sword. That quick tongue; that fiery, temper-driven tongue; that insidious, insinuating tongue; that soft, slimy, slandering tongue; that sharp, sarcastic tongue; it is dangerous to handle such cruel weapons heedlessly. With one of them you may so pierce your mother's soul that she will wish she had never been born; you may so rend your father's heart as to bring down his grey hairs in sorrow to the grave; you may cut the nearest, dearest ties and leave the heartstrings bleeding. Be merciful with your tongue.

Being merciful does not mean merely the performance of acts of benevolence, but being possessed of a spirit of mercifulness. There is as much wickedness in believing a lie as in telling it, if we are always ready to believe it. There would be no slanderers if there were no receivers and believers of slander; for when there is no demand for an article, there are no producers of it; and if we will not believe evil reports, the talebearer will be discouraged and leave off his evil trade. But suppose we are compelled to believe it? Then the merciful man shows his mercy by not repeating it. It is for the Christian not to expose, but to deal ever towards the erring in the gentlest possible manner.

Mercifulness exists not in a series of merciful acts but in an abiding state of merciful feeling, a state of feeling that is just as merciful when there are no such acts to perform.

The mercifulness of Jesus existed, not so much in healing the sick and curing the blind, but in having compassion on the multitude. The faces of the crowd went to His heart; He was touched with the feeling of their infirmities; their sorrows brought heaviness to His soul; and when they wept, it brought tears to His eyes. The fifth Beatitude breathes its blessing on a like simplicity of sympathy, a similar tenderness of heart.

> A soul that can rise above trifles,
> A spirit immovably sweet;
> A soul that can soar high and mighty
> O'er trouble; a soul that can mete
> Out kindness to every other,
> And never the poorer be;
> That can stoop and lift up a lost brother,
> Or sister, or father, or mother;
> Nor forgets as ye love one another
> Even so shall I love thee.

The hearts of men all around us are aching and breaking for that very human touch, the touch that has known the divine touch, the touch of kindness, the touch of sympathy, the touch of mercy.

There is a mystery about true selflessness as there is about real love. Like the river on its way to the sea, the merciful man cherishes in his heart a profound mystery. The river is pouring itself out all the while; yet it is abundantly repaid by the freshness of the fields and the beauty of the wild flowers all along its banks. As the merciful man well knows, "There is that scattereth, and yet increaseth; and there is that withholdeth more than is meet, but it tendeth to poverty" (Prov. 11:24.)

> Not what we give, but what we share,
> For the gift without the giver is bare;
> Who gives himself with his alms feeds three,
> Himself, his hungering neighbor, and Me.

"It is certain that the good Samaritan," says Spurgeon, "got more out of the poor man whom he found between Jerusalem and Jericho than the poor man got out of him. He had a little oil and wine, and twopence, the expenses at the inn, but the Samaritan got his name into the Bible, and there it has been handed down to posterity – a wonderfully cheap investment; and in everything that we give, the blessing comes to those who give it, for it is more blessed to give than to receive."

It is very wonderful, yet it is true, that He who gave us the fifth Beatitude accepts as a sacrificial service rendered to Himself every cup of cold water that merciful hands extend to thirsty lips.

> And still wherever Mercy shares
> Her bread with sorrow, want, and sin,
> And Love the beggar's feast prepares,
> The uninvited Guest comes in,
> Unheard, because our ears are dull,
> Unseen, because our eyes are dim,
> He walks our earth, the Wonderful,
> And all good deeds are done to Him.

And so the waters of the river flow at last into the infinite sea. The trickling fountain at the little pool consisted of water that had come from the ocean. The sun had wooed it into the clouds; the clouds had distilled it over the hilltops; and the mountain torrents had borne it back once more to the sea. So this gracious and all-refreshing stream, having its rise in the Eternal, empties itself into the Eternal again. The divine mercy is its fountainhead; the divine mercy is its goal. Blessed are the merciful, for they shall obtain mercy.

They are not merciful in order that they may obtain mercy. I like to fancy that the rivers, as they pour themselves down through the valleys, gladdening every pasture through which they pass, are not deliberately searching for the sea. They dumbly feel that they sprang from the infinite; they feel that they belong to the infinite and can never be quite at rest until they reach the infinite again. But they think nothing of that. They think only of their mission. It is theirs to give to the grass its greenness and to the trees their beauty. It is theirs to refresh the tired horses that are led at evening to the ford, the sheep that browse at the water's edge, and the cattle that stand among the reeds and rushes. And, busy with their lowly labor, they rush on and ever on, singing as they go. And their song is the song of a joyous surprise. For, to its amazement, the river discovers that, although it is pouring itself out unselfishly and unstintingly all along its course, it gets deeper and broader the farther it goes!

This is the first astonishment, and the second is even more amazing. For, one great day, as the waters turn a bend in the channel, there is the sea, stretching out in its blue immensities, the infinite from which they sprang! So mercy greets mercy. Blessed are the merciful, for they shall obtain mercy. The merciful, made merciful by mercy, find mercy in its fullness awaiting them at the last.

(See F. W. Boreham's article, "The Quality of Mercy," in *The Christian World Pulpit*, Vol 115, pp. 172-4, and C. H. Spurgeon, *The Treasury of the New Testament*, Zondervan, pp. 61-6.)

PRACTICAL SUGGESTIONS
FOR DOING GOOD

To be truly Christian is to be merciful. But life is so complex and difficult sometimes that we do not know just how to go about it. It is then that practical suggestions can be very helpful. To have mercy in our hearts is good, but to know how to express it in the right way is better. The value of something is diminished if we do not know how to use it.

In the practice of mercifulness, we should begin with our own households as our missionary effort. Husbands, be merciful to your wives; and wives, be merciful to your husbands. And how much mercy is needed in the training of children! Actually, the best place for the exercise of any virtue is in the home. Each individual in a household may be tempted to think himself the most perfect member in it. If so, then each should endeavor to outdo the other in the exercise of mercy in the home.

Recently I had the opportunity of conversing with Mrs. May Moody Whittle, D. L. Moody's daughter-in-law. I asked her what was her outstanding memory in the life of Dwight L. Moody. Do you know what she said? "He could tell his children that he was wrong and ask them to forgive him." She went on to tell me that one day the children let the horses out of the stable and it took him a long time to get them back. He really told them off. Finally, at night when the children were in bed, Mr. Moody went up and apologized to them for having spoken as he did. And this trait is what his children esteemed more than anything else in their father. It may be, when all is said and done in this life,

409

yours and mine, that our mercifulness will be the thing that is remembered by those who are left behind.

A minister called at the home of one of the young women of his church. He had never met the girl's people. A tired, worried looking woman answered the door, to whom the minister said, "Mary is one of our young folk, and I felt I should call on her people; she's such a bright Christian."

"Is she?" asked the woman. "Well, sir, Mary is our oldest daughter; we are only too pleased to have her attend church a lot; but I have been sick for a long time, and as soon as Mary gets home from work, she's off again; we see very little of her."

"I'm sorry," said the minister. "She seemed to have such grace."

"Maybe so," said the mother, "but she doesn't show it here. She must keep it all for outsiders." As the minister was turning away in disappointment, she called after him, "Perhaps you can show Mary that it takes great grace for the little things, too."

Are we merciful in the little things of life in our homes? Our mercy at home will become contagious, so that we need not teach it to our children and other members of the family by the imposition of penalties. Here are some practical suggestions to guide you.

1) Be careful about insisting that you are in the right and others are in the wrong. It is possible, you know, that the reverse may be true.

2) Never regard as your due those things that others do for you, even in your own household, but rather as demonstrations of their love and devotion to you. A demanded right, even in the home, is never as pleasurable as natural mercifulness. How well I recall a relative who was infuriated because we always said "please" and "thank you" to each other in our home,

even for small things. She was an autocrat who preferred to demand rather than ask. This woman was miserable all her life and she died miserable, feeling that the world owed her something. She lived a life of demanded rights rather than one of unexpected mercies from God and her fellow beings.

3) Make it a point in life always to outdo others in mercifulness, even in your own household. Don't try to get as much as possible but to give as much as possible. If you simply receive mercy and freeze it within yourself, you will be cold and unloving. J. H. Evans said, "I believe that God often permits me to be chastened by my sin, because I do not make use of my mercies." We often lose our mercies by loving them too well, as the ball of snow is melted by the heat of the hand that holds it; or a rose is spoilt by pressing it too tightly. Theophilus Gale very well said, "Whatsoever I thankfully receive, as a token of God's love to me, I part with contentedly, as a token of my love to Him."

Mercy is like food. It accomplishes its intended purpose when it is transformed into energy and not when it is simply stored away. The reception of mercy from God and others can become a burden instead of a blessing.

But our world must not be just our family, although it seems to me that if we practice mercifulness in the small world of our family we shall also practice it in the larger world outside. As we look upon the world, we see that it is made up of the rich and the poor, the jovial and the depressed. Let us not make the mistake of thinking that only the poor and depressed need our mercy. The rich and the jovial may need it just as much. Sometimes, if we get under the skin of the rich, we catch a glimpse of real misery. Oh, if you and I could only meet the clowns of our day when they are alone in their rooms! Have you ever wondered why so many of them end their lives with an overdose of sleeping pills? The rich and the merry are just as fallen as the down and outs. Those who are poor and depressed have many who are concerned about them and try to reach them with the message of the Gospel – to which many of them marvelously respond. We have rescue missions for alcoholics and the poor, but you never heard of a mission for kings and princes, a mission for the rich, the intellectuals, or for university professors. Do you think that they need the mercy of God, or of us who are the purveyors of God's mercy, any less than the drunks? If Marilyn Monroe had only had someone to tell her of the Lord Jesus Christ and of His ability to satisfy the gap in her life, tragedy might have been averted. There is no mission for movie stars, but they, too, need our mercy and compassion.

Along our way come those who not only need the spiritual salvation we possess, but also our practical compassion. There is always someone in life who is poorer, or sicker, or more depressed than we. We need never feel that there is any lack of those to whom we can show mercy.

4) Be careful not to give the wrong kind of mercy. If bread is needed, don't dismiss a hungry person with mere words. If words of comfort are needed, don't just give money. The Apostle James put it so beautifully: "If a brother or sister be naked, and destitute of daily food, and one of you say unto them, Depart in peace, be ye warmed and filled; notwithstanding ye give them not those things which are needful to the body; what doth it profit?" (James 2:15, 16.)

"Where God has given a man a new heart and a right spirit, there is great tenderness to all the poor, and especially great love to the poor saints; for, while every saint is an image of Christ, the poor saint is a picture of Christ, set in the same frame in which Christ's picture must ever be set, the frame of humble poverty. I see in a rich saint much that is like his Master, but I do not see how he could truthfully say, 'I have not where to lay my head.' Nor do I wish to say it; but when I see poverty, as well as everything else that is like Christ, I think I am bound to feel my heart specially going forth there. This is how we can still wash Christ's feet by caring for the poorest of His people. This is how honorable women can still minister to Him of their substance. This is how we can still make a great feast to which we may invite Him, when we call together the poor, and the lame, and the halt, and the blind, who cannot recompense us, and we are content to do it for Jesus Christ's sake." (C. H. Spurgeon, *The Treasury of the New Testament*, Vol. 1, p. 63.)

Is there no poor, sick, lonely person you can show your God-given mercy to? Never postpone the expression of your mercifulness. The opportunity you have today may be lost tomorrow.

> Said yesterday to tomorrow,
>   "When I was young like you,
> I, too, was fond of boasting
>   Of all I meant to do.
> But while I fell adreaming
>   Along the pleasant way,
> Before I scarcely knew it,
>   I found I was today!
>
> "And as today, so quickly
>   My little course was run,
> I had not time to finish

413

One half the things begun.
Would I could try it over,
But I can ne'er go back;
A yesterday forever,
I now must be, alack!

"And so, my good tomorrow,
If you would make a name
That history shall cherish
Upon its roll of fame,
Be all prepared and ready
Your noblest part to play
In those few fleeting hours
When you shall be today."

5) Above everything else, let us be merciful toward
the characters of others, even as we would like them
to be merciful to our characters. When you hear a
derogatory story about a brother, believe it as readily
as you would like someone else to believe a similar
story about yourself. Search out the truth with all
diligence and be ever ready to believe the best rather
than the worst. "Blessed are the merciful: for they
shall obtain mercy."

SCIENCE AND THE BIBLE AGREE:
GOD IS INVISIBLE

"Blessed are the pure in heart: for they shall see God" (Matt. 5:8).

If you have studied philosophy, you will notice that most philosophers are hesitant to deny the necessity for the existence of the Infinite. And most scientists are ready to concede that man is finite. If man were the creator of his own universe, he would continue to have and manifest at least some of his original creative powers. But man has never been able to create something from nothing. All he can do is to manipulate the raw materials already in existence, according to the ability given to him by his Creator.

To see God has been the ultimate aim of all true philosophy; it is the ultimate hope of all science; and it will remain the ultimate desire of all nations. But God cannot be found in this way anywhere in the wide realms of nature, in the great and wonderful world which we see and touch. Science proclaims that no God can be found on the pathway she has explored. By means of her telescope she has surveyed the heavens, and nowhere among the stars and suns which shine in those infinite depths can she find a God. She has used her microscope for the purpose of examining the minute and astonishing forms of life which she can place in her hands, and in none of them can she detect the presence of God. He is not in the stars of the sky. He is not in the grains of sand; not in the flowers gemmed with dew, nor in the marvelous processes of life which form the basis of our own physical being; He is not to be found far away, or near at hand. (See "The Visible God," by William Dorling, in *The Christian World Pulpit,* Vol. 6, p. 168.)

The Bible long ago declared what science is now finding out, that it cannot discover those things that are known by revelation only. The Bible nowhere intimates that a mere scientific search for God is suitable or likely to succeed. Those who have been looking for God with their natural vision, fortified by telescopes and other scientific aids, tell us that they have not found Him. The Bible could have told them as much. Job bore testimony to this fact when he said, "Oh that I knew where I might find him! that I might come even to his seat! . . . Behold, I go forward, but he is not there; and backward, but I cannot perceive him: On the left hand, where he doth work, but I cannot behold him: he hideth himself on the right hand, that I cannot see him: But he knoweth the way that I take: when he hath tried me, I shall come forth as gold." (Job 23:3, 8:10.)

Any scientist will tell you that neither microscope nor telescope can discover God, this Infinite Power to whom is ascribed the creation of all things. If man were able to see Him, the very fact of His visibility would rob Him of His infinity. The finite can never fully comprehend or view the infinite. Then what did the Lord Jesus mean by this sixth Beatitude, "The pure in heart . . . shall see God"? How is it possible for admittedly finite man to see the infinite God?

We have reached the place in human achievement when man can leave this sphere called earth and travel into space. Yet after all, is this really such a great achievement, in view of the immensity of the universe? A couple of Russian astronauts orbit the earth and, thinking they have explored all the possibilities, contemptuously speak of not having seen God up there.

John Glenn, in a humbler frame of mind, gave God the glory for his success. He did not expect to see Him in outer space, for he knows that God does not dwell in the universe that He has created in such a way as to be seen physically.

The fact that God cannot be seen by our physical eyes is not a recent Russian discovery. By definition, God is a Spirit. We must fully understand what we mean by the words we use. When the Scriptures speak of God, they mean the Creator of the universe, Infinity, Eternity. Paul, speaking to the Athenian philosophers, expressed clearly what we mean by the term God: "The God that made the world and all things therein, he, being Lord of heaven and earth, dwelleth not in temples made with hands; neither is he served by men's hands, as though he needed any thing, seeing he himself giveth to all life, and breath, and all things; and he made of one every nation of men to dwell on all the face of the earth, having determined their appointed seasons, and the bounds of their habitation; that they should seek God, if haply they might feel after him, and find him, though he is not far from each one of us: for in him we live, and move, and have our being" (Acts 17:24-28, author's translation). That God in His eternity and infinity cannot be seen by man must be the conclusion of any thinking person. It is, furthermore, the revealed declaration of the Bible, which tells us, "No man has seen God at any time" (John 1:18; I John 4:12).

"You teach," said the Emperor Trajan to Rabbi Joshua, "that your God is everywhere, and boast that He resides among your nation; I should like to see Him."

"God's presence is indeed everywhere," replied Joshua, "but He cannot be seen. No mortal eye can behold His glory." The Emperor insisted. "Well," said Joshua, "suppose we try to look first at one of His ambassadors."

The Emperor consented. The Rabbi took him into the open air at noonday and bade him look at the sun in its blazing splendor.

"I cannot," said Trajan. "The light dazzles me."

"Thou art unable," said Joshua, "to endure the light of one of His creatures, and canst thou expect to behold the resplendent glory of the Creator? Would not such a light annihilate thee?"

This same thought is expressed in the Bible, in I Timothy 6:16, "Who only hath immortality, dwelling in light unapproachable; whom no man hath seen, nor can see: to whom be honor and power eternal. Amen." (Author's translation.)

It is, in fact, illogical to reject that which one cannot know by his own power and intelligence. Man has always felt impelled to search for that which he neither knows nor can find, and yet that which must be, for it is the only explanation of that which he knows and sees. That is why the Athenians dedicated one of their altars to the Unknown God: the Invisible, Infinite, and Eternal One. But Christ declared that this invisible God is real, knowable, and visible under certain conditions and by certain people. "Blessed are the pure in heart: for they shall see God." This is what Paul meant when he said, "What therefore ye worship in ignorance, this I set forth unto you" (Acts 17:23).

Let us not be like the two little boys on the hilltop, one of whom was up a tree stealing apples and the other watching to make sure they were safe from observation. They were blissfully unaware that someone watched them through a telescope seven miles away, noting each motion and even the guilty expression of their faces as plainly as if he had been in the tree with them. How absurd for the boys to conclude that vision ended with their own vision, and that safety was the result of

418

what they could distinguish! In this universe, which is but the result of God's handiwork, we are no more intelligent than these two little boys, if we conclude that God must not be, since we cannot see Him with our own two eyes.

The finite can neither see nor comprehend the Infinite. The Infinite has to reveal Himself. Henry Ward Beecher said, "When Columbus drew near to the eastern coast of this continent, he could see that there were mountains, but do you believe he knew what minerals were in them? Do you suppose he knew all the trees, all the shrubs, all the vines, all the herbs there? He knew something about the outlying islands of this great continent, but he did not understand the details that went to make it up. I can understand that there is such a being as God, but when it is said that He is infinite, I am so finite that I break down right there. I cannot understand infiniteness. All things in the natural world symbolize God, yet none of them speak of Him but in broken and imperfect words. High above all He sits, sublimer than mountains, nobler than lords, truer than parents, more loving than lovers. His feet tread the lowest places of the earth; but His head is above all glory; and everywhere He is supreme."

Simonides, a heathen poet, on being asked by Hiero, King of Syracuse, "What is God?" desired a day to think upon it. At its end, he desired two. Thus he continued to double the number of days before he could give an answer. The king asked what he meant by this conduct. The poet replied, "The more I think of God, He is still the more unknown to me."

One thing, however, that this sixth Beatitude makes very clear is that a certain group of people, having attained a certain state, can see God. "Blessed the pure in heart," it says, "for they themselves shall see God" (literal translation). Who are these people characterized by purity of heart, and how can they see God? Where, and what kind of being, is the God they see?

WHAT GOD DO THE PURE
IN HEART SEE?

In our previous study, we concluded that the Scriptures fully agree with the process of careful logic and the declaration of the best in science, that God in His infinity and eternity cannot be discovered, known, or seen by man. Yet we are puzzled over the words of the Lord Jesus in Matthew 5:8, "Blessed are the pure in heart: for they shall see God." Let us first determine what is not meant by the term God used in this sixth Beatitude.

God is not a shape or form, as of some mighty and majestic man, visible to the eyes of such beings as have been created to behold Him. Our concept of God must not be anthropomorphic, ascribing to Him the characteristics of human beings. God is not as we are. He is not bound by time and space, for if He were He could not be their Master and Creator. It is impossible to conceive of God as creating that which would become His master, for this would make Him an inferior Being who gave birth to a God superior to Himself.

Why did God, in the second of His Ten Commandments to Moses, forbid the reducing of the spiritual to the material? "Thou shalt not make unto thee any graven image, or any likeness of any thing that is in heaven above, or that is in the earth beneath, or that is in the water under the earth" (Exod. 20:4). There are real created personalities, powers, in the universe and beyond it, to which cannot be ascribed form or shape. Any attempt to do so leads us to the unconscious limitation of the limitless. Unfortunately, many religious persons have formed far too familiar and manlike notions of the Most High. Even in our liturgical worship we must be careful lest any of the spirituality of God be stolen from Him through our material representation of Him and His working.

Such material representations are indications of man's yearning to have God near him, so that he can feel Him and see Him. This is what the Greeks of Athens tried to do, "if haply they might feel after him, and find him" (Acts 17:27). He was not far from them, Paul declared, but He could not be known or His presence realized by man's physical senses. "He is Lord of heaven and earth" and "dwelleth not in temples made with hands" (Acts 17:24). Keep God in the realm of the Spirit, was Paul's admonition to the Athenians. Do not reduce Him to matter. It cannot be done. "In him we live, and move, and have our being" (Acts 17:28). Life is not primarily material. A dead body cannot get out of its casket. God is Life with a capital "L," and life is spiritual, even as God is Spirit.

The Lord Jesus explained this carefully to the Samaritan woman who thought God dwelt only on a certain mountain (John 4:24). "One God and Father of all, who is above all, and through all, and in you all" (Eph. 4:6). The awful remoteness at which some have placed Him has imparted a thrill of cold dread to many human hearts. But we may not, on the other hand, describe Him to our minds as though He were in all respects like ourselves. The likeness that was stamped on man at his creation was of a spiritual, a moral, an intellectual nature. Surely none can suppose that it was physical.

Nor are we to suppose that God has a local habitation, as we human beings have. It is true that we are told in the Scriptures that God inhabits a region called heaven. But heaven is larger in scope than we sometimes imagine.

Heaven includes some human hearts; and while the ideas of place are perhaps necessary to bring it to our imagination, the predominant idea is that of a state of being. Oriental poetry and imagery, aided in the Christian ages by the visions of artists and poets, have given to us a world of ravishing beauty and glory, investing it with the fadeless splendors of a gorgeous scene that captivates and absorbs the fancy. Let us be comforted! Heaven is not less, but more than that. The physical picture only serves to sketch with a few faint lines the glorious home of immortal beings.

The ideas which most devout and reflective minds have associated with their concept of God are that He is a Spirit; He is immaterial; He can be, and is, everywhere present without being seen by the eye of sense. Language imperfectly symbolizes our thoughts, and our thoughts are but poor efforts at conceiving of the infinite God. As soon as we begin to inquire into its meaning, we are involved in difficulties which harass the intellect and perplex the heart.

What, for instance, is a spirit? At least we may say that a spirit is not evident to the eye of sense. It is not subject to the conditions that we attach to matter. A spirit may be possessed of all the qualities of thought, feeling, and suffering; and we are certain that the Eternal is thus rich beyond our computation. His thoughts are a great deep. He is a God of love; He is a consuming fire. We read of His wrath and His hatred, of His love and His pity. He possesses power by which He can deal with all material things, and cause them to accomplish the ends He pleases; but He is not simply a great worker of wonders in the material universe. He is more awful and glorious as we contemplate Him on the throne of the mental and moral world. There He has power over the inner forces and mysterious energy of life. (See "The Visible God," by William Dorling, in *The Christian World Pulpit*, Vol. 6, pp. 168-9.)

When Jesus said, "Blessed are the pure in heart: for they shall see God," to what kind of God was He referring? Wasn't He God who spoke these words? In John 1:1 we read, "In the beginning was the Word, and the Word was with God, and the Word was God." The Word here stands for Jesus Christ, for in John 1:14 we are told, "And the Word became flesh."

Very interestingly, in the Greek text of the Beatitudes, the definite article appears before the word "God." This verse should literally be translated, "Blessed the pure in heart: for they themselves shall see the God." Whenever the definite article is used before the word "God," it doesn't necessarily refer to the abstract totality of Deity, but, the context permitting it, to one of the definite personalities of the Trinity. Let me illustrate by going to the great Christological passage of John 1:1-18. In verse 18 we find this statement, and I translate literally from the Greek text: "God [without the article] no one has seen at any time." The fact that the definite article is omitted here points up the fact that reference is made to God in His general make-up, in other words, to His infinity and deity, to His total being.

William Edward Jelf, one of the great Greek grammarians, says in his *Grammar of the Greek Language*, "The effect of the omission of the article is frequently that the absence of any particular definition or limitation of the notation brings forward its general character." (Vol. II, John Henry and James Parker, 1859, p. 124.) Therefore, what we have in John 1:18 is the declaration that God, in His infinity, in His eternity, in His totality, cannot be seen by anyone; and that includes not only man, but the angels and all created

424

beings. This is fully logical and scientific, nor does it come into conflict with the statement in the sixth Beatitude that the pure in heart can see God. This Beatitude speaks of "the God" and not "God." The definite article here speaks of God the Father, whom Jesus Christ, the God-man, came to reveal.

A literal translation of the Greek text of John 1:1 should help to make this clear. "In the beginning was the Word, and the Word was toward the God, and God was the Word." In the second clause of this verse, the definite article is used before "God." Here we have two personalities, "the Word" and "the God." "The God" in this instance, and in this context, refers to God the Father, as "the Word" refers to God the Son. John wants us to understand that he is speaking about two distinct personalities – the Son and the Father. This is exactly what he declares in the second part of John 1:18, which reads, "The only begotten Son, who has always been with the Father, he hath declared him." Here we find a clear statement of the two Persons involved, the Son and the Father. Therefore, we could safely translate John 1:1b, "and the Word was toward the God," meaning, "and the Son was toward the Father." This indicates to us the eternal interdependence of God the Son and God the Father, two co-equal and co-eternal personalities, both God.

Jelf furthermore states, "Some words are found both with and without the article, and seemingly with but little difference; but without the article they signify the general notion conceived of abstractedly and not in actual existence; with the article the objective existence is brought forward as *theos*, the divinity; *ho theos*, the God we worship." John, therefore, in using the definite article before "God" in this Beatitude does not speak of divinity in general; He does not refer to the Infinite

God comprising all Three Persons of the Trinity: God the Father, God the Son, and God the Holy Spirit; but speaks of God the Father, whom Jesus came as God the Son to reveal and make visible to man.

You remember that the Lord said to Thomas, "If ye had known me, ye should have known my Father also: and from henceforth ye know him, and have seen him." Then, when Philip said to Christ, "Shew us the Father," He replied, "He that hath seen me hath seen the Father; and how sayest thou then, Shew us the Father?" (John 14:7, 9). One of the unique things that the Lord Jesus came to do was to reveal that this infinite God can become our Father. This relationship of man to God, and God to man, as child and Father, is possible only through the Lord Jesus.

PURITY: THE GRACE THAT MAKES GOD VISIBLE

In our study of the sixth Beatitude in Matthew 5:8, we have seen thus far that true science and the Bible agree that the Infinite God is invisible. We have also learned that what Christ meant when He said that the pure in heart shall see God was that children of the new birth would discern God the Father as revealed through His Son, Jesus Christ.

The Apostle Paul touches on the subject of how far man can see when He searches for God. "For the invisible things of him from the creation of the world are clearly seen, being understood by the things that are made, even his eternal power and Godhead; so that they are without excuse" (Rom. 1:20). The word "Godhead" is a mistranslation of the Greek word *theiotees*, which actually means "divinity," not the substance but the quality of God, His attributes manifested in and through the things He has made. The Greek word for "Godhead," which sums up all that deity is – God the Father, God the Son, God the Holy Spirit – is *theotees*, which is used in Colossians 2:9, "For in him [Christ] dwelleth all the fulness of the Godhead bodily." In Christ and for the sake of Christ we can see God, the intricate and undiscoverable and unexplainable Trinity of the Godhead. Nature, apart from the revelation of Scripture, reveals a God, but not the God of the Lord Jesus, a loving Father.

The wonders of the earth, the stars, the sea –
They are of God's full glory merely hints:

427

The lily and the rose, the leaf, the tree —
These are no more than His faint fingerprints.

— Mary S. Smith

The attributes of God are perceivable by man's intellect, as is God in the abstract, but not God as the Father of the man who is purified by His Son, the Lord Jesus. That takes the heart of man to see, and not merely his mind. It takes more than comprehension; it takes belief; and that belongs to the realm of the heart. You grope with the mind; you believe with the heart. "For with the heart man believeth unto righteousness; and with the mouth confession is made unto salvation" (Rom. 10:10). When man believes with his whole heart, he is saved, his vision is purified, the scales fall from his spiritual eyes, and he can see God. The condition, then, for vision with the heart is that the heart be pure.

> Heaven above is softer blue
>   Earth around is sweeter green,
> Something lives in every hue
>   Christless eyes have never seen.
>
> Birds with gladder songs o'erflow,
>   Flowers with deeper beauties shine;
> Since I knew, as now I know,
>   I am His and He is mine.

To see God is so far from being a universal privilege, however, that God Himself could not make Himself visible in the glory of His moral character to any creature whose own moral character was either undeveloped or defiled. We can understand this by analogies within our own experience.

428

A child, for example, may grow up for years in the same house with his father, and know him to be kind and pleasant indeed, and very dear, yet never see him to be a man of exceptional strength and nobleness and completeness of virtue, a rarely heroic or saintly man; for the soul of a little child is not itself grown to such moral stature as to be capable of measuring the morally great.

Again, a bad man with a mean or twisted moral nature may be in contact with a person of almost angelic purity, sweetness, humility, and disinterestedness, yet fail to see or be attracted by the beauty of that lovely life; for the bad heart projects its own badness, and lacks the power to appreciate, or even to discern, unselfish virtue. To see God at all or in any measure in this life requires that such cleanness and sweetness of heart should at least have been begun in us. So long as we are ourselves proud, lovers of evil, with a conceit in ourselves greater than in any other, or possessed by dark, selfish, or vicious passions, we cannot see God's goodness to be good. We love the darkness; and the light which we do not love we cannot see.

A young man attended an informal gathering in a Christian home at which those who attended were encouraged freely to express any perplexities that stood in the way of belief. "I went into the woods one day," this young man said to the group, "and sat down on a sandy patch of ground and said to God, 'God, if you will destroy that little pine tree I am looking at, I will believe in You.' I sat there a long while, but nothing happened. Now, if there was a God, why didn't He reveal Himself to me when I asked Him to?" He was honestly troubled and obviously in earnest, yet not knowing the Scriptures he erred. Man does not set the conditions by which he will condescend to believe in

God, but God sets forth the conditions under which He will reveal Himself to man: coming to Him through the provision He has made in Christ, repenting of his sin, and yielding his heart to the purifying action of the Holy Spirit. Then and only then will he "see God."

Our Lord declared three things in the sixth Beatitude:

1) That the blessed, those in whose hearts God dwells, shall see Him. (See author's booklet, *The Pursuit of Happiness*, in which he discusses the meaning of the word "blessed" *(makarioi* in Greek).

2) That they are blessed, God-indwelt, for the sake of Christ. This is where we relate this Beatitude to its foundation phrase in verse 11, "for my sake." No one can become blessed outside of the person and work of Jesus Christ.

3) That the blessed are also the pure in heart, for the holiness of God cannot co-inhabit with sin. Therefore the phrase, "for my sake," refers to both the blessed and the pure in heart, only because of Christ; and it is as a result of their cleansing by the blood of Christ that God is willing to dwell in their hearts. Neither the blessedness nor the purity of man is possible outside the person and work of Jesus Christ. So the phrase, "shall see the God," refers both to the word "blessed" and the phrase, "the pure in heart." The two are synonymous: blessedness is the result of purity of heart, and purity of heart is the condition of blessedness. God will not indwell an unclean heart. It must first be made pure, and then God will make his dwelling place there. God the invisible, God the infinite, God the eternal, is willing to inhabit the limited confines of human personality. What greater miracle could there be than this? Man cannot ascend to heaven to grasp God, but God condescends to come down to earth and sacrifice Himself on the cross of Calvary in the person

of His Son, so that the heart of man may be purified, indwelt by the Father-God! Here we have a statement of the interplay of the two Persons of the Trinity, God the Father and God the Son. God the Son, through His person and work, makes possible the purification of the human heart from sin and the reconciliation of man the sinner with God the Father.

Therefore we might very well paraphrase this Beatitude, "Blessed – that is to say, indwelt by God – are the pure in heart." These are pure because of Christ – God the Son. These, the blessed and the pure, shall see the Father. And the Father is made visible through the Son. Isn't this exactly what John 1:18 declares? "God [no definite article] in His infinity and eternity no one has seen at any time; the only begotten Son who has been in the bosom of the Father at all times, He hath declared Him" (literal translation). (Also see author's study on John 1:18 in booklet, *Can Man See God?*) The invisible God becomes visible through the Son, Jesus Christ, "Whom having not seen, ye love; in whom, though now ye see him not, yet believing, ye rejoice with joy unspeakable and full of glory" (I Pet. 1:8). This is the basic and comprehensive meaning of the sixth Beatitude.

SORROW: GOD'S PURIFYING FIRE

The Beatitudes in Matthew have a fascinating order. The first three indicate the conditions of blessedness: poverty of spirit, which means human helplessness; mourning, which means sorrowing for our own sins and those of others; and meekness, which means righteous anger, controlled anger, at sin in our own lives and in the lives of others, as well as full and complete acceptance of God's will and purpose in our lives. Helplessness, sorrow, meekness — three conditions indicative of human emptiness. The result of these conditions is in each case blessedness, which means the presence of God within the human heart.

But in each instance there is also a specific filling, along with the general state of blessedness that is the indwelling of God. When the person is helpless and runs to Christ, the Kingdom of Heaven becomes his, taking over from the kingdom of earth. Man becomes a citizen of heaven. When a person sorrows for his sins, he receives divine comfort, the comfort of forgiveness of sin. When a person recognizes the evil of sin and stands up against it, and at the same time subjects himself to the directive and permissive will of God, he can really enjoy the earth, for he is right in the sight of God. Whatever God permits, he considers not as his legal right but as gifts of divine grace. This would apply not only to health, but to sickness; not only to riches, but to poverty; not only to prosperity, but to adversity. Here, then, we have in exchange for helplessness, the Kingdom of Heaven; for sorrow, comfort; for meekness, the enjoyment of the earth.

Immediately after these three conditions of blessedness and their corresponding specific rewards (which are in addition to the general indwelling of God within the human heart), we have a hunger and thirst for a righteousness that is not ours but Christ's. "Blessed are they which do hunger and thirst after righteousness: for they shall be filled" (Matt. 5:6). When a person has recognized his helplessness, his sinfulness, his battle with sin, and his resignation to the will of God, he can never feel self-satisfied. Man's state at that point becomes one of permanent and continuous un-satisfaction accompanied by continuous satisfaction of his spiritual needs. He goes through a constant and uninterrupted process of emptying of self and filling with Christ. The more Christ fills us, the more hungry we are for Him. This is the central and distinguishing feature of the Christian life — a continuous hunger and thirst for the righteousness of God.

Next we have a grouping of the three corresponding results of the state of blessedness. Because a person is blessed under the Kingship of Christ, receives the comfort of Christ, and willingly accepts and uses God's purpose and will for his life, he cannot help but demonstrate three things in his life: mercy, purity of heart, and peace. We must clearly understand that these qualities of blessedness do not at the same time produce our original blessedness. In other words, an unregenerated man who may perform casual acts of mercy, demonstrate apparent purity of life, and act as a peacemaker, cannot claim the blessedness of God in consequence. Mercy shown by man cannot gain the favor of God unless it is mercy first received from God; for human mercy is but the overflow and outcome of God's mercy in a man's own heart.

As Portia so aptly observed in Shakespeare's *The Merchant of Venice:*

The quality of mercy is not strained,
It droppeth as the gentle rain from heaven
Upon the place beneath: it is twice blessed;
It blesseth him that gives and him that takes:
'Tis mightiest in the mightiest; it becomes
The throned monarch better than his crown;
His sceptre shows the force of temporal power,
The attribute to awe and majesty,
Wherein doth sit the dread and fear of kings;
But mercy is above this scepter'd sway, —
It is enthroned in the heart of kings,
It is an attribute to God himself;
And earthly power doth then show likest God's
When mercy seasons justice.

To sum it all up, we are merciful, we are pure in heart, we are peacemakers, because of salvation in Christ, because of forgiveness in Christ, because of subjection to Christ, because of our constant and uninterrupted hunger for Christ.

We noted in our previous studies a beautiful correspondence between the three Beatitudes preceding the fourth (which speaks of the hunger and thirst after righteousness) and the three that follow it. These can be most effectively paired.

"Blessed the poor in spirit: for theirs is the kingdom of heaven" (Matt. 5:3).

"Blessed the merciful ones: for they shall obtain mercy" (v. 7).

Realizing how helpless he has been, the sinner cannot but demonstrate the same mercy that has been demonstrated to him. That which he has received, he gives.

"Blessed the mourning ones: for they shall be comforted" (v. 4).

"Blessed the pure in heart: for they shall see God" (v. 8).

Mourning is pressure from the afflictions of life: above us, around us, within us. God purifies the mourning hearts of His children in the furnace of affliction. He often allows sorrow, pain, sickness, poverty to come upon them. He does not let them suffer longer than is right. When He has made them what He intended, He delivers them. A silver coin or medal is generally stamped with the image of the sovereign. This can be done only when the metal is soft, and it is made soft by the heat of the fire. Even so God's children should bear the likeness of Christ stamped upon them in their conduct. God sends affliction to soften their hearts that they may more easily receive that holy impression, and so become more like Jesus.

When you sorrow over something, your immediate desire is to get rid of the cause of your sorrow. In the second Beatitude, the root of sorrow is mourning over sin, the sin of Adam and personal sin. There is only one way man can rid himself of original and personal sin. That is through the shed blood of Jesus Christ. The result of sin forgiven is the joy of salvation and the comfort of Christ. When this takes place, the human heart becomes pure. Therefore purity perfectly corresponds with the fire of sorrow and mourning. Try as you will, you cannot extricate the pure metal from the lump of ore without some kind of fire.

When God wants to refine a man, he exposes him to the great white heat of the fiery furnace. But this white heat does not injure him; it brings him forth· as pure gold. Through the prophet Isaiah, God said to His people, "Behold, I have refined thee, but not with silver; I have chosen thee in the furnace of affliction. For mine own sake . . . will I do it" (Isa. 48:10, 11).

435

Now we come to the third couplet:

"Blessed the meek ones: for they shall inherit the earth" (v. 5).

"Blessed the peacemakers: for they shall be called the children of God" (v. 9).

Childhood is not perfect without the quality of submission. We attain to the perfect status of children of our Heavenly Father the more actively we resist sin and the more passively we submit to God. In this state of meekness, we do not settle for peace at any price or endeavor to bring about the co-existence of right and wrong. This is a false and deceptive peace. It is a peace that no child of God should seek. The peace the child of God should seek is the one that has its roots in the meekness of the third Beatitude. Active resistance against evil, and submission to God, will put him on the side that is right.

James 3:17, 18 says, "The wisdom that is from above is first pure, then peaceable, gentle, and easy to be intreated, full of mercy and good fruits, without partiality, and without hypocrisy. And the fruit of righteousness is sown in peace of them that make peace." Mercy, purity of heart, and peacemaking, these three distinct qualities of blessedness assume the possession of the righteousness of Christ and do not presume to deserve it. We are merciful, we are pure in heart, we are peacemakers at no sacrifice of holiness, because we possess the righteousness of Christ. We do not become righteous because we are merciful or show an apparent purity of action or a desire for peace.

But why does the Beatitude regarding purity of heart follow that regarding mercifulness? On a memorable occasion, when the Lord Jesus went to luncheon with a Pharisee and scandalized him by omitting the customary ablutions, we read that the Lord said, "Give as alms the things that are within; and lo, all things are clean to you." This is the literal translation of Luke 11:41 from the Greek, and not as it is usually translated, "Give alms of such things as ye have." In other words, the Lord taught that the exercise of a merciful spirit tends to produce purity of heart. In this principle lies the connection between the fifth and sixth Beatitudes. The merciful man not only obtains mercy but also grows toward purity.

S. D. Gordon has a final word for us: "How many thousands of lips have lingered lovingly over Philippians 4:7, 'The peace of God, which passeth all understanding, shall keep your hearts and minds through Christ Jesus.' It is God's peace. It acts as an armed guard drawn up around heart and thoughts to keep unrest out. It is too subtle for intellectual analysis, but it steals into and steadies the heart. You cannot understand it – but you can feel it. You cannot get hold of it with your head, but you can with your heart. You do not get it – it gets you. You need not understand in order to experience. Blessed are they that have not understood, and yet have yielded and experienced."

WHAT THE HEART OF MAN IS

William Lyon Phelps said, "The Beatitudes are in reality Be-attitudes; they are attitudes that come not from doing, but from being." The Lord told us that if we have God in our hearts because of what He is and what He has done for us, the first thing that we shall demonstrate is mercy. We shall be known, both to God and our fellow men, as merciful people.

The second characteristic of our blessedness — the result of our mourning and sorrowing for sin — is the cleansing of that sin. God says to the sinner, "Though your sins be as scarlet, they shall be as white as snow; though they be red like crimson, they shall be as wool" (Isa. 1:18). Again, in I John 1:7, 9, we read, "If we walk in the light, as he is in the light, we have fellowship one with another, and the blood of Jesus Christ his [God's] Son cleanseth us from all sin . . . If we confess our sins, he is faithful and just to forgive us our sins, and to cleanse us from all unrighteousness." He doesn't say "some of your sin" or "a part of your sin," but ALL sin, ALL unrighteousness.

The sixth Beatitude is the assurance that the impure, who recognize their impurity and sinfulness, shall find cleansing in Christ. This Beatitude, as all the others, must necessarily be linked with that foundational phrase of Matthew 5:11, "for my sake." "You are blessed," the Lord says, "because you have God within you. This has been accomplished, not through any effort of your own, but through Me. I have brought God to you; I have revealed Him; I have brought Him out of His hiding place so that you can see Him by possessing Him."

This Beatitude also indicates, like all the others, that

God is more concerned about man's inward state of being than his outward circumstances. Christ did not come so much to bestow happiness, favorable circumstances, as to bestow blessedness, divine indwelling of the heart. He did not say, "Blessed are the rich in circumstances, the prosperous in life," but "the pure in heart." The benediction is not upon outward circumstances but upon inward character; and wherever holy character is, there the benediction rests; wherever the character is not holy, though a man be clothed in purple and fine linen every day, he has no lot or share in the benedictions of Christ.

The heathen were satisfied with external character. To be right in the sight of men was all they wished; to be correct in the outer conduct was the very flower and perfection of heathen morality. The Pharisees, indeed almost the whole nation of the Jews, were more anxious about the outside of the platter being clean than the inside. All excellence was conformity to the letter of the Law; it mattered not that the spirit of it was violated ten times a day. It is of these that Christ speaks when He says, "Except your righteousness exceed," not only in degree, but in kind, "that of the scribes and Pharisees" – that is, righteousness of the letter; rigid, mechanical righteousness, instead of righteousness from the heart – "ye cannot see the kingdom of heaven." (See Rev. John Cumming, *Benedictions or the Blessed Life*, John P. Jewett & Co., 1854, pp. 163-4.)

God is a holy God. He cannot indwell a heart that is uncleansed, unholy, and sinful. "If I regard iniquity in my heart, the Lord will not hear me," said the Psalmist (66:18). Habakkuk 1:13 declares, "Thou art of purer eyes than to behold evil, and canst not look on iniquity." Also God told the Jews in Isaiah's day, "When ye spread forth your hands, I will hide mine eyes from you: yea, when ye make many prayers, I will not hear: your hands are full of blood" (Isa. 1:15).

On the one hand, then, we have the holiness of God, and on the other the sinfulness, the filth of man. This is not a sinfulness of action only but a sinfulness of the seat of action. We must bear in mind that the Lord Jesus Christ did not come to this earth merely to make the thief stop stealing, or the adulterer cease his adultery, or the drunken man abstain from his liquor. He came to remedy the root of stealing, the root of adultery, the root of drunkenness — to cleanse the source. If a stream of water should be found to be impure, wouldn't it be absurd for us to try to purify each pail of water as we got it from the stream? How much better to go to the source of the stream, find the cause of the impurity, and remedy that!

The human heart is recognized in the Word of God as the center of man's personality. But what is meant by this use of the word "heart"? Before we can understand who the pure in heart are, we must know just what this heart is. Is it that vital organ of the body that pumps the blood through the arteries and veins? This is the commonest meaning of the word. In Leviticus 17:11 we read, "For the life of the flesh is in the blood," and we know that the center of the life of the blood is the heart. The brain cannot think except as it is supplied with blood by the action of the heart. Without our physical hearts, we could not conceive of the human organism. But we know that, when the Lord spoke of "the pure in heart," He was not referring to those whose blood was free of disease and whose hearts were functioning normally. We can dismiss the meaning of the word heart here as the physical organism vital to the preservation of bodily life and health.

Another meaning of the word "heart," which has come down to us from ancient times, both in Biblical and secular use, is "soul" or "spirit," to indicate the seat of the desires, passions, sensations, and will. In this sense, the heart is regarded as the seat of life, the center around which a man's personality is oriented and integrated. The Lord consistently spoke about the heart of man as being sinful and in need of cleansing.

A young child was promised a certain book she wanted on condition that she would learn to read the fifth and sixth chapters of Matthew in two weeks' time. She immediately undertook the task and, when she read to the old gentleman later who had promised her the reward, he stopped her at the end of twelve verses, asking her which one of the qualities described in the Beatitudes she would most like to possess. She replied, "I think if I could have a pure heart, I would have all the other good things this chapter tells about."

"The heart is every man's best part — the shrine of his affections, the ocean of his thoughts, the store-house of the energies of his will — insomuch that there is not one of the multifarious responsibilities of life which he can worthily bear, nor one of its great duties that he can effectively discharge, until he has learned to put his heart into it. Least of all is it possible for religion to be of value unless it be suffused with the tenderness, glowing with the ardour, and resolute with the purpose of the heart. As we ourselves know that we have never won a man until we have gained his affection, so He who created and redeemed us insists that we have given nothing to Him until we yield our love. Consent of the intellect alone is nothing. Conviction of the judgment alone is nothing. Service of the hands alone is nothing. His grave, sweet voice still calls to us out of heaven, 'My son, give Me thy heart'; and only when this is done can we be counted among His disciples. The seat of His religion is the heart – its effect is to produce purity of heart – its reward is to open the eyes of the heart." ("The Heirs of the Kingdom," by Rev. W. J. Woods, in *The Christian World Pulpit*, Dec. 31, 1890.)

The Word of God says in Jeremiah 17:9, "The heart is deceitful above all things, and desperately wicked: who can know it?" The heart is constantly used in Scripture in a figurative sense to indicate the hidden springs of personal life. The Bible describes human depravity as in the heart, because sin is a principle which has its seat in the center of man's inward life and then defiles the whole circuit of his action. "For out of the heart proceed evil thoughts, murders, adulteries, fornications, thefts, false witness, blasphemies: these are the things which defile a man: but to eat with unwashen hands defileth not a man" (Matt. 15:19, 20). It is, therefore, at the root of man's personality that the Lord wants to enter. This is actually what the word blessedness means – to be distinguished by the quality of deity. God is pure; He is pure not only in His actions, but in His inner being. When we become blessed by receiving the Lord Jesus as our Saviour, we do not merely perform pure or merciful acts, but we become pure, we become merciful. These are concomitant virtues of blessedness.

The actions themselves may not be, or appear, perfect and absolutely pure, but the heart is pure because of the work of God in the human personality. The Bible tells us that God punished David sorely for his threefold sin of covetousness, adultery, and murder with regard to Bathsheba and Uriah. But when David repented with godly sorrow and genuine remorse, the Lord restored him and called him "a man after his own heart" (I Sam. 13:14). He who controls the heart controls all. That is why the Scriptures, especially the New Testament, are not full of specific and detailed instructions about our actions in life. They are, however, deeply concerned that we shall have the center of the personality, the heart, always purified by the Lord. The Psalmist said, "My heart is fixed, O God, my heart is fixed" (Ps. 57:7).

Why didn't the Lord say, "Blessed are the pure in soul" instead of "Blessed are the pure in heart"? In some passages, the word *kardia* (heart) is used both as heart and soul — *psuchee* (soul) and *pneuma* (spirit) — the latter even more prominently than the former. But with respect to the emotional life, a review of the usage of the words shows this distinction: that the immediate desire which makes its appearance in the form of a natural instinct is ascribed to the soul, whereas the desire cherished with consciousness and expressed with will, reflective volition and resolve, activity of thought is ascribed to the heart. Therefore, the soul is more generally associated with the natural instinct; while the heart is more generally associated with conscious, volitional desire. (Herman Cremer, *Biblico-Theological Lexicon of the New Testament Greek*, T. & T. Clark, Edinburgh, pp. 343-50.)

This indicates that this purity of heart is not something arbitrary and authoritarian, imposed upon us by God. A mother gives her child a bath whether he wants it or not; but it is a "willing" bath that God gives man. Through the miraculous operation of the Holy Spirit, He causes man to recognize his sinfulness, to be sorry for it, and then to run to Christ for cleansing of heart and forgiveness of sin. Man must say yes to God in this matter before God will cleanse him.

It is in this respect that purity of heart differs from pardon of the heart. Let us not confuse the two. Forgiveness is purely an act of God; but purity, although an act of God, must have the obedient cooperation of man. We have no part in securing our pardon. We can have no share in providing for our salvation. It is our Saviour's unaided sacrifice on the cross that makes pardon possible for man. In the matter of purity, however, there must be harmonious cooperation between the sovereign Spirit of God and ourselves – God and man each taking his appropriate part.

Purity is the result of the pardon of God in Christ and is not the pardon itself. A convict, dying of a loathsome disease in the Arizona State Prison at Florence, was given a New Testament one day by a visiting prison worker. He started to read it and became so convicted of sin that he hurled it the length of the cell. When the Book landed on the floor, it fell open to the First Epistle of John. A verse boldly outlined in red caught the angry convict's eye. He stooped down to look at it and this is what he read: "The blood of Jesus Christ his Son cleanseth us from all sin." That message brought him to his knees, crying out to God for forgiveness, for cleansing, for healing. He became a new man in Christ Jesus. He started a Bible class for the convicts, and in time secured an unconditional pardon from the Governor of Arizona. But the pardon the Lord gave brought him purity of spirit, soul, and body, and through him brought many others into the Kingdom.

This is why we repeatedly find in the New Testament that it is with the heart that man believes unto righteousness (see Romans 10:9, 10, and Ephesians 3:17-19). Therefore it is the heart, above all, that is the seat of belief and unbelief.

WHY MAN'S HEART NEEDS PURIFYING

We have seen that the term "heart," both in classical and Biblical Greek, means the center of man's personality, thought, affection, and volitional desire. The activity of the spirit must be especially sought in the heart. What, in the last instance, belongs to the spirit we can attribute to the heart. As the Greek scholar, Hermann Cremer, states: "We find heart and spirit used as parallels, or in the closest character with each other. For as the personal life (of the soul) is conditioned by the spirit and mediated by the heart, the *activity of the spirit* must be especially sought in the heart . . . . As the spirit is specially the divine principle of life, and is therefore particularly employed where manifestations, utterances, states of the religious, God-lived life come under consideration, we can understand why religious life and conduct pertain mainly to the heart. Further, in one case, we find ascribed to the spirit what, in another case, is ascribed to the heart. It is of chief importance to recognize the heart as the seat of the activity of the Spirit, of the divine principle of life." *(Biblico-Theological Lexicon of New Testament Greek,* p. 347.)

In addition to the relationship of the heart to the soul, and the heart to the spirit, we must examine one more relationship. We have seen that the heart refers more to our volitional desires, while the soul refers to our natural desires. When the Lord seeks our hearts in particular, He seeks our assent to His outstretched arms for salvation and redemption. The relationship of the heart to the spirit is that our spirit is the receptive element of the communication of the Spirit of God, but the seat of that communication of our spirit and the Spirit of God is the heart.

The heart, therefore, represents the proper character of the personality – or hides it. The fact that the Lord tells us in this Beatitude that we must be pure in heart to see God is indicative of the inherent sinfulness of man. Only something that is defiled needs purification. Man's defilement of heart is the result of man's fall. Because of his evil heart, his thoughts and imaginations are evil continually (Gen. 6:5). Therefore, when the Lord speaks of the pure in heart, He refers to a very special class of people. As in all the Beatitudes, the definite article is used here. It is *hoi katharoi*, "the pure." This, according to Greek grammar, is restrictive; it refers to a special class of people. (A. T. Robertson, *Grammar of the Greek New Testament in the Light of Historical Research*, Hodder & Stoughton, New York, p. 757.) It doesn't mean those who consider themselves pure, those who have been purified by human means, but those who have been purified by the Lord Jesus Christ.

This sixth Beatitude means nothing apart from its foundation phrase in Matthew 5:11, "for my sake." The purification referred to is restricted to that accomplished in the believer by the Lord Jesus Christ. Thus we could paraphrase this as "Blessed are those who have been made pure for the sake of Jesus Christ: for they, and they alone, shall see God." This is in full agreement with what Christ said on another occasion, "He that hath seen me hath seen the Father" (John 14:9). The Lord is telling us in this Beatitude how blessed are those who have been cleansed by Him, how pure they are, and what the end result of this state is: they can see God.

The expression, "the pure in heart," includes both the result and the condition of blessedness. Blessedness means the dwelling of God in the human heart. This is accomplished through Jesus Christ; but in order that God may dwell in the human heart, it is necessary that it be cleansed. Therefore, before a person is said to be "blessed," he must be "pure." Purity thus becomes a condition of blessedness, as do all the other characteristics mentioned in the previous Beatitudes: humility, mourning for sin, meekness, hunger for Christ's righteousness, mercifulness. All are conditions of that original blessedness which we acquire when we first believe and the further development of the blessedness of the Christian life. To these is now added purity of heart. The conclusion we reach, then, is that blessedness without purity of heart is impossible.

Blessedness, as we have seen time and again, is not something that can be had merely for the asking. It is the end result of the fulfillment of certain conditions. If you are sick, you go to a doctor. He doesn't write out a prescription for health but recommends certain procedures that will lead to health. There are certain medications you must take and certain modifications you must make in your way of living. Then the doctor can say with a measure of certainty, "If you do thus and so, you will get well." The Lord says with absolute certainty, "The pure in heart are blessed." They have God within them; and God, the Holy One, consents to dwell only in those whose hearts are pure. That is why we find so many exhortations to purity in the Scriptures. Paul adjured Timothy, his son in the faith, "Be thou an example of the believers . . . in purity" (I Tim. 4:12), and later on, in the same letter, he reiterated, "Neither be partaker of other men's sins: keep thyself pure" (I Tim. 5:22).

The purity of heart of which the Saviour speaks is also the result of blessedness. It is because of what Christ has done on the cross to make it possible for

God to indwell the human heart that the heart of man is pure. In other words, the blessed are the pure in heart, and the pure in heart are blessed — two interwoven, inseparable qualities that are God-given. Both are totally and exclusively due to the Lord Jesus Christ. It is all "for my sake," the Lord says.

What, exactly, is meant by purity of heart? *Katharos*, the Greek word for "pure" or "clean" used in the Beatitudes, occurs about twenty-four times in the New Testament. It is not, however, exclusively a New Testament word. It was used in classical Greek in a variety of ways. It was used to denote physical cleanliness, and also to indicate that something was free from any admixture, as in speaking of clear water. It also described grain that had been winnowed, or metals free from alloy.

The fact that the Lord tells us that we need to be cleansed before we can see God is indicative of the fact that we are impure when we are outside of Christ. How nonsensical it would be to tell your wife, your daughter, your maid, "Go wash the dishes," if the dishes were already clean. Only something that is dirty needs purification. The basic declaration of this sixth Beatitude, therefore, is that the heart of man is impure, depraved, unable to see God, unblessed unless Jesus Christ purifies and cleanses it.

When God looked down on the earth in Noah's time and saw that man's wickedness was great in the earth, "and that every imagination of the thoughts of his heart was only evil continually," the Book of Genesis records, "it repented the Lord that he had made man on the earth, and it grieved him at his heart" (Gen. 6:5, 6). However, He provided a way out for the one righteous family, and the ark that Noah built is a type of the Ark of

Safety that the believer who is pure in heart has in Christ.

Lot did not entertain angels because he was sinless or perfect, but God saw that his heart was pure toward Him and that the sins of Sodom and Gomorrah brought him grief and vexation of spirit. Then God warned him to flee from the punishment He intended to rain down upon those two centers of iniquity, whose very names will always be synonymous with the total depravity of mankind.

When Christ said, "The pure in heart . . . shall see God," He was declaring that when He becomes part and parcel of the human personality, is accepted as Saviour, it is not merely the external actions that appear Godlike, but the central intellectual and emotional agency of the personality becomes pure and clean in itself. The Lord does not merely look at our acts to find out what the dispositions of our hearts are, nor does He try through the correction of our behavior to purify our hearts. When He wants us to be honest, He doesn't merely influence our specific desires for not stealing, but He revolutionizes our whole concept of life. It isn't the habitual abstaining from evil that makes us good, but the work of redemption in the human heart that causes the cessation of our habitual evildoing. We do not become by doing, or cease to be by not doing, but we become and do. We become Christians in our hearts and then act as Christians in every manifestation of life.

You know, some people try to act like Christians who have never truly become Christians. The fact that the Lord constantly admonishes us to have our hearts purified, instead of giving us specific instructions as to what we should and should not do, is an indication of this. (See Romans 1:21, James 4:8, Matthew 23:27, 28.) The world is a stage on which we observe all kinds

449

of actors. An actor is an individual who impersonates someone else. A great many of the people who call themselves Christians today are only going through the motions, trying to act out what they think should be the manifestations of Christianity, without Christ in their hearts, without having experienced the blessedness of Christ and the purity of heart that He alone can bestow. This often causes a basic antagonism between the inner character and the outward appearances. The only way this spiritual schizophrenia can be healed is through purification of heart. Otherwise we have to confess that we are hypocrites, living a lie, acting a part, trying to appear something that we are not. This sets up conflicts which can cause a definite split in the personality, with sorrowful and inescapable consequences.

GOD THE TRANSMITTER, MAN THE RECEIVER

Man may be pure to all outward appearances; he may be free of the consequences of sin and the overt expression of sin; but that doesn't mean that he is pure in heart. How about those hidden dispositions of heart that, for one reason or another, we prefer to keep hidden? Frankly, there are only two who know what is in our hearts, God and ourselves. Will you pause just for a moment and in all sincerity look into your heart? Can you honestly say that it is pure in all its thoughts, pure in all its dispositions, pure in all its imaginations and motives? Just a little reflection will lead you to the conclusion that you lack the purity of which Christ speaks in the sixth Beatitude. But virtues that are naturally absent from the human heart can be divinely instilled. You may work as hard as you like to try to clean up your own heart, but apart from the person and work of Jesus Christ you cannot be truly pure in heart. Such purity requires the action of an agent outside yourself. Your own standards of purification are unacceptable to God. Only when God, through Jesus Christ, purifies the human heart, can it be said to be truly pure. Self, as sinful, is buried.

John Flavel has said, "If I could be master of myself, my own wit and will, how blessed I would be! We have need to be redeemed from ourselves, as much as from the devil and the world. I would make a good bargain and give old for new, if I could turn out self and substitute Christ my Lord in place of my self; to say, Not I, but Christ; not my will but His; not my desires, not my wealth, but Christ, Christ."

A. B. Simpson re-echoed Flavel's words when he wrote:

Not I, but Christ, be honored, loved, exalted;
Not I, but Christ, be seen, be known, be heard;
Not I, but Christ, in every look and action;
Not I, but Christ, in every thought and word.
Oh, to be saved from myself, dear Lord,
Oh, to be lost in Thee!
Oh, that it might be no more I
But Christ who lives in me.

Human emotions are sublimated by the Divine, and the end and purpose of life is conformity to His image, for His glory.

When St. Paul's Cathedral in England was being demolished to make room for a new edifice, thirty men operated a battering-ram for one whole day on a certain part of the wall. Not seeing any immediate effect, they thought this a colossal waste of time, but they were told nonetheless to continue. On the second day, the wall began to tremble at the top and fell in a few hours. If our prayers and repentances do not appear to overcome our inner corruption, we must still continue to use these battering-rams, for through faith in Christ the power of evil shall be overthrown. This is what the Scriptures call the working out of your own salvation (Phil. 2:12).

Very interestingly, the work *katharos*, "pure," in ancient Greek was used in the sense of "free from debt." A man who was able to pay all his accounts and taxes and on whom no one could lay a claim was *katharos*, "pure." To make someone *katharos* is to give him a discharge from a debt or to acquit him of a charge. This is a beautiful picture of what happens when Jesus Christ enters your life and mine. In our sinful state we were debtors, for "The wages of sin is death" (Rom.

6:23). You and I should have died because of the sin of Adam and our own personal sin. Instead of this, Jesus Christ intervened and died so that you and I could be pure, "without debt," before God against whom we had sinned. "Blessed are the pure in heart: for they shall see God," means "Blessed are those whose debt of sin has been paid for the sake of Christ: for they shall see God."

Tell the truth: when you owe a man a large sum of money and are unable to pay him, you don't feel much like seeing him, do you? You go out of your way to avoid him. When you are free from debt and owe no man anything, it gives you the courage to face the world with your head held high. It is only as you are free of the debt of sin that you can look into the face of God.

The word *katharos* also meant being free from all guilt and pollution. It was used, for example, of innocent hands, of a body and soul that were morally clean. In this sense, Matthew 5:8 can certainly be taken to mean that, when the work of redemption takes place in our hearts through Jesus Christ, we are not only free from the guilt of sin; it is as if we had never had any debt before God, as if we had never sinned or lost the image and likeness of God. If we are pure, it is because we possess a purity that is not inferior to His, which had been given by Him. If you claim to have a purity of your own and not of God, then you can neither hear His voice nor feel the throb of His heart, nor do your prayers get any higher than the ceiling. You cannot see God if you are trusting in your own purity and righteousness.

A New Zealand preacher described a Pharisee as being like a bag tied in the middle. Anything put into the top will not reach the bottom. The Pharisee opens wide his mouth when he prays, but his heart is tightly shut. With his lips he asks for things that his heart does not really desire. If God were to give him the spiritual blessings he asks for, it would only be a waste of good gifts, for they could not get to the bottom of the bag. His pride would choke them off and they would reach no farther than his throat.

The Lord Jesus gave a supreme illustration concerning self-righteousness when He told the story of the Pharisee and the publican. The Pharisee stood where everyone could see him and made his pretentious, lengthy prayer for all to hear. The publican, knowing his unworthiness, smote his breast and asked God to be merciful to him, a sinner. The Lord said that the publican went down to his house justified rather than the other; for "every one that exalteth himself shall be abased; and he that humbleth himself shall be exalted" (Luke 18:14).

It is a law of electronics that there has to be a correspondence between the transmitter and the receiver. You may think that everything in the room you are now in is apparent to the eye. However, there are many things there that you are not even conscious of, unless you bring in something that can detect them. The room in which you now sit is filled with all kinds of radio and video waves. Your unaided eye cannot see them; your unaided ear cannot hear them. You need a radio or television set tuned to the wave-lengths of the transmitters in order to be aware of the reality of the existence of these waves. There has to be a correspondence between the transmitter and the receiver. Now, who can see God? The one whose receiver has been attuned to the transmitter, the one whose impure, filthy, sinful, unregenerate heart has willingly, consciously, miraculously through the operation of the Holy Spirit, been tuned to the transmitter of God. Then, and only then, will there be free communication and a clear vision of God. But this tuning of man, the receiver, to God, the transmitter, can only take place through Jesus Christ. The receiver must be made to correspond with the transmitter. The purity of man must be the purity of God in order for man to be on the same wave-length as God.

The word *katharos*, "pure," also means "ceremonially clean, fit to approach God, or fit for the worship of God." It is used with reference to the altar, to the sacrifice of the worshiper who has carried out the correct ritual of the days on which sacrifice might be ordered, so that such a day can be called a "pure" day. It describes something that is fit for the service of God, fit for communication with God, fit to stand in the presence of God. Isn't this the state of the believer before God?

John Ruskin was walking along the streets of London one rainy day, when he noticed the great quantities of mud at his feet. The thought occurred to him that it would be interesting to have the mud analyzed to find out exactly what inorganic elements were in it. This was accordingly done, and it was found that London mud consisted of sand, clay, soot, and water. Musing upon that fact, it struck him that these are the very substances from which our precious jewels and gems are formed. From the sand come the onyx, agate, beryl, jasper, amethyst; from the clay come the sapphire, ruby, emerald, topaz; and from the soot, the diamond. London mud composed of precious jewels! Man cannot transform the mud into those glittering points of light, but God transforms and recreates the mud – poor, sinful, wayward humanity – into redeemed souls who sing the new song and carry with them glad tidings of great joy!

If God were to look at us as we are, don't you think He'd see the mud in us more plainly than the jewels? That He can make of us something fit to stand in His presence is, in itself, a miracle of miracles! There is joy in coming to God for salvation, to be rescued from sin; but this cannot be compared to the joy of fellowship with God, of being in His presence, of being constantly able to see Him. The purer the heart, the clearer the sight of God in all His manifestations.

In addition, the work *katharos* means "pure in blood" or "genuine." It is used to denote someone whose race is pure. It is used of a saying whose authenticity or veracity cannot be doubted. This suggests to us that when we are purified by Christ we immediately become genuinely pure. We belong to a very special group of people – the pure in heart. There is a tremendous difference between this group and the class of the sinful in heart. We hear of many religions today, but actually there are only two – the religion of the pure in heart and the religion of the impure in heart. It makes no difference to what religious body you belong; the important thing is whether your own heart, individually and specifically, has been purified by the blood of Jesus Christ. Do you belong to the peculiar class of the redeemed? I do not ask whether you are Greek Orthodox, or Roman Catholic, or belong to one of the many Protestant denominations. The important thing is that your heart be pure before God. Christ never said that being affiliated with a particular sect or denomination would enable you to see God. He said, "Blessed are the pure in heart: for they shall see God."

SANCTIFICATION : WHAT IT IS

"Blessed are the pure in heart: for they shall see God." Does this refer to our justification in Christ or to our sanctification? We believe in the Lord Jesus, we appropriate His work for us, and for His sake we are forgiven – pardoned both for our original and our personal sin. This is the beginning of our blessed life. We have become babes in Christ. Our hearts have been changed from black to white. The filthiness caused by sin has been replaced by the pure righteousness of Christ.

As the newborn babe in Christ grows in the Christian life, he will find that he needs constant cleansing of heart. Once he has been purified by the blood of Christ, he is not thereby exempted from the soiling influences around him or from the renewed activity of the flesh and the old nature. The Scriptures tell of an initial cleansing, followed by many subsequent cleansings of the human heart. The first is a radical housecleaning, and the other consequent cleansings are entirely dependent upon that original cleansing. That first purging of the human heart is instantaneous and simultaneous with the forgiveness of our sins by the Lord Jesus. However, the ensuing series of pardons and purifications demands human cooperation. That is why there are various degrees of blessedness, just as there are various states of purity. What this Beatitude means is that the purer a man's heart is the more blessed he is. Purity of heart as stressed in the Beatitudes is a condition that man must meet in order to experience God's blessedness. (See Ps. 24:3-5.)

We have spoken before of the ladder of Christian blessedness that we are ascending. The first step is the recognition by man's spirit of his helplessness or "poverty of spirit." Only the helpless who recognize their condition will go to Christ. "Blessed the poor in spirit: for theirs is the kingdom of heaven – for the sake of Christ."

The second step is man's sorrow for sin. Only as we sorrow for our sins shall we experience the joy of forgiveness. There is no blessing in an empty cup; the blessing is in the filling; but the cup must be empty first. We do the emptying as we are energized by the Holy Spirit, and the Lord does the filling. "Blessed they that mourn: for they shall be comforted." The condition of receiving God's comfort is man's voluntary sorrow for sin.

In our helplessness, we have been taken in by the King. In our sorrow, we have been comforted. The natural reaction to such a wonderful state is to be proud of what we are in Christ. That is why the Lord adds the third step on the ladder, "Blessed the meek: for they shall inherit the earth." We have found among other things that meekness means getting angry over our besetting sin. It's still there and we ought to be actively engaged against it. As we fight against sin, we realize that the full enjoyment of life, even with all its besetting sin and resultant sorrows, can be realized only by complete submission to the Lord Jesus Christ. We thus become heirs of all that the earth offers us because of Christ. Meekness is the condition man must meet so that God's earth may become his to enjoy.

On the fourth rung of the ladder of blessedness we have those who hunger and thirst after Christ's righteousness. Hunger and thirst is man's desire, which can be satisfied only as he appropriates God's provision. The Bread of Life will be given only to those who hunger for it. It will not be forced down anyone's throat.

On the fifth rung we have the merciful Christian. A child of the King; a Christian rejoicing over his God-given sorrow for sin; an active fighter against sin; a man submissive to God's will; one whose hunger is satisfied: all blessings received from God. To keep them for oneself would be to slip down the ladder, not ascend. Sharing of one's blessing is the condition of mounting to the fifth rung of the ladder of blessedness. Hoarding God's blessings reduces their blessed quality; sharing them increases it. This is mercifulness. "Blessed the merciful ones: for they shall obtain mercy." The more we give the more we receive.

The person who has reached the fifth rung now has the opportunity of moving up. The condition for this is purity of heart. But isn't he already pure? Of course he is. His heart was purified when he first recognized his helplessness and ran to Christ. But in his sorrow, in his fight against sin and the struggle to be submissive or meek, in his hunger, in his mercifulness, he has been constantly in touch with the world, with sin. Additional cleansing is needed now. Any house, no matter how clean, gets dirty with use. The Christian who claims the absolute maintenance of that original purity is one whose purity is sterile and isolated. Activity involves getting soiled. That is the inevitable outcome of the Christian's walk as he rubs shoulders with the world and contends with his old sinful nature. He can't help it. Therefore it is necessary for us, even as purified Christians, to recognize our impurities and invite the Lord Jesus to continue His purifying work in us.

In reality, this Beatitude says, "Blessed is he who, having once been purified by the blood of Christ, recognizes and confesses that he still needs purification every moment of his life." That is why we are instructed constantly in Scripture, even after we are saved, to continue to ask for forgiveness. Blessed is he who maintains purity of heart through continuous cleansing by the Lord Jesus and by the continuous appropriation of His cleansing and keeping power.

This is clearly set forth by the Apostle John in his First Epistle. "If we say that we have no sin, we deceive ourselves, and the truth is not in us" (1:8). John included himself in this group. He was certainly purified in heart, yet he recognized the presence of sin. If you don't recognize sin, you won't invite Christ to cleanse you. If you say your house is clean, you will not clean it or engage someone else to do so. Observe what John says in verse 9: "If we confess our sins, he is faithful and just to forgive us our sins, and to cleanse us from all unrighteousness." The condition of our forgiveness by God is our recognition and confession of sin. This is the fundamental meaning of the sixth Beatitude as a condition of blessedness. It speaks of the necessity of purity and therefore of the necessity of our confessing our impurity even in our state of purity. If you feel you have all that is to be had of purity, you will never know the real blessedness of this Beatitude.

The Apostle James summarizes his understanding of the fifth and sixth Beatitudes in his epistle when he says, "Pure religion and undefiled before God and the Father is this, To visit the fatherless and widows in their affliction [that's the mercifulness of the fifth Beatitude], and to keep himself unspotted from the world [that's the purity of heart of the sixth Beatitude]" (James 1:27). Here the word "pure" is the same as that in the sixth Beatitude. Mercifulness is followed by self-examination and the discovery of need for further purification. Recognizing the sin of others and showing mercy toward them must be followed by the recognition of our own sin and the desire to be purified from it. The

Christian should not only cast his eyes around him, but also look within. Don't for one moment feel that it is only the world around that needs mercy and purification. We, too, need it, even if we are on the sixth rung of the ladder of blessedness.

Paul reminded the Corinthians, "Know ye not that the unrighteous shall not inherit the kingdom of God?" Then he named various groups and classes of unregenerate sinners, concluding: "And such were some of you; but ye are washed, but ye are sanctified, but ye are justified in the name of the Lord Jesus, and by the Spirit of our God" (I Cor. 6:9-11). While justification is implied and presupposed in the sixth Beatitude, its real meaning in sequence is that of holiness and sanctification of life. Justification is definite, instantaneous, and received in the hour of conversion; sanctification is a lifelong process in which we are continually becoming more like our Lord.

Blessedness is Godlikeness. Take that oft-quoted phrase in I John 1:7: "The blood of Jesus Christ his Son cleanseth us from all sin." This has nothing to do with unbelievers. Read it in its context and you will find it deals with those in fellowship with Christ, with believers. John declares that even after we have believed we have constant need of cleansing by the blood of Jesus Christ. The present tense of the verb "cleanseth," *katharizei* in Greek, indicates continuity of action.

The Scripture is full of commands for holy living implying activity and dedication on our part. "Keep yourselves from idols"; "Be ye holy in all manner of conversation"; "Keep thyself pure"; "Purify your hearts." The flesh wants to claim us and drag us down, but the Spirit of God desires to possess us and cleanse us. How can we counteract and paralyze the power of the flesh? How can we obtain the mastery over our flesh? How is this experience of purity to be gained? It is a refining process from within accomplished by the Holy Spirit. "Work out your own salvation with fear and trembling, For it is God which worketh in you both to will and to do of his good pleasure" (Phil. 2:12, 13). In the constant working out of our salvation we need constant purification by the blood of Christ. The purer we are the more blessed we are, and the clearer we can see God.

A woman from Berne, Switzerland, tells us this story of her country's flower, the edelweiss. The very name of this plant is a story in itself. Edelweiss is a compound word, which in the German means "noble and white." It is a small perennial herb of the aster family, whose pure white blossom must be sought after, since it nestles in the highest snowy crags of the Alps. It is so absolutely white that it blends perfectly with its environment, losing its identifying characteristics completely in its surroundings. Even when picked and pressed in paper for preservation, it remains free from discoloration for many years. If we would be like the edelweiss, we must keep ourselves pure and noble, striving to attain the heights with God. Then, as He keeps us pure in heart and motive, He will enable us to accept with humility the loss of our own status in the scope of His larger landscape.

THE BLESSINGS THAT RESULT
FROM PURITY OF HEART

Adam was pure. It was at the point of his purity that Satan attacked him. When he fell, thus losing his purity of heart, he became Satan's ally. Satan consorts with the impure, inspiring their actions, but he never ceases to attack the pure. His activity is felt both by the pure and the impure. For the first, his presence means war; for the second it means a friendly alliance.

As God is called the Father of mercies, so the devil is called the father of lies. He was first known as Lucifer, an angel of light; but through pride and rebellion against God became the Prince of Darkness, who by his lies induced one-third of the angels to rebel also. He deceived Eve in the Garden, and she in turn involved Adam in her deception. Satan was once called the "son of the morning" (Isa. 14:12), but Peter referred to him as "a roaring lion," who "walketh about, seeking whom he may devour," and cautioned Christians to resist him, "stedfast in the faith" (I Pet. 5:8, 9).

No heart is so pure that sinful thoughts do not occasionally arise in it. The purer the heart, the fiercer Satan's assault. The choicest fruit in the garden is always the first to be insect-stung. The wasp invariably samples the ripest and most beautiful fruit. It is always the purest heart that is the target of the first line of attack of sin, Satan, and the world.

In the Korean impasse, which was never officially termed a "war," the Eighth United States Army and the North Korean Communists ravaged the city of Seoul three times. It was a battle of wits as well as of arms, because the American soldiers were thousands of miles from the source of their ammunition supply. At the outset of the conflict, they had to be ready to fight, to dig in and hide, or to retreat, if ordered. The very word "retreat" has always had a shameful connotation on the battlefield, so the generals and colonels chose to call it "a strategic withdrawal." Sometimes, when the battle against sin and Satan becomes hot in the Christian's life, discretion is the better part of valor, and a hasty retreat to the place of prayer is not only indicated but wise.

These satanic attacks should in no way frighten or discourage us. It is in this way that our original purity is tested and demonstrated. How can the strength of a warrior be shown if he is not attacked and proven victorious over his adversary? Because the heart is assailed by sin, or even touched by it, or inadvertently a sinful thought finds lodgment in it, you need not conclude that you are not a child of God. The evidence of your sonship lies in resistance to this alien evil. Thrust out the impure thought that, if cherished, will ultimately attain domination and carry soul, body, and spirit with it.

Thomas a Kempis has said, "First there comes to the mind a bare thought of evil, then a strong imagination thereof, afterward delight and evil motion, and then consent." His advice was, "Withstand the beginnings." If you apply a magnet to the end of a needle that moves freely on its pivot, the needle affected by a strong attraction approaches as if it loved it. Reverse the order, applying the magnet to the other pole, and the needle shrinks away trembling as if it hated it. One man rushes into the arms of vice; another recoils from it in horror. According as the nature it addresses is holy or unholy, temptation attracts or repels, is loved or hated. Our Lord Jesus said, "Watch and pray, that ye enter not into temptation: the spirit indeed is willing, but the flesh is weak" (Matt. 26:41).

The pure-hearted are blessed in that they are not deluded into thinking that Satan will never bother them. They are not caught in a state of unpreparedness. To be unaware that you have enemies all the while you are really living in their midst and feeling their onslaughts is dangerous self-deception. The blessedness of the pure in heart is in the knowledge that their purity is under attack. Under what delusion India lived when she was attacked by Communist China! She was unprepared. A heart that is swept and purified never puts away the broom. Although Peter's body was washed, it was necessary for him to have his feet washed also.

This is the kind of cleansing to which James refers when he commands, "Cleanse your hands, ye sinners: and purify your hearts, ye double-minded" (James 4:8). Note that the previous verse tells us of the attacks of the devil and what a Christian should do. "Resist the devil, and he will flee from you." This is the purification of prevention. If the devil were permitted to come in, he would defile the heart. "An ounce of prevention is worth a pound of cure." If you can chase Satan away before he gains entrance, you will save yourself a lot of grief. The least contact with your heart will mean defilement. The pure in heart are blessed, then, in that they are ready to resist the devil, for they are not ignorant of his devices. They are cheered and fortified by this promise: "Greater is he that is in you, than he that is in the world" (I John 4:4).

Furthermore, their blessedness is characterized by a lack of pretension. The pure in heart are basically different from the hypocritical pharisees who are not pure but are trying to appear so. It is difficult to be a pretender, a play-actor. It wears you out; it robs you of your joy. When you look at yourself in the mirror, you avoid your own eyes. It is hard to face yourself alone in your room. That is why so many commit suicide. It is the final outcome of the conflict between reality and pretense.

The pure are free from such gnawing of conscience. Their deeds are a reflection of what they are. They are not suppressing their natures but living them out. They live and act as they feel and think. The hypocrite, who maintains outward appearances to achieve ulterior motives, is always on the watch, always playing an artificial, strained, and mechanical part. Such a life is drudgery. But the person whose heart is right within has no such trouble. It is as natural for him to do justly as to breathe. It is as natural for him to follow all things that are just, honest, lovely, and of good report, as to live. He is not unduly concerned about his outer walk. He is sure it will be right if he only takes great trouble about his inner character, praying God to preserve his pure heart as His possession.

The blessedness of the pure in heart is also evidenced by the pure company he keeps, for in such company the Lord is pleased to dwell. Your blessedness in life depends to a great extent on the company you keep. Your purity will attract pure companions. Otherwise, it may be evidence that you are not pure. There is no greater evidence that you belong to God than that you hate what He hates, love what He loves. Your heart gives hospitality to all that is pure and rejects the presence of all pollution.

The blessedness of the pure in heart is characterized by the fact that to them all things are pure. This does not mean that they will consider sin pure; but all things that in themselves are innocent are to the pure in heart perfectly pure. Conversely, to the sinner, everybody is a sinner. A liar will never believe anybody, because to him all are liars. The thief will never trust anyone, because he suspects everyone. This is a negative attitude — considering everyone our enemy, seeing nothing but the blackness in individuals. The pure in heart are blessed because they can discern both the brightness and the shadows. As far as their lives are concerned, they are committed to Divine Providence.

In 1925, Betty Stam said, "Lord, I give up my own purposes and plans, all my own desires, hopes, and ambitions, and accept Thy will for my life. I give myself, my life, my all utterly to Thee, to be Thine forever. I hand over to Thy keeping all of my friendships; all the people whom I love are to take second place in my heart. Fill me and seal me with Thy Holy Spirit. Work out Thy whole will in my life, at any cost, now and forever. To me to live is Christ. Amen." Nine years later on December 8, 1934, Betty and her husband, John Stam, calmly and bravely laid down their lives for Christ when they were martyred by Chinese Communists.

The pure in heart never consider that God acts in their lives in any other way than for their ultimate good. The Christian's interest is God's interest, once his life is hid with Christ in God. As far as the pure in heart are concerned, then, their estate or the loss of it, their prosperity or their adversity, their illness or their health, all that comes into their lives, comes to them from God, is received by them as such — if prosperity, thankfully, and if adversity, endured by them patiently, for Christ's sake. (See John Cumming, *Benedictions or the Blessed Life*, John P. Jewett & Co., Boston, 1854, pp. 174-6.)

DIFFERENT WAYS OF LOOKING AT GOD

Man has three kinds of sight: physical, mental, and spiritual. Physical sight belongs to the body. Since God, in His infinity and eternity, is not bound by a body, we must exclude the possibility of seeing Him with our natural vision. Physical eyes can see only physical objects. There must always be correspondence of nature between the viewer and the object viewed.

Mental sight belongs to the scientist, the poet, the thinker. It is the sight the Apostle Paul describes in Romans 1:20, "For the invisible things of him from the creation of the world are clearly seen, being understood by the things that are made, even his eternal power and Godhead." What this means is that any thinking man can look upon material things and perceive the invisible mind that made them. Behind every table is a carpenter. The carpenter is just as real as the table. To "see" the thought that went into making the table, you must be a thinking being.

But not all men who can perceive thought behind matter see God. The word "Godhead" in Romans 1:20 is a mistranslation of the Greek world *theiotees*, which means "divinity" or "something pertaining to the divine." It refers only to the attributes of God and not to His total personality. "Godhead" in Greek is *theotees*, as in Colossians 2:9, "For in him dwelleth all the fulness of the Godhead bodily." In Christ, and in Him alone, were the personality and nature of God revealed to man. Christ did not come to reveal that which could be seen in nature and the created world. His revelation was not a duplication, but a completion, of what God wanted to show man.

Beyond the mind is the heart, or spiritual sight. It is with the heart that we can see God as He reveals Himself in His Son. With the mind we can see only that He must be, and that He must be omnipotent, omniscient, and good. But we can never look into His inner being and know the thoughts and purposes behind His manifestations.

In the natural man, this spiritual sight has been lost because of sin. Adam had spiritual sight by nature. That is why he could see, hear, and speak with God. In the blessed man, this sight is restored by grace, for the sake of Christ. With our minds we see the *theiotees*, divine attributes, of God through the created world around us; but with our regenerated, enlivened spirits we see the *theotees*, or fullness, of God. The one is a matter of inference, because it is the product of imagination; the other is a matter of knowing, because it is a matter of revelation. We receive this spiritual sight by faith in the person and work of the Lord Jesus Christ, who said, "Oh, the blessedness of those who can see God because their hearts have been made pure because of Me!" Christ "gave himself for us that he might... purify unto himself a peculiar people" (Titus 2:14), that is, that He might make us pure in heart.

There are some things of whose existence we are satisfied but which have never revealed themselves to physical perception. For instance, who has ever seen what we call truth? Who has ever looked on love? Who has touched the quality of justice, or tasted of righteousness? If physicists have been occupied with the search after God, they might as well have sought to dissect a mother's love under a microscope. Such qualities, in which none of us can fail to believe, are not to be detected by the keenest physical vision, nor can they be subjected to the most delicate forms of chemical analysis.

Since the world began, no one has ever seen or handled a single emotion of the human heart.

If God is the source of those spiritual qualities to which we give the names righteousness, truth, goodness, purity, justice, and love – and the perfect combination of these in His character – then we cannot expect to see God any more than we can expect to behold such qualities elsewhere. If, when we think of them as being present in a human character, we realize we cannot see them with our bodily eyes, let us not expect to see them as they are contained in perfect measure in God. And should it be pointed out that we cannot see these qualities as they are possessed by a human being, yet we can look upon their possessor, our reply is that the Possessor in this instance is a Spirit. It is only through the spiritual faculty that we are able to apprehend the spiritual God. The power which we have for reverence, adoration, praise, all that we mean indeed by worship; desire, sympathy, compliance, wish, all that is involved in love; these we are to cherish because we are spiritual beings. Our bodies can neither worship nor love; they can only become the medium for the expression of the feelings that dwell within the spirit.

The impure in heart do have a certain vision of God. but it contains no blessedness. It is full of terror. The impure in heart apprehend God, and in this they may be said to see Him; but not having become His children, they view Him as a God of wrath. Two classes of people confess to the existence of God: those who see Him as responsible for all the evil in the world and those who see Him as the cause of all that is good. The first group is a guilty group. Their guilt is written in the very depths of their soul and is responsible for their blurred sight of God.

A criminal, knowing he is guilty, greatly fears the

470

judge before whom he must appear. Is this the fault of the judge or the criminal? An innocent man is not afraid. He will appear before any judge without hesitation. The judge is his friend, not his enemy. Thus, the person who has been forgiven by Christ and has become pure in heart does not fear God in a slavish manner. He appears before Him boldly, knocks at His door, communes with Him knowing that God is his friend, not his enemy. His guilt of sin has been taken by Christ on Calvary's cross. The sixth Beatitude does not deny that there is a way in which the impure can see God, though it be unwillingly and inevitably. They fear Him, and with reason. "Blessed are the pure in heart: for they shall see God." If this Beatitude had merely said, "The pure in heart shall see God," it would have excluded the impure from any sight of God. But their sight of Him is not blessed. It is no blessing to the criminal when he sees the judge. It is a calamity, a curse. Blessedness from the sight of God comes only to the pure in heart.

We know from the Scriptures that the impure in heart will see God in the world to come. A day is coming in which they will call upon "the mountains and rocks, Fall on us, and hide us from the face of him that sitteth on the throne" (Rev. 6:16). "Every eye shall see him, and they also which pierced him: and all kindreds of the earth shall wail because of him" (Rev. 1:7). Of these things to come upon them, the impure have some premonition.

The sight of God here and hereafter is for all men. But the holy man sees Him as a holy God. The guilty sinner sees Him as an avenging monster. Both see Him. And to each He is and will be what He is thought of. But He is not responsible for being a lamb to one and a lion to the other. God is to us what we choose Him to be. The judge appears good to the innocent and bad to the guilty. But his apparent goodness or badness depends on what the person who stands before him is.

Two persons stand together on a mountain top. Widely and gloriously the view stretches out across a valley to the distant hills. The lights and the shadows reflect the hues of the overarching sky. A stream runs peacefully down the valley overhung by trees; the hills are bathed in glowing sunlight and wrapped with tender shadows; the air is musical with the songs of birds. All nature bursts with joy. To the one beholder the scene ministers rich and unspeakable enjoyment, to the other only a commonplace sensation that would arise as quickly in a city square or a reedy marsh.

At the Grand Canyon, a guide took a group of tourists to the southern rim. Among the sightseers were an artist, a minister, and a cowboy. After they had beheld the spectacle for a few moments, the guide asked the artist, "Could you paint a picture like that?" "Never!" the artist replied. "Only God could make that scene." The guide then turned to the minister. "Could you describe such grandeur in a sermon, Pastor?" The minister shook his head. "No, sir. Such majesty defies mortal description." Finally he turned to the cowboy. "And what do you think about this Grand Canyon, partner?" The cowboy answered in wonderment, "I was just thinking — what an awful place to lose a cow!"

When Christ was here on earth, He was to many only a Jewish rabbi, to some a deluded fanatic, and to others a son of Belial. A few welcomed His presence and rejoiced at His words. Some confessed, "Thou art the Christ, the Son of the living God." In every age man has apprehended God, but only according to the condition of his spiritual nature. The moral discipline of Christian life ought to be one life-long education of the heart in

472

this faculty that appreciates God, this power of seeing goodness with thorough love and enjoyment. Throughout life, however, we continue to be no better judges of the Divine than the little child of a great father. Something we can see: His kindliness to ourselves; His condescension; His readiness to pardon; His bounty in bestowal; these paternal features as they appear in His treatment of us in Jesus Christ. And this much, when seen by the lowly saint, is quite enough to ravish him with admiration and affection for the Father who is in heaven. But God is vastly more and greater. These qualities themselves, which lie on that side of His nature that He has been pleased to turn toward earth, have a superlativeness about them which we now want width or insight of vision to measure; while above and beyond them lie perfections of a more awful magnificence, of which we here learn the names and little more. What can the best of saints be said to see of the divine holiness, or the divine wrath, or the divine peace, or the divine unchangeableness, or the divine complacency, or the divine interchange of love betwixt the persons, or that divine joy that we call the blessedness of God? What little children are we to have a Father so sublime! How unfit to discern, what He is at no pains to conceal, the lofty and awful parts of His infinite nature! The earth is full of His goodness; but to see His glory we must wait for heaven.

SEEING GOD IN THE HEREAFTER

"Blessed are the pure in heart: for they shall see God." We have seen that the sight of God is possible only through spiritual perception. We see Him with our Spirit as the infinite and eternal Spirit.

But in Scripture we find a differentiation between the quality of sight in this world and the world to come. Our spirits are now in prison. Our vision is somewhat darkened. The material world in which we live hinders our free sight of the full excellency and majesty of God. As Paul says in I Corinthians 13:12, "For now we see through a glass, darkly; but then face to face: now I know in part; but then shall I know even as also I am known." This is the great Apostle speaking whose experiences of the sight of God were probably unsurpassed. He it was who saw God manifested especially and uniquely to him as he traveled the road to Damascus. Later, as Paul was giving his defense before King Agrippa, he told of what Christ had said to him on that occasion. "I am Jesus whom thou persecutest. But rise, and stand upon thy feet: for I have appeared unto thee for this purpose, to make thee a minister and a witness both of these things which thou hast seen, and of those things in the which I will appear unto thee." Paul saw the Lord Jesus after the resurrection. But the Lord told him He would appear to him again. To this unusual man of God, Paul, was given a further sight of God, possibly in the metaphysical realm, as he describes it in II Corinthians 12:2-5: "I knew a man in Christ above fourteen years ago, (whether in the body, I cannot tell; or whether out of the body, I cannot tell: God knoweth;)

... how that he was caught up into paradise, and heard unspeakable words, which it is not lawful for a man to utter. Of such an one will I glory."

It is apparent, then, that the sight of God in this world is limited for the pure in heart because of the material body in which their spirits are imprisoned, and that there will be a full and clear sight of God in the world to come, the metaphysical world, which is shrouded in mystery. The Lord has revealed all that our limited minds can possibly understand. An earthly father knows much more about the mysteries of the natural world than his child can absorb. But the manifestation of his knowledge is limited by the capacity of his child to comprehend. Our spiritual capacities as the human children of God are far less than the natural capacities of our own children. With what language could God possibly describe heaven and its glory, the manner of our life after our spirits are freed from their bodily prisons? Actually, the Lord has to describe the spiritual glories of the world to come in terms pertinent to our physical understanding. Paul says in II Corinthians 3:18, "But we all, with open face beholding as in a glass the glory of the Lord, are changed into the same image from glory to glory even as by the Spirit of the Lord." And in Colossians 3:4, "When Christ, who is our life, shall appear, then shall ye also appear with him in glory."

A Christian military officer, who visited the bedside of a dying soldier under his command, said to him, "I am going to ask you a strange question. Suppose you could carry your sins with you to heaven — would that satisfy you?" The poor dying lad replied, "Why, sir, what kind of heaven would that be to me? I would be just like a pig in a parlor!" He was awakened to a sense of his lost state, "And," the officer concluded, "he was panting after a heaven of holiness, and was convinced if he died in his sin he would be quite out of his element in such a place of purity."

The Beatitudes have their partial fulfillment in this world, but their ultimate fulfillment is in the world to come. The full kingship of the Lord is not known down here, nor His full comfort, nor the full inheritance and enjoyment of life and this earth, nor shall we ever have enough of Christ and His righteousness but in the world to come. The full measure of His mercy will be known later. And so will the full vision of Him. After all, there was some truth in the belief of the ancient Greeks that the *makares,* "the blessed ones," were in the next world and not in this. Heaven is the place of the really and ultimately blessed. This is an indisputable truth of Scripture as well. As Oswald Dykes says, "The perfection of spiritual vision – the sight which supersedes faith, drowns conjecture, and sweeps up doubt in certainty – is kept for the place of the blessed. This deepest and sweetest of Christ's Beatitudes seized the souls of His two noblest scholars. Paul and John alike found in it their ultimate expression for the enraptured communion of the perfected state."

To see "face to face" is the expression of Paul, and to "see him as he is" the way John expresses it. The apostle of ardent logic and the apostle of devout contemplation meet in words like these. Further can neither go than to stand with absorbed, self-forgetting, passively silent ecstasy, gazing forever into that celestial Countenance whose perfection transcends description. Here are mingled the majesty and sweetness of the "King eternal, immortal, invisible, the only wise God." The promise of this vision has passed from Scripture into the most sacred speech of every Christian age; the hope of it is the last longing of the deepest Chistian hearts. To

476

Chrysostom, to Origen, to Augustine, to Dante, to Aquinas, to Bernard, to Calvin, to Bunyan, to all the saints of God, the beatific vision of God has equally meant the perfection of immediate knowledge and the perfection of spiritual rapture. Higher than this desire cannot rise; further than this created capacity cannot go. Nothing sweeter, nothing loftier, nothing more heavenly can heart devise or tongue frame, than to be deemed worthy of that honor of which Jesus spoke when He prayed "That they ... be with me where I am; that they may behold my glory which thou hast given me" (John 17:24).

In all its stages, whether as begun now or as hereafter consummated, this vision of God is a moral act, made possible by the moral condition of the man. It is the act of a soul. Here at least, and in this life, no bodily sight even of the man Jesus is permitted; and supposing that, with resurrection organs, the saints should hereafter behold the resurrection body of Jesus, that by itself would be in no true sense a vision of God. "God is a Spirit," and it is spiritually He must be seen or known. Even Christ we know no more, as St. Paul says, "after the flesh." The invisible Godhead is not to be beheld through material media. It offers nothing of which organs of sense can give us proof. (See *The Beatitudes of the Kingdom*, by J. Oswald Dykes, pp. 121-3.)

The benediction, then, is not only for the present; it is especially in the future. The present benediction is the earnest and foretaste of the harvest of full benediction that is to come. Such, it is said, "shall see God." "Faith," we are told, "is the substance of things hoped for, the evidence of things not seen" (Heb. 11:1). "Faith ... worketh by love," says Paul, and adds that it purifieth the heart. There is the evidence of what the world doesn't see; for God no man hath seen or can see, but all shall see Him perfectly and fully in the life to come. (See *Benedictions or the Blessed Life*, by Rev. John Cumming, pp. 176-7.)

All that we can see of God now is mixed with imperfections, clouds, and shadows. When astronomers look at the sun, through a telescope, they are obliged to look through smoked glass because the intense splendor of the noonday sun would destroy the eye that gazed upon it. At present, we cannot see God as He is; we must look through a glass darkly. But a day comes when the glass will be broken and the smoke shall be removed and we shall see God no longer through darkened or shaded glass, but face to face. Then our purity of heart will be so perfect that we shall be able to gaze upon the noonday splendor of that unsetting Sun and to continue to gaze on Him with perfect joy, peace, and repose. This sight of God which we shall enjoy in the future will prove a transforming one. How expressive is that thought, "We shall be like him." Why? Because "we shall see him as he is." Our justification is complete and needs no augmentation, but our inner character is progressive and, in many of us, it is far, far short of what it should be. But when we reach the gloryland from which no traveler returns, when we appear in the presence of God, the first flash of the unutterable glory will transform by its touch our imperfect character into perfection, and we who have been advancing slowly and with staggering steps toward Christ's likeness here below shall then and there be transformed in the twinkling of an eye into His perfect image. "We shall be like him; for we shall see him as he is" (I John 3:2).

Suppose we could view, on some brilliant moonlit night, the Parthenon in all its flawless symmetry, as beautiful in its perfection as it was in the days of conquering Greece. Surely that would be glorious in a small way; but what a poor simile this is to illustrate the transformation that awaits our vision when we shall go hence! Here we have been picking up fragmentary ideas of God, distorted, exaggerated in one way and shrunk in another. We have hardly been able to put them together, such is the low state of human character in this world; but what will our conception of Him be when we shall see Him as He is!

This sight will be perfectly satisfying. There is no satisfaction, everybody knows, to be gotten upon earth. There is no one attainment upon earth so complete that it will fill the almost infinite capacity of man's soul. It is the proof of man's fall that he gropes for satisfaction upon earth; it is the proof of man's grandeur that he can never find it. Nothing earthly can fill the vast capacities of that great soul which is in the very poorest, lowliest, and humblest of mankind. The Psalmist makes the distinction very beautiful: "Whom have I in heaven but thee?" (Ps. 73:25). Earth is the place of desire; heaven is the place of having or perfect possession. The Psalmist says prophetically, as if he had caught in all their fullness the rays of the future glory, "I shall be satisfied, when I awake, with thy likeness" (Ps. 17:15). What a blessed thought it is that those yearnings after perfection that every Christian is conscious of, those desires and longings after a beauty, a glory, and a repose that grow upon no earthly tree and are thrown out by no earthly fountain, shall all be satisfied and fully met where there is no more want, and therefore no more prayer, but full having, and therefore everlasting praise.

When we shall see God as He is, it will be a joyful sight. "We shall enter into joy." "In thy presence is fulness of joy; at thy right hand there are pleasures for evermore" (Ps. 16:11). May it be true of us, "Whom having not seen, ye love; in whom, though now ye see him not, yet believing, ye rejoice with joy unspeakable and full of glory" (I Pet. 1:8). If the ebb tide of our joy be so rich, what shall the rising tide be? If the earnest be so delightful, what shall the full harvest be? The pure in heart are blessed indeed by and from what they are able to see now. Blessed especially are the pure in heart because they shall see God in all His glory; in the light of God all things, the mere surface of which we see now, the very essence and hidden excellence and latent beauty of which we shall see then as clearly as we are now seen." (See *Benedictions or the Blessed Life,* pp. 132-5.)

Isaiah describes the glory of the New Jerusalem which John the beloved echoes in the Revelation, "And an highway shall be there, and a way, and it shall be called The way of holiness; the unclean shall not pass over it . . . but the redeemed shall walk there: and the ransomed of the Lord shall return and come to Zion with songs and everlasting joy upon their heads: they shall obtain joy and gladness, and sorrow and sighing shall flee away" (Isa. 35:8-10).

"And his servants shall serve him: and they shall see his face; and his name shall be in their foreheads" (Rev. 22:3,4).

SEEING GOD IN THE MANIFESTATIONS OF LIFE

Not all people can see God in the various manifestations of life. Two men looking at the same person may make two quite dissimilar observations; they may form two varying opinions; but their judgments will reflect their differing viewpoints. When Thomas Edison was a young man in school in Ohio, his teacher said he'd never amount to anything because, seemingly, he could learn only science and mathematics. He couldn't pass his other subjects because he wasn't interested in them. The poor fellow nearly despaired when his teacher, at wit's end, recommended his expulsion. He knew he was slow in English and history, but he was sure he WAS going to amount to something in spite of it. This young man, as everybody now knows, was a genius, an electrical wizard, a pioneer inventor, who helped make America's standard of living what it is today.

Thus it is with men's opinions and observations of God as He is manifested in everyday life. The same rain that brings a wealth of verdure and life-giving moisture to crops in arid lands floods already oversoaked ground somewhere else. The same sun that liquefies paraffin wax also makes bricks of clay. The end result of the product depends upon the quality of its composition, for the same trial that melts and molds one heart into a likeness of Christ embitters and hardens another.

It takes purity of heart to see God in our lives and the purity of His intentions in the way that He acts toward us. The pure in heart can see God in life's trials. What consolation it is to see God in the hurricane that sweeps away all the property that our industry has amassed! What comfort it is to see Him in that sickness that befalls us, in that sorrow that breaks our heart, in the storm whose waves and billows pass over us! It is real consolation to recognize that these are from the Father; are chastisement, not judgment; not penal, but paternal; and are working for our good and His glory. "Now no chastening for the present seemeth to be joyous, but grievous: nevertheless afterward it yieldeth the peaceable fruit of righteousness unto them which are exercised thereby" (Heb. 12:11). Thus the pure in heart see that affliction is a purifying agent of the Father in heaven.

Jeremiah, often referred to as "the weeping prophet of Israel," found comfort in affliction. In the third chapter of his Lamentations we read, "The Lord will not cast off for ever: but though he cause grief, yet will he have compassion according to the multitude of his mercies. For he doth not afflict willingly nor grieve the children of men." (vv. 31-33.)

The pure in heart also see God in life's prosperity. It is often more difficult to see God in prosperity than in adversity. It is a strange fact that, when God smites, we see and recognize His hand, but when He blesses, we are prone to take the credit to ourselves. The pure in heart see God in their trials and are prayerful and patient. They see God also in the sunshine of their prosperity, thank Him, and give Him all the glory. They are not like the rich and selfish farmer, about whom our Lord taught, who had "much goods laid up for many years." We hear no word of praise to God from this man whom God had favored with prosperity. Instead, he said, "What shall I do, because I have no room where to bestow my fruits? ... I will pull down my barns and build greater ... And I will say to my soul, Soul, thou hast much goods laid up for many years; take thine ease, eat, drink, and be merry." But he was deluded by his affluence, for God said, "Thou fool, this night thy soul shall be required of thee: then whose shall those things be?" (See Luke 12:15-21.)

The pure in heart see God in all His providential dealings. They have left the region of chance where all is chaos because all is accident. They have entered the region of order, where God is working out His grand designs, often by means inexplicable to us but nevertheless successful because wielded by Him. Paul said in Romans 8:18, "For I reckon that the sufferings of this present time are not worthy to be compared with the glory which shall be revealed in us." And again in verses 28 and 29, "And we know that all things work together for good to them that love God, to them who are the called according to his purpose. For whom he did foreknow, he also did predestinate to be conformed to the image of his Son." To make us like Christ, that we may act in harmony with Christ, is the grandest of all His grand designs!

Let us never forget the contrasting meaning of the two basic words, "happiness" and "blessedness." Happiness results from favorable circumstances — luck, if you want to call it that. Blessedness (makariotees) is the work of God in our own hearts, so that we interpret the circumstances of life as God intends them to act upon us. The happy person is a circumstance-conditioned person; the blessed person is a God-conditioned person. The happy man sees favorable conditions as the result of his own ingenuity, but a blessed person sees the circumstances of life, whatever they may be, as God's divine provision.

The pure in heart also see God in all creation. When they gaze upon the varied magnificence and beauties of the countryside, they revel in the knowledge that the Father made them all. The tendency of the scientist is to investigate nature, and stop after he has discovered her laws. The natural man who is not a scientist looks at nature and admires her charms. The pure-hearted Christian, with clear vision and clean life, will see God in the least, as well as the loftiest, thing. In the wall-clinging herb, in the centuries-old tree, in the soaring butterfly, in the sporting leviathan of the deep, in all things minute or great, in all heights and depths, he will trace the workmanship and see the footprints of the Heavenly Father, and give Him the praise as the Creator and Governor of all. He can say with the poet:

> This is my Father's world,
> And to my listening ears
> All Nature sings, and 'round me rings
> The music of the spheres.
> This is my Father's world;
> I rest me in the thought
> Of rocks, and trees,
> And skies, and seas;
> His hand the wonders wrought.
>
> This is my Father's world;
> The birds their carols raise.
> The morning light, the lily white,
> Declare their Maker's praise.
> This is my Father's world;
> He shines in all that's fair.
> Through the rustling grass
> I hear Him pass;
> He speaks to me everywhere.

The pure in heart will also see God especially and

primarily in the Sacred Page. When the natural man opens the Bible, he may read Paul's writing, but the Christian sees through the veil and reads God's mind. When the natural man opens the Bible, he finds eloquence, poetry, history. But the Christian penetrates the outer wrapping and sees and hears God. Standing in the Rock, he beholds all God's glory sweeping past him. As with Moses on the sacred mount when the Lord passed by before him, he proclaims, "The Lord God, merciful and gracious, longsuffering, and abundant in goodness and truth, keeping mercy for thousands, forgiving iniquity" (Exod. 34:6, 7).

Wherever there is purity of heart, the believer will see God in this life. In order to appreciate character in another, there must be a corresponding integrity in one's own life. Only a truly benevolent man can appreciate a charitable benefactor; only a patriot can understand another's patriotism. Only one who possesses a pure heart can see and value purity in his fellow. Only purity of heart can envision a pure and holy God. (See *Benedictions or the Blessed Life*, by Rev. John Cumming, pp. 177-81.)

THE PEACE THAT IS BORN
OF PURITY OF HEART

Blessedness, the dwelling of God within the human heart, is the natural outcome of fulfilling certain conditions. The peace of God that follows is the crowning experience of man's obedience to Him. Christ's commandments to us, as found in the Beatitudes recorded by Matthew, are humility, sorrow, meekness, hunger and thirst for Christ's righteousness, mercifulness, purity of heart, peacemaking. These qualities, though not perceptible to our physical senses, are nonetheless real, for they pertain to that which is the basis of all physical reality, that unfathomable part of the self called spirit or soul.

Six of these seven spiritual qualities can be set in pairs — three on each side of the central Beatitude that enjoins spiritual hunger and thirst.

Humility and meekness go together. He who humbles himself in spirit will receive such an abundance of God's mercy that he cannot help but share it with others. The helpless, who have recognized their inability to save themselves and sought Christ's mercy, cannot help sharing the mercy received with others.

Sorrow goes with purity of heart. Sorrow is the outcome of recognizing our sinful estate, at which point God steps in to cleanse us and to continue cleansing us. The fire of sorrow purifies the heart and life.

Meekness goes with peacemaking. Without meekness we cannot be peacemakers. Meekness in no way implies compromise with evil, the adoption of evil for the sake of superficial tranquillity, but a demonstration of anger against evil in order to bring it into harmony with good. The meek in Christ are the only ones who enjoy the real peace of God, the smile of God's approval for their submission to all that is divine and their reproof of all that is sinful. The meek have much in common with the peacemakers. Thus, in considering the seventh Beatitude, in Matthew 5:9, we must examine it in relation to its companion Beatitude in verse 5, "Blessed are the meek: for they shall inherit the earth." Peacemaking is inseparably linked to meekness.

In our detailed study of meekness, we saw that it has an active and a passive aspect. Actively, meekness is anger at sin, either in our own lives or the lives of others, always with an unselfish motive. After we have registered our strong objection to sin, and implemented it by whatever action God shows us to be necessary, we have fulfilled the active aspect of meekness. Passive meekness is the joyful acceptance of God's will for our lives. Meekness, therefore, is characterized by war and peace — war with evil and peace with God. It is to proclaim God's demand for holiness, and to accept the price of maintaining holiness in the midst of sin.

Dean Church once sat in the audience at an evangelistic campaign. After the service, the evangelist went to different people in the audience and asked them the rather pointed question, "Have you found peace?" Coming to Dean Church, he asked the same question, to which the Dean replied bluntly, "No, I have found war!" Which of these men was right? The answer is, they were both right.

Peacemaking, too, consists of war and peace — outward objection and inner subjection. This is basic to our understanding of the seventh Beatitude. Peace is not toleration of evil and consent to sin. That would be equivalent to covering a sore instead of healing it. The

487

very word peace speaks of war. It is the end-product of war, the prevalence of good over evil, the reign of God in man's heart and life. But the Christian must wage the right kind of war in order to bring about the right kind of peace. It should not be the kind of peace that is temporarily gained by false meekness. In the great battle of life, there are some men who remain withdrawn from the fierceness of the struggle, in a retired and sheltered part of the field. They think this proves them to be meek, but it is quite possible that it may only prove them to be cowardly; for there is a false meekness that consists in submitting to be driven because we have not the courage to drive. Edmund Burke has said, "For evil to triumph, it is only necessary for good men to do nothing." Our Christian warfare must be motivated altruistically and not selfishly; and then peace will be so abundant in our own hearts and lives that it will become contagious in the lives of others.

In the spring of the year 372, a young man in great distress of mind flung himself on the ground and burst into tears. The sins of his youth weighed heavily on his soul. Overhearing a chance conversation from a neighboring house, he was led to read the thirteenth chapter of Romans, and as a result was gloriously converted. In the language of Gaussen, "Jesus had conquered; and the grand career of Augustine, the holiest of the fathers, then commenced. A passage of God's Word had kindled that glorious luminary, which was to enlighten the Church for ten centuries . . . even to this present day. After thirty-one years of revolt, of combats, of falls, of misery; faith, life, eternal peace, came to this erring soul; a new day, an eternal day, came upon it."

As we look at the command to be peacemakers, we see that an understanding of the word "peace" is central to our discussion. First let us note its meaning in context.

This Beatitude follows immediately after that relating to the pure in heart. The order is first purity and then peace. It is the one who is pure in heart who has peace in his soul. Peace is the natural product of forgiveness of sin, of the cleansing of man's heart by the Lord Jesus Christ. Those whose hearts are not pure have no peace within themselves and certainly cannot impart it to others. It is of this peace that results from purity that our Lord is speaking in this Beatitude, not peace as the world understands it. "Blessed are the peacemakers" does not primarily mean those who negotiate a truce between two conflicting factions, nations, or people, but those who, having experienced the peace of God as a result of forgiveness of sin, preach it to others and become the instruments in God's hands for leading others to experience the same peace. It is the peace that comes as a result, not of a compromise between opposites, but of the purification of the evil heart.

None of the qualities mentioned in the Beatitudes could be acquired by man without the supernatural intervention of God. They are God's gifts for man, the man who believes and is willing to receive them by faith. It is God alone who makes a man realize his complete helplessness and humbles him enough to call upon Christ to save and help him. It is God alone who makes a man sorry for sin. The natural man never considers sorrow a blessing. God alone can make it that. And God alone motivates man to fight against sin and at the same time to resign himself to God's will, to be meek. Man in his natural state does not hunger for the righteousness of God. God works in a man's life by emptying him of self, humbling him, purifying him in the flames of sorrow, and teaching him to conduct his Christian warfare in a spirit of meekness.

There is a calm the poor in spirit know,
That softens sorrow and that sweetens woe.
There is a peace that dwells within the breast,
When all without is stormy and distressed.
There is a light that gilds the darkest hour,
When dangers thicken and when tempests lower.
That calm, to faith and hope and love is given;
That peace remains when all beside is riven;
That light shines down to man direct from heaven.

As a result of all this, man longs to be filled with
something other than self; he desires the righteousness
of Christ. The overflow of that filling is mercy for
others. But in sharing the purifying mercy we have
received from God, we do not become impoverished and
impure ourselves. The more mercy we share with others
the more we experience and the purer we become in
heart. It is the constant and abundant flowing of God's
mercy through us that helps to keep us clean and pure.
A person who keeps God's gifts to himself will lack
purity of heart.

On a farm in New York State is a pond and a little
brook. When I last saw them, it was in the rainy season,
and both were full to the brim of clean, pure water. It
is in the dry season that the difference in their natures
shows up. The stream, constantly on the go to water the
banks all along its course, still keeps pure and sparkling,
for it continues to draw from the underground springs
at its source and to give freely as it goes along. The
pond, neither receiving nor giving, hoards its precious
moisture only to have its waters become foul and
stagnant. It is the same lesson our Lord was always
trying to teach His disciples: We gain by giving and
lose by keeping. After sharing the mercy of God and
thus maintaining and increasing our own purity, we

receive the peace of God in such abundance that it overflows to all around us.

These three Beatitudes, then, that follow the fourth Beatitude of hungering and thirsting after righteousness, may be called the Beatitudes of the abundant life. There are too many professing Christians today whose ultimate goal in life is to have enough for self. They lack the mercifulness, the shining purity of heart, and the peace-making nature of which the Saviour speaks. The enjoyment of peace and the sharing of it seem to be the pinnacle of the beatific edifice. For peace is one of the most potent and forceful things in all the world. It is infinitely alive. It is life at its highest and its best. There is a superficial view of life that leads men to associate the idea of peace with inertia and stagnation. True, a calm day, a waveless sea, grey boulders on the shore, are a parable of peace, if you understand that the hush in the air and the lull of the tide and the stillness of the rocks are the outcome of incalculable forces balanced and coordinated, an omnipotent equilibrium. All the vast powers of Nature go to the making of a perfect calm. And as it is in the world we see, so is it in that unseen world where the soul draws its breath. There is nothing so strong and tense and vital as peace. It is spiritual equilibrium. It is the balance of that soul that is in perfect harmony with the laws of its life. And there is in every life the possibility of such harmony and the duty of seeking it. (See Percy C. Ainsworth, *The Blessed Life*, Charles H. Kelly, London, 1915, pp. 145-6.)

So-called Christians whose goal begins and ends with self-satisfaction lack the abundant life, the overflowing life, of which the Saviour spoke when He said, "I am come that they might have life, and that they might have it more abundantly" (John 10:10). The sharing of the life received from Christ, the sharing of His mercy, His purity, and His peace, is an evidence of our abundant life in Him.

Madame Guyon led such an abundant Christian life. Though persecuted and imprisoned for her beliefs and teachings, she had a deeply spiritual, quietly sanctified life in Christ. During her exile from the French society of her era, she wrote this poem that has since become a hymn:

My Lord, how full of sweet content
I pass my years of banishment.
Where'er I dwell, I dwell with Thee —
In heaven, in earth, or on the sea.

I hold by nothing here below;
Appoint my journey, and I go.
Though pierced by scorn, oppressed by pride,
I feel the good — feel nought beside.

Ah, then, to His embrace repair,
My soul, thou art no stranger there;
There love divine shall be thy guard,
And peace and safety thy reward.

She concluded, "God is not only in the soul itself, constituting its true life, but is in everything else. My soul is in such a state that God permits me to say there is no dissatisfied clamor in it, no corroding sorrow, no distracting uncertainty, no pleasure of earth, and no pain which faith does not convert into pleasure; nothing but the peace of God which passes understanding, perfect peace. Nothing is of myself, but all of God."

You can lead a miserable, predominantly selfish Christian life or an abundant one. Which one is yours?

MAN'S LOST PEACE

Before we can understand what the Lord Jesus Christ meant by the term "peacemakers" in the seventh Beatitude (Matt. 5:9), it is necessary for us to understand the basic meaning of the word "peace." What is peace? We have seen that in its context in the Beatitudes it follows forgiveness of sin resulting in purity of heart.

Peace in its figurative sense signifies "harmony," and figuratively is akin in thought to the Greek *homonoia*, meaning "of the same mind." The Greek word for peace is *eireenee*, from the verb *eiroo*, basically meaning "to join together." Two things, two forces, or two individuals that agree or fit together are said to be at peace with each other.

In English, the word "peace" is derived from the Latin *pax*, "an agreement," from the root verb *pac*. The basic idea is found in our common words "compact" and "pact."

What, then, is the idea of peace? Not stagnation, not stillness, not even rest. We can have rest without peace and peace without rest. Peace in Greek thought is a joining, agreement, harmony, symphony, synthesis.

Let us take an example from the physical world. Light is peace. Look at the rainbow that is the result of storm. Its colors come from the dividing up of light into its essential and constituent rays. Merge the rays and you lose the color, but you have light, and light is peace.

Take music. You hear a soprano, a contralto, a tenor, a bass – all different voices – but when they blend there is harmony, there is peace.

493

Observe a boat as it mightily moves on the sea. That is an illustration of peace. It is the combination in unity and activity of the elements of power. There is static power, the power restraining and holding in place: there is dynamic power, the power equal to accomplishing things; there is kinetic power, the power that lies in action. The three perfectly working together produce peace.

Not stagnation, not stillness, but harmonic realization of all the meaning and mystery of being, and the expression of that meaning and mystery in the grandeur of accomplishment — that is peace.

What is peace — human peace? In the individual life it is balance, proportion, cooperation, and consequently the doing of the things that life is made to accomplish. Balance of what? Proportion in what? Cooperation between what? Let personality be considered as consisting of spirit, soul, and body; or as consisting of intelligence, volition, and emotion. Find me a man in whom these things are balanced, and I will show you a man who is at peace. That man who is cultivating his physical powers at the cost of the mental and spiritual is never at peace. That is a disproportion of personality that means war and ruin ultimately. That man who is cultivating his spiritual activities at the expense of his physical is not at peace. Find me a man in whom these things are perfectly poised, balanced, and adjusted and I will show you a man at peace. He is not a still man, not a stagnant man, not a man at rest. He is a man at peace. Social peace is the commonwealth of gifts and service, realized and yielded. This world has never yet seen it in its perfection. We have had glimpses of it, gleams of it, occasional approaches toward it, but we have never yet seen it entirely. The world came nearest to it in apostolic times in connection with the peace in the apostolic Church. Listen to the infinite music of the declaration: "No man said that aught that he had was his own. They had all things in common." That was peace. It was peace because those men discovered their capacities and gifts, and used them in the interests of their brethren. If a brother lacked something, then his fellow would supply it. In that commonwealth of gifts and service yielded there was peace. That is the only glimpse the world has yet had of what peace really means. (See G. Campbell Morgan's sermon, "The Peace of God," in *The Christian World Pulpit*, Vol. 86, pp. 233-4.)

When God created man, man was at peace with his Creator. This was not because God consented to fit His ideas and purposes with man's, for it was man who was created in the image of God, to fulfill His purposes. "So God created man in his own image, in the image of God created he him; male and female created he them" (Gen. 1:27). God stamped His nature, the imprint of His divinity, upon humanity. As long as man did not seek his independence from God, there was harmony, peace between the two. But Satan intervened between God and man, planting the unworthy thought that God was jealous of man, afraid that if man were to know the difference between good and evil experimentally he would become as great as God. Satan's object was to make man declare his independence of God. And because man believed Satan, he disobeyed the express commandment of God and has lived independently ever since – at war with God. The pact, the peace, was broken. Man no longer agreed with God. His desires were not God's desires. And the penalty was death. Death is the ultimate outcome of this war between man and God; it is the separation of man from God, which in reality is the absence of peace.

We snap the delicate, slender threads
    Of our curious lives asunder,
And then blame heaven for the tangled ends,
    And sit and grieve and wonder.

What does it take to restore this peace between God and man? St. Gregory of Nyssa said, "Peace is the harmony of satisfied union." God must be satisfied in His reunion with man, and man finds his satisfaction in his reconciliation with God. The union must be satisfying both to God and to man. But how can God be satisfied in this union? It was God who was sinned against and in consequence had to impose man's estrangement from Himself. It was man who caused the separation, but God who imposed it. How, then, can man blame his Creator for the warfare between them? This war was of man's making, not God's. "Sin," said St. Augustine, "is the variation of the will of the intelligent creature from the known will of the Creator." The punishment imposed by God is simply the natural consequence of His original law for man. It is only logical to grant the Creator the right to establish laws governing the tranquil maintenance of His creation. Law is a right and necessary thing, and the obedient will rejoice in it. However, we must recognize that laws are both beneficent and punitive. They provide for obedience and disobedience. Obedience spells peace between the creation and the Creator; disobedience means war. There is a sense, then, in which we may say that this war has its inception, not in man, but in God; for He who initiated peace also imposed war as the consequence of man's rejection of His peace.

In this matter of restoring man to God, and thus restoring God's peace in the human heart, God again took the initiative, even as He did in creation – being the beginning, the cause of all things. He sent Christ, the eternal Second Person of the Trinity, to die and thus satisfy divine justice. "He [Christ] died for all," Paul tells us (2 Cor. 5:15). In Christ's death there is sufficient satisfaction to God for the sins of all who come to Him. God descended in Christ to bring peace to the world. But the difference between His first creation and His second is that the latter is only for those who believe, those who accept it. God took the initiative in restoring peace to the world, but since only those who desire it appropriate it, we have a world at peace and a world at war. There are only two classes of people in this world, those who are still at war with God and those who have accepted God's new offer of peace with Him through Jesus Christ, His Son. To which class do you belong? If there is war and disturbance in your soul, the fault lies with you. God has done His part. You must believe. "For God so loved the world, that he gave his only begotten Son." That's God's part in the peace-making between Himself and man. "That whosoever believeth in him ... "; that's man's part, your part, the putting of your confidence in Christ's work. "Should not perish, but have everlasting life"; that is peace fully restored for time and eternity.

Thus we see that the peace of God is a gift to man as long as man bears the image of his Creator and obeys Him. In man's rejection of that peace, we have war, the consequence of man's sin. War is not a gift of God but a consequence imposed by God and brought about by man's sin. Christ came into this world to restore this original peace between God and man, as attested by the angels who proclaimed "Peace on earth" at His birth. "Glory to God in the highest, and peace on earth, in men of good belief" (literal translation of Luke 2:14; see Nestle's text.) The word is *eudokias* in the genitive in Nestle's text (*eu*, meaning "well," and *dokeoo*, meaning "think, believe") and not *eudokia* in the nominative. (Arndt and Gingrich, *A Greek-English Lexicon of the New Testament*.) This indicates that the Lord Jesus came into the world, not to bring both peace and good will among men as is commonly thought, but to bring only His peace, the reconciliation between God and man, in those who will rightly believe on Him. In this verse, only peace is spoken of as coming to earth through the birth of God's Son. This peace becomes the possession of those in whom God is satisfied. His peace is for men of good belief. If you believe well – to His satisfaction, not yours – then His peace will be your portion. Christ came to restore the lost peace of God to the hearts of men who believe. Man, by believing in Christ, is once again at peace with God, his Creator.

PEACE REGAINED

When Christ died on the cross of Calvary, His death paid the penalty of sin for all who would believe. Man, by appropriating by faith what Christ did for him, regains his status before God. His peace is restored. This regaining of status before God is what Christ meant by the new birth of which He spoke to Nicodemus in the third chapter of John. In order for man once again to have the unimpaired image of God, a process of re-creation is necessary. He must be born again. Any other expedient is mere human patchwork. The new birth restores man to God and causes God's peace to reign in man's heart once again.

This is what is troubling most people in the world today; they lack the peace of God. They look for peace everywhere except the right place, in Christ. If you want true peace, that original peace that God meant for you when He created you, you can find it only through the new birth, by believing in Christ and receiving Him as your Saviour and Lord.

In Christ's teaching, whenever He referred to peace in relation to the human heart, He meant this peace of God of which He became the source for all who believe. Only as you remember this fundamental meaning of peace — that it is the result of Christ's reconciliation of man to God — will you understand some of our Lord's paradoxical and seemingly contradictory statements.

Here is one from Matthew 10:34-36: "Think not that I am come to send peace on earth: I came not to send peace, but a sword. For I am come to set a man at variance against his father, and the daughter against her mother, and the daughter in law against her mother in law. And a man's foes shall be they of his own household." Is this the same Christ who said, "Peace I leave with you, my peace I give unto you: not as the world giveth, give I unto you. Let not your heart be troubled, neither let it be afraid"? In one place He declared that He came to bring war, and in another He promised peace. How can we reconcile these statements?

We can resolve this apparent contradiction only by remembering the basic meaning of the word "peace" as harmony or reconciliation between man and God. In the first passage, Christ was speaking to His disciples, whom He had commissioned as missionaries of the Gospel. Previously He had said to them, "Behold, I send you forth as sheep in the midst of wolves: be ye therefore wise as serpents, and harmless as doves. But beware of men: for they will deliver you up to the councils, and they will scourge you in their synagogues; and ye shall be brought before governors and kings for my sake, for a testimony against them and the Gentiles ... And the brother shall deliver up the brother to death, and the father the child: and the children shall rise up against their parents, and cause them to be put to death. And ye shall be hated of all men for my name's sake: but he that endureth to the end shall be saved" (Matt. 10:16-18, 21, 22).

There is no doubt that Christ here assumes the responsibility for this war against His disciples. While they were sinners and therefore did not rebuke the world's sin and apostasy, they were regarded as its true friends. No one will object to you as long as you agree with him. But try to interpose between people and their enjoyment of sin and you will see what happens. The war that the world (whether they be strangers or your nearest and dearest) declares against the disciples of

Christ, especially when they testify of Him, is the result of the peace of God that has come to these disciples as a result of trusting Christ.

Gregory Nazianzen said, "Do they cast us out of the city? They cannot cast us out of that which is in the heavens. If they who hate us could do this, they would be doing something real against us. So long, however. as they cannot do this, they are but pelting us with drops of water or striking us with the wind."

And Leighton observes, "All the peace and favor of the world cannot calm a troubled heart; but where the peace is that Christ gives, all the trouble and disquiet of the world cannot disturb it. Outward distress, to a mind thus at peace, is but the rattling of the hail upon the roof to him that sits within the house, at a sumptuous feast."

This is the kind of peace that the early Christians possessed when faced with martyrdom, or when brought into the arena to face the lions. They came forth from their cells with a song of praise and victory upon their lips.

Generally, when men speak of peace, they do not mean the same thing that Christ means. Though words are thoughts expressed, it is necessary to examine the mind and philosophy behind the words in order to determine their real meaning. When the world speaks of peace, it means the absence of outward disturbance, no matter what the underlying cause or motive for this state of seeming tranquillity. Most of the time such peace is a forced state of acquiescence, born, not of mutual and willing agreement, but of the fear of the consequences of open hostility. It is an ephemeral and shallow peace, akin to the docility on the surface of a volcano. The elements are seething inside, but the explosion is held in abeyance. If "peace is the harmony of satisfied union," what goes by that name in this world is merely co-existence. As long as man chooses to be independent of God, he will have to bear the resultant evils, fear and inner disturbance.

But when Christ speaks of peace, He does not refer to the acceptance of the righteous and pure man by society, but to his acceptance by God, the Author of peace. The sinful world is never satisfied with the righteous saint of God, nor is the saint of God ever able to find peace, harmony, and satisfaction in association with the world. The peace of God comes to man only when he is reconciled to God. And when he is at peace with God, he cannot help being at variance wiht those who are at war with God.

Paul, describing the armor of the Christian soldier, exhorted the Ephesian Christians to take unto themselves the whole armor of God so that they would withstand in the evil day, and to stand with their feet shod with the preparation of the gospel of peace. Even today, centuries later, we still "wrestle not against flesh and blood, but against principalities, against powers, against the rulers of the darkness of this world, against spiritual wickedness in high places" (Eph. 6:12). We not only contend *for* the faith, we contend *in* our faith, and we contend *by* our faith.

Thy hand, O Christ, is light; with sweet caressing
It leads to peace, but only through the fray.

An incident at Valley Forge in the Revolutionary War led General Lee in later years to describe General George Washington as "First in war, first in peace, and first in the hearts of his countrymen." General Washington's Colonial regulars, ill-clad, underfed, and poorly armed, were being mercilessly slaughtered in Pennsylvania. He was so sick of war, and so disheartened by the privations of his forces and the rigorous winter, that he nearly penned his resignation to the Continental Congress who had appointed him. As he walked in the woods, he was so overcome by his grievous burden that he sank to his knees in the snow and poured out his heart to Almighty God. He pleaded for strength to continue, wisdom in directing the battle, and the championship of God on behalf of his stricken men. This was the crisis, and the tide turned for the Continental forces. God had showed George Washington that peace could not come without his execution of the present struggle, but that his heart could be at peace, even in the midst of war.

THE THREE KINDS OF PEACE

The seventh Beatitude, "Blessed are the peacemakers: for they shall be called the children of God," is like the fifth, "Blessed are the merciful: for they shall obtain mercy," in that both speak of sharing God's blessings with others. In Matthew 5:9 it is peace that is shared, and in verse 7 it is mercy. This is not our own peace and mercy but the mercy and peace that we have obtained first from God through Christ.

Let us not forget the basic word "blessed" *(makarioi)* and the basic phrase "for my sake" (Matt. 5:11) in our study of the Beatitudes. We are blessed because of Christ. He brought God to us. We are blessed here and now. War may be raging around us, but this does not affect the peace of God within. In fact, it becomes more pronounced and blessed in times of outward disturbance. The peace of God is not dependent upon our circumstances but is an inner peace of the soul.

A naval officer whose ship was being buffeted by a storm was confronted by his wife, who cried out with alarm, "Oh, how can you be so calm in such a storm?" He arose and drew his sword. Pointing it at his wife's breast, he said, "Aren't you afraid?" She instantly replied, "No, of course not." "Why?" asked the officer. "Because," rejoined his wife, "I know the sword is in the hand of my husband, and you love me too much to hurt me." "Then," said he, "remember, I know in whom I have believed, and that He holds the winds in His fist and the waters in the hollow of His hand."

We do not become blessed basically because of anything we may do to settle disputes in the realm of international or national affairs, or in the fields of sociology, politics, economics, labor, etc., or even between friends. It is because we are already blessed in Christ that we can spread His peace to others. How could we possibly give to others what we ourselves do not possess? Because we are blessed, that is, indwelt by God, and have His peace in our hearts, we can share God and His peace with others. As we do this, our own blessedness increases. It is a great joy when our sins are forgiven, but it is surely just as great a joy to see God forgive others as we introduce God to them. Mercy and peace shared bring far greater joy than if we keep them to ourselves. When we share God's gifts to us, we never need fear that we shall be left with less. We either end up with more or find that we enjoy what is left far more. The life of Christian blessedness is a life of peace, not only for ourselves but for others. Our only care should be to remember that what we have to share was initially given to us by Christ. It is His peace, His mercy that we share.

As in all the other Beatitudes, the class of persons on whom the Lord pronounces His blessing (in this case, "peacemakers," *eireenopoioi)* is preceded by the definite article *hoi,* which is restrictive. It emphasizes that this is a particular class of peacemakers, those whose peace has come to them for Christ's sake and who share it for His sake. The article here emphasizes that this is a particular class of individuals who are peacemakers, distinguishing them from all other would-be peacemakers who ultimately and in reality are not lasting peacemakers. Our Lord distinguishes Christians, who are the real peacemakers, from non-Christians, who are not really peacemakers, even though they might try to be. (See A. T. Robertson's *A Grammar of the Greek New Testament,* p. 757.) This is really the benediction Christ pronounces upon His missionaries whose purpose in life is to share the peace of God with others. If you have never experienced this joy, it may be because you are hoarding Christ's blessings instead of sharing them.

When John Broadus was sixteen he accepted Christ as his Saviour and at once began to introduce others to his new-found Friend. His first convert was a school friend. These two lived most of their lives in the same city, Broadus a professor in the university, the other a truck-driver; and Broadus said that he never met the man during all those years but he touched his cap as they passed and said, "Thank you, John, thank you." "I know just what he will say when I meet him coming down the golden street of heaven," said Broadus. "It will be just what he said this morning, ' Thank you, John, thank you.' "

> 'Tis worth living for this,
> To administer bliss
> And salvation in Jesus' name.

We must be careful not to limit the "peacemaking" of which Christ speaks to the settling of wars and disputes. It refers primarily to sharing God's inner peace with others through proclaiming the Gospel.

That this Beatitude deals with a particular, restricted class of peacemakers, whose peace is God-given and unique, is confirmed by what the Lord Jesus said to His disciples in John 14:27, "Peace I leave with you, my peace I give unto you. Let not your heart be troubled, neither let it be afraid." His peace is a gift. It is far different from the material, worldly concept of peace.

What is the significance of the Eastern salutation, *Shalom*, or *Salaam*, meaning "Peace"? The very existence and frequency of such a salutation is a confession of the turbulence of the human heart and of the world in which we live. We talk about peace in times of war or when rumors of war threaten our security. Christ came into a world of intense turmoil. His Spirit has been at work for 1900 years. Yet there are far more wars today than ever before, and they are far more destructive. Men live in fear of imminent total catastrophe or news about the increased destructibility of atom warfare.

In a recent magazine symposium, young people were asked to write on what troubled them most in their growing years. A large percentage answered, "The threat of the atom bomb." In a world where school children must crouch against walls or beside desks in air-raid drills, it is no wonder that such fears loom large in their lives and in the lives of their parents.

"Peace I leave with you," said the Lord Jesus to His disciples. It was the peace that He had already bequeathed to them by reconciling them to God. His departure from them would not mean the withdrawing of that peace. His peace is not dependent upon His physical presence with us. It is a mystical inner peace that supersedes human attainment and comprehension. Have you ever observed a final leavetaking between two people who love each other? The other day I was called to the bedside of a dying Christian. There he lay in a coma, his wife standing beside him. The only evidence of life was his labored breathing. I held the wife's hand while I prayed with her. She knew that her beloved husband, with whom she had looked forward to taking a trip just two days hence to visit two little orphans whom they supported, was never going to accompany her anywhere ever again in this life. And yet she was supremely peaceful. Her peace was not one that could be stolen by the adverse circumstances of life, or even by death, the sudden death of the husband she loved so dearly. It is this kind of peace to which our Lord refers when He says, "My peace I give unto you: not as the world giveth, give I unto you." This is the peace of blessedness and not of mere happiness; it is the peace of God and not the peace of favorable circumstances. The one is permanent and rides out the inevitable storms of life; the other is temporary and sporadic, and cannot weather the gale.

What does the expression, "Not as the world giveth, give I unto you," mean? "The world" means either mankind in general or the whole external and material order of things. This is what everybody was doing and is still doing in our day, seeking peace on the horizontal level. There are three kinds of peace:

1) Peace from around us, the peace of human friendship — that which comes from others, when they treat us as we want to be treated.

2) Peace from beneath us, the peace of material possessions, which comes from having a sufficiency of this world's goods.

3) Peace from above us, the peace of God.

Our wish for peace usually involves a desire for harmony with our environment and for material possessions. This is a tragic and non-satisfying peace. It leads to destruction. When dying, Mahmoud ordered his treasures, apparel, and other badges of luxury to be brought to his chamber. He wept like a child and said, "What toils, dangers, and fatigues of body and mind the getting and keeping of these have cost me, and now I must leave them all!"

It is inconceivable that the peacemaking to which our Lord refers is the horizontal or earthly peace. It is the heavenly peace that He Himself bestows. It is a peace that transcends the limits of human love and human help. How many times in life we stand helpless

508

before some overwhelming storm. What can we do? What can we say?

A highly successful doctor and his wife had an only child, a son, whom they adored. When it came time for him to enter military service, he became an army officer. One day he was killed in a car accident. From the third floor of their apartment building, the mother saw his casket and realized that her son was dead and not merely wounded, as she had been told. In a frenzy of grief she flung herself out the window and was killed. The sorrowing father later stood between two caskets, one bearing the dead body of his son and the other of his wife. What kind of peace was missing here? Not the horizontal or earthly, for there were many friends to express their sympathy, and plenty of money to take care of the family in great comfort. But the mother could not be reconciled to life either by human or material peace. She could have withstood the shock if she had had that heavenly peace that characterizes the blessed person. Do you have that kind of peace?

SUBSTITUTES FOR PEACE

James, that Apostle of the Practical who could see through all sham and pretense, vividly distinguishes between earthly and heavenly wisdom. The former he calls "earthly, sensual, devilish," while of the latter he says, "But the wisdom that is from above is first pure, then peaceable" (James 3:15, 17). This is the seventh Beatitude according to James. After purity of heart comes peace – both characteristics of heavenly wisdom; and wisdom itself is a figurative name of Christ, as set forth in Proverbs 8.

How deep and impenetrable is the isolation in which each human soul lives! How helpless we are to share another's deepest feelings or to express all that is in our hearts to those closest to us. We wish we could see inside another's heart and soul. But God has not relinquished this prerogative. After we have experienced all the love and fellowship of others, we dwell alone on our little island in the deep, separated by "the salt, unplumbed, estranging sea," and we can do little more than hoist signals of goodwill, and now and then for a moment stretch our hands across the "echoing straits between." Longfellow felt this most keenly when he wrote:

> Ships that pass in the night, and speak
> each other in passing,
> Only a signal shown and a distant voice in
> the darkness;
> So on the ocean of life we pass and speak
> one another,

Only a look and a voice, then darkness
again and a silence.

Men sigh on, not knowing what the soul wants, but
only that it needs something. Our yearnings are homesick-
ness for heaven; our sighings are for God; just as children cry themselves asleep away from home, and sob
in their slumber, knowing not they sob for their parents.
The soul's inarticulate moanings are the affections yearning for the Infinite, and having no one to tell them what
it is that ails them.

On they go, these sobbing children, crying out against
the world's injustices with a sense of personal grievance.
God has not fashioned the world to suit them, so they
refuse to play by His rules. They would rather feel
downtrodden and abused; it suits their self-pitying
natures and gives them an excuse not to have to lift
themselves up to His high level but to wallow in their
own excesses and those of the world around them. "Your
way is a hard way," they say resentfully, not realizing
that their lack of peace comes from their failure to
submit themselves willingly to a higher wisdom than
their own. "Our way is the natural and right way to
happiness — giving free expression to our natural desires
and full scope to our egos." And so we have the rebels,
who in their very defiance proclaim their lack of peace.

As F. W. Robertson says, "This disordered universe
is the picture of your own mind. We make a wilderness
by encouraging artificial wants, by creating sensitive
and selfish feelings; then we project everything stamped
with the impress of our own feelings, and we gather the
whole of creation into our pained being. 'The whole
creation groaneth and travaileth in pain together until
now.' The world you complain of as impure and wrong
is not God's world, but your world; the blight, the

511

dullness, the blank, are all your own. The light which is in you has become darkness, and therefore the light itself is dark."

Nor can outward things give real peace. The world is all for excitement. A young man hearing a sermon on interior peace said, "It's not peace we young fellows want — it's thrills." Is that how you feel? Let me tell you, there is a supernatural thrill in heavenly peace but no peace in worldly thrills. The color of heavenly peace is not a dull grey. It is brilliantly white, even in the darkest night. This is not an outside paint job, it is inlaid. Oilcloth and linoleum may both look bright and shiny, but under the stress of daily wear the cheap oilcloth soon wears out, while the inlaid linoleum gives good service for many years. The stresses of life soon show up the shoddy material of which human peace is made, but they only bring out more brilliantly the divine peace that Christ brings to our hearts.

If a physician should say to a man in a fever, "I cannot give you anything to soothe you; here is a glass of brandy for you," that would not help to allay the fever, would it? The world comes to us and says, "I cannot give you rest; but here is a sharp excitement for you, more highly spiced and titillating to your tongue than the last one, which has turned flat and stale." That is about the best it can do. And eventually man reaches the point of satiety, and everything becomes stale and profitless.

Oh, what a confession are the rush and recklessness, the fever and the fret of our century! You go about our streets and look men in the face, and you see how all manner of hungry desires and eager wishes have imprinted themselves there. And now and then — how seldom! — you come across a face out of which beams a deep and settled peace. How many of you are there that dare not be quiet because then you are most troubled? How many of you are there that dare not reflect because then you are wretched? How many of you are uncomfortable when alone, either because you are utterly vacuous, or because then you are surrounded by the ghosts of ugly thoughts that murder sleep and stuff every pillow with thorns? The world will bring you excitement; Christ, and Christ alone, will bring you rest. (See Alexander Maclaren, *The Holy of Holies*, Hodder and Stoughton, 1905, p. 142.)

Christ could not have pronounced His benediction on the sharing of a peace that is neither real nor lasting. It was His peace, that would be admired by others watching His redeemed children, that He wanted the blessed to share with the troubled souls of men.

But pleasure is only one substitute for peace. The person of a more serious turn of mind, conscious of a vacuum within, may turn to work to fill it. The scientist, the artist, the writer, the poet — even the perfectionist housewife — may seek to find satisfaction for a restless spirit in giving themselves untiringly and devotedly to their work. Again to no avail. Perfection always eludes them; someone is always above them as they seek to scale the mountain; self-doubt insinuates its unsettling question, "Of what use is all this in the end?"

A story is told by William Gilbert of how Dante, wandering one day over the mountains of Lunigiana, eventually drew nigh to a lone, secluded monastery. It was at a time when his mind was wracked with internal conflict and was seeking refuge from the strife. So he loudly knocked at the monastery gate. It was opened by a monk, who in a single glance at the wan, pale face, read its pathetic message of misery and woe. "What do you seek here?" said he. And with a gesture of despair, the poet replied, "Peace." Ah, it was the same old craving followed by the same old search. But neither the solitary places, nor the anchorite's cell ever brought true peace to the afflicted heart. It comes not from without but from within. We can have it in the winter of age or the spring of youth; in the lowly cottage or the stately castle; in distressing pain or in buoyant health. The secret of it is in comradeship with Christ. You can have peace in the midst of the storm, if you have Christ. He is the shelter from the tempest, the soul's haven of rest. If we have learned to value His friendship, we have mastered the secret of the "peace which passeth all understanding."

Perhaps most tragic of all the substitutes for divine peace is that of a false religion. So many voices promise peace: the cults of the East, which are having a fashionable renaissance right now; the claims of one sect or another to be the road to fulfillment and peace with the Infinite; the devotion to one cause above all others that seems to promise a better and brighter world according to its self-styled prophets; and world communism, which produces a fanatical religious fervor on the part of its deluded followers. Even lip-service to the most orthodox Christian doctrine can be a delusion and a snare, for its adherents can claim to be following the truth and yet not attaining peace of heart.

Peace is not primarily in a set of beliefs, however correct. Peace lies in no organized movement, in no program for human or world betterment. Peace lies in a Person; it is His gift to all who will come unto God by Him. Commit yourself wholly to Christ, in all humility and without reservation, to do His will, and "the peace of God, which passeth all understanding, shall keep your hearts and minds through Christ Jesus."

PEACE OR A SWORD?

In Scripture we have reference to two distinct stages of the Gospel. In its first stage the Gospel comes as "a sword." "Think not that I am come to send peace on earth," said our Lord. "I came not to send peace, but a sword" (Matt. 10:34). Contrast this with Paul's designation of it as "the gospel of peace." In its second and final stage the Gospel brings "peace." And the end result? War brings sorrow, peace brings joy.

This process of war and peace in the human heart inaugurated by the same causative agent, Christ, is very clearly demonstrated in the Beatitudes. Evidences of warfare are given in the first half of each Beatitude. They are poverty of spirit or helplessness, mourning or sorrow, meekness — which is anger at sin and submission to God's will, hunger and thirst, the need of mercy all around us, the realization of our need of cleansing, the presence of strife, persecution: all conditions that bespeak war.

The second part of each Beatitude gives the product of this strife — peace. And the peace of God is what we know as the Kingdom of Heaven within us, bringing comfort, the inheritance of the earth, filling with Christ's righteousness, the greater mercifulness of God, the sight of God, being called the children of God, and the reign of God within us. All these experiences speak of the peace of God within the human soul.

It is interesting to note that the word "peacemakers" in Greek is *eireenopoioi*, a compound word derived from two Greek words: the substantive *eireenee* meaning "peace, harmony," and the verb *poieoo*, meaning "to do, to make." There is another Greek word meaning "to do, to make," the verb *prassoo*. This has to do more with the means by which an object is obtained, whereas *poieoo* brings out the object or end of the act itself. The peacemakers *(eireenopoioi)*, then, of whom our Lord speaks are not merely those who make an attempt at peace, but those who establish it. Their efforts lead to results. It is the end effect that Christ refers to. The means can be multiple as far as we, the instruments of God, are concerned. We may make peace in the hearts of men and women by the way we live, simply through our blessedness. There is great power in letting people see how calm the Christian can be in the midst of storm.

I know a very dear couple in Michigan whom I count as real friends in Christ. I've stayed in their home time and again when on preaching missions in their city. The wife was saved first, and the peace of God came into her life. But her husband resisted the wooing of God's Spirit. I asked him what constituted the deciding factor that finally led him to accept the Saviour. Do you know what he said? "One day I came home from work and accidentally dropped my full tool box on the rug in the living room. Not a word of complaint did my wife utter. Before she was converted, she would have raised the roof. Now she was undisturbed. She patiently and smilingly picked up the spilled tools while I stood there boiling. But that was it. I saw what Christ did to her. I took Him, too. He did the same thing to me." And I know He did, because I have never found a more patient and saintly person than he. The means of peacemaking in his life was the patience of his wife.

Then again the means may be the preaching of the Gospel, through radio, the pulpit, the printed page, a personal word of testimony — or anything else. It is not the means and their uniformity or variety that are stressed here, but that, whatever the means, God can use them effectively. This is a real encouragement to all of us, some endowed with great gifts and some with small in making the peace of God known to others. Christ reassures us that it is God who gives the end result, and not the means we employ. We are mere instruments of His peace.

A hold-up man and kidnaper was sent to prison for twelve years, and there he met Jesus Christ. While he was praying, Christ seemed to say to him, "I will come and live in you, and we will serve this sentence together," and they did. Several years later he was discharged, and just before he went out he was handed a two-page letter written by another prisoner. After the salutation, it said in effect, "You know perfectly well that when I came into this jail I despised preachers, the Bible, and everything. I went to the Bible class and the preaching service because there wasn't anything else interesting to do. Then they told me you were saved, and I said, 'There's another fellow taking the Gospel road to get a parole'; but, Roy, I've been watching you for two and a half years. You did not know it, but I watched you when you were in the yard exercising, when you were working in the shop, when you played, while we were all together at meals, on the way to our cells, and all over, and now I'm a Christian, too, because I watched you. The Saviour who saved you has saved me. You never made a slip." Roy said afterward, "When I got that letter and read it through, I broke out in a cold sweat. Think what it would have meant if I had slipped even once."
— *Sunday School Times*

The verb *poieoo* is also used in connection with the doing of miracles (see Matt. 7:22; 13:58; Acts 19:11, etc). And the peacemaking that we are entreated to engage in is nothing less than the performance of a miracle. The greatest miracle that can take place in a man's life is for him to be reconciled with his Creator, God. But we must never forget that it can take place only for the sake of Christ. It is He who speaks peace to the souls of men. You and I are merely channels. In our peacemaking we should have our eyes on neither our methods nor ourselves, but on Christ, and be confident that He will accomplish His work of peace in the hearts of men. Miracles belong to the realm of the supernatural. But what a privilege for us to be counted worthy of being called to be coworkers with God as His peacemakers!

Nothing is inferred in this Beatitude as to what precedes the miracle of peacemaking in the heart of a sinner. We can infer from Matthew 10:34, however, that it is the sword. What happens between the time the Spirit of God begins to act in the human heart until the peace of God is firmly established there? It is the activity of the sword that precedes the establishment of peace. This is a peace by way of judgment. Jesus did not come to sing a lullaby to humanity, or to tell it that sin does not matter and that all its wickedness will eventually be forgotten. He came in the name of God and eternal truth to declare war upon all those things that prevent peace. The sword is necessary in the interests of peace.

When the Gospel first comes to men, it finds them in a state of moral insensibility. "Dead in trespasses and sins" is the apostolic description of our natural condition — not only destitute of spiritual life but morally unconscious. Just as a corpse is insensible to outward stimuli, so are we, in our natural state, insensible to the things of the Spirit. The first effect of the Gospel is to arouse the dormant powers of the soul. It "convinces of sin, of righteousness, and of judgment." It reveals our spiritual bankruptcy and shows us that we are guilty, perishing sinners. It produces alarm, trouble, unrest. Like the flash of lightning that shows the traveler that he is on the edge of a fearful precipice, the Gospel opens the eyes of the sinner to his lost and perilous condition and fills him with anguish and dread.

When the Gospel was preached by Peter on the day of Pentecost, those who heard "were pricked in their heart, and said unto Peter and to the rest of the apostles, Men and brethren, what shall we do?" (Acts 2:37). They were disturbed. The Gospel was a sword-thrust to their hearts.

When Paul had a revelation of Jesus as the Lord, while journeying to Damascus, we read, "And he trembling and astonished said, Lord, what wilt thou have me to do?" (Acts 9:6).

When the Gospel first came to the Philippian jailer, in an agony of fear he cast himself at the feet of Paul and Silas, saying, "Sirs, what must I do to be saved?" (Acts 16:30). Truly, in such cases the words of the Saviour are verified, "Think not that I am come to send peace on earth: I came not to send peace, but a sword."

But after this comes "the gospel of peace." To the troubled penitent Christ says, "Come unto me . . . and I will give you rest. Take my yoke upon you, and learn of me; for I am meek and lowly in heart: and ye shall find rest unto your souls" (Matt. 11:28, 29). The sins of such men are forgiven; their guilt is taken away; they are "accepted in the beloved." "Therefore being justified by faith, we have peace with God through our Lord Jesus Christ" (Rom. 5:1). The believer has the assurance of God's favor; he can take up the language of the Prophet and exclaim, "O Lord, I will praise thee: though thou wast angry with me, thine anger is turned away, and thou comfortedst me" (Isa. 12:1). The "spirit of bondage to fear" gives place to the "Spirit of adoption, whereby we cry, Abba, Father" (Rom. 8:15). How often we have found the air on a summer's day hot, oppressive, and stagnant. Not a breath of wind stirs the leaves that hang parched or weltering in the burning rays of the sun. The very birds are silent, as though unable to breathe. Suddenly the thunder peals, and the great raindrops patter upon the ground. Then the storm bursts forth in all its fury. Flash succeeds flash with startling rapidity, the thunder rocks the very buildings in which we are sheltered, and the rain descends in a fierce deluge. At length the storm ceases, and then what a change has passed over the scene! Before, there was a peace; but it was the peace of inanimation and death; now there is a peace, but it is the peace of blessed life. The air is cool and fresh, the trees assume their verdant hues, the flowers give forth their sweetest fragrance, the birds make the groves echo again with their glad melody; in a word, all nature is peaceful with a deep, exuberant vitality. And so with the Gospel; it arouses men from their deadly lethargy, producing sorrow, distress, and anguish; but after this there comes a peace, even "the peace of God, which passeth all understanding."

PEACE BY WAY OF THE SWORD

Although Christ's coming into a man's life brings peace, it often comes by way of the sword. There are three ways in which His coming into the heart may be likened to a sword-thrust.

First, Christ opens up the depths of sin within us. Oscar Wilde was one of the most brilliant writers of comedy that the Victorian era produced. He made a tour of the United States and lectured more than one hundred times on the philosophy of the esthetic. But morally the man was a degenerate. He could write English of silken delicacy, but he could also write the coarsest stuff. He sowed great fields of literary wild oats. He was sentenced at last to two years imprisonment for the gravest moral offenses, and during his confinement he wrote a little book called *Out of the Depths*. Let me give you the preface:

"The gods had given me everything, but I allowed myself to be lured into sensualism. I amused myself with being a flaneur, a dandy, a man of fashion. Then tired of the heights, I became a malady and a madness. There is only one thing left for me now, absolute humility. I have lain in prison for nearly two years. Out of my nature have come despair, scorn, bitterness, rage, anguish, sorrow."

The man cried out to God in penitence. Whether his penitence was sincere or not, is not clear. Judging from his behavior in prison, according to the testimony of the warden, it was. Let us hope it was.

"O wretched man that I am!" cried Paul. "Who shall deliver me from the body of this death?" (Rom.

7:24). We were tolerably contented with our character once, but when Christ comes we are never complacent again. John reproved the Church of Laodicea because of their smug self-satisfaction in one of the most scathing denunciations of Scripture: "Thou sayest, I am rich and increased with goods, and have need of nothing and knowest not that thou art wretched, and miserable and poor, and blind, and naked" (Rev. 3:17). Like the sheep that look clean enough among the summer grass but against the background of the virgin snow look foul, so you and I never know how vile we are until the background of our life is Christ. You would have thought that when Christ filled Peter's net, Peter would have been ecstatically happy; but instead of that you have Simon Peter crying, "Depart from me, O Lord, I am a sinful man." Christ came to Simon Peter with the sword; showed him himself; taught him how dark he was. And whenever the sword-stroke of an indwelling Saviour cuts into the deeps of a man's heart, the wound is very likely to be sore. Yet it is as necessary as the surgeon's scalpel, which cuts to heal. "Lord, Thy most pointed pleasure take, and stab my spirit broad awake!" prayed Stevenson. Let us therefore not flee the sword but bare our breasts to it. In the hands of Christ, the sword wounds to heal.

Secondly, Christ calls us to a lifelong warfare. The note of warfare rings through the whole New Testament. The spirit is quickened now to crave for spiritual things and the flesh and the spirit must battle till the grave.

> When the fight begins within himself,
> A man's worth something. God stoops over his head;
> Satan looks up between his feet — both tug —
> He's left, himself, in the middle: the soul awakes
> And grows. Prolong that battle through this life!
> Never cease growing till the life to come.
>   — *Browning*

522

We wrestle not against flesh and blood, but against principalities and powers and spiritual darkness. And the evil that I would not, that I do, and the good I would, that I do not. Paul knew the peace of God that passed all understanding, yet to Paul the Saviour came bearing the sword. In the same manner our peacemaking makes a warrior of the person to whom Christ brings peace. It is a war against the evil that seeks to destroy our God-given peace. As we seek to establish the peace of Christ in the hearts and lives of others, we at the same time establish a battlefield. That's the sword the Saviour spoke about as preceding His peace.

Thirdly, Christ's coming brings a sword, because His regenerating peace heightens our ideals in life. Before we believed, we had no objection to anything that was not of the highest moral caliber. But as the ideal is heightened by the acceptance of Christ, the old peace with the low and degenerate things of life goes and the pain of the desire for the highest begins. It is in the new conception of what life may be that the sword-stroke cuts into the heart. We are no more the children of time and mortality. We are the children of eternity and immortality. Wound and pain accompany the accomplishment of the birth of a mighty thought and ideal. Whenever the horizon widens, there is sorrow. The sword of Christ smites through the thongs that bind us. The sword of Christ cuts down the veil that shadows us.

Look at the home of Mary and Joseph at Nazareth. Jesus comes into that home. Till then there was the peace of mutual love and trust. But the announcement that Mary was expecting to give birth to a child that was not Joseph's was a sword to his heart. He was minded to put Mary away quietly, for the great love he had to her. After our Lord's birth came the flight to Egypt;

then Jesus in the Temple – ah, yes! the sword is going deeper now. And when the public ministry began, and He was put to scorn, rejected, crucified, I think the sword had smitten that quiet home. It might have been so peaceful and so happy, with the laughter of children and the joy of motherhood. It might have been so peaceful and so happy if God had never honored it like this. But Jesus was born there, and that made all the difference. It could never be the quiet home again. Gethsemane was coming, Calvary was coming; a sword was going to pierce through Mary's heart. He came not to send peace, the peace of a lullaby and a narcotic, but a sword, the sword of the ideal divine peace penetrating the sinfulness of humanity.

Develop love, and you develop sorrow. Deepen the heart-life, and you deepen suffering. It is by doing that, through all the centuries, that Christ has brought the sword into our homes. The Stoic philosopher of Greece said, "Dry up these fountains of feeling"; so he made a solitude and called it peace. But Christ deepened and cleansed life's well-springs here, and that very deepening has brought the sword. I think it is worth it, not only to experience it ourselves but to bring it to others by being peacemakers, the peacemakers of the seventh Beatitude. I would not be a Stoic. I would not live without the sensibility of a conscience that has been touched and is being worked on by God. I would no live a life of isolation from God. This is the peace o spiritual death. I'd rather be alive unto God and a peace with Him, at war with self and evil. It is bette to live vividly, in spite of the pain of resisting that which seeks to abolish peace, than to have the fingertips of al the angels grope at a heart of steel.

Our duty as peacemakers is to make people aliv unto God at any cost and to cause them to realize th war that the peace of God in the human heart must wage. The peace that comes from above feels, sorrows with the sorrowing, rejoices with the victorious against sin, never lives unto itself, concerns itself with others. That's the blessing received and the blessing given through peacemaking as taught by Christ. (See G. H. Morrison, *Sun-Rise*, pp. 158-68.)

> Outward life is light and shadow,
> Mingled wrong and struggling right,
> But within the outward trouble
> Shines a healing, inward light.
>
> Not to us may come fulfillment,
> Not below our struggles cease,
> Yet the heavenly vision gives us,
> Even here, our inward peace.

PEACE IN AND THROUGH SUFFERING

In this matter of peacemaking, we don't want to fool ourselves or others. We've got to have a clear idea of what peace is not — that inner peace Christ spoke about, which is associated with blessedness. As peacemakers, we want to bring real peace to others and not a counterfeit of it; we want to tell them of the peace that brings tranquillity of soul, and not just a stoical quiet.

First, peace is not immunity from pain and sorrow, nor is it freedom to pursue our own ends. It is not independence from the interference or misfortunes of neighboring nations, and safety from annoyance and attack. Peace, in brief, does not come from having our own way in life. You don't really have peace when you are free to choose the circumstances of your life. Try an experiment with a child. Give him whatever he wishes, do his every bidding. Do you think you will have a contented, peaceful child? You know better. You will have a fretful, bewildered, unhappy little tyrant.

God the Father must often look upon us as spoiled children. We want what we want, and that is not always what He has chosen for us. We rebel against Him. If He were to give us all the desires of our heart, we still would not have peace. Self-satisfaction, maybe — not of the self God wants us to be, but of sinful, fallen self.

Christ's peace has nothing to do with freedom from trial and suffering. He says so Himself, in John 16:33: "In the world ye shall have tribulation: but be of good cheer; I have overcome the world." His peace comes to us, not because of favorable circumstances but in spite of unfavorable ones. That's what blessedness means — a state of inner sufficiency regardless of our outward circumstances, good or bad. Christ not only does not promise us immunity from injustice, slander, hatred, and all other wrongs man may inflict on his fellows; He warns us to expect them. The Christian is always in a small minority. He can never have the pleasure of shouting with the largest crowd. His standards are quite different from those of the world, and our Lord's words remain true for all time: "If ye were of the world, the world would love his own: but because ye are not of the world, but I have chosen you out of the world, therefore the world hateth you" (John 15:19).

Where has the finest literature come from — the literature of peace, joy, light, hope, inspiration, triumph? Has it come from men whose lives were free from suffering, pain, and disappointment? Sometimes, perhaps, but not very often. Most of it has come from prison cells, from blind poets, from disease-racked bodies. From the pens of those who suffered issued the literature of hope, our hymns of joy, our stories of faith. From this we see who really has peace. The outward circumstances and patterns of life are not its real essence. In large measure our outward and inward life are independent of each other. True peace does not come from external situations but from something within us — our inward sense of rightness with God, our consciousness of true purpose and an undivided heart. True peace looks at life from above. It regards heaven not only as a place to go to, but also as a condition to attain. If you possess Christ's peace, you are like a man secure in the comfort of his home while the storm rages outside. The ultimate victory of human life is this triumph of the inner spirit over the outward life. Look around you and you will see that those who are the calmest, the strongest, the most peaceful are not those whose lives have been filled with ease or frivolity. They are those who have known suffering, pain, and disappointment.

Anne Steele was an incurable invalid, in constant suffering, who knew deep sorrow. But the fruit of that experience was a hymn such as this:

> Father, whate'er of earthly bliss
>   Thy sovereign hand denies,
> Accepted at Thy throne of grace
>   Let this petition rise.
>
> Give me a calm, a thankful heart,
>   From every murmur free;
> The blessing of Thy grace impart,
>   And let me live to Thee.
>
> Let the sweet hope that Thou art mine
>   My path of life attend;
> Thy Presence through my journey shine,
>   And crown my journey's end.

Is the peacemaker, then, in his efforts to bring Christ's peace to others, simply to ignore the unhappy circumstances of others? Not at all. There is great value in ministering to the physical and social needs of those in trouble; but we must know that relieving their wants will not of itself bring them inner peace. Each man has two lives: the outward and the inward. Man's spirit can either conquer his circumstances, or his circumstances can overwhelm his spirit. A man's spirit may either humble and degrade itself so that man becomes its slave, or it may override all obstacles in its path and thus prove man a king.

Take a good look at the Lord Jesus in the closing days of His ministry. He grows stronger and stronger the nearer He comes to the cross. And when is it that He speaks most of peace? At the close of His ministry, when the forces opposed to Him were wild with fury and the darkest hour of His life was upon Him. He gathered His little company of disciples about Him in the upper room, and after seeking to prepare their hearts for what was to come, He ended His discourse by saying, "Peace I leave with you, my peace I give unto you: not as the world giveth, give I unto you. Let not your heart be troubled, neither let it be afraid" (John 14:27). Within a week the tragedy of the cross was accomplished and was transfigured by the triumph of the resurrection; and Christ stood among them again, probably in the same upper room, and said, "Peace unto you." Through the turmoil and the temptations of the three years of His public ministry, He had proclaimed the Kingdom of God, which is righteousness, peace, and joy, in the Holy Ghost; and these were the men who had received His word. To them He uttered this final and significant saying, which, in all that it involves, is the central and last word of Biblical revelation on the subject of peace.

When Christ came into the world, the Jews were expecting a Messiah who would free them from Roman domination and establish a Jewish nation. They looked at the promise of peace as a promise from God to smite their enemies and allow them to rule over them. It is evident, however, that the Lord did not mean to establish that kind of peace at all. "Peace as a Messianic blessing is that state, brought about by the grace and loving mind of God, wherein the derangement and distress of life caused by sin are removed. Hence the message of salvation is called 'the gospel of peace' (Eph. 6:15)." Paul calls this peace "the peace of God, which passeth all understanding" (Phil. 4:7). God is called "the God of peace" (Phil. 4:9). And then Paul, writing to the

Thessalonians, gives the full scope of the meaning of the word peace: "And the very God of peace sanctify you wholly; and I pray God your whole spirit and soul and body be preserved blameless unto the coming of our Lord Jesus Christ" (I Thess. 5:23). Peace is not anything less than the sanctification of our entire being by God Himself. It is not something we can acquire through our own efforts. It is a gift of God. It is the power of God that brings harmony to us. This is the real meaning of the word peace.

Nor is peace found in human friendship. You remember, when Job was in trouble, how little his friends did to make his lot more bearable. All their counsel could not bring peace to his heart; not being God-inspired, it merely aggravated his difficulties. Elihu asked Job, "When he giveth quietness, who then can make trouble?" (Job 34:29). For once he hit the nail on the head. Amy Carmichael says, "Not all the Elihus in the world can make trouble when God gives quietness. They can do us no harm, they cannot spoil that inner quietness which must be if God's perfect peace is to be ours. Supposing they do succeed in disturbing us; then there is one certain and swift way back into peace: one upward look — Thy pardon, Lord; Thy stillness, Lord — and that which went from us returns. We have peace from the God of peace."

Look at the Master, fresh from Gethsemane, facing the cross, with not one brave soul to stand by Him to the end. But at the same time hear that calm, majestic utterance, "I have overcome the world." He had; not by outwardly subjugating it, but by bringing His peace — which the world does not comprehend and can neither give nor take away — into the hearts of men and women who would receive Him.

MUST THE PEACEMAKER
SUBMIT TO OTHERS?

To be a peacemaker is to bring the peace of God to others. It is not to secure "peace at any price." Peace is not a state of being resigned to evil, passively suffering the whims and designs of others — whether they be nations, organizations, or individuals — for the sake of avoiding conflict and gaining superficial calm. In this respect the meaning of peace is like that of meekness: It is unalterably opposed to evil. Peace is not patching up a compromise that must ultimately break in pieces. It is not crying "Peace, peace," when there is no peace, but laying the foundations of a just peace in righteousness. "The work of righteousness shall be peace." That is how it is made, and the effect of righteousness is quietness and assurance forever. Peace without heroism is no peace. Peace may actually necessitate war. Peacemaking is not waiting resignedly for peace to come; it is snatching it out of the lion's jaw; it is sculpturing it out of the rough, hard, intractable material.

But immediately someone will confront us with the words of Christ in this same fifth chapter of Matthew, verses 38-42. "Ye have heard that it hath been said, An eye for an eye, and a tooth for a tooth: but I say unto you, That ye resist not evil: but whosoever shall smite thee on thy right cheek, turn to him the other also. And if any man will sue thee at the law, and take away thy coat, let him have thy cloke also. And whosoever shall compel thee to go a mile, go with him twain. Give to him that asketh thee, and from him that would borrow of thee turn not thou away."

How are we to understand this passage? Are these Christ's directions to His peacemakers? Do they produce a sentimental and effeminate type of Christian, a shirker, with no element of the adventurous and heroic in his make-up? The answer is no on both counts. Let us see why.

Although Christ assigns His Church the role of peacemaking in the world, He also marks her out to be the Church militant here on earth. Now this double character — of warlikeness and peacefulness — is not only stamped upon the Church by Christ Himself in her history, but we see it in His own life. Never was there such a peacemaker, and never, on the other hand, was there such a warrior. Never was there one who spoke so sternly as a prophet, so sharply and resolutely as a judge, so keenly, so searchingly, and so provocatively as a reformer, as Christ our Lord, Christ the Warrior, whose warfare is as a consuming fire; Christ the Peacemaker, whose words are all tenderness and love.

Here is a man in a passion. He strikes me, and I stand there and say, "Strike me again." Nine times out of ten he will do it. It is decidedly naive for some preachers to say that such a man will be so touched by my non-resistance that he will blush and let me alone. Man's sinful nature does not usually respond to such incomprehensible behavior; he regards with suspicion such unwonted humility, feeling that it is intended to subdue his spirit of superiority and conquest. What would happen if we as Christians made such behavior the general rule of our life? People would regard it as an invitation to push us around unmercifully. Did the Lord really want us to encourage evil? What would we do when such situations arose in family life?

Here are my seven-year-old son and his ten-year-old sister playing in the yard. Out of a clear sky, the boy hits the girl. Is she to stand there and take it? Is she to say to him, "Go ahead and hit me again. I want to do what the Lord Jesus says, to be hit and never hit back. I want to keep peace at any price." Do you think such an attitude would be helpful to the boy? Not if you know human nature. And what part should I as a parent play in this situation? Should I tell my daughter to go on suffering uncomplainingly at the hands of her brother, that by her passivity she is obeying Christ? In so doing we would both be encouraging my son to become a little monster; it would reduce Christ's teaching to an absurdity; and Christ, the Supreme Intelligence, never taught absurdities, nor encouraged evil.

Neither do we, His followers, under the pretext of peacemaking, have the right to ask others to continue in their evil ways. What right has a Christian to ask his assailant to continue his sadistic brutalities? Why should he ask anyone to hit him again? To do so is to confront him with an additional temptation at the point where he is least able to resist it. If my daily prayer to the Lord is "Lead us not into temptation," why should I think He wants me to lead others into temptation?

Did Christ intend us to take these words literally? We must always ask ourselves what the Lord's basic intent was in His teaching, and what final result He wanted to achieve. If the literal sense of these verses is contrary to His basic teaching, then we must believe He meant them to be understood figuratively. Suppose someone were to strike you on the right cheek. Is all that the Lord requires of you to turn your left cheek and say to your attacker, "Strike me again"? Or if someone takes your coat, is all that the Lord wants of you to give him your cloak, too? As long as we think of Christ's commands in this external, literal way, we may as well ask, "What would be the good of it?" It would be nothing more than a ceremonial act, no different from the offering of the tithes of mint and cummin. If the mint and cummin did no good, at least they did no harm; but if men are left unredeemed, unchanged by grace, would not a literal application of these precepts only encourage them in greed and violence? Does not a bully become more and more a menace to society if no one opposes him? Is it really love to your enemy always to behave as these verses suggest?

Christ's interest is in the conversion of the evildoer. His intent in giving these illustrative commands was to suggest that our willingness to suffer should have such an effect upon the one that imposes the suffering that he will cease for very shame. If this purpose is not achieved, then our submission to further buffetings and robbery does neither the offender nor ourselves any good.

Consider what our Lord says in Matthew 5:40, "And if any man will sue thee at the law, and take away thy coat, let him have thy cloke also." That is, if you are sued at law, you are to give more than is demanded. Is that part of the peacemaking command of Christ? Would it make yourself or the other party more blessed in any way? If this is taken as laying down a universal rule for society, it would mean that we are never to resort to law for any claims made against us. That would practically mean that we are not to have laws at all in so far as it implies that no one is to stand up for his legal rights. The effectiveness of law depends on men being prepared to stand up for their rights. Yet a society in which all men always insisted on their legal rights would be a disgusting society to live in, even if we were content with much less than the spirit of the Sermon on the Mount. "The finest thing about our rights," says George Macdonald, "is that, being our own, we can give them up."

Look at Abraham and Lot. How perfect was Abraham's conduct; how miserable was Lot's! Abraham, the elder, who might have exacted all, conceded all. He said, "Let there be no strife, I pray thee, between me and thee, and between my herdmen and thy herdmen; for we be brethren. Is not the whole land before thee? separate thyself, I pray thee, from me: if thou wilt take the left hand, then I will go to the right; or if thou depart to the right hand, then I will go to the left" (Gen. 13:8, 9). And Lot, with the selfishness that is the peacebreaker, in awful contrast to the love that was in Abraham the peacemaker, made his election, and saw that the plain of Sodom was well watered and abundant; and he pitched his tent there. But he learned that the peacebreaker never can be on earth the peace-enjoyer; and Abraham learned by experience what he held in principle, that a peacemaker was not only a child of God, but was honored also by being called "the father of the faithful." (John Cumming, *Benedictions, or The Blessed Life,* pp. 207-8.)

On the other hand, do we seriously think that we are loving our enemies if we do not resist the claims of legal blackmailers? I don't think we can avoid the conclusion that were we to act in that way constantly we should be making laws and rules impossible; that it is for the advantage of all, even of those who from time to time break rules, that rules should be kept. I am quite clear that we believe that we ourselves should be made to keep rules, and that, if we love our neighbors as ourselves, we should support the maintenance of rules. But here in the Sermon on the Mount we are called upon to fulfill, not to destroy, the law, and to bring love to our interpretation and application of it. We are never to say, "The law is on my side and that is an end of the matter." We are to be ready, not to give up our public concern for law, but to modify our private resentments.

We are to go a long way in not standing up for our rights at those times when without danger to society we are free to do so.

Always to insist upon our rights is as un-Christian as never to do so. If you are one who is ever quick to insist upon your rights, here are a few you might begin with:

> ... What are they?
> The right to labor and to pray,
> The right to watch while others sleep,
> The right o'er others' woes to weep,
> The right to succor in distress,
> The right while others curse to bless,
> The right to love while others scorn,
> The right to comfort all who mourn,
> The right to shed new joy on earth,
> The right to feel the soul's high worth,
> The right to lead the soul to God
> Along the path the Saviour trod.

PEACEMAKING OR COWARDICE?

The blessing of peacemaking has given rise to tremendous misconceptions, the greatest of which is that it provides an excuse to encourage evil. The proponents of such peacemaking make an altogether erroneous application of Christ's words in Matthew 5:39, "Resist not evil." Is non-resistance to evil the duty of the Christian peacemaker?

The nature of rules depends on how men normally behave. In the Sermon on the Mount we are called upon to be better than the norm, to have a higher standard than that of the world. But this does not alter the necessity for having rules. Most men feel that keeping inside the rules set by society is enough guarantee of good conduct. What Christ sought to do in the Beatitudes and in all His teaching was to shake men out of lazy living within fossilized forms. We need a dramatic striking expression like this Sermon on the Mount to pull us up out of that laziness. It says to us, "Your being within your rights and the other person being wrong is by no means an end of the matter. You ought, perhaps, to give in and give in again, even more than he is now asking. You mustn't ever shelter yourself under the guarantee of the law or the ordinary moral code. It is up to you to make the law human." Applying a rule in love is one thing; making a rule of making rules impossible is quite another. It is an easier thing and a disastrous one.

Here is another commandment of our Lord's that is often erroneously applied to peacemaking: "Give to him that asketh thee, and from him that would borrow of thee turn thou not away" (Matt. 5:42). Does that mean we are to pauperize the community, awaken in them passions of greed, indolence, fawning, lying, theft? Already our national economy is overburdened with the consequences of a false welfarism. The lazy and immoral lean heavily on the fact that if they knock hard at the door of the anxious vote-getting politician they will get all they want. And the empty-headed politician feels that he is doing his Christian duty when he gives to him that asketh him. But the more he gives the more he will be asked for. All of us know that there are couples, unfortunately too many of them, who prefer to draw on the welfare treasury for their six or eight children than for the father to go to work. After all, the welfare department pays more than the father could ever hope to earn. And so it goes. Our civilization is developing a society in which those who conscientiously work will have to care for the lazy and demanding. What Christ taught as a voluntary, discreet, and discriminating sense of philanthropy is becoming a forced encouragement of the degenerate human instincts of greed and laziness.

When someone comes to your door and asks for money, what should you do? You must try to determine whether the man is where he is, in a state of beggary, because he cannot help it or because he likes it. If the first is true, it is wrong to refuse him; if the second is true, it is a crime to help him. You must consider the end result of your action, not only on yourself but also on the person who comes to you for help. If your help will only demoralize him further, you should not give it. But if it will tide him over a bad place and help him to get on his feet again, you should do all in your power to give him a hand up.

Suppose you want to start a Sunday school in a needy community and give out handbills offering a dollar to everyone who will come. No doubt you'll attract quite a number. But do you think that you will really be helping those who come, either through the money or through your teaching? Hardly. The money will spoil the teaching, for their purpose in coming was financial rather than spiritual gain. Actually, you would be a public danger and a destroyer of morals if you were to do a thing like that. You would be setting a material goal for people while trying to achieve a spiritual end. And they would stop with what they were trying to achieve, not the good purpose you had for them in the back of your mind.

If in all circumstances of life we are to "resist not evil," why do we have locks on our doors? Isn't this contrary to Christ's command, "Give to him that asketh of thee"? Leave your door open so anyone can help himself. Is every policeman engaged in a business opposed to Christ's teaching in the Sermon on the Mount? Is Christian peacemaking an invitation to housebreaking?

The ancient Greeks chose for the protectress of Athens the Goddess of Wisdom, bearing the olive branch of peace, but they set her image in the Parthenon helmeted and bearing a spear to defend the peace that she brought to earth. This is symbolic of the Greek concept of peacemaking — not the submission of good to evil for the sake of peace, but the defense of the right in wisdom. He is no peacemaker who has no iron in his blood, no hot word of indignation at fitting times on his tongue, who is not ready, when occasion calls, to be a follower of Him who could flash forth, "Woe unto you, scribes and Pharisees, hypocrites!" and who spoke with appalling concreteness of the wrong combination of work and worship — devouring widows' houses and making long prayers. But he who seeks peace at any price must ever resort to the device of sacrificing principle for expediency. He who is adept at that exchange is regarded as a safe man. Nor in any sphere is he thought safer than in the Church. Of such expediency for the sake of peacemaking our churches are alas too full today. Never mind, say the pseudo-peacemakers, about the doctrine of the infallibility of the Bible. Don't trouble new members about the necessity of believing in the virgin birth of Christ, in His vicarious death, in His bodily resurrection, in His deity. All we want is to worship God together in peace, letting every man believe whatever he wants. This is the peace of much ecumenical churchianity. This is why it is failing to bring peace to the souls of men. Peace apart from truth, its appropriation and propagation, is a farce. The peace of the Church of Jesus Christ can only come through union with Him who is the Truth. The spokes of this wheel called church ecumenicity must be joined to Christ. It is in Him that we meet. There may be a group or two that are truly attached to Christ and His basic doctrines, but the rest hold to a union of the rim of the wheel and not to its center. The less spokes that are joined to the hub of a wheel, no matter how perfect and round its periphery, the weaker it is. The least weight will crush it.

History confirms the judgment that the person within the Church who sacrifices principle for expediency in order to promote apparent peace is one of the most dangerous men in it. When will we awake to the fact that peacemaking is not compromising with evil at the expense of righteousness? When will we turn a deaf ear to the false peacemaker who tries to enforce his average opinions, which are not opinions at all; dupe us into the acceptance of his dull, formal decisions, which are not decisions at all; and persuade us to follow his course shaped only to drift with the current, which is a course peacefully leading to the precipice of destruction?

Nor is it only in the Church that such a man is dangerous. Under his shelter all abuses tend to gather. The evil that corrupts the world is not fostered mainly by bad men but by ease-loving men who will never take their stand upon principle and dare the consequences. Evil prospers so abundantly only because it can count so securely on such compliance and cowardice.

There is a very interesting old story in the Book of Deuteronomy that sets forth the instructions to the priests and officers about the preparation for a battle. The officers were instructed to go around among the soldiers and speak with them, and if they found there a man who was a coward, and who was afraid the army was going to be whipped, they were to send him home lest he have a bad influence on the other soldiers and spread his cowardice through the army. Gideon also was instructed to send home all cowards before he went to battle. These two cases show us what God thinks of cowards. He not only considers such a person of no use in a fight but thinks he is dangerous to have along. A coward is like a rotten apple in a barrel; it not only is of no value but it starts the other apples to rotting all around it. Yet courage can be cultivated like anything else. Many people who are naturally fearful have overcome their fears through Christ and have forced themselves to stand bravely for the right.

PEACEMAKING
NOT A COMPROMISE WITH EVIL

"Blessed are the peacemakers," said our Lord. Some people seem to interpret this as saying "Blessed are those who let people get away with murder." The law of liberty in the Church or in a nation is not a license to let evil have full expression along with good. In recent years, evil has even been encouraged by some decisions of the Supreme Court of the United States and by some of its justices. The idea seems to be that if the exponents of the Gospel and morality are free to preach it, so should the proponents of immorality be at liberty to foster baseness. Justice Douglas opposed banning a book because postal officials or "some purity league" considered it obscene. "Should a publication whose main impact is the arousal of sexual desires be banned? A goodly part of life is the arousal of sexual desires ... The real purpose is to make the public live up to the censor's code of morality ... Sex cannot be suppressed in life. Should it be attempted in literature?" *(U. S. News and World Report*, Dec. 24, 1962, p. 12.)

There is a point where freedom becomes license to do evil. Shall good make peace with evil and have it confirmed even in our Supreme Court? How absurd our society is. Justice Douglas says that, since sex finds its expression in life, why should it not find its expression in literature? The implication is that some citizens of the United States can publish obscene literature and we who believe in decency and morality must tolerate it for the sake of peace. This false concept of freedom and peacemaking is the Achilles' heel of this great nation.

It will fall or stand as we privately and nationally tolerate evil for the sake of peace. We need a revolution of morality in this country and this world, even if that means bucking the decisions of our judges. It is better to obey the Supreme Judge of all humanity, God.

It is all right, according to Justice Douglas, to arouse immoral feelings through the printed page; it is only when a man attacks a woman on the street that it becomes a crime. If we were only consistent and punished an act of immorality when televised or printed, the same as when actually perpetrated, we would have a much lower crime rate and it would be safer to walk the streets of our cities. Christians, raise your voices, spend your strength and money in the kind of peacemaking that refuses to tolerate evil or to compromise with those who permit it officially or unofficially, the peacemaking that never sacrifices principle for expediency.

A wholly perverted idea of Christian meekness leads some people to accept things as they are as the will of God. Serious men who have no wish to travesty Christianity believe that it is the Christian temper to sit down and fold one's hands while disease festers in the dark, and injustice makes use of the civil powers, and wars are stirred up from oppression or greed of gold. They have even come to think that this is what Christ meant by being a peacemaker.

"For this purpose the Son of God was manifested, that he might destroy the works of the devil" (I John 3:8). The mission of Christ in this world was the destruction of all evil. All evil, whether it be that of error or of sin in practice, opposes itself to the mission and purpose of Christ and His Church and must be removed if that mission is to succeed. Christianity, as far as evil is concerned, is necessarily an intolerant religion, and as such it provokes strife, and as such we must not fear to provoke it. Christ troubled the State and rent the Church; He created a whirlwind of infinite desire and unsatisfied longing in the heart of man. Those who went out in His name turned the world upside down. And no one has ever truly learned His spirit to this day who is not a disturber of conventions and formalities and "agreements with hell to be at peace with it." "My peace," said the Master, "I give unto you." Yet it was certainly not as the world gives it, but with Gethsemane and Calvary in it, with sin crushed and love victorious, and God's will done on a hostile earth as in a favoring heaven. And His followers are those who resist unto blood striving against sin: and they and they alone are the true peacemakers. The true peacemakers are those who set good where evil was, who establish peace in time of war. When Jesus said that He was come to bring war and not peace, He meant war against evil, against Satan and the world, against evil which is an offense, against Satan the murderer, against the world where strife reigns eternally. In a word, Jesus meant to wage war against war.

And yet we, in our warfare for truth, have need to remember that we are also peacemakers. Though every peacemaker is a fighter, every fighter is not a peacemaker. To be a peacemaker we must fight in peace as well as for it. If we honestly desire truth and hate error, then we must honestly recognize truth wherever we meet it. We must take heed lest with our statement of the truth we provoke and intensify, by any fault in our statement, by any error in our conception of it, the very error that we are warring against. Only when we fight with God to guide and sustain us can we fight in love, without which no fighting is peacemaking. Love must often fight, and sometimes in anger that is part of meekness, but it must never cease to be love. All its warfare is to save, not to destroy; to pardon, not to avenge; to establish mercy and not mere justice, but this mercy not at the expense of justice. Even indignation must not only be akin to pity but be ever ready to change into it; and it must be purged of violence by knowing that sin, being folly and weakness, and not merely aggressiveness and wrong, is to be pitied.

Even for the economic battle, we have to do more than fight self-interest with other self-interests; and for peace in the world we have to do more than oppose violence to violence. No device has ever yet been discovered whereby in such battles the weakest do not go to the wall. To have any hope of success we have to put the whole matter on the level of reverence for man as man, justice as in God's sight, pity as between fellow-travelers from time to eternity, compassion as from those who need compassion, responsibility for talents, wealth, opportunity, privileges, as gifts from God wherewith to serve.

This means that no one can be a true peacemaker who has not God's peace, which is just God's love, in his heart. He must be a man the current of whose life runs too deep for earthly strife to ruffle, because it springs from the perennial fountain of pardon, grace, and eternal life. If that be the source of his power, the first need of his life will be a fellowship in worship, a fellowship where he will unite with all his brethren, master and workman, friend and foe, to look up into the face of their common Father. Especially will it be a fellowship where he will see God's face in the face that was more marred by conflict with the world's sin and sorrow than any man's, and yet in which is seen, as nowhere else, the glory of God. (See *The Speaker's Bible*, pp. 96-8, and *The Anglican Pulpit Library*, Vol. 9, pp. 28-32.)

Moral cowardice – how it infects our pulpits and

pews! How people will often declaim at home about what ought to be done; about what a shame such and such a situation is; about what is wrong with this, that, and the other. But when these same men and women have an opportunity to speak up where it counts, how studiously self-effacing they suddenly become, how quiet, lest someone might think they held a contrary opinion! And so wrongs go unrighted, the weak go unchampioned, the brave man must stand alone while those who were so outspoken in private hold their tongues in public. For shame! Where would the Church be today if Martin Luther had acquiesced in the evil practices of his day? When Luther said to Erasmus, "You desire to walk upon eggs without crushing them, and among glasses without breaking them," the timorous, hesitating Erasmus replied, "I will not be unfaithful to the cause of Christ, *at least so far as the age will permit me.*" Is that your philosophy? If so, how can you face yourself in the mirror?

Be strong!
We are not here to play, to dream, to drift.
We have hard work to do and loads to lift.
Shun not the struggle, — face it: 'tis God's gift.

Be strong!
Say not the days are evil. Who's to blame?
And fold the hands and acquiesce, — O shame!
Stand up, speak out, and bravely, in God's name.

Be strong!
It matters not how deep intrenched the wrong,
How hard the battle goes, the day how long;
Faint not, — fight on! Tomorrow comes the song.

— *Maltbie D. Babcock*

546

PEACEMAKING
AND PERSONAL RETALIATION

Christ's teaching to turn the other cheek, resist not evil, go the other mile, as found in Matthew 5:39-42, may seem absurd in our present-day civilization, but it would be normal, natural, and logical in a different order of things, when the reign and righteousness of God is pre-eminent, as it will be in the coming millennium. Twentieth-century man may be advanced in science and technology, but he is still a sinful, selfish being. Man in his fallen state loves to take rather than to give, to hurt rather than to suffer, to gain rather than to relinquish his rights, to rest rather than to work, to borrow rather than to lend. We live in a state of civilization where self is the central consideration, not God and others.

That has been the situation ever since man disobeyed God and fell in the Garden of Eden. Self has been placed above God, so that man's primary interest has been to enhance man. To be independent of and equal to God was the greatest allurement Satan could place before Adam and Eve. "For God doth know that in the day ye eat thereof [of the forbidden fruit], then your eyes shall be opened, and ye shall be as gods, knowing good and evil" (Gen. 3:5). It was too good an opportunity to miss. Why should we not be equal to God? The promotion of self: you can see it ever since in every field of human endeavor. We are blinded by self, smothered by self, buried in self — and God and others can take the leavings.

But could things be different under conditions where

self took a back seat? Can you conceive of an order of things under which, if a man did so forget himself as to strike you, and you offered the other cheek, it would so shame him that he would repent of his aggressive temper? Or, under some circumstances, borrowing or asking may be such a delicate matter, and cost a man so much to dare to ask, that if you did refuse you would indeed be committing an un-Christian act. When has real Christianity and its principles ever had a chance since the first days of the Church, when men had all things in common and shared with those in need? We have had a little Christianity here and there in churches and among small groups, but we have never had a Christian state or a Christian country. We have never had a civilization that was based upon the principles and passions and purposes of our Lord Jesus Christ. It is only when Christianity is being tasted, where Christianity is the dominating factor, that you can decide whether it is a permanent and vital thing.

"Why are we angry?" asks Epictetus, the Stoic Greek philosopher. "Is it because we value so much the things of which ... men rob us? Do not admire your clothes, and then you will not be angry with the thieves. They are mistaken about good and evil. Ought we then to be angry with them, or to pity them?" Our resistance to evil is wrong when it arises from our having placed too high a value on self and its possessions.

God gave the Law to Moses so that self and its manifestations might be kept within bounds. If I push my own self interests without control and restraint and you do the same, what will happen? There will inevitably be a clash. Self-centeredness is the greatest peacebreaker there is. It broke the peace between man and God and it makes peace impossible between human beings.

Somebody hits you a blow. What is your instinctive

reaction? To give him only one blow in return? No, when he gives you one, you feel like giving him five. Self wants to retaliate out of all proportion to the injury done to self. If one man strikes another so that he loses an eye, the injured party feels like killing him, not merely plucking out his eye in return. The Jews believed in the latter course. When our Lord spoke of this law, He was referring to the commandments given to the Hebrews in Exodus 21:24, Deuteronomy 19:21, and Leviticus 24:20. "If a man cause a blemish in his neighbour; as he hath done, so shall it be done to him; breach for breach, eye for eye, tooth for tooth: as he hath caused a blemish in a man, so shall it be done to him again." And also, "If a false witness rise up against any man to testify against him that which is wrong... Then ye shall do unto him, as he had thought to have done unto his brother: so shalt thou put the evil away from among you... And thine eye shall not pity; but life shall go for life, eye for eye, tooth for tooth, hand for hand, foot for foot." The Mosaic Law did not exact a head for a tooth, a leg for a finger, but directed that there should be a correspondence between the harm done and the penalty inflicted. This is what our courts of law endeavor to do today: first to find out whether a person is guilty and then to impose an equitable punishment.

This determination of guilt and punishment is not a matter of private initiative but of public justice. We must not take into our hands what belongs to the courts. In Old Testament times the people had a system of public justice even as we have today. Some of the proud religionists of the day of Christ, the scribes and the Pharisees, usurped this prerogative for themselves, making the law a weapon for private revenge. But the law never gave a license to retaliate to any private

549

individual. This would result in despotism and chaos rather than law and order.

The peacemaking our Lord taught to His disciples did not entail the abolition of courts of justice or even of the law. Civilization would degenerate to anarchy if every man were his own judge and free to mete out his own brand of justice to others. There would be as many dictators as there are men. The end result would not be peacemaking but peacebreaking. "Think not," the Lord said, "that I am come to destroy the law, or the prophets: I am not come to destroy, but to fulfil" (Matt. 5:17). Our Lord wanted to forestall any misconceptions along this line, and perhaps to refute what some were already saying about Him. The Lord came to supplement the law. He was the grace added to truth and justice (John 1:14, 17). Without truth – a standard to measure by – there could be no guilt; and where there is no guilt no grace is needed. Grace, which is Christ, stands on truth and justice. And justice demands the punishment of the evil and the reward of the good.

But how are we to answer those who make the peacemaking of the seventh Beatitude equivalent to Christ's command in Matthew 5:39, "Resist not evil"? First we must bear in mind that no statement should be lifted out of context. These words taken in isolation from their context would result in absurd deductions. For instance, no parent should ever scold his child. We should stop locking our house and cars. The police force should be dismissed. People who drive through red lights should be able to do so with impunity. This would be a utopia for those who put self and its interests above everybody and everything else. That is, up to the point where they found out that it just wouldn't work.

Or take the words of Christ in Luke 14:26, "If any man come to me, and hate not his father, and mother, and wife, and children, and brethren, and sisters, yea, and his own life also, he cannot be my disciple." Taken as an independent, unrelated, universal statement, it imposes an immoral requirement, unworthy of the general character and purpose of Christ. But His hearers understood what He was saying. It was an extreme statement indicating that our primary love must be for Christ, and, in any conflict of interests between earthly loves and love of Christ, we must be willing to put Him first.

He spoke of faith removing mountains. But the removal of huge masses of rock and earth would be an unrealistic object for most people's prayers. Mountains stood for obstacles; and we pray, not to demonstrate that our prayers can move them, but for the accomplishment of some good purpose in accord with God's will.

It will help us to remember that Christ and His disciples all spoke in what may be called the Oriental idiom. They spoke as the people of Eastern lands always do, with what seems to the Western mind an exaggeration of expression, but is perfectly comprehensible to the native Easterner. Sometimes this Oriental manner of exaggeration for effect made it necessary for Christ, as He saw men taking Him literally, to modify His expressions and explain His meaning. He declared that a rich man could no more enter the Kingdom of Heaven than a camel could pass through a needle's eye. But when the disciples exclaimed, "Who then can be saved?" He said that only God could make it possible, implying that a special miracle would have to take place before a rich man could be saved.

An English teacher at Beirut, Lebanon, once said that the Bible needed little explanation to her scholars; they understood its idiom far better than she. A native of the East could tell in a few words far more clearly what Christ's command, "Resist not evil," means, than Tolstoi did in a whole book devoted to the subject. I certainly find my having been born and having lived for the major part of my life in the East extremely helpful in understanding the New Testament, which, when you come right down to it, is an Oriental book.

When you read the Bible, try to put yourself in the place of the one speaking, then in the place of the ones spoken to. Imagine yourself back in that time in history, under the circumstances and customs that prevailed in that day. Then ask yourself, "What do these particular words of Scripture mean in relation to the purpose of the one speaking, considering the condition of those spoken to, and the times and circumstances?" And the final question to ask yourself is, "How does this teaching harmonize with all the rest of Scripture?" Never try to apply a verse in isolation; you must understand it in relation to its particular context and to the whole context of Scripture.

RESISTANCE
OR NON - RESISTANCE — WHICH ?

"Resist not evil," said our Lord in Matthew 5:39, and many people have felt that this is connected with the seventh Beatitude in verse 9, "Blessed are the peacemakers." But what is the context of the whole passage in which this admonition is found (vv. 39-42) ? The Lord is contrasting the Christian life with the Old Testament Jewish ideal, as embodied in the law of Moses, and pointing out how that ideal had degenerated in actual practice. The Jewish ideal was to impose an equitable punishment upon the evildoer, not by the injured party but by the judges or the law of justice. The consequences of lawbreaking were inexorable. Pity was not to enter into it. There was no thought of winning over the evildoer and converting him. When Christ came, He introduced a higher concept — that of peacemaking. The Lord wants the blessed Christian to act as a peacemaker in the face of evil. How does He want us to do this?

1) By standing up for truth and seeking by all means to win others to the same Christian blessedness that we ourselves enjoy.

2) When someone attacks the truth, to resist him, but in a proper spirit and with a right motive. Christianity is predominantly a religion of the motive behind the action. We are not to do good with the expectation of attracting the favor of God, but to do God's will because of our love for God Himself and for His glory. It is not just what we do that counts in Christianity but why we do it.

3) Our non-resistance to evil must be on the same basis — because of God and for His glory. When should

we not resist evil? When no principle is at stake; when by our kind and unimpassioned behavior we can win the erring one to a softer frame of mind, in which the claims of the Gospel can be presented.

When Southey was a small boy, he tells of another boy in his neighborhood by the name of Jim Dick. A number of children began tormenting him one evening, calling him names because of his racial origin. The poor little fellow was reduced to tears and slunk away. One day Southey wanted to go skating, but his skates were broken, and the only boy from whom he could borrow a pair was Jim Dick. "I went to him and asked him for them," said Southey. " 'Oh, yes, Robert, you may have them and welcome,' was his answer. When I went to return them, I found Jim sitting by the fire in the kitchen reading the Bible. I told him I had returned the skates and was under great obligations to him for his kindness. He looked at me as he took his skates and with tears in his eyes, said, 'Robert, don't ever call me names again,' and immediately left the room. The word pierced my heart; and I burst into tears, and from that time resolved never again to abuse a member of a minority group."

We resist evil only so that the truth may be maintained, not that we may get even with the enemy of truth. Retaliation, or besting another in an argument, should never be the motive of our resistance against others. The Lord never retaliated against His enemies but died that He might redeem them. If His voluntary sacrifice in going to the cross were not to be of benefit to His enemies, it would be a wasted effort, a senseless tragedy. He did not die only to satisfy the justice of God but also for the eternal welfare of others. There was no selfish motive in His death. It was actually His resistance against sin, the evil in man. His death was the only means by which man could be redeemed. His resistance to evil could have taken the form of destruction of His enemies. And one day in the consummation of the age this will happen. But during this dispensation of grace, the central purpose of God through Christ and His followers is redemption, not punishment. That redemption can take place because of Christ's sacrifice.

If we resist evil only for the sake of seeing punishment meted out and retaliating for wrongs done to us, we are not being Christlike. We are like the Pharisees of old, who were vindictive in their application of the law. That is why the Lord had to tell the men of His day not to resist evil, since their motive was to get even rather than to reclaim the sinner to righteousness.

Here is an illustration that has made this practical in the experience of some with whom I have been associated. A man had funds entrusted to him for the purpose of spreading God's Word. But instead of purchasing Bibles and Testaments to distribute, he was appropriating the money for himself. When his embezzlement was discovered, what was the Christian who entrusted him with the money supposed to do? Forget it? This would only embolden the embezzler to try the same thing on others. The Christian had certain responsibilities in this case. They were toward God, toward the embezzler, and toward the original donors of that money. He was faced with a conflict of responsibilities. If he let the embezzler go, and he continued to defraud others, the Christian would bear part of the blame. He would actually be an accomplice. And since he allowed his donors to be defrauded, he must either make good himself what had been embezzled or try to recover it from the thief. Now in all this he was never possessed with the spirit of retaliation, but while justice was satisfied, the redemption of the soul of the culprit was sought diligently and prayerfully.

Actually, the law of the Old Testament not only asked for an equitable punishment of the evildoer in Leviticus 24:20, "Breach for breach, eye for eye, tooth for tooth," but also the absence of hatred in the execution of such punishment. "Thou shalt not hate thy brother in thine heart: thou shalt in any wise rebuke thy neighbour, and not suffer sin upon him. Thou shalt not avenge, nor bear any grudge against the children of thy people, but thou shalt love thy neighbour as thyself" (Lev. 19:17, 18). The religionists of Christ's day, however, conveniently ignored this latter injunction.

But the Lord went further in asking us to seek the conversion of the evildoer. The verb "love," in the command, "Love your enemies," is *agapate* in Greek, which speaks of a love that is unselfish, a love that is attached to its object because of the latter's need. God loves us in our sin, but His love does not pursue a policy of non-resistance toward that sin; it implies pity for us. God's love for mankind is not a compromise of holiness with sin, but the pity of holiness for sin. When in His love He resists our sin, and us as we persist in sin, it is because He wants to win us.

Loving our enemies does not mean that we submissively consent to their hating us, but that we consider their enmity toward us pitiful, and seek to convert it into love. This is also true of resistance to evil. When the Lord says "Resist not evil," He means that we are to love those who try to do evil to us, by earnestly yearning and working for their conversion — even if that may involve personal suffering and loss. The motive is the same whether we resist or do not resist: the conversion of the evildoer.

Mere non-resistance to evil does not result in peacemaking as the Lord Jesus taught it; it does not bring the peace of God to the heart of the evildoer. It takes more than that. The same is true of resistance against evil. Merely to be against somebody or something is not what Christ teaches; nor does He teach that it is enough not to be against people and things. The Lord does not condone either opposition or apathy toward evil. Our Christian attitude toward it should be remedial. If it is not, our motive is wrong. It is also wrong to go on sacrificing yourself, either in resistance or nonresistance to evil, if you have ample evidence that the evildoer is resolute in his persistence in evil.

This is what the Lord meant when He said, "Give not that which is holy unto the dogs, neither cast ye your pearls before swine, lest they trample them under their feet, and turn again and rend you" (Matt. 7:6). Our Lord recognized that there are some people who are no better than pigs. It would be dangerous not to resist them. We are never to be quick to place anyone in the category of "dogs" and "swine," brutish souls who will trample our sacrifices underfoot and turn and rend us, thus becoming more confirmed in their bestiality. But neither are we under obligation to expose our tenderest relations with Christ to the spiritually coarse and rejecting. "Pearls before swine" are uncalled for sacrifices, serving no good purpose, and subjecting us to useless suffering.

On the other hand, there are those to whom kindness brings compunction and consequent conversion. Thus in our peacemaking it is necessery to practice both resistance and non-resistance, with discrimination, judging each situation on its merits, as guided by the Holy Spirit.

CHRIST OUR EXAMPLE IN PEACEMAKING

The words of Christ may sometimes be misunderstood, but, when taken in conjunction with His actions, they will be strikingly illuminated. As we try to comprehend what He meant when He said, "Blessed are the peacemakers: for they shall be called the children of God," we shall do well to examine His life and study His example of peacemaking. The Lord Jesus went a good way along the path of non-resistance, but He was far from being what Tolstoi imagined Him to be — completely opposed to setting the record straight.

The Gospels give no instance of Christ smiting when smitten, or injuring when injured. He could have struck back had He wanted to, but He did not will to do so. Herein lies His greatness, His superiority over man. We would strike back and take justice into our own hands if we could, but He would not though He could. Great power not controlled by the divine will is a dangerous force indeed. Fear the person who has tremendous power and a sinful, greedy, revengeful, hate-filled nature. The will of the divinely indwelt person will exert a restraining influence on his capacity to strike, but the will of the unregenerate will misdirect his power. Power that seeks to destroy before it has tried to redeem the evildoer is not Christlike. The word "perfect" in Greek is *teleioi*, which comes from *telos*, meaning "end, goal, purpose." The test of our perfection, referred to in Matthew 5:48, is whether we are reaching God's goal for every human soul, his salvation. We must try in every way we can, including personal sacrifice, to bring this about, without compromising principle or doctrine.

The Lord could have descended from the cross when challenged to do so. But He did not want the manifestation of His power to be simply in response to human challenge, but the natural outcome of His eternally appointed task. He refused to come down from the cross in defiance of man's hate and revenge, but He arose from the grave while no man was conscious of what was going on. In the same manner we should be resistant to evil in our peacemaking because of our blessedness in Christ, rather than in defiance of the evil that confronts and challenges us. It is not to be resistance for its own sake, or in retaliation for personal affronts, but because of our belief in justice and right, for the sake of Christ.

> Am I a soldier of the cross,
>   A follow'r of the Lamb,
> And shall I fear to own His cause,
>   Or blush to speak His name?
>
> Are there no foes for me to face?
>   Must I not stem the flood?
> Is this vile world a friend to grace,
>   To help me on to God?
>
> Since I must fight if I would reign,
>   Increase my courage, Lord.
> I'll bear the toil, endure the pain,
>   Supported by Thy Word.

Christ did resist His foes, by word, by look, by gesture. And yet He permitted Himself to be sentenced, mistreated, and crucified. He could have struck them all dead in an instant, but He chose not to do so, because then there would have been no possibility of their ever appropriating His peace through His own cross and resurrection. His was a merciful mission, offering opportunity before condemnation, salvation before judgment. He deliberately set the bounds of His resistance or non-resistance as a matter of His discreet choice. This was part and parcel, not of a prescribed philosophy of non-resistance, but of His mission of fulfilling His Father's will to save and redeem mankind. One of the focal verses of the New Testament is John 3:17, "For God sent not his Son into the world to condemn the world; but that the world through him might be saved." Striking His enemies dead would certainly not be accomplishing this purpose. He had to suffer at the hands of evil men in fulfillment of His mission. This was not submitting to their evil but to God's justice, which required the payment of the penalty of sin. Had Christ fully resisted evil, it would have been tantamount to the destruction of evil men by force. But His purpose was the redemption of evil men through whatever personal sacrifice was necessary. In His first coming, Christ resisted evil only to the degree necessary to show people that He was neither the author nor the supporter of it. He did not resist beyond the point where His resistance would hinder the purpose for which He came. We see, then, that He came to resist evil and at the same time to redeem men from it. He would not allow His first purpose to hinder His second, nor the second to cancel out the first.

This is why we find Christ seemingly acquiescent toward evil on occasion. He forbade force to be employed in His defense against His cruel foes. "Put up again thy sword into his place: for all they that take the sword shall perish with the sword" (Matt. 26:52), He said to Peter, who had cut off the ear of one of the soldiers who came to arrest Him. This was useless resistance. Its end result could not have been the redemption of the Roman soldier. And Christ, in spite of constant remonstrances from His disciples, did not wish to be spared from the cross. He could have avoided it but He would not, for your sake and mine. Praise God that He didn't! He surrendered Himself and was led away. He could have summoned twelve legions of angels to rescue Him, but He would not.

Our resistance to evil must fit within the framework of God's purpose. It should not be aimless. It should lead to peacemaking, that is, reconciling men to God. Was Christ referring to Peter when He said, "They that take the sword shall perish with the sword"? It is more likely that He was referring to the armed soldiers who came to apprehend Him. Leave them alone, said Christ. They rely on the sword; they hate Me and reject My salvation; their final end shall be judgment — the sword.

Observe Christ in court. His accusers were unable to find any two witnesses whose testimony against Him would agree. Finally the High Priest called Jesus to the stand and administered the oath. "I adjure thee by the living God, that thou tell us whether thou be the Christ, the Son of God" (Matt. 26:63). Jesus protested, "If I tell you, ye will not believe" (Luke 22:67). Yet He freely bore His testimony, declared that He was the Son of God, and was led away to His death.

One day Jesus wanted to travel from Galilee in the north to Jerusalem, where He would ultimately die — not because of His inability to resist and subjugate evil, but because it was His Father's will for Him to do so. As Samaria lay between Galilee and Judea, He sent messengers to Samaria, who asked the inhabitants of a certain village to make ready for Jesus' passing through. They refused to receive Him, which greatly angered His disciples. James and John returned to Jesus and said, "Lord, wilt thou that we command fire to come down from heaven, and consume them, even as Elias- did?" Now, they could have done this, if Jesus had given them the power, and He had it to give them. Observe how He rebuked them: "Ye know not what manner of spirit ye are of. For the Son of man is not come to destroy men's lives, but to save them" (see Luke 9:51-56).

Notice that these incidents were connected with His death at Jerusalem for the sake of reconciling man to God. He would let nothing stand in the way of the perfect consummation of His life in death – an end that would be the beginning of eternal life for you and me.

A Chinese Emperor, upon being told that his enemies had raised an insurrection in one of the distant provinces, said, "Come, then, my friends, follow me, and I promise you that we shall quickly destroy them." He marched forward, and the rebels submitted at his approach. All now thought that he would take the most signal revenge, but were surprised to see the captives treated with mildness and humanity. "How!" cried the First Minister; "is this the manner in which you fulfill your promise? Your royal word was given that your enemies should be destroyed, and behold you have pardoned them all, and even caressed some of them!" "I promised," replied the Emperor, with a generous air, "to destroy my enemies; I have fulfilled my word; for, see, they are enemies no longer: I have made friends of them."

Christ has two ways of destroying His enemies: one is to win them by love, as exemplified in His death on the cross; the other is to let them reap the consequences of their rejection of Him in the final judgment. "Greater love hath no man than this, that a man lay down his life for his friends ... But God commendeth his love toward us, in that, while we were yet sinners, Christ died for us" (John 15:13, Rom. 5:8). What more can

He do to make peace with His enemies? Yours is the choice: Will you be won over by love through accepting His atoning work on the cross for you; or must you await the final judgment in fear and trembling?

RESISTING IN LOVE

Though Christ protested against evil on many occasions in His life, and even took action against it, His resistance to man and man's wickedness was never such as to hinder Him from being completely subject to the will of His Father. He had come into the world to save sinners, to destroy the works of the devil, and nothing must be allowed to divert Him from His mission. When you remember this, you will see where His resistance found its place in the total framework of His life. Christ resisted evil and rebuked His foes by look, by word, by gesture. Think of His words to Ruler and Pharisee and Scribe. They were awful in their severity – among the sternest ever spoken. Did He always quietly submit to the anger of His foes? No, only if that submission would further the total plan and purpose for which He came into the world.

And as He is, so are we in this world, the Bible tells us. Our resistance or non-resistance to evil must have the same motivation – to win souls and overcome wickedness for Christ's sake. We not only have no right to resent and avenge personal affronts, but we also have no right to let affronts to God and others go unchecked and unchallenged. We are to have neither the "tit-for-tat" spirit nor the *laissez faire* spirit.

On one occasion, when His countrymen sought to cast Him from the brow of the hill whereon their city stood, we read, "He passing through the midst of them went his way" (Luke 4:30). Did He always offer the other cheek when He had been smitten? He did not do so in the presence of the High Priest, but asked in remonstrance, "Why smitest thou me?" He wanted to submit, and He did, but not without a protest. We, too, should be true protestants in the presence of evil, remembering, nevertheless, that we have a God above to whom we owe submission. Never yield to evil, but to God, who may permit it to accomplish His divinely and mysteriously appointed will. We may be sure that even the most literal-minded of our Lord's hearers would not have felt bound to offer his cloak to one who had stolen his coat. He understood that our Lord meant to apply a principle here, that we are not to value our material possessions above winning over an enemy for Christ. In this connection, I like a little motto that used to hang in the lobby of Shelton College:

> Hail, Guest, we ask not what thou art;
> If friend, we greet thee, hand and heart;
> If stranger, such no longer be;
> If foe, our love shall conquer thee.

When Christ went up to the Temple, a corrupt and wicked government had put cattle in the one court where the Gentiles might go. He did not merely utter a verbal protest against it; He wove a whip of small cords of the straw that was at His feet and, with flashing eye and with thunderous tones, drove the frightened traders from the Temple with their cattle, and overturned the money-changers' tables, leaving the money to roll about the floor.

When the Temple band came to arrest Him, and His disciples were defenseless in Gethsemane, Christ went forward and put Himself between the band and the disciples. They fell backward to the ground. For the moment, He confronted them and held them at bay, that His disciples might escape, and then, and not till then, surrendered Himself. Christ used force to defend others but never to defend Himself. The fundamental principle in Christ's teaching is this: Love may use combativeness; selfishness may not. The wrath, says the Book of Revelation, is the wrath of the Lamb. There is a combativeness motivated by love that is legitimate. If the highwayman demands my purse, I may hand it over to him rather than take his life, and frankly confess, were I ever so brave, I think I would rather go without my purse than have the blood even of a guilty man on my hands. But if he assaults my wife or my children, whom God has put in my keeping, that is another matter; then, if I do not defend them, I am a coward and a criminal. Our lives are so intertwined with one another that it is often impossible to tell whether we are defending ourselves or another. It is spirit, not rule or regulation, which Christ prescribes, and this is the spirit: Love may fight; selfishness may not. To a considerable extent modern civilization accepts this principle. In a barbaric community every man carries a pistol in his hip pocket. We civilized communities do not. We trust other men to be our defenders and protectors. (See Lyman Abbot's sermon, "War or Peace," in *The Christian World Pulpit*, Vol 49, p. 132.)

As we saw in our studies on meekness and in our examination of Christ as the meek and humble One, the divine method is not passive but active in relation to evil. God resists evil, not passively, watching it without involvement and hoping for the best, but by doing something for its reversal, for the establishment of righteousness in its place. There is a moral order in the world, which, if we go against, will slowly but surely bring retribution upon us.

> Though the mills of God grind slowly,
>   Yet they grind exceeding small;
> Though with patience He stands waiting,
>   With exactness grinds He all.

Surely we are in line with that order when, with pity in our hearts for the sinner, we resist his sin. This is what is involved in our peacemaking. Christ Himself looked round upon His foes "with anger, being grieved for the hardness of their hearts" (Mark 3:5). That is the point at which we so often fail. We become angry, not just against the sin, but against the sinner, often without pity for him in our hearts. What is right in God cannot be wrong in man insofar as he moves along the same lines and is touched by a like spirit. A mother shows more love in reproving her child than in permitting him to grow up with a disregard for the rights of others. A doctor shows more love in causing pain to a patient that will ultimately be to his benefit than in letting him die of his malady. A judge shows more love in imposing a corrective sentence on an offender than in letting him continue in a life of crime. There may indeed be more love in resistance than in yielding to the evildoer. There may be more love in the sentence against than in indifference to his offense. But in both the heart of love must beat, and our resistance to evil or our judgment upon it must be directed against the sin, not the sinner.

Let us permit the life of Christ to cast light upon His words. He is the best interpretation of His teaching. We are not merely to obey the words, but to follow the speaker of them; we have not only a guide-book but a guide, and it is by both of these, not merely one, that we should be led. Orthopraxy — right doing — is our exegesis of orthodoxy — right thinking. (See "Non-Resistance," by W. Garrett Horder, in *The Christian World Pulpit*, Vol. 49, pp. 117-19.)

"The words that I speak unto you, they are spirit, and they are life," said Christ (John 6:63). Letter-of-the-law Christians are as deserving of censure as were the letter-of-the-law scribes and Pharisees whom Jesus rebuked. It is possible to obey Christ's commands to the letter and totally fail to discern their original intent or the spirit that should motivate them. You can turn the other cheek in a spirit of self-righteous martyrdom that will only infuriate your assailant further. Or you can with perfect propriety rebuke him in love, and in a kindly spirit even restrain him physically from inflicting injury on you, without violating the spirit of Christ's commandment. It is retaliation that is forbidden, meeting anger with anger. By refusing to respond in kind, you demonstrate that you obey a higher law, the law of love. Take this, then, as your guiding principle in seeking to carry out the will of God with respect to resistance or non-resistance: It is the spirit that counts; love may combat, but selfishness may not.

DO YOU HAVE PEACE OF SOUL ?

When we read "Blessed are the peacemakers," in Matthew 5:9, we take it for granted that we understand what Christ meant by these words. But there are many facets to this simple injunction. For instance, what direction does this peace take? Can you bring peace to others if you yourself are not at peace with God?

Your peace must first have an inward direction. Your initial concern should be to have peace in your own soul and life, for you cannot share what you do not possess. To try to do so is hypocrisy. Pity the poor souls who go to church looking for peace and have the misfortune to sit under a preacher who preaches the peace of God but has never experienced it. His words lack conviction because they are not mirrored in his life. Those who possess peace show it through their lives as well as their words. But the trouble is not altogether with the preacher. There are many sitting in the pews who know the peace of God, realize that the preacher neither has it nor preaches it, yet make no effort to share their peace with him or others who are in need of it. A peacemaker must have firm convictions about God's way of peace and be willing to do something about them. As someone has said, "It would be a great mercy if every converted person would positively refuse to listen twice to any minister who denies the inspiration of the Bible, or to give a penny to a church or missionary society that gave the right hand of fellowship to men of this type. If this were done, there would be less people in the pulpits and on the mission field whose preaching brings everything but peace to the souls of men."

What Woodrow Wilson said about preachers is worthy

of the careful consideration of every one of us: "When I hear some of the things which young men say to men by way of putting the arguments to themselves for going into the ministry, I think they are talking of another profession. Their motive is to do something. You do not have to be anything in particular to be a lawyer, and I know. You do not have to be anything in particular, except a kind-hearted man, perhaps, to be a physician, nor undergo any strong spiritual change in order to be a merchant. The only profession which consists in being something is the ministry of our Lord and Saviour — and it does not consist of anything else. And that conception of the ministry which rubs all the marks off and mixes him in the crowd so that you cannot pick him out, is a process of eliminating the ministry itself."

Our job as preachers is to share the peace of God in our own hearts. If we do not possess it, we ought not to waste the time of others by offering them empty words, deceiving them into believing that they can find something worthwhile in our well-turned but hollow phrases.

A young preacher fresh from seminary went to the front as a chaplain. He announced to the soldiers that he would let them choose whether they wanted him to preach a sermon or tell them funny stories. A tall, blunt-speaking fellow arose and said, "If you have come three thousand miles to talk to a bunch of soldiers, some of whom are going into eternity within three days, and you don't know whether to preach to them or tell them funny stories, I suspect you had just better go ahead and tell something funny." Think of it! No wonder men faint from fear, when no one is willing or able to share with them the peace of God.

The Beatitudes, including the injunction to peace-making, are addressed primarily to Christ's disciples.

who had already experienced the peace of God as a result of the forgiveness of their sins by Christ. Because this is the only way peace can come to us, it should form the basis of our preaching. Any book on peace for the troubled man of the twentieth century immediately becomes a best seller. There is a great uneasiness in the souls of men. Let's not tell them that this disturbance is the result of unjustified guilt-feelings, that it is all the product of man's sick imagination. The cause is real; the Bible calls it sin, rebellion against God. Unless man makes peace with God, he will never know peace of heart and mind.

It is said of a famous preacher that he always preached "as a dying man to dying men." Such preaching is effective. A minister visiting a penitentiary one Saturday was invited by the Christian warden to speak to the inmates the next day. That evening the minister felt that he should return to the penitentiary to learn the details regarding the service. Noting two chairs draped in black in the main assembly room, he inquired as to the reason. Said the warden, "These two chairs are draped for death. Your sermon will be the last these men will ever hear." Do you think that a funny story would have helped these men? What they needed was peace with God; they needed Christ as their Saviour before they met Him as Judge. I am very conscious as I preach that there are chairs in most audiences draped for death. The peace of God in my own soul is the most precious possession I have. Like Peter and John, "Such as I have give I thee: In the name of Jesus Christ of Nazareth rise up and walk" (Acts 3:6). Sin paralyzes and deforms. Christ releases us and heals our spiritual wounds. In His healing of our souls we find peace.

We must preach what has passed through the crucible of our own experience. We shall never produce conviction in others until truth is a burning conviction in our own souls. And genuine peace can only be based upon truth. If we do not practice and preach the truth, we cannot hope either to enjoy peace or be peacemakers. Bunyan says, "I preached what I did feel, what I smartingly did feel." When David Hume, the philosopher, had listened to John Broun of Haddington, he remarked, "That's the man for me; he means what he says; he preaches as if Christ were at his elbow."

Are you at peace in your own soul? The first exercise in peacemaking is to look inward. You may be in the best of circumstances, and yet there is a secret pang that makes you ill at ease; there is a bitter thought that comes across you when first you wake in the morning; there is a something of which you do not like to speak, of which you do not like to hear, and of which, if possible, you would rather not think. That is your alienation from God. You are at war with your Creator. You need to make peace with Him through Jesus Christ, who is our peace. It hurts to recognize your sin; it is like submitting to the surgeon's knife. But look at the results — healing, forgiveness, and the peace that passeth all understanding.

For those who have already made peace with God through Jesus Christ, there is still an inward look to take. We may be going through a time of suffering, pain, sorrow, illness, and yet be in perfect peace because we are doing our God-appointed duty. It may be that our duty is only the duty of endurance, resignation, and submission. Never mind. If this be clear before us. and if we resolve upon this, it is enough. "They also serve who only stand and wait." Or it may be that our duty involves business, or public cares, or private ministrations. That, too, is enough. It shows the path before us straight and clear; it makes us indifferent to what people say or think of us; it makes us forget ourselves; it makes life worth living; it makes death welcome. "Mark the perfect man, and behold the upright," says the Psalmist, "for the end of that man is peace" (Ps. 37:37). To have said the right thing, though it cost us an effort; to have done the right thing, though it seemed hard at the time; this, you may be sure, leaves a tranquillity behind that long outlives the moment and makes us feel as if we were in a haven of rest, because the peace of conscience is indeed the peace of the Holy Spirit of Christ. (See *The Anglican Pulpit Library*, Vol. 9, p. 28.)

The fact that Christ said, "Blessed are the peacemakers," shows that though it is God's desire for every one of His creatures to possess His peace, this is not the actual state of affairs. No man is born with the peace of God in his heart. The natural man is not in harmony with God; he is a rebel. God has taken the initiative of bringing us back to Himself by sending His Son to die for us. But that does not automatically save all. We must appropriate God's offer. It takes two to make peace: God offers it and man accepts it. Salvation is all of grace, but man must have faith to receive it. Blessed are those who make peace with God — their own peace, yet not their own but based on the peace of God that by faith they make their very own.

Isn't it strange that when we read the words of our Master, "Blessed are the peacemakers," we think only of the role we should play in the lives of others. But we cannot play that role until we have first applied the lesson to our own hearts. Blessed is the man who has made his peace with God. No matter how long you have been at war with Him, if you will only believe on Christ, for His sake you can experience that peace for yourself. This personal peacemaking is for the passionate, the fretful, the ill-tempered, the selfish, and the sinful. It begins with your own life.

The work of peace is neither superficial nor external. It is as deep as the human heart. We are accustomed to look upon the restlessness and the strife of the world as something about us, but the secret of it all is within us. It is written in the inner place of every man's life. Men are wrong with each other because they are wrong with God. Sin is the one and only disturber of the peace, and sin is the transgression of the infinite law of righteousness and love under which the soul lives. The way to peace lies through the cleansing of the inward life from all impure and selfish thoughts and purposes. It lies through the vision of God that brings with it the true vision of life. The peacemakers are to be called the sons of God because they are, indeed, the children of their Father in heaven, living out their lives in simple obedience to His will. They are not so much the sons of God because they make peace; rather they make peace because they are living in realization and acknowledgment of that sonship. The peace that a man is able to minister to the world about him is just the measure of the peace that is ever being ministered to his own heart in response to his reverence and faith and obedience and spiritual earnestness.

Entering into peace is entering into life as God means it should be lived, understanding its true significance, its priceless spiritual values, and its real issues. The peaceful — and therefore the peacemaking — life is one lived in harmony with the divine order. And the way into such harmony is a blood-stained way. The world's true peace grows out of the world's supreme tragedy. "Having made peace by the blood of his cross." The hands that are stretched forth to still the passions and the strifes of men are nail-pierced hands. The feet that

574

go before us in the way of peace are wounded feet. The divine Peacemaker was crucified. And it is at the cross, with its awful indictment of human selfishness and its tender mercy for every sinful life, that the work of peace begins. It is not possible to set forth the nature and scope of this work of peacemaking in anything but general terms. It is not a duty in life, it is a whole duty of life, to seek peace and pursue it. Every effort to be what God means us to be, and to do what God means us to do, is a real part of the high service of peace. (Percy C. Ainsworth, *The Blessed Life*, pp. 147-150.)

THE FIRST QUALIFICATION OF A PEACEMAKER - UNSELFISHNESS

Christians have to get along with two classes of people in this world: those who, like themselves, are blessed because of Christ, and those who have never come to know Him as Saviour. Their peacemaking activities are related to both. Sometimes it is harder to live at peace with those within the fold of Christ than with those without. Paul had his differences with Barnabas, John Mark, Peter, and James; and we, too, will experience personality clashes in our dealings with other Christians. We tend to expect perfection from those in Christ, and they expect perfection from us, but as we rub shoulders in the exercise of our daily tasks we find out that we are still human beings who are pressing toward the mark but have not fully attained. Of course, it is much easier to see the imperfections of others than our own. A Christian really needs a pair of two-way spectacles that would enable him to look as clearly inside himself as outside. There would be much more peace in the family of God if you and I started wearing such glasses.

Modern psychologists say that sometimes the faults we are most intolerant of in others are those that we secretly or unconsciously harbor in our own hearts. We have two sets of value-words in dealing with the shortcomings of others as compared to our own. We say: They are stubborn; we are firm. They are badtempered; we are righteously indignant. They are greedy and grasping; we are prudent and foresighted. They sometimes cut corners or are downright dishonest; we are businesslike and practical. They tell lies; we are tactful.

We all know and are amused by the overweight person who wants everyone else to go on a diet, but claims he cannot lose weight himself because overweight runs in his family. But on a larger scale this sort of self-deception is not amusing, and among Christians it makes our testimony valueless in the eyes of our brethren and the world. "Why beholdest thou the mote that is in thy brother's eye," asked our Lord, "but considerest not the beam that is in thine own eye? Or how wilt thou say to thy brother, Let me pull out the mote out of thine eye; and, behold, a beam is in thine own eye? Thou hypocrite, first cast out the beam out of thine own eye; and then shalt thou see clearly to cast out the mote out of thy brother's eye" (Matt. 7:3-5).

Yet the Christian peacemaker cannot remain indifferent to his adversaries. At the funeral of the late great Greek Evangelical leader, Dr. Constantin Metallinos, it was said that what stood out about his life was that he had no enemies. But that was only a half-truth; it described his personal attitude toward others, believers and unbelievers alike. But that could hardly have been the attitude of all others toward him, for that would have contradicted the experience and words of Christ, who said, "Ye shall be hated of all men for my name's sake" (Matt. 10:22). When Thomas a Kempis was negotiating with the proud religionists of his unevangelical day, we hear him saying, "Jesus Christ was despised of men, forsaken of His friends and lovers, and in the midst of slanders. He was willing, under His Father's will, to suffer and to be despised, and darest thou to complain of any man's usage of thee? Christ, thy Master, had enemies and backbiters, and dost thou expect to have all men to be thy friends and benefactors? Whence shall thy patience attain her promised crown if no adversity befall thee? Suffer thou with Jesus Christ, and for His sake, if thou wouldst reign with Him. Set thyself, therefore, to bear manfully the cross of thy Lord, who, out of love, was crucified for thee. Know for certain that thou must lead a daily dying life. And the more that thou diest to thyself all that the more shalt thou live unto God."

The Christian hates no man, but he is often hated for the sake of his principles. It is the duty of the peacemaker, short of sinning and compromising principle, to win his adversaries over by love.

Observe that the Greek word used in urging us to love others is the verb *agapaoo*, which means to love someone, not because of what he is, but in spite of it, because of his need. God loved us, not because we were good, and pure, and lovable, but because in our sinful, lost estate we needed Him. That is the kind of love He wants us to demonstrate to others. Where would we be if God loved us only when we deserved it? We are to love our adversaries, not because they deserve it but because they need it.

Another Greek word for love used in the New Testament is *phileoo*, which refers to a love based on common interests rather than the unselfish sacrifice implied in *agapee*. In our peacemaking, the Lord does not want us to love the world in the sense of *philoumen*, accommodating our principles to its sinful indulgences, but in the sense of *agapoomen*, for the sake of winning men to Jesus Christ. This love "seeketh not her own, is not easily provoked, thinketh no evil; rejoiceth not in iniquity, but rejoiceth in the truth; beareth all things, believeth all things, hopeth all things, endureth all things" (I Cor. 13:5-7). It "suffereth long, and is kind ... envieth not ... vaunteth not itself, is not puffed up"

(v. 5). The Christian cannot sit contentedly under the rapture of God. He cannot keep it selfishly for himself. God loved and He gave. Have you that kind of love?

A state of alienation is too painful to be borne when it can be mended. If, without loss of true honor, or practical injustice, or any other greater evil following, the offender can be won to penitence or the offended to pardon by any humbling on our part or by personal loss and pain, the pure heart will be pressed out of itself to win its brother, as God in Christ has won us. The peacemaker then loves with a divine love that is not won over to sin but that woos the sinner to Calvary.

In our mission of peacemaking, as we seek to demonstrate love to those who rub shoulders with us in life, whether they be believers or unbelievers, we must recognize and correct those tendencies in ourselves that would break the peace rather than promote it. The first direction of our peacemaking must be inward.

There must be no stinging conscience, there must be no unsatisfied desire, there must be no inner schism between inclination and duty, reason and will, passion and judgment. There must be the quiet of a harmonized nature which has one object, one aim, one love, without contradictions running through the inmost self. There is only one way to get that peace — cleaving to Jesus Christ and making Him our Lord, our righteousness, our aim, our all. Your conscience will sting, and that destroys peace; or, if it does not sting, it will be torpid, and that destroys peace, for death is not peace. Unless we take Christ for our love, for the light of our minds, for the Sovereign Arbiter and Lord of our will, for the home of our desires, for the aim of our efforts, we shall never know what it is to reproduce His gentleness, sympathy, compassion, insight into men's sorrows, patience with men's offenses, and all which makes, in our relations to one another, the harmony and the happiness of humanity.

The primary disturber of the peace in our own lives and the lives of others is our lusts and passions, our appetites and desires. If we are greedy and are not satisfied with what God has been pleased to give us, and we place our passions first, we will disturb the peace of contentment within ourselves and the peace of others. We may thus destroy the peace of our own homes, of wife, of husband, of children. The craving for self-satisfaction, the desire to have everybody contribute to our physical or spiritual wants, is the greatest peacebreaker imaginable. Peacemaking love must attend a funeral — the funeral of its own self — before Christ can work in and through us and His glory be reflected in us and by us.

A selfish man can neither be peaceful nor a peacemaker. He cares intensely and continually for his own wants, however minute, and nothing for the greater distress of his brother, however pressing. He seeks his own advantage; and if the way to it should lead through chaos, amid bloodshed, a universal disquiet, it matters not to him. His object is to gratify himself, and he is prepared to sacrifice others in the process. Abbé Grou says, "Self-love makes us touchy, ready to take offense, ill-tempered, suspicious, severe, exacting, easily offended; it keeps alive in our hearts a certain malignity, a secret joy at the mortifications which befall our neighbor; it nourishes our readiness to criticize, our dislike at certain persons, our ill-feeling, our bitterness, and a thousand other things prejudicial to charity."

Let it be stated, then, that the first qualification of a peacemaker is unselfishness, for only in the spirit of Christ can he bring Christ's peace to others.

THE CHARACTERISTICS
OF THE PEACEMAKER

We have seen that a selfish man can never be peaceful or a peacemaker. The first Beatitude establishes the basis of all our peacemaking — poverty of spirit or humility. Without humility no one can be a peacemaker; and no selfish person can be humble. The would-be peacemaker cannot mount to the seventh rung of the ladder of Christian blessedness without having taken the first step of humility, without having fulfilled the first condition of blessedness — humbling himself before God. There can be no skipping of rungs on this ladder, though many Christians have tried and are trying to do just that. That is why so many undertaking the professional task of peacemaking turn out to be peacebreakers. As Alexander Whyte says, "Every man who is to be the minister of a parish should make his own heart and his own life his first parish. His own vineyard should be his first knowledge and his first care. And then out of that and after that he will be able to speak to his people, and to correct, and counsel, and take care of them. In Thomas Boston's *Memoirs* we continually come on entries like this: 'Preached on Ps. xlii 5, and mostly on my own account.' And, again, we read in the same invaluable book for parish ministers, that its author did not wonder to hear that good had been done by last Sabbath's sermon, because he had preached it to himself and had got good to himself out of it before he took it to the pulpit."

If you are not humble, you cannot fulfill the rest of Christ's commandments in the Beatitudes. You cannot mourn, you cannot be meek, you cannot hunger and thirst for a righteousness that is not your own, you cannot be merciful, you cannot be pure in heart, and finally you cannot be a peacemaker.

When we know ourselves as we are, and see ourselves in the light of God, we learn to lie low in the dust, to think others better than ourselves, and to wonder that so great grace has been manifested by God to us so unworthy. When one thus feels humbled in the sight of God, he will show himself most tender, most unselfish, in the sight of and in his relationships to man. He feels that his own place is larger than he deserves; his own fame much louder than he merits; his own blessings far richer than he ever dreamed of; and he will be so overwhelmed by the sight of the good things that he has, and a sense of how little he merits them, that he will have no time to pick quarrels with a brother. He rejoices at the prosperity of every one who he thinks is better than himself, and of whom he can only entertain the most charitable and kindly apprehensions.

The second trio of Beatitudes following the fourth Beatitude of hungering and thirsting after righteousness has to do with our relations to others. Before God we have to be humble, mournful, meek; and before men we have to be merciful, pure, and peacemaking. As Alexander Maclaren says: "The climax of Christian character, according to Jesus Christ Himself, is found in our relations to men, and not in our relation to God. Worship of heart and spirit, devout emotions of the sacredest, sweetest, most hallowed and hallowing sort, are absolutely indispensable. But equally, if not more, important is it for us to remember that the purest communion with God, and the selectest emotional experiences of the Christian life, are meant to be the bases of active service: and that, if it does not follow these, there is good reason for supposing that these are spurious, and worth very little. The service of man is the outcome of the love of God. He who begins with poverty of spirit is perfected when, forgetting himself, and coming down from the mountain-top, where the Shekinah cloud of the glory and the audible voice are, he plunges into the struggles of the multitude below, and frees the devil-ridden boy from the demon that possessed him. Begin by all means with poverty of spirit, or you will never get to this — 'Blessed are the peace-makers.' But see to it that poverty of spirit leads to the meekness, the mercifulness, the peace-bringing influence which Christ has pronounced blessed." *(The Beatitudes and Other Sermons, pp. 66-7.)*

"That man knows little of himself," says Alexander Whyte, "who does not despise himself for his secret self-seeking even in the service of God. For how the love of praise will seduce and corrupt this man, and the love of gain that man! How easy it is to flatter and adulate this man out of all his former opinions and his deepest principles, and how an expected advantage will make that other man forget now an old alliance and now a deep antipathy! How often the side we take even in the most momentous matters is decided by the most unworthy motives and the most contemptible considerations!"

From selfishness springs covetousness. The covetous person cannot be a peacemaker, because he thirsts to fill his coffers with the riches of the world. Gold is his God. What fills our calendars with crime? What makes our courts of law echo with ceaseless lawsuits? The love of money. Probably the love of money is the greatest peacebreaker upon earth. There is a pathetic passage in Dicken's *Christmas Carol* in which Scrooge, escorted by the Ghost of Christmas Past, sees himself as a much younger man. "His face had not the harsh and rigid lines of later years; but it had begun to wear the signs

583

of care and avarice. He was not alone, but sat by the side of a fair young girl in a mourning-dress, in whose eyes there were tears, which sparkled in the light that shone out of the Ghost of Christmas Past.

" 'It matters little,' she said softly. 'To you very little. Another idol has displaced me; and if it can cheer and comfort you in time to come, as I would have tried to do, I have not just cause to grieve.'

" 'What Idol has displaced you?' he rejoined.

" 'A golden one.' "

Although Scrooge tried to protest that his love for his betrothed was as strong as ever, his words were lame and half-hearted; and she gave him back his engagement ring. So Scrooge shut love of humankind out of his life and gave himself wholly over to love of gold.

If you wish to be a peacemaker, begin by being loving and generous. We are each different from the other. Some of us are naturally generous and some of us are misers. But whatever our natural dispositions, we must remember that when we become Christians we are supernaturally transformed into new beings in Christ Jesus. By your generosity you manifest your degree of blessedness and peacemaking.

In your selfishness you may not be thirsty for gold but for glory. This, too, can shatter the peace of your own soul and of others. What causes wars? Ambition for glory. Hitler was driven by it to the slaughter of millions. Communism is ambitious and therefore reckless. Analyze the wars within the portals of our churches. The cause will be found in the inordinate selfish ambitions of some individuals, the pastor not excluded. Let one man, one woman acquire the thirst for glory in a congregation and peace disappears.

The Apostle John, in writing to Gaius, in his Third

Epistle, speaks of such a one: "I wrote unto the church," he says, "but Diotrephes, who loveth to have the preeminence among them, receiveth us not. Wherefore, if I come, I will remember his deeds which he doeth, prating against us with malicious words: and not content therewith, neither doth he himself receive the brethren, and forbiddeth them that would, and casteth them out of the church" (vv. 9, 10). How many like Diotrephes disrupt the peace of the Church today! Let them take heed to the word of the Lord in Jeremiah 45:5, "Seekest thou great things for thyself? seek them not."

The thirst for power, for aggrandizement and renown, has been one of the greatest peacebreakers in the history of mankind, internationally, nationally, and within our communities, churches, and families. And sometimes peacebreaking ambition is very viciously and deceitfully disguised as service to mankind. The ambitious man wants to become as powerful as possible so he can dictate peace. But the peace of the ambitious is usually the peace of tyranny; and war, open war for individual freedom, is far better than the uninvited peace imposed by an ambitious tyrant.

LIVING AT PEACE WITH OTHERS

When we have made peace with God in our own souls through receiving Christ as our Saviour and yielding to Him as Lord, we are ready to direct our peacemaking outward, toward others. As we apply this Beatitude inwardly, it is evangelism for our own hearts; and as we direct it outwardly it is a missionary message for others. We are to proclaim to the world that Christ has made peace through the blood of His cross, and we are to be willing to share this peace at all costs.

A business girl who was having a very hard time among her friends, and suffering much persecution for her Christian testimony, came to an evangelist who was holding a series of special Sunday evening services in a large public auditorium and told him she was afraid she must give it all up. He said to her, "Tell me, where do we put the lights?" She looked puzzled at his question, so he answered it for her: "We put the lights in a dark place." In a moment she saw his meaning and realized that God had put her in difficult surroundings that she might shine for Jesus in the midst of darkness. She went back determined to be more courageous than ever in her witness for Christ. A few weeks later, after the evening service, she came to him with a group of other girls, all radiant with joy. "Oh," she said, "the thirteenth from our office has decided for Christ tonight!"

It would certainly be a watering down of Christ's message to conceive of this Beatitude in its outward expression as merely an endeavor on our part to live agreeably with others. A person who possesses the peace of God is also possessed of divine principles. And where there is principle there must be division when these principles are transgressed. This is what the Lord intimated when He said, "I am come to send fire on the earth; and what will I, if it be already kindled? But I have a baptism to be baptized with; and how am I straitened till it be accomplished! Suppose ye that I am come to give peace on earth? I tell you, Nay; but rather division: For from henceforth there shall be five in one house divided, three against two, and two against three. The father shall be divided against the son, and the son against the father; the mother against the daughter, and the daughter against the mother; the mother in law against her daughter in law, and the daughter in law against her mother in law." (Luke 12:49-53.)

Compromise with sin and the sinner can never be conceived of as New Testament peacemaking. Our peacemaking efforts must go far deeper than that, not simply seeking to change the circumstances of people's lives but their very hearts, through leading them to Christ, so that they can see God and cooperate with His will in the circumstances of their lives. Then, instead of grumbling, we shall have praise, and instead of rebellion, peace. The circumstances remain the same, but the person is changed. Blessed are the peacemakers and also those to whom they bring peace. They cannot bring peace to others by sharing their material possessions or providing for their bodily needs — although Christ's peacemakers will want to relieve human need and suffering — but by proclaiming the Gospel of reconciliation. Remember Christ's eternal words, "A man's life consisteth not in the abundance of the things which he possesseth" (Luke 12:15). "Godliness with contentment is great gain" (I Tim. 6:6).

This is how it worked with Aquilla. He was lame from birth, and as he sat by his window propped up in a chair and watched the other boys playing in the

587

street, he asked, "Why has God made me thus? Why have I not feet and legs to run and jump as other boys? O God!" he exclaimed, "I am angry with you! Away with God! Away with religion!" He was full of sharpness, and sourness, and complaint. His disposition was bitter, and this bitter disposition shed bitterness on all the world around. But a friend came in one day who loaned him a Christian book. Aquilla read this book, and it opened new thoughts to him. Step by step he was led along until he saw himself as a sinner and his faith laid hold on Christ. The burden of sin was removed; his heart was renewed; the love of God was shed abroad in his heart by the Holy Ghost; and now, as he saw the people passing his window while he was confined to his chair, he said, "It is all right. God has done it. My Father has done it. I love Him. He loves me. He can but do all things for my good." Where there had been war there was peace, with a friend and a book as the peacemakers.

This Beatitude not only means that we should bring the peace of God to those who know Him not; it has a bearing on our day-to-day relations with them. Short of compromising with sin, we who are blessed in Christ are admonished, "as much as lieth in you, live peaceably with all men" (Rom. 12:18). This means that the Christian should strive for the highest possible degree of peaceful co-existence consistent with not sacrificing principle or allowing evil to overrun good. There is a point at which the Christian must break with the world; he is to live in the world but not become worldly. Men and women cannot become one outside of Christ; but we must relate to them in such a way that they will desire the peace that we manifest. The Christian should seek, "as much as lieth in him," to be attractive and not repulsive to those who are not Christians. The way we live should cause others to be disturbed and at the same time drawn to us.

This injunction to live peaceably with all men also applies to the household of faith. Christians are to live at peace with one another. Though members of the same family of God, and redeemed by the same blood of the cross, we are all different in appearance, in the way we think, speak, and act. The Christian who wants everyone else to be like him is a peacebreaker. In his spiritual pride he wants to set himself up as the model Christian. If the other person does not think as he does, he is not spiritual. Beware, you who set yourselves up as a standard of spirituality to which you feel others should conform. The greatest peacebreaker in Christendom is he who appoints himself judge over others. No one is comfortable in his presence. On any committee he wants to run the whole show or he will not cooperate. He is heady, intolerant, harsh, dogmatic, censorious. Young Christians are discouraged by his constant faultfinding. Older Christians are repelled by his demand that they concur in his unkind judgments. He is an irritant wherever he goes. Inward peace and outward peacemaking are foreign to his nature. How different was the spirit of Alexander Pope, who wrote:

Let not this weak, unknowing hand
    Presume Thy bolts to throw,
And deal damnation round the land
    On each I judge Thy foe.

If I am right, Thy grace impart
    Still in the right to stay:
If I am wrong, oh teach my heart
    To find a better way.

Save me alike from foolish pride
    Or impious discontent,
At aught Thy wisdom has denied,
    Or aught Thy goodness lent.

Teach me to feel another's woe,
    To hide the fault I see;
That mercy I to others show,
    That mercy show to me.

    Let us recognize the diversity in our physical and spiritual make-ups, even as in nature there is diversity with over-all harmony. The world would be a dull place, indeed, very different from what God intended it to be, if all of us thought, spoke, and acted alike. The world of nature derives its beauty and its grace from the ups and downs, and rents and fissures, and straits and seas which cut it asunder, and give it all its various shapes and forms. And so it is with the world of man. We must allow men to differ. We cannot force everyone into the same mold of character, pursuits, tastes, and opinions. But here, as in the natural world, we can and should prevent any difference, except the difference of sin, from becoming a separation.

    The word "pontiff," used to designate the highest religious order of the Roman Catholic Church, namely the Pope, has an interesting history. This was the name which, in the old pagan religion of ancient Rome, was given to the chief priests. The pontiffs were those who were invested with pontifical power. The name as it was first applied meant "the makers of bridges." Why it was so used in the first instance we hardly know. Those old Roman pontiffs were, perhaps, specially employed in consecrating those mighty instruments of earthly peace and civilization, the great roads and bridges by which the old Romans tamed and subdued the world. But in a moral and spiritual sense we ought all to be makers of bridges. Pontiff or no pontiff, minister or no minister, every Christian who walks in his Master's steps ought to make it his special business to throw bridges across those moral rents and fissures which divide us one from the other. Across these various gulfs and chasms let every one lend a helping hand to build such bridges as best we can. There cannot be a more truly pontifical work.

PRACTICAL POINTS ON PEACEMAKING

"Though I speak with the tongues of men and of angels," said Paul, "and have not love, I am become as sounding brass, or a tinkling cymbal. And though I ... understand all mysteries ... and have not love, I am nothing" (I Cor. 13:1, 2). Likewise, if you and I understand all that is involved in Christian peacemaking, and do not apply it, it is useless knowledge. Therefore I would like to offer a few practical suggestions for those who want to take this task of peacemaking seriously.

Cultivate a forgiving spirit. Be "easily entreated," as Scripture puts it. Anger is not sinful when it is for the right cause and at the right time; but when it degenerates, or rather kindles, into revenge, then it becomes one of the most hateful occupants of the human heart. It supposes it meets with insult where insult may not have been designed; and if it burn in an individual soul it challenges to a duel; if in a nation, it instantly provokes or challenges to war. Revenge, whether in individuals or nations, becomes one of the great peacebreakers.

Cultivate a spirit of contentment. Where envy reigns, there is a man prepared to quarrel; and of all passions it is the most contemptible. Envy is not a desire that I should be blessed or benefited, but that my brother should be dragged down from his eminence, even if I should remain on the same dead level to which I would reduce him. And when this passion gets full possession of the human heart, its corroding pain within and its calamitous consequences without are too frequently seen; they are written in some of the darkest pages of history.

Be slow to resent slights or injuries. When men speak

ill of you, unless it be something that demands instant and public reply, let it alone. "Every time," says J. R. Miller, "we keep silent under insult, and loving and sweet under provocation, we have made it easier for all about us to do the same." Especially exercise the grace of silence or the power of gentleness in your own home. Your wife or husband or child or mother says something to you that kindles resentment. Don't ask for an explanation and apology. Find a way to show that Christ dwells in your heart, not by descending to the level of the offender, but by identifying with Christ in attitude and word, so that the peacebreaker cannot but look up to you as an example of forbearance, patience, and long-suffering. Words spoken in anger and resentment are like rubber balls thrown against a wall. The harder the surface you bounce them against the harder they fly back at you. Love seeks to find justification for many actions that grieve it. If you really love your wife or husband or pastor or friend, you'll try to justify the motivation although you will condemn the act. But let the condemnation remain unspoken, and at the same time let a prayer ascend to God for the offender's correction. You don't really want to destroy the person you love, but win him over.

Be slow to listen to rumors, above all about a brother; and when these reach you prophesying evil, when others only look at the bad side of his conduct, reject all at once, until incontrovertibly demonstrated to be true. Suspect the person who always whispers in your ear something he does not want anyone else to hear. In reality it is the opposite that he desires. In every community there are whisperers who go about retailing gossip, the tendency of which is to separate friends. Every Christian should be a discourager of talebearing. Too many people encourage it. They are glad to hear something unpleasant about another and are quick to pass it on. Such eagerness is not commendable and does not have upon it the blessing of peacemaking.

If you are tempted to reveal
    A tale someone to you has told
About another, make it pass,
    Before you speak, three gates of gold.

Three narrow gates: First, "Is it true?"
    Then, "Is it needful?" In your mind
Give truthful answer. And the next
    Is last and narrowest — "Is it kind?"

And if to reach your lips at last
    It passes through these gateways three,
Then you may tell the tale, nor fear
    What the result of speech may be.

Refrain from sowing doubt and suspicion of others in people's minds. That is not the office of a peacemaker. One often learns, in close fellowship with others, that two neighbors or friends are in danger of becoming enemies. Now is the opportunity for the peacemaker's ministry. Instead of aggravating the little beginning of bitterness, as he may do by a word of encouragement, he should set about to try to heal the breach and restore confidence. Usually it is not hard to do this. Many quarrels begin in a slight misunderstanding, and a few words spoken by a true-hearted peacemaker will show, first to one and then to the other, that there is really no cause for ill feeling, that the doubt of loyalty is unjust, and that a separation or an estrangement is not only unnecessary but would be positively sinful.

When over the fair fame of friend or foe
  The shadow of disgrace shall fall; instead
Of words of blame, or proof of thus and so,
  Let something good be said.

Forget not that no fellow-being yet
  May fall so low but love may lift his head;
Even the cheek of shame with tears is wet
  If something good be said.

And so I charge ye, by the thorny crown
  And by the cross on which the Saviour bled,
And by your own soul's hope of fair renown,
  Let something good be said.
                              —*James Whitcomb Riley.*

A true peacemaker, going about thus, trying to draw
people ever closer together and to heal all threatened
contentions and quarrels, is doing a divine work of love
in the world. The great majority of strifes among men
are needless. They are caused by the meddlesomeness of
outside parties. Or they come from hasty words or acts
unconfessed and unrepented of. The peacemaker's word,
spoken at the right moment, would prevent all this.
(See J. R. Miller, *The Garden of the Heart*, pp. 250-9.)

Those who have been estranged for one reason or
another stand very little chance of ever establishing
peace between themselves because they tend to avoid each
other. The Christian peacemaker can at least try to bring
about a meeting between them. Use your home as a house
of peace. Within its portals let there reign the peace of
God, so that when others come in they cannot but be
awed by it. Those at war with their relatives and fellow
men will see that peace is not an impossibility and that

the absence of it from their particular environment may be their own fault.

All true peacemakers think things through. It does not take brains to destroy, but it does take thought to build. A housewrecker needs no university training, but an architect does. Think before you speak, and your speech is more likely to promote peace. Forbear in speech when a word is ready to escape from your lips that would kindle a conflagration. Stop to think before you lift your hand to strike. Count the reaction and the end result. Forbear in hand, when your action might be violent and destructive. Think your thoughts over when they might prompt to revenge. Very high in the records of peacemaking stand the names of those who in every age have brought to the problems of life the acumen of a finely-tempered reason, yoked with the simple and safe instincts of a clean heart. These have ever given to the world true views of God and life, and we are called to share not merely in the gains of their toil but in the toil itself. There is a scholarship of sanctity, a wisdom of the heart, within reach of us all; and so far as we learn to think truly about our Father in heaven and the life He would have us live on the earth, we may find some place in the ministry of light that leads to the way of peace. (See Percy C. Ainsworth, *The Blessed Life,* p. 152.)

It is thought, sanctified thought, that will show us when to resist and when not to resist, when and how to speak and strike. When Christ said, "Give to him that asketh thee," was He advocating indiscriminate charity? We should not allow ourselves to be deceived by impostors, but neither should we harden our hearts and do nothing. In my life, I prefer to be deceived than to deprive a worthy individual of help. We must exercise judgment, thought, both in peacemaking and in charity.

"The easy wrong things to do," says A. D. Lindsay, "are to give without thought, and not to give, again without thought. We owe people our clear thought as well as our kind heart. We ought to give to him that asketh us, but not always what he asks; and it often takes a great deal more pain and trouble and thought to give people what they need than to give them what they wish. To take these verses as simple rules, requiring of us lots of will to do, but no thought to interpret, is really moral laziness, and can clearly do much harm." *(The Moral Teaching of Jesus,* pp. 107-8.)

CHILDREN OF GOD

Each of the Beatitudes of Christ contains a condition to be fulfilled in order to attain the blessedness it promises, as well as a reward for its fulfillment. In the seventh Beatitude the condition is peacemaking and the reward is to "be called the children of God." This may not sound like much, but there are great spiritual riches involved in it. The greatest award that can come to any man is to receive recognition as a child of God. Paul tells us, "And if children, then heirs; heirs of God, and joint-heirs with Jesus Christ" (Rom. 8:17). Such men are the most blessed, the richest, the most joyous creatures of earth. They dwell in this world, but they are really citizens of heaven.

Who gives this recognition to the peacemaker? First, God Himself. To consider yourself a child of God proves nothing. People's estimates of themselves are notoriously untrustworthy, as witness the mental patients who harbor delusions of grandeur about themselves and their friends. A man may call himself the closest friend of the President of the United States; but that is really up to the President to say. Many people who think they are the children of God, God never recognizes as such.

We see, then, that God does not recognize as His children all whom He has created. Unregenerate men have broken their filial relationship to God. That is why, after the fall of man, you find man possessing little consciousness of God as Father. He calls Him Jehovah. God, on the other hand, has never considered Himself anything but a Father to all His creation. But to estranged children, the feelings of God have little value. The light falls everywhere, but only the eye drinks it in. The lower orders of creatures are shut out from all participation in the gifts that belong to the higher forms of life, simply because they are so made and organized that these cannot find entrance into their nature. Always and necessarily the capacity for reception must precede and determine the bestowment of blessings. Thus we have the peculiar situation that God is always the Father but men are not all His children. This is why we hardly ever find it stated in Scripture that, when man believes and accepts Christ as Saviour and Lord and is thus born again, God becomes his Father, but rather that man becomes His child.

Thus, in this seventh Beatitude, the reward of peace-making is not stated as God becoming the Father of the peacemakers, but as the peacemakers being known as the children of God. The change is on man's part and not on God's, for God is ever unchangeable in His character. What He bestows here is divine recognition of the change in man. When you and I become His children through faith in His Son, He recognizes us as such. He treats us like sons. He makes us heirs of all that He is and all that He possesses.

This recognition by God is progressive. It comes to us first when we are born again. "But as many as received him, to them gave he power to become the sons of God, even to them that believe on his name" (John 1:12). That capacity to believe is a distinct characteristic of men and it is distinctly a gift of God. Actually it is the only possible sensibility upon which the Spirit of God can work to woo us back to His Fatherhood. The prodigal son knew instinctively that he would be accepted by the father when he returned home repentant. The moment you, as a sinner, do the same, God will accept you with great joy. He will say, "You are my child now, since you have come back to

Me through My Son, the Lord Jesus Christ, whom I sent to reconcile you to Me."

After this initial recognition by God, there is a growing consciousness of our sonship to God and His kinship to us. We find a parallel here with the physical relationship between a child and his parents. As the child grows, he realizes more and more that he belongs to his parents. And the more he realizes the love, power, and provision of his parents, the greater his attachment to them and the boldness of his expectations of them. This is why, in the maturity of our Christian life, we are admonished to approach the throne of God's grace boldly. Also, with growth comes a progressive increase in likeness. When does a child look more like his parents, at birth or in later life? Family resemblance develops with growth.

When this Beatitude states, "Blessed are the peacemakers: for they shall be called the children of God," it makes it plain that the family likeness will be recognizable. Note that it does not say that peacemakers shall *be* God's children; rather it says that they shall be *called* by that name. If a man is not a child of God to begin with, he cannot be a peacemaker, for how can he bring the peace of God to others if he does not possess it himself? No one can be a peacemaker who is not "blessed" – that is, indwelt by God – to start with. If he is not blessed, he cannot be a peacemaker; and if he is a peacemaker, he is already a child of God.

Here we have sonship verified through likeness, as when children grown to age reproduce the parental characteristics and tread in the father's footsteps. If God's children are not only to be, but to be declared, His sons, it is not enough to be secret disciples, hiding their vision of Him. Forth into the evil, hostile world they must go, as did the proper Son of His love. Into the Son's task they too must enter. Possessing purity of heart may make us like God inwardly, but actively engaging in a ministry of peacemaking and reconciliation of mankind to God will be following in our Lord's footsteps.

It is your likeness to Christ when you are a peacemaker that is readily recognized, not only by God Himself, but by all who observe you. The child bears the likeness of the Father. God does not have to walk the streets of your town and mine; He has you and me to bear witness to Him. Do those who watch us and listen to us find it easy to tell who our Father is, whose likeness we bear? When you make the very work that Christ came to do — bringing peace to sinful men and women — the passion of your life, how can others refrain from calling you a child of God? From the time of His prophesied incarnation, Christ was called the Prince of Peace. And not until you become the bearer of His peace to others can you have this unique distinction, not of becoming a child of God, but of being called a child of God. Not until you come to the seventh Beatitude do you have this reward. You can exemplify all the graces of the preceding Beatitudes: you can be poor in spirit (humble), mournful, meek, hungering and thirsting after righteousness, merciful, pure in heart. But not until you assume this holiest and highest task of peacemaking are you most discernible as a child of God. You have been His child ever since you received Christ into your heart by faith, but now, when there is an identity of vocation between you and Christ, you are the most Christlike.

It is said of Fenelon that he had such communion with God his very face shone. Lord Peterborough, a skeptic, was obliged to spend the night with him at an inn. In the morning he rushed away, saying, "If I stay another night with that man I shall be a Christian in spite of myself."

Fenelon's manners were full of grace, his voice full of love, and his face full of glory. The invitation, "Come to Jesus," was in every act. He was a "spiritual magnet." That is what we all can be, by just yielding up all to Christ, and letting Him live again in us. Under no other condition can this transforming power fulfill its peacemaking mission to our own souls or enable us to bring peace to the souls of others.

This recognition of our Godlikeness is by no means general. It is primarily a recognition by God Himself in this life and more especially in the day when we shall appear before Him in heaven. Every time you engage in bringing the peace of God to some heart and life, you may have the witness of this in your own soul. "You are My child," He says to you. "You are like Me; your work is the same as Mine." There can be nothing more satisfying in life. It is more to be desired than anything else. In fact, if we have that, we have everything.

A little lad stopped at a door and heard a young man singing, "My Father is rich in houses and lands." Disgusted that anyone should brag about his father's wealth, the child was about to turn away when the rest of the song caught his ear. "He holdeth the wealth of the world in His hands! Of rubies and diamonds, of silver and gold, His coffers are full; He has riches untold."

"Boy, I wish his father was mine!" said the boy.

"I'm the child of a King, the child of a King," the song went on.

"Now, how can that be?" wondered the child. "We have no king, and I know good and well his father isn't the President."

"With Jesus, my Saviour, I'm the child of a King," concluded the singer.

Then the lad knew he was singing of God. Yes, our

Father is rich, and all His riches are ours. Therefore, no matter what our suffering or privations for His sake now, we can still sing:

> A tent or a cottage, why should I care?
> They're building a palace for me over there!
> Tho' exiled from home, yet still I may sing,
> "All glory to God, I'm the child of a King."

John perceived the greatness of this privilege when he wrote, "Behold, what manner of love the Father hath bestowed upon us, that we should be called the sons of God" (I John 3:1).

THE CHRISTIAN'S HIGHEST CALLING

The peacemaker has the supreme joy in this life of hearing God's whisper in his heart, "You are my child, in whom I am well pleased." Others in the family of God will also recognize him as one of themselves, for spiritual things are spiritually discerned. But to the world peacemakers may look like fools, passing up the opportunity to acquire riches, fame, and secular recognition for the sake of serving God. This should not surprise us. Paul has warned us that it would be so. "But the natural man receiveth not the things of the Spirit of God: for they are foolishness unto him: neither can he know them, because they are spiritually discerned" (I Cor. 2:14). And some not only fail to recognize the Godlikeness of our peacemaking efforts, not only call us fools, but actively persecute us, as we see in the next Beatitude (Matt. 5:10). Our peacemaking interferes with their warmongering and the profits derived therefrom. Yet this can in no way take away from the joy of our reward.

Though God will call us His children, and other Christians will recognize us as such, His enemies will fight against us. Our peacemaking will awaken hostility. This is the sword aroused by peace. They will hate us as they hated our Master, who came not only to bring peace but a sword. They will take up stones to cast at us just as they did against Him. But this will only serve to manifest afresh our Godlikeness. It is really an indirect recognition of our likeness to Christ. As we actively engage in peacemaking, there will be crosses for us even as there was a cross for Him. That will be the zenith, the apex of our peacemaking. That is when our spirit is closest to His, and safest in His keeping. The nails driven by the crucifiers only drive us closer to the heart of God, bringing more clearly to us His whisper, "You are my child; that is why you are here, suffering as I suffered."

There is no definite article before "God" in the expression, "children of God," in this Beatitude. It does not read, "They shall be called the children of *the* God." In English, of course, you could not use such a construction, but in Greek it would have been grammatically possible to say *huioi tou theou,* "children of *the* God." Instead it says *huioi theou,* "children of God." Why in the immediately preceding Beatitude does the Greek construction read, "Blessed are the pure in heart: for they shall see *the* God," and here say, "Blessed are the peacemakers: for they shall be called children of God," omitting the definite article? When the definite article is omitted in such cases, it is God in His totality, in His general make-up and infinity, that is meant. (See *Grammar of the Greek Language,* Vol. II, by William Edward Jelf, John Henry and James Parker, 1859, p. 124. Also see the author's booklet, *Can Man See God?,* an exegesis of John 1:18, where the definite article before the word *theou,* "God," is also omitted: "God no one has seen at any time.")

We are called children of God as we engage in peacemaking. But the word "God" does not merely refer to one of the three personalities of the Godhead but to all three together. It refers not only to the visible manifestations of deity but to deity itself, to God in His unity, in His eternity, and in His infinity. We are the visible peacemakers, the children of the invisible God, the only true Peacemaker, the eternal and infinite Prince of Peace. What a suggestive thought this is. In the work of salvation, of bringing peace to the heart of man, all three persons of the Triune God take part. God the Father welcomes the repentant sinner, God the Son paid the penalty of his sin, and God the Holy Spirit woos the sinner, convicts him of his sin, and brings him to a realization of his need of a Saviour.

Similarly we, in our task of peacemaking, need the supernatural activity of God the Father, God the Son, and God the Holy Spirit. How confident and fearless the assurance of such eternal and infinite power operating in our behalf makes us as we declare and apply the peace of God. No wonder it passes all human understanding. No human agency, psychological, philosophical, or theological, can bring God's peace to man's soul. It requires the converging of all the faculties of the eternal Godhead — Father, Son, and Holy Spirit. What a privilege is ours even to be given the opportunity of having the least share in this divine peacemaking. And because of the greatness of our small part we are called the children of the infinite and eternal God.

The Greek word used for children in this verse is *huioi* rather than *tekna*. Lexicographer Hermann Cremer tells us that frequently *teknon* is distinguished from *huios* in that *teknon* expresses the origin, *huios* the fellowship of life. (*Biblico-Theological Lexicon of New Testament Greek*, p. 554.) *Huios*, the word used in this Beatitude, stresses the dignity and character of the relationship. *Tekna*, as used in John 1:12, stresses the initial establishment of a relationship to God as a Father, a matter of belonging to Him. The peacemaker is recognized as a Christian of growth and maturity, although in his relationship to God he is still characterized as a child. The Christian peacemaker enjoys the highest degree of fellowship with God. He can feel God's passionate throb for the sinner and share in it. He is a child with mature understanding of the innermost feelings and desires of God as they pertain to His creatures. He understands the dignity and character of his relationship to God and honors it. He is a child who has become a worker together with God, a partner in the salvation of disturbed and guilty sinners.

The definite article is also omitted before the word *huioi*, "children." The English translation is inaccurate when it says, "Blessed are the peacemakers: for they shall be called *the* children of God." In the Greek text it is simply "children of God." If the definite article had been used, emphasis would have been placed on the origin and the belonging instead of on the fellowship of life. It would carry the connotation that only the peacemakers are the children of God, while we know that peacemaking is a high calling and development of those who are already children of the new birth. It is not merely because we are peacemakers that we are called children of God. Many born-again Christians are not peacemakers. In fact, very few in the redeemed and regenerated family of God are peacemakers. Of those who are, it was not their peacemaking that made them God's children initially; they were already that or they wouldn't have become peacemakers at all. These are children of God *par excellence,* accorded that recognition here and now, who will be more fully rewarded when the final accounting of our being and doing is held in heaven. The peacemakers are not the only children of God, nor are all the children of God peacemakers. Peacemaking is a high distinction of fellowship and a fuller realization of our relationship with God as Father. When any of us are so distinguished of God, He calls us in a special way His children. This is most satisfying and rewarding.

The demonstrative pronoun *autoi* is used in this

seventh Beatitude, as in the previous one, further to emphasize this distinction of the peacemakers. Blessed are the peacemakers; for they themselves *(autoi)* shall be called children of God. It is they above all, so to speak. To them especially is afforded this great honor to be called children: not only partakers of God's nature but also sharers of His concern for sinners, and naturally sharers also of His sufferings. With all this in mind, we find Romans 8:17 taking on added meaning: "And if children, then heirs; heirs of God, and joint-heirs with Christ; if so be that we suffer with him, that we may be also glorified together." The peacemaking of which the seventh Beatitude speaks elevates the child of God to the position of sharing not only in the accomplished work of Christ, but also in the process and method by which that accomplishment was achieved. The peacemaker takes advantage of the offer of salvation as all who wish to become Christians must; but he goes on to accept the responsibility of the suffering that is involved in the sharing of that blood-bought peace.

> Suffering together in fellowship holy,
>   Sharing His sorrows, His treatment, His shame;
> Though man despise me because I am lowly,
>   Mine is an honor which no one can name.

> I am an heir to all treasures immortal,
>   Heir to the Father, joint heir with the Son;
> And just beyond, where I stand on the portal,
>   I shall reign with Him, because we are one.

> Lord, grant that now I may faithfully serve Thee,
>   Since I am one with Thee, help me, I pray;
> That by my life, and my words, I may praise Thee,
>   And may exalt Thee, dear Saviour, each day.

AFTER PEACEMAKING - PERSECUTION

The fact that we engage in the divine task of peace-making does not mean that we shall lead a peaceful existence. Recognizing this, the world cynically para-phrases the seventh Beatitude in Matthew as "Blessed are the peacemakers: for they shall get it in the neck." Our Lord did not promise happiness to peacemakers, but bless-edness — that is, His indwelling presence, approval, and felicity. It is very significant that the eighth Beatitude, "Blessed are they which are persecuted for righteous-ness' sake: for theirs is the kingdom of heaven," immediately follows the one about peacemaking.

Christ wants us as His followers to bring the peace of God to others, but not to expect peace in return from all to whom we preach it. It is inevitable that the peace-maker shall be hated by some and loved by others.

Isn't it strange that the Beatitude regarding peace-making is not followed by a Beatitude that speaks of those who are loved for their peacemaking efforts? This would seem to be the logical and natural order of events — that those to whom we have brought peace should show love and gratitude in return. It is blessing and refreshing for the peacemaker to see the seed of God's Word bring forth the peaceable fruit of righteous-ness. Yet our Lord made no mention of this obvious fact, perhaps because He felt it would have been unnecessary to do so.

What is not logical or expected is to be hated and persecuted for trying to bring about peace. Supernatural grace is needed to withstand persecution for the sake of Christ. Read these two Beatitudes together, in the order in which our Lord gave them, to see how He tells us that when men from whom we should naturally expect love and gratitude turn against us because of their naturally sinful dispositions, we who are supernaturally blessed must accept this joyfully. "Blessed are the peacemakers: for they shall be called the children of God. Blessed are they which are persecuted for righteousness' sake: for theirs is the kingdom of heaven" (Matt. 5:9, 10).

Another reason that our Lord may not have stressed the blessedness of those who are loved for their peacemaking efforts is that the zeal for persecution of the sinful is often more pronounced and determined than the dedication and love of those to whom we have brought the peace of God. Take our Lord's life as an example. He came to bring peace, and did so in the troubled and sinful hearts of His disciples. But when He hung on the cross, whose feelings and words were more pronounced — those of His disciples, who were enjoying His divine peace, or those of His enemies? No word of "dedication to death" is now heard from Peter or John or James, of the inner circle of discipleship. It is not recorded that a cup of fresh water was offered to Him by any of the women who had been cleansed from their sins. Instead, His persecutors offered Him vinegar mixed with gall.

The absence of Christ's friends is felt by any observant reader of this tragic scene of peacemaking on the cross. There seemed to be no "protestants" at Golgotha. One wonders whether many who bear that name today are really worthy of it. The jeer of the thief who was crucified with Jesus is heard louder than any protestation of loyalty from His followers: "If thou be Christ, save thyself and us" (Luke 23:39). The passersby join in the chorus, "Thou that destroyest the temple, and buildest it in three days, save thyself. If thou be

610

the Son of God, come down from the cross" (Matt. 27:40). Where was the hymn of faith of the First Apostolic Choir in Jerusalem? Instead we hear the mocking refrain of the scribes and elders: "He saved others; himself he cannot save. If he be the King of Israel, let him now come down from the cross, and we will believe him. He trusted in God; let him deliver him now, if he will have him: for he said, I am the Son of God" (Matt. 26:42, 43). No flaming words of heroism burst from the lips of His disciples; only ridicule and vituperation from His enemies. What a sad commentary.

But are we any better today? Our courage as children of God should far outshine the courage and audacity of the children of the devil. Are we losing the war for men's souls by default? Is the invitation to "go to the devil" via modern philosophy louder than the call to "come to Jesus"? Is communism outshouting Christianity? Shame on us, if this be so.

The Lord knew from personal experience that His peacemakers would meet with disappointments at times. Many to whom they brought the peace of God would not be as ready to stand up for the truth as sinful men would be to attack it. Therefore the Beatitude of the persecuted ones needed to follow on the heels of the injunction to peacemaking. In this way Christ undertook to encourage His peacemakers, lest they become discouraged, not only by those who actively opposed the Christian faith, but also by the silence or indifference of those to whom they had brought peace.

Who makes the most fuss in our day about Bible reading and prayer in the public schools — those who oppose it or those who are in favor of it? Have Christians been as vigorous in their efforts to establish firmly and irremovably those Christian practices that have existed ever since our godly founding fathers first stepped on the free soil of these shores? Or is it predominantly atheists and non-Christians who give so freely of their time and money to appeal to the Supreme Court, urging them to abolish every public recognition of our godly heritage? Where are the great bulk of the Christians? Are they asleep? Why do they allow the jeers of the persecutors to be heard above the cheers of those who know the peace of Christ? No wonder wrongs flourish, and the minority group of active peace-makers need a benediction to hearten them under persecution.

A few years ago, an orphan girl from Greece came into our home. She went to our town high school, where she did fairly well, despite the fact that she could not speak English at all fluently. But one day she came home in tears. Her gym teacher had tried to force her to take part in mixed dancing, though she had protested, "I am a Christian; I cannot dance." The next day I went to see the principal. He called the gym teacher, who said that dancing was part of the curriculum and therefore compulsory. I said, "If I went down the street of our town and embraced a woman, I would be arrested for assault. Yet you force my child to do in school what would be considered a crime outside. What kind of society is this?" And do you know what the principal said? That as long as he had been at that school, no one had ever objected to mixed dancing. Yet several boys and girls went to that school from sound evangelical churches where the peace of God is proclaimed. No wonder immorality is rampant in our schools. Yet what classification do you think I found the Bible under in that particular school library? Mythology!

Why no protests from God's people? Surely we have as much right to speak out as those who protest against all that is godly — and with far greater justification.

Would to God that all who have and proclaim the peace of God considered it such a blessed privilege that they would be willing to defend it to the death.

If you want to find an example of God's children who had the courage of their convictions, you should get acquainted with Shadrach, Meshach, and Abed-nego, whose story is told in the Book of Daniel. Those young men did not take the time to consider what was offered them when they refused to worship the golden image. They knew they would not change their minds, and might as well have the thing over with at one time as another. After they had made their courageous answer, Nebuchadnezzar seemed to go wild with fury. He ordered the furnace to be heated seven times hotter than usual and commanded the soldiers to bind the brave young men and cast them into the fiery furnace. The soldiers shoved them along, with great boldness, no doubt, and show of strength and authority, and cast them headlong into the seething hell of flame. But though the furnace was so hot that it slew the soldiers that cast them in, the three young heroes walked unharmed in the midst of the fire. Not only were they unharmed, but a fourth figure, "like the Son of God," walked with them in cheering fellowship through all their fiery trial. God is as faithful to give the comfort of His presence to people who have the courage of their convictions today as in the days of Daniel and his friends.

PERSECUTION INEVITABLE

Some people say there are eight Beatitudes in Matthew, some only seven. The latter group exclude Matthew 5:10, "Blessed are they which are persecuted for righteousness' sake: for theirs is the kingdom of heaven." Perhaps they cannot conceive of persecution as a condition of blessedness or a characteristic of the blessed Christian life. How can persecution be a blessing?

Admittedly, this Beatitude is somewhat different from all the others. It involves a state not directly brought about by the Christian's volition. Who would choose to be persecuted? Yet in choosing to do God's will, as opposed to the world's will, every Christian in a sense chooses persecution. To that extent, volition is involved. Persecution, then, is the inevitable consequence of his choice manifested in the seven previous Beatitudes. Patiently, by God's grace, he has ascended the ladder of Christian blessedness rung by rung.

First, he has chosen to be poor in spirit. He has recognized his spiritual helplessness and has turned to Christ. This has brought him into the Kingdom of Heaven through the new birth.

Second, he has chosen to mourn — to sorrow over his own sins and the sins of others. Once within the Kingdom, he becomes deeply conscious of the sinfulness of sin. He recognizes all deviation from the will of God as sin in His own life and in the lives of others. He no longer indulges in it but weeps over it. Once a sinner has entered the fold of Christ and has had his sinful nature redeemed and purged, though he does not become sinless, he discerns sin and sorrows at its every recurrence.

Third, a Christian who is blessed has chosen to be meek: that is, he is actively angry at sin but at the same time submissive to the sovereign will of God. A man who thus becomes intolerant of sin and submissive to God inherits the earth. He is the only one who can really enjoy life.

Fourth, a Christian who has become disgusted with sin in himself and in the world yearns for something outside himself that can satisfy his spiritual nature. Since he is now spiritual in his make-up, he naturally hungers and thirsts for righteousness. Seeking after God is no longer an effort for the Christian who has reached the fourth rung of the ladder of blessedness, but a part of his regenerated nature. And God "satisfieth the longing soul, and filleth the hungry soul with goodness" (Ps. 107:9).

Fifth, the Christian who has been filled with God will overflow to others. God never fills us just enough to satisfy ourselves, but blesses us so that out of our abundance we may bless others. This over-abundance of the supply of God in Christ is expressed in mercifulness. A merciful Christian is one who has received such a full measure of God's mercy that he cannot help but share it with others. Yet as he empties himself of the mercy of God, he is never found wanting. New mercy constantly comes down to him from above. He early learns that his replenishment depends upon freely giving of what he has received. The inflow is proportionate to the outflow.

Sixth, the Christian must realize that he is not a vessel in which the peace of God is stored, but a channel through which it flows. If God's mercy were simply poured into him for his own spiritual enjoyment, it would become stale for lack of an outlet, and there would be no possibility of his receiving fresh cleansing

But as God's mercy flows through him to others, he is made purer and purer. Our purification does not take place once and for all but is a continuous process of the grace of God. And as we have a constant intake of God, we see Him more clearly with each inflow. That is why our purification in the sixth Beatitude is connected with seeing God.

Seventh, the Christian who has chosen to fulfill all these conditions of blessedness is now qualified to become a peacemaker. He feels the divine imperative to share with others that peace that has come to him as the direct product of his regeneration and purification by his Heavenly Father.

But he will get into trouble by this peacemaking. It will disturb the free and uncontrolled exercise of sin in the world. As meekness will not tolerate sin, so sin will not tolerate Christian meekness or Christian peacemaking. The Christian actively opposes sin, but sin also actively opposes righteousness. Satan is a jolly good fellow with tolerant fellows, but if we declare war against him, he will declare war against us. As we demonstrate all the characteristics of the blessed life, and more especially meekness, purity, and peacemaking that follow spiritual hunger and thirst, we shall find ourselves in trouble with the world around us as well as with Satan, "the god of this world."

Note that the word *dedioogmenoi*, "persecuted ones," is a perfect passive participle. It is not *hoi diookomenoi*, "those who are being persecuted," but "those who have been persecuted." In all the previous Beatitudes, present participles are used. This is the only one in which the perfect passive participle is used. Therefore the translation of the Authorized and the Revised Standard Versions is wrong. "Are persecuted" should rather be "have been persecuted." This process of persecution did not start on the seventh rung of the ladder of righteousness. It began the moment you decided to put your foot on the first rung and be clothed in Christ's righteousness. It has been present all along, increasing in intensity with each step upward on the ladder, until when you have reached the status of a peacemaker it is your daily portion. The Lord does not say, "Blessed are those who shall be persecuted or are being persecuted," but "those who have been persecuted" from the very beginning of their Christian experience. They are now full-fledged *dedioogmenoi*, "persecuted ones."

And yet there is more than the perfect passive, "have been persecuted," involved here. This Beatitude does not refer solely to the blessedness of those upon whom God permitted persecution to come, but also of those who are inwardly disposed to the acceptance of persecution, as a blessing rather than a curse. Beyond the fact of persecution spoken of here lies the glad disposition of the believer toward persecution. It is possible to suffer persecution as a believer and receive no blessing from it. The value of an experience depends to a great extent upon our attitude toward it. Our joyous experiences may be marred by a disposition to complain, and our sorrowful ones may teach us nothing of dependence upon God. Christ's blessing here is pronounced not so much on the fact of persecution as on our inner attitude toward it. Does your attitude in trial contribute to your blessedness or detract from it? We might render the sense of this Beatitude as "Blessed are they in whose lives persecution was permitted to become a blessing." Such Christians did not merely accept it; they used it.

In one sense, this eighth Beatitude is not a separate one, for it is inherent in every one of the other Beatitudes. In each of the previous conditions of blessedness there is something that stirs up resentment and persecution in the sinful world. Take the second Beatitude as an illustration. Is the world in agreement with your sorrow for sin? No, they would rather have you enjoy sin, be jubilant over it, for that entails profit-making. A bartender does not like your sorrow over the consumption of liquor. He may agree that people ought not to drink too much; but he will never agree that the source of all the misery caused by drinking should be cut off. He will persecute any Christian who tries to put a stop to drinking. In like manner there is persecution against the meek Christian, the Christian who hungers and thirsts after the righteousness of Christ, the merciful, the pure, the peacemaking Christian.

But finally, on the eighth rung of the ladder of Christian blessedness, we have the accumulation of the world's reaction to the Christian. If you are characterized by all the conditions of blessedness, you cannot help but be the focal target for the enemies of the Gospel. "Blessed are they which are persecuted for righteousness' sake: for theirs is the kingdom of heaven," contains a special recognition of your cumulative treatment at the hands of the world when you have reached the highest degree of blessedness.

As in all the other Beatitudes, the class spoken of is not a wide, general one, but a very particular and rather small one. The restriction is indicated first of all by the use of the definite article *hoi*, "the," before the word *dedioogmenoi*, "persecuted ones." Not all persecuted people are blessed, and not all blessed people are persecuted. It depends on how actively they oppose evil and how pure they are in themselves.

The restricted nature of the group of persecuted ones who are blessed is further indicated by the specific reason for their persecution, "for righteousness' sake."

It sometimes happens that there are other reasons for which a blessed person is persecuted. He may bring persecution upon himself because he is selfish, hard-headed, determined to have his own way, unwise in his life and testimony. There are any number of reasons why he may bring down the wrath of others upon himself, not without justification. After all, isn't our own Christian opposition to evil a form of persecution in reverse? Of course it is. But persecution of evil is not evil *per se*. It all depends on the motive and method. Through selfish motives or unwise methods, our fight against evil may only serve to make it worse. For instance, we as parents, in fulfilling our obligation to correct our children, may go about it in such a tactless or bad-tempered way as to produce the opposite result of what we intended.

The fact that you are persecuted does not necessarily mean that you are very close to the heart of God and enjoying the utmost in blessedness. Look deep within your heart and see whether the cause of persecution does not lie within yourself rather than in the righteousness of Christ. Is it really Christ you have been seeking to exalt, or yourself? Is it the attempt to establish your own righteousness that is causing all the trouble, or your efforts to promote the righteousness of Christ? The scribes and Pharisees who vaunted their own righteousness were rebuked by Christ. Sometimes, by the way we act, we give grounds to others to feel that even God must be against us. Self-righteousness is a noxious weed that needs divine uprooting, that it may be replaced by Christ's righteousness.

UNNECESSARY PERSECUTION

Persecution is a blessing in the Christian life only if we suffer "for righteousness' sake." We are not to invite persecution for discreditable reasons. If we do, our suffering cannot contribute to our blessedness, but will only serve to make us feel martyred or resentful. Only persecution "for righteousness' sake" carries a blessing with it. Indirectly, then, Christ tells us to avoid being persecuted for any other reason. What might some of these be?

The commonest are self-importance and self-righteousness. We may place ourselves on such a pedestal that we become obnoxious to others. We fail to realize that we have been put here, not to perform a solo in life but to contribute to the over-all harmony of differing individuals, each seeking to serve the Lord. Nor should each one who takes part in the chorus seek to drown out all the others, but so subordinate his own notes as to produce a melody that will attract others to the Lord he serves. A great many people are repelled by Christians whose personalities give the lie to the doctrine of Christ's righteousness that they preach. Before you look any further for the reasons you are persecuted or spoken evil of, take a good, hard look at yourself. It may be that you are like that little girl who prayed, "O God, bless Harry and make him as good as me!" People are repelled by self-righteousness, and God sternly warns us against it throughout Scripture. Carlyle made a telling point when he said that the greatest of faults is to be conscious of none. If people discover that you are living primarily for self, they'll despise you as a hypocrite when you preach to them. Don't, in such circumstances, pose as one who is persecuted for righteousness' sake.

Once in a dream a man was haunted and thwarted by a mysterious veiled figure. As soon as he had managed to amass a fortune, the veiled form snatched it away from him. When he was about to enter into peace and joy, the veiled figure attacked his mind with anxiety. When he was hungry and sat down to eat, it took away his appetite. When he was overcome with weariness and lay down to rest, this enemy of his life filled his mind with thoughts that banished sleep. When he had won fame, the veiled figure took away his reputation. When he stood at the open door of a great opportunity, the hand of the veiled one slammed it shut in his face. When he stood at last at the marriage altar and was about to take the sacred vows, the veiled one strode forth and, lifting up his hand in protest, said, "I forbid the banns!" Enraged, the unhappy man cried out to his adversary, "Who art thou?" In his fury he ripped the veil away; and lo, the face that he saw was his own!

This dream sets forth the well-known truth that man is his own worst enemy. "The fault," said Cassius to Brutus, "is not in our stars, but in ourselves." Man in a measure can make or mar his own destiny.

Alcibiades, the gifted but unscrupulous Greek general and politician, was known as an unhappy man. Someone asked Socrates why it was that Alcibiades, who had traveled so extensively and seen so much, was still so melancholy. The sage answered, "Because wherever he goes, he always takes himself with him." Do you often have the feeling that your neighbors, your business associates, your relatives, are all against you? That if you could live elsewhere, get a different job, travel in distant lands, you would be happier? Maybe so, but it is just possible that the center of your difficulties lies within yourself.

But how can we know whether we are suffering because self gets in the way, or for righteousness' sake? Here are some danger signals to look out for:

Do you think that everyone is looking upon you with disfavor, though you feel you have done nothing to draw their criticism? "It's not my fault if everybody singles me out!" protested someone to me recently. This reminds me of the childish refrain of that once-popular song, "Why is everybody always picking on me?" Because you overrate your own importance, because you are so concentrated on yourself, you think that everyone is aware of and commenting on your every move. If, as sometimes happens, you are not wanted or needed because you do not fit the requirements of a particular situation, you call it persecution. This is not the kind of persecution the Lord is speaking about. A self-centered person is little interested in helping others, although he may love to tell them off. An outgoing Christian concentrates on others for the sake of Jesus Christ. He is not interested in being the center of attention.

Phidias, the great sculptor, was employed by the Athenians to make a statue of the goddess Diana, and he succeeded so well as to produce a masterpiece. But he became so enamored of his own work, and was so anxious that his name should go down to posterity, that he secretly engraved his name in one of the folds of the drapery — an act of sacrilege, as he well knew. When the Athenians discovered this, they indignantly banished the man who had dared to pollute the sanctity of their goddess. So do the self-righteous act with the pure, spotless robe of Him who knew no sin. As we proclaim the righteousness of Christ, let us beware lest we start taking a share of the credit to ourselves. And if we do, let us not be surprised if nobody wants us around.

A second danger signal to look out for is the feeling that you are the sole possessor of truth and righteousness, or that you know all the truth that is to be known. "No doubt but ye are the people, and wisdom shall die with you," said Job to his know-it-all friends (Job 12:2) Being right is good, but believing you cannot be wrong steals the "right" from righteousness. If you are adamant about things that to many Christians seem small, you may be acting out of a desire for self-distinction. Watch yourself when you harp on one verse of Scripture, in complete disregard of the rest of the Bible. Fixed ideas may be symptomatic of opinionatedness, prejudice, or even insanity. People who suffer from persecution complexes cannot get along with others and often have to be removed from society for treatment. This is not the kind of persecution our Lord pronounced His blessing upon.

Another symptom closely akin to this is making mountains out of molehills. A man attacked by two highwaymen put up a terrific fight. Finally he was subdued and searched. But all they found on him was a dime. "Do you mean to tell me," demanded one of the bandits, "that you put up a fight like that over a measly dime? Why, we almost had to kill you!" "Well," answered the victim, "the truth of the matter is, I didn't want my financial condition exposed." People who put up a fight for a dime, so to speak, in the Christian Church, are actually exposing their spiritual poverty. This is certainly not suffering for righteousness' sake. "If you want to realize your own importance," said Robert Burdette, humorist and preacher, "put your finger into a bowl of water, take it out, and look at the hole." It was to Christians that the Apostle Peter said, "If ye be reproached for the name of Christ, happy [literally "blessed," *makarioi* in Greek — the same word that is used in the Beatitudes] are ye .... But let none of you suffer as a murderer, or as a thief, or as an evildoer, or as a busybody in other men's matters. Yet if any man suffer as a Christian, let him not be ashamed; but let him glorify God on this behalf" (I Pet. 4:14-16). These early Christians, freshly converted out of a wicked and pagan civilization, needed to be warned against gross crimes; but notice that the word "busybody" is included in this list of serious offenses. Perhaps the word "busybody" should be written in capitals as the cause of disturbance in the lives of many Christians.

As you examine the Scriptures and study the life of Christ, you will discover that our Lord was never persecuted for standing up for His personal rights, but always for the sake of others. The cross He bore was not for His own sins but for the sins of others. Is your cross one of your own making, or are you enduring persecution for the sake of others? It makes a difference, you know. "Blessed are they which are persecuted for righteousness' sake: for theirs is the kingdom of heaven."

THE BENEFITS OF PERSECUTION

Some people suppose that sorrow or persecution always does good, blesses the life, enriches the character. But, if we do not submit ourselves to God in grief and persecution, if we resist and rebel, if we chafe and repine and go on grieving inconsolably, it often hurts our lives irreparably. It mars the beauty. It hushes the song. It dims the eye. It robs the heart of its love. If, however, we reverently accept our sorrow as a messenger from God, sent on a mission of love, bearing gifts and blessings from heaven for us, then we shall get good and not evil from our pain and loss.

Blessedness means the indwelling of God in the human heart and the consciousness of His sufficiency. We must always bear this in mind if we are to understand the logic of the Beatitudes. When Matthew 5:10 speaks of "they which are persecuted," it employs the Greek verb, *dedioogmenoi*, in the passive voice. Persecution is caused by others. This verb does not refer to our own inner tortures of soul that result from the mind and its imaginations, but the suffering that results from the actions and attitudes of others outside ourselves. The Greek word for "blessed," *makarioi*, stands in sharp contrast to "happy," which means joyous because of the circumstances of life. *Makarioi*, "blessed," are those who are not affected in their inmost beings by circumstances. They can continue to be blessed when persecution is directed at them. It is not the persecution that makes them blessed. They are already blessed, and that is why they are persecuted. Their persecution only results in further blessing. They were not persecuted when they were not blessed, that is, before Christ dwelt in their hearts by faith and they found their sufficiency in Him. It is God within who is the target of the persecutor — not the person persecuted. The enemy of the Gospel loves us enough to try to win us over to Satan but cannot abide the God within us. Failing to win us, he persecutes us.

One reason the Lord calls the persecuted Christians "blessed" is that persecution is a sure proof that we are God-indwelt. When we realize this, we cannot help but stand up and be counted for Christ. God within us is a reproof to the evil works of darkness. Darkness hates the light and tries to extinguish it. Persecution is also a proof that we are not merely "happy" or circumstance-conditioned Christians, but "blessed" or God-conditioned. Persecution tests the reality of our Christian faith. True Christians will welcome persecution and refuse to compromise with sin. Those whose profession of Christianity is rooted in shallow soil will shrivel up under the heat of the noonday sun. Only those who are rooted and grounded in Christ will continue to grow and produce fruit. In the absence of persecution, it is not always possible to tell who are true Christians and who are not.

Persecution is one form of tribulation that God permits for our own good. The word tribulation comes from the Latin *tribulum*, a threshing sledge or flail. The thresher uses the flail to beat and bruise the sheaves, that he may separate the golden grain from the chaff and straw. Tribulation, persecution, is God's threshing, not to destroy us but to separate what is good, heavenly, spiritual in us from what is wrong, earthly, and fleshly. Nothing less than the blows of adversity will do this. The evil clings to the good; the golden wheat of goodness in us is so wrapped up in the strong husks of the old life that only the heavy flail of suffering can produce the separation.

Some years ago in Dublin, a company of women met to study the Bible. One of them was puzzled by the words of Malachi 3:3, "And he shall sit as a refiner and purifier of silver." After some discussion, a committee was appointed to call on a silversmith and learn what they could on the subject. The silversmith readily showed them the process. "But, sir," said one, "do you sit while the refining is going on?" "Oh, yes, indeed," he said. "I must sit with my eyes steadily fixed on the surface, for if the time necessary for refining is exceeded in the slightest degree, the silver is sure to be injured." At once they saw the beauty and comfort of the Scripture passage. As they were leaving, the silversmith called after them, "Oh, one thing more! I only know when the process is complete by seeing my own image reflected on the silver." That is what the Lord Jesus wants to see in you and me as He refines us by fire — His blessed image. And it will be reflected to others, too. In this is persecution blessed, that it allows Christ to see Himself in us, and others to see Christ reflected through our lives.

The Lord mentions the blessing of persecution at the very end of the Beatitudes, perhaps because it is the test of every other condition of blessedness. Persecution, ridicule, slander, tribulation will separate the chaff from the wheat.

God never would send you the darkness
    If He felt you could bear the light;
But you would not cling to His guiding hand
    If the way were always bright,
And you would not care to walk by faith
    Could you always walk by sight.

So He sends you the blinding darkness
    And the furnace of seven-fold heat.
'Tis the only way, believe me,
    To keep you close to His feet;
For 'tis always so easy to wander
    When our lives are glad and sweet.

God is like a photographer who carries his film into a darkened room to develop it. He leaves the developing to the very end. It will be the test of the previous exposures to the light.

Our Lord once bade His disciples consider the lilies, how they grew. Where do they get their beauty? Down in the darkness of the soil the roots lie, hidden, despised, amid clods; but there they prepare the loveliness and the sweetness that make the lilies so admired as they emerge into the light of day. Once an ugly bulb, but in it there lay hidden colors that no human artist could reproduce. First it must be buried. The choking soil must cover it. But if it is a real lily, it will come up: it will blossom; it will attract others.

Persecution, affliction, permitted by our Saviour, test the reality and fidelity of our profession. But they also leave a beneficent imprint on the character. Notice how the Apostle Paul viewed his persecutions and afflictions. Few of us could equal them in number or degree. In II Corinthians 4:8-11 he says, "We are troubled on every side, yet not distressed; we are perplexed, but not in despair; persecuted, but not forsaken; cast down, but not destroyed; always bearing about in the body the dying of the Lord Jesus, that the life also of Jesus might be made manifest in our body. For we which live are always delivered unto death for Jesus' sake, that the life also of Jesus might be made manifest in our body." To the Apostle Paul, troubles caused by others only served to bring the life of Christ to the fore in the Christian's life. The manifestation and working of Christ in and through us should not fill us with dismay but with joy. That is why Paul further states, "Most gladly therefore will I rather glory in my infirmities, that the power of Christ may rest upon me. Therefore I take pleasure in infirmities, in reproaches, in necessities, in persecutions, in distresses for Christ's sake: for when I am weak, then am I strong" (II Cor. 12:9, 10). Sufferings are multiplied for Paul, but he looks upon them, not as problems to worry about, but as opportunities to be seized.

"Unless a grain of mustard seed be bruised, the extent of its virtue is never acknowledged. For without bruising it is insipid, but if it is bruised, it becomes hot, and it gives out all those pungent properties that were concealed in it. Thus every good man, so long as he is not smitten, is regarded as insipid, and of slight account. But if ever the grinding of persecution crush him, instantly he gives forth all the warmth of his savour, and all that before appeared to be weak or contemptible is turned to godly fervour, and that which in peaceful times he had been glad to keep from view within his own bosom, he is driven by the force of tribulation to make known."

Do you suffer persecution for your Christian faith? If you can accept it as being God's will for you, a necessary part of your Christian training and purification, and rejoice in it for His sake, then "Blessed are ye."

DOES ALL PERSECUTION
RESULT IN BLESSING?

What is so blessed about being persecuted? If you have an enemy who makes your life miserable, is that supposed to make you happy? It all depends. In order for persecution to result in blessing, it must be for the right reasons. As we have said before, persecution that you bring on yourself because of your own faults, your all-too-human bad temper, flaws of character, self-righteousness — these bring you no blessing whatever, unless to teach you that you need to go to Christ for further purification of your heart and life.

In order for persecution to result in our own blessedness being increased, it must be "for righteousness' sake." Matthew 5:11 ends with the phrase "for my sake" when speaking of the persecution that shall come to the Christian. Christ equates the word "righteousness" with Himself: "For righteousness' sake," "for my sake," are interchangeable. The one equals the other. Righteousness is Christ and Christ is righteousness.

Sometimes we may be tempted to ask, "Why am I being persecuted for doing what is right?" Right in whose estimation? The word "right" is a relative term, depending on whose viewpoint you are looking at it from. Have you ever thought that what you call "right" may only be what you think is right; that others, looking at it differently, might think it wrong? Who is the judge of absolute right and wrong? Righteousness is to be found relatively in man and absolutely only in God. Everybody has a sense of right and wrong, because he is created in God's image. But this is further conditioned not only by his finite and sinful nature but by his upbringing, his education, his temperament and character – any number of things. Since righteousness is absolute only in God, the measure in which we understand righteousness is the measure in which we know and possess God. Righteousness is equivalent to God Himself. Therefore, when Christ equates Himself with righteousness in its absolute sense, He equates Himself with God. In saying, "for my sake" when giving the motive for accepting persecution, He really declares, "I am God manifested in the flesh." He said this on another occasion with indisputable clarity, "I and my Father are one" (John 10:30).

What, then, is righteousness in man? It is adjustment to God, thinking with God, feeling with God, willing with God. It is man identifying himself with God through Jesus Christ. In the measure that you and I willingly submit ourselves to God are we righteous. Righteousness is an adjustment of the whole life to God, every day, in every place, under all conditions, in all our attitudes. Though it is true that we cannot include God in the same list with our material possessions, or with human beings, it is also appallingly, tragically true that many of us put our material possessions and our loved ones where God ought to be. Although the comparison may sound frivolous, there are men and women who are entirely adjusted to their houses, automobiles, bank accounts, and relatives who are still basically maladjusted people. Socially, righteousness is that relation between man and man that is the outcome of the adjustment of individual lives to God. A man whose relationship with his fellow man is wrong at any point is a man whose relationship with God is wrong in spite of his avowals of faith. To be adjusted to God in all truth is to be true, and the man who is true cannot lie to his fellow man. To be adjusted to God in grace is to be gracious, and the man who is gracious cannot be mastered by malice in his dealing with his fellow men. (See G. Campbell Morgan, *The Westminster Pulpit*, Vol. 9, pp. 150-3.)

Righteousness in man is Christlikeness. The more like Him we are, the more certain it is that we shall be persecuted. He who indwells us is a rebuke to others through the way He lives and works through us. He is our righteousness, a manifest condemnation of man-made righteousness. The result can only be a clash, as with Christ and the Pharisees. That is why He said in John 15:18-20, "If the world hate you, ye know that it hated me before it hated you. If ye were of the world, the world would love his own: but because ye are not of the world, but I have chosen you out of the world, therefore the world hateth you. Remember the word that I said unto you, The servant is not greater than his lord. If they have persecuted me, they will also persecute you; if they have kept my saying, they will keep yours also." To persecuted and puzzled Timothy Paul wrote, "Yea, and all that will live godly [that is, righteously] in Christ Jesus shall suffer persecution" (II Tim. 3:12).

What is it to live godly in Christ Jesus? This supposes that we have been made the righteousness of God in Christ, that we have been born again, and are made one with Christ by a living faith and a vital union, even as Jesus Christ and the Father are one. Unless we are thus converted and transformed by the renewing of our minds, we cannot properly be said to be in Christ, much less to live godly in Him. To be in Christ merely by baptism and an outward profession is not to be in Him in the strict sense of the word. They that are truly in Christ Jesus are new creatures; old things are passed away, and all things are become new in their hearts. Their life is hid with Christ in God; their souls daily feed on the invisible realities of another world. To live godly in Christ is to make the divine will, and not our own, the sole principle of all our thoughts, words, and actions; so that, whether we eat or drink, or whatsoever we do, we do all to the glory of God. Those who live godly in Christ may not so much be said merely to live as Christ to live in them. They are led by His Spirit, as a child is led by the hand of its father, and are willing to follow Him wherever He leads them. They hear, know, and obey His voice. Their affections are set on things above. Their hopes are full of immortality; their citizenship is in heaven. Being born again of God, they habitually live to, and daily walk with God. They are pure in heart; and, from a principle of faith in Christ, are holy in all manner of conversation and godliness.

This is to live godly in Christ Jesus; and hence we may easily learn why so few suffer persecution; because so few live truly godly lives. You may attend on outward duties; you may live morally; you may do no one any harm, and avoid persecution. But they that live godly in Christ Jesus *must* suffer persecution. (See *Memoirs of Rev. George Whitefield*, by John Gillies, "Persecution Every Christian's Lot," p. 329.)

Notice that Paul did not say, "All that lead good lives shall suffer persecution." People are usually highly respected when they conform to the highest moral standards of the day and scrupulously observe the religious practices of their particular faith. It is "living godly in Christ Jesus," depending on Him for all the grace whereby to serve our God, and giving to Him the glory of all that we do that will involve us certainly in persecution. This is what the Gospel invariably requires and this will still give the very same offense which it gave in former days. St. Paul and all the rest of the Apostles suffered on this account. And at this day,

633

wherever salvation by faith in the atoning blood of Christ is proclaimed, as opposed to salvation by works, there is a division among the people, "some saying of the preacher, He is a good man: others saying, Nay, but he deceiveth the people." (See *Expository Outlines on the Whole Bible*, by Charles Simeon, pp. 63-4.)

Pierre Dumoulin expressed the feeling of all true Christians back in 1620 when he said, "If we must be persecuted, all those who fear God desire that it should be for the profession of the Gospel, and that our persecution should truly be the cross of Christ."

If it is your righteousness that you are persecuted for, you will feel hurt; but if it is the righteousness of God in Christ, then you'll be blessed. The way you react to persecution may well be the criterion of what kind of righteousness you possess – your own or God's.

"You are blessed because of Me," Christ said, "but you are also persecuted for righteousness' sake." If you are not, there is something wrong with your blessedness. Your lamp is hidden under a bushel. Your salt has lost its savor. The more blessed you become because of Christ the more persecuted you will be, and the more persecuted the more blessed. It is a perpetual feedback system.

THE COST OF BLESSEDNESS

Christ did not want His hearers to gain a wrong impression of all that was involved in becoming a follower of His. As He proclaimed the blessedness of those who would fulfill the spiritual conditions in each of the Beatitudes, He did not want His hearers to be under the delusion that the moment they believed and testified and sought to declare His peace all would be well with them. The blessedness He proclaimed, with all its wonderful privileges, such as having God within them here and hereafter and experiencing His all-sufficiency, would lead to certain seemingly unpleasant consequences. Blessedness, which is concerned with God dealing with us, involves our vertical relationship. But on the horizontal plane we live in a world that is not blessed and neither knows God nor recognizes His authority. Christ wanted to warn His hearers that those who are not of the world, though still in the world, will find themselves in conflict with the world and the world with them.

A fire captain was killed in a conflagration in New York City. In commenting on his death, the chief of the Fire Department said something like this: "Firemen have been killed in this city before and firemen are being killed in this city right along. The fact is, fighting fire in New York is a dangerous, hazardous occupation. Now every man in this department knows that. He knew it before he joined the department. Consequently, when he joined up, he had already performed his act of bravery. Anything that follows, even death, is just in the day's work. This man did not go in there intending to die. He went in to put the fire out – and he died, and that is all there is to it."

One could hardly describe in better words the Bible conception of a yielded servant of God, a truly dedicated follower of Jesus Christ, a blessed person. To be a soldier of the cross is a hazardous and dangerous calling. Everyone should thoroughly understand that before he joins up. If, then, he joins that army, his act of bravery may be said to have been already performed. Whatever comes after that, even death, is just in the line of duty. Men and women who are Christians have not gone looking for persecution and suffering; they have gone into the thick of the conflagration to fight against sin and shame and have suffered and died. That is about all there is to the truly Christian life.

Christ wanted to paint a realistic picture of what awaited those who committed themselves wholly to Him. As far as their relationship with God was concerned, peace, joy unspeakable and full of glory, would be their portion. But not where their relationship to the world was concerned. Their position would be like that of the oak tree, which sets its roots deep in mother earth and soars high into the sky, but must suffer the buffeting wind and the storms that try their best to uproot it. The sturdiest oak is the one that has withstood the strongest winds.

God of the gallant trees,
    Give to us fortitude;
Give as Thou givest to these
    Valorous hardihood.
We are the trees of Thy planting, O God.
    We are the trees of Thy wood.

Now let the life-sap run

636

Clean through our every vein;
Perfect that Thou hast begun,
    God of the sun and rain;
Thou who dost measure the weight of the wind,
    Fit us for stress and for strain.
                    — *Amy Carmichael.*

We are just like that, the Lord said. Our persecution is the result of our blessedness in Christ, the result of our peacemaking efforts "for righteousness' sake," and for no other reason. We do not become blessed because we are persecuted; but, because we are blessed, persecution follows. Nor does our persecution detract from our blessedness, but rather adds to it.

Our Lord's purpose in being truthful about the dangers involved in the Christian life was not to frighten people away from Him but to present a challenge. True Christian men and women are not looking for a soft and easy life. Any demagogue can get a loose, temporary following by appealing to people's love of ease or desire to avoid pain. This is the psychological basis of some present-day preaching. Christ is presented as the way of escape from all earthly troubles. Actually, when we receive Him as Saviour, our fundamental problem is resolved, that of our relationship to God, including forgiveness of sin. But it is also true that a host of troubles begins when, through regeneration, we become "different" in the eyes of the world. That is why Paul says to young Timothy, "Thou therefore endure hardness, as a good soldier of Jesus Christ" (II Tim. 2:3).

But simply appealing to the desire to escape from trouble is not enough. If you want to secure the permanent loyalties of men, you must appeal to something deeper and finer — their ability to endure and to suffer. That is one reason why young people generally go in for the more hazardous sports, why our young athletes find football more appealing than croquet. They like to pit their strength against the element of danger and hardship. The same is true of men's occupations. The more perilous an occupation is, the more brave men compete for the honor of engaging in it. Look at our test pilots and astronauts. What courage, arduous preparation, and endurance they exhibit. It is such men and women the Lord is looking for.

> Must I be carried to the skies
>   On flowery beds of ease,
> While others fought to win the prize
>   And sailed through bloody seas?

Here is the answer that comes from the brave hearts of the blessed in Christ:

> Since I must fight if I would reign,
>   Increase my courage, Lord!
> I'll bear the toil, endure the pain,
>   Supported by Thy Word.

The fact is that, since this old world, with all its glad and beautiful aspects duly acknowledged, is still so full of sorrow and inequity and tragedy, coziness and comfort can never be tolerable for an unspoiled human heart. Someone once wrote: "Beholding the appalling sufferings of my fellow creatures, I should feel myself guilty, possessing abundance and leaving them in hunger, nakedness, immorality, deepest crime, and deepest ignorance, if I retired into domestic quiet and left the struggle to be carried on solely by others." The greatest men and women in this world have found that what seemed most intolerable to them was that their lives seemed condemned by Providence to be too easy and comfortable.

> If He could doubt, on His triumphant cross,
> How much more I, in the defeat and loss
> Of knowing all my selfish dreams fulfilled —
> Of having lived the very life I willed?
> My God, my God, why hast Thou forsaken me?

It is simply a crime for Christians to enjoy their blessedness in quietness and ease while the world is perishing. Avoiding a fight with evil for the sake of superficial and selfish peace is cowardice. "I believe in Christianity," said Matthew Arnold, "because I do not know of a single acre of ground which is not a better acre of ground the moment Christianity touches it." "I believe in foreign missions," declared President Taft, "because where missions go there goes civilization." Are you content, beholding the millions without Christ, and retiring into domestic quiet, leaving the struggle to be carried on by others lest you be persecuted? (See Raymond Calkins' sermon, "Suffering Hardship," in *The Christian World Pulpit*, Vol. 93, pp. 302-5.)

The five young missionaries who went into the jungles of Ecuador to bring the Gospel to the Auca Indians were not looking for a soft and easy life. They had accepted the challenge, counted the cost, and finally paid it in martyrdom. Their loved ones who remained did not cry out against their hard lot; they, too, accepted the cost, took up the challenge, and went forward in complete surrender to God's purpose in bringing them to this hard field. We wipe away a tear when we read of it and go on hugging our blessedness to ourselves. No wonder it proves less rewarding than we expected. This is one commodity that, the more you spend it, the more you have. Naturally, God doesn't want everyone to go storming into heathen jungles to convert wild savages; but I'm sure that He wants each of us to be willing to forgo selfish ease and comfort, get out and take an active part in making His Word known to others. Even a shut-in can have an active ministry of prayer, you know. "What is that in thine hand?" God asked Moses (Exod. 4:2). Whatever God has given you in the way of blessedness, share it with others, and you will be surprised at the blessedness that will result in their lives and at the increase of blessedness in your own.

CHRIST WARNS OF PERSECUTION

Persecution is a distressing experience. When it descends upon us because of our wrong actions and attitudes, it entails no rewards. But when borne "for righteousness' sake," it increases our blessedness in Christ. Our Lord announced a definite reward for all who endured persecution for their faith.

Although Christ was surrounded by the inner circle of His disciples, who were undergoing persecution at that time, He did not say to them, "for yours is the kingdom of heaven," but "for theirs." In this way He indicated that His message was not for them exclusively. He wanted the others listening to Him on the mountainside, the outsiders, so to speak, to learn the conditions of blessedness and the world's ultimate reaction to active blessedness. The Christian life, He declared in effect to those who were wondering whether to follow Him, is not all sweetness and light. It is, as far as our relationship with God is concerned, but not where the world is concerned. It was as if the Lord were telling His disciples, "I want any who are thinking of joining our ranks to know that, if they come to Me, I will make them members of the Kingdom of Heaven, I will comfort them, enable them to enjoy the earth, fill them with My righteousness, continually pour My mercy into them, show Myself to them, recognize them as My children – BUT the world on which they turn their backs will persecute them. That is inevitable. They might as well know it beforehand."

This was Christ's warning as to the price of following Him. He recounted all the blessings first, leaving the Beatitude of persecution to the very end that people might see how worthwhile it is to suffer for Christ. Persecution cannot detract one iota from our blessedness, but rather increases it. Christ truthfully represents both the blessing and the cost of Christianity. Though there is a cross to be borne, it is worth it because of the resurrection. Without the resurrection, the cross would be shame. Christ's service, as outlined in the Beatitudes, is seven times blessed; and when it comes to the hostile reaction of the world, it is still blessed. Praise God! The disciples knew all this, but not those still outside their circle who had not yet experienced the blessing of God through faith in Jesus Christ.

There is a significant variation in the tense of the verb in this eighth Beatitude. Christ does not say, "For theirs will be the kingdom of heaven," but "for theirs *is* the kingdom of heaven." Only in the first and last Beatitudes do we find the promise given in the present tense. All the verbs of promise in between are in the future tense. Read them over again and see if this is not so. Here are Matthew 5:3 and 10, the first and last Beatitudes:

"Blessed are the poor in spirit: for theirs *is* the kingdom of heaven.

"Blessed are they which are persecuted for righteousness' sake: for theirs *is* the kingdom of heaven."

And here are Beatitudes two through seven:

"Blessed are they that mourn: for they *shall be* comforted.

"Blessed are the meek: for they *shall inherit* the earth.

"Blessed are they which do hunger and thirst after righteousness: for they *shall be* filled.

"Blessed are the merciful: for they *shall obtain* mercy.

"Blessed are the pure in heart: for they *shall see* God.

"Blessed are the peacemakers: for they *shall be called* the children of God."

Now why this variation in the tense of the verbs? In both cases where the present tense is used, it is "the kingdom of heaven" that is possessed. A king can grant no greater gift than to share his kingdom with us. Here we see a declaration of the sovereignty of God.

Let us go back to the first Beatitude, which speaks of being "poor in spirit," utterly helpless to help ourselves spiritually. You reach the place of realizing your inner poverty and acknowledge that there is absolutely nothing you can do to help yourself. You know that rescue has to come from outside yourself, from the Lord Jesus Christ. No spiritual struggle will help you; in fact, like a drowning individual whom someone is trying to save, the more you struggle the less likely are your chances of rescue. The blessedness of which Christ speaks can come to you only as you completely abandon yourself to Him. This is what is meant by salvation. It is yours the moment you believe and receive Christ as Saviour and Lord. "Blessed are the poor in spirit: for theirs *is* the kingdom of heaven." It is now and ever will continue to be yours. Salvation is not a reward promised for the future, but a present, immediate, and lasting gift of God.

Now let us look at the eighth Beatitude in the light of the first. The struggle with evil and the resistance of the evil one to the believer does not start at the end of the Christian life. It starts immediately we believe. That is why the promise to the persecuted ones is also given in the present tense. The world will begin to hate us, persecute us, call us crazy the very moment we become children of the Heavenly Kingdom. Expect it, be prepared for it, says our Saviour. As it comes, it is an affirmative demonstration of what you are – children of the King of Kings. Persecution is an integral part of belief and a proof of its genuineness. There is a cost to blessedness. No, you can't pay for your salvation, but when you become a partaker of Christ's blessedness you also become a partaker of His persecution at the hands of His enemies. Your identity with Christ in the glory of His salvation is precious, but your voluntary identification with Him in His sufferings is even more precious.

By a sure instinct the early Church discerned in the death of the martyr the repetition, not the less real because faint, of the central Sacrifice of Calvary. "As we behold the martyrs," writes Origen, "coming forth from every Church to be brought before the tribunal, we see in each the Lord Himself condemned." So Irenaeus speaks of the martyrs as "endeavoring to follow in the footsteps of Christ," and of St. Stephen as "imitating in all things the Master of Martyrdom." In the early Church the imitation of Christ, as a formal principle in ethics, played but a secondary part, so far, at any rate, as the average member was concerned. The martyrs and confessors alone were thought of as actually following and imitating Jesus; they alone were the "true disciples" of the Master. It was enough for the servant that he should be as his Lord. (See *Persecution in the Early Church*, by H. B. Workman, pp. 21, 22.)

Someone may object, "But I don't deserve this suffering." Of course not. Deserved suffering is the portion of the disobedient, the ungodly, the criminal. No one ever bore such undeserved sorrow as did Jesus of Nazareth. Even of Him, the spotless, the sinless, it was said that He was made perfect through suffering. He bathes our eyes with tears until by faith they can behold that invisible land where tears shall be no more.

PERSECUTION BY CHRISTIANS

The 11th and 12th verses of the 5th chapter of Matthew are an amplification of the 8th Beatitude in verse 10, dealing with persecution. The Lord changes from the third person now to the second person. In verse 10 it was "Blessed are *they*." Now it is "Blessed are *ye*, when men shall revile you, and persecute you, and shall say all manner of evil against you falsely, for my sake" (v. 11). Christ turns to the disciples personally and tells them that they are counted among the blessed since they are presently being reviled, persecuted, and evil spoken of. "Blessed are ye, in spite of what you are going through," He says; "your blessedness is not affected by the persecution you are experiencing." Could the Master turn to you and me and say, "Blessed are ye"?

Our Lord wanted to prepare His disciples for the fact that persecution is not a momentary thing, that it would continue. The Greek word *hotan* here, incorrectly translated "when," should be "whenever." Actually the verse should read, "Blessed are ye *whenever* men shall ... persecute you." It would be a recurring experience. Their lives would not be all persecution, but occasional persecution would be unavoidable — in their lives and ours. "Which of the prophets have not your fathers persecuted?" Stephen asked when he was about to be stoned to death. "Yea, and all that will live godly in Christ Jesus shall suffer persecution," Paul warned Timothy (II Tim. 3:12). Not constant persecution, but occasional outbursts of it, are sure to arise against the active peacemaker as he goes counter to the accepted philosophy of the world.

This is further supported by the tense of the three

plural verbs in verse 11. They are in the aorist in Greek, which indicates, not a constant and protracted action, but one that takes place within any prescribed time, point, action. In other words, although our Lord wanted us to know that the blessed life involves persecution, He also wanted us to know that this would not be a constant state of affairs. The three aorists express actuality but not constancy.

Who are those who will revile us, persecute us, and speak evil of us? Our Lord does not specify. No doubt they will be mostly the enemies of Christ; but sometimes they may be those who profess to be our brethren.

A young man came to me with his prospective wife for counsel recently. He had at one time lived in deep and hideous sin, but he had confessed it before the Lord and his brethren and had gained the victory. When we confess our sins to God and turn from them, He forgives and forgets; but men are not always so magnanimous. This young man told me with deep grief, "No one to whom I confessed my sin ever treated me the same after that." They insisted on prolonging the agony of the memory of past sin, instead of rejoicing in present victory over daily temptation and trusting in God for future deliverance. It is in this manner that Christians may be said to persecute the brethren, refusing to recognize the work of grace God has wrought in them as genuine; discouraging the weak when they ought to encourage them. Remember, it is only by the grace of God that we are able to withstand in the day of temptation. Let us not, by our unforgiving spirits, be included among those unnamed ones whom our Lord said would persecute His children.

The first mate on a certain vessel, yielding to temptation, became drunk for the first time in his life. The captain entered in the ship's log, "Mate drunk today."

The mate implored the captain to remove it from the record, saying that if the ship's owners saw it he would lose his post, and the captain well knew it was his first offense. But the obdurate captain refused, saying, "This is the fact, and into the log it goes." Some days afterward, the mate was keeping the log; and after giving the latitude and longitude, the run for the day, the wind and the sea, he made this entry: "Captain sober today." The indignant captain protested, saying that it would leave an altogether false impression in the minds of the owners of the vessel, as if it were an unusual thing for him to be sober. But the mate answered as the captain had, "This is the fact, and into the log it goes."

We smile at this, but something very like it can creep into our own conduct without our being aware of it. Before going to God in prayer about those who persecute you, examine your own heart to see if you are persecuting anyone else. We expect this of enemies of the Gospel, but it is a sinful contradiction when Christians persecute each other. As in the case of the captain and the mate, such persecution is usually based on a half-truth, not taking into account all the facts. Something like this could easily have happened to me recently. I was flying to London, but because of fog the plane had to go on to Frankfurt, Germany. It was around two in the morning when we were finally taken to a small town and provided with lodging. Everyone complained of hunger, but on this cold winter night all the restaurants were closed. I went to bed, but at three a. m. the telephone rang. It was the airline stewardess calling to say that they had found a place where we could get something to eat if I wanted to come. I declined because I was more tired than hungry. Imagine my surprise next morning when I found out that it was a night club that my fellow passengers had been taken to. Suppose I had gone, and another Christian who knew me had seen me there. If he told others that he had seen me in a night club, he would have been telling the truth, yet only a half-truth, as when the mate stated that the captain was sober, implying that this was an exception to the rule. Many slanders can start with a true statement that does not present a balanced, accurate picture. Truth told with the intent to deceive is a lie; half-truths are falsehoods.

Those who spoke only of the sin of the young man who came to me, and not of his subsequent victory, were malicious, untruthful, un-Christian. In God's sight, such a persecutor may well be the more sinful of the two, though he be a Christian of many year's standing. God deliver us from such pharisaical conduct.

God's mercy is big enough for all. It can save you and your sinful brother, too. A Russian Christian tells a parable of a man in hell who prayed earnestly to be released from torment. At last a voice said, "Rescue will come," and a carrot held by a slender thread was let down into the abyss and he was told to grasp it. He did so, and weak though the thread seemed, it began to draw him up. But others, seeing his ascent, seized upon his garments that they also might be rescued. The man kicked them off, crying, "The thread will break!" And break it did, alas! And again the voice spoke: "The thread was strong enough to save both you and your brothers, but it was not strong enough to save you alone."

In your selfishness, do you think that you alone are saved by the mercy of God and made righteous before Him; that the thread of redemption is too thin to save those who come out of gross sin, those who have not attained to the eminence of respectability on which you fancy yourself to stand? As in the parable of the Pharisee and the publican, it is often the self-righteous who persecute the truly righteous who confess their sins.

Part of the cost of being true to God is that some of your own brethren may never let you forget how sinful you were and will not give you a chance to live on an equal footing with them. They think that the scarlet thread of redemption is only sufficient to save them.

It goes without saying that a blessed Christian will never persecute non-Christians, either. The inquisition is a black page in the Church's history. Christ never persecuted anyone; and when His disciples asked if they should command fire to come down from heaven and destroy those who rejected Him, He said, "Ye know not what manner of spirit ye are of," plainly implying that such promptings were of the devil.

> That man is happy, Lord, who love
>   like this doth owe:
> Loves Thee, his friend in Thee, and,
>   for Thy sake, his foe.
>
> — *Richard Chenevix Trench.*

THE JOY OF BEING PERSECUTED

What is involved in being persecuted for righteousness' sake, that is, for Christ's sake? One thing that will happen, our Lord said, is that "men shall revile you." The Greek word is *oneidisoosin*, the same word used in Luke 6:22, but there translated "reproach." Reviling, reproaching, is what we Christians are to expect as the crowning experience of our blessedness in Christ.

To revile or reproach someone is to abuse him in speech because you despise him. Sometimes taunting is involved, a cruel form of making fun. The persecuted ones are the victims of name-calling. That men will scoff at what is pure and noble and admire what is low is a proof of the degeneracy of the human race. The names the ungodly call us manifest the nature and degree of our blessedness. No follower of Christ has been called by worse names than his Master. But hostile taunts are really tributes; the reproaches of our enemies reveal our true character; and it is in this that we should rejoice. "Blessed are ye, when men shall revile you . . . Rejoice, and be exceeding glad."

In the eighth chapter of John's Gospel we find the Lord in the temple arguing with the Jews. They claimed to be patriots, children of Abraham and therefore children of God. The Lord, discerning their sinful hearts and the consequent falsity of their claim, did not hesitate to rebuke them. "Ye are of your father the devil," He said (v. 44). How could a true Jew speak thus of His fellow Jews? They felt that any breach in religious unity was tantamount to the breaking of the nationalistic spirit and entity. They hurled an accusation at Him that would brand Him as a traitor: they called Him a

Samaritan. "Say we not well that thou art a Samaritan, and hast a devil?" (v. 48). You're an enemy of the Jewish nation, they told Him. They could not recognize the love that underlay His sternness, His longing that they should not be Jews outwardly, but as Paul put it, "circumcised in heart." Nations, like individuals, too often think that the man who tells them the unpalatable truth must be their enemy, when he may be the greatest patriot of them all. These people, misunderstanding the motive that lay behind Christ's words, and feeling keenly their sharp edge, could only suppose that anyone who would speak thus to them must be a bad Jew and an enemy of his race.

God has permitted me to feel something of this even in this day and age. It has been my privilege to write a Gospel message each week, printed as a paid advertisement in nearly every Greek newspaper and secular magazine. Through this medium I tell my people, the Greeks, that natural descent is not a ticket to heaven, that being a Greek does not automatically make one a Christian. Because, for reasons of conscience, I do not belong to the State Church of Greece, I have been branded a heretic and a traitor. In recent years the reproach has been hurled against Greek Evangelicals that they are not true Greeks. The Holy Synod of the State Church even issued an official encyclical against me and circulated it widely. The whole basis of this four-page defamatory document is their contention that the unity of the nation depends on unity of church affiliation. Deflection from the faith of the majority means defection from patriotism.

Here are parts of this encyclical: "According to Article One of the Constitution, the prevailing religion in Greece is that of the Eastern Orthodox Church of Christ, proselytism and every other intervention against the

651

prevailing religion being forbidden. The Greek Nation, finding in the Hellenic Christian tradition the unity, the fighting spirit on behalf of truth and freedom as the power of the Creator, cannot permit the subversion of the religious conscience of its people. This is why it enacted the above Constitutional provision, according to which it forbids proselytism and every other intervention against the prevailing religion ... Of course, we are a free Nation, and we have a fully free press. We respect every heterodox person in our Country. But since these take advantage of the freedom which the Country gives to them and endeavor through propaganda to break the unity of the Faith and the very coherence of the Nation ... we are obliged ... to defend ourselves, to raise a voice of protest and to protect the Faith of our Fathers, our Nation, ourselves. If this sect leader sincerely desired to preach Christ, he could go to Nations and people to whom the Gospel has not yet been preached, so that he might enlighten and lead to Christ these semi-savage and uncivilized ones, and not us Orthodox Greeks, in whose country the Gospel was preached by the Apostles and where Christianity developed ... Every divider of the Ecclesiastical unity is also an enemy of the Nation ... Do not read the heretical articles of the sect leader Spiros Zodhiates and of the other heretics. Do not receive into your hands anti-Orthodox tracts, printed materials, books; and if you have such, burn them. Close your doors to the visits of the heretics."

Sad, isn't it? But under the guise of patriotism a great many missiles are being hurled at those who have the courage to proclaim that salvation is a personal and not a national matter. Christ was called a Samaritan; He, a Jew, was accused of being anti-Jewish because

He dared to call Jewish sinners the children of the devil. I, too, have been called a heretic and a traitor because I tell my people the Greeks that being born into a particular church will not save them, but only their personal faith in Jesus Christ. This runs counter to national and religious pride and therefore arouses the persecutory spirit. It is a defense mechanism on the part of those who feel threatened. In order to make their position believable to the public, they will formulate all sorts of half-truths about the person persecuted. He will be ridiculed, disparaged, slandered — all because he chooses to spend his life for righteousness' sake, for Christ's sake, rather than for self-gratification and advancement. The world little realizes that the joy of sacrificing for Christ far outweighs the pleasure of selfish enjoyment of this world's goods. Such an attitude is foolishness to the world. The joys of the world are external, those of the Christian internal. To see a soul saved produces greater joy than to inherit great riches.

Bunk! you say. Well, don't knock it if you haven't tried it. Saint Augustine tells of a certain pagan who showed him his idols, saying, "Here is my god; where is thine?" Then, pointing up at the sun, he said again, "Lo! here is my god; where is thine?" So, showing him divers creatures, he still upbraided him with, "Here are my gods; where are thine?" But Saint Augustine writes, "I showed him not my God, not because I had not one to show him, but because he had not eyes to see Him."

Thus the joys of a Christian, though not discernible to natural vision, are incomparable in the delight and comfort they afford, as witness that joy in the Holy Ghost that is so inexpressible, which eye hath not seen, nor ear heard, neither entered into the heart of man to conceive of. This explains why the joys of the Christian are ridiculous in the eyes of the world, and the joys of the world are so little thought of by Christians.

Another basic teaching of our Lord in Matthew 5:11, 12 is that the blessedness of persecution for the sake of Christ is greatly increased when it produces joy and gladness. That is why our Lord added these two verses to the 8th Beatitude. We can rejoice in the midst of persecution for two reasons: because the accusations hurled at us are false, and because instead of persecution hindering the Gospel it prospers it. It may kill us, but the Gospel will flourish. In this we are to rejoice and be exceeding glad.

During the months that Saint Francis went up and down the streets of Assisi carrying in his delicate hands the stones for rebuilding the St. Damiano Chapel, he was continually singing psalms, breaking forth into ejaculations of gratitude, his face beaming as one who saw visions of inexpressible delight. When questioned why he sang, he replied, "I build for God's praise, and desire that every stone shall be laid with joy." In such a spirit should we bear our burden of persecution, rejoicing at being counted worthy to suffer for Christ's sake.

NOT PERSECUTION BUT GOD OUR SOURCE OF JOY

When our Lord said, "Blessed are they which are persecuted for righteousness' sake: for theirs is the kingdom of heaven," He was not setting a premium on persecution for its own sake. Many who have mistakenly thought that joy and gladness are inherent in persecution have deliberately set out to cultivate martyrdom. Men are motivated in their actions by the result they hope to achieve. If they think that the end product of something is joy, they will deliberately seek it. But this will not work where persecution is concerned. We are not to hunt for opportunities to suffer, for this has no value for the cause of Christ nor does it increase our own blessedness. The desire for martyrdom can even be sinful if the basis of it is a desire to attract attention to ourselves and merit salvation or reward from God. There is an insidious aura of self-glorification about it, whether we are conscious of it or not. The acid test is, are we accepting inevitable persecution for the glory of Christ, or are we courting martyrdom and deriving secret satisfaction from our own supposed holiness? Let us examine our hearts and ask ourselves why we are being persecuted. Have we brought it upon ourselves, or is it the natural outcome of our blessedness in Christ as we have sought to exalt Him in the sight of men? Others have a way of discerning our motives, and they judge us by these rather than by the face value of our actions. We are not blessed because we suffer persecution, slander, and ridicule; we are blessed because of God's presence within us. Persecution must come only as a result of Christ living out His life in us and through us.

It is enlightening to note that the Greek verb *diookoo*, "to persecute," from which the substantive *dioogmos*, "persecution," is derived, also means "to hasten, to run, to press on, to run after, to pursue, to strive for, to seek after." On two occasions the Apostle Paul uses it in connection with something desirable for Christians. In Romans 12:13 he writes, "Distributing to the necessity of saints; *given to* hospitality." "Given to" in the original Greek is *diookontes*, "chasing, seeking after." It is the same word that refers to persecution. And in I Corinthians 14:1 Paul adjures the Christians, "*Follow after* charity." *Diookete*, "follow after," is also derived from the root verb "to persecute." This will help us to understand what our Lord meant by persecution, that it involves the world running after us to cause us suffering, not we pursuing them to bring suffering on ourselves. Persecution must come about naturally, through others, solely as the result of God's life within us. We are not to draw it upon ourselves by any eccentricity of ours, or by a desire for favorable attention from God or man.

It is also significant to observe the tenses of the verbs used in verses 11 and 12. In verse 11 the aorist is used: *oneidisoosin*, "shall revile you"; *diooksoosin*, "shall persecute you"; *eipoosin*, "shall say." These refer to certain attitudes and actions of others against us within a limited and prescribed period of time. Limited and prescribed by whom? In the Christian's life, it is not those who persecute us who prescribe either the intensity or the duration of their hostile actions, but the overruling and omnipotent God. No man's strength or will supersedes God's. Not even Satan can tempt us beyond the point that God has set for the accomplishing, not of our desires, but His own eternal purposes. Only as we comprehend this fundamental truth will joy accompany the experience of persecution and even outlive it. Whatever God permits in our lives is never purposeless, although the purpose is not always immediately or fully manifest to us.

Those who heard Jenny Lind, the sweet singer of Stockholm, have written of the wonderful quality of her voice and the charm of the songs she sang. Yet few realize that she owed as much to the school of suffering and sorrow as to the academy where her powers were developed. Her childhood was full of sadness. The woman with whom she lived locked her in her room each day when she went to work; and the only means the child found of whiling away the long hours was to sit by the window and sing to herself. One day a passerby heard the voice of the unseen singer and detected its possibilities, for he was a music master in the city. He called a friend to his side, and together they listened to the wonderful voice within. They got in touch with the child's guardian and made arrangements for the almost friendless girl to be given her chance. There were many difficulties to be overcome, but step by step she mounted the ladder of fame. She astounded London and Paris, Vienna, Berlin, and New York. Some say there never was such a voice, trilling like the thrush, pure as the note of the lark. But those who knew her best realized how the sorrows of her childhood gave a richness and depth to her song that otherwise would have been unattainable. She herself once wrote:

> In vain I seek for rest
>   In all created good:
> It leaves me still unblest,
>   And makes me cry for God.
> And safe at rest I cannot be
>   Until my heart finds rest in Thee.

Yes, there is a purpose in what God allows us to suffer. His sovereignty has not been usurped by evil or evildoers. He is still on the throne working our good through the persecution directed against His Son and His blood-bought children.

Now observe the tense of the verbs in Matthew 5:12. These are imperatives, commandments. "Rejoice, and be exceeding glad." Both these verbs in Greek, *chairete* and *agalliasthe*, are in the present tense. They refer not to temporary joy and gladness limited to the here and now, but to a permanent state, a constant attitude, not necessarily produced by the present experience of being persecuted, reviled, and slandered. These are but incidental experiences in the permanent, constant, eternal life of joy and gladness that is ours in Christ. He is our joy, He is our gladness — not the persecution, or the reviling, or the slander.

In fact, the actions of our enemies ought to bring sorrow to our hearts; we should mourn because of the sinfulness of those who persecute us. The sins of others should not produce joy in us. We must weep, as Christ wept over unrepentant Jerusalem.

It is God's indwelling — constant, unaffected, and uninterrupted by any persecution, reviling, or slander — that is the basic source of all our joy and gladness. We weep over the sinfulness of our persecutors, but mixed with these tears of compassion are streams of joy resulting from God's presence within us. Persecution proves the fact of our blessedness, and it is this assurance of God's reality and sovereignty in and over our lives that causes us to "rejoice, and be exceeding glad."

We must learn the lesson that we are not our own, but God's, and that in this lies our joy and gladness. The idea of the eighth Beatitude is that we can be joyful, not because of persecution, but in spite of it.

Men may rob us of our possessions, do us bodily injury, even kill us; but they cannot touch our real life, for this is hid with Christ in God. All the wrongs they can inflict upon us cannot work us lasting harm. But if we give way to anger, if we let bitterness creep into our hearts, if we grow unforgiving and resentful, we have hurt ourselves. If, on the other hand, we keep a loving spirit through all the wrongs we suffer, we shall have won the victory over all wrong.

> Here, and here alone,
> Is given thee to suffer for God's sake.
> In the other worlds we shall more perfectly
> Serve Him and love Him, praise Him, work for Him,
> Grow near and nearer to Him with all delight;
> But then we shall not any more be called
> To suffer, which is our appointment here.
> Canst thou not suffer, then, one hour or two?
> If He should call thee from thy cross today,
> Saying, It is finished! — that hard cross of thine
> From which thou prayest for deliverance,
> Thinkest thou not some passion of regret
> Would overcome thee? Thou wouldst say, "So soon?
> Let me go back and suffer yet awhile
> More patiently: — I have not yet praised God."

— H. E. H. King.

HOW CHRISTIANS SHOULD REACT
TO PERSECUTION

When others persecute us, malign us, make fun of our Christian testimony, what should our reaction be? Hurt feelings are human, and perhaps we cannot altogether help them; but resentment, bitterness, the desire to defend ourselves, to retaliate — how far should we let ourselves go in this direction? In a world where we are urged to stand up and fight for our rights on the one hand, and compelled to knuckle under by force of circumstances on the other, this can be a very disturbing problem.

You may say, "It was all very well for Christ to command us to rejoice and be exceeding glad when we are persecuted, but Matthew 5:12 doesn't seem a very realistic solution to the problems I face in my home, at work, in my community, in my country. in my twentieth-century world." Well, let's try applying these words to our lives in a practical way.

Most of us have to work for a living, which involves taking orders from others, some of whom are not easy to get along with. The kind of world we live in today, as in Christ's day, contains good, bad, and indifferent masters. True, we are not slaves, but bosses can sometimes be tyrants. Strength ought to be gentle, but there are strong men who use their power brutally. There are none of us who do not, at some time in our lives, have to suffer unjustly. Justice is not a universal human characteristic. We as Christians can expect to be misjudged and misunderstood. We should not wonder at it when others repay our kindness with unkindness, our self-sacrifice and love with ingratitude and neglect. There have always been good men who suffer for their goodness. That's what the Lord is talking about in this Beatitude.

The problem is how to maintain a Christian spirit, how to be Christlike when others are unreasonable, exacting, unkind, or unjust. Peter, in writing to Christian slaves, who often found their position very hard under severe or cruel masters, said, "Hereunto were ye called." That is, they were called upon to suffer wrongfully, to submit quietly, not only to the good and gentle, but also to the oppressive. "If, when ye do well, and suffer for it, ye take it patiently, this is acceptable with God. For even hereunto were ye called" (I Pet. 2:20).

Here is the Christian spirit: to manifest the patient, gentle nature of Christ whatever our hardships and wrongs, realizing that back of the human masters stands another Master, and it is for Him that we are really working. This changes the character of all service, so that we will do our work conscientiously, without skimping, without bitterness under unjust treatment, knowing that by so doing we are pleasing Him. A Christian is not called to an easy, comfortable, self-indulgent life but to one of self-denial, sacrifice, cross-bearing. "Blessed are they which are persecuted for righteousness' sake: for theirs is the kingdom of heaven. Blessed are ye, when men shall revile you, aud persecute you, and shall say all manner of evil against you falsely, for my sake. Rejoice, and be exceeding glad: for great is your reward in heaven: for so persecuted they the prophets which were before you" (Matt. 5:10-12).

Our Lord always practiced what He preached. The lessons He taught He illustrated by His own example. We say we want to be like Christ, to live as He did, but do we really mean it? When we examine His life, we find that a large part of it was the enduring of wrong.

He was the love of God incarnate, offering mercy and heavenly gifts to all who would open their hearts to receive them, yet "He came unto his own, and his own received him not" (John 1:11). Most of our Lord's sufferings were at the hands of men. He went among them as a friend, seeking always to do them good, only to have His kindness met with unkindness in return. The greater part of those He sought to save rejected Him. He never ceased doing good, and men never ceased persecuting Him, until finally they nailed Him to a cross. In reality, they had been crucifying Him, driving nails into His hands and feet, piercing His heart with a sword, all during the three years of His public ministry. Yet His love was never chilled by their enmity and cruelty. He bore it all with never a bitter thought in His heart. At His trial, when falsely accused, He held His peace. Even on the cross, when human hate had done its worst, He loved as tenderly, as patiently, as forgivingly as if He had been receiving only love from the world all these years. His anguish found vent, not in imprecations against His enemies, or cries of pain, but in a prayer of love. "Father, forgive them, for they know not what they do."

There was never a moment in our Lord's life when bitterness or resentment found lodgment in His heart. His answer to all the unkindness, the enmity, the plottings, the denials, the treason, to all the cruelty, the brutal accusations, and the terrible wrongs inflicted upon Him was love. Thus it is that we should bear all that is unjust, unkind, and wrong in the treatment we receive at the hands of others. We are to keep love in our hearts through it all.

In Northern Greece we have a beautiful summer camp at the foot of Mount Olympus. It is right on the shores of the blue Aegean Sea, whose water is very salty. But stand where the water has just receded and dig a few inches, and the hole will fill up with the most refreshing sweet water you have ever tasted. It has come from the hills and hidden itself out of sight, to be discovered only by digging. When the sea rolls in and pours its bitter flood over the little hole, though it covers it with a shroud of brackish waters, the stream of sweet water is still there. Such should the stream of love in our hearts be. When the floods of unkindness and wrong pour over us, however cruelly we may be treated by the world, and whatever injustice we may have to endure from others, the well of love within us should never retain a trace of bitterness but remain pure and sweet.

We cannot avoid suffering at the hands of others, even as the stream of sweet water could not escape the engulfing waters of the sea. In the truest and most congenial friendships there are things that sometimes cause pain. In the happiest homes there is frequent need of mutual forbearance and forgiveness. And there are many who have to suffer continually, ofttimes cruelly and bitterly, at the hands of others.

Here, then, is the problem — how to keep love in our hearts through all unkindness, ingratitude, and injustice; not to allow bitterness to creep in; not to give way to feelings of resentment; always to be forgiving, loving, ready to help. It was thus that Christ went through life to the very end, praying for His enemies even on the cross, and giving His life to those who sought to thrust Him out of His own world.

"But why did Christ submit to this terrible treatment?" you ask. "Have we not a right to demand justice in this world? Must wicked men be allowed to go on forever in their wickedness and cruelty?" Do not look for all wrongs to be righted in this present world. "In the world ye shall have tribulation," our Master told us. "But be of good cheer; I have overcome the world" (John 16:33). And that is what we, too, must do. Here, then, is how to endure wrong and not be hurt by it:

First, we must commit ourselves and our distresses to Him who threatened not when He suffered, "but committed himself to him that judgeth righteously," to His Heavenly Father. He did not take the righting of His wrongs into His own hands, though He had the power to summon legions of angels to fight for Him.

Second, we must realize that God has a purpose in our suffering. When Pilate spoke to Jesus of his power to crucify or release Him, Jesus said, "Thou couldest have no power at all against me, except it were given thee from above" (John 19:11). God could build a wall about us if He would, so that no enemy could touch us. That He does not do so should make us realize that all that comes to us in the way of suffering at the hands of others is permitted by God, and therefore comes from Him. It is not an accident, a lawless occurrence, something that has broken away from the divine control, a catastrophe that God could not prevent. In nature, not a drop of water in the wildest waves of the sea ever gets away from the leash of law. Law reigns everywhere, in things small and great. And this is as true of men's lives as it is of matter. God's hand is in all things. When someone oppresses you, remember that God permits it, and therefore it is one of the "all things" that work together for good in your life. What you are called upon to endure may be designed to make you better, holier, richer in life and character, gentler, more patient.

Thirdly, we must leave to God the matter of the evil committed against us. When we realize that persecution of the blessed Christian is really a demonstration of enmity against God within, we will understand that the wrong is against Him far more than against us, and He will judge the matter. Our only concern should be to learn the lesson He wants to teach us.

Men seek to destroy what they cannot conquer. They may break your heart into a thousand pieces. But God can take those pieces and make from them a life that glows with the radiance of His love and compassion for others. A musician ordered a violin-maker to construct for him the finest instrument he could make. But when he came to test it, his face clouded with anger at the tone. Lifting the violin into the air, he dashed it to pieces on the table. Then, paying the price he had agreed upon, he left the shop. The violin-maker shrugged his shoulders, gathered up the broken pieces, and set to work to remake the instrument. Again the musician was sent for and drew the bow across the strings as before. The violin was perfect. When he asked the price, the violin maker replied, "Nothing. This is the same instrument you broke to pieces. I put it together, and out of the shattered fragments made this perfect instrument." That is how God often works in our lives. He suffers others to break us to pieces that He may remake us. (See J. R. Miller. *Finding the Way*, pp. 179-187, and *The Lesson of Love*, pp. 31-41.)

THE AIM OF PERSECUTION

When the ungodly persecute us, what is it they are really after? If we were not what we are, blessed Christians, upholding righteousness, would we be persecuted, reviled, slandered? In reality they are not so much against us as against our Lord and the Christian convictions with which He has imbued us, because they stand in their way. Their goal is to remove anything that hinders the full expression of their own unrighteousness.

Our Lord told us to rejoice and be exceeding glad, because they will never succeed in doing this. In fact, by opposing the Gospel, they really cause it to spread further. "But I would ye should understand, brethren, that the things which happened unto me have fallen out rather unto the furtherance of the gospel," said Paul as he wrote to the Philippians in whose city he was imprisoned (1:12). I don't like the verb "happened" in the English translation. In isn't there at all in the Greek text. Things don't just happen in the Christian life.

The last clause of verse 12, "for so persecuted they the prophets which were before you," invites us to look back for a demonstration of the truth proclaimed. The prophets were persecuted, maligned, and killed; but the prophecy of God continued. The truth of God marches on in spite of the persecution and death of the truth-bearers, the prophets. Their persecution meant the advancement of the cause for which they gave their lives.

Lord Kelvin, on one occasion when he was lecturing to his students and an experiment failed to "come off," said, "Gentlemen, when you are face to face with a difficulty, you are up against a discovery." That is true not only in science but in our daily experience. The discovery that opposition to the Gospel has meant its advancement has been made over and over again throughout the Church's history. Christians have been imprisoned and put to death, but not Christianity itself. If the enemies of the Gospel really understood how to hurt us, they would ignore us instead of opposing us. Learn a lesson from history: Your opponents most advance the cause of Christ when they think they are inflicting most damage upon it. Only if it's your own cause you're promoting can they hurt it. Although a very few may oppose the Gospel out of mistaken zeal for God, as in the case of Saul of Tarsus, the majority of those who do so are acting from selfish motives. Be careful that your reaction to such opposition is not selfishly motivated, also.

Look for a moment at the first outburst of persecution against the Christians as described in Acts 4. The priests and the captain of the Temple were annoyed by the very fact that Peter and John taught the people – the former, because they were jealous of their official prerogative, and the latter because he was responsible for public order, and a riot in the Temple court would have been a scandal. The Sadducees were indignant because the resurrection of the Lord Jesus disproved their denial of the possibility of the resurrection. Before the resurrection, it was mainly the Pharisees who opposed the Lord, but after His resurrection it was the Sadducees also. It is a fearful thing to fall into the hands of wicked people who have been proven wrong. They did not care to ascertain whether the teaching of the apostles was true or false. They were simply guided by expediency. Toleration of Christ's teaching was not expedient to the perpetuation of their own beliefs and practices. By falsehood, therefore, they sought to put an end to truth. This is always an impossibility. Men can kill the truthful but not truth.

Here, then, we find Peter and John in prison, the first of thousands who have suffered bonds and imprisonment for Christ and have therein found liberty. What lofty faith, and what subordination of the fate of the messengers to the progress of the message are expressed in that abrupt introduction, in verse 4, of the statistics of the increase of the Church from that day's work! "Howbeit many of them which heard the word believed; and the number of the men was about five thousand." This was ten times the total number of those who viewed the Lord after His resurrection, which we may assume to have constituted the total number of believers during Christ's earthly ministry, since if there were more they surely would have done everything in their power to see the risen Lord. So what did it matter that it ended with the two apostles in custody, since it ended too with five thousand rejoicing in Christ? Wasn't this enough to make any suffering believer leap with joy? In the first round of the world-long battle between the persecutors and the persecuted, the victory is all on the side of the latter. So it has been ever since, though often the victors have died in the conflict. The Church, it has been said truly, is an anvil which has worn out many hammers, and the story of the first collision is, in essentials, the story of all. (See Alexander Maclaren, *Expositions of Holy Scriptures*, "The Acts of the Apostles," Vol. 1, pp. 130-136.)

Sundar Singh once was put in prison in Nepal for preaching Christ; so he preached to the other prisoners, as did Paul on a similar occasion. The governor then had him thrust into solitary confinement, in a foul-smelling cowhouse, tied hand and foot, naked, with leeches thrown on his body. He lifted up his heart to

God and sang His praises, "Though I am a very poor singer," he adds. His accuser said to the jailer, "What do you think of this man? He is so happy though he is suffering." "He must be mad," the jailer replied. The jailer then went to the governor. "Our purpose is not being fulfilled," he said. "We hoped with this punishment to make this man sorry and leave off preaching, but we are only adding to his happiness." Then the governor said, "He is only a madman; let him go."

The sooner we, too, realize that Christ will live though we die, the more joyously we suffer for His sake. And the way to the cross on behalf of others will not be a street of mourning but a thoroughfare of joy. As Beecher said, "In this world, full often our joys are only the tender shadows which our sorrows cast." "Remember," said Philip Henry, "the wheel is always in motion, and the spoke which is uppermost will soon be under; therefore mix trembling with all your joy." We often lose joys because we are afraid of deep sorrows.

We must school our hearts not to rebel against suffering, for "Hereunto were ye called." There must be a benevolent purpose for this in God's plan for us. So often we find that we cannot reach the best things in life but by the paths of pain. All the richest blessings of grace lie beyond lines of suffering, which we must pass to get them. Even of the Lord Jesus it is said that He was made perfect through suffering. There were attainments which even He could reach in no other way. All that is worthiest and most Christlike in good men bears the marks of pain upon it. We must pay the price if we would get the blessing.

But mixed with the blessing for ourselves is a blessing for others also. Christ suffered for all men as no other one ever can suffer. The influence of His unspeakable sorrow is renewing and refining the whole race. Sorrow in any life softens other hearts. How you stand and rejoice under it speaks volumes to others who would not hear you otherwise. We are all woven together into one mystic web of humanity, so that no man can live to himself. We must be willing to suffer that others may receive blessing from our pain. We never can become largely useful without suffering. We cannot get the power of sympathy which alone will fit us for being helpful to others in the best ways, save in the school of pain. We never can do anything worth while for humanity without first learning in suffering the lessons we will teach in song and hope.

The Christian does not live either unto himself or for himself. Persecution and suffering should be welcome, not because we feel it ennobles and refines us, but because our deportment in suffering may win someone to Jesus Christ who is looking for more than words to prove to him the reality of our faith. God permitted the terrible crime against His Son for the good of the world. Human redemption came out of it. When He permits us to suffer for righteousness' sake, we are in a little measure sharing the sufferings of Christ, and out of it all will come something to make the world better. Paul speaks of being crucified with Christ. When someone has treated us unkindly, wrongfully, because of our stand for Christ, it is a comfort to think that in a small way, at least, we are being crucified with Christ, and that blessing and enrichment will come to the world from our suffering.

We dread suffering in any form. It seems to us something evil which can only work harm. Yet the truth is that many of God's best benedictions and holiest mercies come to us in the garb of pain. We especially dread the suffering that men's wrong or cruelty brings upon us. We resent it. But no other experience brings us so fully into companionship with Christ; for all that He suffered was unjust, and out of His untold sufferings have come all the hopes, joys, and blessings of our lives.

When a great building was about to be erected, a certain artist begged to be permitted to make one of the doors. If this could not be permitted, he asked that he might make one little panel of one of the doors. Or if this, too, were denied him, he craved that he might at least be permitted to hold the brushes for the artist to whom the honor of doing the work should be awarded. If so small a part in a work of earth were esteemed so high a privilege, it is a far higher honor to have even the least share with Christ in His great work of human redemption. Everyone who suffers any wrong patiently and sweetly, in love and trust, is working with Christ in the saving of the world. (See J. R. Miller, *Finding the Way*, pp. 179-87, and *The Lesson of Love*, pp, 31-41.)

BIBLIOGRAPHY

Abbott, Lyman, "War or Peace," *Christian World Pulpit*, vol. XLIX. London: James Clarke and Co., 1896, p. 132.

Ainsworth, Percy C., *The Blessed Life*, London: Charles H. Kelly, 1915, pp. 117-27, 145-50, 152.

Arndt, W. F., and Gingrich, F. W., *A Greek-English Lexicon of the New Testament and Other Early Christian Literature.* Chicago: University of Chicago Press, 1957.

Arnot, William, *Illustrations of the Book of Proverbs.* London: T. Nelson & Sons, 1858, pp. 68-73.

Barclay, William, *The Gospel of Matthew*, vol. I. Edinburgh: Saint Andrew Press, 1958, p. 98.

Beecher, Henry Ward, "Meekness, a Power," *Christian World Pulpit*, vol. VII. London: James Clarke and Co., 1875, pp. 179-84.

Boreham, F. W., "The Quality of Mercy," *Christian World Pulpit*, vol. CXV. London: The Christian World, Ltd., 1929, pp. 172-4.

Bruce, Alexander Balmain, *The Kingdom of God.* Edinburgh: T. & T. Clark, 1909, pp. 166-86.

Calkins, Raymond, "Suffering Hardship," *Christian World Pulpit*, vol. XCIII. London: James Clarke & Co., 1918, pp. 302-5.

Cremer, H., *Biblico-Theological Lexicon of New Testament Greek.* Edinburgh: T. & T. Clark, 1954, pp. 343-50, 454, 554, 777.

Cummings, John, *Benedictions: or The Blessed Life.* Boston: John P. Jewett & Co., 1854, pp. 72-83, 136-61, 163-4, 174-81, 182-5, 207-8.

Dorling, William, "The Visible God," *Christian World Pulpit*, vol. VI. London: James Clarke and Co., 1874, pp. 168-9.

Douglas, William O., *U. S. News and World Report*, 24 December 1962, p. 12.

Dykes, J. Oswald, *Beatitudes of the Kingdom*, pp. 121-3.

Gillies, John, "Persecution Every Christian's Lot," *Memoirs of Rev. George Whitefield.* p. 329.

Horder, W. Garrett, "Non-Resistance," *Christian World Pulpit*, vol. XLIX. London: James Clarke and Co., 1896, pp. 117-19.

Howard, Henry, *The Raiment of the Soul.* London: Epworth Press, pp. 160-1, 170-6.

Hubbard, William, "The Blessed Poor," *Christian World Pulpit*, vol. XV. London: James Clarke & Co., 1879, p. 49.

Jelf, William Edward, *A Grammar of the Greek Language*, vol. II, Syntax. Oxford: John Henry and James Parker, 1859, pp. 124, 196, 567-8.

Jones, J. D., *The Inevitable Christ*. London: Hodder and Stoughton, 1928, pp. 299-316.

Jowett, J. H., "The Anger of the Saints," *Christian World Pulpit*, vol. LXXXIII. London: James Clarke & Co., 1913, p. 158.

Liddell, H. G., & Scott, R., *A Greek-English Lexicon*. Oxford: Clarendon Press, 1958, p. 1073.

_____, *A Greek-English Lexicon*. New York: Harper, 1889, p. 1160.

Lindsay, A. D., *Moral Teaching of Jesus*. London: Hodder & Stoughton, 1937, pp. 107-8.

Macdonald, George, "Sorrow, the Pledge of Joy," *Christian World Pulpit*, vol. XLII. London: James Clarke & Co., 1892, pp. 47-8.

Matheson, George, *Leaves for Quiet Hours*. London: James Clarke & Co., 1904, pp. 99-101.

_____, *Rests by the River*. London: Hodder and Stoughton, 1906, pp. 115-18.

McLaren, Alexander, *The Beatitudes and Other Sermons*. London: Alexander and Shepheard, 1896, pp. 66-7.

_____, *Expositions of Holy Scripture* (Acts of the Apostles, chapters 1 to 12:17). London: Hodder and Stoughton, 1907, pp. 130-6.

_____, *The Gospel According to St. Mark*, chapters 1-8. New York: A. C. Armstrong and Son, 1907, pp. 94-104.

_____, *Holy of Holies*. London: Hodder and Stoughton, 1905, p. 142.

Mellor, Enoch, *The Hem of Christ's Garment and Other Sermons*. London: Richard D. Dickinson, 1883, pp. 87-109.

Miller, J. R., *Finding the Way*. pp. 179-87.

_____, *Garden of the Heart*. pp. 250-9.

_____, *Lesson of Love*. London: Hodder & Stoughton, 1903, pp. 31-41.

_____, *The Master's Blesseds*. London: Hodder & Stoughton, pp. 44-6, 55-6.

Moberly, George, *Sermons on the Beatitudes*. Oxford and London: J. H. and James Parker, 1860, pp. 63-4.

Morgan, G. Campbell, "The Peace of God," *Christian World Pulpit*, vol. LXXXVI. London: James Clarke & Co., 1914, pp. 233-4.

_____, *Westminster Pulpit*, vol. IX. Old Tappan, New Jersey: Fleming H. Revell Co., 1954, pp. 150-3.

Morrison, George H., *Sun-Rise*. London: Hodder and Stoughton, 1903, pp. 158-68.

_____, *The Wings of the Morning*. London: Hodder & Stoughton, 1907, pp. 256-9.

Moulton, J. H., & Milligan, G., *The Vocabulary of the Greek Testament, illustrated from the Papyri and other non-literary sources*. Grand Rapids, Michigan: Wm. B. Eerdmans Publishing Co., 1957, p. 386.

Nida, Eugene A., "Meaning and Translation," *The Bible Translator*, vol. VIII, No. 3 (July 1957). pp. 97-108.

Robertson, A. T., *A Grammar of the Greek New Testament in the Light of Historical Research*. New York: Doran, 1923, pp. 513, 757-8, 785-8, 872, 891-2.

Sauer, Erich, *The Triumph of the Crucified*. London: The Paternoster Press, 1951, pp. 22-5, 142-3.

Simeon, Charles, *Expository Outlines on the Whole Bible*, vol. XIX. Grand Rapids, Michigan: Zondervan Publishing House, 1955, pp. 63-4.

Speaker's Bible, The, vol. XXIX, The Gospel According to Saint Matthew, vol. I, "The Peacemaker and the Peaceable," Hastings, Edward, editor. Aberdeen: The Speaker's Bible Office, 1938, pp. 96-8.

Spurgeon, C. H., *Treasury of the New Testament*, vol. IV. Grand Rapids, Michigan: Zondervan Publishing House, 1950, pp. 61-6.

_____, *Ibid.*, vol. I. p. 63.

Stanley, A. P., "Peace," *Anglican Pulpit Library*, vol. IX. London: James Mackenzie, Ltd., pp. 28-32.

Trench, R. C., *Synonyms of the New Testament*. Grand Rapids, Michigan: Wm. B. Eerdmans Publishing Co., 1953, pp. 152, 169.

Warschauer, J., "Nabal and Abigail," *Christian World Pulpit*, vol. LXXXIII. London: James Clarke & Co., 1913, p. 117.

Woods, W. J., "The Heirs of the Kingdom," *Christian World Pulpit*, vol. XXXVIII. London: James Clarke & Co., 1890, pp. 3-6, 95-6, 135-6, 418.

Workman, Herbert B., *Persecution in the Early Church*. London: Charles H. Kelly, 1906, pp. 21-2.

Wynn, Walter, "The Mourning Heart," *Christian World Pulpit*, vol. XXXIX. London: James Clarke & Co., 1891, pp. 179-81.

Zodhiates, Spiros, *Can Man See God?* (booklet). Ridgefield, New Jersey: AMG Press, pp. 9-13, 30-8.

_____, *Mercy: God's and Ours* (booklet, now appears in this volume, pp. 355-82). Ridgefield, New Jersey: AMG Press.

_____, *Persecution* (booklet). Ridgefield, New Jersey: AMG Press, 1962, pp. 14-17.

_____, *Pursuit of Happiness, The* (booklet, now appears in this volume, pp. 1-33). Ridgefield, New Jersey: AMG Press, 1967.

_____, *The Work of Faith* (now part I of this volume), pp. 190-3.

I
INDEX OF SUBJECTS

II

INDEX OF ENGLISH WORDS

English	Greek	Scripture	Page
love unselfishly	*agapa-oo*	Matt. 5:9, 44	556, 578
man(kind)	*anthroopos*	Luke 6:22, 26	137, 155, 219
mature, perfect	*teleios*	Matt. 5:9, 48	558
meek	*praus*	Matt. 5:5	278
meekness	*praotees*	Matt. 5:5,	263, 267, 268
	prautees	7	278, 279, 285
			286, 288
			291, 356
merciful	*ele-eemoon*	Matt. 5:7	380, 390
mercy	*eleos*	Matt. 5:7	373, 375
mercy, show	*ele-eeoo*	Matt. 5:7	391
middle, a	*mesotees*	Matt. 5:5	267
minister to oneself, a	*autodiakonos*	Matt. 5:3	58
moderation (of one's passions)	*metriopatheia*	Matt. 5:5	267
mourn	*penthe-oo*	Luke 6:25	202, 203, 225
		Matt. 5:4	226, 239
			250, 257
mourning	*penthos*	Matt. 5:4	225, 250
needy one	*ende-ees*	Matt. 5:3-11	
		Luke 6:20-22	18
nevertheless	*pleen*	Luke 6:24	186
now	*nun*	Luke 6:25, 26	195, 202
obedience, ready	*eupeitheia*	Matt. 5:5	268
occupation	*ascholia*	Matt. 5:5	267
pain	*ponos*	Matt. 5:3	57
pain, suffer	*pone-oo*		
	poneomai	Matt. 5:3	57
passion	*pathos*	Matt. 5:4	225
peace	*eireenee*	Matt. 5:9	493, 515
peacemaker	*eireenopoios*	Matt. 5:9	505, 515, 516
persecute	*diookoo*	Matt. 5:10,	616, 617, 618
		11	625, 656
physician	*iatros*	Luke 6:22	157
poor	*penees*	Matt. 5:3	57, 58
poor	*ptoochos*	Matt. 5:3	57, 58
poor, be	*penomai*	Matt. 5:3	57
poverty	*penia*	Matt. 5:3	57
poverty	*ptoocheia*	Matt. 5:3	57, 59
pride	*hupseelokardia*	Matt. 5:5	291
pure	*katharos*	Matt. 5:8	446, 448, 452
			453, 455, 456
receive in full	*apechoo*	Luke 6:24	188, 189
		Matt. 6:2,5,16	190, 195
rejoice	*chairoo*	Luke 6:23	
		Matt. 5:12	160, 162, 658

English	Greek	Scripture	Page
reproach	oneidizoo	Luke 6:22	
		Matt. 5:11	145, 650, 656
righteousness	dikaiosunee	Matt. 5:6	342
sameness of mind	homonoia	Matt. 5:9	493
satisfy	chortazoo	Luke 6:21	
		Matt. 5:6	102, 349, 353
say	legoo	Matt. 5:2, 11	7, 82, 215
		Luke 6:20,26	216, 656
see (perceptively)	hora-oo	Luke 6:23	167
self, same	autos	Luke 6:23	172, 349, 390
		Matt. 5:6, 9	607, 608
shepherd	boskos	Matt. 5:4	249
son	huios	Matt. 5:9	605, 606, 607
soul	psuchee	Matt. 5:8	443
spirit	pneuma	Matt. 5:3, 8	58, 443
straining, a	epitasis	Matt. 5:4	226
teach	didaskoo	Matt. 5:2	
		Luke 6:20	7
thanks, give	euchariste-oo	Matt. 5:3-11	
		Luke 6:20-22	32, 33
the	ho	Matt. 5:3-11	13, 18, 59
		Luke 6:20-23,	94, 96, 106
		26	137, 157, 158
			172, 219, 220
			226, 250, 338
			342, 349, 390
			424, 425, 446
			505, 605
			616, 618
think	doke-oo	Matt. 5:9	498
thirst	dipsa-oo	Matt. 5:6	338, 349
this	houtos	Luke 6:20	135
weep	klai-oo	Luke 6:21, 25	106, 202
well	eu	Matt. 5:9	498
when	hote	Luke 6:22	97, 135
whenever	hotan	Luke 6:22, 26	97, 135
		Matt. 5:11	215, 645
with	meta	Matt. 5:4	226
woe	ouai	Matt. 5:3	
		Luke 6:24-26	57, 185
wrong, be/do	hamartan-oo	Luke 6:22	135
you	su	Luke 6:25	202
yours	humeteros	Luke 6:20	75

III

INDEX OF GREEK WORDS

Greek	English	Scripture	Page
agallia-oo	be extremely joyful or glad	Matt. 5:12	658
agalliasthe, see *agallia-oo*			
agapa-oo	love unselfishly, etc.	Matt. 5:9, 44 I Cor. 13:5-7	556, 578
agapate, see *agapa-oo*			
agapee	love (unselfish, etc.)	Matt. 5:9 I Cor. 13:5-7	578
agapoomen, see *agapa-oo*			
an	if	Luke 6:22	97
anankazoo	force, compel, urge	Matt. 5:3 Luke 6:20 Matt. 14:22	41, 42
anexikakia	forbearance of evil	Matt. 5:5	267
anthroopoi, see *anthroopos*			
anthroopos	man, mankind	Luke 6:22, 26	137, 155 219
aorgeesia	angerlessness	Matt. 5:5	263, 267
apechein, see *apechoo*			
apechete, see *apechoo*			
apechoo	receive in full	Luke 6:24 Matt. 6:2,5,16	188, 189 190, 195
aphechousin, see *apechoo*			
aphorismos	excommunication	Luke 6:22	142
aphorisoosin, see *aphorizoo*			
aphorizoo	exclude, separate	Luke 6:22	142, 144
apo	away from, from	Luke 6:22, 24	142, 188
ascholia	occupation industry business want of leisure	Matt. 5:5	267
auta, see *autos*			

Greek	English	Scripture	Page
echoo	have	Luke 6:24	188
edidasken, see *didaskoo*			
eenangasen, see *anankazoo*			
eidon, see *hora-oo*			
eipoosin, see *legoo*			
eireenee	peace	Matt. 5:9	
		Matt. 10:34	493, 515
eireenopoioi, see *eireenopoios*			
eireenopoios	peacemaker	Matt. 5:9	
		Matt. 10:34	505, 515, 516
eiroo	tie, join together	Matt. 5:9	493
ekballoo	cast out, expel throw out	Luke 6:22	156
ekbaloosin, see *ekballoo*			
ele-eemones, see *ele-eemoon*			
ele-eemoon	merciful showing pity	Matt. 5:7	380, 390
ele-eeoo	show mercy have pity on	Matt. 5:7	391
ele-eetheesontai, see *ele-eeoo*			
elegen, see *legoo*			
eleos	mercy, pity	Matt. 5:7	373, 375
empepleesmenoi, see *empi(m)pleemi* and *empipla-oo*			
empi(m)pleemi, *empipla-oo*	fill, satisfy, enjoy	Luke 6:25	193, 194
ende-ees	needy one	Matt. 5:3-11 Luke 6:20-22	18
epieikeia	gentleness	Matt. 5:5 II Cor. 10:1	285, 286, 288
epitaseoos, see *epitasis*			
epitasis	a stretching straining	Matt. 5:4	226
epoioun, see *poie-oo*			
eu	well	Matt. 5:9 Luke 2:14	498
eucharisteesas, see *euchariste-oo*			

Greek	English	Scripture	Page
klaiontes, see *klaioo*			
klaioo	cry, weep	Luke 6:21, 25	106, 202
klausete, see *klaioo*			
legoo	say	Matt. 5:2, 11	7, 82, 215
		Luke 6:20, 26	216, 656
legoosin, see *legoo*			
lupe-oo	grieve	Matt. 5:4	226
lupoumenoi, see *lupe-oo*			
makar	blessed	Matt. 5:3-11	9, 12, 231
		Luke 6:20-22	476
makares, see *makar*			
makaria, see *makarios*			
makarioi, see *makarios*			
makarios	blessed	Matt. 5:3-11	9, 10, 11
		Luke 6:20-22	17, 18, 19
		Matt. 28:20	23, 24, 37
		John 16:22,33	38, 43, 52
			56, 58, 72
			130, 131, 229
			231, 238, 279
			327, 355, 430
			504, 623, 625
makariotees	blessedness	Matt. 5:3-11	12, 56
		Luke 6:20-22	231, 483
makarious, see *makarios*			
makaritees	blessed	Matt. 5:3-11	
		Luke 6:20-22	13
makarizomen, see *makarizoo*			
makarizoo	bless	Matt. 5:3-11	
		Luke 6:20-22	
		Luke 1:48	
		James 5:11	23, 24
megalopatheia	fortitude	Matt. 5:5	267
mesotees	a middle a mean (between two extremes)	Matt. 5:5	267
met', see *meta*			
meta	with	Matt. 5:4	226
metriopatheia	moderation (of one's passions)	Matt. 5:5	267

Greek	English	Scripture	Page
nun	now	Luke 6:25, 26	195, 202
oneidisoosin, see *oneidizoo*			
oneidizoo	insult	Luke 6:22	
	reproach	Matt. 27:44	
	revile	Matt. 5:11	145, 650, 656
orgee	anger	Matt. 5:5	267
orgees, see *orgee*			
orgilotees	excessive anger	Matt. 5:5	263, 267
ouai	woe	Matt. 5:3	
		Luke 6:24-26	57, 185
pantes, see *pas*			
parakale-oo	summon, call to one's side, call upon for help, request, encourage, comfort, cheer up	Matt. 5:4	256, 257
parakleesin, see *parakleesis*			
parakleesis	comfort consolation	Luke 6:24	189
parakleetheesontai, see *parakale-oo*			
parakleetos	advocate	Luke 6:24	
	attorney	John 14:16, 26	
	comforter	John 15:26	
	helper	John 16:7	189, 255
pas	all, every	Luke 6:26	219, 220
pateer	father	Luke 6:26	220
pateres, see *pateer*			
pathos	passion	Matt. 5:4	225
peina-oo	be hungry	Luke 6:21, 25	94, 96, 197
	hunger	Matt. 5:6	338, 349
peinasete, see *peina-oo*			
peinoontes, see *peina-oo*			
penees	poor	Matt. 5:3	
		Ps. 112:9	
		II Cor. 9:9	57, 58
penia	poverty	Matt. 5:3	57
penomai	labor, be poor, be needy, etc.	Matt. 5:3	57
pentheesantes, see *penthe-oo*			

663

Greek	English	Scripture	Page
pentheesete, see *penthe-oo*			
penthei, see *penthos*			
penthein, see *penthe-oo*			
penthe-oo	mourn	Luke 6:25	
		Matt. 5:4; 9:5	
		I Cor. 5:2	
		II Cor. 12:21	202, 203
		James 4:9	225, 226, 239
		Rev. 18:11,15,19	/250, 257
penthos	mourning	Matt. 5:4	225, 250
penthountes, see *penthe-oo*			
peri	around, about, near, as to, in reference to, with regard to, etc.	Matt. 5:5	267
phile-oo	love, like, be fond of	Matt. 5:9	578
philoumen, see *phile-oo*			
pleen	but, however nevertheless	Luke 6:24	186
pneuma	spirit	Matt. 5:3, 8	58, 443
pneumati, see *pneuma*			
poiee, see *poieoo*			
poieoo	do, make	Luke 6:22,23,26	
		Matt. 5:9	
		Matt. 7:22	
		Matt. 13:58	135, 176, 217
		Acts 19:11	515, 516, 517
poneeron, see *poneeros*			
poneeros	evil	Luke 6:22	
		Matt. 6:13	
		Eph. 6:16	157, 158
pone-oo, *poneomai*	toil, suffer pain, labor, etc.	Matt. 5:3	57
ponos	labor, pain	Matt. 5:3	57
praotees	meekness		263, 267, 268
prautees	mildness	Matt. 5:5,7	278, 279, 285
	gentleness	II Cor. 10:1	286, 288
			291, 356
prassoo	do, make	Matt. 5:9	516
praus	meek		

694

Other Books by Dr. Spiros Zodhiates

Studies on Luke

Studies in John's Gospel

Studies on James

Three-Volume Set in handsome slip cover

Miscellaneous Titles